HOME GUNSMITHING DIGEST

Second Edition

By Robert A. Steindler

Edited By Jack Lewis

Follett Publishing Company / Chicago

T - 1212

Production Editor
BOB SPRINGER

Technical Editor
DEAN A. GRENNELL

Research Editor
ROGER COMBS

Art Director
MALCOLM WILSON

Staff Artists
LORIE DISNEY
JOHN VITALE
SONYA KAISER
FELICITY WHITER

Production Coordinator
BETTY BURRIS

Associate Publisher
SHELDON L. FACTOR

Produced by

ISBN 0-695-81212-2   Library of Congress Catalog Card Number 71-118931

CONTENTS

INTRODUCTION

UNFORTUNATELY FOR me — and fortunately for a number of gunsmiths — I was not born with the gun tinkering smarts. My gun tinkering began some twenty-five or so years ago when a friendly gunsmith drilled and tapped an action of a rifle for me, then handed me the scope, rings and mounts with the casual observation that I could do the rest of the job myself.

I had seen the gunsmith casually — and with great economy of motion — slap a scope on anything from an M52 Sporter to a Remington Model 30-S, and I figured that I, too, could seat a couple of screws.

Let me recap that tragi-comedy briefly. I was using Weaver blocks and rings, the rear block being slightly higher than the front one. Therefore, the suitable screws for the rear block were longer than those for the front base. Knowing no better, I grabbed the first screw that came to hand and ran it into the forward hole of the front mount. Everything went fine. Seating four screws should take just that many minutes, I figured, and I was rather proud of having saved myself two whole bucks, the standard scope-mounting charge at that time.

I seated the front mount screws, ran those for the rear block into the mount, and the damn block slipped right off the receiver! I had left the bolt in the rifle, so now I decided to take it out of the action. But the bolt was locked up tighter than Fort Knox's main gate. The long rear screws in the front block had bottomed out, made contact with the bolt, and now held it there very, very firmly.

Nobody had told me to make sure that the base screws would not work loose eventually and, after getting bases and screws sorted out, I seated the screws the way any home handyman would. Not owning a collimator, I took the finished job to the gunshop where there was a range. On the second shot I was still on the paper, the third shot missed the fifty-yard target completely, and after the fourth shot, the scope, rings and bases were laying on the shooting bench, next to the rifle and the box of ammo.

It took me three evenings to get that scope mounted, and in those evenings, I developed a passionate dislike for that gunsmith.

This book differs, in one or two major aspects, from others on gunsmithing. I never had had any formal gunsmith technical training. Therefore, I made all of the mistakes the beginner makes, plus some of my own which surely would entitle me to some kind of an award were one given in the category of home gun tinkering. Hopefully, you will be able to benefit from my past mistakes, and perhaps we can also forestall some future ones.

Over the years I have encountered a number of tools, jigs, gizmos and gadgets for the gun tinkerer which, at first glance, seemed to be the answer to some particular problem. However, many of these items seem to have been designed to create eye appeal, and to relieve me of some hard-earned money. Not being overly endowed in that department, I learned to improvise, and my experiences in this area will also prove to be of value to you.

With my early mistakes, I also learned to do a number of jobs the right way. The late John Riley Buhmiller, a friend of many years, introduced me to the world of machine tools and to the making of rigs and jigs that cannot be bought. Dan Bechtel of B-Square Company, a designer, engineer, machinist and gun crank, was helpful above and beyond the call of duty when it came to questions — and of those I must have had a couple of million. Bob Brownell, with his vast gunsmithing experience, was more than happy to share his knowledge and expertise. Dave Corbin and Jerry Yorks, a crackerjack gunsmith of the old school, always were available for endless questions and a couple of rescue missions.

And my special thanks to Jack Lewis, who got the ball rolling.

Bob Steindler
Erewhon Farm, Illinois

Chapter 1

YOUR BASIC TOOLS & EQUIPMENT

What To Buy, What To Pay, What To Make — And The Differences!

PRECISELY WHAT tools you will want or need depends on just how much gun tinkering you want to do and what type of work you want to tackle. If you merely want to keep your guns in tip-top shape and install an occasional scope on a rifle, you can get along with a minimum of tools. If you're only interested in making your own stocks, then you'll need more stockmaker's tools and not much in the line of metalworking tools.

Tools, for most men, hold a fascination that is hard to resist, therefore overbuying of tools is not uncommon. A friend of mine stood by one day to watch me install a scope and fix the trigger pull of a rifle. He got the gun tinkering bug and the next thing I knew, he had more tools in his shop, including a twelve-inch lathe, than most well-equipped gunshops have.

Traditionally, this chapter should start with a learned discourse on where to set up shop, benches, lights, ventilation, tool storage and other such gems of wisdom, but since this is not a book about advanced gunsmithing, we'll start with the tools. A bench, if need be, can be improvised, you can even hang a bare bulb over your work area — but the tools are the important investment, since they will govern the quality of your work and the ease with which you get a job done.

One piece of advice about tool buying that has been passed on for many, many years is: Buy the best you can afford, even if it means you cannot buy all the tools you want right away.

Take the matter of the simplest of all tools, the screwdriver. I have seen screwdrivers sold in drug stores, supermarkets, hardware stores, automotive supply houses, chain stores, hock shops — you name it, but the screwdrivers you need are best bought from a specialty house such as Brownell's or Mittermeier. Why pay slightly more for those tools than you do in the local hardware shop? Gunsmithing screwdrivers are specially hardened, have blades that are designed to fit the screwheads found on screws used in and on guns, and these special screwdrivers will outlast the run-of-the-mill tool by ten or more years. I have gunsmithing screwdrivers that have seen much hard use for the past twenty years, and none of them have ever needed regrinding.

Just as an auto mechanic or a watchmaker gets his tools from a specialty house, so does the gunsmith. Some tools you can either improvise or make yourself, but this requires a bit more skill and equipment than you are likely to have when you start your gun tinkering, so this aspect of home gunsmithing is best left alone for the time being.

A list of basic tools would be quite short and would include a set of screwdrivers, perhaps one or two small watchmaker's screwdrivers, one 1/8 and one 5/32-inch pin punch, one 1/16 and one 3/32-inch starter punch, a brass and a nylon drift punch, a light hammer with a brass face and perhaps one with a nylon face. To these, add an Arkansas or India stone, a sight-base file for cutting dovetails by hand, a wood rasp for shaping or reshaping a stock, and an eight-inch pillar file with at least one safe or noncutting side.

Also include a metal scribe, a center punch, and perhaps

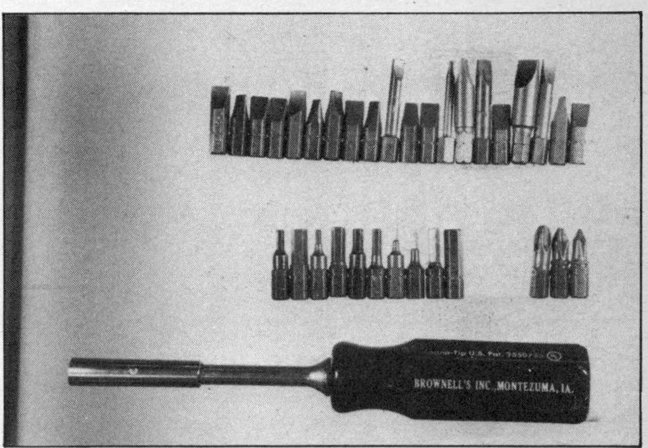

(Above) Brownell Magna-Tip holds bits in shank of tool by magnetism, allowing a wide range of shapes, sizes. (Below) Watchmaker's screwdrivers also have many uses.

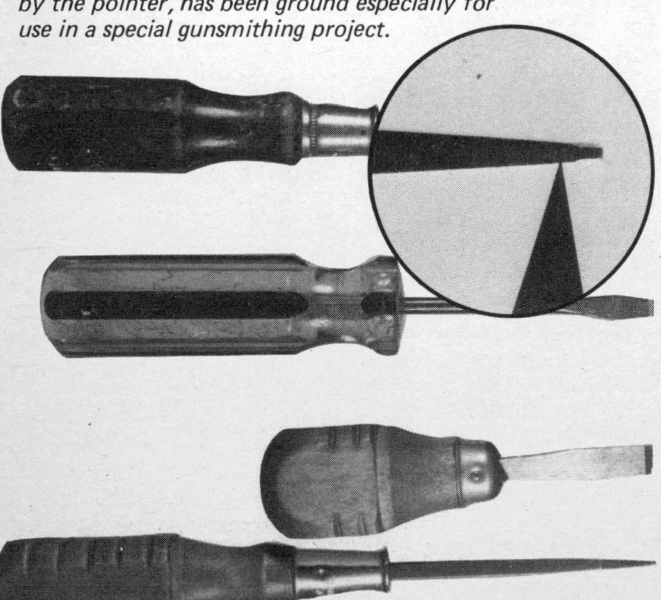

Gunsmithing screwdrivers come in a variety of shapes, with many of them being made for special jobs and uses. For example, the blade shown in the inset, marked by the by the pointer, has been ground especially for use in a special gunsmithing project.

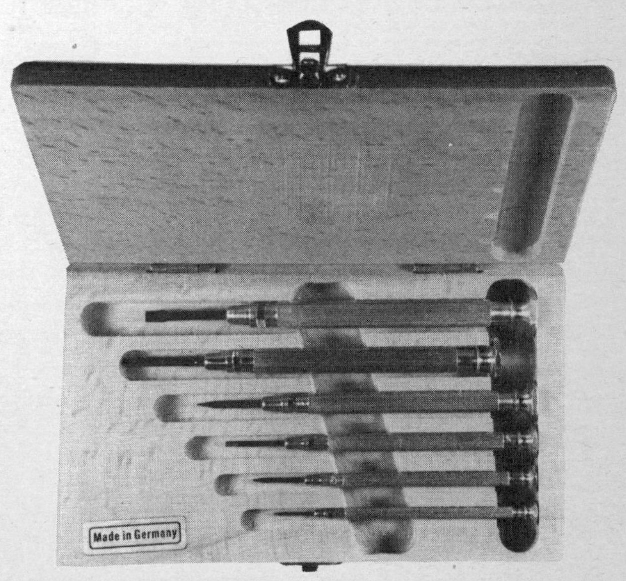

one pair of parallel jaw pliers which are a modification of the angler's pliers, and a couple of needle nose pliers, either the standard type with the wire cutting edge or the type sold by Brownell's without the wire cutting edges. The small parallel jaw pliers, when tied up with a couple of heavy rubber bands will double as a small parts vise in a pinch, in the shop and on the range.

Sooner or later, you will need a vernier caliper and a micrometer. While an adjustable depth gauge is nice to have, I have been doing without one simply by using the vernier caliper. On both these precision measuring tools, I favor the direct reading ones — they are simpler and faster to read. A small machinist square is helpful, but for the time being, any square can be used. One handy item is the bench block, and once you have used one, you will find many uses for it.

You also will need a fine-toothed jeweler's saw and a gadget called a Screw Gizzie — the simplest and also the most effective way of holding a screw while you grind or file away on the screw. I don't know who the genius was who dreamed this one up, but you can get it from Brownell's for about five bits, and it's worth its weight in gold. A set of fine Swiss files is handy, especially for the finer and somewhat touchier jobs, and I find them valuable when ruined screwheads have to be repaired.

Although you can buy special handles for these files, I find that I can control the file just a bit better without a handle, hence would not suggest that you buy or make handles for these files.

If woodworking — that is, stockwork and checkering — is to your liking, you'll need the various inletting tools as well as checkering tools, perhaps a small checkering cradle, stockmaker's screws and more wood files and rasps than already suggested. Specialized tools and gadgets will be discussed later on wherever these tools become important.

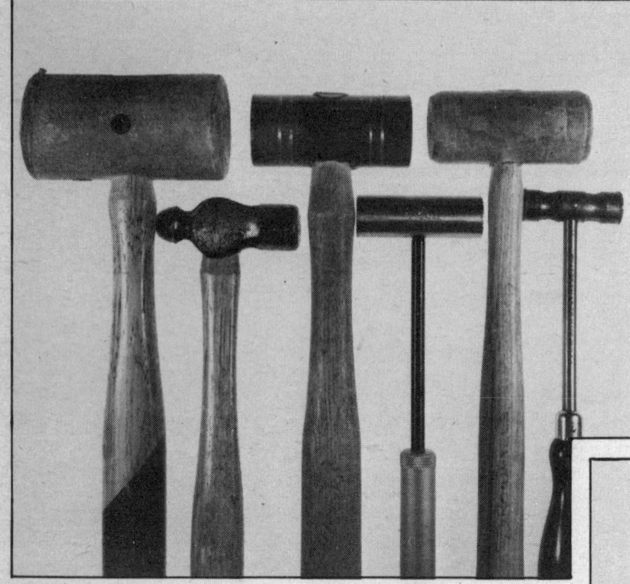

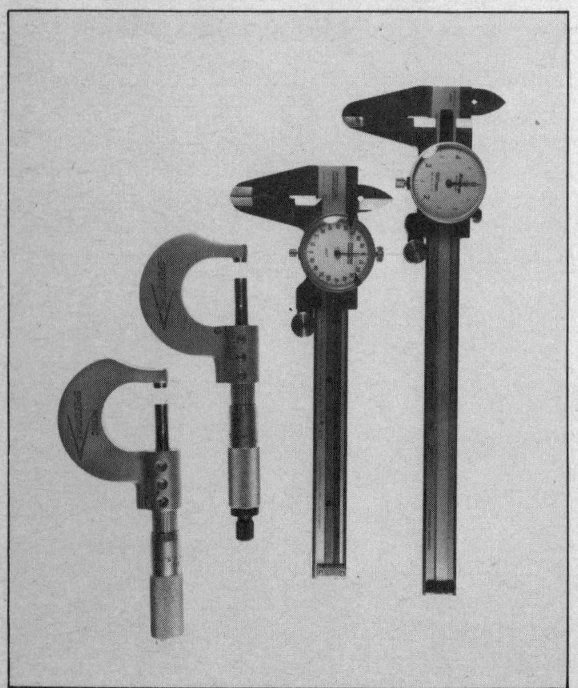

(Left) Rawhide, plastic, brass hammers are used in nearly all gunsmithing work. (Lower left) Direct reading vernier caliper, micrometer can make life easier for the beginner. (Below) Mixture of pin and starting punches are a requirement. Pin punches tend to break, must be replaced. (Bottom) Pin punches are of the type with quickly replaceable tips if damaged.

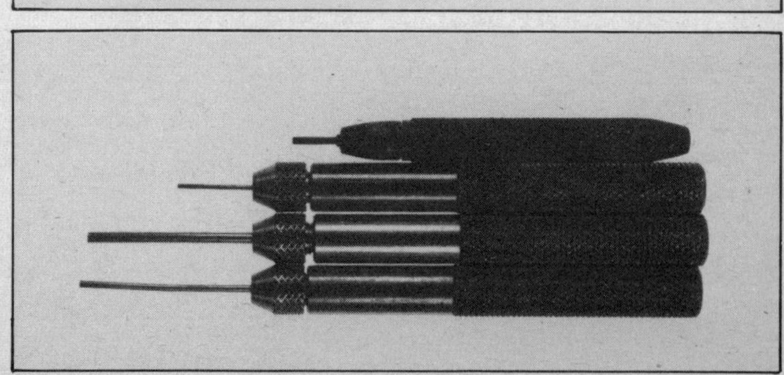

Most of the suppliers of gunsmithing tools are not the manufacturers of the products they sell, therefore you will see the identical tools in the various catalogs. Because of this, these houses always are on the lookout for better and more suitable tools. In the section on *Trade Sources,* you will find the addresses of the various companies mentioned throughout this book. Write for catalogs and do some comparison shopping — the same tool often is priced differently and you can save a few dollars here and there, providing you are certain that you are not about to get stuck with a poor copy of a quality product. You should, for a starter, have the catalogs from Brownell's, B-Square Company, Frank Mittermeier, Corbin Manufacturing & Supply, Incorporated, Brookstone, and Manhattan Supply Company.

Some tools you may have already, or they can be bought at most hardware stores. An adjustable hacksaw frame with at least three blades, with eighteen, twenty-four and thirty-two teeth per inch, should be on hand. While the ten-inch blades are handy in some work, I favor the twelve-inch blade.

If you happen to break a couple of blades, don't pitch them out. Properly heat-treated, they can be used for a multitude of jobs, as will be described later. And while on the subject of busted and worn-out tools, never toss any of them out! Worn-out or broken Swiss files can be converted easily to scribes, flat and even curved files are changed into chisels for stockwork, and even the lowly Allen wrench has its uses as a scratch awl or scribe once it is set into a homemade dowel rod handle.

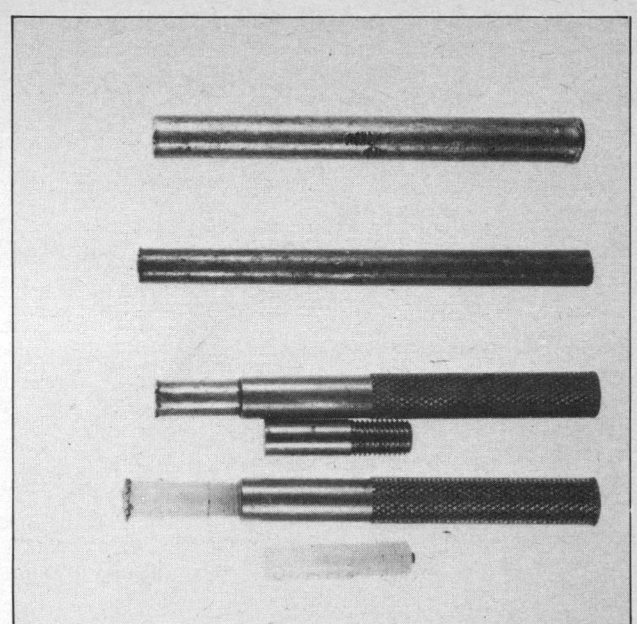

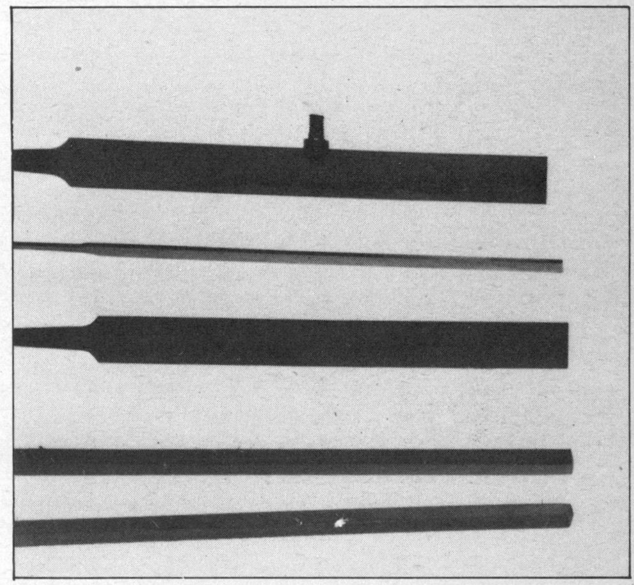

(Top) Brass drifts can be made from scrap rod, but the Brownell drift punch with interchanging brass/nylon tip is made specifically for gunsmithing. (Right) Sight base or dovetail slot files have one cutting surface; screw slot files cut metal on their narrow sides. (Lower right) For grinding down over-long screws, use either the two-piece B-Square screwholder or a Brownell Screw Gizzy. (Below) Brownell's parallel jaw pliers, when used with hefty rubberband, convert into hand-held vise for filing screwheads or screw slots.

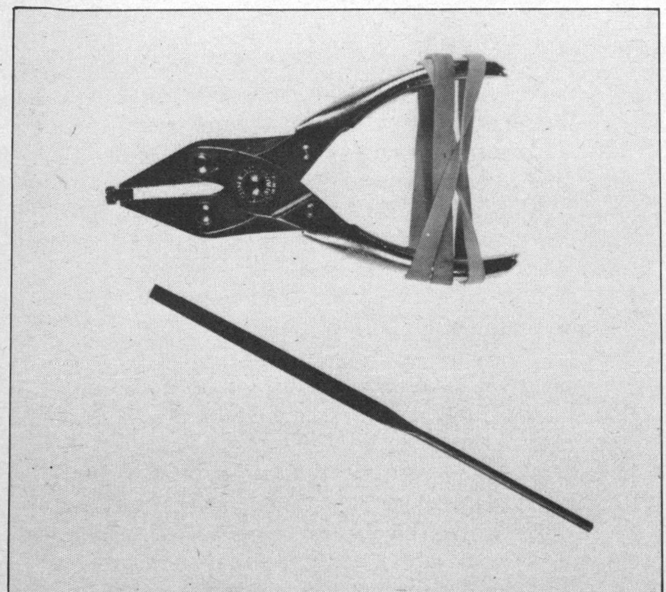

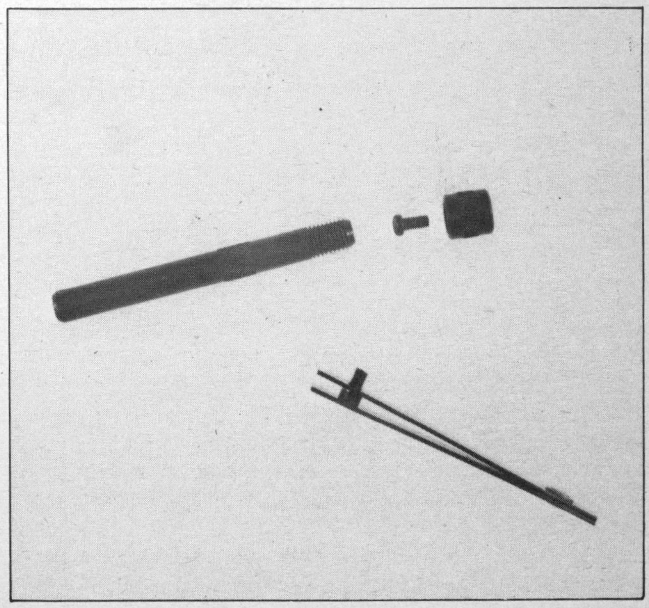

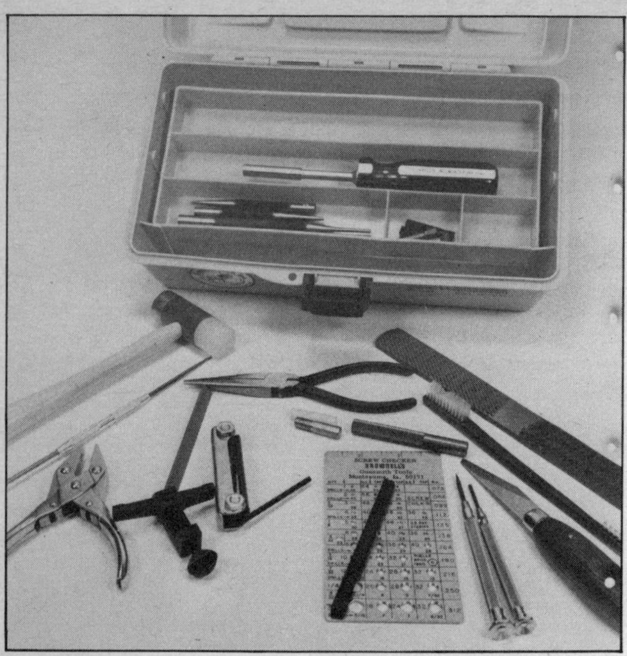

Brownell's now markets this beginner's kit, which comes complete with plastic tool chest. A more advanced kit is available for those who take down guns for blueing.

Other tools that you may have already and which you will sooner or later find useful in your work on guns include an eggbeater drill, a pair of tin snips which are usually referred to as aircraft snips, countersinks for metal and wood, a brace with suitable bits including a countersink bit and a dowel pointing bit, a standard crosscut and a fine-toothed saw for stockwork, some wood chisels, C-clamps in various sizes, and a steel rule, preferably one marked in tenths and hundredths of an inch.

Some files for wood as well as a few for steel are handy to have on hand, along with a file card, of course. One trick when it comes to draw filing and any other finish filing is to rub some plain blackboard chalk across the teeth of the file — this prevents clogging of the teeth. I also have found that a small soldering iron is a welcome addition, not so much for my gun tinkering, but for making various supporting structures and for jerry-rigging jigs of one sort or another.

A small ballpeen hammer is handy, and to make certain that a gun is locked into the vise properly, you will want to use a small level. A torpedo level can be used or even a small line level will do the job.

When shopping for drills, it is best to concentrate on the boxed sets, and don't buy anything but the best high-speed steel drills. Regrinding a drill tip is an art, even when you use a jig. Good drills, though costlier at the outset, will easily outlast the cheaper ones that look so good in the store or the catalog. Drills come in three different specifications — the letter size, the fractional size and the number system, the latter being the most versatile and most widely used standard. Solid carbide twist drills are essential when you have to drill into very hard steel, but chances that you will need one of them is fairly slim.

Taps and dies come in a wide variety of makes, and costs vary greatly. A complete set looks impressive on the bench, but it has been my experience that you need only a few of these taps and dies. Some of the taps needed are special sizes and should be bought from one of the gunsmith supply houses. All other taps and dies can be bought piecemeal from the local hardware or machinist supply store for little money. This means that you won't spend a pile of dollar bills on something you really don't have to have.

While on the subject of drills, taps and dies, you should have some good-quality cutting oil handy. Even if you use a hand drill or an electric drill, cutting a good, clean hole into metal — any type of metal — will be made easier when you use a few drops of cutting oil as the tip of the drill or tap enters. Running a tap into a drilled hole and keeping the blamed thing one hundred percent vertical is somewhat of an art. If the tap enters crooked, the tapped hole will be useless for scope mounting, so it becomes essential that the tap runs true. B-Square has a tool they call the Tru Tapper which, when chucked into a drill press and operated manually, does the perfect vertical tapping job.

You will have to have a bench vise with at least three-inch jaws and a swivel base. This type of vise most often is called a machinist vise, and is quite heavy. When setting it in your bench, be sure to locate it in such a manner that you won't run into trouble when it comes to fastening the vise with bolts. Depending on the location of your workbench, the vise can be mounted either on the left or the right forward corner. Be sure the rod that moves the jaws of the vise back and forth does not interfere with the opening and closing of a drawer or with an electric outlet.

Once the vise is installed, make up the padding needed for the vise jaws. If you have access to the lead sheathing used on some of the telephone cables, cut two pieces of it so that they overhang the jaws of the vise, then contour the lead sheath with a ballpeen hammer so it fits the vise jaws. This makes a nearly ideal surface for gripping small metal parts such as screws, followers and floorplates. The lead will protect the metal parts and blued parts locked into the vise will not be damaged. If you cannot get lead sheath, you can buy brass or copper jaws for your vise. For holding stocks and long guns in the vise, make up two pieces of scrap wood or hardened Masonite to fit the jaws, cut some heavy felt to fit, and glue the felt on the facing sides of the boards; you have a pair of vise jaw pads that will last for years.

Your bench and work area layout will depend on a great many things. If you have the space and can use a hammer and saw, you can build a small workshop that will be the envy of everyone. But let me caution you about space and shop layout. I have had to move my shop twice since the original setup, and each time I have taken great pains with the layout. That is, the location of the lights and the benches, positioning my power tools, and shelf and storage space. Somehow, after a few months, I always have ended up with a shop that is not large enough and does not allow unlimited movement and handling of equipment.

A lot of professional gunsmiths use one bench for everything, yet those who are doing metalwork as well as stockwork will tell you there should be a special bench set aside for stockwork.

A friend of mine has what I consider the best of all possible shop layouts. Not having space in his house, he bought a used travel trailer, set it on blocks, and now does all his work there. His woodworking shop is at the stern end where the bunks used to be, the kitchen and dining room area contain most of

the power tools, while the forward end houses a large lathe and a bench made from 4x4 oak timber. Electricity is run in from the outside feed line and the shop has heat, air conditioning and a stereo radio. There is even space for a compressor and oxy-acetylene equipment.

Contrast this with the first gunsmithing bench I made: A couple of saw horses, plus a handful of 2x4s laid lengthwise and nailed down. The 2x4s were topped off with a sheet of three-quarter-inch marine plywood. Another bench consisted of a reinforced kitchen cabinet, repainted and topped off with hardwood tongue and groove flooring. With lumber costs going up and up, I have found that the steel workbench legs, topped with 2x6 boards bolted down, are just right. Don't make the bench longer than six feet, or if you do make it longer, be sure to have a support in the center so that the bench won't develop a sag. Benches made with these steel legs, obtainable at most hardware stores, can be equipped with drawers, and the legs also have provisions for a shelf below and cross braces. If the bench, after being assembled, develops a wobble, it is time to put on back braces. These can either be wood, like 1x3 braces, or 1/8x1-inch bar stock drilled for bolts which fasten onto the legs.

If you decide to have shelves over such a bench, you can fasten them to the wall with lead mollies or toggle bolts, or if these shelves are to stand on the top of the bench, be sure to make provisions to bolt the shelf structure to the top of the workbench and also to the wall.

Covering the bench top is essential. Hardwood flooring is great and gives the bench an elegant appearance, but it is also quite expensive. The next best thing is tempered hardboard which is nailed down. Tempered hardboard must be pre-drilled for the nailing, while the softer type can be nailed without pre-drilling. A good many years ago, when machines in factories still were running off belts, worn-out canvas belting often could be had for the asking. A double layer of twenty-inch wide drive belt made an excellent bench cover, especially in those areas where blued gun parts were put down or where scopes were installed.

If you don't have adequate space for a bench and shop setup, you can make do with a sturdy old kitchen table or even a dining room table. Such furniture often can be found in outlets like the Salvation Army. Make certain that the piece is sturdy and made from solid wood. Thin woods covered with verneer cannot be used too easily since they don't take kindly to the installation of braces and other supports.

You may encounter problems with such an arrangement, since mounting a heavy machinist vise may not be practical. In this case, you'll have to make do with one of the small ball-joint vises, mounted on a separate board and held down with clamps onto the bench when in use. You can, with some juggling, learn to do most of the smaller jobs with such a setup, excepting clamping stocked rifles or barreled actions.

Storing your new tools will depend on the place where you will be working. Most of these shops find a home in the

Heavy lathe accessories should not be hung up, as an accidental drop could ruin them. Lathe and hand tools are racked so they are handy without endangering hand in reaching for them when the lathe is in operation.

basement, but for some years I used a spare bedroom. The attic is another good choice, providing you can insulate it so the winters are tolerable and you have at least an even chance of surviving the heat of summer. I have seen shops in a converted chicken coop, a garage, a converted summer kitchen — almost anywhere where you can bring in an electric line and get heat.

Ventilation is important for some jobs, and depending on the location of your shop, you may be able to get all of the necessary ventilation by opening a door or a window, or by installing a small exhaust fan in a window. I like to have my guns, ammunition and loading gear near the shop or right in it. If you are setting up new quarters, do not mount your guns near the workbench. Dust from sanding, grinding and other debris will settle all too quickly on uncovered guns and keeping sliding glass doors passably clean is more housekeeping than I care to do.

Bare light bulbs or bulbs with some sort of cover give, at best, a mediocre light. Daylight fluorescent lights, or the same in what is called egg crate housing, are much better and cost less to operate than the incandescent bulbs. When a fluorescent tube begins to flicker constantly, replace it — it uses more electricity than a new tube will cost you, and such a tube adds little to eye comfort when you are working. You will want some bench lights, with one of them located near or slightly above the bench vise. One light that swivels can be used on the bench where your grinder and drill press will be, and you also should have a light over your bullet-casting

This simple shelf over the bench holds all the tools needed for the lathe. A similar shelf on the workbench can hold micrometers, calipers, other fragile tools.

bench and one over the powder scale, with the latter arranged so that the light hits the scale and not your eyes.

If you are going to use your shop more or less daily, then your hand tools should be hung up or stored so you can see each one and choose the right one without having to look at five or six of them to be sure you have what you need. If the bench is backed against a wall, you can use peg board with the suitable hangers, but be sure to install 1x2-inch strips of wood to hold the peg board or you'll find that the hooks for the board won't slide through. Moreover, if basement walls have a tendency to be moist or there is a seepage problem, you'll forestall early rusting of your tools by keeping away from direct contact with the wall. One worthwhile investment is a dehumidifier, especially in areas where the humidity is high.

You can also build boards with pre-drilled holes for holding tools. When arranged in a step-like fashion, this makes a good arrangement, providing of course that you put all your tools back where they belong as soon as you are through with them. Although some like the magnetic tool holders, I cannot work up much enthusiasm for them. They are relatively expensive, especially when you have to store a fair number of tools, and I don't like magnetized tools.

If you must store tools in drawers underneath the bench, here is a trick that saves a lot of clutter and allows you to store more stuff in one drawer. Depending on the depth of the drawer, make up a shallow tray using pressboard as base and ½x½-inch or similar scrap, cut on your bench saw, as sides. The tray slides back and forth in the drawer on runners which also are made from scrap wood and are nailed to the sides of the drawer. Such trays are usually about half the length of the drawer from front to back, thus allowing easy access to the contents in the lower part of the drawer.

I don't like to have mikes, vernier calipers, magnifiers and other delicate tools and instruments bounce around on the bench. Borrowing an idea from the big industrial lathes, I have made a couple of stands for my workbench and the lathe bench, and you are more than welcome to copy the idea. The size of the tray depends only on you and the amount of scrap lumber you have on hand. You may want one or two supports which consist of twelve inches of three-quarter-inch

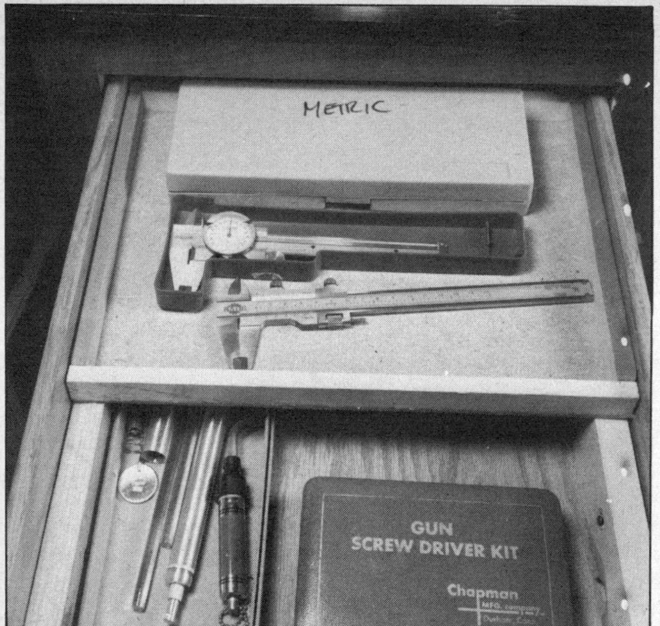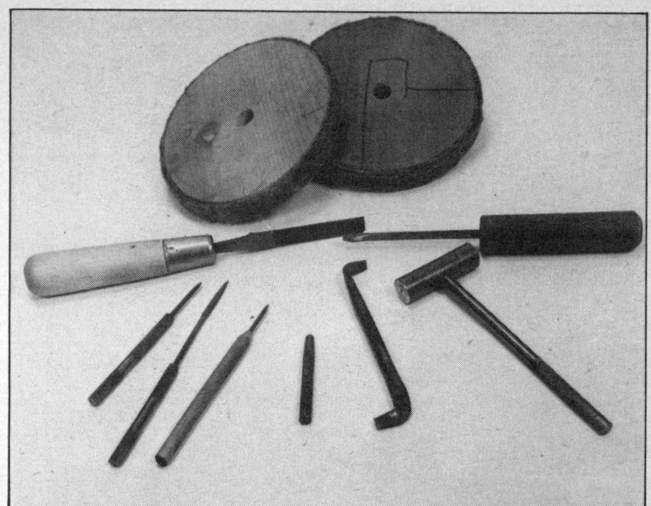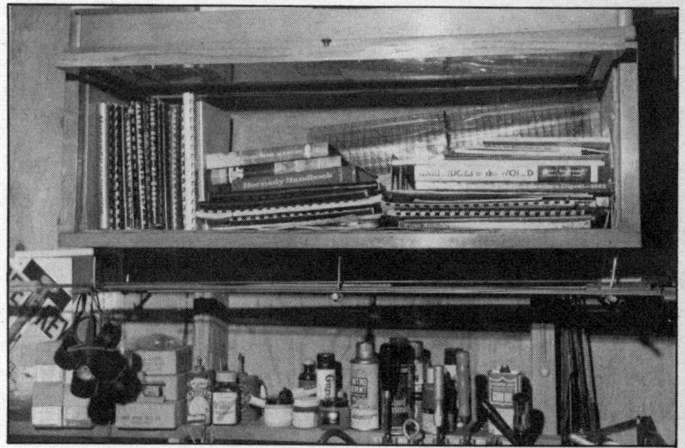

(Above) Converting a deep drawer into a shallow one is simple. This can double the storage area. (Upper right) Homemade tools include chisel from a file, scribes from Swiss files, hammer made from scrap, screwdriver made with broomhandle grip. Wheels are cut from pine, felt edges glued on for buffing. (Right) Old bookcase is mounted on shelf support brackets, anchored by screws.

galvanized pipe threaded on both ends and equipped with flanges.

Especially in temporary arrangements, where you cannot set up your workshop and leave the tools on a wall board or somewhere near or on the bench, you may want to fall back on the use of some sort of tool chest for housing your gunsmithing tools. Brownell's basic gunsmithing tool kit is a self-contained little shop, except for the vise. As you add tools, you can add another tool kit or chest, thus protecting your investment from those who need a tool in a hurry and don't care about returning it.

By the way, I would suggest that you make it clear to all those who have access to your gunsmithing tools and equipment that borrowing a little bitty screwdriver for just a little bitty minute is okay, as long as the borrower is either willing to face the firing squad in the morning or is able to leave a $1000 cash bond with you. That sort of thing tends to discourage tools and other gunsmithing paraphernalia from wandering off into Never-never Land.

In my years of wandering through gunshops and home workshops, I have seen only one other shop where the owner made provisions for book shelves and storage for other literature. You'll collect all sorts of takedown instructions, operating instructions, books and pamphlets which you want near the bench so that you can refer to them easily.

Another gimmick that seems to have passed from favor is the overhead rack that allows you to store shipping boxes, gun stocks and even a few long guns you are working on or want to work on. If you have a special place where you'll clean guns, do touch-up bluing and other such jobs, you will need not only a bench light, but some means of storing your cleaning rods. If the bench is deep enough, you can install cup hooks on the side of the bench, or install a shallow shelf under

the bench top, or dream up some other way of storing cleaning rods — but do all this before you drive the last nail and set the last lag bolt.

Some tools can be made in your home workshop. Scribes can be made from Allen wrenches which are ground to a fine point, then set into a handle made from one-quarter-inch dowel rod. Broken or worn out Swiss files also can be converted easily into scribes, and broom handles, chopped into suitable lengths, make good handles for files. You can make your own screwdrivers, and if the handle of one of the store bought ones breaks, don't fret — you can easily fashion your own plastic handle at a fraction of the cost of a new handle from the hardware shop. Worn-out files make admirable chisels and stock scrapers.

You can make your own sanding wheels and even some polishing wheels. A piece of drill rod, slotted at one end and set into a handle at the other makes a great inside polisher with a strip of emery cloth. You can make your own centering punches and, later on, learn to make your own brass hammer.

There is no end to the things you can make or do once you have learned the basics of shopwork. One friend of mine, not satisfied with the tool holder of his twelve-inch lathe, made his own quick-change holder that, when bought over the counter, would have cost close to $150. Another friend developed a liking for machine working. Not being able to afford a new lathe, he bought a badly abused one, cleaned and rebuilt it, and now makes his own barrels and even chambers them.

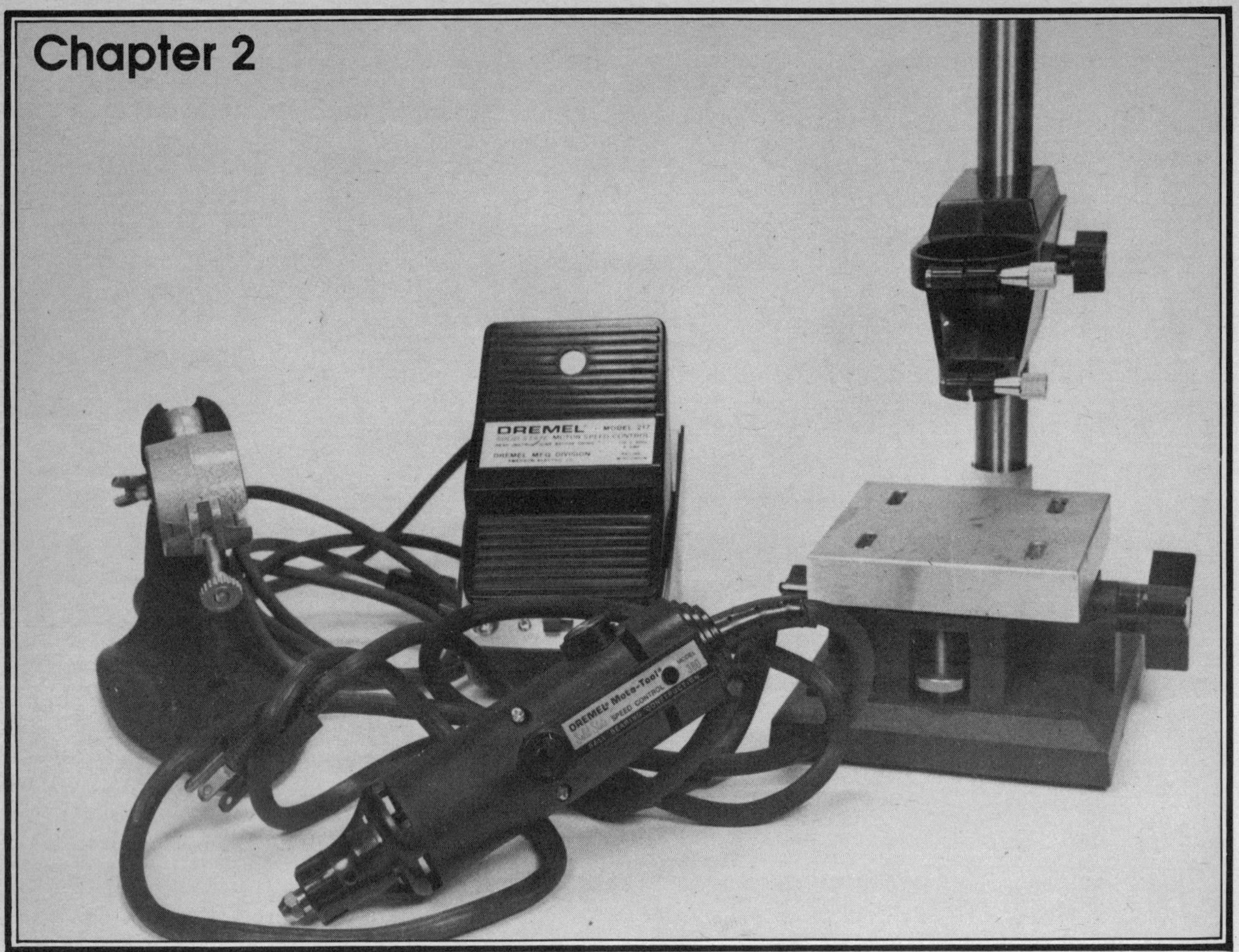

Chapter 2

Although it is the least expensive power tool of all, the Dremel Moto-Tool is the most versatile and useful.

POWER TOOLS FOR THE GUN TINKERER

IF YOU have heard that the old-timers in the gunsmithing field got along without power tools, excepting perhaps a lathe, you heard right. But talk with some of these old gents and you'll find that they were mighty happy to get their first grinder, buffer or drill press. Most of today's amateur gunsmiths have better equipment in their shops than did the old gunsmiths, and while there is no doubt about the convenience and ease with which we can do a job today, somehow those old guys not only were fine gunsmiths, but first-class artisans.

Apprentice machinists had to file their own V-blocks and true-blocks, often made their own tool chests, plus other tools we would not even consider making ourselves. That power and machine tools are handy was proved to me some years ago. A machinist had loaned me a set of V-blocks which he had filed by hand from two chunks of steel forty years

It Doesn't Require A Full-Scale Machine Shop To Do Your Thing!

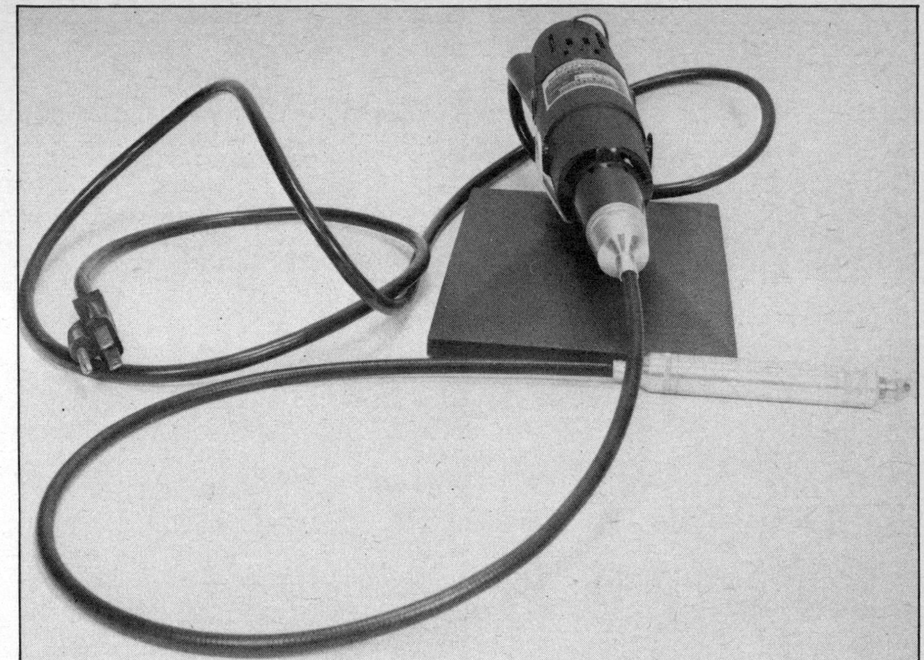

Another handy device from Dremel is the Moto-Flex. Smaller hand piece is easier to use, but requires more precious bench space.

earlier. I used these blocks as patterns for blocks I was making, the only difference being that I first used a milling machine, then a surface grinder. In less than one evening's work I had completed copying those blocks that my hunting crony had made in two months of steady filing.

When you start thinking about power tools, and before going shopping for one or more of them, consider first how much you really will need the tool, and secondly, whether or not the tool has some versatility for your gunsmithing hobby. A milling machine mills, and that is all it will do. In contrast to this, a drill press can be made to drill holes, to tap, grind and polish. It can be used to engine turn parts, and with some patience, you can even use the drill press as a substitute milling machine for such jobs as dovetail slot cutting. Remember what was said about shop layout in the first chapter. If you are thinking about adding power tools eventually, you will need more floor space, more electric outlets, and perhaps even a special line run into the shop area. Trying to find room for a twelve-inch lathe in a crowded room is impossible, especially if you want to be able to use the lathe for cutting long stock.

Some sort of hand grinder/polisher is a worthwhile investment. The Dremel Moto-Tool, the most readily available of these tools, is reasonably priced and, thanks to the many attachments available, has the greatest degree of versatility of this type of power tool. Moto-Tool accessories can be bought in many shops, including hardware and discount stores, and because of its popularity, there is never any shortage of accessories, parts or service. When mounted in the Dremel stand, it becomes especially versatile since your hands are free to hold and manipulate the work.

If a flexible shaft tool is more to your liking, the Dremel Moto-Flex, running at 20,000 rpm, is an excellent choice, but this tool cannot, for instance, be chucked into the Dremel mini drill press stand. With one of the regular Dremel tools in such a stand and with a board clamped onto the table of the drill press stand, you can even do a limited amount of engine turning.

Power sanders are useful for stockwork. I favor the belt sander for any work that can be sanded, buffed, polished,

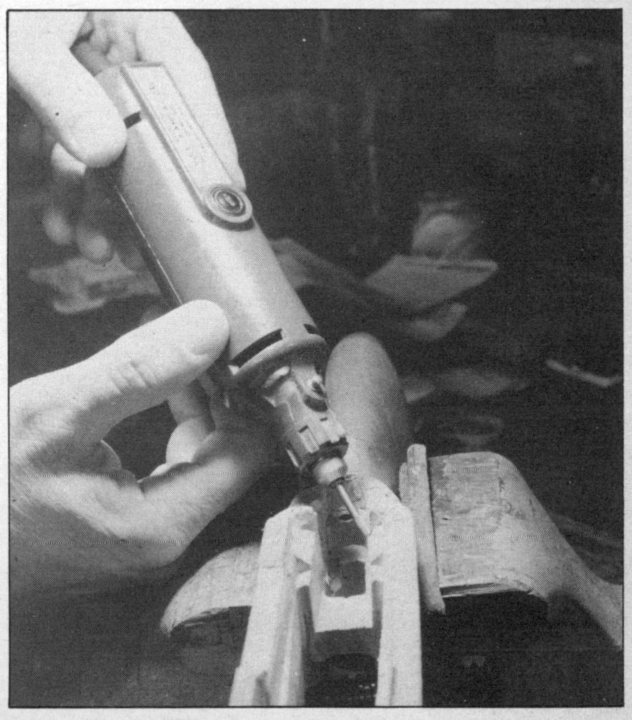

Final inletting of rifle stock is a skill which may be mastered in but a few hours' practice with the Dremel Moto-Tool, available at many retail outlets.

A belt sander does much more than sand. It may be used to polish metal, sharpen knives and other tools and is essential for much of rifle stockwork including recoil pad installation. Variety of grits adds versatility.

shaped. Such a sander can even be used to form and sharpen tools. Since belts with four different grades of grit are offered, the belt sander has many uses and has become, at least in my shop, one of the most important tools.

A tool grinder should be on hand, and it is best to buy one with at least six-inch wheels. If you shop around, you may be able to find a used unit and perhaps replace the old wheels with new ones, or you may also be able to find an arbor and either buy a reconditioned motor or liberate one from an old refrigerator. The small four-inch wheel grinder is too small for some of the larger jobs for which you will need a grinder, but for touching up screwdriver blades and other such jobs, it will do the trick, providing you install a better light source than the one usually installed on these small grinders.

While the smaller grinder can be bench-mounted, the larger units should be fastened to a separate stand. This either can be bought or homemade if you have access to welding equipment. Larger welding shops usually have enough scrap pipe and flat stock on hand to weld something together. If you go this route, make a small sketch indicating height, size of top plate, and all other essential dimensions. Such a sketch will save time and labor in the shop, hence will help to keep costs down. If you have the top steel plate, predrill or at least mark all the holes, and indicate front and back so the job does not come out backwards.

Doing a little work yourself, you can have a buffer for about $20. Buy a polishing head or arbor and the needed buffing wheels — more about these later. If your bench layout permits, you may be able to take power off one of the electric motors already in use. If not, scare up another refrigerator motor. You'll need a pulley for the motor and a belt to link motor and polishing head. To keep the belt under tension, mount the motor so that the weight of the motor will put just the right amount of tension on the belt. Buffing wheels are

Large grinder with six-inch wheel will grind, shape and sharpen many tools and parts. Stand is welded from scrap.

Small grinder may be mounted on bench and is handy for reshaping screwdriver blades and other lightweight sharpening chores.

relatively inexpensive, so buy enough that you never mix two different grits of buffing compound on the same wheel. Use a felt marking pen to mark the grit grade on both sides of each wheel. This will save a lot of guessing later on and will speed the job of buffing gun parts and tools. A couple of wheels used only for rouges, such as rust removal rouge, jeweler's rouge and so on, make it much easier to keep other tools in good order. Similarly, a fine, medium and a coarse wire wheel should be on hand for the sundry cleanup jobs you will no doubt run into.

There is no trick to making a number of wood wheels which become real handy polishing wheels when the edges are surfaced with felt or leather. Years ago, it was the accepted way of doing things — you made your own buffing wheels, and leather wheels were very much in vogue. A special binding glue was required to glue the circles of leather together to form the buffing surface. I made one up some years ago, but discarded it after one use and spent the rest of the week cleaning up the shop.

In using a buffing wheel, remember that even the finest of the final polishing grade of any buffing compound is abrasive and that it will cut steel. More than one sharp edge on the slide of a Colt .45 or a Mauser action has come out rounded and out of whack. The secret of good buffing is to keep the work moving with smooth, even strokes.

A drill press — a table model is fine and there is no need for a floor model — is a nice luxury. But you can do a great deal of drilling, buffing and even engine turning without one. Most every home handyman has an electric drill. The standard one-quarter-inch drill will do in a pinch, but I favor the three-eighths or even the one-half-inch drill. When such a drill is mounted in one of the many available drill stands, it is converted into a drill press, lacking only the adjustable table and perhaps also the speed control of the drill press.

Mounting electric motor on hinged board allows weight of motor to maintain belt tension, above. Cloth buffing wheels are marked with felt tip pen indicating grade of grit. Three grades of wire wheels is adequate.

For engine turning, you will need one of the engine-turning jigs or fixtures. If a drill press is used, a compound or universal compound drill press vise is needed for such jobs as engine turning, while the drill and stand arrangement requires only a previously scribed plate that is bolted to the base of the stand, with the jig being indexed and clamped into place manually. A drill or bench vise — and this is not the same as a machinist vise — is essential for drilling, so be sure to have one before tackling any job with either a drill press or the drill-in-stand system. The drill and bench vise should be bolted to the table of either drilling setup.

A bench drill press, having more power, will do more jobs faster and also somewhat better than a drill mounted in a special stand. On the other hand, one of the best gunsmiths I know uses nothing but a three-eighths-inch electric drill in a stand — he sold me his drill press some ten or so years ago, and both of us have lived happily ever after. If you do buy a drill press, you have to decide whether or not you need a tilting table model. My second-hand press does not have this feature, and so far I have not missed the tilting table arrangement.

A lathe can easily become the most important of the power tools for the home gunsmith. The choice can be somewhat bewildering and, as I learned from sad experience, you had best study the available machines before spending your hard-earned money.

The small model maker's machines are great for doing little jobs such as turning a firing pin, but they are way underpowered and much too small for most of the gunsmithing jobs. The Unimat, the Maximat, the Machinex and other such combination tools that convert into miniature drill press, milling machine and lathe are not adequate for gunsmithing. In addition to being underpowered, the holes through the headstock are not large enough.

The six-inch lathe is the smallest one that should be considered, and even here you are severely limited in the jobs that can be done. The ten-inch lathe is probably the one most often seen in nonprofessional shops, and will do most, if not all, of the jobs you are likely to tackle, including tapering barrels, chambering and threading the barrel shank. The twenty-inch lathe, essentially, is nothing more than a beefed up and larger edition of the ten-inch lathe, but it would be my choice if I were to re-equip my shop. A quick-change gear box is highly desirable and though a lathe with this feature is quite a bit more expensive, believe me when I say that you should definitely go that route — changing gears with the other type is a time-consuming and ornery chore.

Depending on the tool and where you buy your lathe, you will have to face several questions. Most machines come with electric motors, but without any of the attachments. Since costs of machine tools keep going up and up, it is a good investment to buy whatever extras you want for your lathe at the time you order the machine. A steady rest and follow rest, as well as a four-jaw chuck, are essential. A face plate and

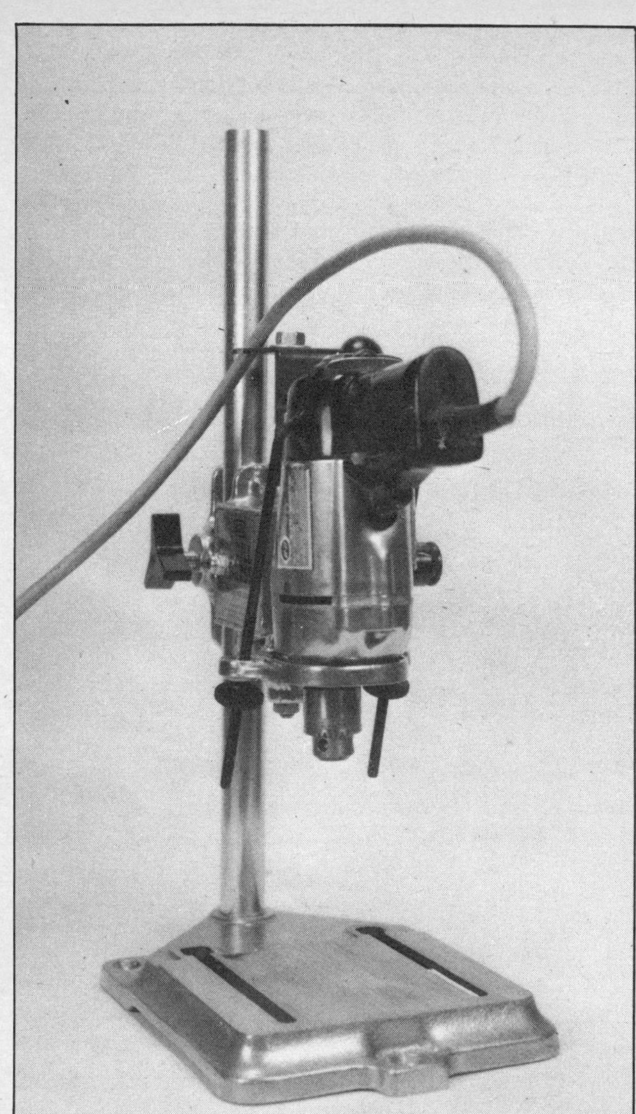

back plate, complete with dogs, should also be ordered, but I would pass on the metric gears if they are offered as extras. The milling attachment has some merit, especially if you do not have a drill press, but a tapering attachment is not really required since a certain amount of taper is built into the tail stock of most of these machines. Dave Corbin of Corbin Manufacturing imports a number of quality machine tools, from drill presses to production lathes which are ideally suitable for the hobby and small production shop.

Although learning to run a lathe is not difficult, there are a number of finer points which are a bit difficult to figure out alone. If there is a school near you that offers machine shop courses, by all means, take a course or two. You will not only learn the finer points of operating machine tools, but will also have a chance to see some of the more complex tools in use.

As mentioned before, a drill press and also a lathe can be used for some milling jobs. Corbin offers two combination machines which not only function as precision drill press, but also as full-fledged milling machines. Such a machine can be used to mill scope bases and dovetail slots with ease, and is

Unimat power tool, above, will handle small jobs only. Six-inch lathe, right, is a bit small for barrel work but is essential for many home gunsmithing jobs.

Corbin combination drill press and milling machine is for advanced worker who has the space and the need.

The Corbin ten-inch lathe has
the power and size to handle
all types of gunsmith work,
including barrel chambering.

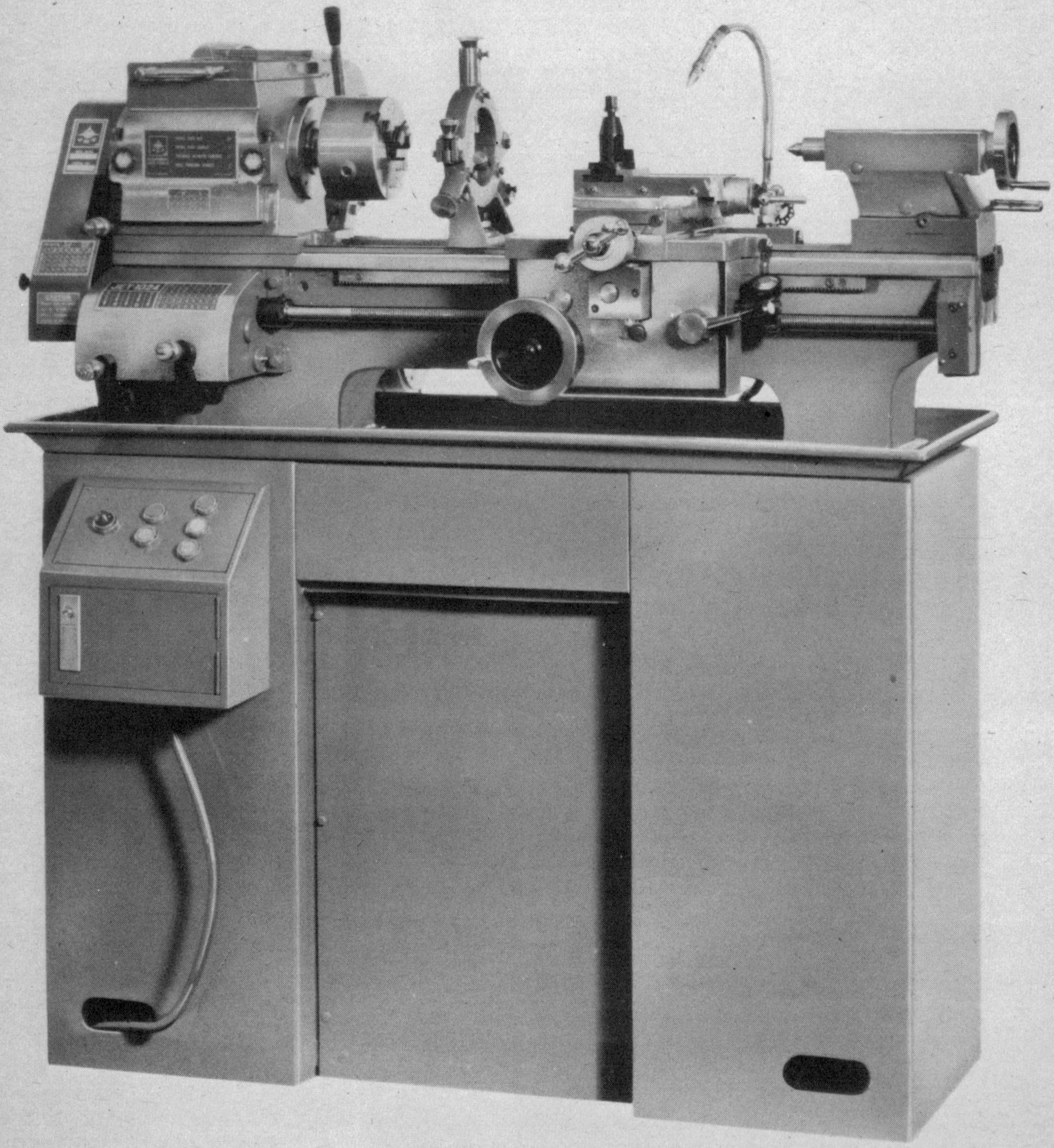

also capable of some of the more complex machine jobs which are usually reserved for the large milling machines.

Valuable only in the larger professional shops are power hacksaws and powered cut-off wheels. A one-quarter-inch or a three-eighths-inch electric drill, especially when mounted in a horizontal stand, can be used with the smaller cut-off wheels, but these shop refinements are really not essential, especially since such stock as solid rod can be cut on the lathe and the cut can then be shaped or contoured.

If working with wood is to your liking, you will want to make stocks, often cutting them from stock blanks. A table or radial arm saw can be used for some of the roughing jobs, with a band saw being used for the finer cuts. With a fine-toothed wood saw on such a machine tool, installation of recoil pads is greatly simplified, while the same band saw with a metal-cutting blade, running at a much slower speed, can be used for cutting metal, from sectioning cartridge cases to cutting cleaning rods and scope mounts. A band saw that is destined to see use on wood and metal should have easily accessible pulleys for the blade so that changing is simplified. Changing the speed of the saw can either be done by changing the belt arrangement between the pulleys or by adding a countershaft between the motor and the saw which automatically slows down the speed of the saw when a metal-cutting blade is installed.

Although not essential, one convenient extra is a spare drill chuck, either one with the key arrangement or a keyless one. The latter, though a bit more costly, is that much more handy. This chuck can quickly be threaded onto the shaft of your buffer or the grinder and, depending on the length of the shaft, you may even be able to leave whatever wheel is on the tool in place.

If you have an electric drill, you will find many uses for it in your shop. If you don't have one, I suggest that you don't buy one of the cheaper and usually very light drills, but one that, without load, runs 2000 rpm. As mentioned earlier, I prefer the three-eighths-inch drill, but with a speed-reducing attachment, the smaller drill can be used with drill bits measuring up to one-half inch. While a reversing gear is handy, it is not essential for your gun tinkering. A rubber sanding disc and a small arbor that can be chucked into the drill makes it possible to tackle jobs which cannot be handled on the larger tools.

All of the power tools and, for that fact, all of the electrical outlets in your shop should be properly grounded. The adapters that allow you to use a male plug with ground in the standard two-prong outlet are useful, but all possible care must be taken to see that they are properly grounded. Failure to do so can result in an electrical fire.

Time-saving trick is to mount extra drill chuck onto threaded end of buffer spindle.

TOOLS FOR THE ADVANCED TINKERER

Your Efforts May Be Advanced, But The Tools Remain Relatively Simple

IN THIS CHAPTER, you will find a number of tools, gadgets, jigs and gauges you should know about. Some of them you may need some time in the future, others perhaps will hold little interest for you, now or later. But you should be aware of these tools, partly so that when you decide how to acquire one, you will know what to get, and partly to show you that others before you also have encountered a specific problem in the shop.

The most common problem must be the frozen screw. Later you will learn how to freeze a screw so it won't work loose under recoil. In freeing stuck screws, if a properly fitting screwdriver blade won't budge the screw, first try holding the screwdriver blade in the slot of the sticking screw, then whack the handle of the screwdriver with a rawhide mallet. If this does not break the bond, you have to try either the B-Square screw jack, an impact driver or a ratchet. Before resorting to any of these tools, try applying a few drops of a product called Bust Rust. Found in most hardware stores, this miraculous stuff will often help loosen a frozen screw.

If scope ring and scope base screws look like they have been chewed up by a bunch of mice, you can replace them with new screws, either with the conventional slotted head ones or with Allen head screws. Complete assortments of both can be ordered from Brownell's. Incidentally, Allen

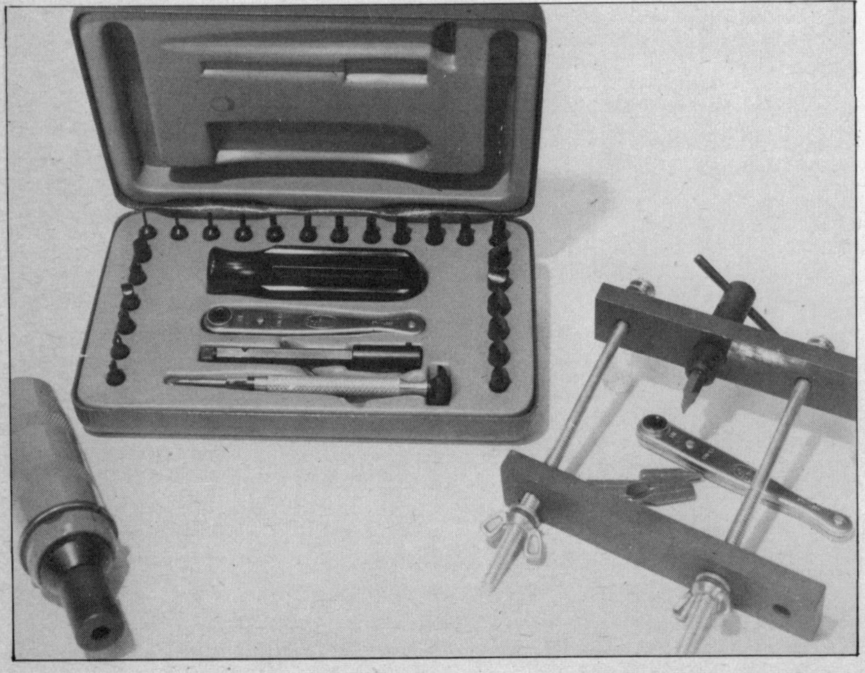

When the day comes that a stuck screw will not budge, these tools are available. From left: Impact driver, special screwdriver set with ratchet handle, and B-Square screw jack. All will work well.

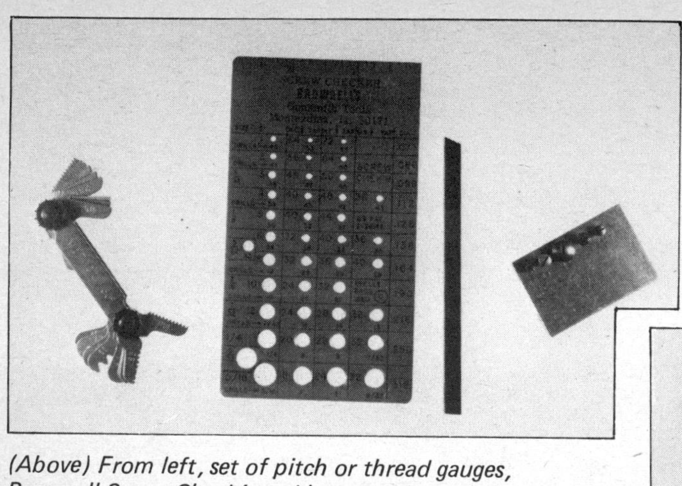

(Above) From left, set of pitch or thread gauges, Brownell Screw Check'r and homemade steel block that allows quick checking of thread on screw.

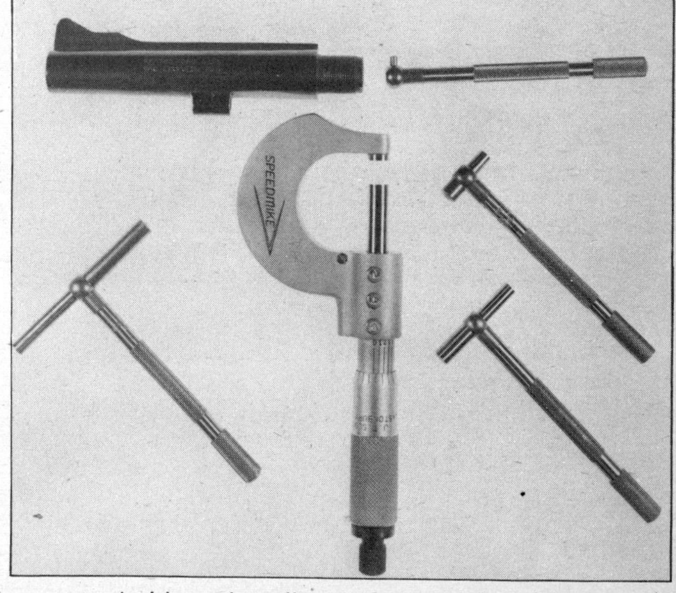

(Above) Depth to which hole is drilled in six-gun frame can be measured with vernier caliper, saving cost of special gauge. (Top right) Machinists clamps at left of photo were purchased, but a set can be made from scrap stock. A piece of heavy glass doubles as surface plate; here it is supported on test tube corks, holding it level. V blocks are sold with or without clamps and are best purchased with the clamps, as these can be quite difficult to make. (Bottom right) If vernier caliper cannot be used, set of telescoping depth gauges can come in handy for such work.

head screw heads are also known as socket head or hex head socket screws.

If you run into a screw which seems to have an odd-ball thread and therefore does not seat easily, you need to check the thread on the screw. This can be done with the help of a Screw Check'r or with screw pitch gauges. For bench use, you can make up a small test block with the help of the suitable drill and tap for specific screws, such as those used in scope rings and mounts.

When drilling and tapping any round object, from gun barrel or receiver to drill rod stock, secure clamping is important. The V-block, with or without the special clamps, is essential. As you get into metalworking, you will find literature that makes mention of these blocks, as well as something variously called a true plate or surface plate. These plates are needed for tool and die makers, pattern makers and others who do precision work. Few professional gunsmiths have one, so don't rush out and buy one — they are expensive and require considerable care. But for a dollar or two you can have something made that is almost as good, although somewhat fragile. The nearest commercial glass shop can cut a piece of plate glass, about eight inches square. The glass should be at least one-half-inch thick, and when the corners are trued and the edges bevelled, you have a dandy surface block. Such a hunk of glass can be used to see if a cartridge is out of round by simply rolling it across the glass while watching from the front — any wobble in the bullet as the cartridge is rolled across the glass will indicate that the case is not round or the bullet is seated crookedly.

A pair of machinist's clamps have saved the day for me more than once. While you can buy them from any of the supply houses, with a little bit of work and a few files, you can make your own. The required threading can be done with a drill and tap, or on a lathe.

As indicated earlier, you won't need a depth gauge, since the moving scale of the vernier caliper can be used, giving you a direct readout. To measure the diameter of a hole, small or large, the telescoping and small hole gauges come into play. Once the gauge has entered the hole, the head of the gauge is expanded so there is just enough play to be able to slip the locked gauge out of the hole. The expanded head of the gauge then is measured with a micrometer.

Bullet and cartridge case spinners which check concentricity are nothing new to the handloader and benchrest shooter. A dial gauge on a stand, though not needed too often, can save the day for you. I did not believe this, but learned differently in a hurry when I tried to run a short piece of stock in my lathe which then developed an awful wobble. My lathe had not gone haywire, but the piece of stock was out of whack. Scribe or line-marking stands, and

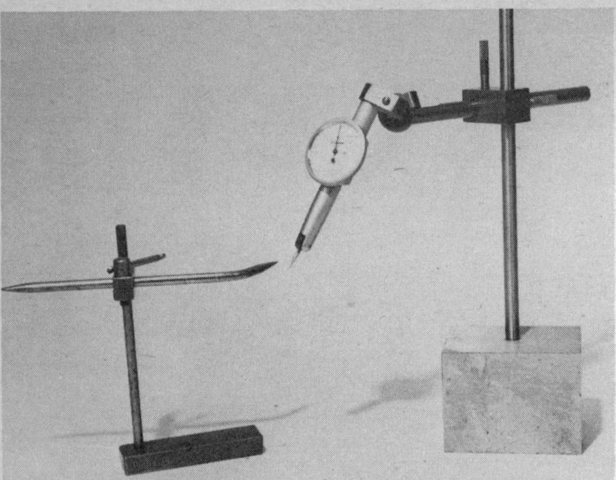

Stands such as these can be made from salvaged scrap. Machine shops are good sources for such materials. (Right) Trigger pull scales come in many sizes, shapes. Weights are better, but thus far, author admits, he has not found the right set for use on double actions.

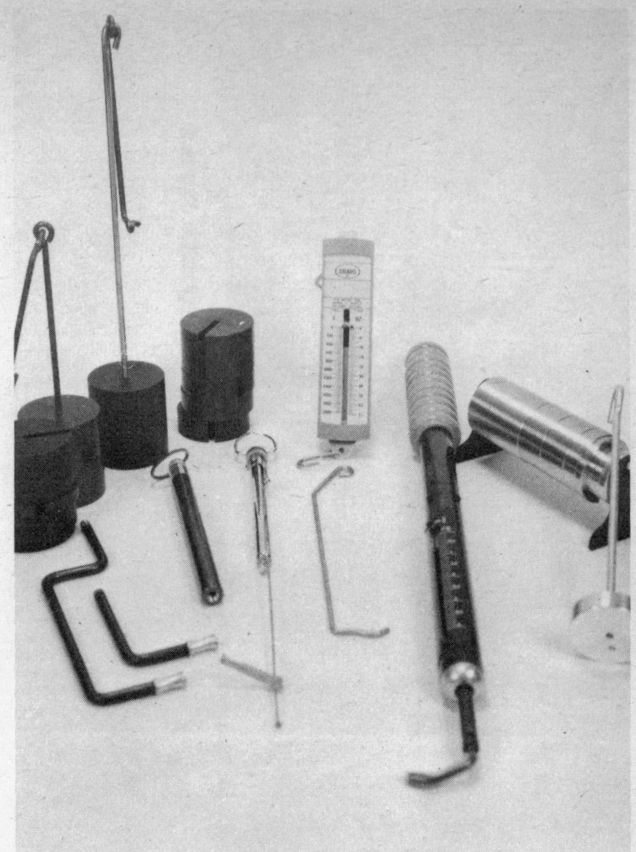

clamps and stands for the dial gauge can be bought, but you can make them just as easily yourself.

In making such a stand, you can use any scrap block of steel and either paint it or engine turn the surfaces for eye appeal and to reduce chances of rusting. The height of the upright rod is governed by the use the stand will see, and the size of the base depends on the height of the rod and also on the weight of the object that will be attached to the upright rod. In deep hole drilling, be sure to run the drill at a fairly slow speed, using plenty of cutting oil, and be sure the drill size and tap size agree.

Should the fit of the rod in the block be a bit on the loose side, the hole being a thousandth or so undersize, you can wrap a piece of fine steel wool into the thread on the bottom of the rod, add a couple of drops of Loctite, then turn the rod in that way.

Drill grinding jig is mounted on the base plate of the power grinder. Before first drill sharpening job, study surfaces of new drill, then attempt to copy these cuts on the bit that is being sharpened. It takes practice.

Expert machinists have another trick which requires some skill on the lathe. They cut a slight oversize thread, then force the thread into the tapped hole. Another and much simpler way of getting a tight fit is to freeze the part that is oversize, wrap the male thread with either a bit of steel wool or the joint tape used by plumbers, and thread the male part into the frozen part. Once the latter thaws and warms to room temperature, you have a tight fit.

Trigger pull scales and weights present a problem in some cases. The spring scales, generally not considered as reliable as the weights, go only to a limited amount of weight, thus are suitable for rifles, shotguns and single-action revolvers. But the pull of most double-action six-guns will defeat the spring scales. Although I have bought a set of each of the weights commercially available, they too fall short of expectations when it comes to measuring the DA pull of a revolver. Go to one of the larger-scale houses and buy a set of slotted weights and, with the help of a length of rod, you can make your own set of trigger pull weights.

A front sight pusher is a handy gadget, but you won't need one often enough to warrant the cost. By using a brass drift and a small brass or ballpeen hammer, you can achieve the same result. The brass drift you can buy, and if there is a brass foundry near you, you may be able to pick up some pieces of scrap. If one or two of the pieces of scrap brass measure more than one-half inch in diameter, you can make up your own brass hammer by drilling a hole into the piece of brass rod stock and threading a length of drill rod on it. The handle of the drill rod either can be left plain or can be knurled on a lathe prior to installation, or you can make a plastic handle for your new bench tool.

When drilling an action or the muzzle of a barrel to install a

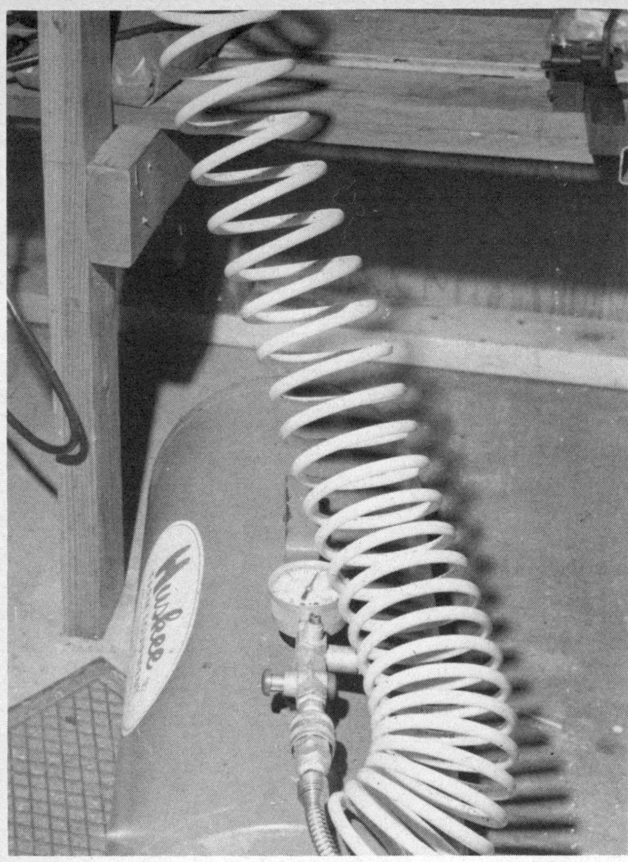

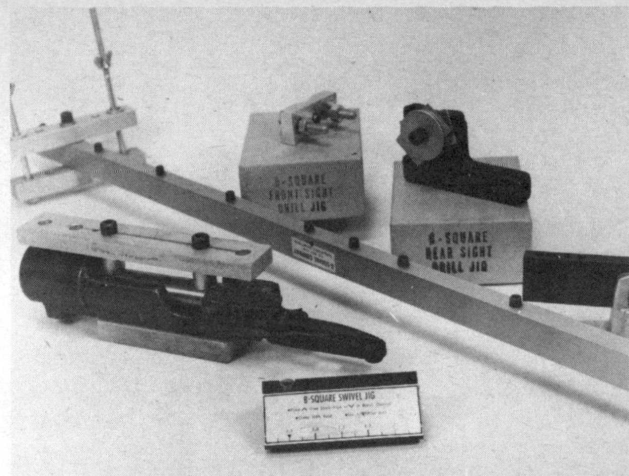

(Left) Compressed air tank with hose is helpful in shop. Blow out air occasionally to do away with condensed moisture. (Above) Selection of the jigs from B-Square have specific uses. Firm's catalog explains uses and tells how to set up each jig for specific application.

front sight, it is all too easy to have something slip in the last second. The result, almost invariably, is a messed-up piece of work that cannot be repaired easily. You are not going to lose any of your macho image by using a jig for the drilling — lots of the top-ranking pros do it, having learned their lesson years ago.

In any drilling, you must measure precisely the location of the hole to be drilled. If you are working on blued steel, you can make it fairly easily, but lines are hard to see on unblued parts. A thin coating of layout blue will save a lot of eyestrain. Apply it, let dry for a while, then draw all your lines on the dye. When the job is finished, the dye can be washed off. A scribe, either bought or made in the shop, is needed to mark lines, and a center punch is required to mark the point where the tip of the drill starts into the metal. The work will have to be held under the drill, whether you use a drill press or the special stand with an electric drill. What looks to be safely locked into the jaws of the machinist vise often will slip the moment pressure is put on the work by the rotating drill, so be sure to lock and support the work properly. When working on a barrel, support the end that extends out from the drill press table.

In learning to drill metal, start with some scrap. A piece of flat bar stock, even aluminum, can be used. This is a good way to learn how to mark the location of holes to be drilled; then you can use the same piece of scrap to learn how to set up the job and finally drill it.

Feed the drill slowly and use cutting oil to prevent the drill from burning up and to help in the removal of chips. If your drill bit has been used, look at the tip under a magnifying glass. If there is the slightest bit of rounding of the tip, either regrind the drill or get a new one.

Regrinding or sharpening a drill bit is an art that can only be learned by practice. The electric drill sharpeners which resemble an electric pencil sharpener are toys and have not worked out in my shop. A drill grinding attachment added to your grinding wheel will be helpful, but by no means guarantees that you will get correctly ground drill bits — only experience will teach you this trick.

The B-Square Company is probably the biggest maker and supplier of gunsmithing jigs. There is a jig that makes it easy to install a recoil pad; a sling swivel installation jig and kit; a jig for installation of a scope on the Ruger Mini-14; a jig for the M94 side mount; a sight soldering jig and a rib soldering fixture; and there are jigs for drilling sights, for drilling most any rifle action. And if B-Square does not have what you need — and that would indeed be a rare instance — Dan Bechtel, the head honcho, will dream one up for you and the others who need or want such a jig or fixture.

One item of shop equipment I consider important is seldom seen anywhere except in professional shops — a compressed air rig. These are quite expensive, and there is no way that I know of that you can cobble one together yourself. If budget and space preclude an air compressor, you still can have a limited amount of compressed air in the shop by buying one of the portable compressed air tanks sold in farm supply stores. These tanks hold air fairly well, are light enough to be taken out of the shop, put into the car, and air, of course, can be had from the local gas station. Compressed air is great to blow out chips from a deep drilled hole, to remove filings and other chips from the bench and tools, and it is handy to get wood dust and shavings out of the work area while chipping away on a gun stock.

Although I do little checkering, I have found that a checkering cradle is a great help. For cleaning up checkering, repairs or recutting impressed checkering, I lock the stock into the checkering cradle, and the cradle itself is locked either into the swivel base machinist's vise or the woodworking vise which, however, does not have a rotating base. A serviceable and quite inexpensive checkering cradle is sold by Brownell's, and is more than adequate for most stockworkers.

To practice laying out a drilling job, use scrap stock to determine the center of a spot, how to mark it, how to drill.

It does not happen often, but often enough to give you fits — you get the bases mounted, the rings and the scope installed, then find that one of the bases is a thousandth or more too low.

One way of taking care of this problem, and I have not seen it used for many years, is to apply a thin layer of solder, what is called tinning. But that's a lot easier said than done. A much simpler way to taking care of this one is to insert a shim. Brownell's not only has precut scope mounting shims, but also steel and brass shim stock. A small assortment of shim stock, once it is on hand, has a surprising amount of uses, and one use I recently learned was to shim a piece of work in the headstock of the lathe that had to be trued and faced off.

When working on actions of guns, and while testing the functioning, **never** use live ammo! Sometimes the suggestion is made that removal of the firing pin is enough as far as safety is concerned. At first glance, that sounds like a reasonable suggestion, but removal of the pin from certain actions is a

Brownell checkering cradle is adequate for most jobs, but locked into a woodworking vise, movement of the cradle is somewhat limited, since it does not permit rotation of the cradle and stock. Author discusses technique in text.

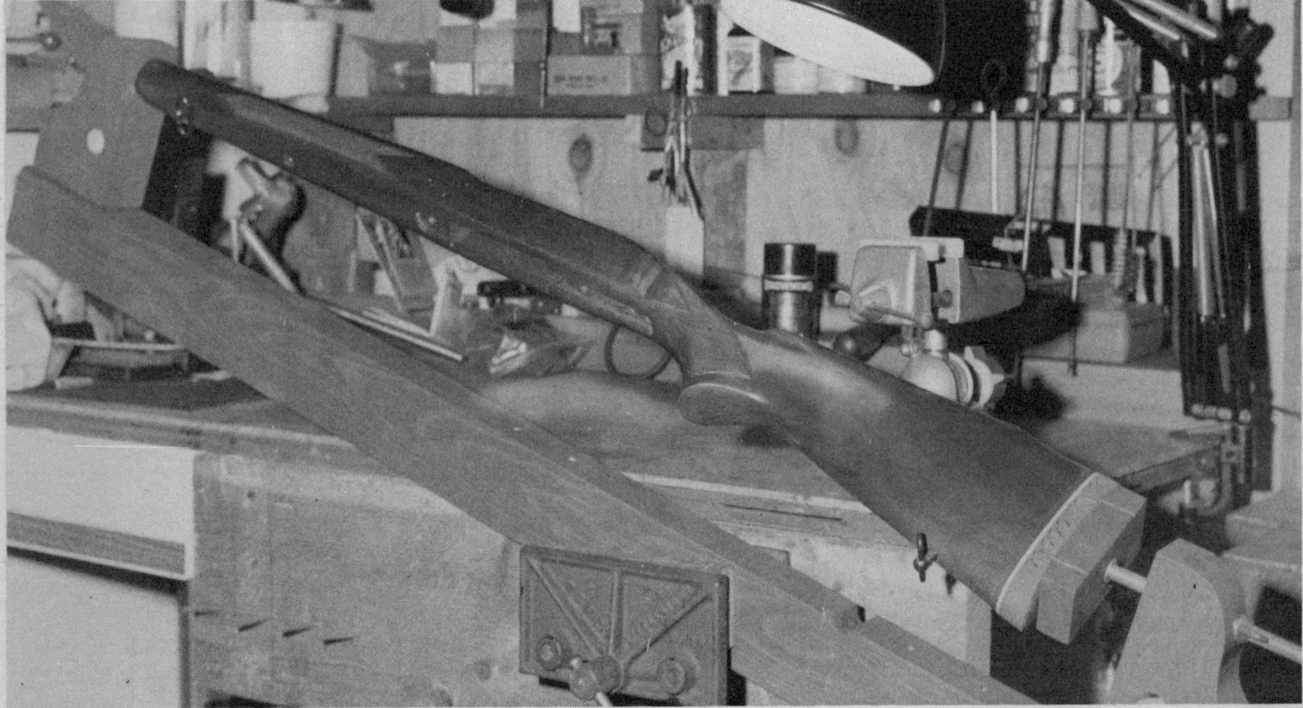

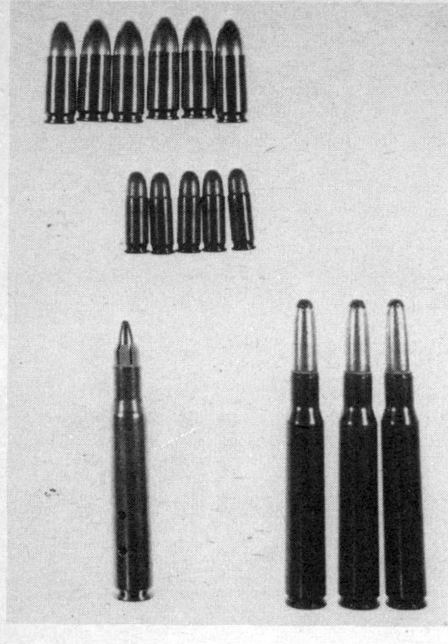

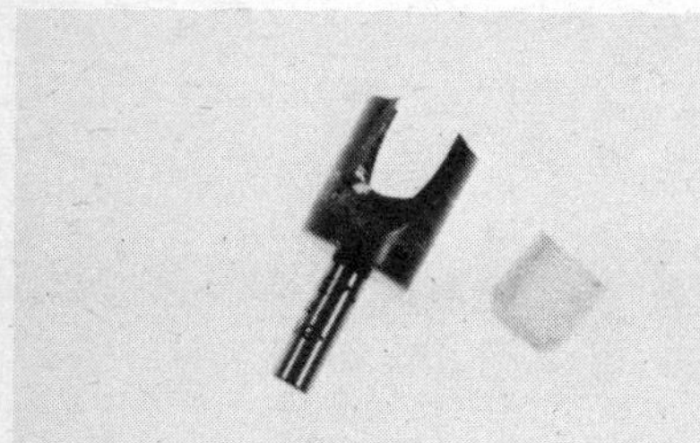

(Above) A short length of scrap I-beam is used in the author's shop in place of an anvil. (Upper left) Winchester dummy rounds can be ordered or made up by handloading. If the latter, drill with a hole to identify as a dummy. Shown are (from top) 9mm Luger, .25 ACP, three rounds of .30/06 dummies. The Remington Accelerator was drilled out as author suggests in the text. (Left) Plug cutter with a plug cut from soft pine. A quarter-inch drill can be used. For larger plugs, author recommends using jig saw.

first-rate headache for most home gunsmiths. It is far easier and safer to use dummy rounds. If you are a handloader, you can make those up yourself, leaving a spent primer in the primer pocket of each case and seating the bullet so that the finished round has the factory spec overall length. To prevent mistakes, drill each case. If you don't handload, you can buy dummy rounds which are made by Winchester. These dummies are offered in many calibers, both in rifle and handgun.

When working with any kind of power tool, eye protection should be worn. This can be either in the form of regular industrial safety glasses, shooting glasses or a plastic face shield. If you are wearing corrective glasses, check with the man who made up your glasses — a number of the newer glasses, especially those with plastic lenses, meet the safety specs.

When operating a grinder, lathe, drill press or buffer, roll up the sleeves of your shirt well above the elbows, take off rings, bracelets and your watch. Power equipment, even when controlled by a dead man's switch, can catch clothing and jewelry; serious injuries can result if such items are caught in machine tools.

Stockmaker's hand screws, sometimes also known as action screws or bolts, are essential when you begin to stock your own rifles. Made for a variety of actions, both military and sporter, these screws will enable you to fit action and stock accurately.

When salvaging old military stocks — and some of them have surprisingly fine wood underneath all the crud — the military hardware is removed. To fill in the holes, I cut suitable plugs from either the forend or the handguard wood.

Smaller plugs are cut with plug cutters on the drill press, larger ones are cut with a coping saw. Plugs need not be overly deep or long, and the wood should be lined up, if possible, so the grain of the plug and the grain of the stock coincide. Glue the plug into place with a good wood glue, then, after the job has dried and the plug has set, sand smooth, fill in edges if need be, and finish the stock.

Every so often a tiny screw will fall off the bench or from the screwdriver. You can either get down on your hands and knees and hunt for the escapee, or you can use a magnetic picker-upper. These come in many shapes and sizes, can be bought in most hardware stores, and save lots of time and also your temper.

Where do you pound metal joints together? All too often the machinist's or bench vise is used for that purpose, a punishment for which the vise was not designed. If you have a drill press or lathe, never use the table of the press or the bed of the lathe to pound on, and never leave tools on either one. If pound you must — and there are not too many jobs where this becomes necessary — get a short length of I beam. These cutoffs from structural steel often can be found in the local scrap yard. If you have more money than you know what to do with, you can buy an honest-to-gosh anvil, but as far as I am concerned, the I beam does just fine.

There are a great many other tools, gadgets and gizmos which are nice to have. Some are worth their weight in gold the one time you have to use them, but more often than not, you can improvise. There is little use in spending six or eight bucks for a tool that you will use once for two minutes, especially if you can improvise or have the job done at the gunsmith's for five bucks.

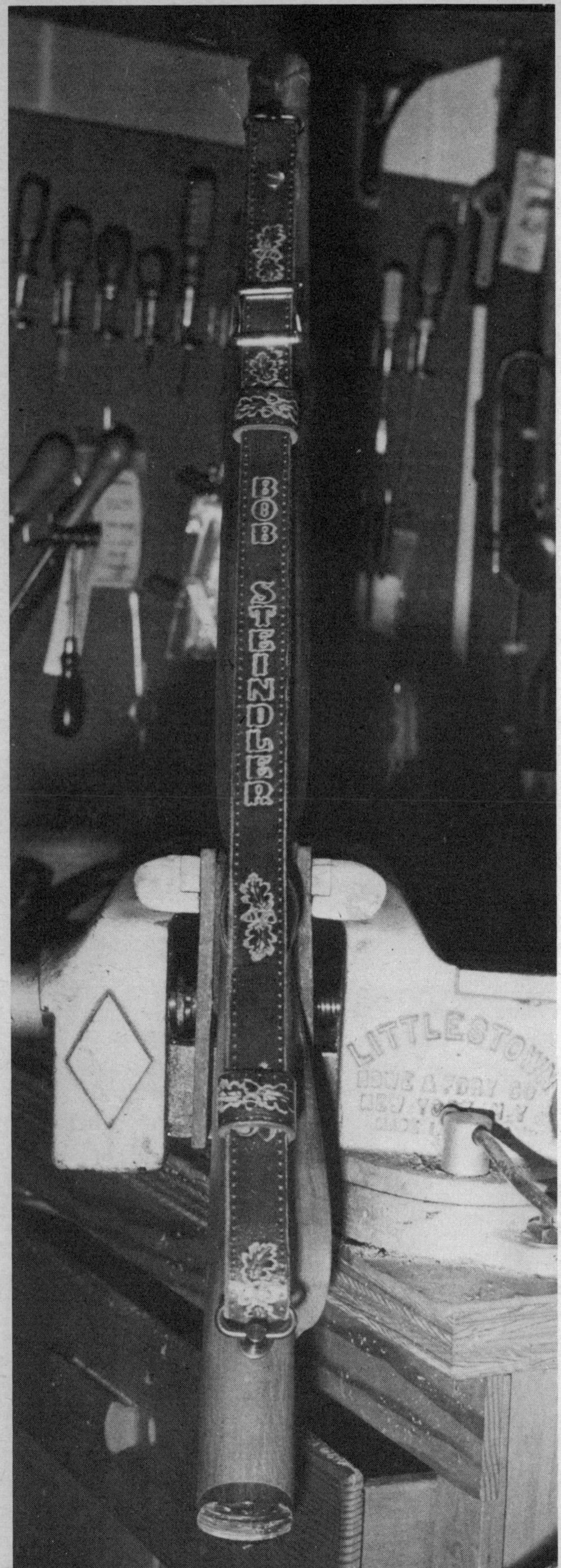

Chapter 4

With sling attached, the gun is ready for the field.

INSTALLING YOUR OWN SLING SWIVELS

You Can Do A Professional Job In The Time It Takes To Read This Chapter

The PRICE OF a pair of sling swivels ranges from $1.25 to about $8, and if you have a gunsmith install them, you might as well add another $8 to $10 to the cost, not counting the tab for the sling or carrying strap. With the help of a one-quarter-inch electric drill, three different-size drills, two screwdrivers and a rawhide mallet, I installed a pair of sling swivels on a wildcat rifle stock in twenty minutes, and this included lighting my pipe a couple of times, scratching the ears of my dog, and digging up the right drills.

The major trick in installing sling swivels is to get them located in the precise center of the stock. The method of installation may vary a bit from one brand of swivels to the other, and if you plan on installing a sling on a Winchester M94 or a Marlin M336, you'll need to drill only one hole into the butt of the gun, with the forward swivel being located around the magazine tube. By the same token, if you plan to hang a sling or carrying strap on a shotgun — and I have often wondered why so few hunters avail themselves of the convenience of a sling — your installation will vary somewhat, not only with the make of the swivels, but also with the make of the gun. All of the sling swivels on the market come with installation instructions, and you should read those first to make certain that you have the needed drills, tools and jigs on hand.

You will need a bench vise that is equipped with some sort of pads for the jaws to prevent stock damage. A small level, such as the line level sold in hardware stores, will help you to level the stock in the vise. After you remove the barreled action, trigger guard and all other such hardware, set the stock in the vise and tighten the jaws of the vise gently. If you must lock the stock into the jaws of the vise in the magazine area, be careful not to apply much pressure on the wood — it's thin there and too much pressure can crack the stock. If you are starting with the forend swivel, lock that section of the stock into the vise and support the butt, either by means of a free-standing support or, if you have a vise with a swivel

Spirit level must be used to correctly level stock in padded vise jaws. With the help of a B-Square swivel jig, below, the position of the rear sling swivel is determined with sharp scribe. After drilling appropriate size hole, the rear swivel stud is seated with nonmarring rawhide mallet.

After rear sling swivel has been seated, installation is completed, above. Next step is to relevel the stock forend, using spirit level as before, and locate forward swivel hole as outlined in text.

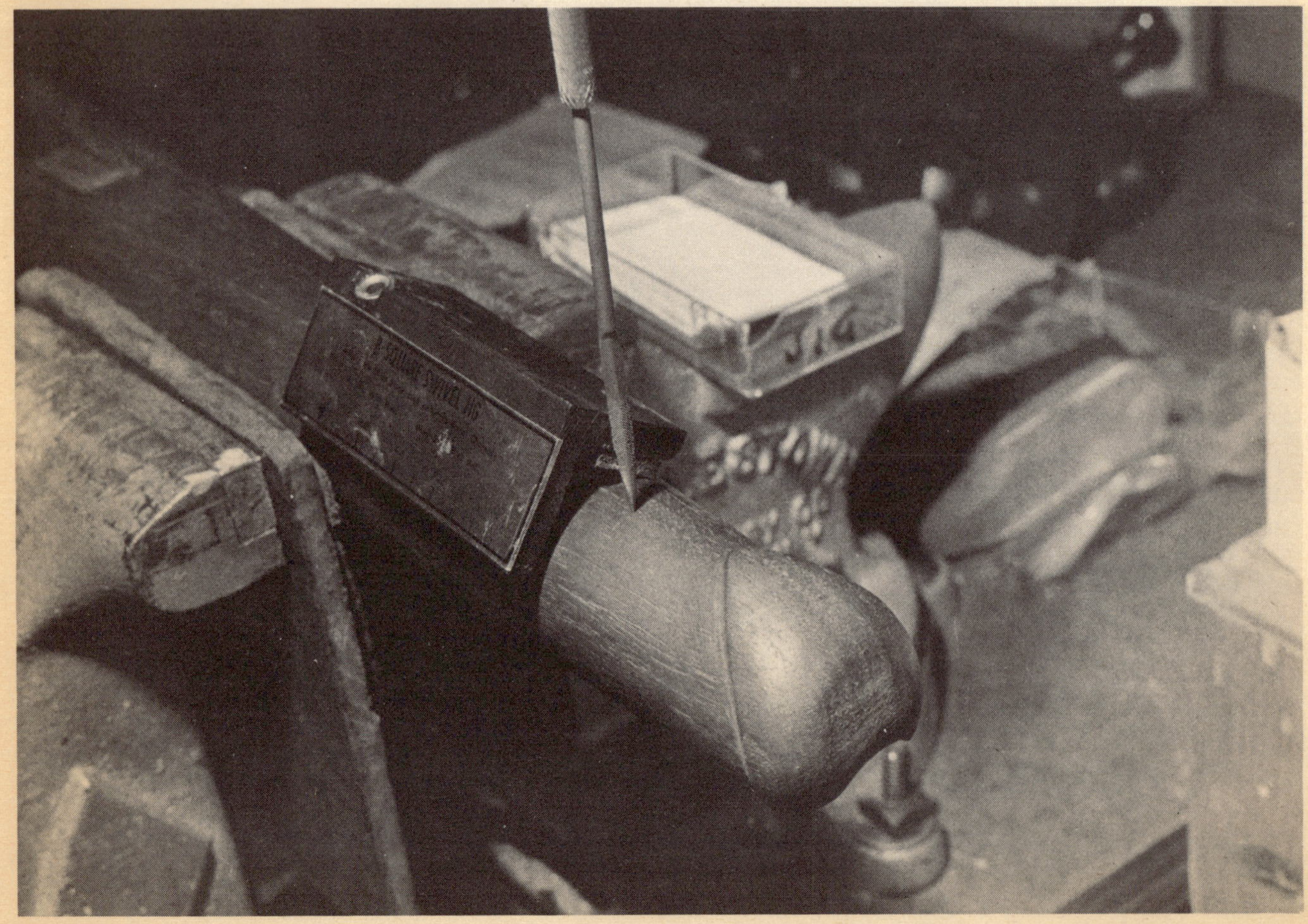

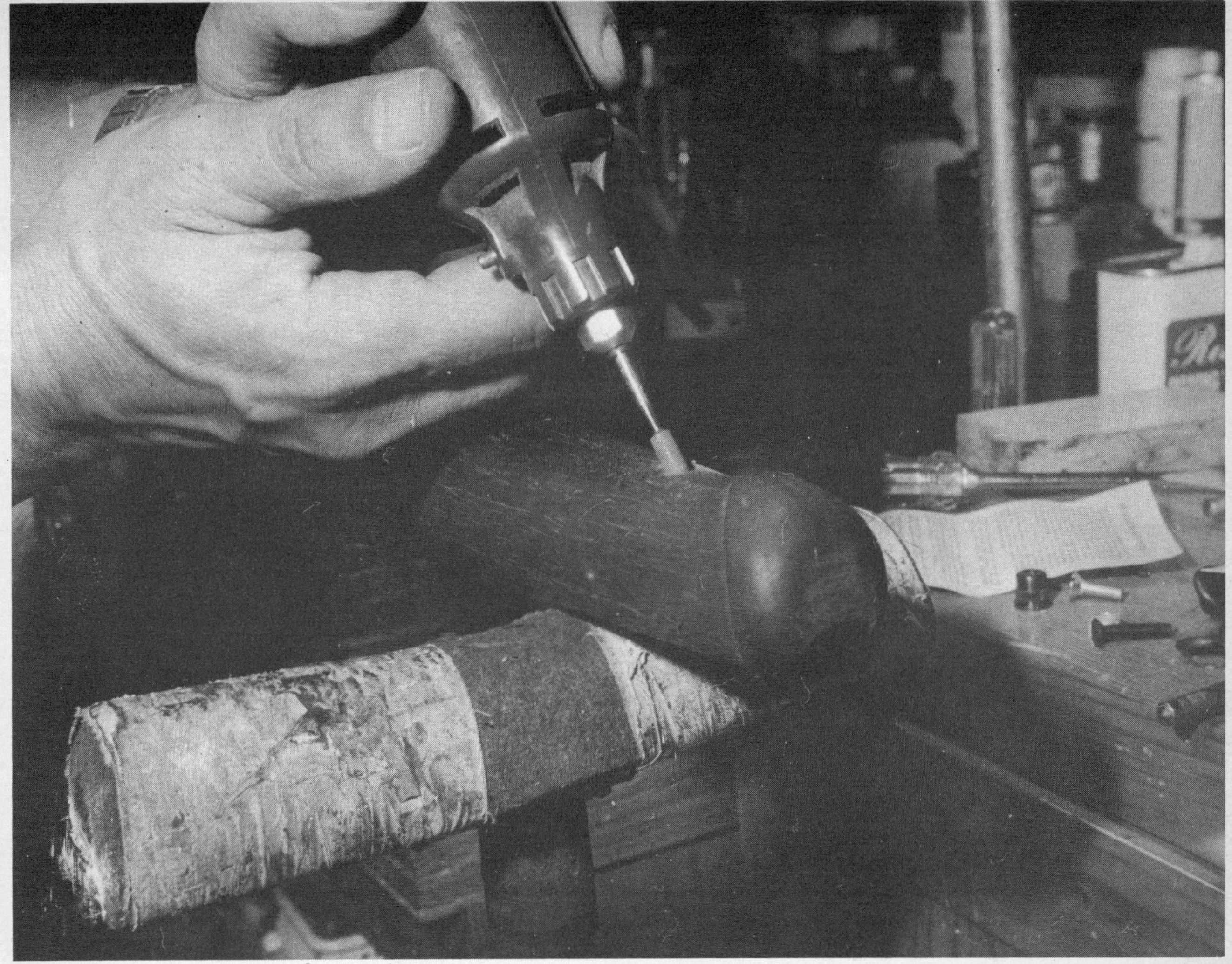

If swivel stud will not fit easily into drilled hole, use of a Dremel Moto-Tool is fast and easy way to correct fault. Absolutely sharp drills are essential to avoid splintering wood around holes as drill wanders or jumps.

base, rotate the base of the vise so that the butt is supported on the bench. You may either want to block the butt with some scrap wood or perhaps with a small sandbag or two. If you are working on the butt, support the forend of the stock in a similar way.

It is a relatively simple matter to drill the needed hole into the forend, providing the electric drill is held at a precise ninety-degree angle to the wood. When drilling the butt stock, level the lower or underneath line of the stock so that your stud or base of the swivel will be at right angles to the stock in all four directions.

If the stock you are working on has not yet been finished, you can possibly get away with using drills that are a bit on the ancient and dull side, but if the stock has been finished fully, use only sharp drills, either resharpened or new ones. If there is any doubt in your mind about the drill, drill a hole into a piece of scrap wood — if the point wanders or the drill does not cut easily into the scrap, then the drill is dull and should be reground or replaced.

Of the various sling swivel installation jigs that I have either seen or used over the years, I find that the one made by the B-Square Company (Dept. GW, Box 11281, Fort Worth, Texas 76109) is the most versatile, simplest and easiest to use. It allows you to locate the hole in the butt as well as in the forend where it can be used either in the barrel channel if the stud goes through the wood there or on the underneath part of the forend.

It makes little difference whether you start with the front or the rear swivel installation. Installation of the forward swivel base on tubular magazine rifles and most shotguns may not require drilling, and Uncle Mike's swivels for such guns come with a ring arrangement that is similar in nature to some scope rings. As a general-rule-of-thumb, thick forends have the base of the sling swivel installed from the underneath side of the wood only, while stocks that are less than one-inch thick are drilled from underneath and then the base is anchored by means of a countersunk screw in the barrel channel.

Locating the spots where you want to place the forward and rear swivel is quite simple. The forward swivel is usually located between thirteen to seventeen inches from the trigger, while the rear swivel is spotted between two to 3½ inches from the toe of the buttstock.

With the help of the B-Square Swivel Jig, locate the holes as outlined. Decide where you want to locate the front swivel, then measure the distance from the tip of the forend. With the jig, spot the location on the outside of the stock and in the barrel channel, if wood thickness and the swivel maker's instructions so specify. I use a homemade, sharply pointed scribe that easily passes through the hardened bushing in the jig. The jig can be held in place manually or lashed down with a broad rubber band. When the scribe bottoms, I tap it once with a mallet to leave a small mark. Thanks to its true ninety-degree angle, the jig will center the bushing, and therefore the scribe, in the center of the stock. If you have to drill through the barrel channel, simply flip the jig over so that the rubber padding on it faces you. The bushing in the jig is located precisely 2½ inches from its right end, and this automatically gives you the right distance from the toe of the buttstock.

Here is a trick that will help you to avoid marring the stock finish. Before using whatever drill is needed to make either hole, start the hole with a smaller-size drill. This not only enables you to set the tip of the drill on the scribe mark, but will also prevent the drill from wandering off dead-center, especially on the butt.

The swivels I used on the stock shown are Uncle Mike's Model DD200 which are not of the quick-detachable type, but installation differs little between this type swivel and others. The base for this set of swivels calls for a three-eighths-inch hole in butt and forend, and since the forend of this stock is just over one inch thick, there was no need to drill completely through the forend and anchor the base with the countersunk screw in the barrel channel. Both

Larger drill is used for body of swivel stud. Drill hole just deep enough to hold stud and avoid bottoming out if possible. Work carefully and check hole depth frequently with vernier caliper, as described in text.

B-Square and Uncle Mike's (Dept. GW, Box 13010, Portland, Oregon 97213) offer special step drills, and these are a good investment if you plan on doing more than one or two swivel jobs a year.

If you have a sling already, be sure that the swivels you buy will accept that width sling. For seven-eighths-inch slings, you will find that the one-inch swivel will be just right, and most swivel manufacturers offer one-inch and 1¼-inch swivels. If you want to give a swivel job that custom look, Uncle Mike's even offers prefinished white spacers that you can place between wood and swivel base.

If you are a squirrel hunter and like to use Remington's Model 66 Nylon, you can now install swivels on that handy and accurate little rifle. Similarly, black powder buffs can install their own sling swivels on a number of different models of black powder rifles, thanks to the efforts of Michael's of Oregon, better known as Uncle Mike's. And Uncle Mike's has even gone one step further — you can now buy and install swivels for over/under shotguns with a ventilated rib!

A sling, whether it is a simple carrying strap or a sophisticated carrying and shooting sling such as Brownell's Latigo sling, can be worth its weight in gold. This has been recognized by many of the rifle makers, both here and abroad, and most current rifle models come with simple screw-in swivels. These can, of course, be replaced with the quick-detachable, or QD, kind with some simple stock-patching work. Usually, it is best to fill in the hole where the original swivel was installed, then, when the filling has hardened, redrill for the new swivel base.

Ithaca recognized that a sling has a definite value on shotguns, especially on those meant for duck and goose shooting, when they equipped their excellent and quite unique 10-gauge autoloader with swivels. Just think of it — a sack or two of decoys, lunch, shell box and perhaps a parka, and where are you going to find that extra set of five fingers to lug that scattergun along?

There is no trick to installing your own swivels if you level the stock before drilling and locate the holes accurately. Then simply follow the swivel maker's instructions and you are home free!

With front swivel stud seated, the installation is nearly complete. Note that forend is supported on scrap wood crosspiece which has been heavily padded to avoid marring wood. Stand is adjusted for height.

Chapter 5

HOW TO MAKE A CHAMBER CAST — AND WHY

Here Are The Reasons, The Materials And The Technique!

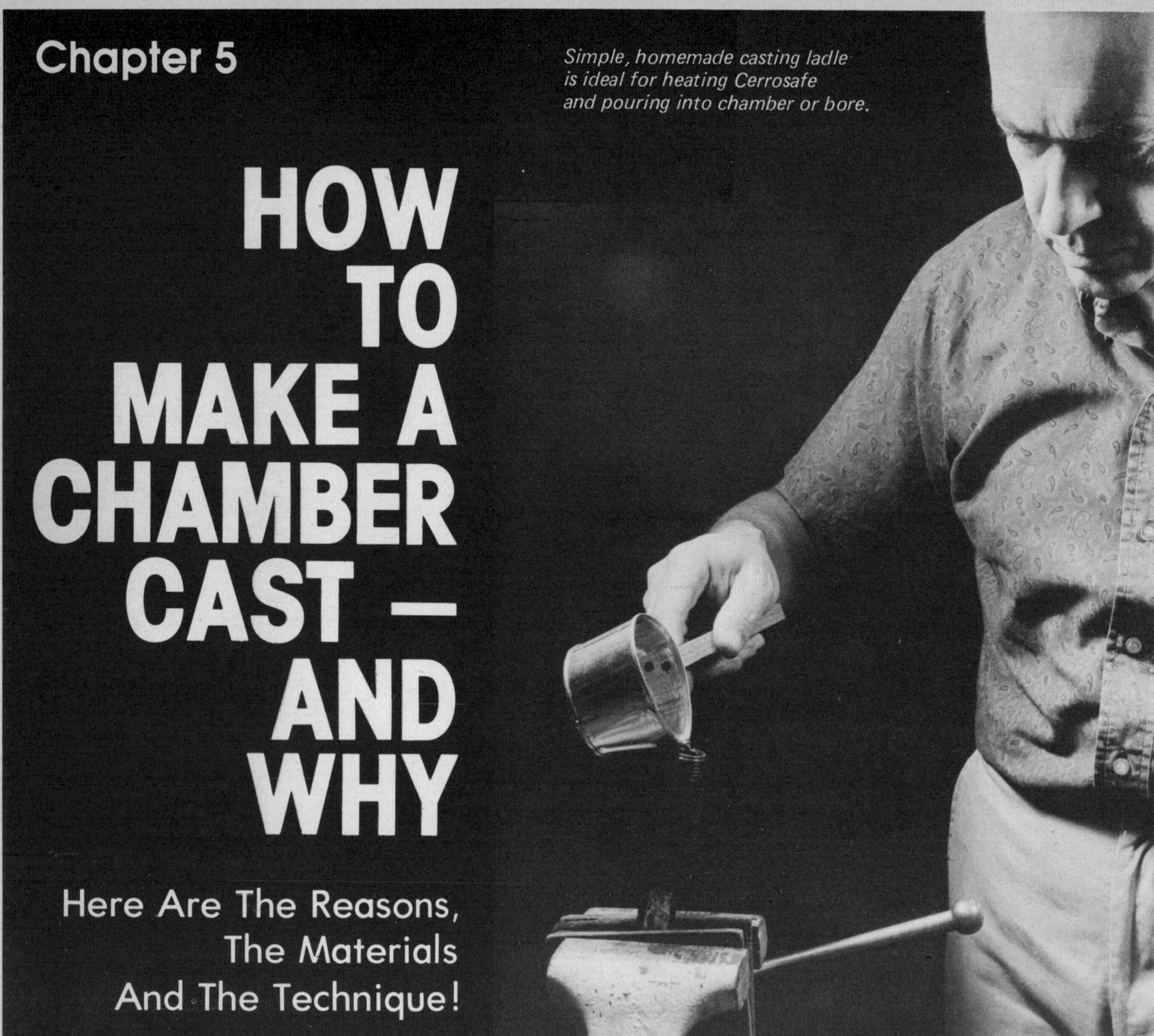
Simple, homemade casting ladle is ideal for heating Cerrosafe and pouring into chamber or bore.

NOT LONG AGO, three totally unrelated incidents occurred that, combined, reminded me of the days when I was a lot younger and greener as far as gun savvy goes.

Incident One: A neighbor had bought a used .30/06 and a range session convinced him he had been played for a sucker. That deer rifle for next year's Western hunt did not group at any range with any of the factory ammo he had on hand. Someone at the range pulled the bolt out of the rifle, peered down the barrel sagely and stated the tube was hopelessly shot out. Stock and action were in good shape and my neighbor pondered the cost of replacing the barrel.

Incident Two: A local varmint shooter had bought a Remington rolling block rifle, complete with scope and custom stock. The rifle was chambered, according to the seller, for either the .218 Bee or the .219 Donaldson Wasp, or was it the .219 Zipper Improved?

Since neither seller nor buyer had any live rounds in those calibers on hand, how could anyone tell what caliber the beast was chambered for?

Incident Three: A Winchester Model 94 that had seen much better days always had been cleaned from the muzzle in its younger years. The gun had been reasonably accurate until the owner began to note, during several target sessions, that accuracy seemed to have gone to pot. The gun no longer delivered the bullets to point of aim and the target looked more like a piece of patterning paper than a rifle target. He noted some slight muzzle wear and wanted to know what could be done about this sudden loss of accuracy.

The answer to those and related questions is simple: Make a chamber or bore cast. A cast, if properly done with suitable casting material, will indicate a lot of things that even a close visual examination won't show. Although making casts is a

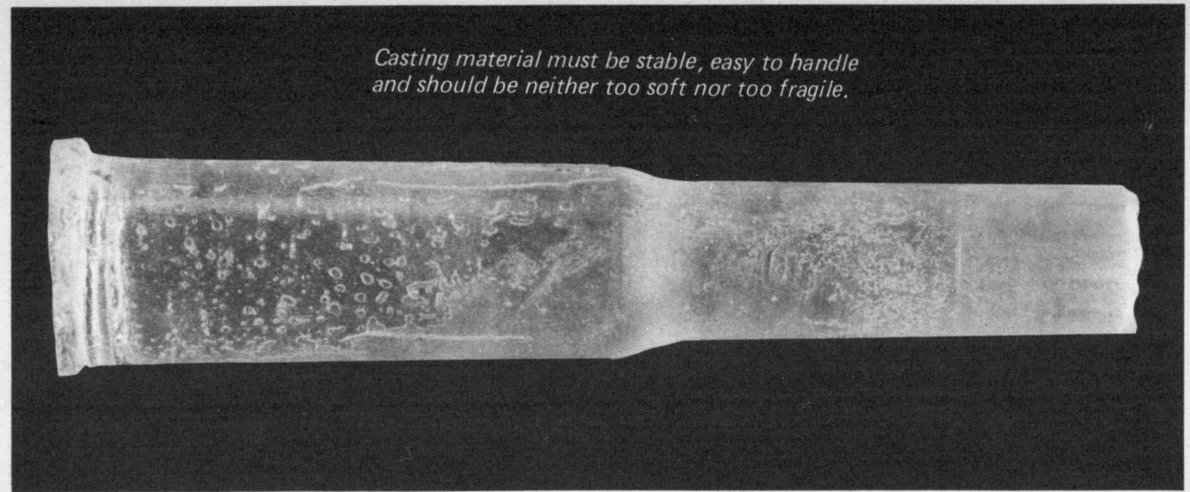

simple matter, it has been shrouded in such mystique that many gun owners think making a cast also requires incantations in some weird tongue when the moon is high and owls and bats are flying. Nothing could be further from the truth.

Basically, you have the choice of a temporary or a permanent cast. Whatever the casting material, it must have a low melting point to prevent possible changes in the metal with which it makes contact; the casting material should undergo a minimum of shrinkage or expansion, should not be hygroscopic — that is, absorb moisture — should be chemically inert and, lastly, should be easy to cast without stinking up the whole house or apartment.

Ideally, whatever material you use for your cast should also be stable, not just for an hour or two, but for the next ten years. This means that the casting material should not react unduly to heat or cold in your gunroom or shop; nor should its configuration change with continued exposure to air, moisture, lack of moisture and other atmospheric conditions.

Of course, the cast should not be so brittle that it breaks when used to make measurements. It also must be hard enough to allow you to bring a micrometer or vernier calipers to bear without denting the cast and therefore getting a misleading reading from your measuring tool. This also means that the material must permit handling and should not crumble in your fingers as you handle the cast.

Making a barrel or bore cast, for instance, does replace the ornery job of slugging a barrel. Gunsmiths talk blithely about slugging a barrel, but for the home gun tinkerer such an undertaking can become a nightmare. Slugging is done with a pure lead slug that starts out slightly oversize for the anticipated bore diameter. Thus, if you want to slug a .30 caliber barrel, you'd start with a .31 or .32 slug.

You can cast a pure lead .38 Special wadcutter, but trying to force that one through a .30 caliber bore not only becomes a chore, but prospects of ruining a perfectly good cleaning rod are excellent. Ideally, the slug is driven through the bore by means of a drill rod of suitable size to which a flat button or platform, slightly undersize from the bore diameter, is welded or brazed. See what I mean when I say slugging a barrel can become a nightmare? These days, I don't even slug easy barrels. I simply make a bore cast in less than ten minutes, without fuss or bother.

Making a chamber or bore cast costs only pennies, but

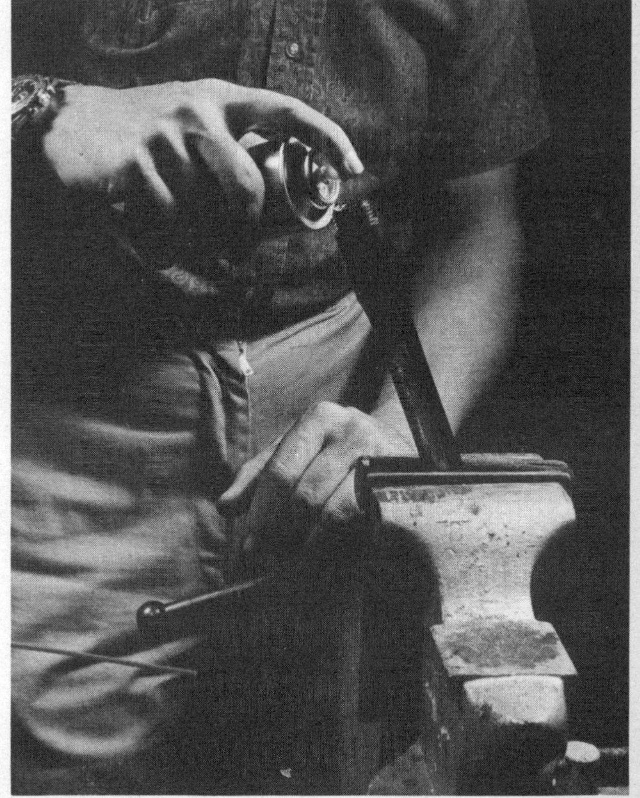

Before casting chamber or bore, a liberal coat of fine gun oil is sprayed on metal as release agent.

some gun tinkerers are not inclined to spend that much money and have tried various inexpensive casting media. Here are some of the more common casting materials and their pros and cons.

Crayon: Marking crayon or even a child's crayon can be used, if nothing else is available. Remove all the paper wrappings and dump the crayon into a small, shallow tin can that can be fitted into another can that contains water. I strongly urge the use of such a double-boiler system since some crayons contain flammable materials. Heat the double boiler over a camp stove or even the kitchen stove. Be sure to have tongs or pliers on hand to handle the container that

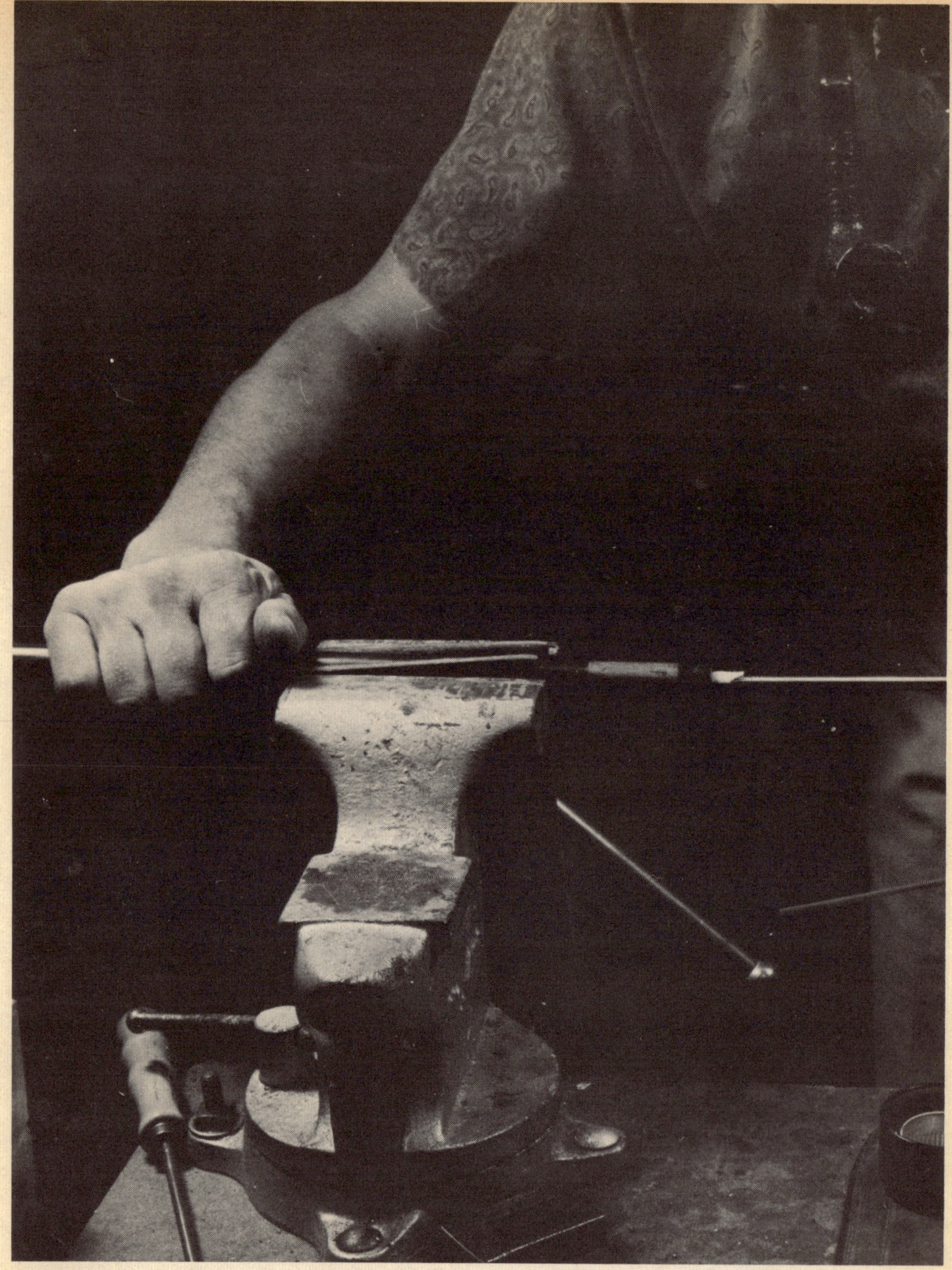

With rifle barrel locked in padded vise, bore cast is carefully pushed out with cleaning rod or drill rod.

contains the molten glob of crayon. Some crayons smell like the devil when melting, and it takes quite awhile for the cast to set before it can be driven out of the barrel or chamber. Crayon casts cannot be handled too easily, since they are fragile and also tend to melt when the room is too warm. Freezing the cast is no good, since too much cast shrinkage occurs.

Sulfur: When heated too much, powdered or molecular sulfur becomes a brownish and sticky mess. A double boiler is suggested, though not essential. If the molten sulfur turns brown and gooey, you have gone too far. Trying to make a cast of this glob is almost certain to result in disaster, since the usual release agent — oil — does not always release the amorphous sulfur. The ensuing mess is enough to teach a

Cerrosafe is an ideal casting medium, is easily melted in clean bullet casting ladle over small camp stove flame.

Marine Drill Instructor some new four-letter words! If you can catch the sulfur as it becomes liquid and before it turns brown, you can make reasonably good casts this way. The trouble with sulfur is the stench that goes with heating it, so I suggest the garage, barn or chicken coop if the kitchen is outlawed. These casts are quite brittle, so handle them with due respect and care.

Lead: Pure lead has a melting point that is higher than that of crayon or sulfur. If you cast your own bullets or balls for your black powder shooting, you need only get some pure lead to make your casts. When it splatters, hot lead can cause deep and painful burns, so caution is in order. A lot of gobbledygook is being bandied around about the dangers of casting bullets — acute lead poisoning is being blamed primarily, but other gases of combustion also get their share of the blame. Don't let that scare you from making a chamber

cast or two and don't stop casting your own bullets because of this ballyhoo. I have been casting bullets for over twenty-five years and pass my annual physical without trouble.

Plastics: Some plastics melt at relatively low temperatures, but can be used to make chamber or bore casts. The problem is that the composition of plastics change and new ones pop up all the time and, unless you are a chemist or have someone who knows his plastics, it is best to steer away from them as a casting medium. Some plastics begin to melt nicely, then burst into flames. Some smell worse than a convention of skunks; still others pour fine, but getting the cast out usually results in barrel damage.

Dental Impression Material: Somewhere I had heard that this is great stuff. Fortunately, I tried it first on an old hunk of barrel that I use as a paperweight in the shop. The stuff —

and there is a wide variety of such materials on the dental market — casts superbly, releases easily and the casts are fairly easy to handle, except that most of the impression materials are too soft to permit measurements. If you have a tank of liquid air handy and the suitable safety equipment you can freeze the cast, thereby shrinking it a bit. You sit and wait until it begins to thaw, then measure at just the right moment. What's the right moment? Beats me, but that was the suggestion of my dentist!

Cerrosafe: This is a special casting alloy, sold by Brownell's. This is the best and most reliable casting material, and since discovering it some years ago, I have given away all of my other casting materials. Cerrosafe shrinks somewhat during the first thirty minutes of cooling, then expands again.

Casts are permanent if you care to save them and can be measured anytime with precision tools; expansion, even two hundred hours after casting, is no greater than one quarter of one percent. The only drawback of the stuff is the cost. A half-pound ingot sells for about eight bucks. The stuff can be used over and over again; I have been using one ingot for over ten years and expect to use it for another ten years.

Woodsmetal: Often touted as an excellent casting medium, this is best consigned to the scrap bin if you want to make casts. It handles well, but casts swell after casting and, unless you are very quick in getting the cast out, you may have to have the thing drilled out. Even liberal applications of a release agent — oil or graphite are suitable — won't always release such a cast. Whoever started the rumor about this

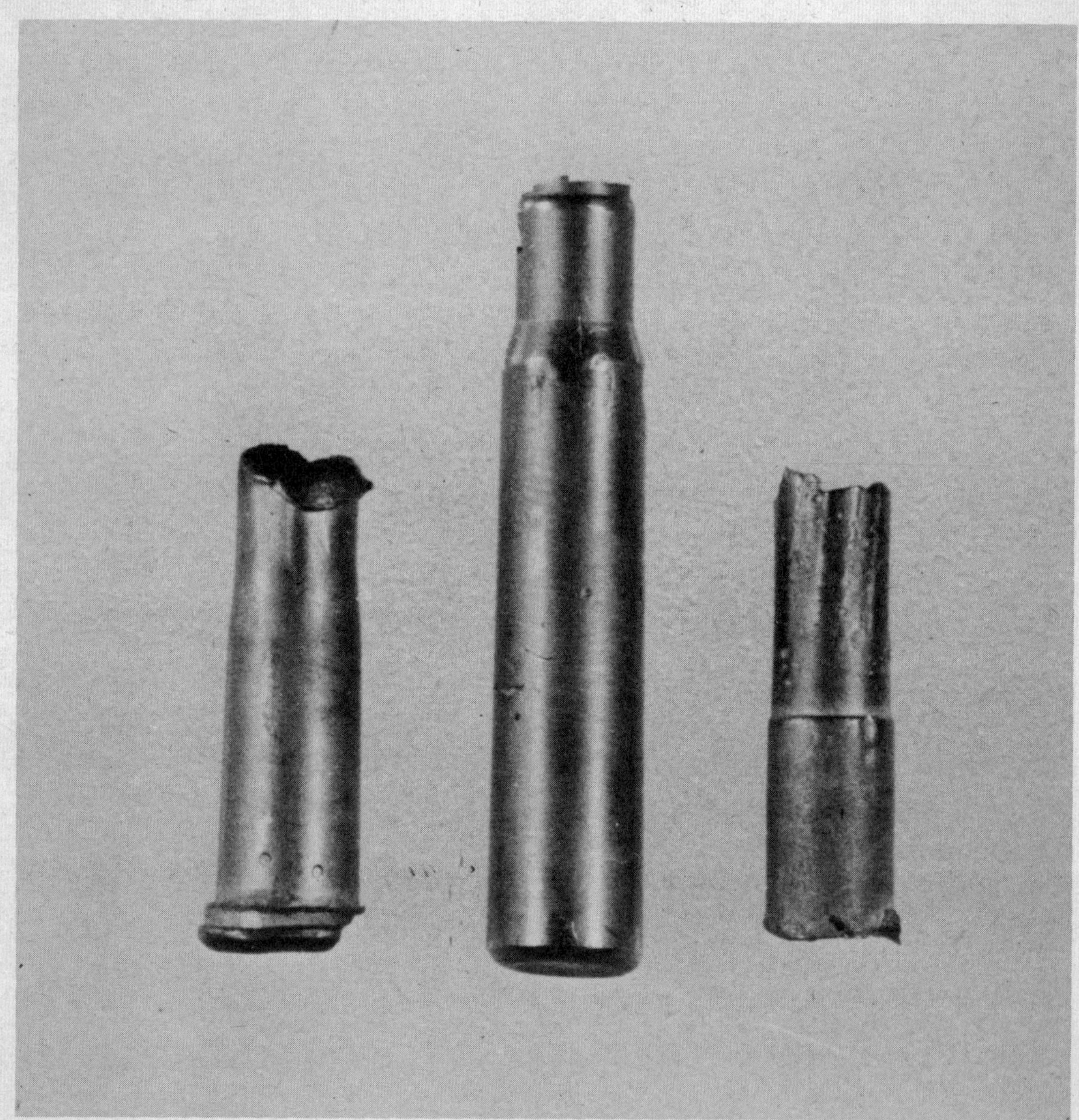

Chamber and throat cast of wildcat chambering tells shooter caliber and condition of internal areas.

being ideal material for chamber or bore casts better not tell me about it. It cost me $50 for a new barrel.

Preparations for making a cast are quite simple. Clean the bore or chamber thoroughly, not just with a couple of patches soaked in a solvent; use a brush to remove all loose fouling, dirt and other foreign matter. Dry the bore or chamber thoroughly and completely with dry patches.

If you are trying to make a bore cast of the muzzle end, plug the barrel with the patches an inch or so below the muzzle. If you are making a chamber cast, plug the bore in the throat area of the barrel. In making these plugs, be sure to seat the plug tightly, but not so tight that it cannot be pushed out with either a wooden dowel, cleaning or drill rod.

Install the gun barrel or the entire gun in your bench vise

Muzzle cast of rifle barrel proved that rifling at that point was still in good condition and not worn.

Bore and chamber cast from old Luger barrel quickly shows that barrel needs only a good cleaning to be serviceable.

and be sure to pad the jaws of the vise so that neither bluing nor wood will be damaged.

You can use graphite as a release agent and, thanks to the small atomizers, it is not too difficult to get an even layer of graphite into the casting area. I prefer to use a fine gun oil, such as Browning's, in the aerosol can. If I get a dab too much oil in the chamber or bore, the patches in the plug absorb it, making removal of the plug that much easier. The addition of the thin plastic spray tube to the aerosol can makes an even distribution of the Browning oil still easier.

Cerrosafe melts between 150-190 degrees Fahrenheit. A clean metal ladle is usually recommended, but you can make your own ladle quite easily by forming a spout on a small tin can, then attaching the can with a couple of screws to a wooden handle or the remnants of a broom handle. I melt my Cerrosafe over a small camp stove, and in a pinch you can even use the flame of a candle for the melting. As soon as the alloy becomes liquid, remove the ladle from the flame and pour the metal into the oiled chamber or bore.

There is one trick to get the alloy into the chamber or bore: use a small aluminum funnel with a piece of surgical tubing attached. Insert the tubing into the bore or chamber and start pouring the molten alloy. As the space fills up, raise the funnel and tubing. If you don't want to bother with this refinement, be sure to spray some oil on the surrounding area so that the cooled Cerrosafe can be picked off later on.

It is best to bring the gun or barrel into a warm room where the casting will be done. If the metal of the gun is too cool, the casting material will solidify prematurely and you may get an incomplete cast. The cast should be removed from chamber or bore as soon as it cools off to room temperature. I prefer to use a wooden dowel or drill rod of suitable diameter to pound out the cast, although a cleaning rod will do in a pinch. Some rods don't have enough "body" and will start to bend. While this won't affect the cast, it may ruin a rod for further use.

If a Cerrosafe cast is left too long in the gun, you may find it difficult, if not impossible, to dislodge the cast, even if the casting area had been coated liberally with oil. If your first casts looks like the mice dined on it, simply wipe it off to get rid of the surplus oil, remelt it and try again.

In reading bore casts or those made from a throat, remember that the cast is the mirror image of the inside of the barrel. A good magnifying glass will help you to read the cast,

Vernier scale calipers measure chamber cast to determine which improved version of the .30/06 the reloader is dealing with.

and if the barrel is really shot out the cast will tell you so. A bore cast can immediately resolve the question: What 8mm tube do I have? Some of the older German 8mm barrels are .318-inch, while others mike .323-inch, and shooting the larger bullets in the tighter bore is almost certain to lead to trouble.

If you — like the fellow down the road — bought a rifle and are not certain about the chambering, a chamber cast will quickly tell you what that smoke pole is chambered for. A cast also will tell you quickly if the tube is really shot out or whether you had better check the rifle. It could be a loose scope block or poor bedding. A worn muzzle can be cured by either recrowning or by removing an inch or two of barrel, provided such surgery does not make the barrel too short.

If you are a reloader, sooner or later you will encounter various versions of improved cartridges. As you know, this means that every gunsmith makes his own improved version, and the only difference between most of them may be a ½-2 degree of shoulder slope. Then a chamber cast will quickly show you with what you are working.

If I sound prejudiced in favor of casts, you are right! I have found them invaluable in many jobs, and it's nice to know how to tackle such a complex job with ease and get results that make you look like a pro!

BORE CARE & CLEANING

A Bit Of Maintenance Can Reduce Problems, But There Are Cures For Extreme Cases!

Bore cleaning and lubricating products seem almost endless in variety as new products are offered each year.

Before any attempt is made to recrown muzzle of any gun, barrel must be squarely and firmly mounted in padded vise.

FASHIONS CHANGE AND so do attitudes about bore cleaning. While shooting for record during a four-position, small-bore rifle match — when every point counted toward winning a trophy or coming in as second best — some clown down the range broke me up by stating that he had just cleaned his .22 caliber match rifle.

Cleaning the bore of a rimfire match gun then was somewhat akin to heresy or disliking apple pie and girls. Anyone who ever ran a patch through the barrel of a match rifle was suspected of having softening of the brain and was in dire need either of pity or a swift kick in the pants.

Some years later I was bitten by the benchrest bug. Just for the record, benchresters clean the bores of their rifles after firing only one or two relays, and certainly after every fifteen or twenty shots. Cleaning rifle bores with that bunch of super-accuracy shooters is tantamount to a ritual, except that the incantations are missing.

Back in the Fifties and Sixties, when surplus GI ammo

Muzzle is recrowned using roundhead brass screw chucked in eggbeater hand drill. Mixture of valve grinding compound and cutting oil is applied to muzzle, care is exercised that drill is held level before turning begins. Check work frequently.

Schukra cleaning rod, imported from Germany, may be used to clean all calibers or gauges.

bounced all over every range in the country, the rule of thumb was to clean rifle bores, since most shooters were not sure whether or not the GI fodder they were using had corrosive primers. Since those days, we have been blessed with noncorrosive primers and powders that are not supposed to foul the innards of a barrel or action. The use of lead bullets, though still popular, is no longer in vogue as it was some fifteen years ago and lead fouling has taken a back seat when the talk turns to gun cleaning.

Badly fouled rifle tubes, if they resisted all cleaning attempts, used to be taken to the gunsmith for something called barrel lapping. Depending on the gunsmith, lapping was done one of several ways. Wrapping some fine steel wool around the roughened outside of a suitable-caliber drill rod running slowly in a drill press was one way of getting the assorted gunk out of the lands and grooves of the barrel. Others tackled the job on a lathe, while those who enjoyed getting a hernia and callouses on their hands did the job with a leather patch and lots of elbow grease. Fouling was removed with mercury, an ammonia mix which I'll discuss later, fine valve-grinding compound or anything else the particular gunsmith fancied.

There still may be a few gunsmiths around who do lapping, but as a routine method of cleaning a badly fouled barrel this process has been almost completely abandoned. Power equipment — a lathe or drill press — even when operated slowly and with care, tends to mess up the lands, often making the cure worse than the original complaint.

Keeping the bore of a shotgun in pristine condition does not present too much of a problem, although plastic shotshells have produced some rusting. I favor the one-piece wood cleaning rods for shotgun care, but those of jointed aluminum also are suitable.

You should have a rod for each gauge, at least one slotted tip, one wool mop and one wire brush. I like the French Tornado brushes, especially if fouling is severe and does not respond to the usual bronze-wire brush treatment.

In cleaning a smoothbore after shooting it, a couple of patches moistened with any of the commercially available gun cleaners or bore solvents should do the trick. As with rifles, work from the breech after removing the barrel or barrels if the gun is a takedown model. Shotguns that cannot be taken down must be cleaned from the muzzle.

Shotgun barrels should not be locked into a vise, as they

are too fragile for this sort of treatment. After one or two solvent-soaked patches are run through the bore, hold the barrel up to a good light and check whether all the fouling has been removed. If there is residual fouling, use a wire brush until the bore shines clean and bright.

Two pieces of equipment always on my bench, but seldom mentioned in print, are a dental mirror and a bore light. The dental mirror is a freebie from my friendly dentist who must replace one every so often. Since handles don't come on dental mirrors any more, drill and tap the cut-off handle of a toothbrush or use a dowel rod as a handle; or, if you have a lathe, make one from a drill rod and decorate it with a metal checkering wheel.

A small bore light not only makes gun care easier, but also is handy for many other jobs. A plastic rod attached to the light serves to concentrate the light and is a worthwhile investment.

While on the subject of fouled bores, a word about light surface rust is in order. Light rusting can happen to anyone, especially on hunting guns which do not always receive enough care in the field. Before contemplating a rebluing job, and instead of wailing and gnashing your teeth, here is the way to handle that light rusting. Get the finest steel wool you can find and make a small ball of it, then soak the ball with fine gun oil. Rub the affected area, using a fair amount of pressure — the rust spots will disappear and this treatment will not harm the bluing.

The recommendation is often heard that severe fouling is best and most quickly removed by running a piece of drill rod or some other steel rod with a steel wool pad through the bore, either on a drill press or a lathe. This can be done of course, but it requires an expert's touch, since too much of a good thing can wreck the choke or rifling quickly.

A light coating of oil is recommended, even if you will be using the gun next weekend. The wool mop is my favorite way of getting an even oil coating into a shotgun barrel. For cleaning shotgun barrels — as well as some rifles that I can't lock into the vise — I cobbled together a padded rack that can be locked into the vise. Cleaning only the barrel and leaving the action full of fouling is done all too frequently, since shotguns usually are harder to take down than a bolt-action rifle or a semiautomatic handgun.

In any gun cleaning, remember that bore solvents can and possibly will mess up the stock finish, and that too much oil can be more ruinous than no oil at all. As long as you take the time and the trouble to clean the bore and the action of a gun, why not also take care of the stock and some of the accessories — such as the sling or the scope? A silicone-impregnated cloth wiped over a scope's metal surfaces and the stock helps to maintain your gun in top condition. Once in a while, especially on guns that have seen hard use, I take the time and trouble to apply some stock wax and then rub it down well — this adds years to the life of the wood and the finish and helps to protect your investment.

Cleaning any type of action is simple, thanks to the gun cleaners now sold in aerosol cans. Rather than a couple of heavy blasts of the stuff, use the small plastic tube that comes with most of the cans. This allows you to control the amount and the direction of the spray better than dousing the whole action, and since the spray is more concentrated in form, it

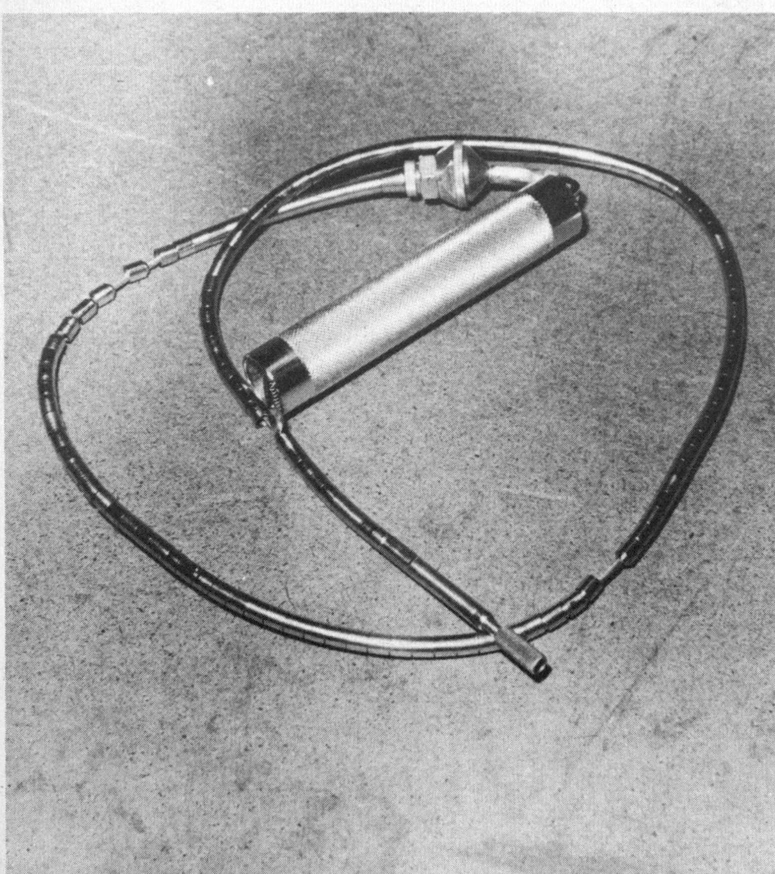

Same cleaning rod as shown on opposite page may be coiled up and carried in pocket or kit.

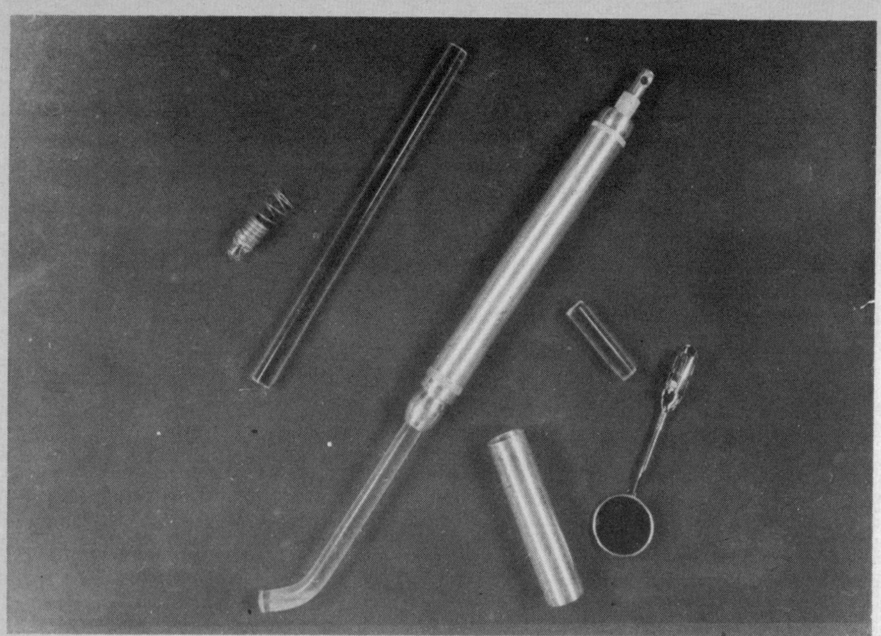

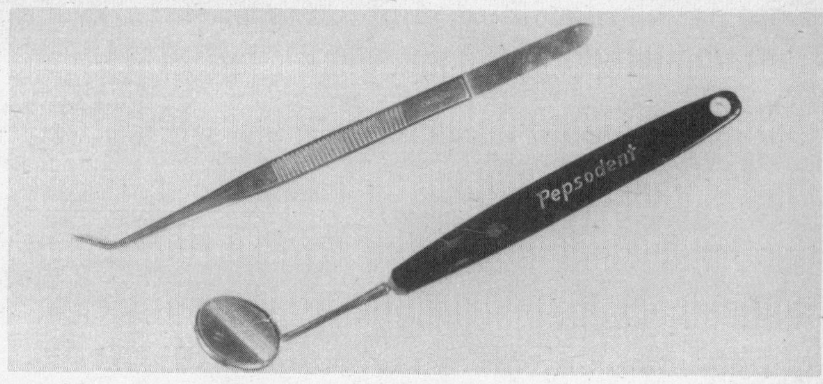

(Above) Combination bore light with plastic rod to direct light makes Brownell instrument ideal for gun tinkerer. Dental tools, right, have use by gunsmith.

also often washes crud out from its hiding places. After one or two shots with the spray, use a cleaning patch held in forceps to dislodge the last of the fouling.

Gun oil in aerosol cans is also available, too, but use it sparingly. Despite modern chemistry, oils still gum up after a while and it's hard to imagine the mess you face when too much of a good thing gets gummy and hard.

In cases of severe and badly neglected fouling and leading, and after everything else has failed, I resort to J-B Bore Cleaner. This mildly abrasive cleaner, applied either on a suitable mop or bristle brush, does wonders for a neglected shotgun barrel. Use this treatment sparingly in the choke area of the barrel, but in the rest of the barrel push and pull the cleaning rod back and forth until satisfied that all fouling is gone.

Bolt-action rifles and others that can be taken down easily should be cleaned from the breech. You'll need cleaning rods in the various calibers and, again, I opt for the one-piece rod. The rod should have a handle that allows rotation of the rod as it is pushed through the barrel. Steel rods are by far the best and the newer ones with a plastic coating are even better.

When it comes to cleaning-rod tips, there are five basic choices. The button tip requires that the tip be placed in the center of the patch, while the spear and worm-type tips are not as critical since, once impaled, the patch cannot slip off the moving rod.

Although tip selection for the cleaning rod and how the patch is fastened to the tip does not appear to be of major importance, any gunsmith will tell you differently. Should the patch slip the slightest bit off the button, spear or worm tip, the rifling is exposed to the abrasive pushing action of the metal tip. Even if the cleaning rod is perfectly straight, pushing a rod through the bore while the tip makes contact every so often with one or more lands is asking for trouble.

In precision shooting, cleanliness is next to whatever comes in second place, but keeping the innards of a barrel undamaged is just as important. For this reason, I strongly recommend that you push the rod with the patch or brush through the bore, then unscrew the tip, bring the rod back out of the action, attach the tip again and keep going that way. Just two strokes of a cleaning rod, when the tip makes contact with the rifling, are enough to damage the rifling beyond repair.

Normal rifle care includes not only bore cleaning, but also care of the external metal parts, stock and such extras as scope and scope caps. Although the external appearance of a gun is important, the condition of the bore is paramount. If

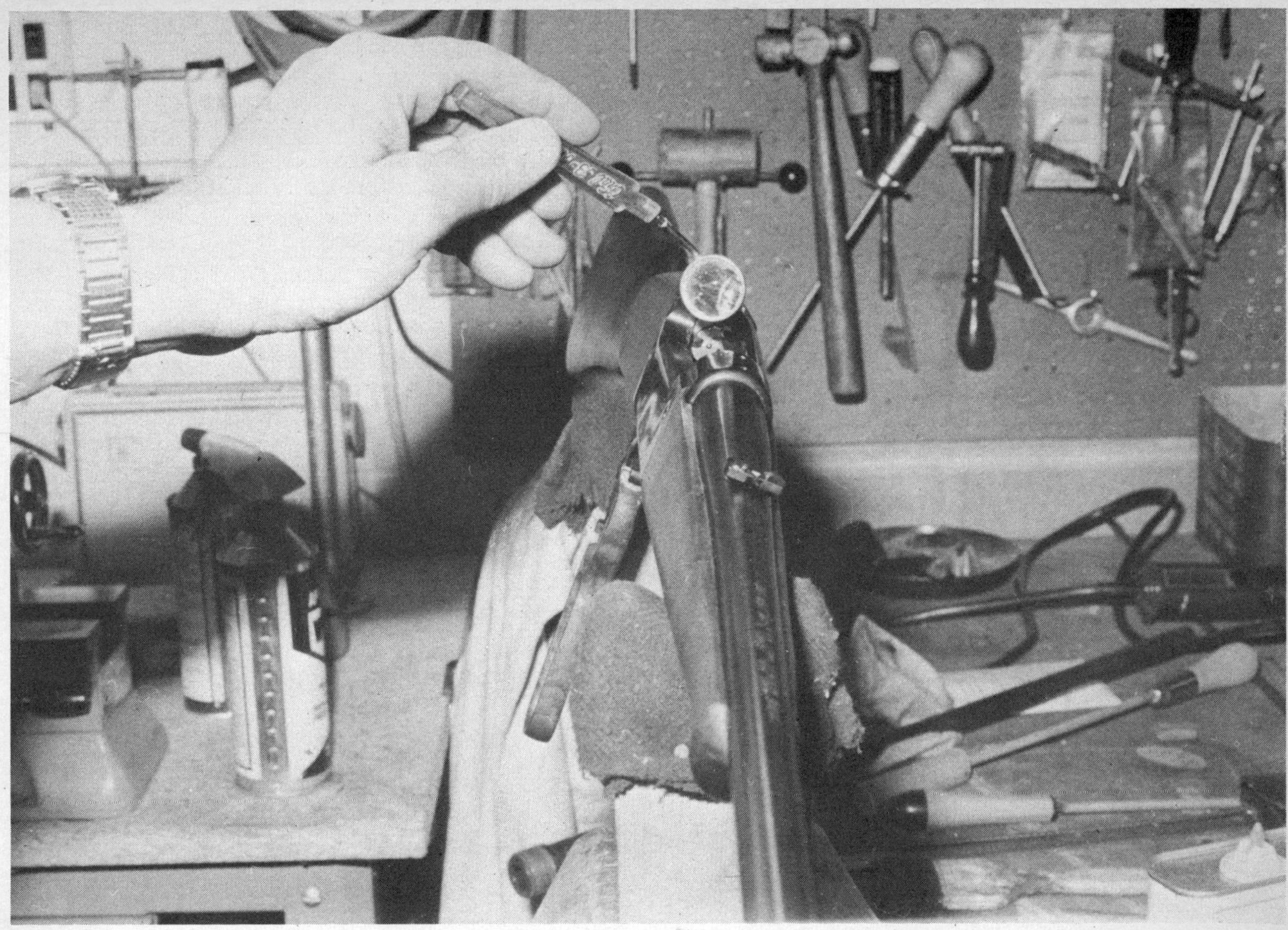

A dental mirror used to reflect light into the rifle's receiver area will indicate cleanliness of chamber and action.

you cannot pull the bolt on your rifle or take it apart, as you would a British double rifle, then you must clean the rifle from the muzzle. A wobbling cleaning rod, introduced into the barrel from the muzzle, is twice as bad as a wobbly rod operated from the chamber end of the tube.

Taylor and Robbins, custom gunsmiths, manufacture a throat and bore saver that is worth its weight in platinum when it comes to keeping the cleaning rod centered in the bore. Inserted into the chamber — the bore saver is only usable with bolt-action rifles — it is long enough to prevent even a rod with a set to touch the lands of the barrel as the rod is moved back and forth. A similar product, this one from MTM Molded Products and therefore made from a plastic material, is available in several calibers.

In a pinch, you can even make your own rod guide with some copper tubing and a suitable cartridge case. Cut off the case head with a tube cutter, silver solder a length of copper tubing to the case neck, making certain that the tubing is a bit undersize for the bore of the barrel.

Should suitable copper tubing not be available, you can get along by simply using a cut-off cartridge case. Buff, file or polish the cut-off so that there are no burrs or rough edges, ream the inside edge of the cut lightly, just as you'd chamfer a

case mouth while handloading, then slip the whole thing gently into the action and chamber.

Make up several of these guides, one for each of the various calibers of your bolt-action rifles, label them and keep them with your gun care equipment. In using any kind of rod guide, be sure to remove the rod tip when it exits from the muzzle, then pull the rod back with the guide and start all over again. It may take a few extra minutes, but it is well worth the trouble and time.

If you must clean the bore of a rifle from the muzzle, the Saunders Sav-Bore is the perfect answer to the problem of keeping the cleaning rod centered in the bore of the barrel. These plastic gadgets are offered in all calibers, including .17, and if the local gun shop does not have them they can be purchased directly from Bob Saunders (see the directory in the back of this book for the address).

In using the Sav-Bore, it is important to have the rod and the Sav-Bore of the correct caliber, although I have managed to clean a .25 caliber rifle with the right-size rod and a .30 caliber Sav-Bore without having the rod make contact with the lands.

The .17 caliber rifles need tender, loving care and special pains must be taken to keep the bore clean. Metal fouling in these rifles, when it becomes severe, can be a real pain. Parker

Ackley, the noted gunsmith and writer, some years ago cooked up a good antifouling solution that, applied liberally to those small bores, does miracles. He suggests mixing the following in a large glass jar: one ounce of ammonium persulfate, 200.0 grains of ammonium carbonate, four ounces of water and six ounces of "stronger" ammonia from the local drugstore.

Rather than using this on a patch, plug the barrel at the muzzle with a cork and, with the help of surgical tubing and a small funnel, pour the solution into the bore, keeping it away from blued gun parts and stock finish.

Stand the rifle muzzle-down and then let the solution work for about twenty minutes. Let it drain, then pour hot water into the barrel, letting the water remove the remnants of the solution. You can either dry the barrel with successive patches or with hot water, then lightly oil the bore. Incidentally, the hot water treatment accorded to black powder rifles is equally as effective on center-fire rifles.

Handgun care is quite similar to that of rifles. Semiautomatic pistols should be stripped as far as possible, as should single-action revolvers. Clean not only the bore, but also all chambers and the forward face of the cylinder, paying particular attention to the area where the barrel is screwed into the frame.

In cleaning pistols and double-action revolvers, it is a good idea to tip the gun so the bore solvent and gunk cannot run into the action. Single-action revolvers can be stripped, the grips removed, then boiled in water to which some detergent has been added. Rinse in hot water, again change the water and bring to a boil, remove gun and parts and hang them up to dry. The heated metal will evaporate the water, and the gun will be ready for reassembly and oiling in a few minutes. To fish gun and cylinder out of the bucket of hot water, I use a hook fashioned from a wire coat hanger.

For gun care afield, a small plastic bottle of bore solvent, some patches and either some silicone oil or one of the lubes containing molybdenum will do for the cleaning of a rifle or shotgun that gets wet, dirty or is fired a lot. Takedown cleaning rods sometimes are packed along, while the pull-through gun cleaning system is favored by some.

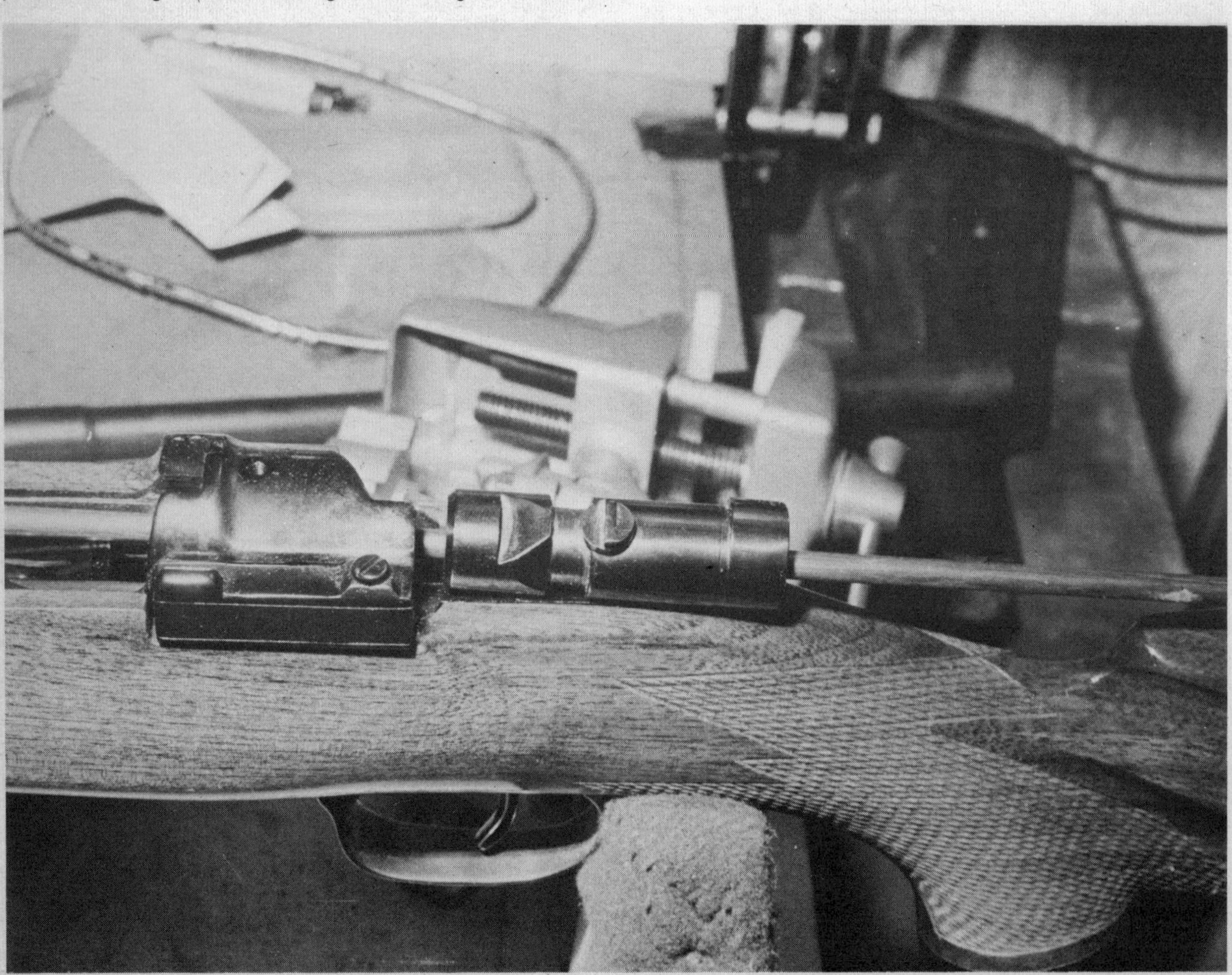

Taylor & Robbins Throat Saver is a device designed to prevent cleaning rod from wearing chamber edge and bore throat.

Three pieces of scrap wood and padding material will produce a handy gun cleaning cradle freeing both hands for rifle work. Uprights have deep V cuts to hold firearm as cradle is clamped in vise jaws at desired angle.

Somehow, many hunters and shooters have overlooked what some consider the best of all cleaning rods for field use — the Schukra collapsible cleaning rod imported from Germany by Kleinguenther's. This rod, when coiled up, can be carried in a shirt pocket, and with one twist of the rod handle you have a rigid cleaning rod. One such rod can be used for all calibers, from .22 to the big .45 caliber bores, plus all shotgun gauges.

Brief mention was made earlier of bore solvents and oils. The J-B Bore Cleaner and a product called Gunsoap have proved effective in removing serious fouling. Other bore solvents are legion, with G-96, Hoppe's No. 9 and Birchwood-Casey bore solvents being the most widely available ones.

Silicone oil is something fairly new and there is no gumming with this product. Molybdenum greases also are excellent, but for long-term storage of guns in humid conditions I stick to the Rig treatment. If you do a fair amount of gun cleaning, do not buy the small boxes of patches. Trade packs, sometimes sold in plastic bags and sometimes in large boxes, are less costly and you'll find that such a pack lasts a lot longer and you won't run out of patches as quickly as you do with the standard-size packages or boxes.

A gun that has become wet or damp must be dried. A couple of clean patches or the remnants of a worn-out flannel shirt should be used to dry off all parts of the gun, including scope mounts, stock, sling swivels and other such oft-forgotten areas as floorplates. Dirty stocks should be wiped down with a soft piece of flannel, using hot water and detergent. Do a small section at a time, dry with another piece of cloth, then apply one of the stock waxes. In a pinch you can use any good furniture wax, but stay clear of the household spray cleaner-waxer products since some of them do attack the bluing. In the cleaning ritual, include the magazine or clip, excepting of course the tubular magazine which should be wiped on the outside only. If the gun has a sling, a couple of drops of Lexol or saddlesoap should be used.

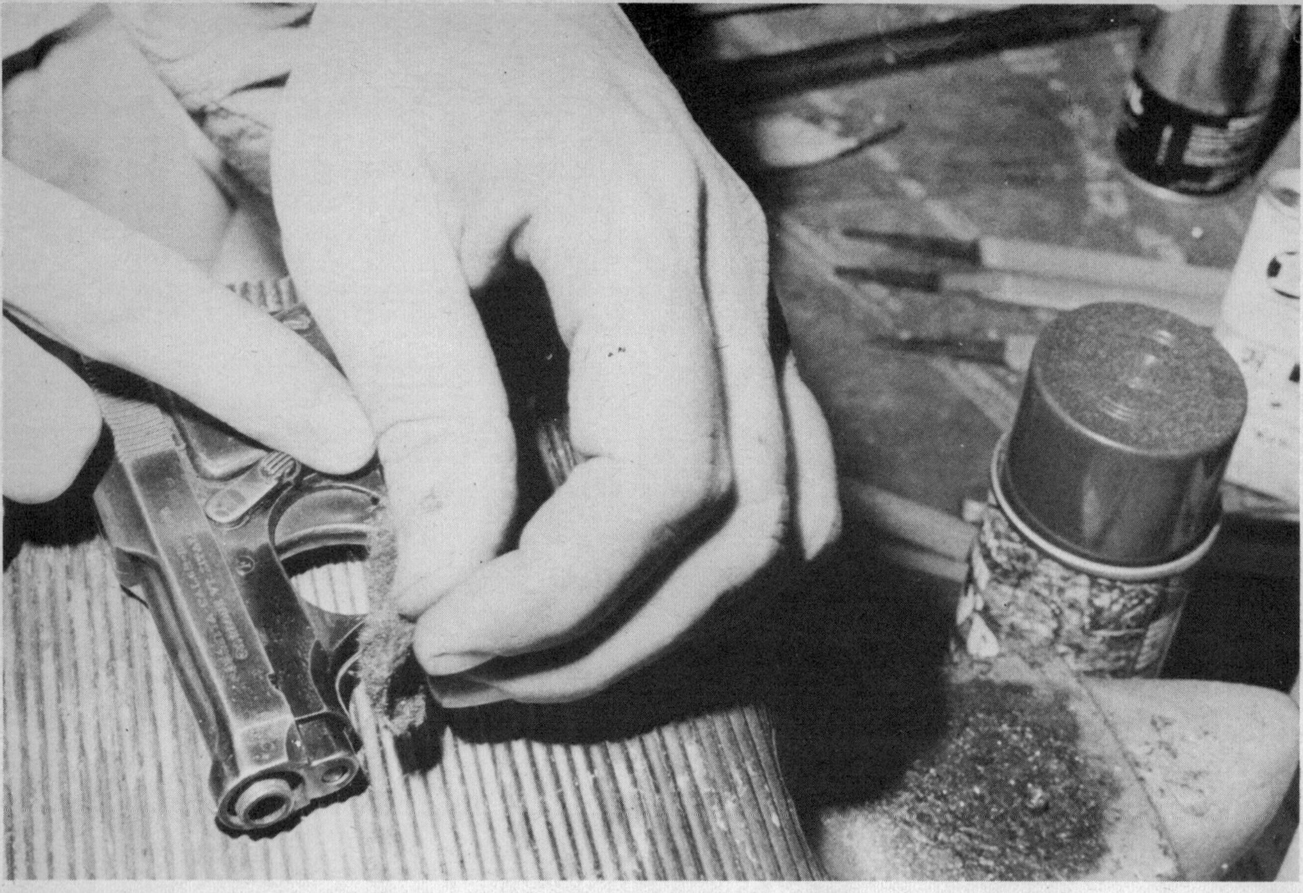

Small ball of finest steel wool dipped in gun oil is easy way to remove light rust. Rubbing only until rust is gone, above, should not damage bluing. When cleaning guns from bore, Sav-Bore will prevent damage to muzzle, below.

The skyrocketing number of gun thefts has led a lot of gunowners to mark their guns in some way, with either their name, social security number or even their vehicle license number. The small electric engravers, such as the one manufactured by Dremel, are quite suitable for this sort of job and can be used to mark many things, from televisions and guns to stereos and tools. In marking guns, apply the mark so that it is not readily seen or found. Unfortunately, this can lead to some rusting in areas of high humidity, since the engraving tool goes through the bluing and into the steel. I marked one of my S&W six-guns that way, placing the engraving under the grip which was removed for this purpose. A few months later I noted rusting in that area. Now when I mark a gun, I polish the engraved area lightly with fine steel wool, then apply touch-up bluing. When this is dry, I finish the job with a swipe or two of an oily patch.

Damaged rifling messes up the accuracy of a rifle or handgun. Since some guns must be cleaned from the muzzle, damaging the lands at the muzzle will affect the performance of the gun. Depending on the degree of damage, the gun will lose some of its accuracy or, more likely, groups won't be anywhere near where the scope or sights tell you they should be. Damaged rifling is repaired by recrowning of the muzzle, and although this is basically a job for a gunsmith, the shooter should know how to do this in case no gunsmith is available.

Go to a hardware store and buy a handful of the large, roundhead brass screws, preferably an assortment. When chucked into your eggbeater hand drill and liberally doused with your favorite polishing goop, you are ready to recrown a barrel — just be sure to hold the drill at the ninety-degree angle to the horizontal of the muzzle. Some gunsmiths prefer to use a hand-held power tool, but I feel that these churn up too many revolutions per minute and that it simply is too darned easy to mess up a muzzle even more. Various grades of valve-grinding compound work well for touching up the crowning, but it must be mixed with a good-grade cutting oil.

A properly maintained gun, even when it shows external signs of wear and usage, indicates that the owner cares about his equipment. In these days of inflated gun prices, you may have more of an investment in your gun cabinet than you realize. Any gunsmith will tell you that neglect is responsible for a large part of his repair business.

Wood parts and leather slings should not be forgotten in cleaning program. Wipe down wood and scope with silicone cloth.

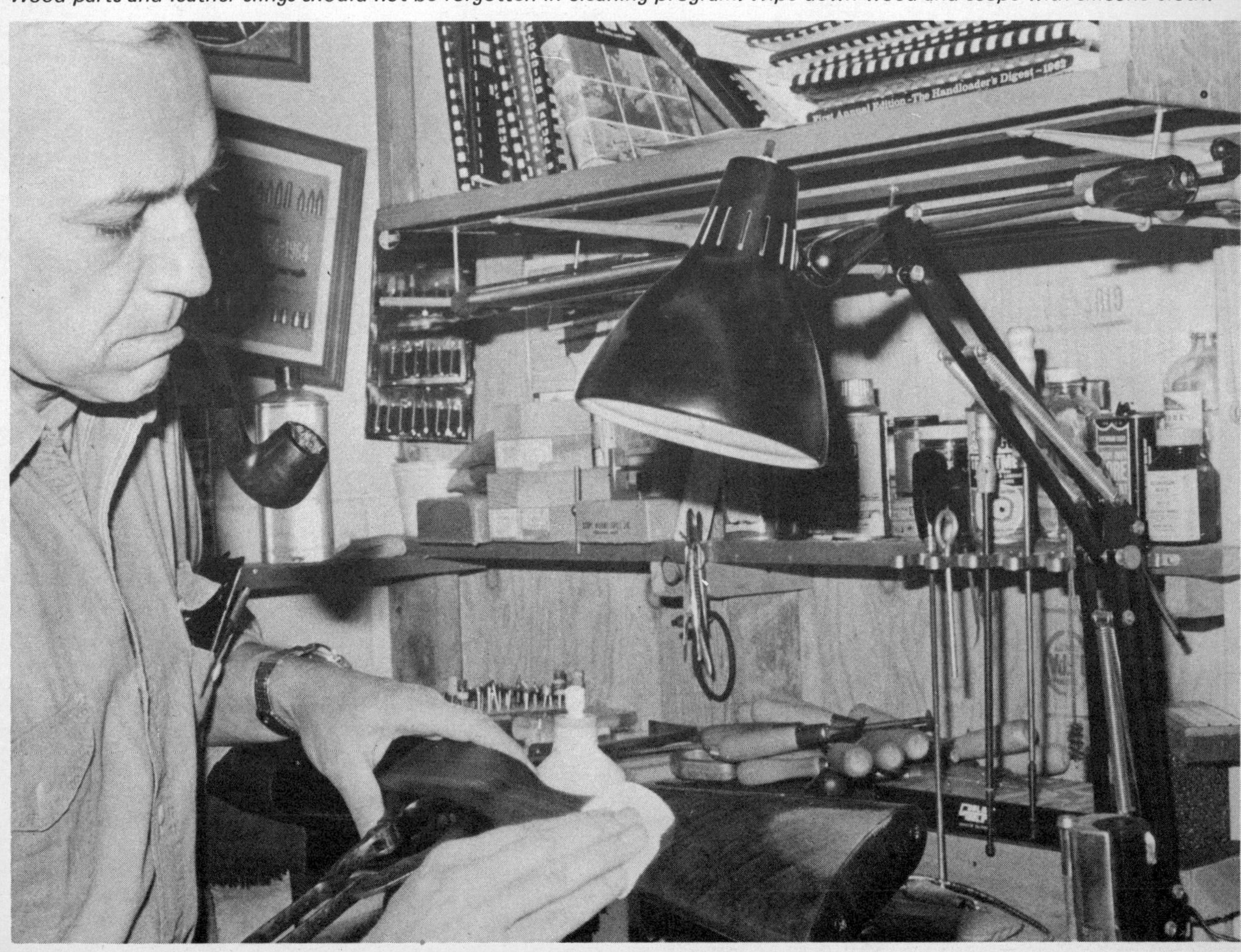

Chapter 7

BUILD A TARGET PISTOL OVERNIGHT

Step-By-Step Conversion Of That Military Autoloader Into A Competition Handgun!

SOME YEARS AGO, I bought one of the South American .45 ACPs that were sold by Centennial Arms for relatively little money. These were used guns and the importer made no claim about the guns being perfect or tuned for match shooting.

When the gun arrived, I fired a couple of boxes of ammo through it. It functioned about as smoothly as any .45 and the trigger pull was about the same as you get on a GI gun. The blue was worn in spots, but after stripping and cleaning the gun, I put her aside.

Later, when I resumed firing the police combat course, I decided to use that .45. Although combat shooting does not call for an adjustable sight, I wanted one on the gun since it also would double as a practice gun for target shooting, where an adjustable sight becomes a necessity. After shopping around and looking at a number of the available sights, I settled on the one made by the Micro Sight Company. Complete with a new front ramp sight, the package cost at that time was $18.50. I had an old Pacific trigger shoe that fit the trigger of that .45, and in one evening's work I converted the gun from military issue to something that shoots as well as a new commercial gun.

When I have a bit more time, I keep telling myself, I'll strip the old bluing, polish and buff her with some TLC, then reblue with Brownell's cold blue, which does a tremendous job.

To install the Micro Sight, one should have no trouble doing the job in one evening. Begin by taking the gun down. You'll need a pair of padded jaws for your bench vise. If you don't have any, cut two pieces of pressboard to fit the vise and get some of the heavy automotive felt used in firewalls, under hoods and, in older cars, even under the floor mats and carpeting. The local car junkyard yields hunks of felt and usually one can get all the felt needed for about thirty-five cents. But don't try and stockpile the stuff: I once did that in a garage and found that moths and mice liked it for breakfast, lunch and dinner. Glue the felt to the pressboard and you have a pair of padded jaws that will last for quite a spell.

With the slide carefully locked into the vise, use a fine hacksaw or jeweler's saw to cut off the front sight. In my gun, the base of the front sight was press-fitted into the slide, then peened a bit. When locking the slide into the vise, don't tighten the vise too much. A little bit of tightening will get rid of the slop or play between slide and frame, but too much tightening will hamper slide travel to the point where you actually put the gun out of commission.

Now turn the slide around in the vise and, using a punch, knock out the remnant of the front sight. Measure your new

Installing an adjustable rear sight on the typical autoloader requires but a few tools and a couple of hours of work at the bench. Typical modification at left. Below: Removing the original front sight is accomplished with fine jeweler's saw. Hold saw level and take care not to contact slide with teeth.

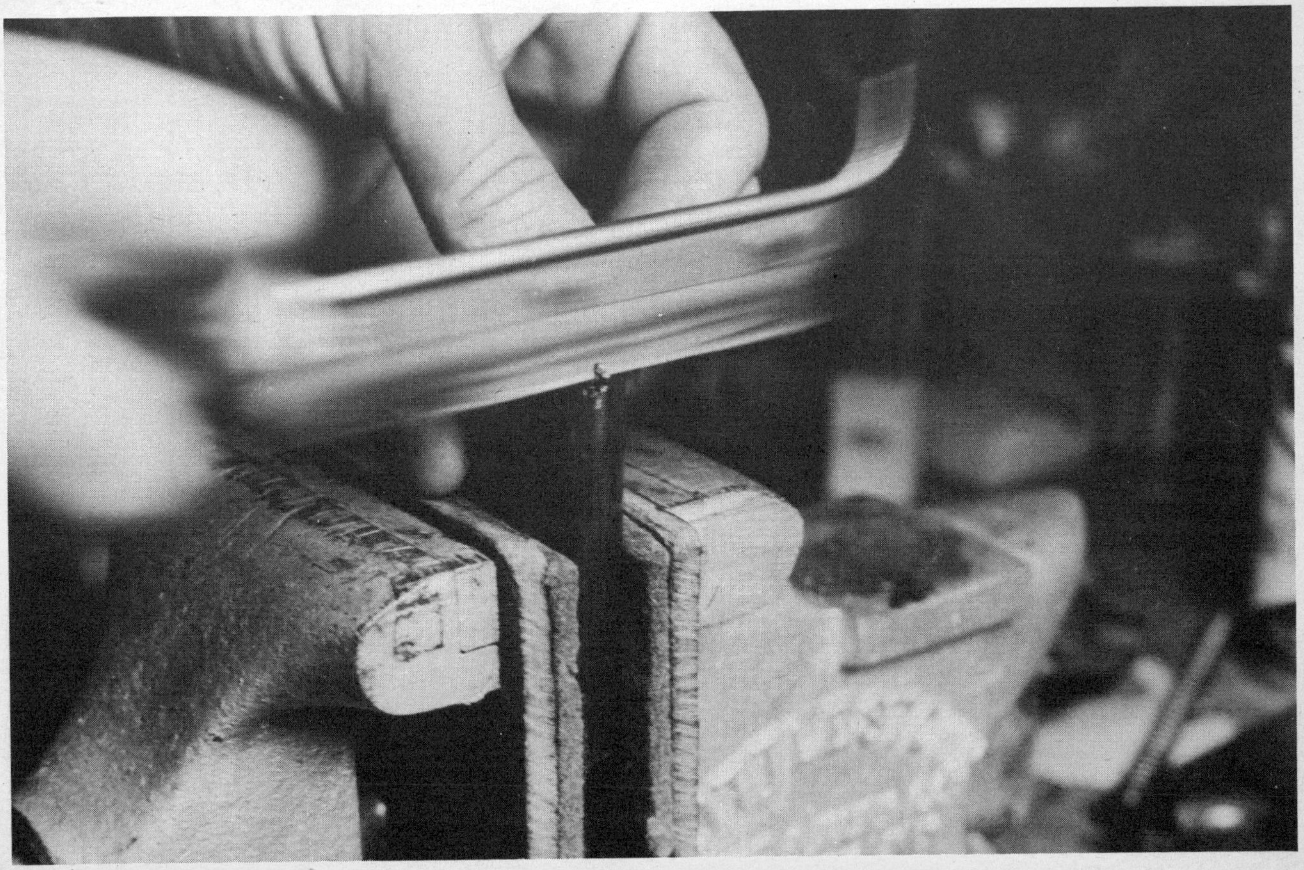

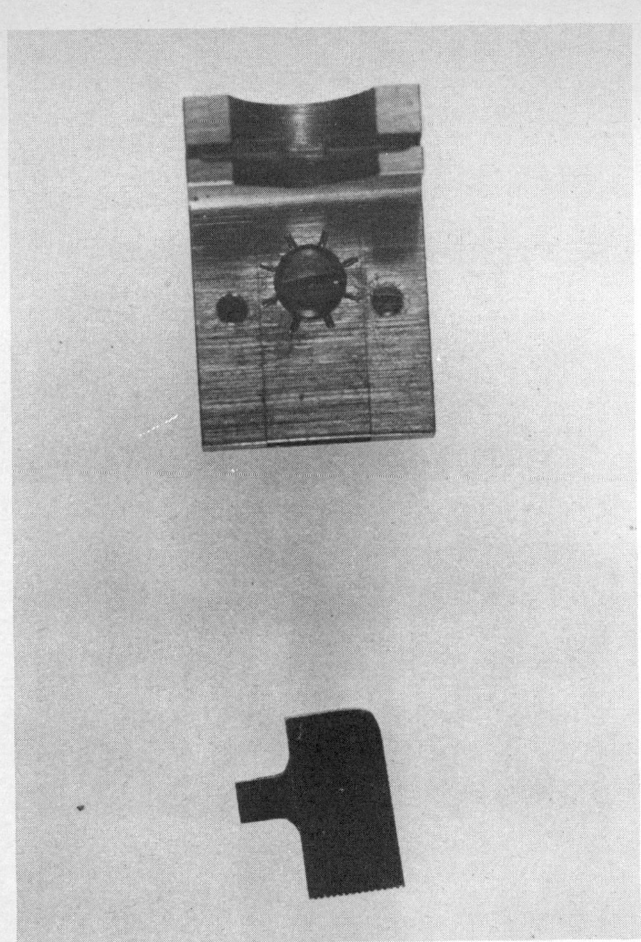

front sight and place it into the position of the old sight. With a sharp scribe, mark the outside edges of the new ramp sight, but be sure not to wiggle the sight as you scratch your lines. These will be your guidelines and a poor fit means that you'll have to file, then fill in with silver solder what has been cut away.

This is not too much of a tragedy, since you have to silver solder the ramp into place, anyway. When the lines are scribed, get to work with a fine Swiss file and gently clean up the area. Work slowly, until you can get a tight press-fit between the cut in the slide and the base of the ramp sight. Depending on the slide of your .45, the base of the ramp sight

Removing front sight base from most military semiautomatic pistols may be done by punching at base of old sight, using light taps of a small ball peen hammer.

Final step before installing new front sight, above, is to Swiss file slot, removing all burrs. After drifting out old rear sight, Swiss or dovetail file is used to slightly enlarge slot for new adjustable rear sight base.

may or may not bottom out. If the base does bottom out, be sure that it is perfectly flush with the inside curve of the slide; if not, use the fine Swiss file until it is.

To silver solder you'll need a propane torch, such as the Bernz-O-Matic unit and I suggest Brownell's Force 44 solder with the Blitz soldering flux. Don't worry about applying too much heat to the slide — silver solder melts at about four hundred degrees and that is way below the range where your heating would affect the temper of the slide metal. If there is a drop or two of silver solder left on the inside of the slide where the ramp sight bottomed out of the slide, file the spot smooth with the Swiss file.

Now put the slide into the vise so that you can drift the military rear sight out of the dovetail slot. While the old sight is hardly worth saving, don't try to beat the sight out of the dovetail with any old hammer. If you should miss, you'll bang up the sight and leave an unsightly mark on the slide which may be difficult to get out. Instead, use a brass drift. If you don't have such a drift — and brass rod is hard to come by

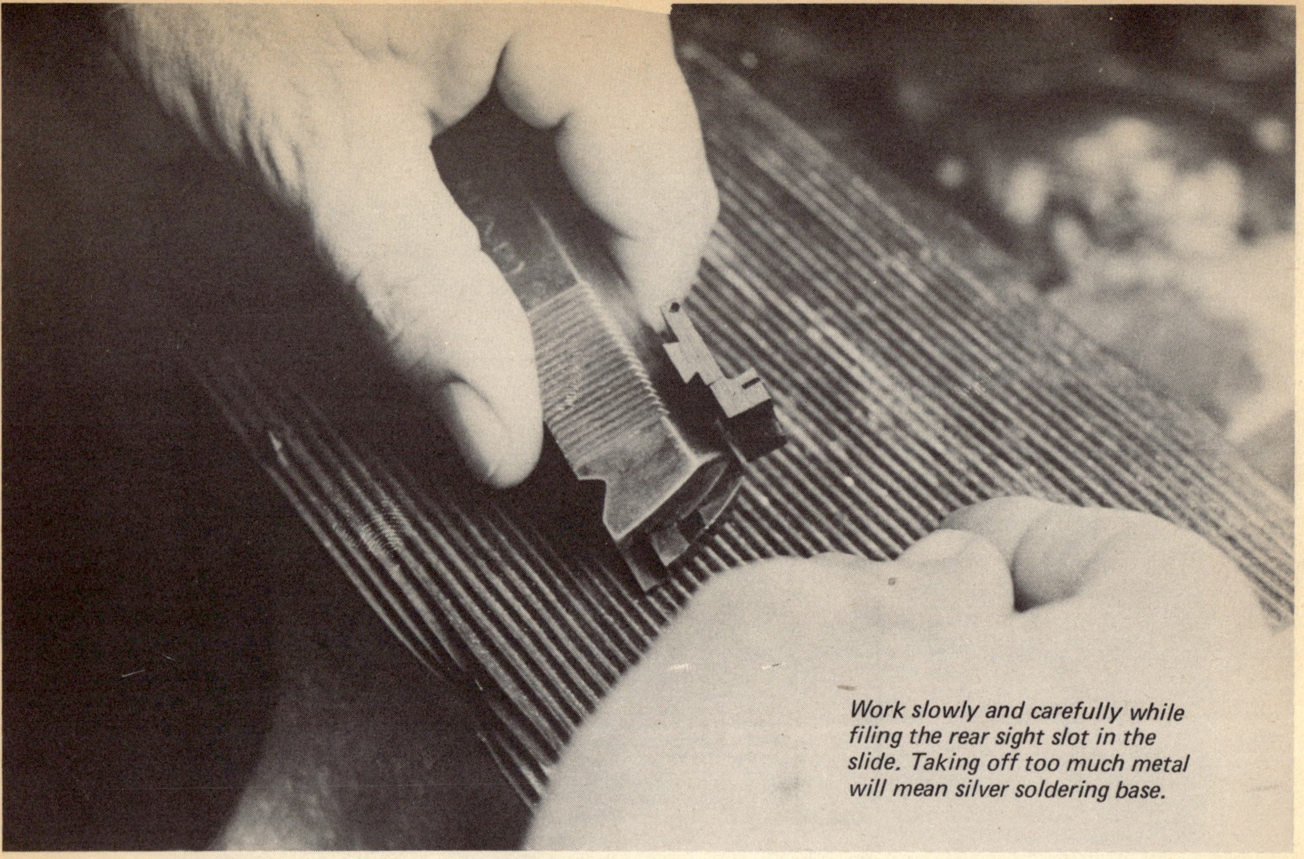

Work slowly and carefully while filing the rear sight slot in the slide. Taking off too much metal will mean silver soldering base.

New front sight may be silver soldered in cleaned-up slot with small flame that will not affect slide metal.

these days — invest in Brownell's nylon-brass drift punch. This drift has an interchangeable tip and will last at least as long as a solid brass drift, and has the advantage of being more versatile.

Now take the new rear sight and place it into the dovetail slot on the slide. I never have encountered a slide where the slot did not need a bit of widening to accept the base of the new sight. Do the widening with care and check the fit frequently. This fit should be tight and the final seating of the rear sight should be accomplished with the brass drift and hammer, with the slide locked into the padded jaws of the vise.

Most slides have an index mark that tells you when you have seated the sight correctly. If your slide does not have such a mark, check the alignment of sight and slide often; not only while the work is locked into the vise, but also by picking up the slide and sighting it the way you would the complete gun.

Once the rear sight is seated, assemble the gun and sight her in. You now have a .45 ACP, or whatever gun you equipped, with an adjustable sight that should give you better accuracy, thanks to a better sight picture.

A word of caution about bluing: If you attempt to reblue your autoloader, be sure to keep the work moving on the buffing wheel at all times. A smooth finish is essential for a good bluing job, but if you keep the work too long on the buffing wheel, you'll round the sharp corners of the metal.

While this won't affect the performance of the gun, the overall appearance will immediately spell amateur gun tinkerer — a label that you can avoid with a bit of care and foresight!

Installation of new front sight and adjustable rear sight transforms old .45 ACP into range-ready targeter. By assembling the proper tools and working carefully, as outlined in text, conversion job can be done in an evening.

Chapter 8

METAL JEWELING MADE EASY

This Inexpensive But Effective Home Shop Method Can Add Elegance And Smooth Functioning To Your Favorite Firearm

FACTORY ENGINE TURNING, jeweling or damascening — whatever term you use — has gone the way of the nickel cup of coffee. Although done by means of power tools, engine turning still must be considered a hand job, with one burnishing mark after the other being applied either in straight rows or in some other sort of eye-pleasing pattern.

Since it is a slow and painstaking job, little jeweling is found on factory rifles, and most gunsmiths will charge at least twenty bucks to decorate the bolt of an M98 action. Even at that price, most smiths steer clear of such jobs, for it takes considerable time to do such work properly.

More complex engine-turning jobs, calling for disassembling and later reassembling the newly decorated part, can cost even more. So, if you want to give your gun or guns that extra-special custom look, doing your own jeweling is the only way to get the job done without having to dig deep into your wallet.

Aside from its eye appeal, jeweling has some real functional advantages. The burnishing creates high and low spots on the metal, thus lubricants are retained on the burnished metal to a greater degree than possible on a smooth piece of steel.

A nonjeweled bolt, for instance, has more friction than a jeweled one. Moreover, although an engine-turned job appears to reflect ambient light more than a similar piece of steel that has not been treated in such fashion, the many small burnishing marks actually serve to break up light reflection. A well-polished but nondamascened bolt can be spotted at considerable distances, while one that has been engine-turned reflects little or no light. A flat part such as an action block, once engine-turned, appears to resist rusting better than an identical part that has not been damascened.

There is yet another reason why a great many sporterized military rifles display some degree of jeweling. Slight pitting

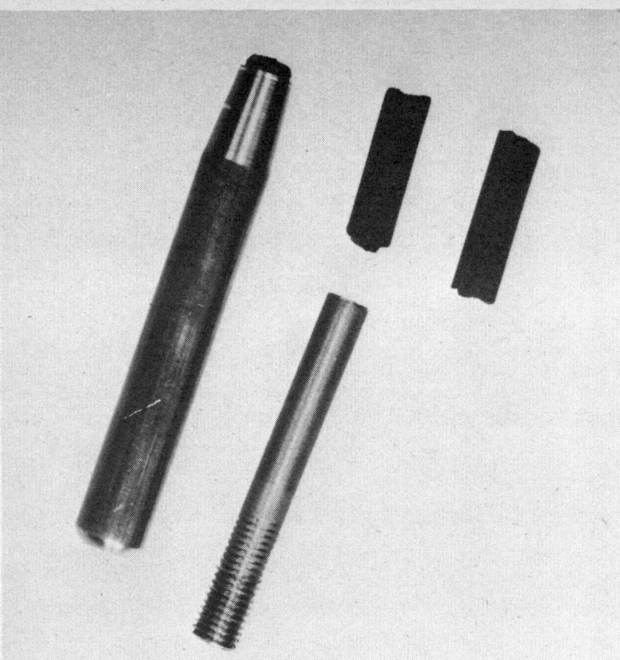

Rex tool is designed for the task of jeweling metal and is a versatile addition to the gunsmith's supply of gadgets. Refills are available but not always on the market locally, must be ordered by mail.

on bolt body or bolt handle is hard to eliminate in most instances, but a quick trip through the jeweling fixture not only will get rid of these blemishes but also will add elegance to a customized and sporterized rifle that, at one time, was a military clunker you picked up inexpensively.

Engine turning may, therefore, also be used to hide or remove other blemishes and minor defects. If desired, such parts can be blued — more or less successfully — after being engine-turned. More about that later.

Engine turning essentially is an abrasive process. The burnishing marks most often are applied in rows, with each mark overlapping on its neighbor — as well as on the marks above and below — in a precise and uniform manner. Unless you have the patience of a saint and the eye of a skilled tool and die maker, this calls for the use of an engine-turning or jeweling jig. However, I have done the inside of several magazine floor plates freehand, the work being guided only by a piece of flat bar stock clamped to the table of a Dremel Moto-Tool stand. This brings us to the tools needed for such a job.

A drill press with an Atlas universal compound vise or even a rotary compound table is ideal. Lacking either of these or some other type of table or vise that permits perfect indexing of the work, a drill press with a length of bar stock clamped to the drill-press table as a guide will also do very nicely.

Different materials and tips will produce different jeweling configurations. An old rifle floor plate was used to test the pattern of the Rex tool, a wire brush and two hardnesses of typewriter erasers, below.

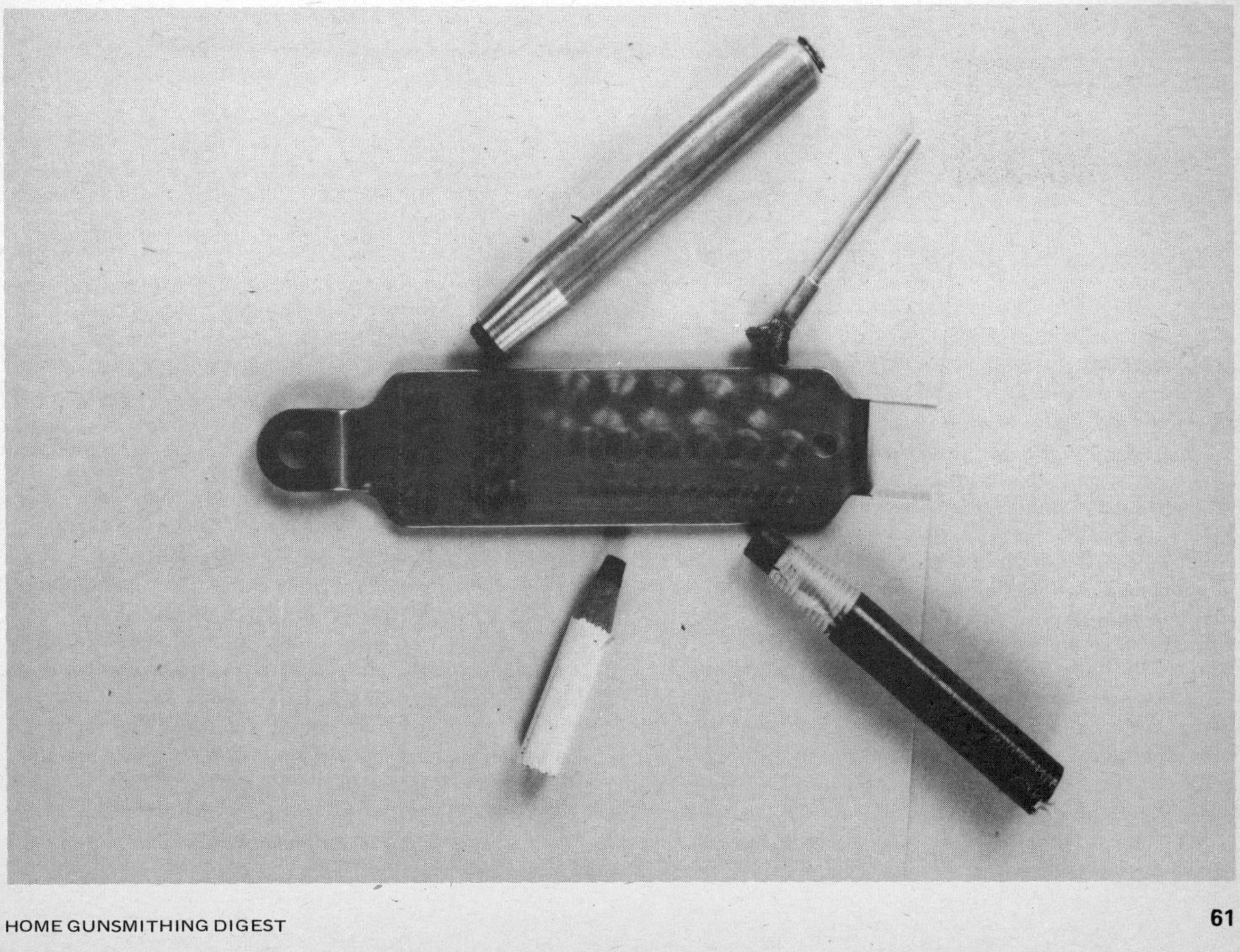

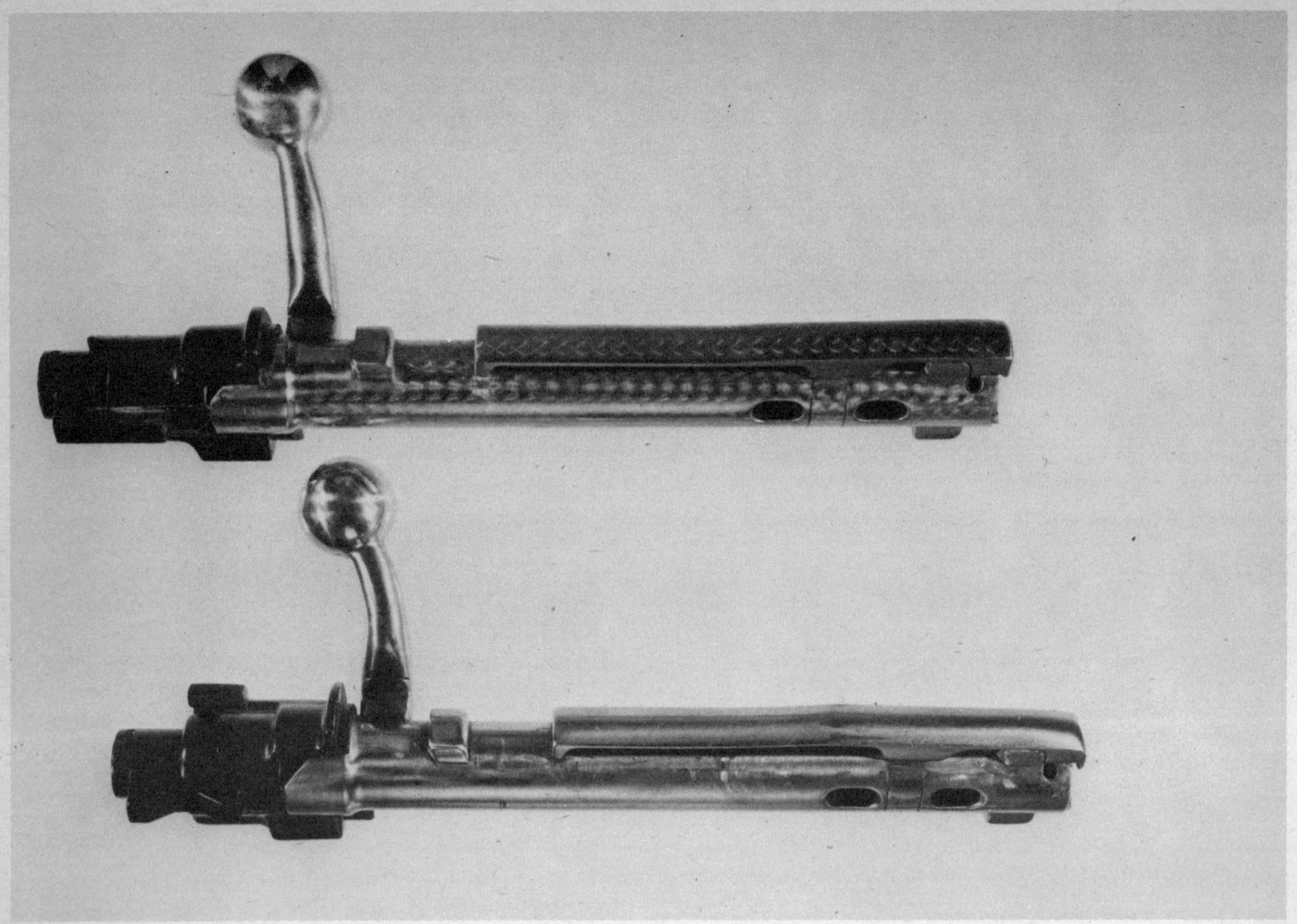

Aside from the attractiveness of the jeweling, an engine turned bolt will function considerably more smoothly.

Lacking an electric drill with stand, it also is possible to use a Dremel Moto-Tool locked onto the Model 210 Dremel drill-press stand. This Dremel setup works essentially in the same manner as a drill press, except that the unit does not have the power of a drill press and you bring the work upward instead of the spindle downward.

If you don't have a drill press, don't give up yet. You can do some neat-looking work with a portable, electric drill that is clamped into a stand. Such a stand, in effect, converts the drill into a drill press. I don't recommend the usual one-quarter-inch drill for this, but if that is all you have, you can get by with it.

If you must use either a portable drill or a Moto-Tool, you will have to clamp some guides to the table. Most of the auxiliary drill stands don't come with a table, but you easily can improvise a small, wooden platform that will hold the work. Ensure that the platform on the Model 210 Dremel stand does not move while you are engine turning a job. A couple of large C-clamps will do the trick and, when properly set up, they won't get in the way.

Do not attempt to use an electric drill freehand — that is, without a stand — as it is impossible to hold the drill perfectly perpendicular to the work at all times. Goofs have to be polished out, and this gives the work an uneven appearance that is almost impossible to correct in a home workshop.

If you are using a drill press, adjust the belts so that the spindle runs at medium speed. Smaller electric drills and the Dremel tool are best run at full speed for satisfactory burnishing, while heavy-duty drills are best run at one-half or two-thirds speed.

Incidentally, if you can make a suitable holder for the work to be jeweled, you can even use a lathe — with the polishing head being locked into the chuck on the headstock and the work being moved toward the rotating burnishing head. A six-inch lathe, such as the one sold by Sears, is suitable, but the smaller Unimat won't do since holding the work calls for extensive machining of clamps and holders, and this, in the long run, costs more than a drill with the stand.

As mentioned before, engine turning usually is done in rows, with the polishing marks overlapping on all four sides. This calls for precise control of the movement of the work. Proper alignment before making contact between job and abrasive point is important for a neat-looking job. The final appearance hinges on the even and uniform positioning of the lap marks, and it is for this reason that I favor a compound vise.

If you can take the time for practice on some scrap bar stock, by all means do so. With some experience, you will soon learn that you can create different patterns, especially when the burnishing head is given a shape other than the customary round one.

Flat work, such as magazine floor plates, triggers and other small pieces can be locked into a vise or some other holding device. Bolts are best stripped or taken down; and here a bolt jeweling jig is a worthwhile investment.

All of the tools and supplies, including vises but excluding drills and drill stands, can be ordered from such suppliers as Brownell's. Dremel products are sold by most hardware stores, while drill presses and vises can be obtained locally from Sears or Montgomery Wards.

The choice of burnishing head depends to some extent on the type of engine turning you want to do. Your selection of

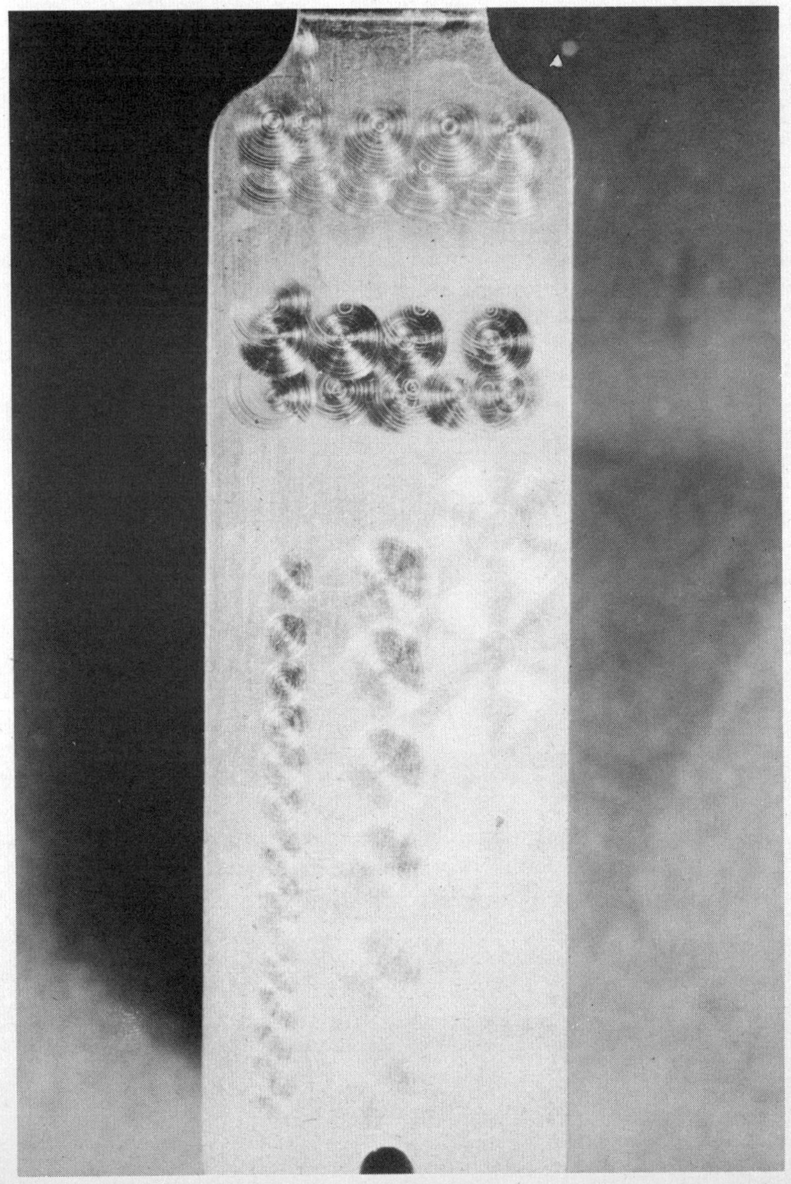

Metal floorplate used for testing various patterns and styles of tips. Note how each mark may be arranged to overlap on either side, above or below.

Abrasive paste should be mixed to fairly stiff consistency before being applied to metal, above. Typewriter eraser, mounted in electric drill or Moto-Tool is brought carefully into contact with paste and metal and operated at slow speed. Twenty or thirty seconds at each application will give the desired uniform results. See text for details.

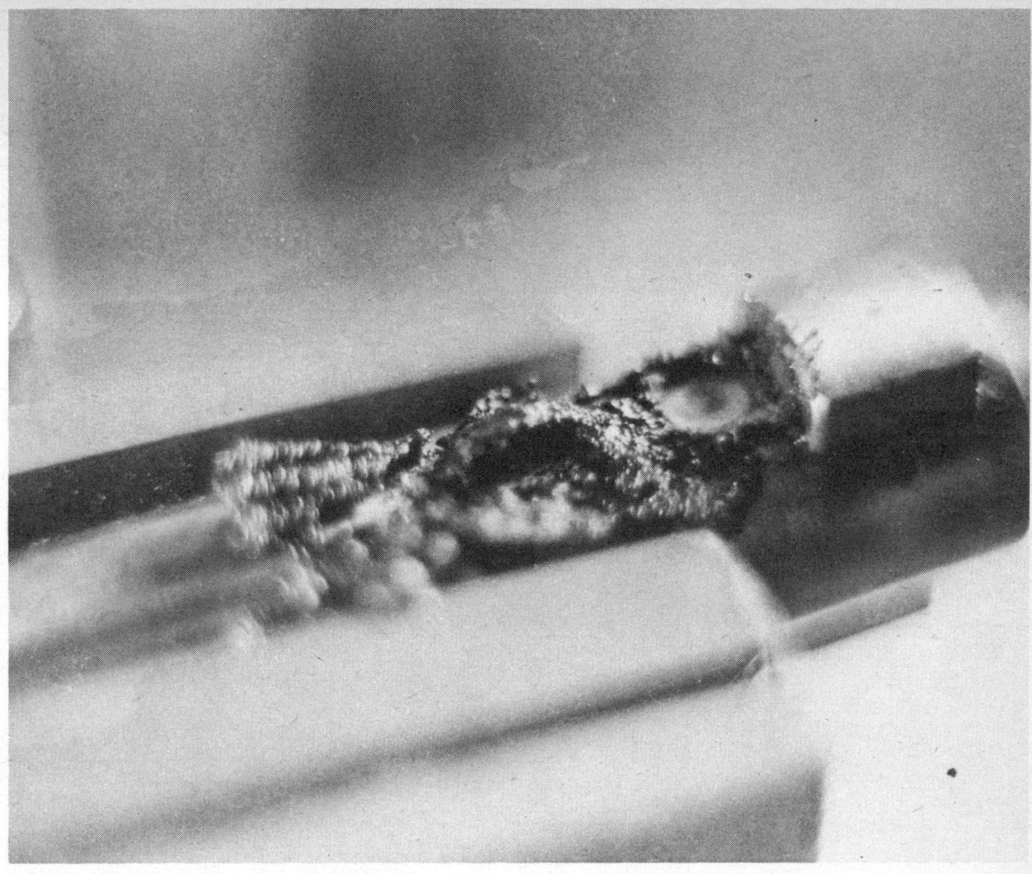

First engine-turned mark on rifle bolt is visible through abrasive paste mixture. Uniform pressure and contact time will produce attractive custom appearance.

the head also depends on the flatness or roundness of the part to be jeweled. For flat work, the Rex engine-turning tool sold by Brownell's is a good choice. This consists, basically, of two threaded metal tubes that contain a replaceable rubber-bonded abrasive tip.

Nearly the same results can be obtained with the pencil-like typewriter erasers that come in different sizes and degrees of hardness. Cut one or more of these into two-inch lengths and peel back the protective paper covering. Do not attempt to shape the exposed rubber into a finely pointed tip, but leave the exposed area fairly round and flat. If the tip is cut at an angle, some interesting engine-turning designs and patterns can be developed. These burnishing heads will fit into all drill presses and drills, but will not fit into the Moto-Tool.

Some gunsmiths use small wire brushes in a drill press and, although they wear much faster than other burnishing heads, they are just the thing for such contoured areas as bolts, where the flat and rather rigid Rex tool or the typewriter erasers don't have the needed give to mold themselves to the shape of the work.

Unless you are going to use the Rex tool exclusively — this tool contains its own abrasive mix — you will need an abrasive compound to apply to the work. You can buy already-mixed emery flour paste, but I prefer making up my own; since I can control just how liquid or stiff the paste will be. For most jobs, a medium-thin paste consisting of cutting oil and abrasive emery flour, about 120 grit, is made up. However, a stiff paste works best with the wire brushes and a slight reduction in spindle speed is suggested, unless you want the abrasive gunk flying all over you and the shop.

The paste can be reused and if it has to be stored for any length of time a tightly sealed, screw-top jar is best. If abrasive paste has been applied to a job and you have to interrupt your work for some time, it is best to remove as much paste as possible from the work and replace it in the jar, then wash the work with a solvent.

The degree of burnishing depends not only on the speed at which the spindle rotates, but also on the duration of the contact between work and burnishing head and the amount of pressure exerted. The degree of engine turning also depends on how much of the abrasive goo is used. Some workers favor using two different mixes, one with a finer grit emery to give the job a second going-over or to touch up corners and edges.

Author Steindler uses drill press with Rex tool to engine-turn metal.

Compound vise on table of drill press with drill or bench vise is the easy, albeit expensive, way of tackling the job. Compound vise allows precise alignment of each burnishing mark with its neighboring patterns.

Special jig is less expensive than compound vise and will produce attractive jeweling. Clamps and guides on drill press table ensure all marks fit chosen pattern.

To get the hang of it, I suggest a bit of practice. You will soon learn how long and how much pressure is needed to achieve the results you are seeking. A piece of scrap or even the inside of a floor plate can be used for experimentation, as well as to determine the method of aligning the rows so that coverage of the work will be even. If your first project is a bolt and you want to be sure of your engine-turning skills before tackling it, remove the handle from one of your loading presses and practice on that. A contact period of ten to fifteen seconds with a shaped typewriter eraser and a paste consisting of 600 grit mixed with Brownell's Do-Drill cutting oil worked perfectly on intricate areas of a Mauser bolt. Using the Rex tool with its self-contained abrasive mix required only a ten-second contact on flat action bars to achieve a satisfactory burnishing mark.

If your first engine-turning effort does not look professional enough, you always can go over the work a second time, using a slightly coarser grit paste. A fine grit used on such repairs, especially when used in conjunction with an angled eraser tip, also gives some interesting results, particularly when patterns are allowed to overlap by about fifty percent.

If you cannot find emery flour locally, get some very-fine and some medium-fine valve-grinding compound. These work nearly as well as the emery paste and have the advantage of always giving the same degree of abrasiveness as long as your stick to the same brand of valve-grinding compound.

When you have completed a job of jeweling, wipe all surfaces containing the emery paste, then wash the engine-turned part in a solvent, being certain that no abrasive paste or residue remains, especially on such functioning parts as bolts.

Hammers of single-action revolvers should be pinned in place with a slave pin and the gun checked for functioning. Similarly, bolt travel and the mechanical performance of any part that has received the beauty treatment should be checked. You will be amazed how much smoother an engine-turned bolt will travel and how much slicker all such parts will function.

Once your first engine-turning job has been completed, you will start looking into your gun cabinet for other guns that could stand such a beauty treatment. Not counting your time and perhaps the cost of the bolt-jeweling jig, giving one of your guns a damascening job will cost you about ten to fifteen cents worth of emery flour and cutting oil — a bargain any way you look at it!

Chapter 9

DO YOUR OWN METAL CHECKERING AND STIPPLING

Here Are Tips And Techniques For Adding That Extra Touch Of Class To Your Personal Firearm!

Five metal checkering files are adequate to do most gunsmithing jobs, available from either Brownell's or Mittermeir, by mail order. Handles are not included.

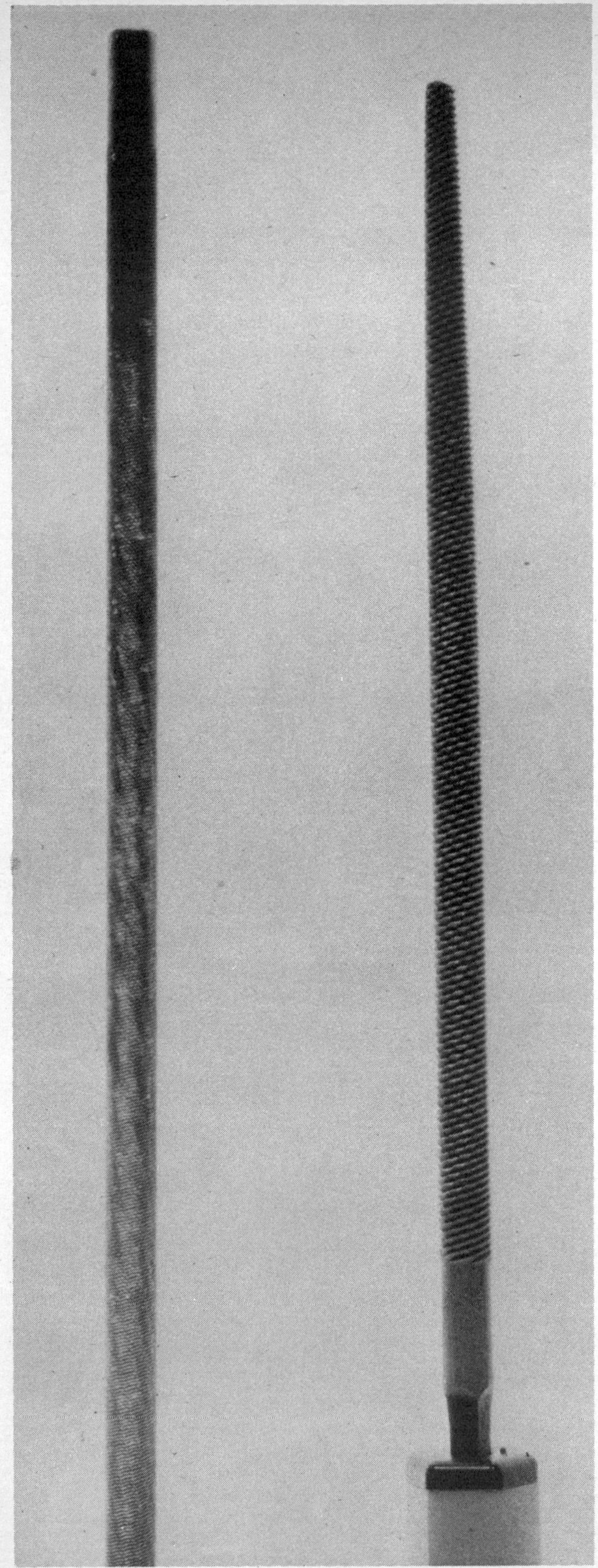

Chainsaw files come in a variety of cuts. The home gunsmith can produce various patterns from each file.

THE METAL CHECKERING seen on hammers of handguns, bolt handles of rifles, trigger guards, and even on other items, has a lot of eye appeal. Some of it also has practical value. With some practice and care, you can learn to do your own checkering.

Unlike wood checkering, where mistakes and runovers often are corrected easily, mistakes on steel are not corrected easily. For this reason — as I found out the hard way — I recommend some practice sessions before tackling your first steel-checkering job. Extra-hard steels are almost impossible to checker and you may have to fall back on stippling, which is easier to learn. The most frequently seen type of stippling is on the front and sometimes the backstrap of match .45 ACP guns. Here, stippling prevents the gun from riding out of the shooter's hand, thus shortening recovery time, an important consideration during timed-fire shooting.

Since the Gun Control Act of '68 has reduced drastically the number of good military surplus actions suitable for custom rifles, I've found that stippling will also convert a cruddy-looking action into something people admire. One such M98 action which I wanted to use for a custom wildcat was so badly pitted that even prolonged buffing and chemical treatment left the action looking like a sad souvenir of years past. After a little lapping of the action rails and engine turning the bolt, the action was slick enough for my wants, but still looked like something the cat dragged in.

Out came the stippling punch and, after stripping the action of whatever bluing was left, I stippled the pitted surface of the action. Since I did not need the gripping surface of the sharp stippling as on the front strap of my match .45 Colt, I used a large center-punch without modifying it in any way.

By holding the punch almost vertically to the surface I was stippling, I got almost none of the hooks which are so undesirable on front and backstraps. The few hooks that were made by not holding the punch directly above the work were knocked off with a mill bastard file. Smaller hooks, created either by angling the punch as you hit it, or by altering the tip of the punch at a forty-five-degree angle, can be made. If these are not desired, the hooks are knocked off with a file. The smaller the tip of the center-punch, the smaller the marks left on the metal.

Before you even consider doing your own metal checkering or stippling, here are a few tips. Strip the gun or action down as completely as possible. If, for instance, you have a pitted receiver that needs a face lifting, do this job before the barrel is installed. The .45 ACP should be taken down completely, the grips removed, so that you can handle the frame more easily in the vise. A rotating base or swivel vise is almost essential and, of course, the jaws of the vise must be well padded to prevent damage to whatever gun parts you are working on.

It is best to remove all bluing, then degrease and polish. After polishing, degrease again and, if you have decided on a pattern, lay out the pattern on the bare, polished metal. If you feel you should or must lay out your checkering, use either a lead pencil or a finely pointed felt pen. Scribed lines are hard to see unless they are made on a layout blue, of which Dykem is probably the best. However, the use of a layout blue also means that, when the job is completed, you have to clean off the blue. Reblue the finished job and be sure the bluing enters into the checkering or stippling.

When you begin to think about checkering steel, here are some suggestions you might keep in mind. As mentioned, stippling is easier than checkering and can be applied to any surface, flat or round. In contrast, the checkering, done by means of special files, is best applied to absolutely flat surfaces, at least at the beginning of your checkering career.

Before you spoil the frame or trigger guard of a gun, practice on some short pieces of aluminum bar stock. Center

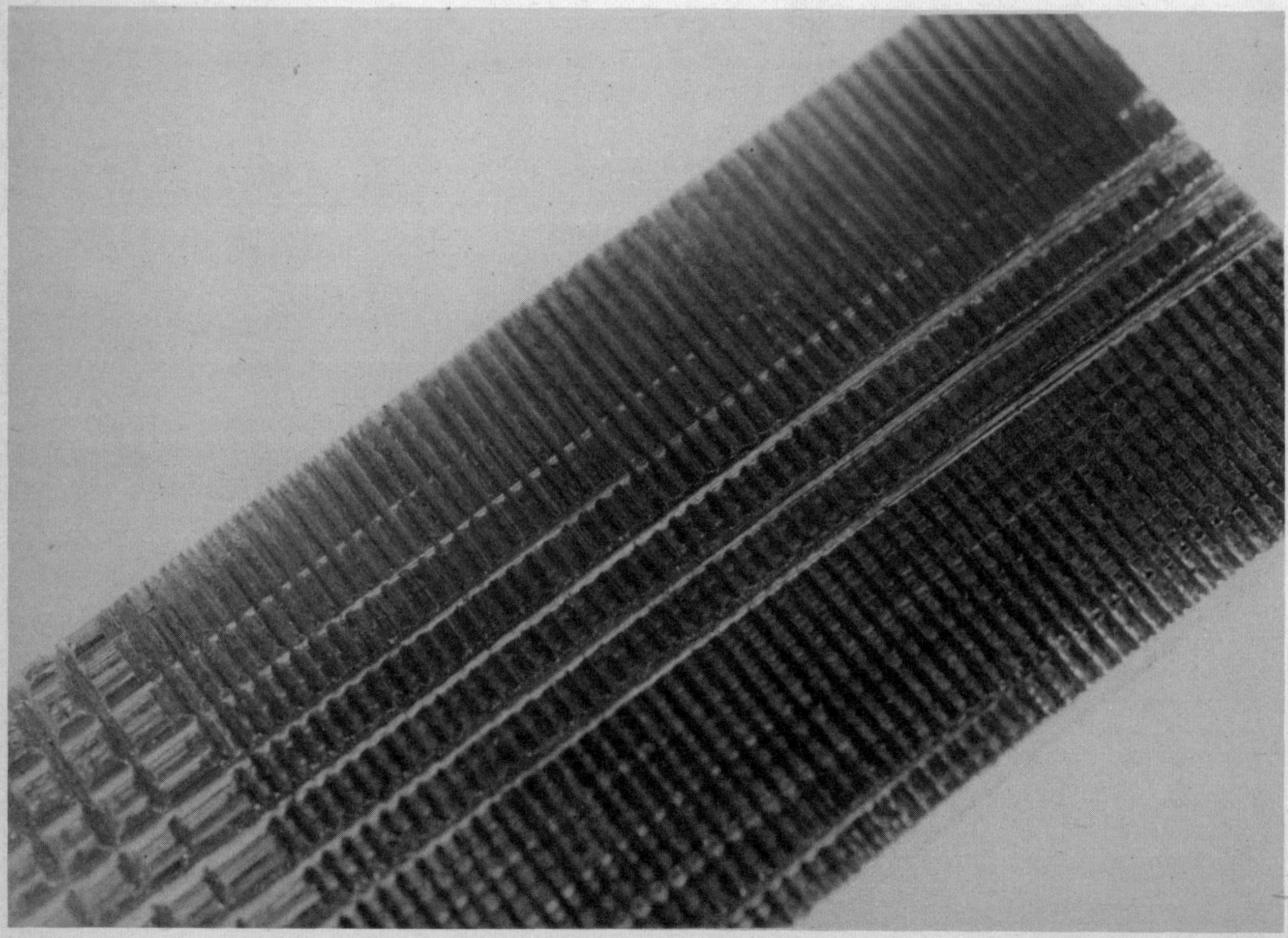

Practice on a piece of aluminum bar stock, which is readily available at most retail hardware outlets around the country. Many patterns of checkering may be practiced and learned, using a coarse pattern file at right angle cuts.

punches, a small machinist square, a small ball-peen hammer and the needed bar stock can be obtained in most hardware stores. The special metal checkering files can be ordered from Brownell's, and five such files are offered. These are graded according to the number of teeth per inch: The No. 00 makes twenty lines per inch, the No. 0 cuts thirty, the No. 1 makes forty, the No. 2 cuts fifty, while the No. 4 is the finest of the lot, cutting seventy-five. Available from either your hardware store or Brownell's are two additional items — a file cleaner and a chainsaw file. The latter comes in various diameters and also with several different patterns.

The checkering files should be equipped with handles; these can be bought or fashioned easily enough from a piece of broom handle. When seating any file in a handle, never use a hammer or mallet on the tip of the file to seat the stem of the file in the handle. Insert the tang of the file in the handle, then push the file into the handle as far as you can, exerting a straight line push only. Then grab the handle, file upward, and pound the handle on the workbench or concrete floor. Should the file be loosened eventually, either repeat the pounding or simply tap the base of the file handle with a hammer once or twice.

The chainsaw file may not come with a handle. Make an extra handle, and seat it on the tip of the file. More about using such a file later. Chainsaw files, as well as checkering files, must be cleaned more frequently than a mill bastard or drawfile. One old machinist's trick to keep the file teeth from clogging is the liberal application of blackboard chalk to the teeth. Simply run a piece of chalk over the file three or four times and clogging will be reduced considerably.

Many machinists have the habit of knocking the edge of the file they are using against the vise, a steel block on the bench or, worse yet, against the bed of the lathe. It looks like the guy knows what he is doing, but in reality, he is merely ruining a good piece of shop equipment. A file cleaner, sometimes called a file card, is the only reliable way to clean

Fine line metal checkering files are a bit more difficult to use than the coarse, as all cuts must be parallel.

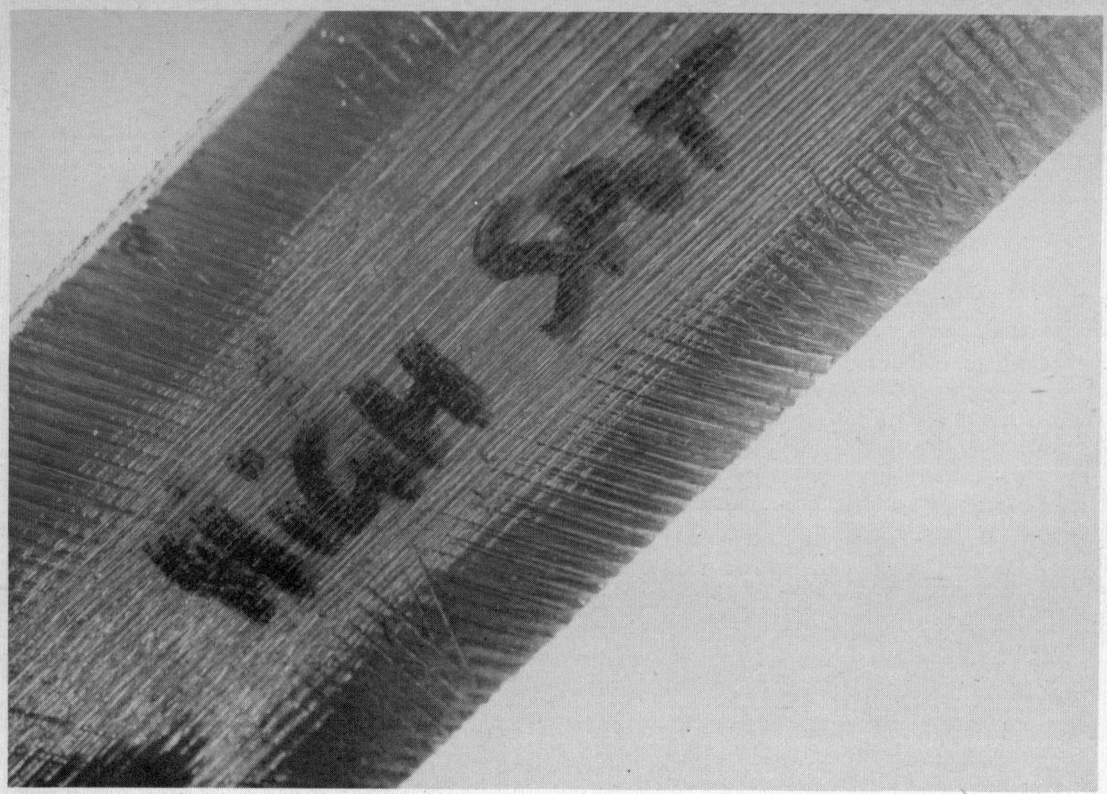

Bar stock, above, was purposely cupped before checkering
to illustrate effect of not having perfectly flat surface
on which to file. Coarse file, when not used in a straight
line, will produce lopsided checkering. Practice on scrap.

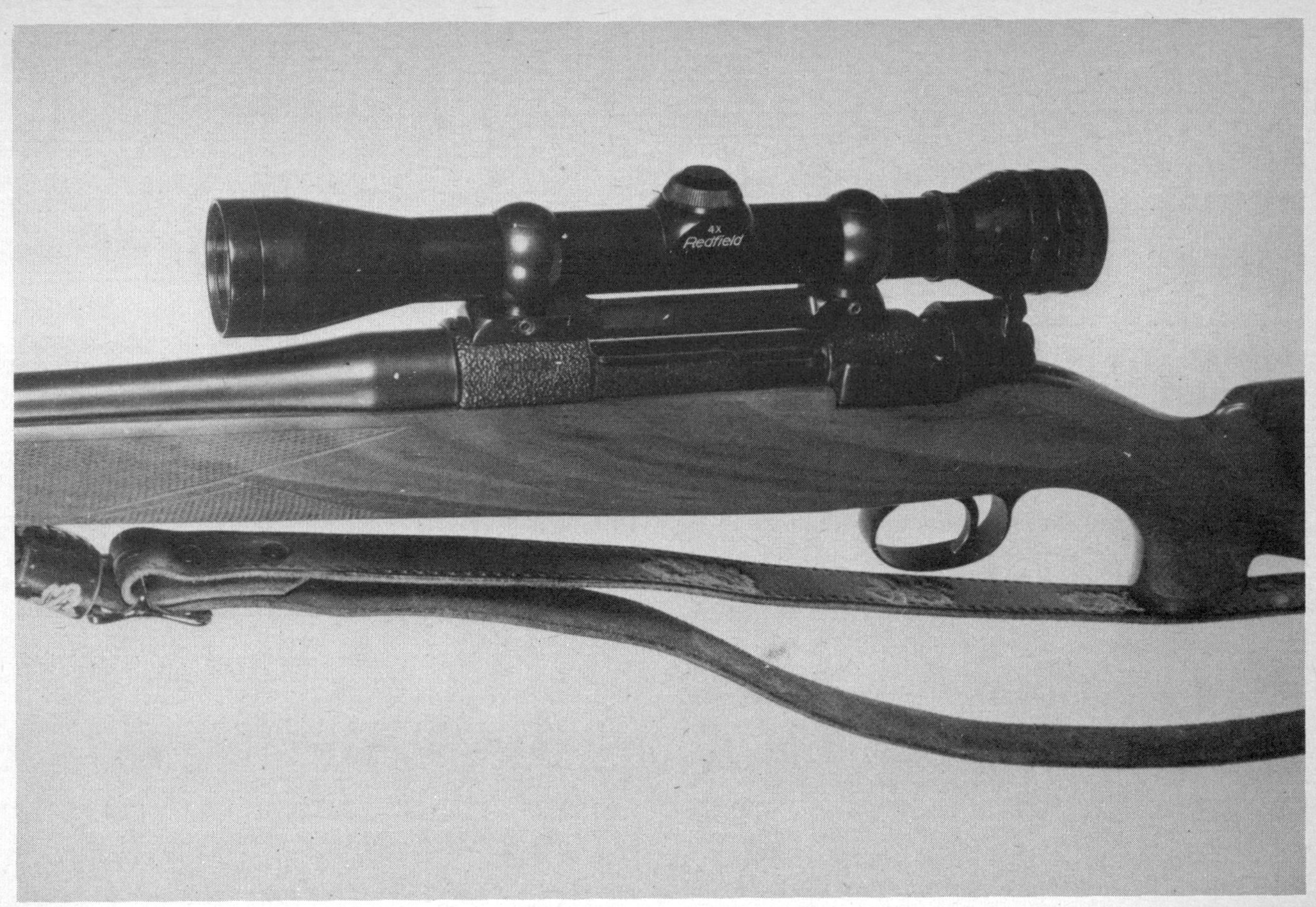

Elderly military action looks like a custom job after facelifting, buffing and bluing. Total cost was under a dollar for a punch, plus about two hours of buffing. Rounded center punch, carefully applied, rejuvenated this M98.

the teeth of any file, for wood or steel. A clogged file will not cut evenly and you have to work twice as hard with a dirty and clogged file than you would with one that is cleaned every so often. Cleaning becomes especially important if you practice on aluminum bar stock, since the metal tends to foul the teeth quickly and completely.

If you have a lathe or access to one, a knurling tool or wheel can be used to good advantage. Although patterns are limited, it is possible to obtain some degree of variation in the pattern being cut by running the work in the lathe at varying speeds and applying varying pressure on the crossfeed.

As mentioned, a center or prick punch is used for stippling. Shop around for one that either has seen better days or one that you can grind down. A lightly rounded tip can be used for attractive stippling on surfaces where stippling or checkering is usually not seen or expected. If possible, stay away from the punches that are thin and shorter than 1½ inches. Holding such punches quickly becomes tiring and your hand will cover the work too often to get a clear picture of what is going on.

The simplest decorative filing is done with a chainsaw file. Lock a piece of the aluminum bar stock — flat side up — in your vise, then roll the file across the surface while exerting pressure. Let the handles of the file rotate in the palms of your hands as you move the file back and forth, maintaining even pressure. Try several such cuts on the piece of aluminum stock and note how the pattern suddenly emerges. Learn to keep the file going so that the marks left by your previous file strokes coincide or run parallel to the next marks left on the metal.

By angling the file to the work, you can create a slanted pattern of lines, and by crossing the original lines made by the file, you can form a distinctive checkering pattern. Try such a cross-cut by intersecting the lines first at ninety degrees, then on another trial piece of aluminum stock by holding the file so that the lines intersect at a forty-five-degree angle. Keep the work clean by using a stiff brush rather than by blowing the filings all over the bench.

In using the Brownell metal checkering files, remember that you not only must move the file back and forth, but you should exert downward pressure on the forward part of the file. Some experience in drawfiling, even if it's practice on a piece of scrap metal, will pay off by giving you a better-looking job with less work. Leave the file on the work for the return stroke and clean the file every few minutes, especially if you practice on aluminum stock. If your work surface is wider than the file itself, be sure to align the file so that the finished lines will be parallel. If you should run into trouble — and this can be avoided by checking your work frequently — there is little that can be done in the way of correcting your goof.

The No. 0 and the No. 1 file can be used to make parallel lines. By angling the next cut, you can create a distinct pattern. An interesting variation is the use of one of these files, with the crosscuts being made by a chainsaw file. You can either try to match the lines per inch you get from the checkering file with the line per inch of the chainsaw file, or you can use a different cut — finer or coarser — to obtain yet another checkering pattern.

Depending on the metal you are checkering and the condition of your files, you may find that the final pattern is just a bit too rough for comfortable use. A few light strokes with a mill bastard, or any other file suitable for drawfiling, will easily smooth out those rough areas of the checkering.

Once checkering of flat and level surfaces has been mastered, it becomes easy to go on to the more complex jobs such as checkering a hammer spur. The easiest, fastest way to tackle this type of surface was taught me by a top-notch machinist and gunsmith.

Remove the part to be checkered from the gun, de-blue and polish it smooth. Then lock the part into the padded jaws of the swivel vise so that part of the area to be checkered is level and parallel to the jaws of the vise. Checker this small section, then rotate the part so the next area is level and parallel to the jaws of the vise. Checker this small section, then rotate the part so the next area is level and checker

this. Keep going around until you have decorated all the surface you wanted to dress up. If there are spots into which you cannot get a checkering file, mark the lines you want to cut and use either a watchmaker's file or a screwhead file. Both are available from Brownell's.

As mentioned, start on flat work for practice. However, some of the bar stock you can pick up for pennies only looks flat. Once a square is put on it, you will notice almost invariably that the outer edges are higher than the center section. Run one of your checkering files across this several times, then make a crosscut with the same file. The center portion of the metal will be devoid of file marks. If you can find a chainsaw file that is narrow enough, you can then make some parallel grooves in this untouched area. If you have either a watchmaker's file or screwhead file, you can make the grooves with that, but be sure to mark guidelines first so your finished lines come out parallel.

If adept at handling a fine-toothed jeweler's saw, you can use this instead of the screwhead or watchmaker's file to create lines, but again, the work will have to be flat. For areas where it is difficult to get a full-length file to bear, one neat trick is to use a cut-off Swiss file of the suitable shape, size and width. Forget about using a hacksaw to cut off a piece of the file. Use the edge of a fine grinding wheel and cut the file so the handle portion of the file can be used, with or without the wood handle.

Hard steel will not allow a file to bite and the file will

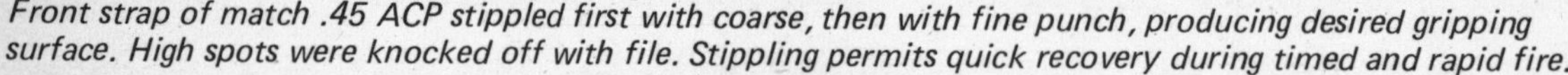

Front strap of match .45 ACP stippled first with coarse, then with fine punch, producing desired gripping surface. High spots were knocked off with file. Stippling permits quick recovery during timed and rapid fire.

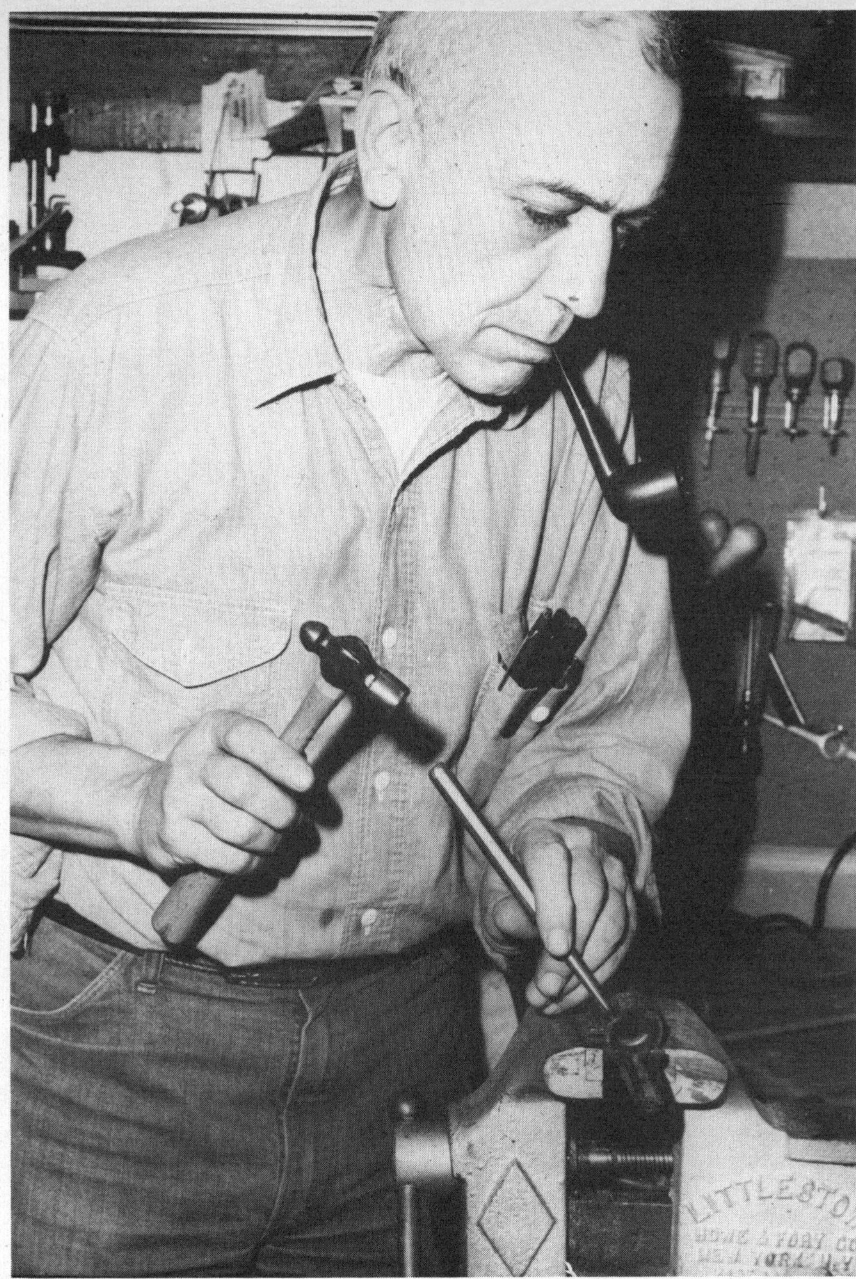

Light ball peen hammer applied to blunt coarse punch is used to stiple Mauser M98 action which was too badly pitted to be buffed out.

simply slip over the surface, often not even leaving a scratch mark. If uncertain about the quality of the steel you want to checker, before removing all the bluing and buffing, find a spot where you can test the ability of the metal to take a file mark. On handguns, removing the grips will give you adequate space for testing.

In the case of rifles, remove the barreled action from the wood and do your testing on the underneath section of the action.

Both stippling and metal checkering can be used effectively when converting an old military steel buttplate into a modern and rather luxurious one. After filing or even sawing the buttplate to fit the new stock, lay out a border that remains uncheckered, then checker or stipple the center section of the buttplate. Other custom touches that you can

apply without too much trouble include checkering screwheads and bolt handles. Even scope bases have not escaped the tender, loving touches of a steel checkering file.

In metalworking, mistakes cannot be corrected as easily as when working with wood. Practice makes perfect and starting with easily filed aluminum bar stock is one way to gain experience without too much hard work.

Metal cutting files are hard, but there is one easy way to wreck any such file: toss it into a drawer with a dozen or so other files and watch them bounce around.

When done for the day, clean each file, apply a new coating of chalk then hang them up on a wall or pegboard. This enables you to see the file and identify the cut it will make. Handled in this way, a good file will outlast most other tools on your bench.

Chapter 10

SILVER SOLDERING MADE SIMPLE

With A Bit Of Effort And Experimentation, You Can Master The Mystics Of Soldering, Brazing, Sweating And Welding

BASIC TO ALL of the metal-bonding methods is the use of heat. In addition, most methods also require a chemical cleaning and antioxidation agent known as flux, and a special metal that, when molten and cooled, will firmly bond the two joints.

Soft soldering requires the least amount of heat, while oxy-acetylene welding requires the greatest amount. The types of metals being joined, the stress the new joint will have to withstand, and the size and shape of the new joint govern the method used. Soft soldering, as used in electrical connections, gives relatively weak joints that cannot withstand pressure or stress, while oxy-acetylene welding makes a strong joint.

No matter what metal or what type of heat is used to make the joint, the most important point to remember is that only clean — and I am talking about almost surgically clean — metals can be joined successfully. With any of the mentioned methods, chemically similar as well as chemically dissimilar metals can be joined, providing the edges of the areas to be bonded are clean.

Before anyone wonders why I left out fusion, it should be understood that fusion is really the melting and combining of metals. Brass, by definition, is a mixture of copper and zinc, the result of the mixture being a fusion. Similarly, if you have a short in an electric wire, the metal of the wire may have

been fused together — but certainly not soldered, brazed or welded together. Some expert welders feel that welding, by whatever means, is really a fusion or melting process, with the welding rod merely supplying the extra metal needed to form a bonded joint.

Providing the surfaces to be joined have been cleaned with a file, wire wheel, brush or by chemical means, the method of joining becomes surprisingly simple. Heat both of the cleaned surfaces until the solder or welding rod melts, and make the joint or junction in such a manner that the molten solder or rod metal fills all hollow or uneven spots in the joint, with the excess easily running off. Only practice will show how much solder is needed to fill the gaps so that there is only a minimal runoff of solder. Let the work cool completely, then remove the overrun metal.

On large joints, reheating the surplus makes removal of that metal easy, but when sweating on a sight, heating the surplus means that the metal under the sight will also melt and the process may have to be started all over again. If the joint comes unglued, remove all of the solder, clean the area completely, and start all over again, this time using less solder to avoid overruns. Somewhere along the line of applying heat, solder, and moving the parts to be joined, you'll suddenly discover that you need at least one or two extra hands. Before you scream for help, let me assure you that ninety-nine

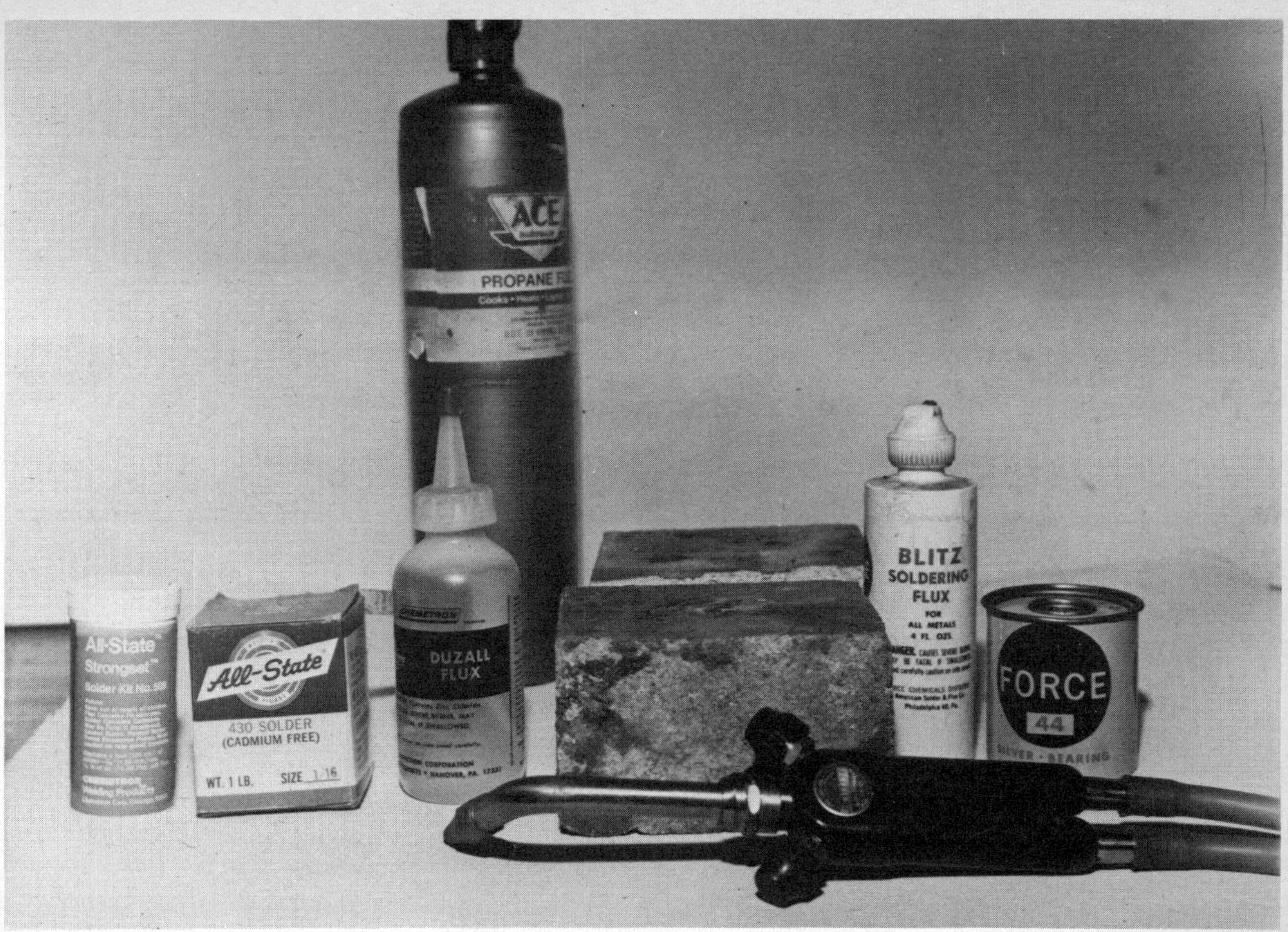

Basic silver-soldering equipment includes torches, flux and solder. For portability, the small propane torch with tank is hard to beat. For prolonged use, a mixture of oxygen and LP gas is ideal and inexpensive.

percent of the welding and soldering jobs can be done by one man.

Obviously, you will need a source of heat. In addition, I suggest a fair-sized piece of asbestos sheet to cover your bench and at least one whole and two half firebricks. Wire wheels, files and steel brushes are also needed. Some experienced guys use muriatic acid (hydrochloric acid) for cleaning metals to be joined. This works fine, but hydrochloric acid is tricky stuff to work with; therefore, I don't recommend it for general shop use.

Failure to get a good soldering job or weld can invariably be traced back either to incomplete cleaning of metals or inadequate heating of the parts to be joined. In contrast to other shop jobs, soldering or any kind of welding requires some extra caution. Fluxes and solders contain chemicals that raise hell with gun bluing, and some parts of the job cannot be heated too much since this would affect the crystalline structure of the metal and therefore its hardness. If there is residual flux on the surface of a newly soldered job, remove it by washing the part in hot water. The flux, sold in either liquid or paste form, prevents the oxidation of the newly cleaned metal before the molten metal begins to flow. Once the solder flows under work, it runs into the joint — thanks to the capillary action.

Soft solder is almost useless for gun work; however, some gunsmiths prefer it over silver solder for installing ventilated ribs. It is mostly used in electrical and radio connections. Mastering soft soldering means that other sweating or brazing jobs will be a lot easier later on. Some electrical solder wire contains the flux, but I favor a separate fluxing agent, especially when using an electric soldering iron.

Sweating, silver or hard soldering is also known as brazing. The joints are somewhat stronger than those made with soft solder, but are considerably weaker than a joint made either by arc, helio arc or oxy-acetylene welding. If brass is to be joined with brass by means of sweating, a brass spelter or solder cannot be used since the heat required to heat the solder is identical to the heat of the metals to be joined and hence those parts will melt at the same time as the solder or spelter rod. Brass has a melting point of 1700 degrees Fahrenheit, so that the silver solder with a melting point of 1100 degrees Fahrenheit should be selected when bonding brass with brass becomes essential.

Silver soldering is, undoubtedly, the most useful of the metal joining processes. Silver solder can be used to join ferrous as well as nonferrous metals. As with cold and hot bluing, two cautionary notes are in order. Once the metals have been cleaned, keep them that way and avoid touching them with bare hands or tools. The U.S. Department of Health has issued cautionary statements regarding the use of silver solder. Solder containing cadmium has been blamed for two deaths due to inhalation of the fumes. As in bullet casting, be sure to provide adequate ventilation while doing any soldering, sweating, brazing or welding job.

When getting ready to install a ramp sight, be sure to level the work in the vise both ways. Then place the sight on the barrel, making certain that it is in the optical and physical center of the barrel. Holding the sight in place with a machinist clamp, scribe a line around the base of the sight. After completely cleaning the metal, and that includes removal of the bluing, apply some French chalk or Solder Talc around the outside of the scribed line to prevent the solder from flowing. Solder will not run over the talc, and this saves a lot of cleanup work later on. While heating the barrel for such a job should not produce enough heat to affect the hardness of the barred steel, take steps to prevent scale from forming inside the barrel. Apply a thin coat of a mixture of bone black and melted paraffin, applying this gunk while the paraffin is still liquid. A pistol cleaning rod with a couple of patches, working from the muzzle with due care, will do the trick. Apply this only where heat is going to be applied to the barrel, and clean with Hoppe's No. 9 after the job has cooled off.

When silver soldering, keep in mind that many fluxes, as well as some solders into which the flux has been incorporated, remove gun bluing quickly and messily. Experienced hands at this kind of work remove the bluing from the area where the sight is to be installed, and start their job with bare metal on the barrel.

If you are going to install one ramp or one sight only once or twice a year, the standard propane tank with a torch that screws right onto the tank will prove adequate. If you are planning on a fair amount of sweating, silver soldering and brazing, you should check into somewhat more sophisticated torches, such as Brownell's Mini-Torch and Rigid Torch. The low pressure gases used in operating kitchen stoves, dryers and other appliances vary regionally in their chemical composition. For this reason, gas mix recommendations are difficult and may not be suitable for the gas you can get locally.

I have used a National Welding Equipment Company Orthodontic No. 3A blowpipe for some years with complete

After covering your workbench with asbestos sheets, hot work is held on firebrick. In this instance, a large nail and a flat-headed wood screw are being joined to produce a worm to remove a stuck lead ball lodged in a black powder gun barrel.

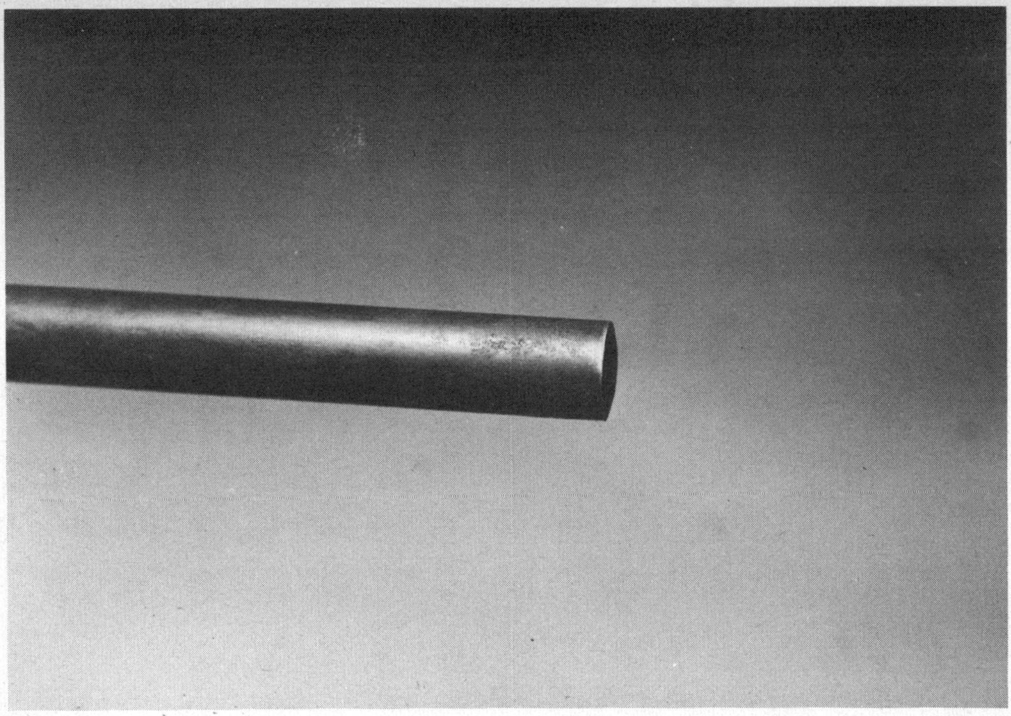

To make certain of good bonding, all of the parts must be cleaned thoroughly, bluing removed and the area must be degreased. Muzzle of this gun has been treated in that way, especially in area where new sight will be installed.

satisfaction. I use a mix of oxygen from a small steel tank and the local brand of low pressure gas, and have found that, with some care, I can even do some limited heat treating with this torch. The greater the control you have over flame movement and the flame itself, the better your soldering jobs will become.

I believe there are as many solders and fluxes as there are rifle calibers, and the choice is indeed a bewildering one. Your best bet is to try several brands and then stick to the one that gives you the best results.

On the whole, the worst place to get advice about silver soldering is from local welding supply houses. They are more familiar with the methods of joining a couple of foot-wide I beams than with delicate soldering jobs. After a great deal of conflicting information and a couple of boxes of so-called silver solder and fluxes, I did what I should have done in the beginning — shop where the gunsmiths shop. The prime source for all sorts of equipment, from fluxes to heat-treating ovens, is Brownell's. I like Brownell's Force 44 solder and the Blitz Flux, and had excellent results with All-State (not related to Sears and Roebuck) 430 solder and Duzall liquid flux. For some delicate work, after you have gained some experience, you may want to try Silvaloy silver solder and Amco's 45 Silver Brazing flux — both are quite expensive, but terrific stuff once you have learned the basics of silver soldering.

As in soft soldering, follow these steps. Clean thoroughly, apply flux, heat both surfaces until the solder flows easily between the joints of the two pieces to be joined. In many cases, it is best to tin the mating surfaces first. This means that after the metal has been cleaned and fluxed, it is heated alone until a small amount of solder sticks to the surface that is to be joined with another piece. Let this tinning harden, and while waiting for that job to cool, you can tin the other part. In joining those parts, it is best to apply heat to the adjoining parts rather than directly on the solder or tinned area.

The best advice anyone can give you is to work slowly and think each step through. Be sure to anchor or clamp parts into place. Heating is best done while the work rests on or just above a piece of firebrick. Should hot solder or a heated piece of metal fall off the job, it won't hurt the bench top and will reduce any existing fire hazard. Remember what was said about ventilation and be sure to support your work. Special soldering clamps can be bought but a couple of small Vise-Grips can be used for other shop jobs. In clamping sights, such as rifle sights on a smoothbore barrel, be sure that you don't get carried away with the tightening of the clamp — pinched barrels, even rifled ones, are more common than most think possible.

Arc welding — sometimes called electro welding — is an advanced system of welding, but does not have wide application in gunsmithing and is not suitable for silver soldering or brazing. Arc welding gives strong joints, and joint strength is almost on a par with oxy-acetylene welded joints. I have used an arc welder to make stands and shelves with angle iron plus supports for my bluing tanks that I use as bathtubs for cleaning guns, barrels and gooked-up parts. In short, the arc welder has a multiplicity of uses, except in the gun field.

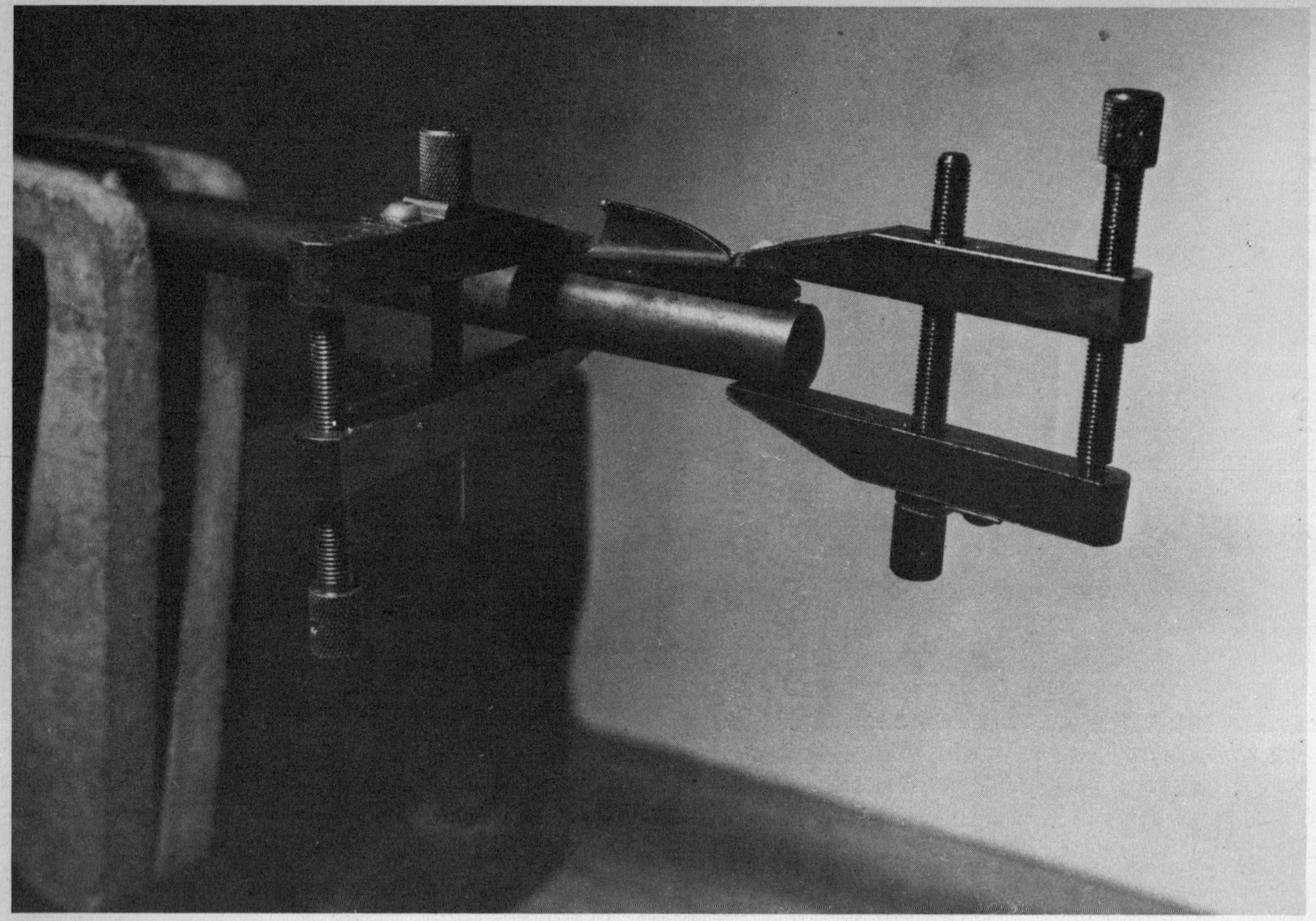

Set the sight in place, clamp it with small machinist clamps. Outline the location of the base on the barrel with a scribe, then check that ramp is located properly in relation to the rear sight. After tinning the area, a little heat should be applied to the sight base. This will allow the solder to flow between the barrel and the sight base for perfect bond.

Oxygen-acetylene welding, though usually considered a craft, is really more of an art. A great deal of specialized knowledge about welding and metals is needed before you can become a fair welder. If there is a trade school or community college with shop courses near you, see if a welding course is offered. This is by far the best way to learn the basics and then some, and you'll be studying under experienced men.

While torches, gauges — one is needed for each tank — helmets, goggles, gloves and other sundries needed for oxygen-acetylene welding are within the reach of most gun tinkerers, the tanks for the gases have gone up and up. Years ago, both tanks could be rented for a few bucks a year, but this has become so costly now that I recommend buying the tanks. You'll get ownership certificates with the tanks, and if you ever want to sell the tanks, you must be able to produce the certificates. Quite often the classified section of the local newspaper is a good source for used tanks, and sometimes even for complete welding outfits. Since tanks have become so costly, there usually is a rush for such secondhand

equipment. Most of the torches are for heavy-duty work and you may want to get some lighter ones, but most of the buyers of used equipment don't care about torches, hoses and the like — it's the tanks they're after! If you do buy tanks this way, be sure to get the needed certificates and find out, if possible, where the previous owner bought his gases. Some welding supply houses are sensitive about refilling someone else's tanks.

For gunsmithing jobs, a relatively small torch with delicate flame control and properly functioning valves for the tanks are a must. In handling tanks, gases and torches, be sure to follow the safety instructions you get with your equipment. If you are uncertain about these safety rules, any welding supply house can furnish you, free of charge, with the needed brochures and folders.

Arc and oxy-acetylene welding produce a fair amount of sparks and hot slag. Select your work area so that there is no dust, wood shavings or powder near the welding area, and keep the place clean and well ventilated.

Experienced gunsmiths can use oxy-acetylene equipment

for everything, from installing a sight to a ventilated rib. I don't recommend that you use one to install a ventilated rib on any kind of double, either stackbarrel or side by side, since many of the joints between the barrels are still made from soft solder that melts all too readily. I use my National torch for this sort of work since I found that it is easier to control flame and heat with this torch than with the oxy-acetylene torch. If you have a ventilated rib that has come unglued, remove it completely from the gun. Some gunsmiths simply resolder the busted joints without removing the entire rib, but I believe complete removal and complete resoldering a fast and easy way out of a fairly tricky job.

Look at the joints where the sight has separated from the barrel. Chances are there is dirt, rust, crud and other foreign matter there, and this is one cause of the separation. Clean all contact points on rib and barrel, then tin these areas lightly. If the tinning does not hold, you did not clean that spot well, so start all over again, and do it right. Once all the areas have been tinned and cooled, install the rib, using the B-Square Rib Soldering Fixture. Heat each area slowly and carefully and when the solder begins to flow into the joint, go on to the next spot. Work from breech to muzzle. Ersin Multicope sixty percent tin solder is said to be good for this type of work, but I have been sticking to the Force 44 solder and the Blitz flux.

As with every acquired skill, it takes time and patience to master soldering, brazing, sweating and welding. Of course, it is best and also least expensive in the long run to latch onto an old barrel somewhere, and to install and reinstall the same sight a dozen or more times on this practice tube. Your first efforts probably will look like the job was done by six mischievous gnomes but, with some experience, you soon will become the envy of your shooting cronies when you casually say, "I silver soldered that sight on myself."

If ventilated rib on a shotgun comes loose, it can be reinstalled with little trouble. But go easy with the torch, the author advises, as too much heat does more harm than good. Details are included in chapter text.

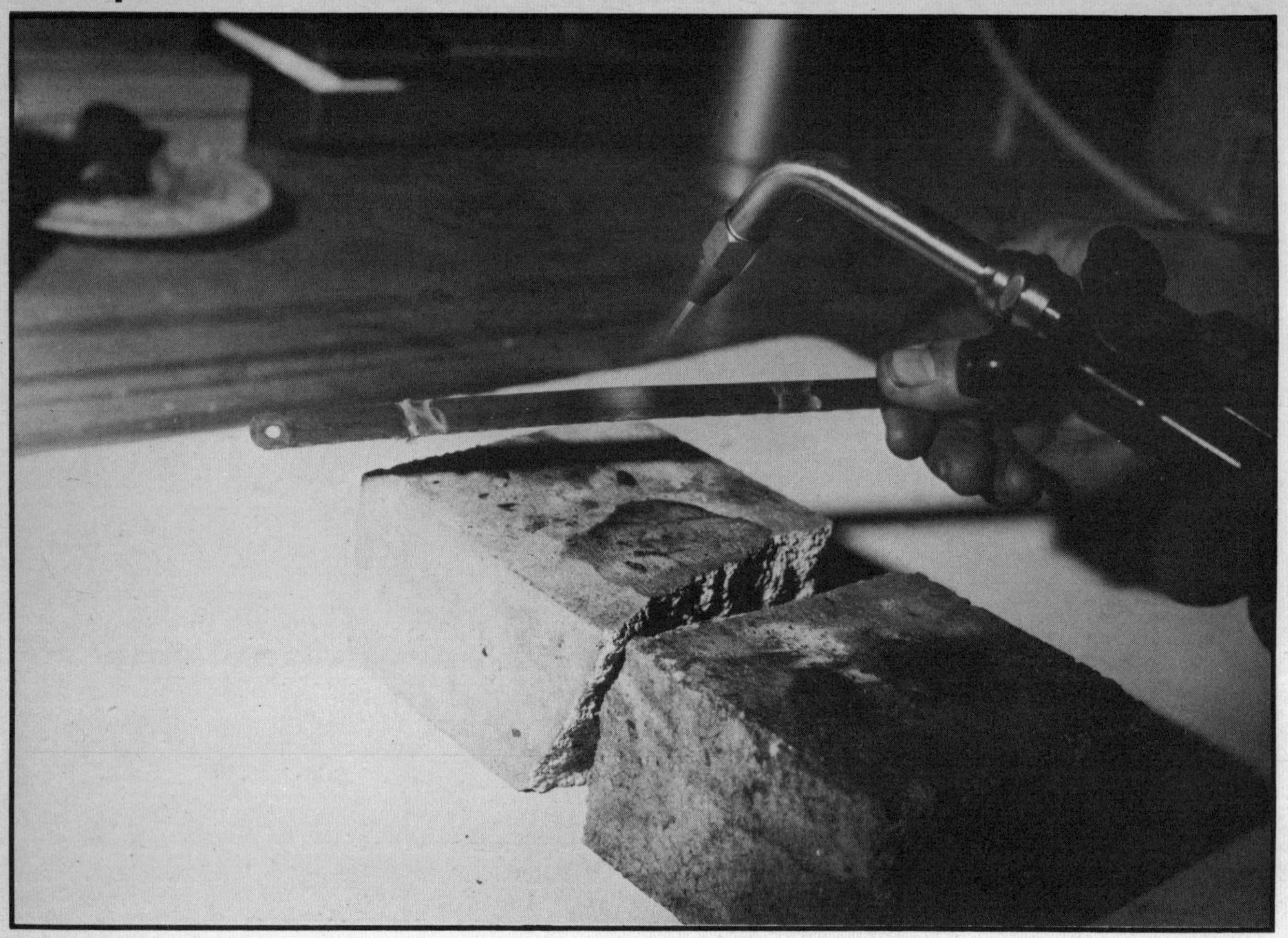

THE BASICS OF HEAT TREATING

With Minimum Tools, The Do-It-Yourself
Type Can Accomplish Some Jobs

Essential first step in heat treating process is to clean up all metal surfaces with high-speed buffing wheel.

ALTHOUGH FORGING — that is, heating a hunk of iron or steel until red-hot and then beating it into the desired shape and form — is still practiced to some extent, it is a thing of the past in the gunmaking field. To be sure, some gunsmiths may well be using this method to shape a

Brownell's Hard-N-Tuff material is applied to hammer of black powder gun before heating with torch. See text for additional case-hardening techniques.

part or two but, on the whole, modern steels call for vastly different treatments.

Heating and forging steel alters the crystalline structure of the metal, producing a coarse grain structure. To reduce strain that eventually leads to metal fatigue and fracture, the shaped and heated steel is reheated and softened, the crystalling structure is refined and the stresses are removed. The most commonly known method of accomplishing that is known as annealing.

Reloaders are familiar with annealing cartridge cases. The procedure is to stand decapped cases in a pan of water, play the flame of a low pressure torch over the case neck and shoulder and, when the brass turns red, tip each case over so that it is quenched in the water. The most recent wrinkle in annealing brass cases and other small parts comes from Dave Corbin of Corbin Manufacturing and Supply, Incorporated (Dept. GW, Box 44, North Bend, Oregon 97459). Corbin now offers an electric blower-type heat gun that is hot enough to anneal brass and other small parts quickly and without the danger of an open flame.

In contrast to brass that is water-quenched, steel is heated to a dull cherry-red color (about 1475 degrees Fahrenheit), and then cooled slowly. Mention should be made here of annealing brass in a pot of molten lead. This suggestion keeps appearing in gun literature and the idea harks back to the time when some metals were annealed successfully this way. However, it was found that only the purest of pure lead could be used, that it had to be fluxed with special chemicals, and that the slightest impurity in the lead was then transferred to the metal being annealed, often leaving the newly annealed material sadly weakened and contaminated. Since case annealing is meant to impart new strength to the brass and few of us have access to chemically pure lead, this method of annealing cases should be abandoned.

There are two basic methods used to give steel added strength: a surface treatment and a heat-treating that essentially rearranges the molecular structure of the steel, thus strenghtening it. The surface heat-treating is known as case-hardening.

The carbon content of steels varies widely, the low-carbon content steels being relatively soft. Case-hardening adds carbon to the steel, and in gunsmithing, only the outer layers — the case — are so hardened, with the core of the steel remaining soft. The heat penetration and change of carbon content usually extends only a few thousandths of an inch into the metal. Besides giving the case or skin extra hardness, this process also adds coloring to the steel treated in this manner, and the result of this is known as color case-hardening.

The majority of heat-treating methods used are not suitable for the gun tinkerer. Many of the chemicals used in treating steel are toxic, and heating methods often call for forced air, special ovens and the like. However, the do-it-yourself gun tinkerer can, with some practice and study, learn to do a few jobs, providing some sort of torch is available that is capable of heating metal quickly and uniformly. Case-hardening, for instance, calls for the use of potassium cyanide, a potent poison. However, with the help of a low pressure oxygen torch or oxy-acetylene torch and some of the newer chemicals, some creditable case-hardening can be done with a minimum of equipment.

The internal hardening of steel by means of heat is known as hardening, and new hardness is the result of heating steel to its proper temperature which is governed by its chemical composition, then quenching the heated metal in cold or hot water, brine or oil. Steel manufacturers specify the temperatures for each lot of steel made — steel composition varies widely depending on the ultimate use of it — and they also color code all stock. As a general rule, steel that is simply permitted to cool off in air has the least amount of hardening. Oil quenching imparts somewhat more hardness, a water quench gives still greater hardness and brine gives the greatest degree of hardness. A dab of blue color on a length of drill rod or flat bar stock indicates that a water quench will produce a relatively high degree of hardness. Green also indicates a water quench, while red means an oil quench is called for. The dab of yellow paint means that the material can be quenched in either oil or air.

Steel that has been heated and quenched is harder than it was before, but it is also somewhat more brittle. To overcome this brittleness, the steel is tempered. This

Annealing cartridge cases is another term for heat treating brass. Corbin's electric heat gun is ideal for this and other jobs which require only medium heat. Simple enameled pan is used to trap heat around brass.

process is also known as drawing the temper or simply as drawing. In tempering, the steel is heated again, but to a lower temperature than for hardening, and is then cooled by quenching in the suitable quenching medium. Over the years, inventive gunsmiths have used many quenching media, including flour, salt, charcoal and sundry combinations of these and other preparations.

If you want to temper a piece of steel or a spring, try and get the manufacturer's specs for the correct heating level and the appropriate quenching medium. Experienced hands at this hardening business can judge the temperature of the steel by its color. If you lack this experience or a thermostatically controlled heat-treating oven, your best bet is a product called Tempilaq. This is a heat indicator substance that melts suddenly when its temperature has been reached. Tempilaq is available in over twenty-five temperature determination points and works like magic. In use, a small and thin smear is applied to the work and permitted to dry to a dull finish. When the metal being heated reaches its appropriate hardening temperature, the Tempilaq suddenly melts and the work is then quenched immediately in the suitable quenching medium.

There is more to quenching and handling hot metal than simply dumping the work into a can of oil or grabbing it with a pair of pliers. A scrubbing motion, a figure eight motion or a simple up-and-down motion is often best when inserting the hot metal into the quenching medium. The liquid medium heats up from the metal, and cool medium must be brought into contact with the metal. If you simply stand a screwdriver in the medium, for example, the heat dissipation will slow down and cooling off will be uneven — and so will the results of your work.

If only a small part of the job, like the blade of a screwdriver, is being heated, the other end of the work may not get very hot; in this case, you could use a pair of pliers to move the work from the firebrick to the quenching medium. If, however, you are making a follower spring for an M98 action from an old hacksaw blade, as I did recently, it becomes essential that the work be handled for bending without pliers drawing off heat from the work. HCP70 Heat Control Paste then will save the day — and your fingers. All of the chemicals needed for any type of heat-treating can be ordered from Brownell's, which is the best source for the stuff, especially in the quantities you are likely to need or want.

I have not tried this trick but have been told by some top-notch gunsmiths that it does work. To determine if steel being heated has reached the correct hardening temperature, place a magnet near it. The moment the correct temperature is reached the magnet is no longer

Construction of a new follower spring begins with removal of hacksaw blade teeth on grinding wheel. Use smooth, continuous movement and grind sharp edges by turning blade several times as you would sharpen a knife.

Use the old follower spring as guide in construction of replacement. Note firebrick behind springs.

Tincture of Benzoin or a liquid touch-up bluing applied to gun part will produce satisfactory amount of color after heating. However, appearance is not as deep as color case-hardening process and may be buffed or worn off.

attracted to the steel. The trick is to keep the magnet away from the steel while it is being heated.

To prevent scale formation while the metal is being heated and to protect the finish of the metal, use a paste of sperm oil and bone black, or if the work is large and being heated in a furnace, wrap the job into a sheet of stainless steel foil, also available from Brownell's. Be sure to follow directions on the handling of the foil and watch those edges — they are razor sharp! By far the easiest and least messy way of preventing scaling, decarburization and pitting during heat-treating is with PBC Non-Scaling Compound. This stuff is especially valuable when heat-treating something that already has been shaped to precise dimensions and where normal heat-treating would change those dimensions.

If a piece of steel is too hard to be filed, sawed or otherwise worked, it must be annealed. Heat the work red-hot on a firebrick, then quickly cover it with wood ashes, letting it cool slowly in this manner. Should this be of no avail and the steel still resists a file or saw, the part was probably from air-hardened steel and that means that you can look forward to a great deal of hard work with file and saw. After whatever alterations you want to make have been done, the work will have to be tempered.

Not all case-hardening will give that mottled color and, on the other hand, not all mottled coloring is really the result of case-hardening. For general case-hardening, I suggest Kasenit — it's better and easier to use than many of the homemade gunks often suggested. After polishing the work, heat it, then quickly insert it into the Kasenit. Let it rest there for a minute, then reheat until the Kasenit melts and begins to bubble. Now dip the job into the can of Kasenit again and repeat the heating. I had good results when dipping the work into Kasenit three times and, after the last heating, quenching the job in tap water.

If you are looking for color when case-hardening a job, simply add about a teaspoonful of potassium nitrate to one-half gallon of quenching water. One old-timer some years ago showed me a neat trick to give the work even more color. He used potassium nitrate and, while quenching, blew a vigorous stream of bubbles into the quenching batch with the help of a piece of garden hose.

Almost traditional for case-hardening is the use of heat, bone meal and charred leather. However, some sort of furnace is needed and the stench is enough to choke a skunk. It has often been said that necessity is the mother of invention and I believe that the coiner of the phrase was a gunsmith. To add color to a case-hardening job that did not develop much color, or to color a piece of steel that was not case-hardened but should appear to have been treated that way, use either of the following procedures:

As surface finish, polish the job, then coat the areas you

want to color with tincture of benzoin from the drugstore. Heat those areas with the torch, and the burning tincture will give a coloring like the finest case-hardening job. Birchwood-Casey's Perma Blue can be used this way: Heat the metal part until it's too hot to handle, then with a cotton swab, simply dab Perma Blue on the heated parts. According to Bob Brownell, Oxynite 122 does the same, and chances are that some of the other cold bluing preparations will also work.

Here are some tips that should enable you to tackle some of the heat-treating jobs you have been thinking about. When you heat a fairly large piece of work, start with the flame playing over much of the work and hold the torch some distance away from the steel. As the steel heats, you can move the flame closer to the area you want to heat. Intensify the heat when the first sign of color appears. This, of course, does not apply if you want to bend a spring or to shape your own screwdriver blade where only the tip is being tempered.

Carbon steels should not be heated above 1650 degrees Fahrenheit and then quenched in water — this is an almost sure way of making the steel brittle, and it will develop cracks. Only low carbon steels can be treated this way.

This hacksaw blade follower spring was not properly heat treated and promptly snapped when compressed.

When you want to make a follower spring, start with an old hacksaw blade. Remove the teeth by grinding them off on the wheel, then polish. Heat evenly but only in the area where you want to bend the steel. Use Heat Control Paste so that you can handle the steel for bending — remember what I said about the use of pliers, they draw heat off the work quickly.

If the recommended quenching medium is water, try hot water. Hot water is less likely to cause cracking than cold water.

If Kasenit does not give a hard enough surface, try Brownell's Hard-N-Tuff. This stuff contains chromium, and carbonizes, nitrides and chromizes the job all at once.

The home gun tinkerer must, by necessity, rely on the available sources of heat. If you have adequate ventilation and have either a small tank of oxygen or air piped into the place, you can construct a small forge with a dozen or so firebricks. Do not use the ones sold for fireplaces but find the ones used in welding shops. Such a forge or oven is best set on a cart made from angle iron. The smallest of the electric furnaces sells for over $200 and I have never felt a crying need for one. I cover the bench top with a sheet of asbestos from the hardware store, and then use two halves or a couple of whole firebricks, depending on the size of the work.

Your oxy-acetylene or oxy-low pressure torch will do most of the jobs you want to tackle. The small low pressure torches are adequate for many small jobs, but for larger jobs, be sure that you start with a full tank. Nothing is more frustrating than to have the gas supply peter out when the metal is just getting the right color.

Speaking of color, here are the tempering colors and temperatures you are likely to need or want.

420 degrees F. — Faint yellow for drawing dies, punches and gun parts that will be exposed to friction but little or no shock.

430 degrees F. — Pale yellow for checkering tools and wood gravers.

440 degrees F. — Light yellow for chambering reamers.

450 degrees F. — Pale straw yellow for action pins and hand reamers.

460 degrees F. — Deep straw yellow for the points on sears and triggers, milling cutters and reamers used in power machines.

500 degrees F. — Yellow brown for firing pin body only and for twist drills.

550 degrees F. — Dark purple for flat springs, extractors, cold chisels and screwdrivers, gun hammers.

570 degrees F. — Dark blue for small screwdrivers, light flat springs and firing pin noses.

Although I have done a fair bit of my own hardening, I have never quite learned the proper judging of colors, hence I rely heavily on Tempilaq.

Flat springs are the easiest to fashion and finish, and just the other week I tried something that is often called blazing off. After the spring is heated and oil quenched, lower it gradually into the flame of the torch and let the oil burn off. This will temper the spring and give it the strength you want. But before you install it, check the performance of the spring in your vise. I have found that sometimes this works and sometimes the spring just snaps. In that case, you start all over again!

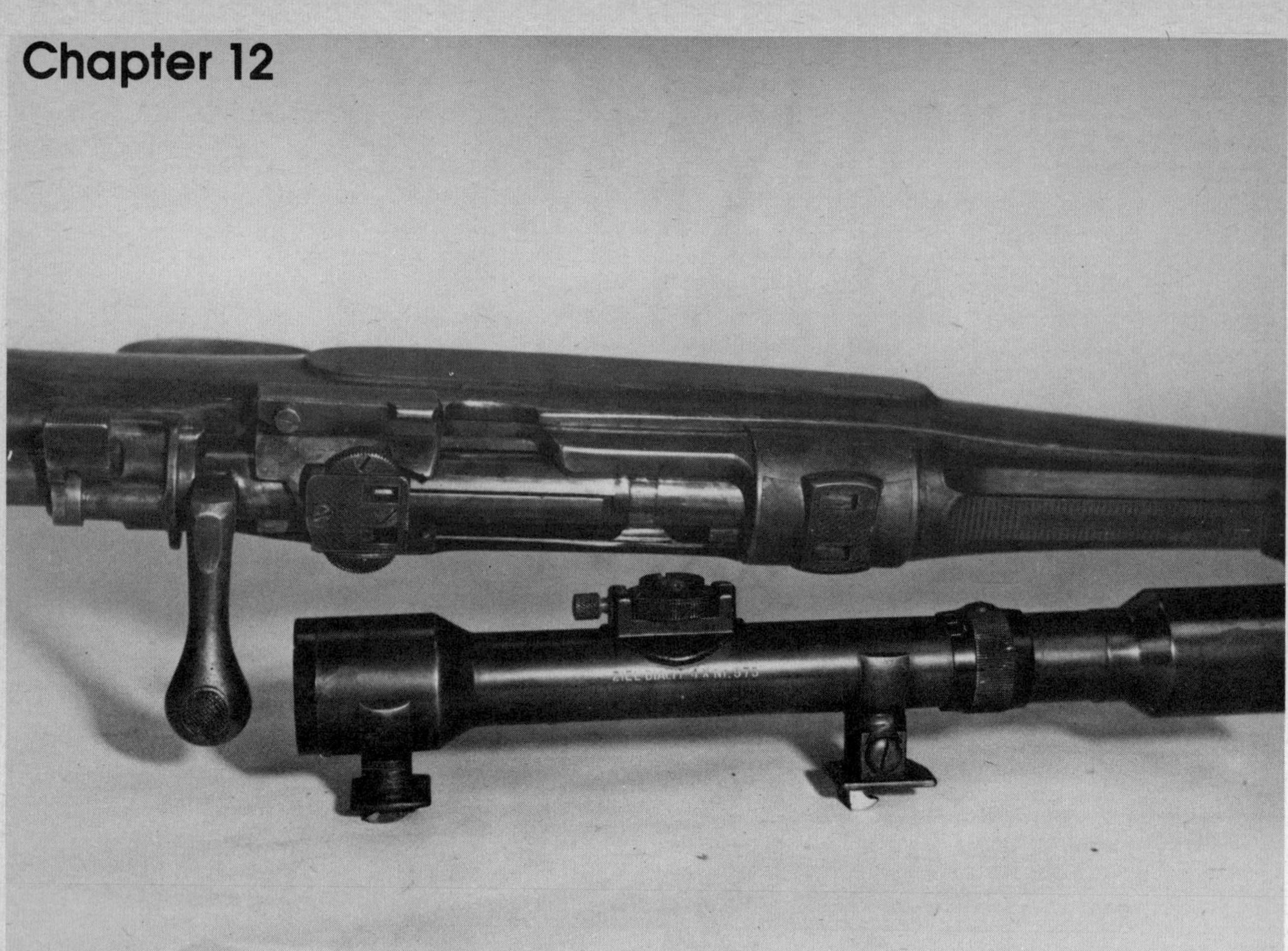

Chapter 12

Case-hardened claw mounts on an early 8mm Mauser rifle which dates back a good many years are still functional. Mounts did not gain popularity in the United States, yet allow quick scope removal, return scope to zero each time.

SCOPE MOUNTING MADE EASY

Almost Anyone Can Mount A Scope, But Doing It Correctly Does Wonders For Accuracy!

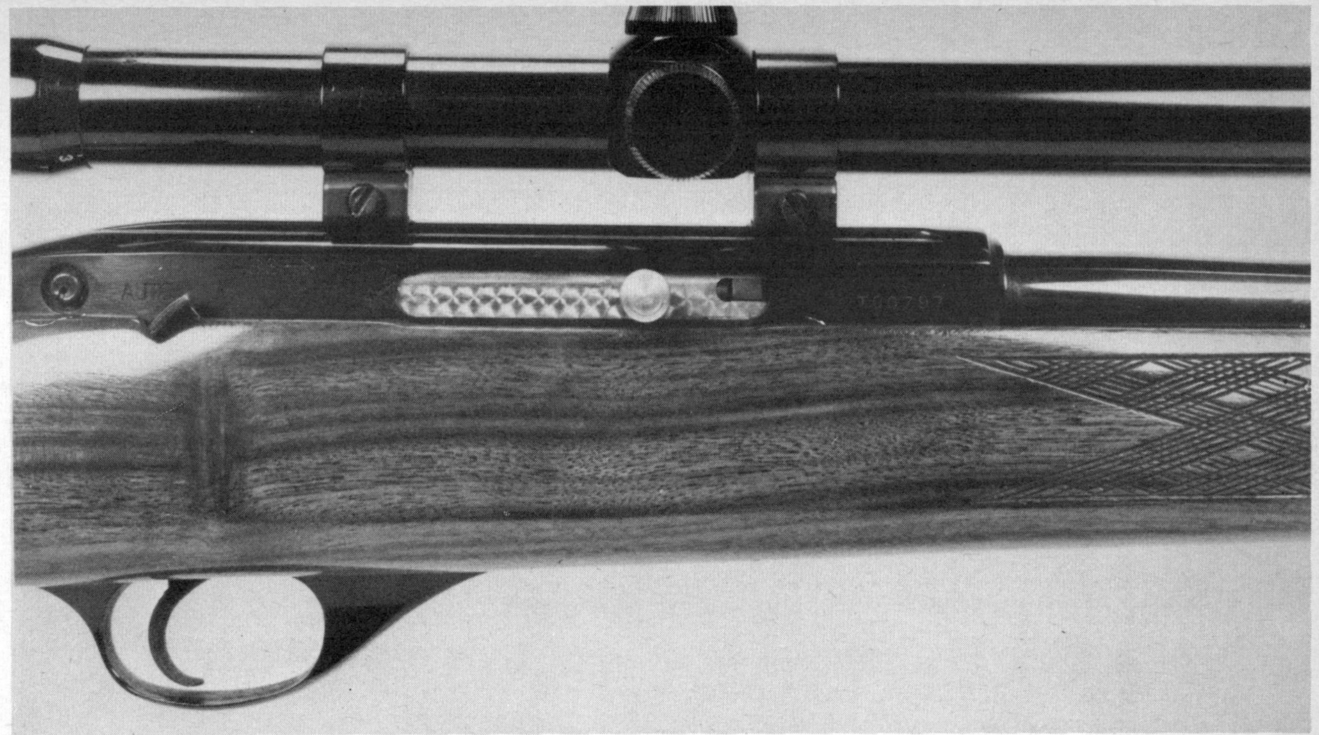

Rail-mounted .22 scope may be attached or removed in matter of few minutes, requiring no gunsmith skills and few tools.

Collimator will save a great deal of time and ammunition when it comes to sighting in a newly scoped rifle. After presighting with collimator, only a few shots need be fired to zero in scope to rifle perfectly.

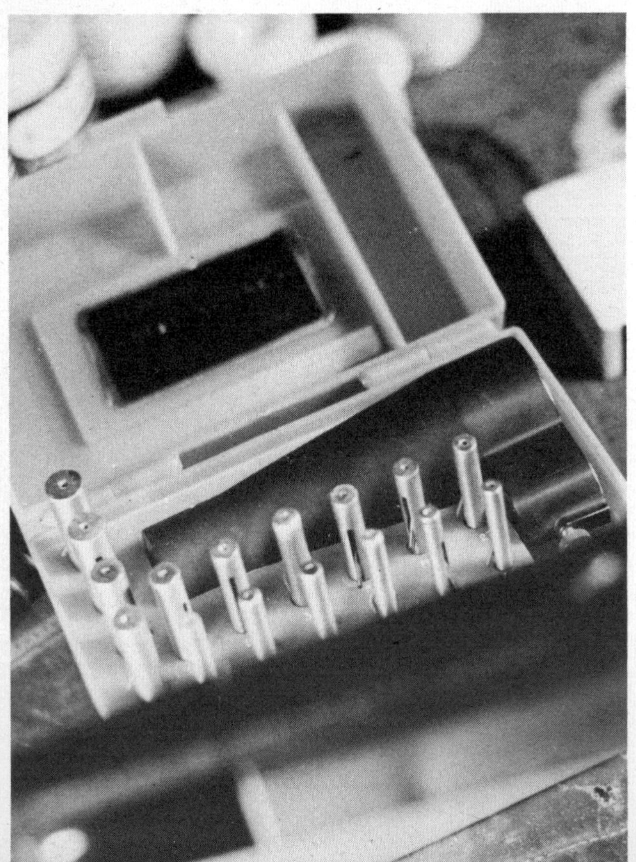

WITH THE EXCEPTION of a few foreign-made guns, all center-fire and rimfire rifles reach the consumer so that scope installation is simple and really does not require the services of a gunsmith. Such rifles can be scoped by most anyone who can handle a screwdriver and follow some simple directions.

The foreign guns which should be scoped by an expert gunsmith, or better yet, scoped in the factory, are the German drillings. These combination guns require the use of claw mounts and considerable skill and care in drilling and tapping. I never have understood why the German claw mounts never became popular here; they not only always return the removed scope back to zero, but also make scope removal and remounting fast and easy.

Prior to World War II, few of the commercial rifle actions were drilled and tapped for scope mounting and when you bought a rifle, you had the 'smith install the scope and mounts of your choice. After WWII, when sporting rifle production had not caught up with the demand, military surplus rifles still were abundant and inexpensive. Sporterizing these rifles was worthwhile and installation of new sights — either metallic or scope — was part and parcel of the conversion process. Since these military actions were not drilled and tapped for scope or sight installation, it remained the job of the gunsmith to mount sights on these rifles.

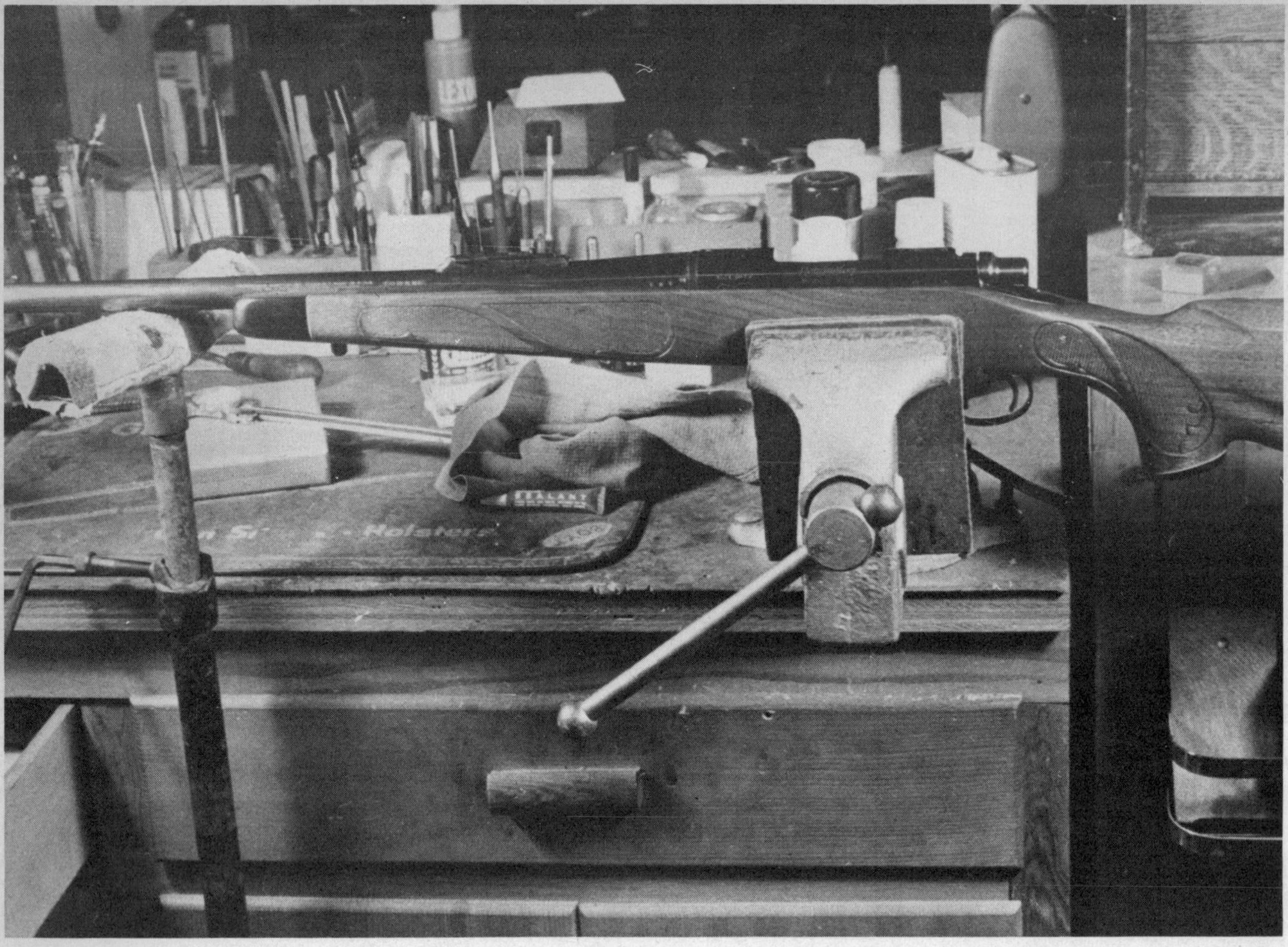

Adjustable tee stand, made from scrap and welded, is an invaluable aid for the home gunsmith. Well padded on top, the stand is ideal when scoping rifles, working on actions or stocking rifles requiring perfect leveling.

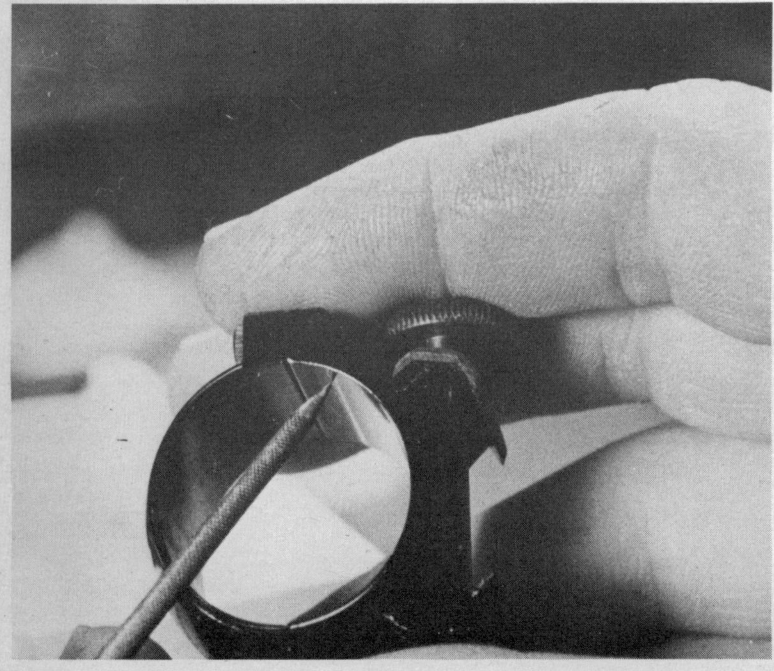

Inside of scope rings are first scribed and then assembled so that lines match, ensuring good fit of rings around scope tube. Degrease metal first.

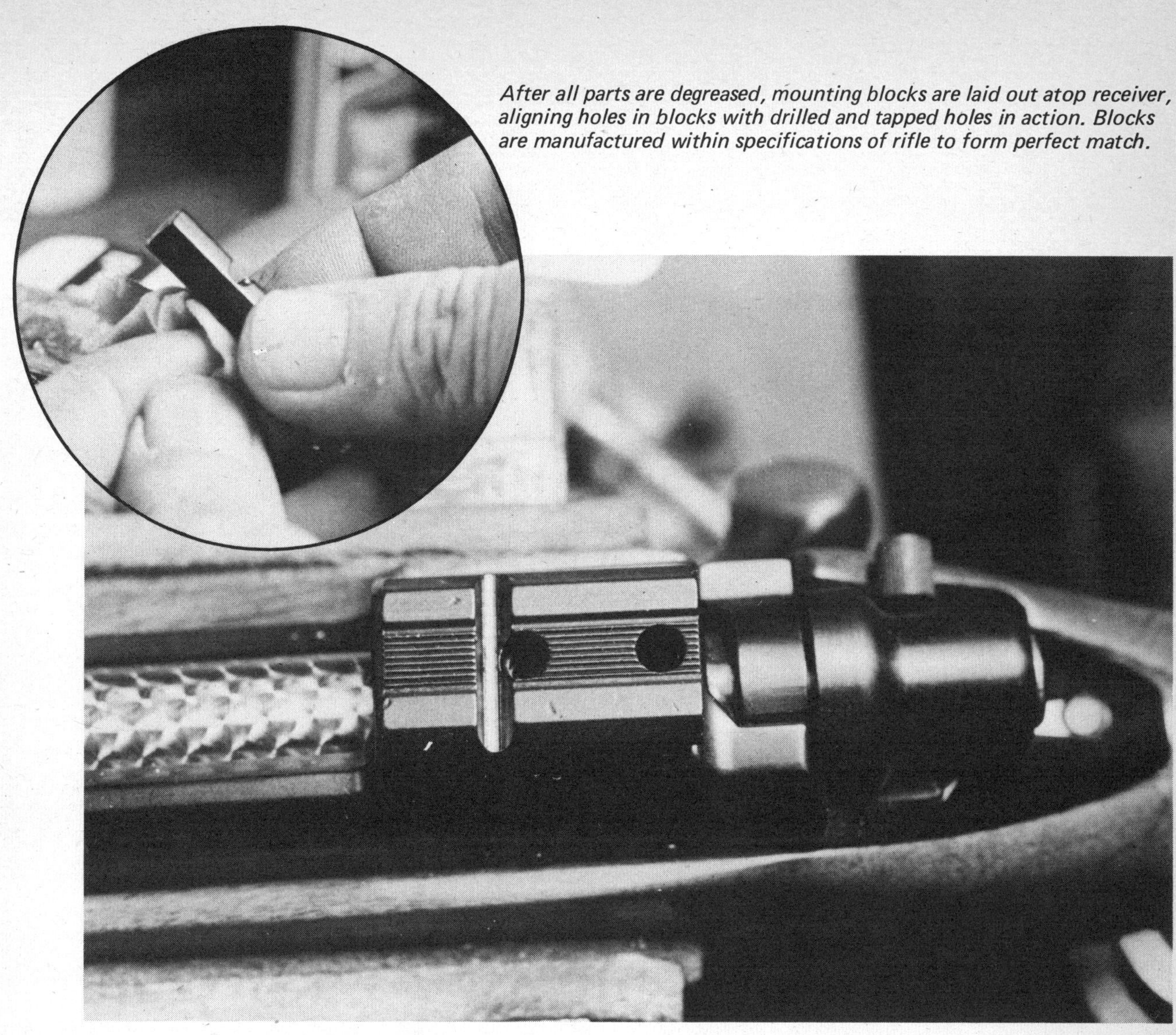

After all parts are degreased, mounting blocks are laid out atop receiver, aligning holes in blocks with drilled and tapped holes in action. Blocks are manufactured within specifications of rifle to form perfect match.

Years ago, it was customary to use mounts and scopes from the same maker, excepting a few instances where a maker, for instance, would make mounts only and you mounted any make scope you wanted on that rifle. Buehler mounts and those then made by Kuharsky were typical, while some scope makers only made scopes and did not produce rings or mounts. In the past several years, a number of mounts which at one time could be used only with the scope rings of the same maker, have been introduced so that, in some instances, you can use the bases of one maker, the rings of another maker, and the scope of yet another company.

Some of the mounts and rings were of questionable value or were so complex shooters simply did not want them. Today's mounts and rings are good and, with the exception of target mounts, I don't foresee many changes in the scope mounts of tomorrow. The same goes for rings. Now the main question seems to be whether rings and mounts, as well as scope tubes, should be made from aluminum to reduce weight, or from steel to make them more resistant to strains and torque.

In scope mounting, one generally breaks mounts and rings down into two groups: hunting or target, also differentiating between rimfire and center-fire scope mounting.

Scoping a rimfire rifle is simple and the whole job should not take you more than a few minutes. Dovetail rails are built into the vast majority of the rimfire rifle actions, so all that needs to be done is to clamp the base onto the dovetail rail. Some scopes come with rings and mounts, others require the purchase of suitable rings where the base may or may not be integral with the rings. If you obtained your scope before you bought the rings, make certain you have measured the diameter of the scope tube — it may be seven-eighths-inch, but a lot of gunsmiths see nothing wrong with using a one-inch tube scope on a rimfire rifle.

A simple and foolproof device to insure crosshairs are perfectly vertical and horizontal is the B-Square Cross Hair Square.

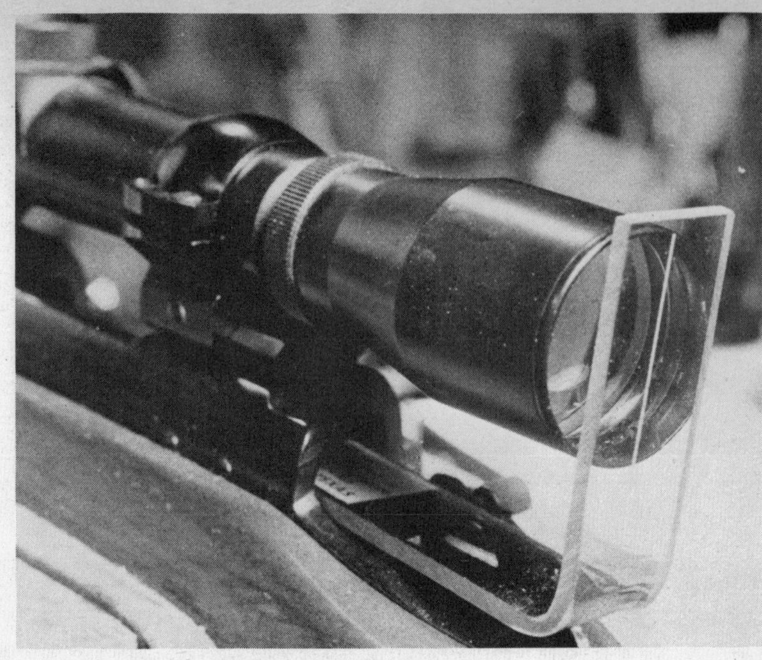

Before finally tightening all screws, verify that scope is level with round spirit level.

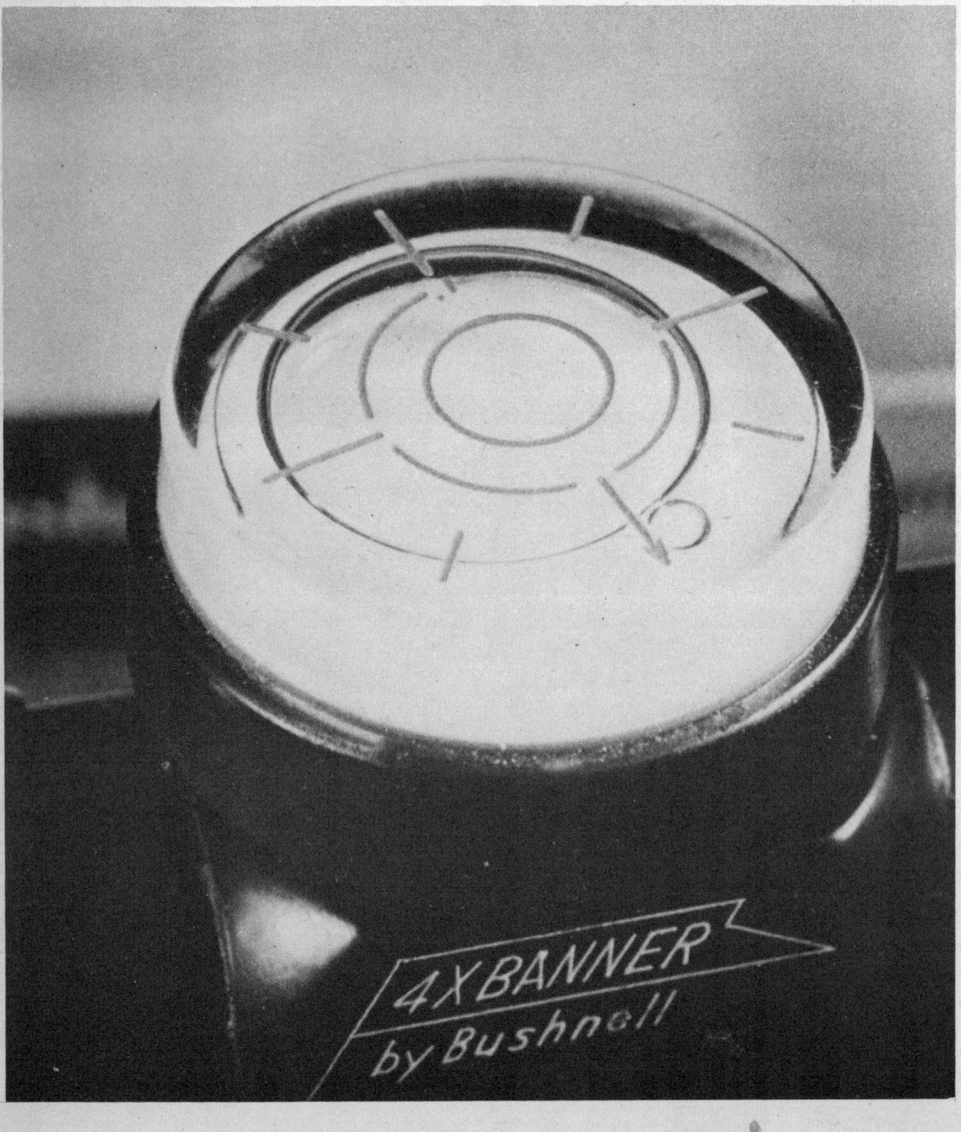

Once you have suitable rings, you can proceed with the scope installation. There is no difference between the front and the rear rings or dovetail clamps, but there is a trick that will forestall any possible ring problem.

When you take the rings out of the box or package, decide which one you will place in front and which in the rear. With the rifle clamped into a vise and supported at the forend with the stand, take a metal scribe and mark each ring on the inside. One set gets one scribe mark, the other gets two such marks. A number of rings are ground and finished so that the two halves of the rings mate precisely, and the marks are put on the inside of the rings so you can tell at a glance which bottom goes with which top.

After marking the rings, disassemble them, remove all the screws and lay them out so you reduce any chance of mixing them up to the irreducible minimum.

Scope rings and bases come from the manufacturer with anti-rust coatings and this must be removed completely. Lighter fluid will do the trick, or a dab of acetone on a cleaning patch does a fine job. Use any degreasing agent you have handy, but stay away from carbon tetrachloride! Degrease all surfaces of the rings and bases, also removing all grease from all screw threads. Assemble the scope in the rings and lightly tighten the screws. Now slip the dovetail base clamps on the dovetail and tighten those screws lightly. If your rings have the conventional screws with the slotted top, make sure that the blade of the screwdriver fits the slot of the screwhead. The trend is now toward the hex head screws, and most of those are sold with the suitable wrench.

Slide the scope back and forth in the rings until you are satisfied that the eye relief is right for you. For this, it is best to remove the rifle from the vise and shoulder the rifle, make

Use of screw sealant, such as LocTite, is an absolute necessity for all scope-mounting work, according to author.

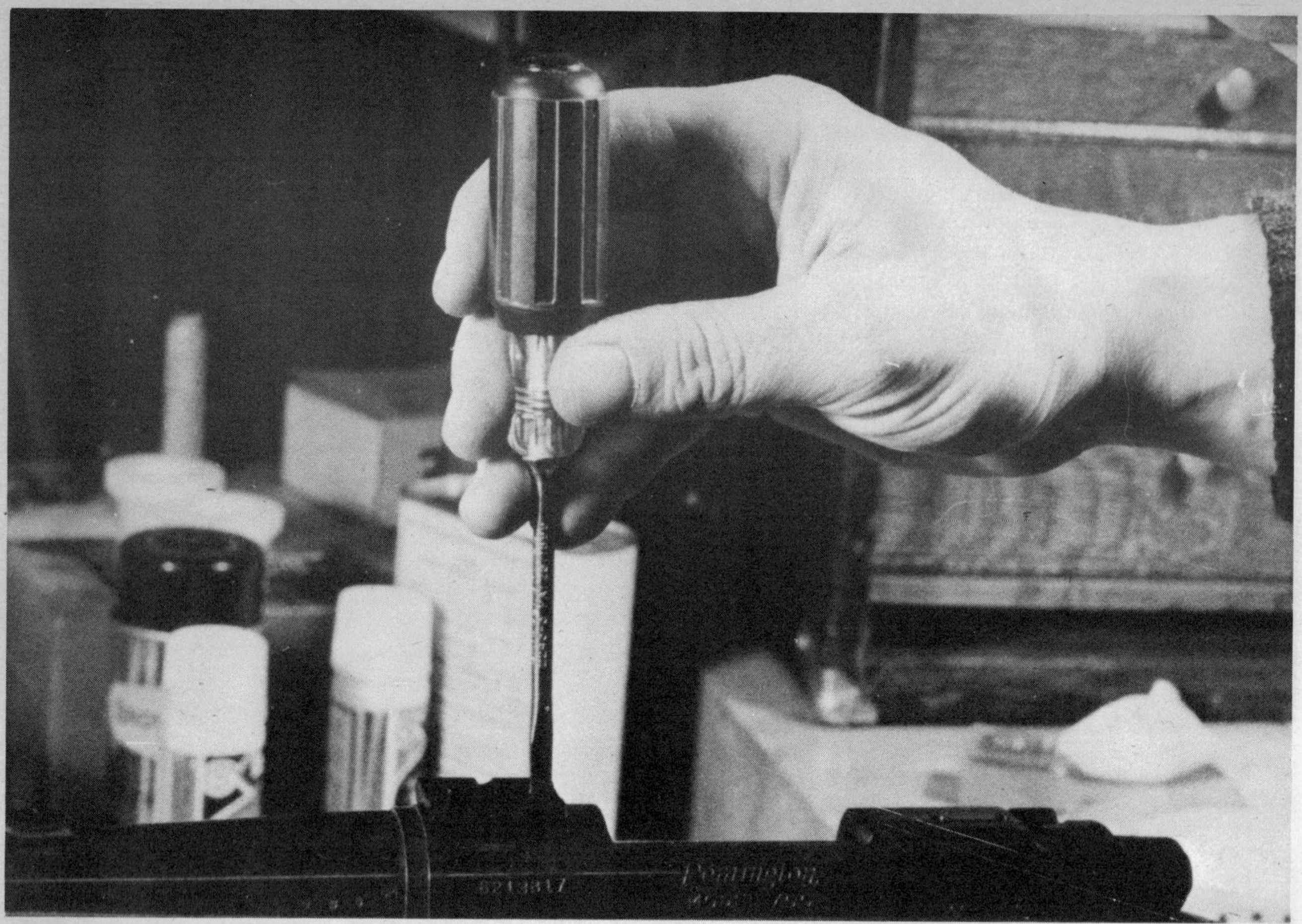

After mounting screws have been tightened down to maximum, leave screwdriver in slot and tap handle with mallet. This should allow screw to be retightened by at least one-quarter turn. Loosen screw in same manner.

sure that the chamber is empty and the action is open. Hold the rifle as you always do, taking into account any stock crawling tendency you might have. Once the eye relief is adjusted, adjust the scope in the rings so the crosshairs are truly vertical and horizontal.

Cinching the various screws tight comes next. For plinking a simple tightening of the screws is often considered adequate. For rifles that will be used for hunting small game and some pest shooting, as well as for target rifles where the scopes do not ride in the special target mounts, I prefer to use a drop of LocTite on each screw.

Set the screw in the usual fashion, leave the blade of the screwdriver in the slot of the screw and give the handle of the screwdriver a whack with a rawhide mallet or a plastic mallet. Then turn the screws in as much as possible, usually about a quarter turn. The newest of the LocTite products, Wick N' Lock, readily flows into the threads of the incompletely set screw. If such a screw must be removed at some time in the future, set the blade of the screwdriver into the slot of the screwhead, whack the handle with the mallet, and turn the screw out. If you ever need to clean a screw that has been held in place with LocTite, you can either use a fine wire wheel to clean the threads, or simply drop the screw for a minute or two into some paint stripper.

Mounting a scope on a centerfire rifle is almost as simple. After you have selected your scope and know which brand of rings and bases you want to use, check the manufacturer's list for the right base designation or number. You have to know the model designation of the rifle, such as Marlin 336 or Remington 700, and in some instances you also will need to know if yours is the short or the long action.

The mount maker's list will indicate which scope block is mounted forward and which goes to the rear of the action. Higher blocks require longer screws.

I learned my scope mounting the hard way some twenty years ago, and my mentor insisted I level each gun in the vise by means of a small line level and that the forend of the gun be properly supported. A pipe stand is handy, but if that is beyond your capabilities, you can do what I did for years.

Your swivel base vise can be turned so the rifle action is held just above the center of the vise. If you clean the clutter off your bench, that part of your work area now can be used to support either butt or forend by means of some wood blocks which are padded with felt, or some sandbags which later can do double duty on the range as rifle rests.

The screws holding the bases to the action and the rings together should receive the LocTite treatment when you mount a scope on a centerfire rifle. Commercial sporting rifle receivers come drilled and tapped for scope mounting, and the filler screws are best removed with a small-bladed watchmaker's screwdriver. There is little sense in saving these screws. I did for years, then one day managed to spill all of them all over the shop. I picked up those little devils on shoe soles, my dogs picked them up on their pads and distributed them throughout the house, and now I pitch them unless the gun is a loaner and must be returned in the condition in which it was received.

when all of us decided to burn up some ammo. On the second shot, I had the feeling that something had just flown over my head and when I looked at the gun I found that my scope and base had shot loose — the scope from the base and the base from the gun. Since then I have carried on a passionate love affair with LocTite.

Once the scope is mounted, it's up to you to sight it in. For years I used to trot to the range to check the setting of a scope or sight, but this was too time consuming, so I now do all my pre-sighting with a collimator. For most of the scope and

If bench stand is not available, vise may be swivelled until rifle butt or barrel rests on bench and adjusted to level attitude.

What was said about degreasing in the discussion on scope mounting for rimfire rifles goes here, too. Remove all grease from the rings and the blocks, as well as from the drilled and tapped holes in the receiver. Adjust the scope for the correct eye relief, then level the crosshairs. Once this is done, tighten the screws with LocTite as mentioned.

It's possible that I am overdoing that LocTite matter a bit, but some ten years ago I learned a hard lesson. I was destined to head West to hunt grizzlies with a handgun. I scoped the six-gun, then shot up a storm on the range to work up loads, and get used to some long-range handgunning. The gun, the mount and the scope survived the range punishment. Out West, I never even fired a single shot until the last day in camp

sight adjustments you will need or want to make, a simple bore sighter is a good investment. The Bushnell TruScope is the simplest and the least expensive of the collimators, and if you have rifles in several calibers, the Bushnell bore sighter with the three expandable arbors is a good bet. The larger collimators are excellent, but are costly and therefore are most often found on the bench of a gunsmith.

There are a number of rifles and handguns which can be scoped without having to drill and tap holes into the receiver or frame of the gun. The Thompson-Center Contender is such a gun, and scoping one of those barrels is less difficult than dialing the phone. The B-Square Contender mount, for instance, utilizes the four drilled and tapped holes, so all you

From left: Two models of front sight soldering jigs and B-Square sight drill jig are designed to hold barrel and work firmly in proper alignment. Before drilling or soldering, work must be precisely laid out and checked.

need to do is install the base and lock the screws in place. Similarly, the B-Square scope mount for the AR-15 Sporter uses the hole in the handle to anchor the base which slips into the handle of the rifle.

Weaver's side mount for Remington's Model 1100 and the Model 870 scope system depends on the removal of the two original trigger plate pins. These are replaced with two pins furnished with the scope mount, and installation of the side-mounted scope plate is so simple that a 10-year-old can manage it. Attempts to scope Winchester's Model 94 had not been too successful until B-Square developed a side-plate mount which, in installation, is similar to the Weaver mounting system for the Remington guns. This will be discussed at length later in this chapter.

The popular Charter Arms AR-7 Explorer was not scoped until the B-Square company developed another side mount system. For installation of this mount, the side plate screw is removed — do not, however, remove the side plate itself — and once the plate is mounted on the side of the action, the original screw is replaced.

On Smith & Wesson revolvers, scope bases are anchored to the top strap by first removing the rear sight, then setting the rear base screw into the machined slot that formerly held the rear sight.

Revolvers which do not have an adjustable rear sight usually require removal of the rear sight, then drilling and tapping of the top strap. Such a mounting system is used for the B-Square scope mount designed for the Ruger Blackhawk model. Here it becomes necessary to drill and tap two holes into the top strap so that the base can be held in place securely. This base then is equipped with two bolted rings to hold the scope.

Installation of metallic sights, either peep or open sights, may be a bit more complicated, especially when a new front sight has to be installed. The installation of a front sight on a rifle barrel can be accomplished either by soldering or by means of some adroit drilling and tapping of the barrel. As a rule, I do not suggest that you attempt to install any kind of sight on a shotgun barrel since drilling and tapping must be done with extreme care so that you don't go clear through the wall of the relatively thin barrel.

The same, incidentally, goes for installing a new or an additional bead on a shotgun with a ventilated rib. Ribs are soldered or screwed onto the barrel, and one careless moment can mean a messed up rib which then needs professional care and attention.

If you decide to solder a front sight onto a rifle barrel, I suggest that you use a jig. A jig, such as the one offered by

HOME GUNSMITHING DIGEST

B-Square, is simply a mechanical means of holding the sight, ramp, or blade securely in its place while you solder or braze. The B-Square jig can be used on handguns, rifles and shotguns, and once you understand how it works, you will use it time and again. If you decide to drill and tap, a jig becomes vital since the location of the screw holes is important. A hole that is not aligned with another hole means a major repair job or, in the worst cases, cutting off a piece of the barrel, which then means recrowning and touch-up bluing at best.

Skilled machinists can do the drilling and tapping with little trouble, but setting such a job up with V blocks, clamps and levels requires not only a fair amount of skill, but also the needed clamps and blocks which are fairly costly. Again, B-Square comes to the rescue, and these days very few gunsmiths bother with setting a barrel drilling and tapping job up the way it was done fifteen or twenty years ago.

The B-Square barrel sight drill jig can be used on any type barrel up to one inch outside diameter, and can even be used for drilling holes into a shotgun tube for bead mounting.

In general, if a jig is used and you have a new or properly sharpened drill bit, center-punching is not essential. Before you get carried away with the idea of mounting a front sight or any other sight, and start to drill and tap your own holes, be absolutely certain layout of the location is correct. It is much easier and less time-consuming to lay out the work first with a scribe or even a plain lead pencil, then check that the job is square. Don't rush ahead with the drilling or even the center-punching, only to find that sight base and line of bore are out of alignment.

Drilling and tapping a non-military action is not difficult. The increased use of slug barrels on shotguns also means more hunters will want to use a low-power scope on their shotguns for their annual deer hunt. Actions such as that of Ithaca's

If drilling jigs are not used, it becomes essential to level the action in drill press vise. Support action with scrap steel and check level in all directions. Grind away hard steel skin or center punch screw hole locations carefully.

Before bringing the drill down
onto the action, check and
recheck the location and
angle of the intended holes.

Drilling jig, such as this one made by B-Square, will save a lot of blood, sweat and tears if correctly used.

Model 37 can be drilled and tapped with the help of a suitable jig. Early Savage M99s sometimes are found which have not been drilled and tapped for scope mounting. Again, a suitable jig will make the job easier. Bolt-action drilling and tapping is a relatively simple matter, but in all such drilling and tapping remember that you are working on a curved surface, not a flat piece of steel.

If you are not certain your layout is correct, here is a trick I picked up from a very experienced gunsmith: If the layout does not look right, he lays the job out on a piece of flat bar stock, using any piece of scrap that can be locked into a machinist vise. He then drills and taps the holes in the scrap and lightly mounts the bases. With the help of a machinist square or a V block, he checks to see the center line of the mounts is really in the center of the action.

The most often used jig in my shop is the Pro scope mount jig made by B-Square. This jig is suitable for bolt actions primarily, since the bolt must be removed before the jig can be used. The design of this jig is based on the fact that the jig is set and centered by means of a precision-ground arbor, so you can use it for drilling and tapping a barreled action as well as an unbarreled action.

The use of any type of jig offers several advantages. It saves time and also avoids measuring errors where you have to work on a curved surface, such as a receiver bridge. Since the jig is squared off before it reaches you, it must be square against the action on which you are working. If you have the slightest suspicion it is not, take the action to a gunsmith and let him check it. Since the vast majority of the currently available jigs also have drill bushings, you can save not only layout time, but also the problem of properly locating, then center-punching the spots where you want to drill. However, the use of a jig does not mean that you simply slip the jig on the job, then shove the whole shebang under the drill press.

Receivers are hardened, and some are so hard one cannot even scratch a line with a scribe on any part of the action. This makes center-punching impossible, and trying to drill into steel treated in this manner is an exercise in futility. The hard skin of steel must be broken or interrupted if you have to scribe, punch and drill into the steel.

The simplest, easiest way of getting rid of the hard skin is to grind it away. If you have a jig with or without drill bushings, you can use it to locate the holes that need to be drilled for scope or sight mounting. A drop of white typewriter correction fluid can be used to spot the location of the required holes, the brush of the bottle cap being inserted through the holes in the jig. Wait a few minutes for this to dry, then remove the jig. Should the first treatment not take, try to degrease the steel, then repeat the white-out liquid treatment again. With the holes located, place the mounts on the areas where they will be fastened and take a close look at the whole arrangement.

Remember how I mentioned any mounting job should be levelled in the vise? Well, this sort of marking an action makes this step mandatory, so be certain the gun is level, square and properly supported at all times. A Dremel tool can now be used to grind off small areas of the hardened skin of the steel. Use the smallest grinding point that you have, wear eye protection, and only grind away enough of the metal for the drill bit to enter the steel. Some gunsmiths feel it is permissible to leave the unblued metal at the location since that area will be covered with the base or mount. I favor drilling and tapping, then degreasing, then using any of the touch-up bluing compounds on these areas where the bluing has been interrupted and where there is the likelihood that rust can begin its dirty work under the mounts.

Here are a couple of tricks that you want to remember when it comes to drilling into hardened steel. Make sure your drill bit is sharp, and if it had been reground, double check to see that the angle was properly ground. The larger the bit, the more difficult it becomes for the bit to enter steel. In such cases, start with a drill that is at least two or even three sizes smaller, then either try the larger bit again or resort to the Dremel tool again. Use a finely pointed grinder and just touch the edges of the hole you started with the smaller drill.

When using a drill press, or even a drill mounted in a stand,

Extra-hard steel skin may be ground off by judicious use of Dremel Moto-Tool with stone grinding tip.

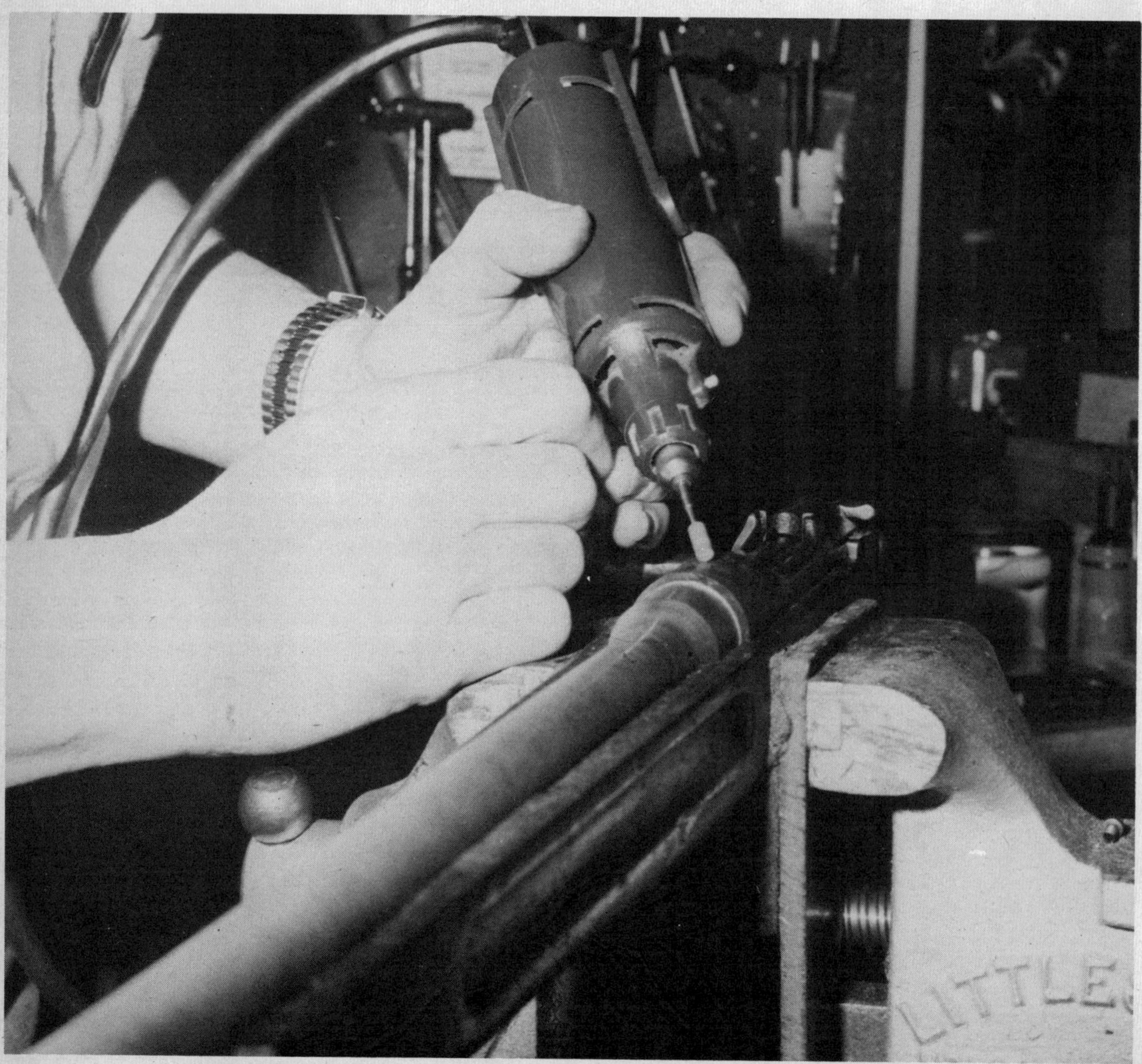

Brownell's Screw Gizzy is ideal gadget for grinding down screws too long or dressing up screwheads damaged by careless screwdriver.

apply just enough pressure to the lever handle to make the drill bite into the metal. Feeding too fast will burn up the drill, especially when the steel is extra hard. Machinists and gunsmiths do not always agree about the use of a good cutting oil when drilling. It is true that the oil will make it a bit more difficult to see what is going on, and oil and chips have the tendency to fly all over the place, especially if too much oil is used. On the other hand, this oil makes the drilling a lot easier, especially when drilling into hard steel.

If you have located the holes correctly, then drilled them, you should be able to follow the earlier instructions about mounting the scope bases or sights. Sad to say, you suddenly find that the holes in the mounts and the holes in the receiver are not lined up. If one or more of the holes don't line up and you are out just a couple of ten-thousandths, you probably can enlarge the hole in the block so that the holes in the action and in the block then line up.

In such instances, it is best to enlarge the hole in the steel also, but only after you've made certain that you have a suitable screw for the job and that the correct tap is on hand. If the hole in the mount is out of alignment only a tiny fraction, enlarge the hole — use a round Swiss file for all this work — then use the original screw. A drop or two of LocTite will help to anchor the threads, and the enlarged hole in the mount then can be filled with a product called Lab-Metal, obtainable from the Brookstone Company and others who specialize in mail-order tools and shop supplies.

Assuming you have your holes drilled and the blocks and the holes in the blocks line up, there are a few more points to check and remember. When drilling metal, do not wear your best shirt and stay clear of those materials in which metal chips seem to find a permanent home. Either roll the sleeves up above the elbows, or better yet, amputate the sleeves. Long sleeves, jewelry and watches should not be worn when

Special screw slot file cuts only on narrow edge, works well on damaged screw slots. Method is described in text.

Many deer hunters are mounting scopes on their slug barrel shotguns. Weaver mount, complete with scope installed on Remington Model 1100, took but two minutes to install. Project is easy for relative beginner.

using a drill press, lathe or saw. Remove all the oil from the drilling area with acetone, alcohol or any other grease and oil solvent, then remove the chips from the hole and the work area. If you have compressed air, fine, but be sure to wear safety glasses. If you don't have compressed air, clean the holes with a fine wire brush. Should that fail, try flooding the chips out of the holes with cutting oil which, has to be removed before seating the screws.

Once the holes are drilled, tapped and cleaned, set the blocks or mounts into place, then lightly run the screws through the mounts into the holes. Tighten just enough so there is no play in the mounts, then use two steel straight edges to check the alignments of the blocks. I have seen factory-drilled rifle actions that, when the blocks were installed as outlined here, were so badly drilled that the job had to be turned over to a gunsmith.

Should you find that any of the scope block screws are too long, first measure the overall length of the screw, then the depth of the hole and the block, keeping in mind that nearly all blocks are countersunk for the head of the screw. Using either a Brownell or a B-Square screw holder, hold the end of the screw against a fine grinding wheel — until the desired overall length has been reached. Hold the screw dead square against the wheel, and you won't have to dress the bottom of the screw.

A stuck screw combined with an improperly ground screwdriver blade results in a mutilated screwhead. If you have spare screws on hand, you can pitch the old one and use a new one in its place. If you have to use the damaged screw, use a fine Swiss file and file off the burrs on both edges of the screwhead slot. File until the surface is smooth. Chances are that this filing messed up the contour of the screwhead as well as the slot. Deepen the slot with one of the special screwhead files sold by Brownell's, then contour the head with another Swiss file, polish smooth, degrease and use touch-up bluing.

B-Square scope mount is specially designed for Winchester Model 9422 lever-action, .22 caliber rifle.

Mentioned earlier were receivers which are especially hard. The hardening, usually an annealing process, hardens not only the top of the bridge of the action, but also the inside. If you have been reading some of the gunsmithing books, you will have noted that everyone seems to have his own way of getting through that tough inside skin on the action. After trying three or four of the suggested methods, I decided to adopt the one proposed by Bob Brownell. He suggests setting the spindle of your drill press to maximum speed, then simply drilling through. If the hole is a big one, use a smaller size drill and make certain that the bit is sharp. If the revolutions-per-minute of the spindle are low, the drill bit will grab when you attempt to break through the tough skin.

Some commercial rifles have scope-mounting holes which go clear through the action; others penetrate only partially, leaving solid steel at the base of the hole. I prefer the latter way, but when properly done, the through-and-through drilling apparently doesn't affect performance of a rifle.

To predetermine the depth of the hole to be drilled, proceed as follows: Measure the overall thickness of the action, add to it the thickness of the mount or block, taking into consideration that the screwhead is countersunk. Now subtract about one-third of the action thickness from this total figure, and you have the overall length of the screw. But check to see if your measurements were correct by measuring the screw itself. Adjust the stop or depth gauge on your drill press for the actual depth of the hole you want and go ahead with the drilling.

Most of the mount makers offer high and low rings. Ideally, the scope is mounted as low over the barrel or action as possible. But there comes the day when you have done everything right, got the scope locked into place, then find you cannot lift the bolt handle up and move the bolt rearward since the handle bumps into the ocular bell of the scope. If you were using low rings, try a set of the high ones. Chances are that this will take care of the problem. If it does not, you may have to resort to higher blocks, but this has happened to me only once and I discovered later that I had simply used the wrong blocks for the action.

All of the jigs, bases, mounts and even the scopes, come with instructions which are all too often laid aside or pitched out before the job of mounting a sight or scope is started.

Maynard Buehler, the mount maker, has a fitting piece of advice in his instruction sheet: *If all else fails, read the instructions.*

Mounting a scope sight on Colt AR-15 is fast and simple. Scope base slips into handle frame and anchoring screw is then threaded through factory drilled hole and into base. Rings and scope are then added to complete job.

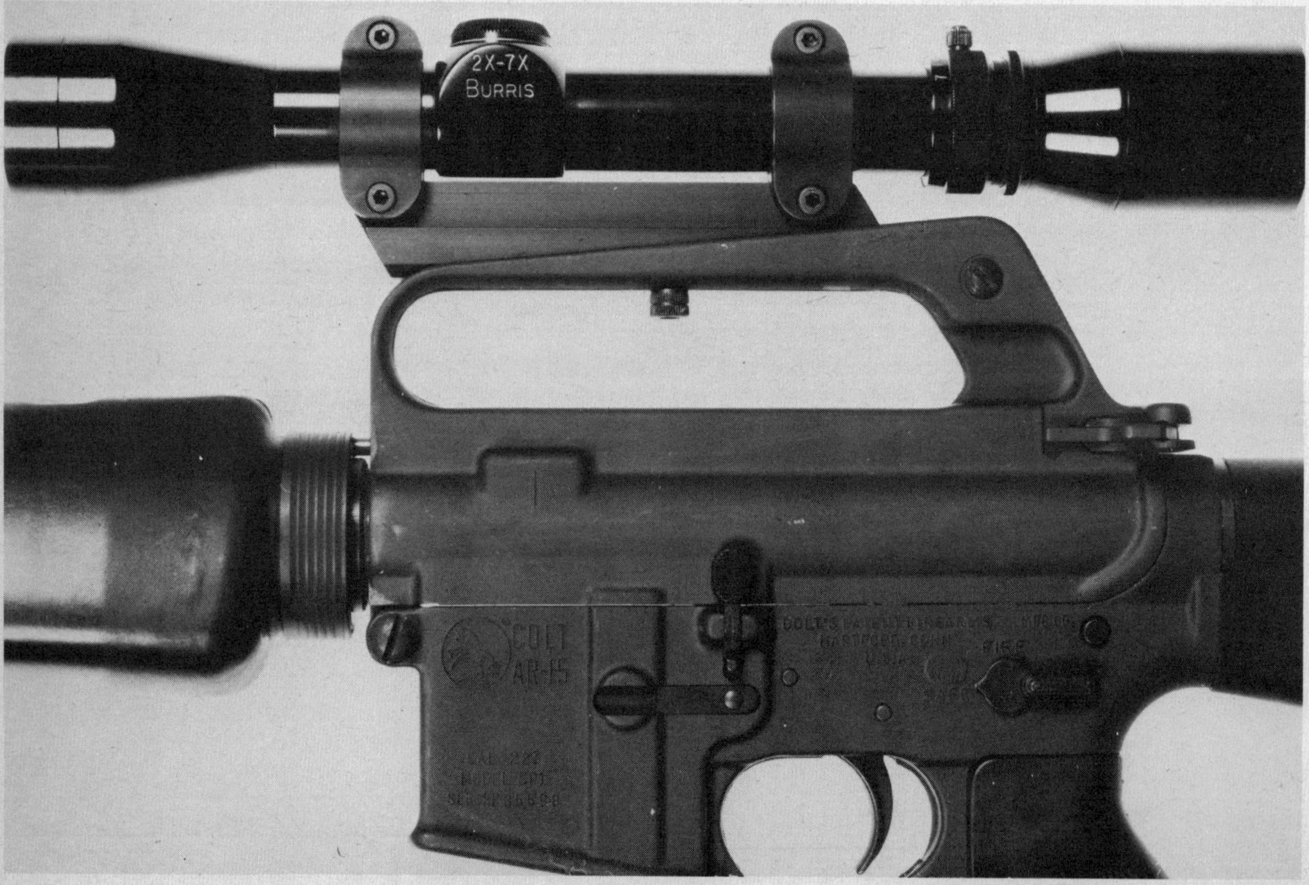

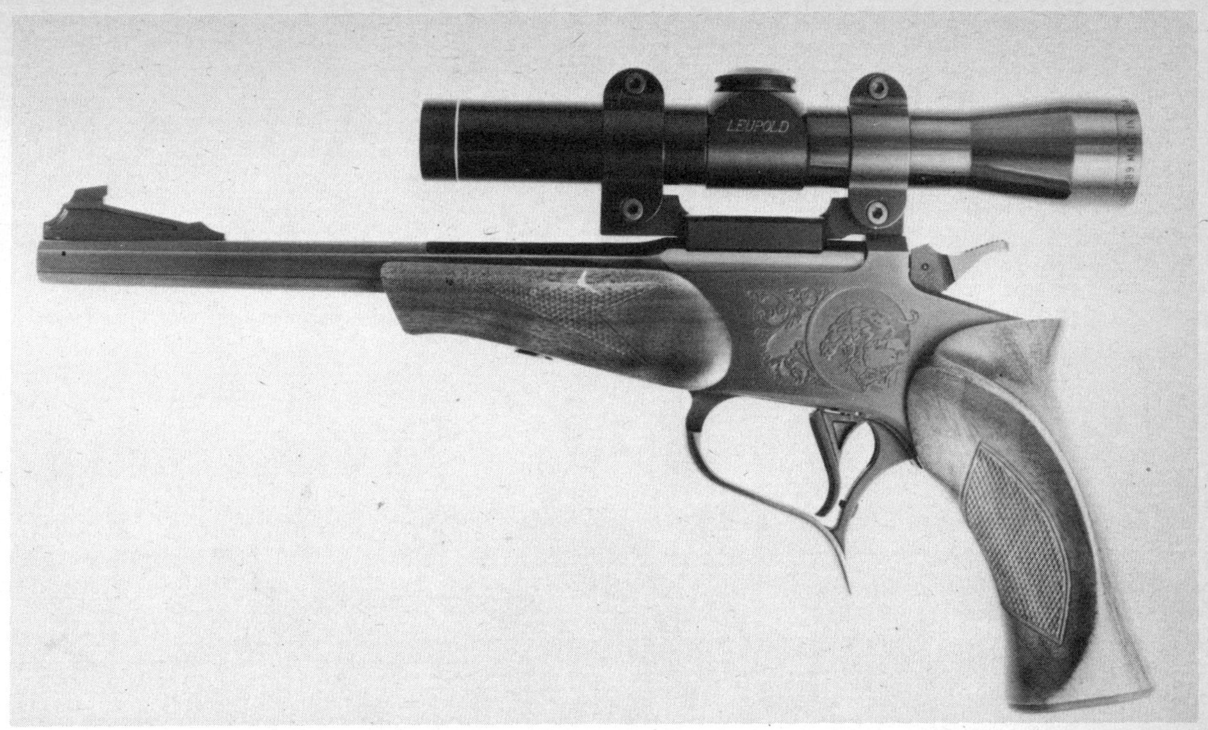

Installing B-Square mount on Thompson/Center Contender is matter of utilizing factory drilled and tapped holes.

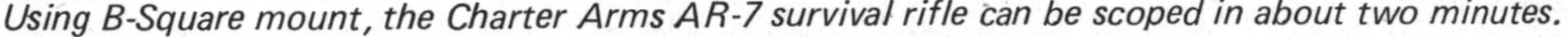

Using B-Square mount, the Charter Arms AR-7 survival rifle can be scoped in about two minutes.

Scoping Lever-Action Rifles But These No Longer

Presents Special Problems,
Are Insurmountable

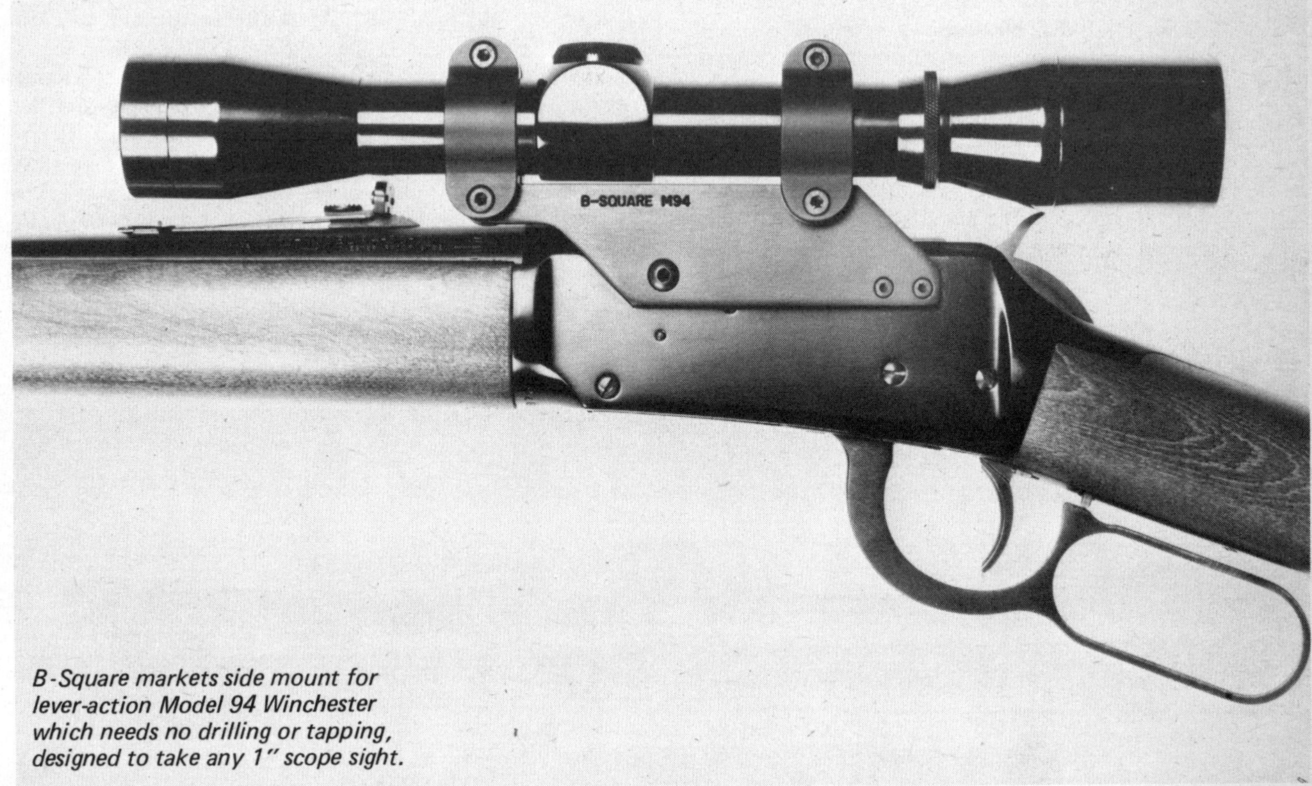

B-Square markets side mount for lever-action Model 94 Winchester which needs no drilling or tapping, designed to take any 1" scope sight.

LEVER-ACTION RIFLES have been with us for well over a century, and even with the fine bolt, semiauto, pump and single-shot rifles currently on the market, the old lever action remains popular. Those models from Winchester, Marlin, Savage and Browning must still be capturing a sizable percentage of total sales or they wouldn't be in their lines.

While these rifles aren't basically improved over their counterparts of twenty-five, fifty or seventy-five years ago — and, in some instances, are inferior to earlier versions — they're popular as a saddle gun, one to carry in a pickup or four-wheel drive vehicle, and as a handy, fast-action brush or timber gun. And quite possibly nostalgia plays a part in their popularity today. Even though they lack the flat-shooting qualities, capabilities of handling modern magnum cartridges, and are inherently less accurate than many modern rifles, they are, in many instances, most practical.

Telescopic sights also have been with us for over a hundred years; hunters of the 1870s used long, crude scopes atop their heavy rifles to decimate the buffalo population.

The lever actions are much the same as they've always been. The new ones handle such cartridges as the .243 and .308 Winchester, sure. There have even been versions with the .44 magnum and larger cartridges, but scope sights have undergone far greater improvements. It's just been in the past couple of decades that the scope has come into its own, being accepted as a great sighting advancement, rather than a frail gadget as so many riflemen once regarded it.

For years, riflemen — realizing the added benefits of a

scope — have made attempts to scope that good, old lever action they've had for decades. The Model 94 Winchester was the most popular of the levers and, because of its top ejection system, successful and practical mounting for use with a scope was near impossible.

Some years ago Redfield came out with their Frontier scope, specifically designed for lever actions. It had great eye relief and was designed to be secured on the barrel near the muzzle. It was awkward, cumbersome and added unwanted weight to the muzzle of the little carbines. Though it worked satisfactorily and improved sighting, it never met with any degree of popularity and public acceptance. I have one on a Remington Fireball .221 single-shot handgun and it's great there, but I was never enthused about one on a 94 Winchester.

Let's look for a moment at the problem of scoping the .22 rimfire lever actions that are enjoying popularity today. The Browning BL-22, the Ithaca Model 72, and the Winchester Model 9422 and 9422M all have grooved receivers to accept the tip-off scope mounts which were introduced by Weaver many years ago. These mounts are available either in the seven-eighths-inch diameter to accommodate the more conventional .22 scopes, or in one-inch diameter.

Marlin offers both the Model 39A rifle and 39M carbine with receiver tapped for scope mounts, which are supplied with the gun. As Browning, Ithaca, the Winchester 9422 and the imported Navy Arms Model 66 all feature side ejection, the prime handicap of scoping these rifles is eliminated. However, the Navy Arms isn't tapped for mounts.

Jerry Holden of the J.B. Holden Company in Plymouth, Michigan, has been making his Ironsighter mounts for some time and has recently come out with designs for the grooved .22 rifle. Each is a good, heavy mount and ring combination, in some ways similar to the Weaver Tip-off, but made of an alloy. They are available in two sizes; one for one-inch scopes, and the other for those seven-eighths of an inch in diameter. The latter comes with a ringed plastic insert so it also may be used with the smaller three-fourths-inch .22 scope. Mounting the scope high, with an arched base, affords the use of either the scope or the iron sights already on the rifle.

But I'm certainly not the first to ponder the problem and come up with a solution of sorts. Gene West's first attempt to scope a center-fire lever action was about some eighteen years ago on an old Model 92 Winchester converted to .357 magnum. For this, he tapped the right side of the receiver and, with a Weaver N2 mount, put an old Weaver 29-S scope on the carbine. Mounting in this manner requires that the shooter's face be to the right and above the stock. In rifles of heavy recoil, this wouldn't be practical, as it would be most abusive to the right cheekbone, though it should work fine for the left-handed shooter. With the light recoil of the .357, it created no problems and increased the accuracy of the gun.

Another lever-action rifle scope mount is designed to fit on grooved receivers. Rings are held with socket screws. Note lack of protruding edges, knobs and sharp edges which may otherwise catch on clothing or branches in field use.

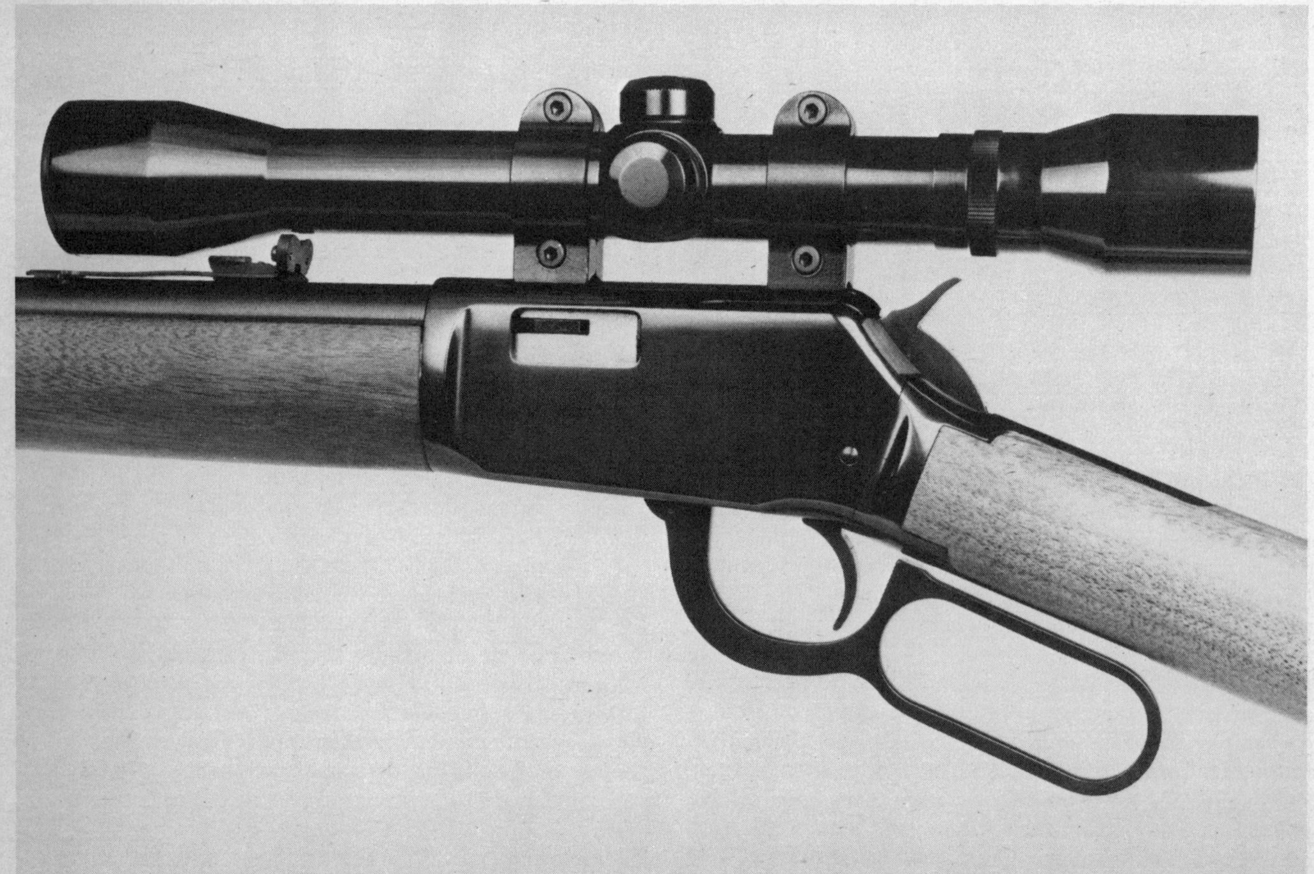

Finger lever stop screw and peep sight rear screws are used to fasten B-Square's Model 94 scope mount. See text for details.

The earlier-mentioned Holden Company, Williams and others have introduced side mounts for the Model 94 and 64 Winchesters. These mounts are secured to the left side of the receiver with three screws. On newer guns, all that is required for mounting is to remove three presently installed screws and attach the mounts. Some older guns require drilling and tapping.

The Williams mount is straight; it goes straight up from the side of the receiver and it is for the conventional one-inch scopes. Due to the way it's positioned, the windage adjustment knob on most scopes is right over the top ejection port. Empty cases, as ejected, hit it and drop back into the action. The solution is simple: rotate the scope a quarter turn and have the windage knob on top, the elevation adjustments on the left side. It's just as easy to make adjustments that way. With this mount, you simultaneously have the use of either the scope or the garden variety iron sights.

The Holden mount is similar, but mounts at an angle, putting the scope more above the barrel, making it easier to get onto quickly when you shoulder the rifle. It, too, allows use of either the scope or iron sights. It has two positions for the front ring for versatility in positioning the scope. This is beneficial from the eye relief point and makes it easier not to have the windage knob protruding above the action, interfering with ejection.

For the Browning BLR, the Marlin 336, 444, 1894 and 1895 models and Savage's Model 99 series, scope mounting offers no problem. These rifles are all side ejection models and manufacturers have tapped them for top-mount scopes.

Why scope a lever action? Isn't it supposed to be the fast handling, slab-sided, saddle and brush gun? True, but far more of them are carried by hunters either on stand or prowling the woods on foot today than are carried in saddle scabbards on Old Paint.

Advantages of scoping a lever action are as great as they are for scoping any other rifle. If you can't see it, you can't hit it and scopes offer a well-known advantage in the poor light of dawn and dusk. With failing eyesight, which catches up with all of us, the single aiming point afforded by the scope makes sighting far easier and more accurate than lining up the old iron sights. A scope adds a bit of bulk to the handy little carbine, as well as a little additional weight, but attributes greatly outweigh the shortcomings, and the latter won't slow you down on a fast shot in heavy timber.

If you've shot open sights all your life, you may have to take the old rifle out several times prior to opening day and get well acquainted with the scope. Make sure the scope is mounted correctly and has proper eye relief. With a bit of practice, you'll find that, as you shoulder the rifle, you'll be looking through the scope and at your target as naturally as you will over the irons. And your shooting should improve.

What scope should one put on a lever action? On the market today is a wide, often bewildering selection. For any centerfire rifle, we'd recommend only a one-inch scope. While some of the less-expensive scopes are quite good, others leave a great deal to be desired. A good scope, cared for properly, will give a lifetime of service. Some of the cheaper models can leave a decided sour taste in your mouth.

If scoping a Browning or Savage lever action chambered

for the .243 or .308, a good variable scope — a 2X-7X or 3X-9X — will cover most situations nicely and there's little need to go to anything more powerful.

For calibers such as the .30-30, .32 Special, .35 Remington, .444 Marlin and .45-70, which are used primarily as short-range brush guns, low-power scopes are the order of the day. A 2.5X or 4X will work well under most circumstances, as will a 1X-4X variable. Most of the shots taken with these will be under one hundred yards and they'll do all you need, without the added bulk of their bigger brothers.

We're blessed with an ever-increasing number of reticles from just about any scopemaker. For most uses, you'd probably be wise to stick to standard crosshairs. In variable scopes of 2X-7X or 3X-9X, one might consider the newer Dual X reticles, which have heavy crosshairs most of the way, suddenly tapering to medium to fine near the juncture. These do a good job at longer ranges, while the heavy wires frame your target at short woods' ranges. If hunting is going to be in heavy brush and timber, perhaps the heavy post reticle would be best. But circumstances under which the rifle/scope combination will be used can vary greatly and reticles are a matter of personal preference.

Although, as mentioned, a number of scope mounts for the Model 94 have been available off and on for years, they either mounted the scope in some odd way, required considerable work on the part of a gunsmith, or allowed little windage or elevation adjustments once mounted on the rifle.

The new B-Square M94 Side Scope Mount overcomes these objections. Dan Bechtel, who heads up the B-Square Company of Fort Worth, Texas, overcame the problem of the top ejection by mounting the scope base on the left side of the action, thus neither obstructing the ejection or feeding port. This allows almost forty inches of windage and elevation adjustment at one hundred yards in the mount — plus whatever adjustment is built into the scope. The mount rides high enough to permit the use of the iron sights and also makes possible the use of the variable power scopes with their larger ocular bell. Some scopes with large scope adjustment turret caps may hamper ejection of spent cases. As mentioned earlier, this is overcome by simply rotating the scope counterclockwise ninety degrees.

The B-Square mount is the least offset of the M94 mounts to date and weighs only 2½ ounces. Since the mount is fastened to the flat side of the action, the mount is locked securely into place and scope slippage is eliminated because

Close-up view of left side of receiver of M94 mount appears streamlined and compact despite size.

Note how low the 4X Burris scope is mounted over the bore, without hindering use of iron sights, when necessary.

there are no dovetails. In keeping with current trends, Bechtel uses socket screws; screws as well as wrenches are furnished with each mount. The B-Square M94 side mount will accept any scope with a one-inch tube.

Despite the fact that this is a fairly large mount and a good-sized chunk of metal is used — actually a high-strength alloy is utilized for the base and rings — it is an eye-pleasing mount without sharp edges or projections to hang up in a scabbard or on clothing while the gun is being mounted hurriedly.

If yours is a model 94 made after 1964, remove the finger lever pin stop screw from the left side of the action. Also remove from the left side of the gun the two plug screws used to hold the peep rear sight in place. Simply install the B-Square mount with the screws that come with the mount. Two large screws are furnished with each mount, and you have to use the one that fits the finger lever stop screw threads on your gun.

Next remove the scope rings from the mounting plate and install the scope in the rings. There are two small half-moon shims on each side of the mounting plate; these should be reinstalled when settling the scope in place. Adjust the scope for eye relief and turn the scope until the horizontal crosshairs are truly horizontal. Of course, one also can use the vertical crosshairs for this purpose. Next tighten the front ring halves, but leave the rear ones loose so that the rings can be moved back and forth until the desired elevation adjustment has been made, then tighten the rear ring halves. If extra windage is needed, switch the shims from one side of the plate to the other in either ring or in both rings. Each of the shims moves the point of impact about ten inches at one hundred yards.

If your gun was made prior to 1964, it will be necessary to drill and tap two rear holes. The B-Square M94 mount can be used as a drill jig and the standard 6-48 scope-mounting screw thread is used.

Thanks to the top ejection of the M94, over-the-bore mounting of the scope is not practical or feasible. The B-Square way of handling the problem appeals to the eye since it is streamlined, unobtrusive and not bulky. Once the screws have been cinched tight, the mount does not develop any looseness in its mounting.

Chapter 13

HOMEMADE TOOLS AND THEIR USES

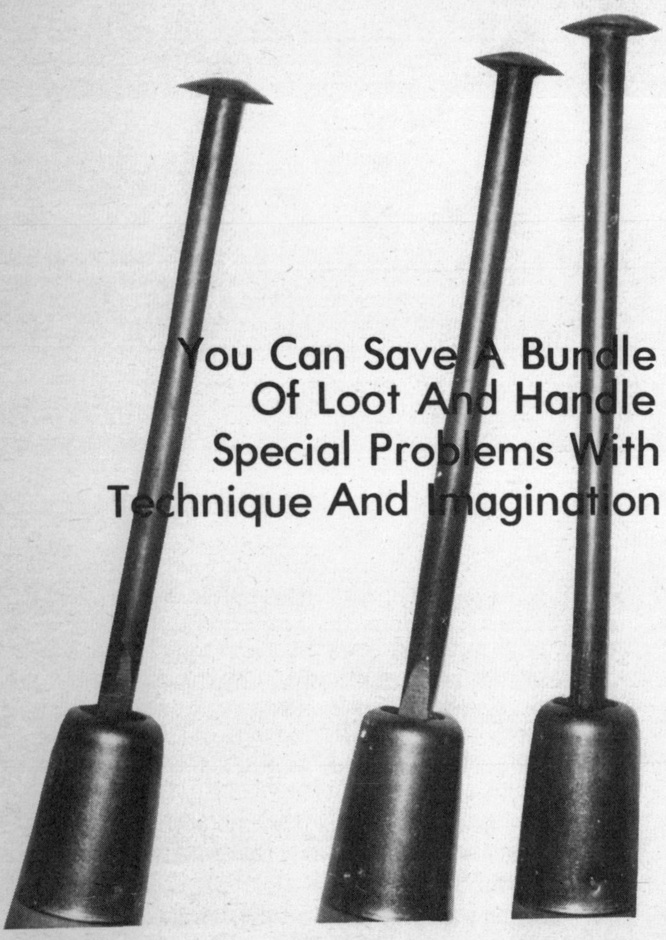

You Can Save A Bundle
Of Loot And Handle
Special Problems With
Technique And Imagination

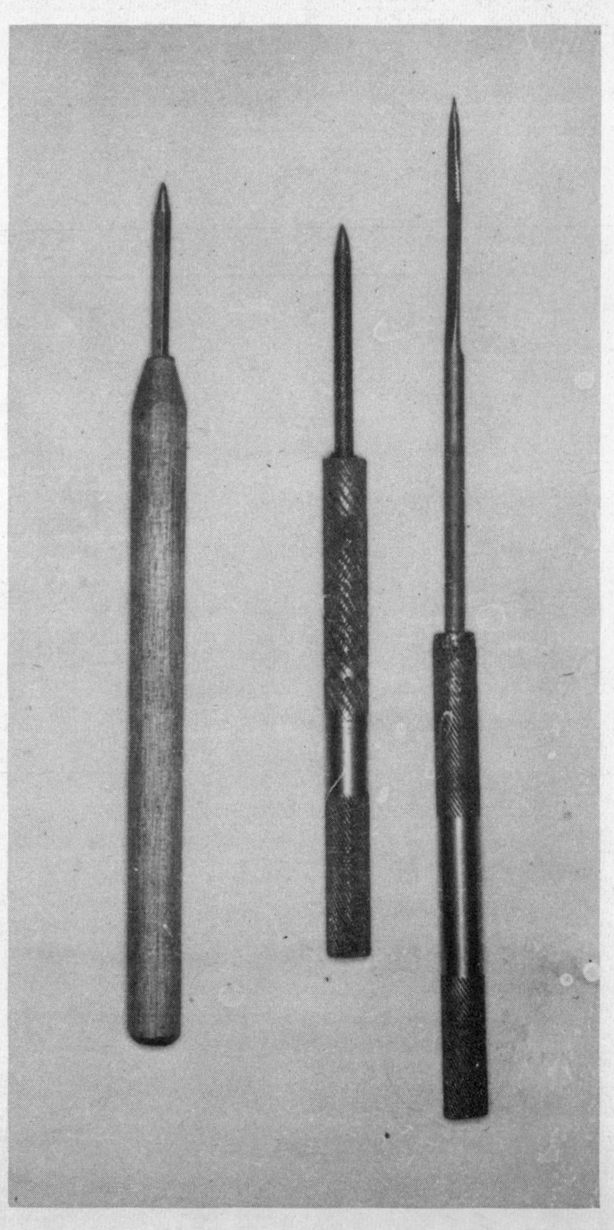

*Some ingenuity and a supply of old tools and parts
are all that are needed to produce special tools
for the home gunsmith. The stock scrapers, above,
may be produced following directions in the text.
Worn-out Swiss files and Allen wrench were basic
materials used to produce drill rod-handled scribes, right.*

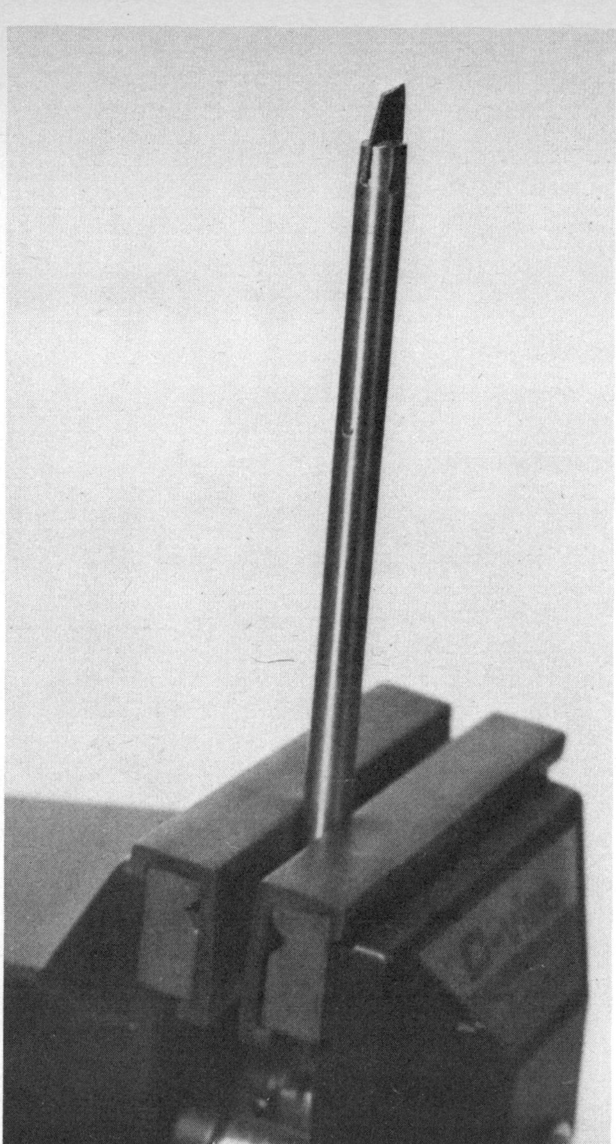

ONCE YOU HAVE collected most of the power tools and have learned how to use them, you will find that you also can make a number of the tools you need or want. Take a look at the bench of a professional gunsmith; it's an even bet you will find he made a lot of his own tools, from simple screwdrivers and scribes, to thread gauges.

Willingness to try something once, discarding the not-so-good results of that experiment and starting afresh is the key to success. Access to the scrap bin of a machine shop helps, but you can collect enough discarded files, Allen wrenches, and hacksaw blades to keep you in homemade tools for quite a spell.

Allen wrenches are hardened and are converted easily into scribes for marking all sorts of metals. Cut off the right angle leg of the wrench, either with a hacksaw or on the grinding wheel. On the wheel the steel will get hot, so use a pair of pliers to hold the wrench during that cutting-off step. You can make a wooden handle from a piece of dowel rod, or for a metal handle, use any round stock that is handy. If you have scrap drill rod stock, this converts into a good handle.

For a wooden handle, grind first one end into a point, pre-drill a hole into the dowel, then seat the scribe-to-be with a hammer. Once this is done, the point that will be used to scribe the metal is ground down. If you are going to make a metal handle, and you have a lathe, drill a slightly undersized hole in one end of the handle-to-be.

If you have a knurling attachment for your lathe, you may want to give the handle that beauty treatment. Break the cut-off edges with a mill bastard file. This is done best while

To produce special narrow-blade screwdriver, left, split drill rod was used for handle and broken-off hacksaw blade inserted as blade. Note beveled and angled blade to protect wood surrounding recessed screwhead. Homemade handles are easily knurled with lathe and knurling tool, set up as shown below.

Handy set of bluing forceps may be produced from old hacksaw blades. Knock off teeth on grinder, heat, bend to shape, quench in oil, grind desired shape to tips and the forceps are ready to pick up most shapes and sizes of material.

Worn-out files, obtained from professional shops, may be ground into excellent chisels which will last a lifetime.

the piece of rod stock is locked into the headstock of the lathe. Grind the end of the wrench that will fit into the handle round, then measure the diameter. Select a drill that is one size smaller, then make a hole into the handle with this drill, either on the drill press or the lathe.

The use of either of these power tools will assure that you are drilling a straight hole into the round stock, but if you can drill offhand with the work locked into the vise and you have the hand-drill that will do the job, you can go that route.

Now stick the scribe-to-be into the deep freeze for several hours. This will shrink the metal, permitting you to seat the former Allen wrench into the handle. To seat, you can drive the round end of the wrench into the handle by hitting with a hammer, or use an arbor press if you have one. In a pinch, one can even use a bench vise for this. Once the frozen steel has thawed out, you will have a tight fit and then can grind the tip down for your scribe.

If you can buy some brass rod from a brass foundry, you can make your own drift punches as well as your own brass hammers. Again, you use a metal handle from any round stock available, break the cut-off edges with a mill bastard file, knurl if you care to, then fasten the brass head to a length of handle. Fastening can be done as outlined above, or you can drill a hole into the brass head, run a tap into it, then

thread the handle. If you find that the thread is wobbly, wrap some plumber's tape around the thread, or use some strands of steel wool in the threads. A couple of drops of Loc-Tite also will help, used with or without the steel wool.

A trick I picked up from a machinist is handy to keep in mind. Drill the hole one size under what the specs call for and tap it with a smaller tap. Once the threads of the rod are forced into the hole in the brass head of the hammer, they won't budge.

Worn-out hacksaw blades should be saved. They can be converted into follower springs, bench tweezers and I have used bits of them as shims here and there. When a blade wears out, I simply grind the teeth off and stick the blade into the scrap bin. Then, when I have time, I convert the blade into some useful items.

Old, worn-out files, often discarded by professional shops and machinists, can be made into chisels for stock work. To convert a file into a chisel, first forge the file into the shape of the chisel you want. Grind off the teeth all around, then grind the shape of the chisel edge. Follow the contour of a commercially made chisel for the shape of the edge. Heat the steel until it is red hot, then quench it in water. Draw the temper when the steel reaches straw color.

Since scrapers for wood removal fall into the same tool

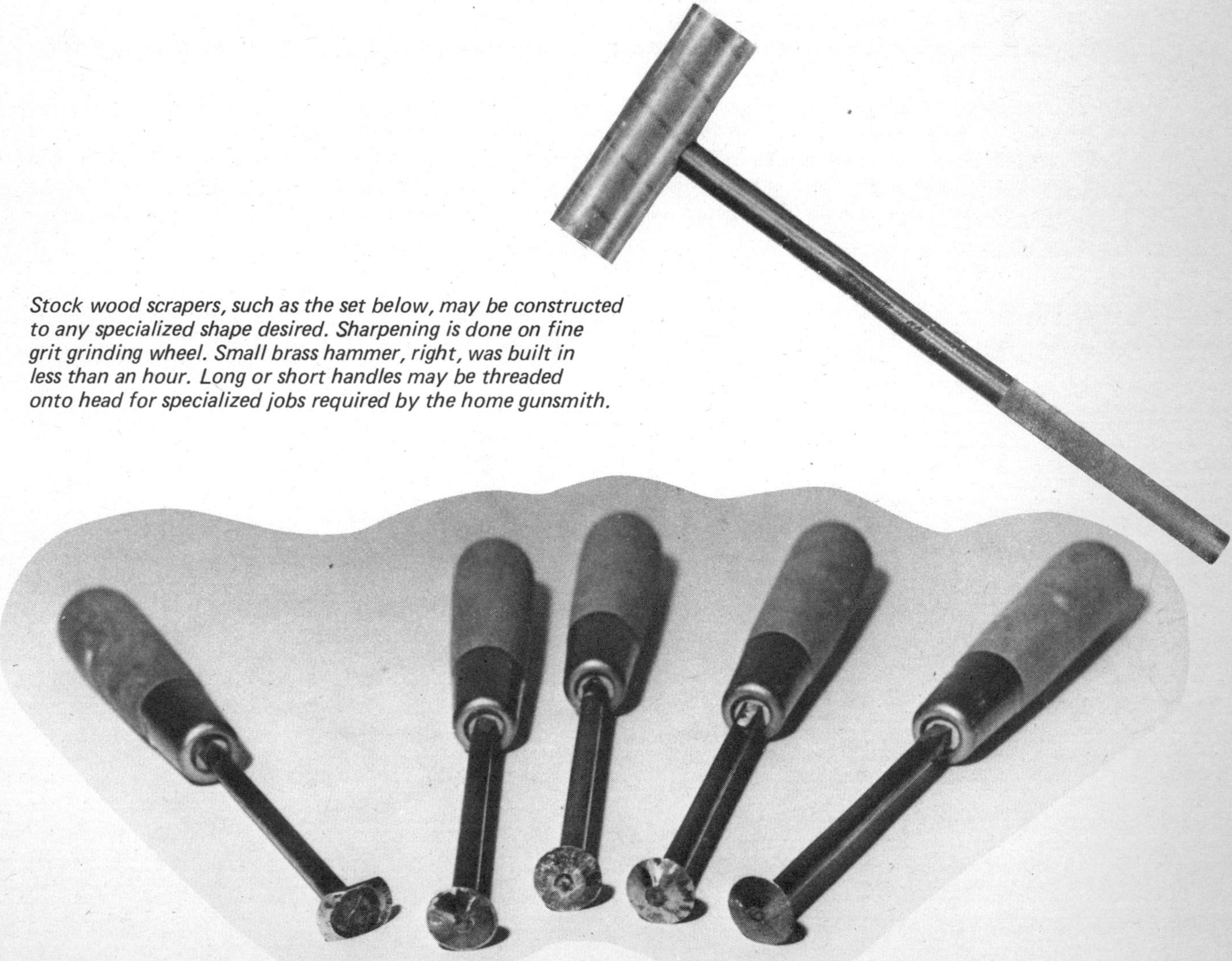

Stock wood scrapers, such as the set below, may be constructed to any specialized shape desired. Sharpening is done on fine grit grinding wheel. Small brass hammer, right, was built in less than an hour. Long or short handles may be threaded onto head for specialized jobs required by the home gunsmith.

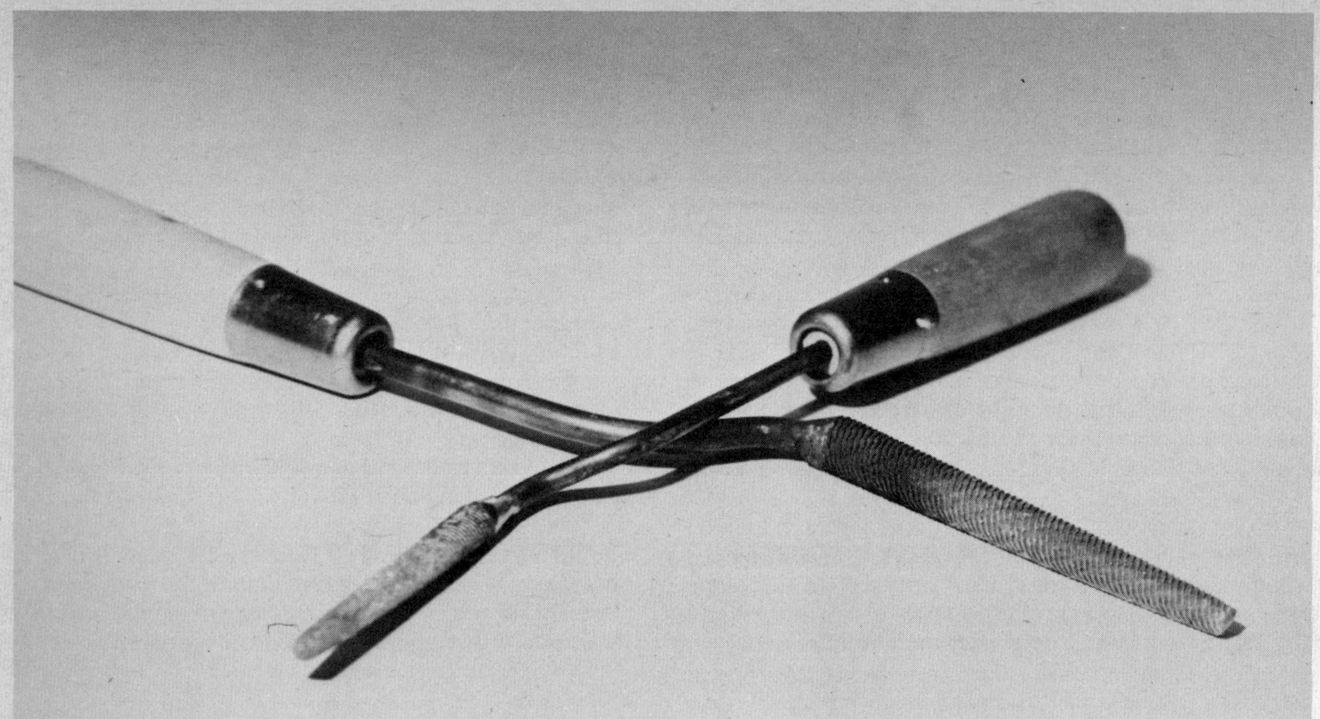

To remove wood from barrel channel, nothing beats a set of fine and coarse files which have been bent to the proper curve and mounted in safety handles. Unable to buy what was needed, the examples above were home produced.

classification as chisels, making a bunch of scrapers should present no problem. In one set I made for my shop, the holes were drilled before the steel was heat treated. Once the edges had been sharpened, the tips of the drill rod handles were heated, then pushed through the holes into the scraper blades, and the ends of the rods were pounded down so that the blades are held tightly in place.

Regrinding screwdriver blades requires either the touch of some highly skilled hands or a jig sold by the B-Square Company. Blades that bend or break must be reground, then

Tenite II was used for handle material of two screwdrivers lying down. Third driver utilized broken screwdriver handle.

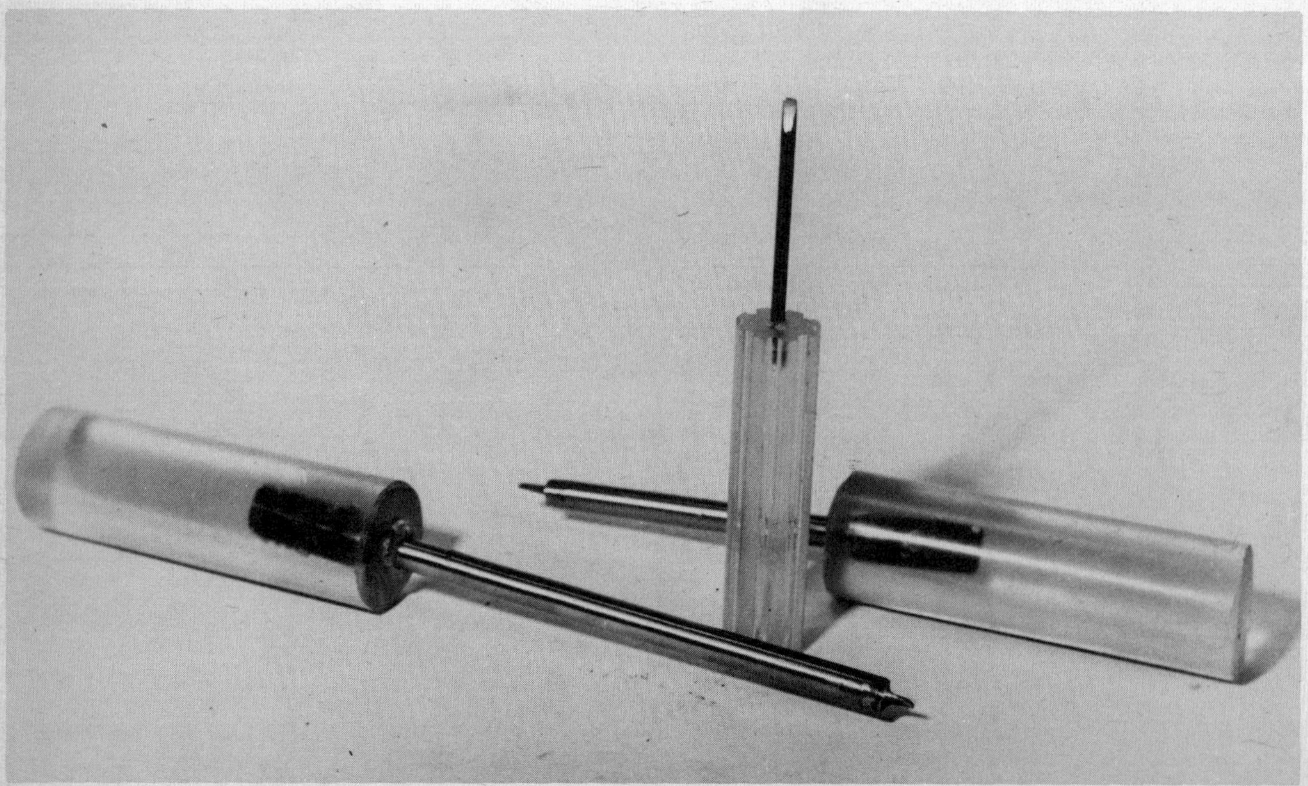

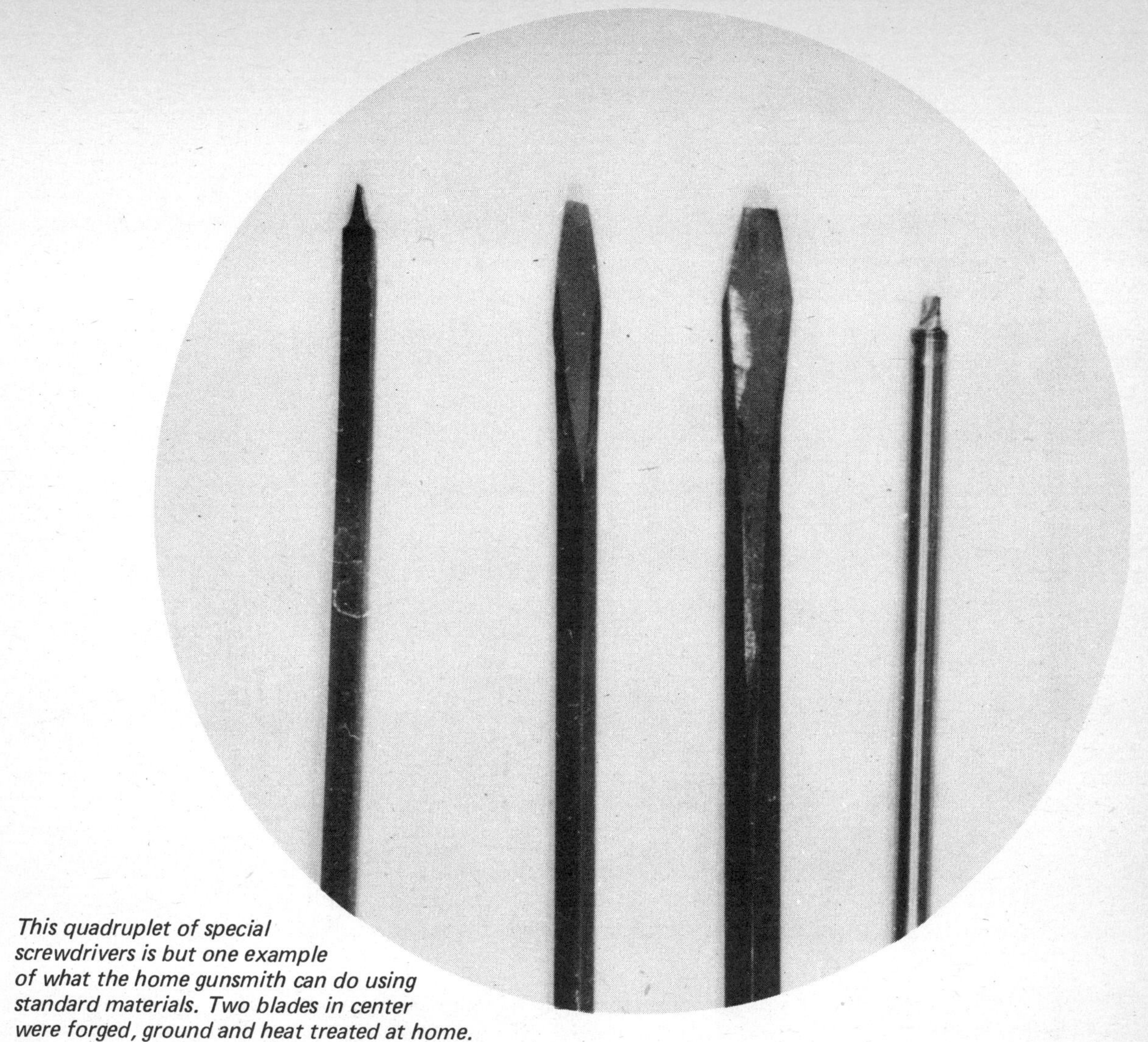

This quadruplet of special screwdrivers is but one example of what the home gunsmith can do using standard materials. Two blades in center were forged, ground and heat treated at home.

heat-treated to give them the needed strength. The jig also can be used when you make your own set of screwdrivers. Drill rod is the best choice for screwdrivers, but if you have the heat-treating equipment you can make some nice screwdrivers from key stock. Grinding blades into the desired shape is probably the easiest way to get the job done, but draw-filing them is the touch of a professional. It takes longer, but it is also a good way to learn how to draw-file properly. I am convinced that more files are ruined and wrecked by improper use than by filing.

Allen wrenches — especially the larger ones — can be converted into screwdrivers. You can either grind them or forge them, leaving the right-angle leg to use both ends of the wrench as driver blade. Ground down and set into a handle, these Allen wrenches are just the ticket for scope-mounting jobs.

Another way to make up small blade drivers, especially those which will be used with the narrow-slot screws found on most of the European guns, comes from Harold MacFarland a gunsmith and author. He suggests the use of drill rod. Slot one end, cut off a piece of used hacksaw blade, insert into the slot, and your basic screwdriver is made. The other end can be set into a handle or squared off for use with a socket wrench.

For inside polishing, either by hand, in a drill press or on a lathe, simply take a length of drill rod and slot it, making the cut with the hacksaw at least one-inch deep. By threading emery cloth or a strip of E-Z Flex Metalite into the slot, you have the near-perfect way of inside polishing. If drill rod is not on hand, you can use dowel rod, but this is used best by hand and if chucked into the drill press, reduce the spindle speed. Be sure the dowel rod does not have a set and that it is straight. This is especially important, if you use the drill press for the job.

Fine scribes and small chisels can be made from worn-out needle files. In making chisels from tired Swiss or needle files, follow the instructions outlined for using large files. To make scribes, simply grind them down on the wheel, with the rough shaping being done on a coarse wheel, while the final shaping is done on a finer wheel. These Swiss files, when converted into a scribe, can be used without a handle since the handle part of the original file has remained unaltered.

Handles for screwdrivers, files and other handtools can be bought from most of the larger hardware shops or from such trade sources as Brownell's or Mittermeier's. Broom handles can be used, if you are interested in utility and don't worry about appearance. Cut off and drilled, these makeshift handles can be left as is or you can sand the sawed corners,

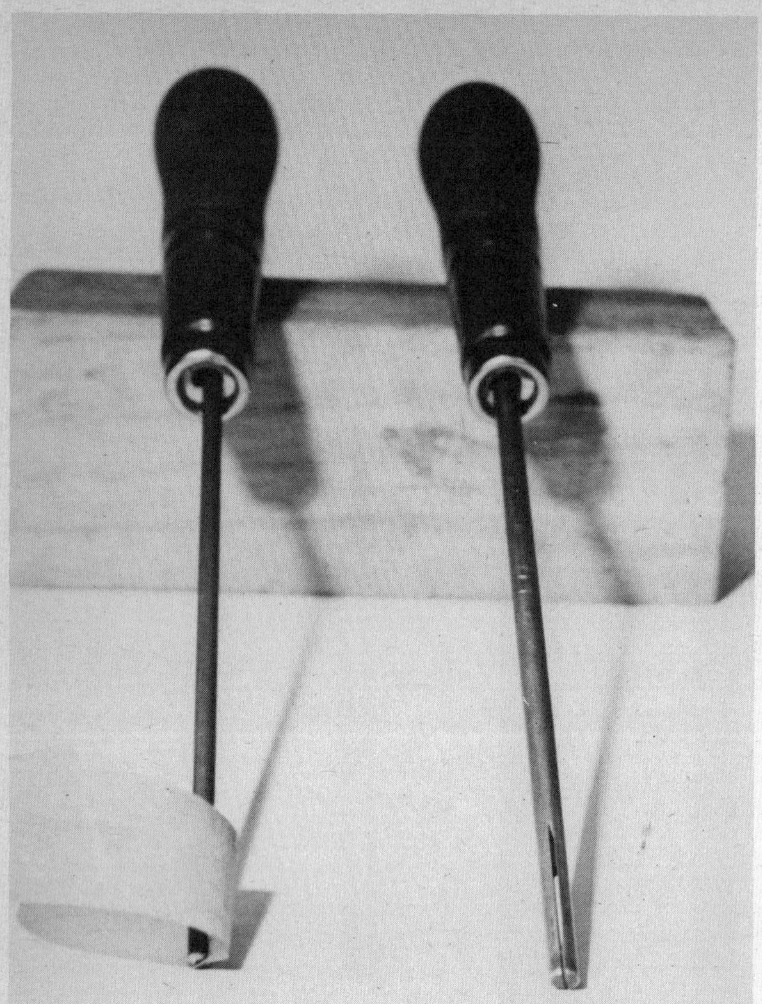

Drill rods, slotted with hacksaw and mounted on handles represent quickly-made inside polishers.

Ground down Allen wrench with Tenite II handle proves ideal for removing factory installed screws from receiver.

paint the handles or dress them up any way you want. Most broom and mop handles are made from hardwood, hence can be used with handtools. Some handles, closet rod and other round stock from the lumber yard is made from soft woods, and usually won't last too long.

Perhaps the best way to make tool handles is to fall back on the plastic material from which most of the commercial tool handles are made. Tenite II is the name of the stuff and the only source I have found for it is Brownell's. Tenite II can be sanded, machined, ground, polished and shaped. It is tough and impact-resistant. Short lengths can be used as bench blocks, or when still shorter, for facing on a hammer that won't mar blued steel, brass or even silver inlays.

To make handles from Tenite II, cut to length with a crosscut saw — the finer the blade, the smoother the cut — then drill a slightly undersized hole into the handle with a slow-running drill or even an eggbeater drill. Measure the tang of the tool you want to seat first to get the size of the drill bit. Wrap the tool into a damp rag. Leaving only the tang exposed, heat the tang until hot; before it begins to turn color, seat in the handle and let cool. Once cooled, the handle is fastened to

the tool. The wet rag is suggested so the temper of the tool is not being drawn, while you heat the tang of the tool.

Felt and muslin buffing wheels are available commercially. Leather wheels no longer are manufactured, although you may be able to find a saddlemaker or leather worker who is willing to make one. I did without one for years, but made one up along the lines shown me by the late John Buhmiller, the barrelmaker from Kalispell, Montana.

Cut some wooden wheels from three-quarter-inch soft pine, with most of the wheels having a six or eight-inch diameter. Drill a three-quarter-inch hole in the center, sand the edges smooth, then glue sandpaper on the edges. Felt weather insulation strips or even a well-used strip of belt leather can be used. The wheels with the garnet or sandpaper are used to dress down wood; the felt wheels are used for polishing, since the felt holds any of the polishing compounds. One veteran gunsmith I know uses such a leather wheel for sharpening his chisels. This provides an edge on the cutting surface that is better than he can get from sharpening his chisels on a stone.

Once you learn how to use the various hand and power

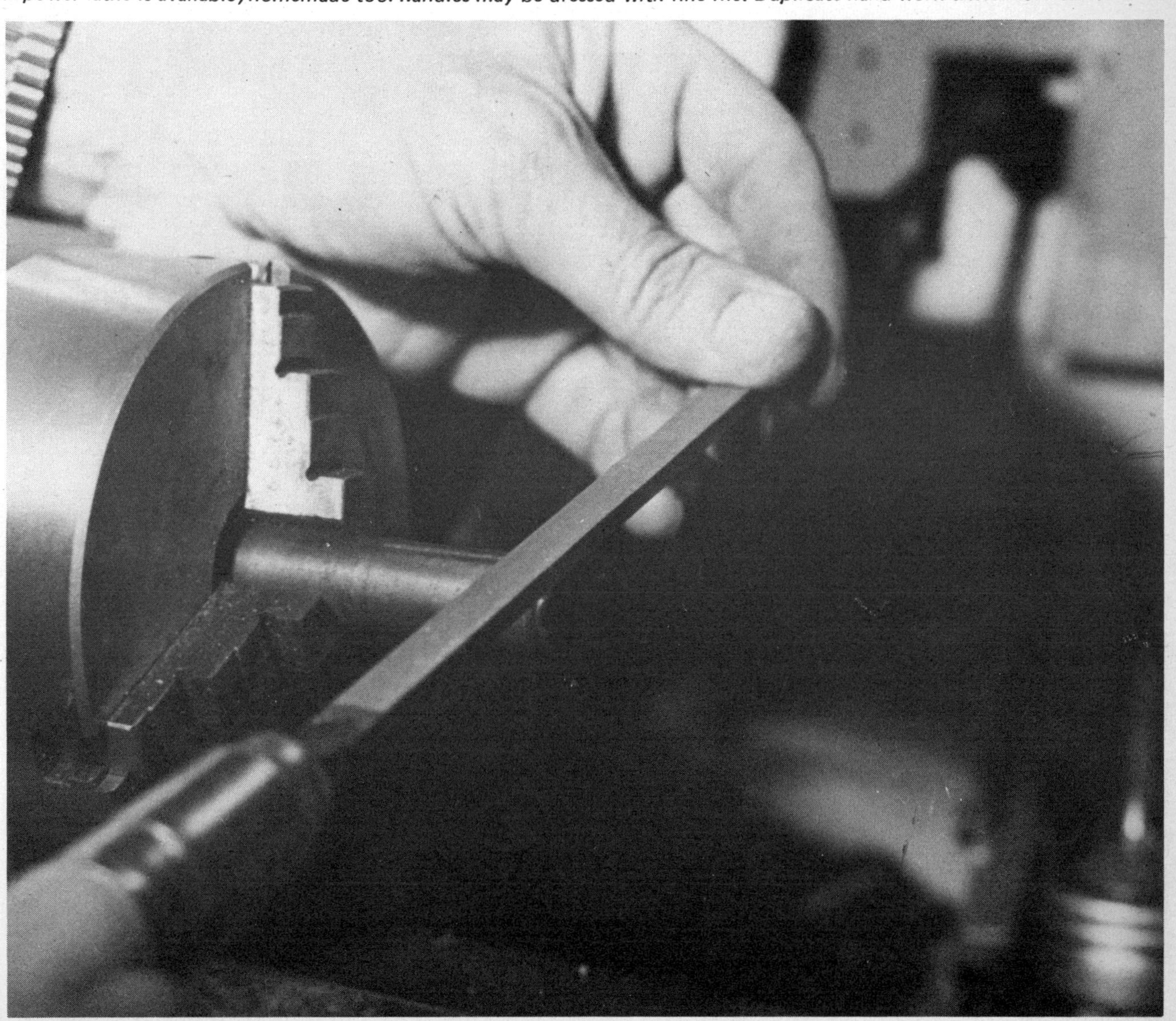

If power lathe is available, homemade tool handles may be dressed with fine file. Duplicate hand work takes more care.

tools, you will find you can make specialty tools. You can make many of your own jigs for the drill press and the lathe, plus fixtures for welding and brazing. Two pieces of square stock, drilled and tapped, plus two pieces of drill rod — each threaded on one end — will convert into a tap wrench handle. The list of tools you can make yourself is limited only by your skill, ambition and ingenuity.

Harold Johnson in his book, *General Industrial Machine Shop,* lists some thirty-five different shop projects of which better than half are tools you will need sooner or later. Included are hammers, squares, V blocks, bench blocks and a number of other tools mentioned earlier in this chapter.

Tools not normally found on a gunsmith's bench include those dental drills the chopper doctor likes to use. Even when he pitches them out, they have at least six to twelve months of life left in them for gunsmithing use. Chucked into the Dremel tool, the drills and grinders are just right for some of the more intricate stock work when you have to remove small amounts of wood, or when you have to grind off a hunk of steel somewhere that a hacksaw cannot be used.

Earlier mention was made of homemade center punches. Remember, the punch must be hard enough to mark extremely hard steel, so it becomes important to prepare the metal correctly. Grind to sixty-degree angles, then polish smooth on a sanding wheel. I prefer to polish tips absolutely smooth, since any imperfection on the exterior can shatter the tip when the tool is struck a hard blow while resting on an equally hard surface. Although not really essential, I treat most of my homemade tools this way. It seems to add extra life to them.

Most of the stockmakers I know make their own checkering tools, the majority of them starting with drill rod. About eight inches of rod is needed to make a tool that will be comfortable to handle. Heat one end cherry red and forge it flat, then bend that end to the angle seen on commercial tools. The checkering pattern on the checkering tools is made by filing. Before tackling such an undertaking, it is best to

Handle for homemade tool may be drilled with handle locked into headstock three-jaw chuck, as shown below.

learn how to use a file properly. Making the needed checkering tools is not too difficult, but requires considerable care, since any mistake will be reflected in a botched job on a piece of good wood.

Some handy knives and small scrapers can be made from discarded hacksaw blades. To give longer life to these blades, shape and grind the blades, then heat them, using an oil quench to harden them.

If you get into stock work, you will need a bushel basket full of clamps. I have yet to see a shop where someone complained bitterly that there were too many clamps on hand. Clamps can be made from 3/4x5/8-inch cold-rolled steel that is heated, then bent to the desired shape. This usually takes the form of a C-clamp. The fastening screw to use on this job is a three-eighths-inch cup point set screw three inches long. Clamps of all kinds can be improvised for welding, brazing and soldering, and a supply of cold-rolled steel helps no end when you want to make up a jig or clamp.

When taking a shotgun stock off the action, you can find a long enough screwdriver and grind the blade and often the handle down, or you can improvise and, sooner or later, wreck the slot in the bolt that holds the works together.

You can make a special stock screwdriver by using five-eighths-inch drill rod. Forge one end to the desired shape, grind the blade level and square, then harden and draw it to a dark blue. Make the tool long enough to clear the stock by at least three inches. Drill a hole through the upper part of the drill rod, insert a short length of drill rod, and use this to apply pressure on the blade. You get plenty of torque this way and few of these bolts can resist the force that can be exerted this way.

Thanks to my shop and the equipment I learned to use, I have been able to make up custom loading dies, dies that swage down bullet diameters, swages that convert spent .22 rimfire hulls into bullet jackets.

I also have revamped and largely rebuilt a microscope and microscope stage, built a macro camera and done a few dozen other jobs I would not have dreamed of tackling before I began doing some of my own gunsmithing.

One of author's more ambitious made-from-scrap projects is this bullet carrier, designed to hold spent bullets for micro-examination or for macro-photography work.

Don't discard those expended .22 cases, if you're a reloader. Brass may be swaged in set of homemade dies and converted into jackets for .22 caliber bullets.

Chapter 14

TOUCH-UP AND COLD BLUING

Here Are The Techniques And Pitfalls Of A Mystery That Has Been Reduced To Following The Rules!

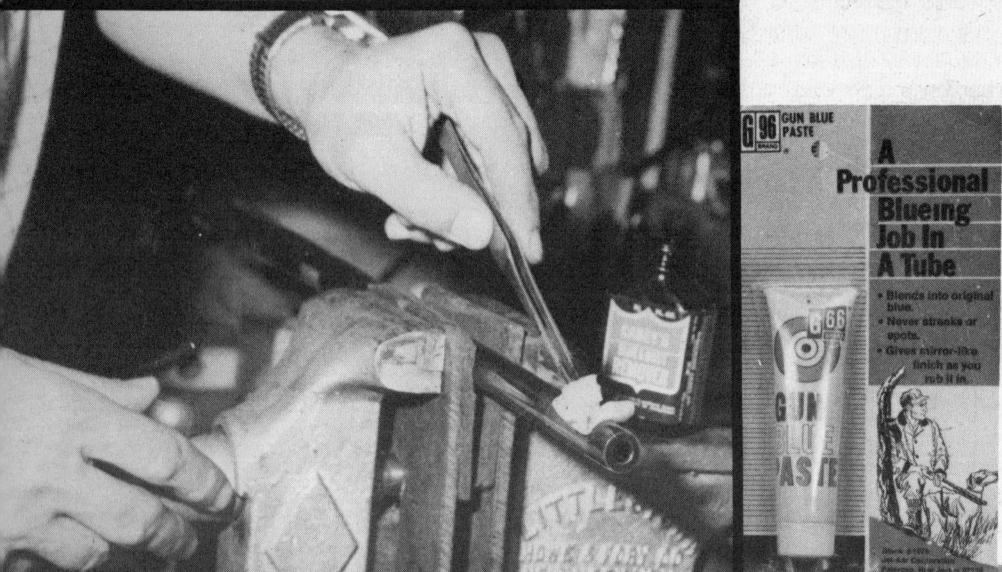

Available touch-up and bluing materials come in all shapes and sizes. Not every product will work on every type steel.

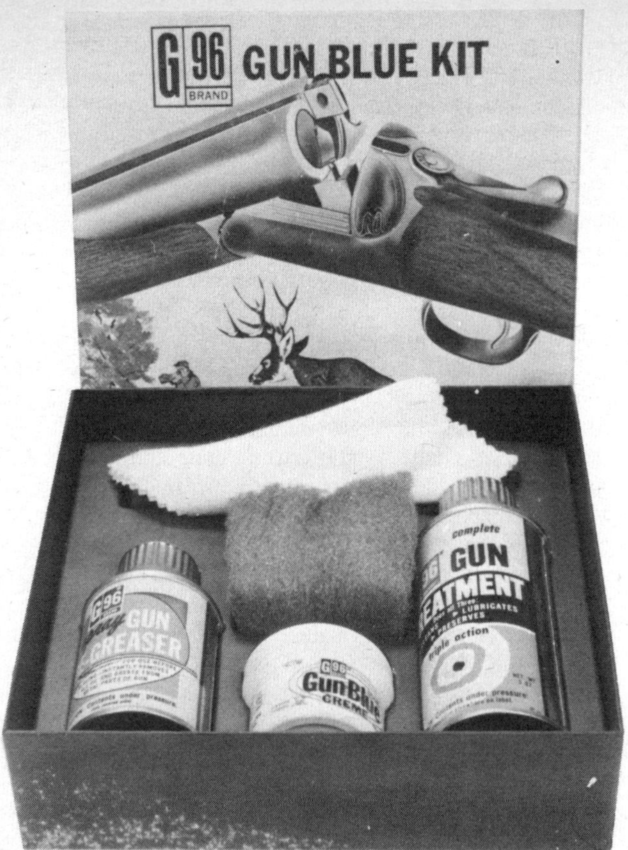

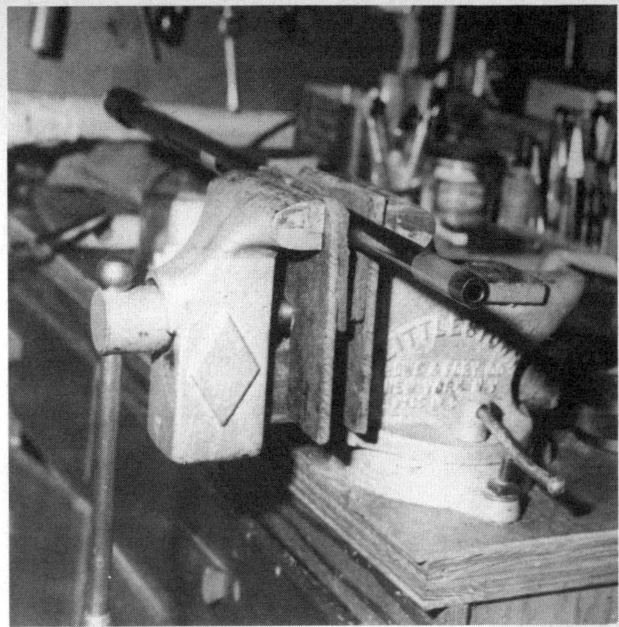

The G96 bluing kit at left contains needed materials for cold bluing one gun, or for touching up worn spots. Above: After removal of front sight band and solder, white band required touch-up bluing.

NO SHOOTER I know would spend good money for a new rifle that is as rusty as a barndoor hinge, except perhaps when he wants either to salvage the beast or salvage parts.

But I know a lot of shooters who are willing to spend a lot of money to have a gun reblued or have a special bluing job done on a custom rifle. What's the difference between the rusty gun and the blued one? Aside from a handful of ten-dollar bills, there isn't any. The rusty gun has been oxidized; the blued one also has been oxidized!

If I could find someone who would be willing to pay me a buck for each printed page that has been published about bluing and the preparation of metal prior to bluing, I could retire and live an indecent life of leisure. Sad to report, I have not been able to find such a sucker so far. Professional gunsmiths and those fabulous guys who do gun bluing for a living should have all the answers to the problems that can be encountered in bluing a gun. But every gunsmith and bluer I have talked with in the years past was quick to admit that (a) in most cases he didn't have too many problems and (b) that he had nothing but problems with that so-and-so gun. In short, bluing is not predictable, no matter how long even an expert has been at it.

Take, for instance, that nice, shiny factory rifle that arrived in my shop a few months ago when the weather was so miserable that not even my dogs wanted to go out. I slapped a scope on the rifle, then set it aside for better weather to arrive since I had better than forty inches of snow on my range. Just a day or two ago, I checked the gun over prior to collimating the scope. Deposits of white crystals were evident where the barrel is screwed into the action, around the ramp front sight, as well as around the rear sight. These oxidizing salts will hold moisture like a sponge and this, of course, is an open invitation for rusting. The bluing shop at the factory must have been overworked the day the gun went through the bluing tanks there, and the collection of the white crystals simply meant that the finished bluing job had not been sufficiently washed or rinsed in hot water to get rid of all the salts that are used to produce that nice, shiny blue you see on the rest of the gun.

Commercial bluing is done by either the hot or the cold method, both of them fairly messy and corrosive. Any such bluing operation must be set up with considerable care, since the hot bluing tanks cannot be located anywhere near tools, guns or any other metallic objects which could rust and/or corrode. As long as bluing has been around, there seems to have been no end of bluing salts, tricks to get the job done better and, as a good many professionals have found out, the bluing salt that worked miracles on one gun will not do a job on the next gun.

Although the method of bluing and the chemicals to which the to-be-blued steel is exposed are important, the most important aspect of bluing is in getting the metal ready for the bluing bath. If you have a gun blued with the standard finish that usually is referred to as "hunter's bluing," you must figure that better than half the charges for the job go to the buffing and polishing that is needed. The finer, and therefore the costlier the bluing, the greater the care that has been taken during that buffing and polishing.

You'd think that shoving a piece of steel against a spinning buffing wheel is the simplest job in the world and you may be tempted to try it yourself. Let me clue you in on a little secret. I thought so, too, and fortunately mentioned that urge to a gunsmith. Reaching into the scrap parts bin, he invited me to use his buffing wheels and compounds, and happily I went to town on a cracked Enfield action. You know how squared off the forward edges of the famous Enfield ears are? Well, about three minutes after I started the buffing wheels,

those edges were lopsided, round and looked like a hungry beaver had chewed on them for a week or two.

Buffing and polishing constitute an art. It also calls for progressively finer polishing compounds, a series of wheels, plus the patience of a saint. Then, when you have it all done, you degrease the job, for the slightest trace of grease will negate all the efforts put forth during the buffing and polishing. If you can sneak a look into a professional bluing shop, you will note that white cotton gloves are the rule when final polished and cleaned parts are handled. Bluing will not take if there is the slighest trace of grease on the steel, hence extra care must be taken to get every part to be blued absolutely clean and grease-free.

Before tackling any kind of bluing job, one or two other points must be made lest you run into trouble. First of all, not all types of steel blue alike — and here I am talking about the standard steel grades most often encountered in actions and barrels. Nickel steel requires a different method of bluing, while stainless steel gives even the professionals ulcers and gray hairs. While hot and cold bluing call for degreasing all metal parts which are to be blued, in touch-up bluing, some of the products work just a shade better when there is a trace of grease left on the steel. This does not mean that you should put a couple of drops of gun oil on areas to be treated in this manner, but the grease left on your fingertips is enough. When degreasing, the question of which solvent to use must be resolved first. Denatured alcohol and lighter fluid are most often thought of as grease dissolvers. They are, but they also leave a film or residual chemicals that often make it difficult, if not impossible to remove the grease or effect a good bluing job.

Since gun bluing, by either the hot or the cold method, requires a considerable cash outlay for equipment and chemicals, and since it is a fairly complex operation, I do not recommend you attempt this.

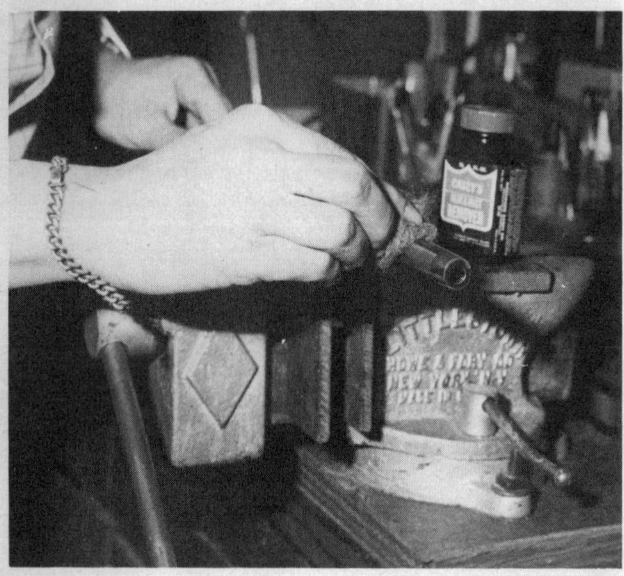

Old bluing on barrel could not be removed with fine steel wool and oil. Eventually, barrel was heated with blow torch and bluing applied to hot metal.

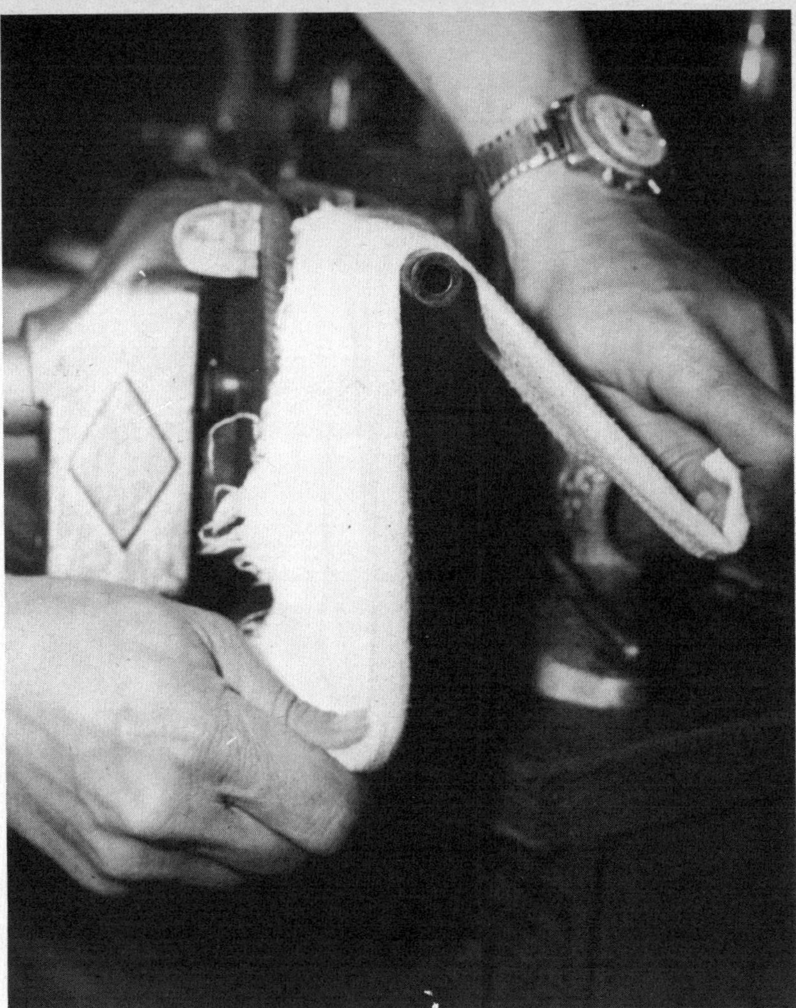

Some metals require considerable effort to reblue. This rifle responded to hot-applied Brownell's Oxpho-Blue, polishing, rebluing, buffing; steps repeated four times.

Muzzle of Smith & Wesson showed holster wear, easily touched up with G96 bluing stick. To ensure reuse of stick, cap of tube must be tightly replaced.

The picture changes when touch-up bluing is considered. Experts at the bluing business seldom are chemists, but thanks to long experience and an inherent willingness to try this or that, quite a few of them have developed pet methods of getting a job done. More often than not, those methods are highly unorthodox. For instance, heating a gun barrel or stripped action in water prior to applying a cold-blue sounds about as crazy as taking a gun part from the hot bluing solution, dumping it into ice water until cold, then sticking it back into the hot solution until hot and then back to the cold bath. Do this three times and the blue is said to be better and more permanent than that you get from the regular methods of hot bluing.

When tackling any kind of bluing, from the hot bath method to touch-up bluing, whatever rust there may be on a gun or part of a gun must be removed. Light surface rusting is best removed with the help of a small pad of fine steel wool which is moistened with some fine gun oil. Rub the rust spots until they disappear; this treatment will not harm the bluing that is on the gun or part now. Years ago, rust was removed by various chemical means, all of them more or less dilute acids, and while most of these older methods worked, they also entailed some dangerous stuff, such as fifty percent solutions of potassium cyanide. Potassium oxalate was one of the milder rust removers and worked quite well.

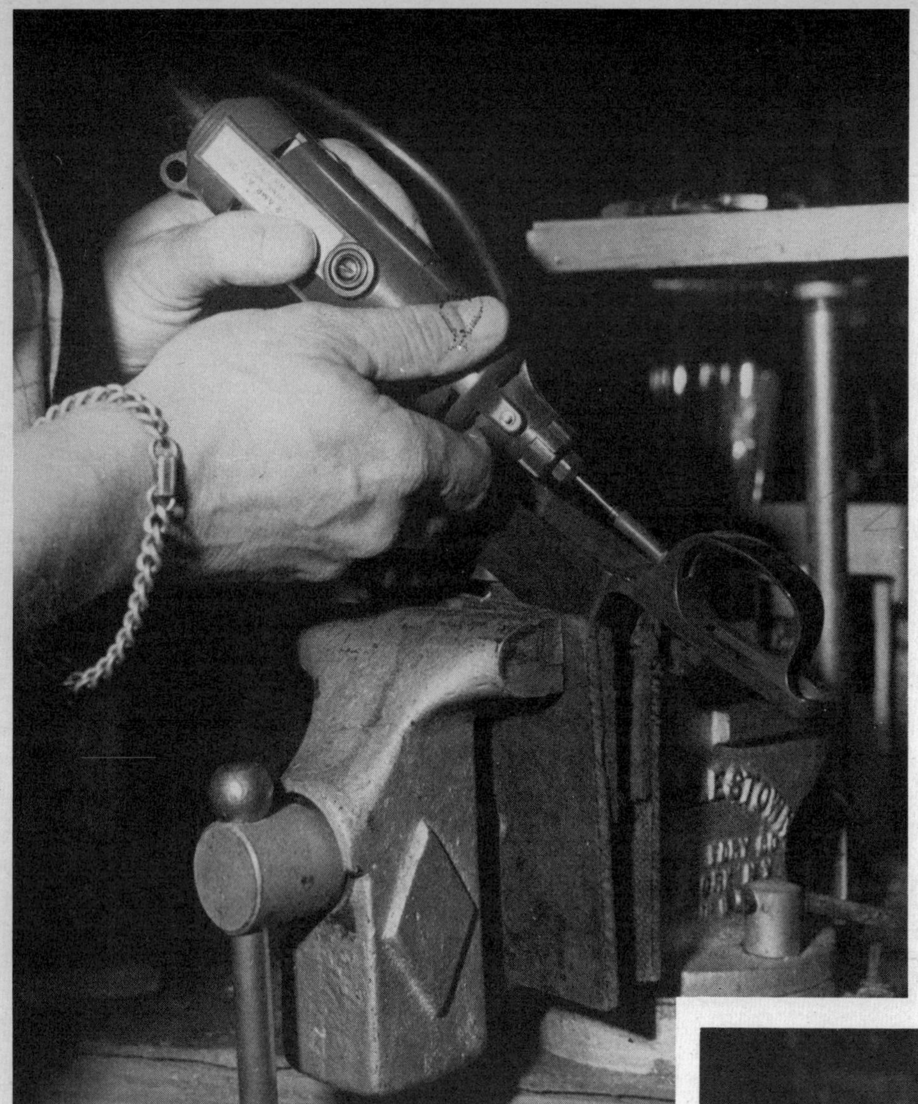

Tough-to-reach areas of Mauser trigger guard and magazine were polished by careful use of Dremel Moto-Tool, left. Bluing solution must be applied to entire surface of metal, which is then wiped dry.

When rust is more severe, but still localized, try first a piece of emery cloth, then the steel wool treatment. One variant of that one is to use Brownell's Oxpho-Blue instead of the oil. If one of the commercial rust removers won't touch the rust, you can, with a great deal of care and a fair bit of mess, use the professional method of rust removal. Make up a ten percent solution of sulphuric acid, then place the stripped and rusty part into the acid bath and heat. Be sure to rinse in cold, running water, then reheat the metal in a hot water bath.

If you must use any of the strong acids, be extremely careful. Use eye and face protection, wear rubber gloves, and when mixing water with sulphuric acid, always pour the acid into the water. If the water is poured into the acid, the heat generated can splatter the still-concentrated acid all over you and your work area.

Most of the commercial rust removers will be able to

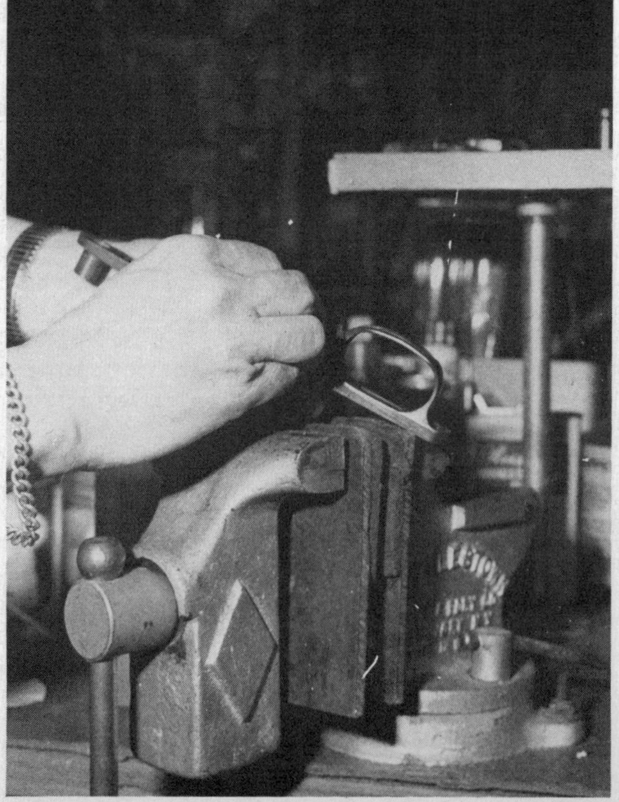

handle all but the most severe rust, and if things have reached that stage, I suggest you let a gunsmith handle the acid treatments. He knows what he is doing and has the needed equipment.

Some users of touch-up and cold bluing have found they get a somewhat better finish when the dried bluing is steel-wooled or carded. Since steel wool as it reaches you contains some oil, this oil must be removed. Get a couple of steel wool patches ready for use, then soak them in denatured alcohol and burn the oil and alcohol off. Do this outdoors to eliminate the fire hazard in the shop; the fumes created by this burning are toxic, so watch yourself.

An excellent grease solvent is household ammonia if you can stand the burning eyes and the runny nose. Household bleach also will do the job, and if you have sensitive skin, wear rubber gloves while using the bleach. The commercial degreasers and cleaners are excellent, but the problem is that you cannot buy them too readily in small gallon lots, while the smaller bottles, such as those marketed by G-96 or Birchwood Casey, just cost too much when you need a gallon or more.

You will need some small tanks for some of the gun cleaning and degreasing jobs, as well as for major rust-removal

If deeper bluing effect is desired, application of cold bluing process may be repeated, left. Final step is to polish with soft cloth, imparting deep sheen.

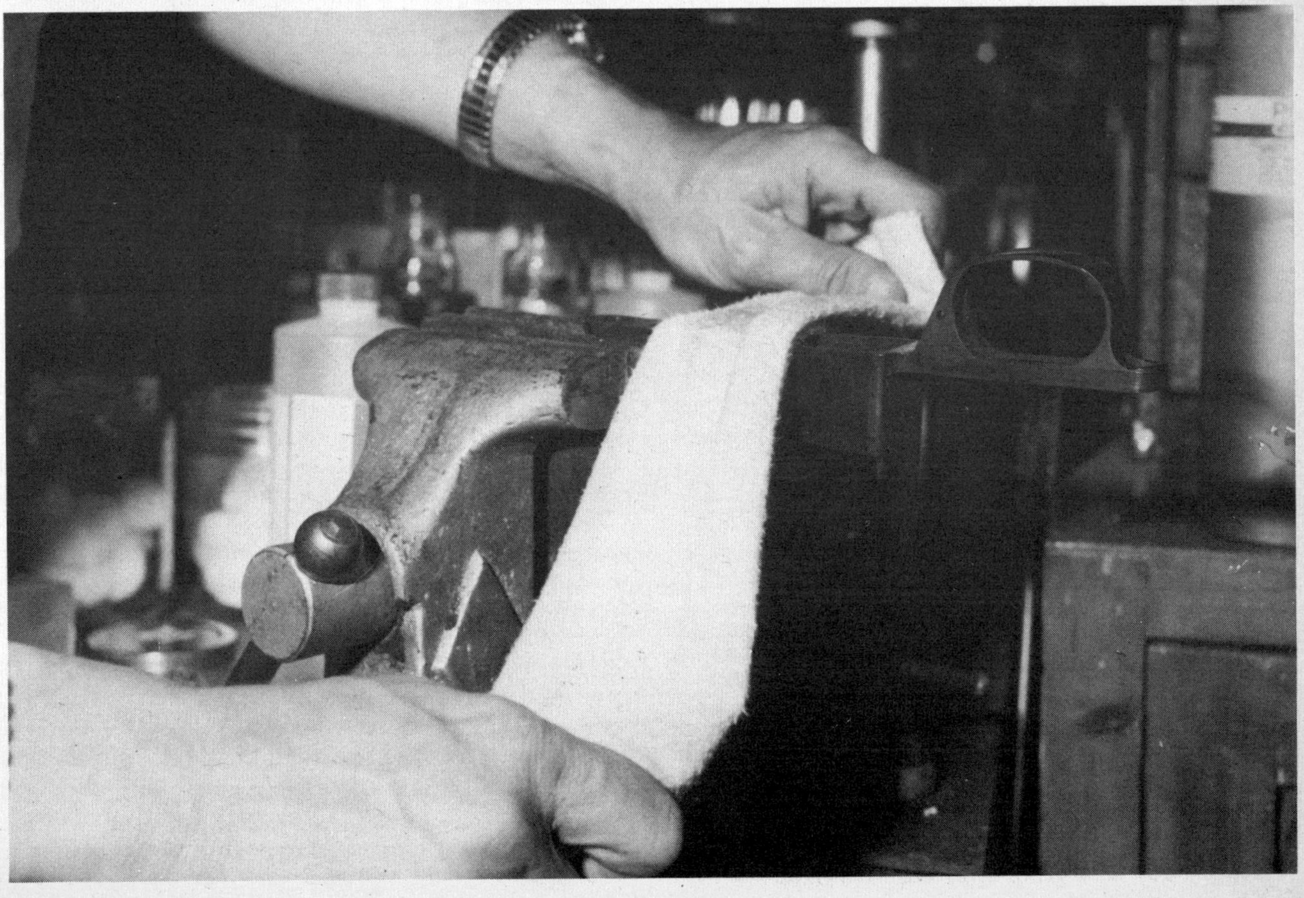

A pad of fine steel wool dipped in good gun oil is used to go over newly blued metal for added protection.

tanks, such as sold by Brownell's, can be heated, and two sources of heat (three are even better) should be used for those 6x6x40-inch tanks.

Cold bluing is not difficult and can be done in the home workshop provided you can have the polishing done for you. If you merely want to reblue a gun and the original polishing and buffing was done well, you probably can get away with merely stripping the original bluing, degrease, then cold blue. The instructions for these products vary somewhat, with some of them insisting that all grease and oil be removed, while Bob Brownell suggests that the excess oil and grease be wiped off, without attempting a complete removal of the stuff before using his Oxpho-Blue.

Most of the liquid touch-up bluing solutions have quite similar chemical compositions, hence instructions for these products are quite similar. The G-96 touch-up bluing stick is good for small jobs, such as holster wear on a six-gun and other small repairs. Be sure to cap the container well since the content tends to dry out as I learned from sad experience.

I have used touch-up bluing products for years and have found that all of them work well, providing the steel is pretreated as suggested in the instructions and the steel you are trying to blue or touch-up is not of some ornery strain of steel. If the bluing does not take, try some other product. Usually one or the other will produce satisfactory results, but every so often, a barrel or action will resist all attempts.

The usual method of touching up is to handle the solution cold, or apply the room temperature solution to steel with the same temperature.

If this does not work, try heating the metal with a torch. In 99.9 percent of the cases this will do the trick. Sometimes all rust and bluing must be removed, and if the steel still won't hold the blue, then degreasing is in order. However, I ran into a barrel that had been hot-blued and a wide front sight band had been removed. The band originally was silver soldered, this was removed by means of a torch, the barrel was polished, degreased and the touch-up bluing solution was applied.

Nothing.

I then swapped solutions and the results also were zilch. I then tried a reliable rebluing solution that had always done the trick for me. Again, nothing.

I finally heated the muzzle end of the barrel, applied hot bluing solution and the results were no better. I then polished the steel with fine, then still finer steel wool, applied bluing again, first cold and then hot. The stuff barely stuck to the steel. Rinsed in water, the bluing washed right off the steel. Since then I have tried just about every cold bluing product on the market on that barrel, and not one of them will take.

Double-barrel shotguns cannot be hot blued, since the solder holding the barrels together would come unglued. In recent years, Brownell's has introduced a cold bluing solution that works like a charm. Dicropan IM requires the use of an acid bath and the space to dump all gun parts into a tank and heat the contents of the tank.

Barrels blued that way can be touched-up when the need arises with Brownell's Dicropan T-4 with ease. The next time I have to blue a barreled action, I might try Dicropan IM, since I was satisfied with the results I got with a side-by-side smoothbore.

In general, I have had better results with liquid touch-up or bluing agents than with the paste or creme compounds.

tasks. Depending on just how many guns you anticipate having to clean and degrease, and whether you will be working with small parts only or with barreled actions, your search for tanks suitable for the jobs probably will be difficult. The large stainless-steel tanks are costly and usually are too big; the usual bluing tanks often are too long, and having smaller ones made up in the local welding shop is a costly proposition these days.

The best tanks that I ever have had are those I made up. Using half or three-quarter-inch exterior grade plywood, I cut the boards, then assembled the boxes with the help of Acraglas and some nails. When the glass had set, I covered the inside and the outside of each box with marine-grade fiberglass, using the same stuff that you can buy in most boatyards and at ship's chandlers. The boxes or tanks are not the lightest ones, but for a total cost of less than five bucks I got the tanks I needed. The outside layer of fiberglass can be colored, so that you can even add a touch of color to your shop.

The only real drawback of these homemade tanks is that they cannot be heated. For instance, when you acquire some type of military surplus rifle, rather than spend hours and hours with cleaning patches, brush and some solvent, it is nice to be able to strip the rifle down, dump the parts into a tank, with the barreled action, then cook the degreasing solution or at least bring the solution to a good, hot temperature. Bluing

Aluminum may be blackened to reduce light reflection. Process is similar to bluing. Below, first coat produces imperfect appearance. Second coat gives smooth look.

Before you start any touch-up bluing, read the instructions on the container. Should the preparation you are using call for the blued parts to be washed in water, and you have no running water in or near the shop, you probably can get along with two buckets of water, using the first one for the first rinse, the second one to make certain all of the bluing solution has been washed off and neutralized. A clean, soft cloth is suggested for the wiping down jobs. The best I've found are the remnants of a well-washed flannel shirt.

Aluminum is blackened rather than blued. There are several such compounds on the market and all work in a similar manner. If that is too much like work, you can resort to Aluma-Hyde, which is being sold by Brownell's. Birchwood Casey has a brass blackening agent that does the job quickly and reliably.

Nearly all of the touch-up and bluing products sold are toxic. A pair of long forceps will be helpful when you have to moisten patches or cottonballs in the bluing solution. A pair of rubber gloves, either the type sold for dishwashing or the very light ones used in hospitals, are a good investment since the bluing solutions leave fingers and nails with a hard-to-remove coat of telltale gray.

Removing the white crystals sometimes found on hot-blued barrels and actions is best done by totally disassembling the gun. Rinse all parts under a strong stream of water. Dry, then see whether this has taken care of the problem. If not, use 00 steel wool with fine oil to remove the rusting salts. When all of these salts have been removed permanently, a light coat of fine oil applied with steel wool will prevent further salt formation.

I believe that too many shooters who do some of their own gun work have steered clear of bluing and anything that is even vaguely related to it. Bluing has the advantage that you can actually see how the appearance of a gun or action part changes. If you goof, you simply use some bluing remover and start over again.

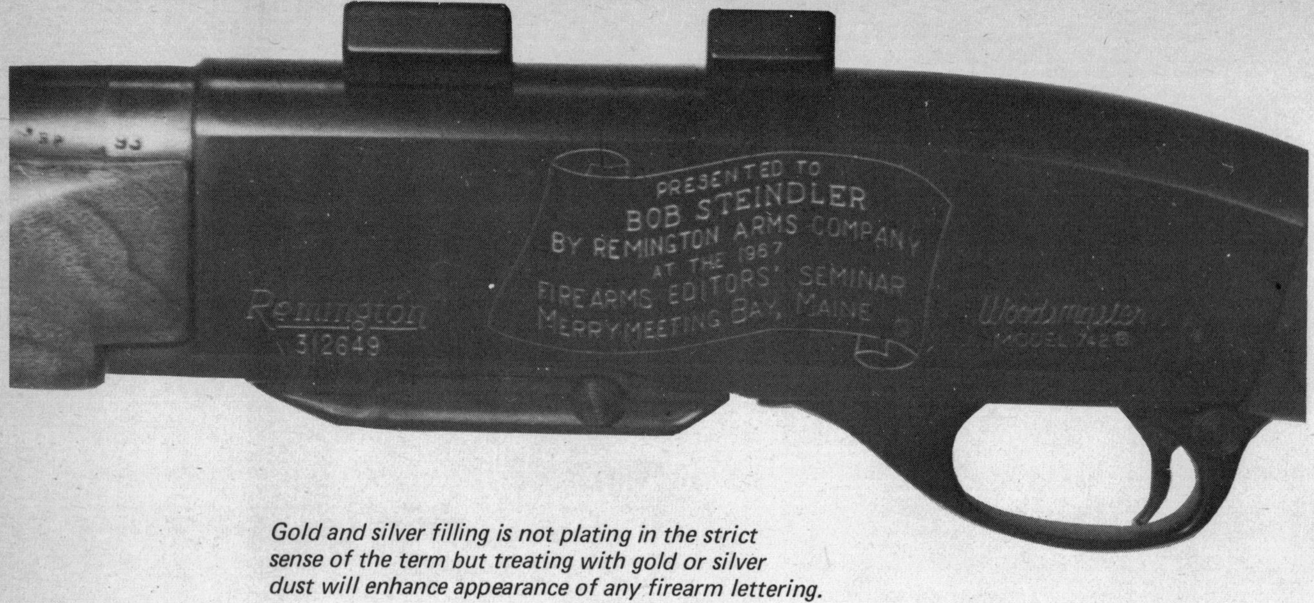

Chapter 15

Gold and silver filling is not plating in the strict sense of the term but treating with gold or silver dust will enhance appearance of any firearm lettering.

THIS THING CALLED PLATING

This Can Be A Worthwhile Project If You Don't Get Carried Away And You Can Follow Instructions

THERE WAS the time when nickel-plating guns was considered quite the fashion. Then came along something called black-nickeling, later came chrome-plating. Plating is essentially a chemical process usually stimulated by electric currents, the plating process depositing a metal skin over all metal parts treated in this manner.

Plating, if done properly and if the metal being plated has been prepared correctly, forestalls rust while giving the plated item a higher degree of appeal to some eyes. In the gun field, more handguns have been plated than either rifles or shotguns, and many of the handguns treated this way have been put out of commission.

By plating moving parts, you add as much as 0.002-inch metal thickness to each surface plated, so that you add 0.004-inch to the thickness or width of a single-action hammer. If the camming surfaces of a sear are plated, the extra thickness being added raises hell with the clearances, since extra thickness has been added to critical dimensions.

Unless performed by a gunsmith or in the plating plant where a qualified technician is keeping an eye on things, plating — including plated holes in a frame, screw threads or pins — more often than not can make reassembly of a gun a nightmare. Indiscriminate plating of guns also has led to the devaluation of good collector pieces. Of course, the most famous case involves a beautiful plating job that froze up a .45 ACP Colt autoloader.

As with bluing, proper metal preparation is important. For instance, the inside of a grip frame of a pistol or the inside of the backstrap of a revolver frame, must be completely polished before that gun part is plated. Rough areas which

Charter Arms' Bulldog was given Bonanza gold inlay treatment, requiring but a few minutes of work.

have not been polished to perfection will not permit the plating to hold, and sooner or later — more often sooner — the plating will flake off.

Before any plating is done, all of the old plating and bluing must be removed. An old plater once told me that preparing metal for plating is like the old-time burlesque shows where the battle cry was: "Take it off, take it all off!"

If remnants of plating are permitted to remain, one of two things invariably happens: The old plating, though not fully removed, will be loosened just enough so that new plating enters some areas, while areas where the plating is retained also accept extra metal from the plating. The net result is not only an uneven finish, but whatever plating did stick eventually will flake off, since no proper bond between plating and plated material has been established.

Removal of old plating is called stripping, and once any metal has been stripped, it becomes prone to rusting. According to one gunsmith, if you strip the parts of a top-break revolver in the morning and plan to plate in the afternoon, you will have extensive rusting by plating time, unless you clean and oil the parts of the gun. A word of caution is in order when considering any kind of stripping.

Old-time gunsmiths and professional platers, use strong acids for stripping. These acids do the job in a hurry, but you have to know the signs which indicate that a part has been stripped or is nearly stripped. Leave the part in the stripping solution a bit too long, and chances are the acids will have worked too well and the parts end up as nothing but scrap.

The home gunsmith should not attempt to strip a chrome-plated gun. Stripping a nickel-plated job is not too difficult, provided you follow directions to the letter. In plating, as well as in stripping, keep in mind that some areas of any gun should not be treated with either stripping solution or with plating. Firing pin holes and firing pin bushings should not be plated, and if plated and stripping is called for, this must be done with care to maintain tolerances.

Barrels must be removed and plugged. The wooden plugs often suggested for this job are useless, since the wood will soak up the solution with which you are working. By far the most satisfactory plugs are are the rubber stoppers obtainable from scientific supply houses or from a chemistry lab. These stoppers come in a wide variety of sizes, and to trim one to fit, use a sharp razor blade, removing rubber the way you'd peel an apple.

Once both plugs fit tightly, make up two L-shaped hooks from a wire coat hanger and insert one of these hooks into one stopper, the other into the other stopper. Be careful not to have the hooks bottom out at the base of the plugs. You don't want to have any of the stripping solution or the plating solution enter the barrel. The hooks are needed to permit you to fish the barrel out of the solutions.

Once they have served their purpose, wash the plugs in water and dry, then rinse and clean the hooks and oil them. Keep the oiled hooks away from the rubber stoppers, since the latter don't take kindly to oil. Before using plugs and hooks again, remove all oil from the latter and rinse the rubber plugs in water.

If you want to try your hand at plating, but want to stay clear of stripping whatever you want to plate, you can find plating houses in most towns. If you can take down a gun completely to its last screw and component, do so, then personally take the completely disassembled gun to the foreman of the plating shop and explain that you want all parts stripped, cleaned and oiled. Make sure it is understood that you want all of the parts and pieces back — loss of one or perhaps two screws is not usually considered as a major tragedy in such shops, but it could be in your case.

If you find it impossible to take the gun down completely, or have trouble getting the barrel out of a frame, take the gun to the local gunsmith. Some of them not only will disassemble the gun for you, but will handle contact with the plating shop which might save you time and trouble.

To strip a nickel-plated gun, the following method has been shown to be the best and easiest way of getting the job done: Stripping is done best in a glass container which should be large enough to accommodate all parts of the gun in such fashion that none of the parts make contact with each other. The glass dish should be at least three inches deep; if there is a tightly fitting glass lid, so much the better. A deep baking dish does the job nicely for some smaller handguns. If there is no lid, a piece of ordinary plate or window glass can be used. Glue a strip of foam rubber on the glass where the cover and the top of the dish make contact. Tight closure of lid and container is important, so check this carefully before beginning the stripping operation. The dish must be deep enough to allow you to cover the gun parts with at least one-eighth inch of solvent. One-quarter inch of solution is better.

This solution, based on that developed by the King's Norton Metal Company, Limited, strips nickel and copper plating from most steels and iron, and is considerably stronger than the original one which was granted a British patent: ammonium persulphate, 7 ounces; ammonium carbonate, 3.5 ounces; liquid 28% ammonia, 2 quarts.

The original solution called for: ammonium persulfate, 5 grams; ammonium carbonate, 1 gram; ammonia D. 0.935, 100cc.

The solution is relatively stable, but is highly light sensitive, hence must be kept in a glass-stoppered brown bottle and kept away from all sunlight.

The rate at which a plated part is stripped depends not only on how well the original plating was done, but on thickness of the plating and on freshness and potency of the stripping solution. Keep the bottle tightly stoppered at all times, and make certain that there is minimal air access to the solution while it is in the glass jar doing its job. Place parts to be stripped in the glass container, add the solution, close both the bottle and the jar, then sit back and wait. Once a uniform gray color appears — which is the color of the underlying metal — the parts are removed from the bath, rinsed in hot water, then dried and oiled. A two-quart batch of solution should strip several handguns, thus the solution can be salvaged if it has been used only once. If, on the other hand, you expect a long storage period, you are better off discarding the used solution and start with a fresh batch the next time a stripping job comes along.

Before oiling each part, examine it critically. If rust spots or shiny spots are visible, the part should be put back into the de-plating solution. As mentioned, plating over residual plate only leads to problems later.

At one time, a great many gunsmiths not only stripped, but also plated guns. Since the demand for gun replating has fallen off, few shops today offer a plating or stripping service. For a fast stripping job, fuming nitric acid was used which did the trick quickly; sometimes a bit too quickly. Nitric and hydrochloric acid fumes raise the devil with any metal, blued or unblued, and one sure way to rust everything, including the light switch, is to have the acid fumes spook around. Moreover, these potent acids are nasty to handle, therefore I *don't recommend* them unless you are a trained chemist or enjoy getting severe acid burns in your clothing and on your hide.

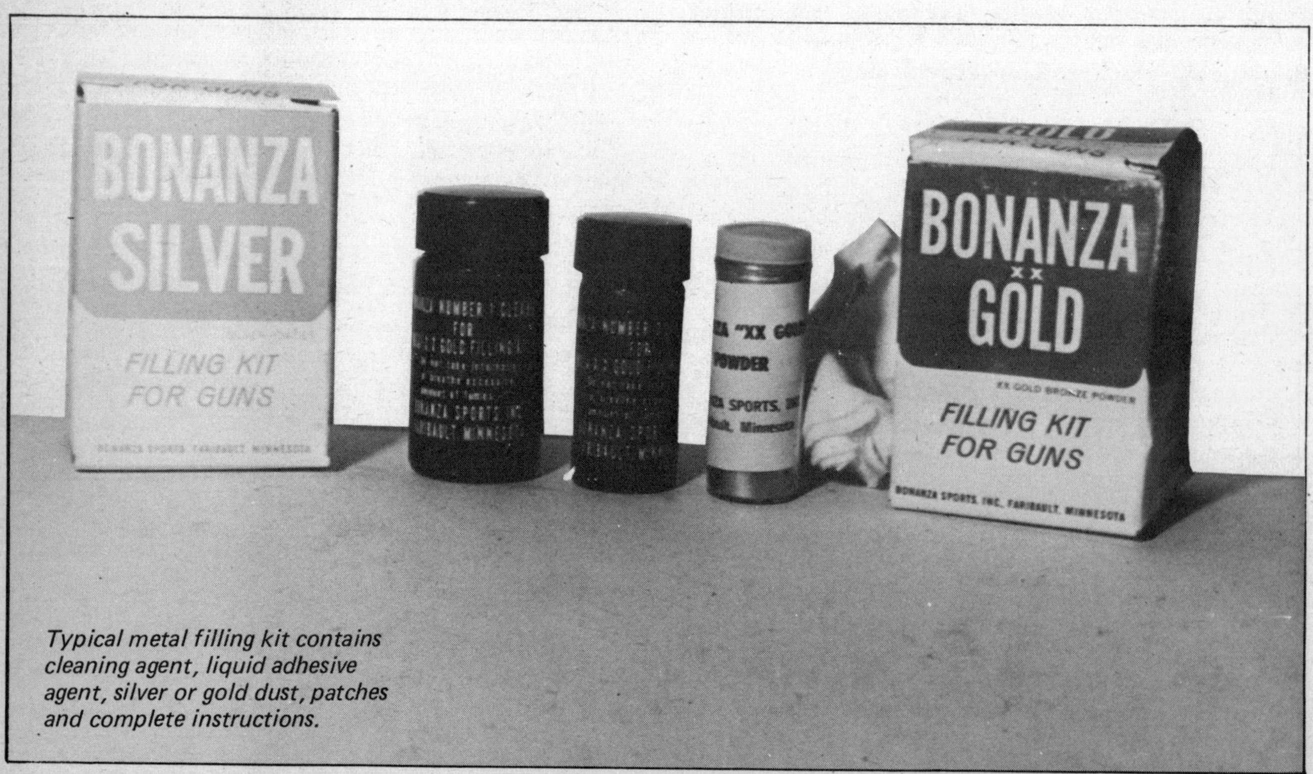

Typical metal filling kit contains cleaning agent, liquid adhesive agent, silver or gold dust, patches and complete instructions.

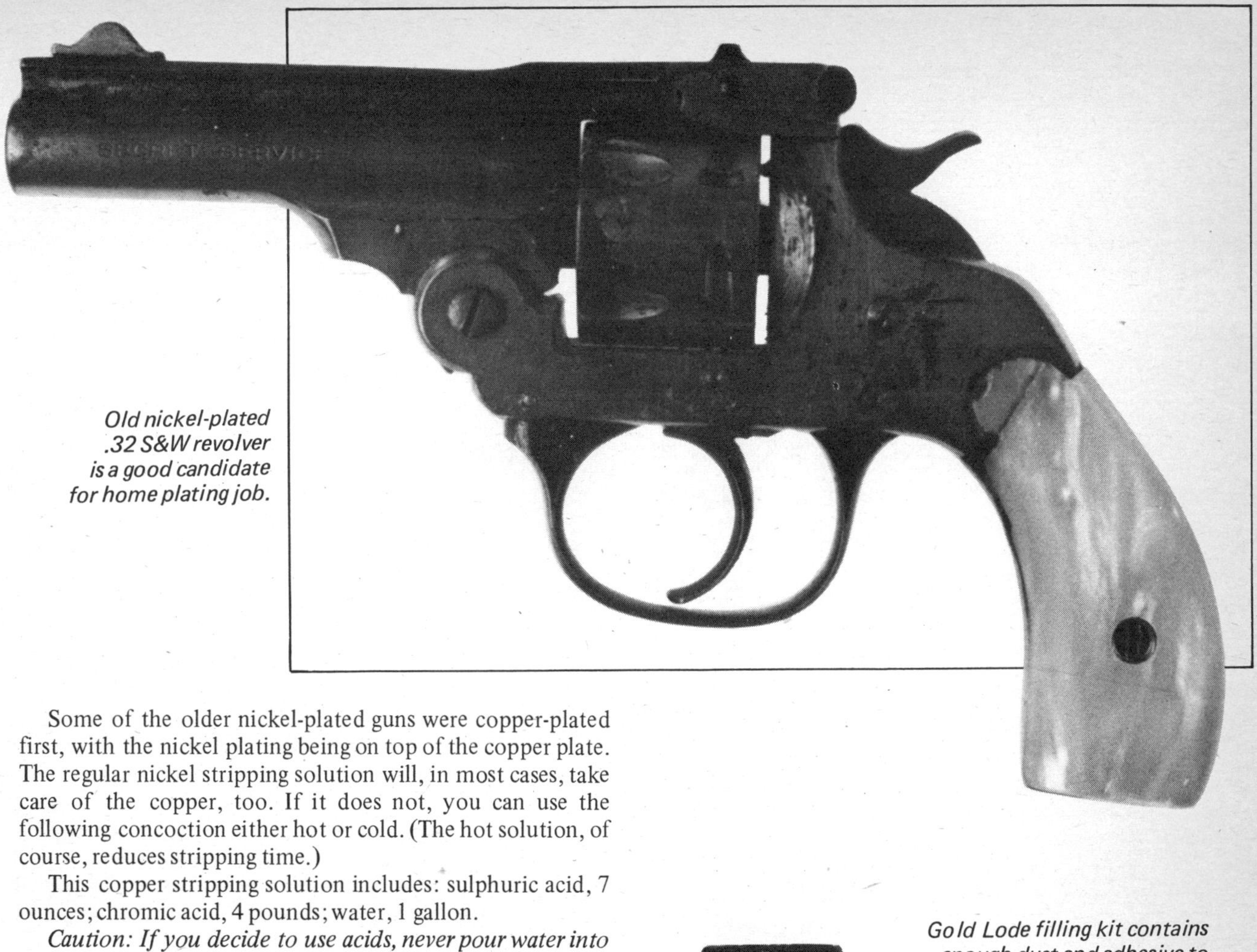

Old nickel-plated
.32 S&W revolver
is a good candidate
for home plating job.

Some of the older nickel-plated guns were copper-plated first, with the nickel plating being on top of the copper plate. The regular nickel stripping solution will, in most cases, take care of the copper, too. If it does not, you can use the following concoction either hot or cold. (The hot solution, of course, reduces stripping time.)

This copper stripping solution includes: sulphuric acid, 7 ounces; chromic acid, 4 pounds; water, 1 gallon.

Caution: If you decide to use acids, never pour water into the acids. Always pour the acids into the water. For instance,

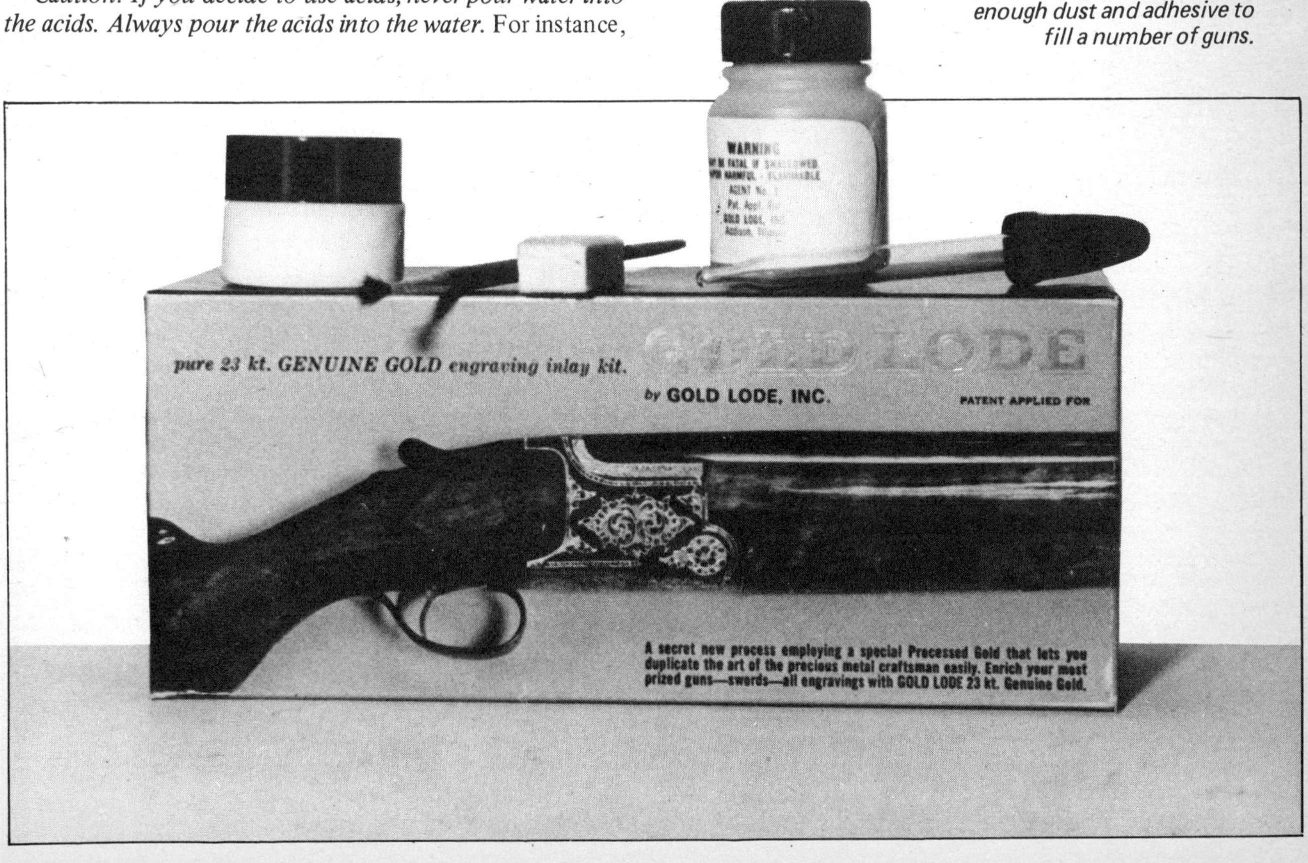

Gold Lode filling kit contains
enough dust and adhesive to
fill a number of guns.

Container for stripping metal parts should be of glass but must be tightly covered. Stripping solution darkens and clouds as chemical works on metal finish.

water poured into sulphuric acid, not only will create heat, but the hot acid will splatter all over the place.

Any kind of plating is an excellent means of preventing rust, and like in bluing, the finish of the metal to be plated must be perfectly smooth and polished. Light pits often will fill in when plated, but they will not fill completely, hence you will have plated high and low spots. Deep pits with rust at the bottom will not take plating, so a successful plating job depends on a thorough buffing and polishing job.

A poor plating job can mean trouble. Not long ago a police officer brought me a .357 magnum revolver that failed to fire every second round. After testing the gun with some of my ammunition and having the same problem, we took the gun apart. A vital part of the sear group had been chromed and the plating was flaking off, effectively locking up the gun.

When talking about plating, it is generally understood that the discussion is about electro-plating, where an electric current induces a solution containing a metal to deposit that metal by means of a chemical reaction. This means that the object being plated ends up with a thin coating of a metal, with the entire object being plated or coated with metal. Adding silver and gold dust to engraving or to the markings on a gun is not really plating, but rather a selective depositing of metal particles. These are held in place by means of some sort of adhesive. The enhancing of engraving patterns and perhaps logos, model designations, maker's name is limited to a small area in contrast to plating. Gold and silver are the metals of choice used for this type of gun decoration. Such gold-filling kits are offered by Gold Lode and Bonanza Sports, the latter supplier also offering a silver kit.

Buffing and polishing is not required when using any of these kits, but the engraving or stamping must be perfectly clean and grease-free. It is important to avoid getting either silver or gold dust into screw holes or screw threads, and when decorating engraved areas, only a small area at a time should be worked on, since both of the products set fairly quickly.

Until last year, home plating was made fairly simple since two sources supplied plating materials and equipment. Bob Brownell for some years offered the Hoover plating outfit. Although designed for the jewelry trade, it had found good acceptance in gun shops and with amateur platers. Since then,

the Consumer Product Safety Commission has ruled that the Hoover Plater cannot be shipped to a residence address, that the unit is to be used for commercial jobs only, that it can be shipped only by truck and that UPS no longer can handle this product.

Texas Electroplaters Company is the only current source for small amounts of plating materials and a small kit for home plating, as far as I have been able to determine. The power source comes from two No. 6 dry batteries available in any hardware store. The system is easy to handle, but if areas larger than four square inches must be plated, an extra battery is suggested. If three batteries are used for a small job, the plating will be done that much more quickly.

With the Texas plating system, special brushes become electric conductors when hooked up with the batteries. As with all other metal bluing or plating, it is important to have the work properly buffed and polished. Once the positive and the negative poles of the batteries have been connected, wires with alligator clips, furnished with the kit, are hooked up so that the positive (+) connection goes to the brush, while the negative(-) wire is connected with the work. After the wiring is done, simply dip the plating brush into the compound so that the brush and the underside of the anode are well covered with the plating compound. Start plating by making short circular motions with the anode brush on the work, making certain that the brush's bristles are pressed lightly against the piece being plated. It takes about thirty seconds for light plating, ninety or more seconds for a heavier plating job. Be sure to replenish the supply of plating solution on the brush as necessary.

When coated with more than a skin of nickel plating, bare metal appears to have a dull, almost foggy finish when plating is completed and while the brush is still in position. Disconnect one of the alligator clamps when the job has reached this stage, then wash the job in running water. If this is not available, use a wet rag to remove all of the residual compound. Then dry with a soft, dry cloth.

A flat finish does not require any polishing, but if a satin gloss is desired, it can be accomplished by polishing lightly with a fine abrasive such as crocus cloth or fine emery paper. Polishing strokes must be in the same direction as the original

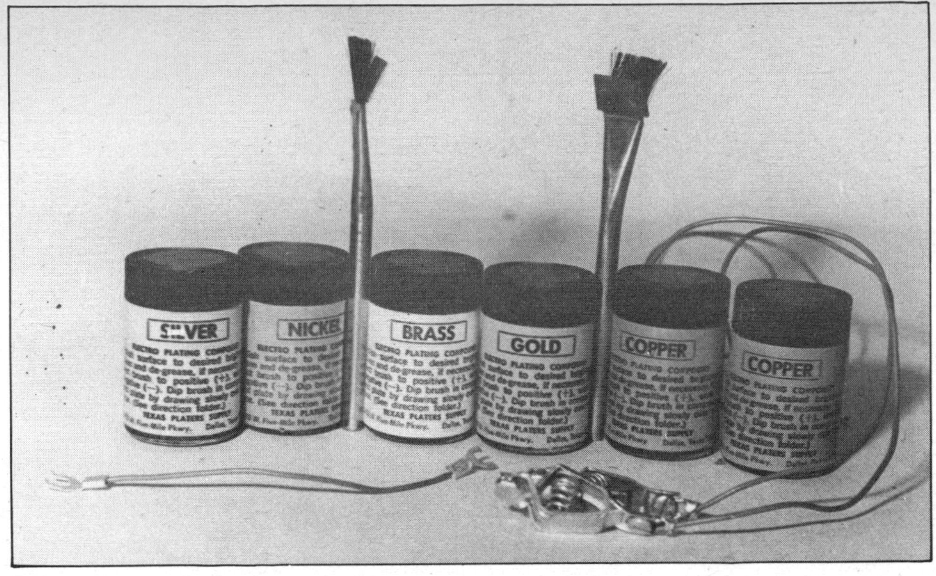

Texas Electroplate kit contains all essentials for first home plating job, except batteries.

buffing and polishing. Bright finishes are achieved by using a polishing wheel and a metal polish. In buffing or polishing after plating, remember that the layer of electro-plating is relatively thin, so be careful on edges and rounded surfaces. It is possible to damage any kind of plating by too zealous buffing.

Clean-up of the brushes is done with water, but be certain to wash all compounds out of the brush and make certain that electric contacts are clean.

To prevent tarnishing and undue wear on plating, the finished job can be given a coat of clear lacquer, similar to that used on some silverware. Worn spots on plating can be repaired if the spots are still small. Chrome-plating cannot be done with the brush application, but cadmium can be used instead, especially for touch-up repairs. Repair of chrome-plating with nickel is not satisfactory since copper, brass and bronze bases will not take the nickel color so that it will blend in with the chrome plating being repaired. Again, cadmium can be used on steel and iron for touch-up jobs on chrome-plated parts. The brush application of plating outlined here works well on small parts, but is not suitable for large parts such as the frame of a .45 ACP pistol.

Should you encounter troubles with your plating while using the Texas Electroplaters kit, check the following points:

1. If the current is reversed, clean the brush being used.

2. Check your wiring, for a loose clamp or a defective wire.

3. Weak or worn out batteries.

4. The work may have been lacquered previously and not all the lacquer removed. The plating will not take except on bare metal.

Texas Electroplaters offers gold, silver, nickel and brass plating compounds, as well as one for copper undercoating.

As with all other metal finishing, the smoothness of the surface is vital to a good plating finish. Proper degreasing is essential, and if you follow those points, you should encounter little or no trouble in plating small parts with these kits. Plating will make metal more rust and wear-resistant, but it does not cover deep pits, nor will it hide goofs committed on the buffing wheel.

This kind of plating is worthwhile, if you understand its limitations and need only small parts plated. Attempting to plate large surfaces is difficult and should be left to the professional plater.

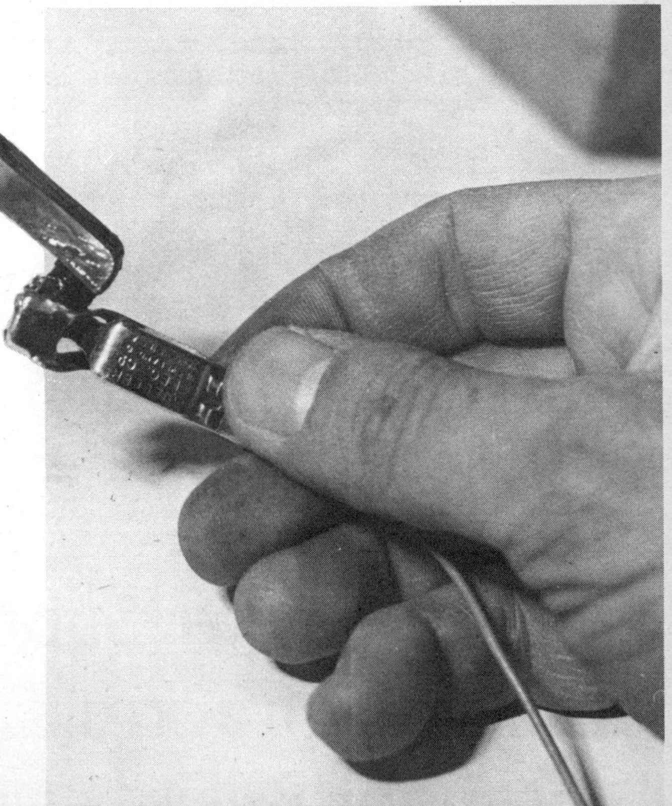

Freshly plated part out of the first rinse and buffed takes on such a polish that photography was difficult. Texas Electroplaters kit was used.

Chapter 16

Left: Winchester Model 70 with 24-inch slightly-tapered barrel weighs in at just under nine pounds without sling or ammo. Custom rebuilt Remington Model 600, right, scales 6¾ pounds, including steel scope and base.

A MATTER OF OUNCES

Adding Or Subtracting Weight From A Firearm Can Be A Problem-Frought Business, But It's Possible

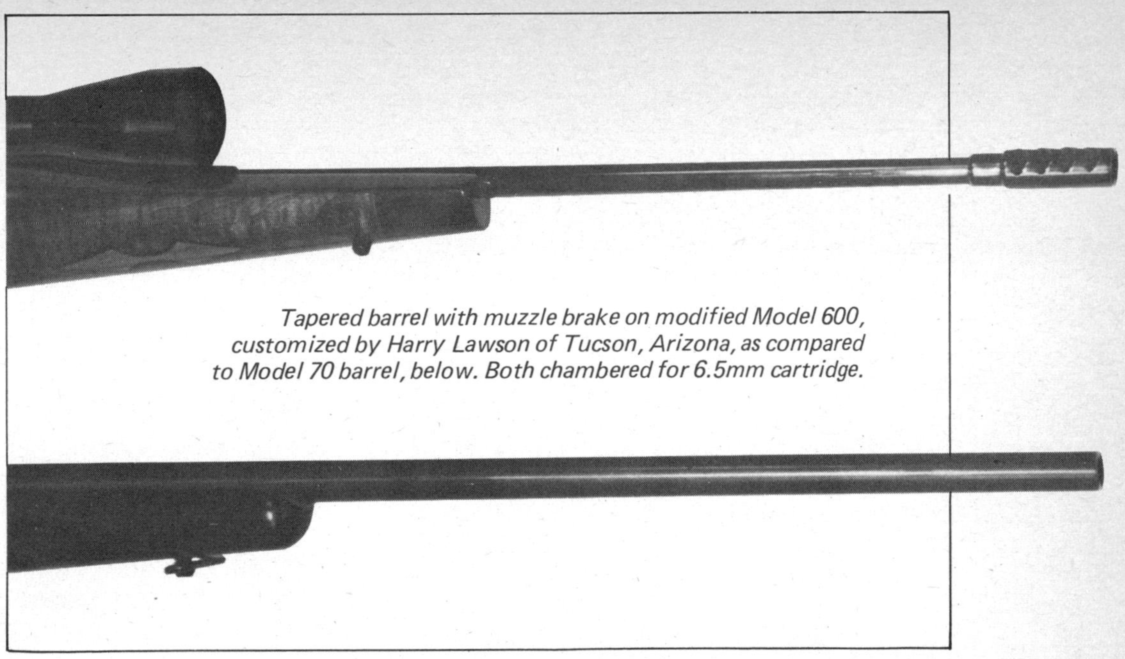

Tapered barrel with muzzle brake on modified Model 600, customized by Harry Lawson of Tucson, Arizona, as compared to Model 70 barrel, below. Both chambered for 6.5mm cartridge.

THE HEAVIER A gun, the less likely one is to feel the recoil and a heavier gun also will settle faster on the target. Certain calibers and gauges are offered only in the heavyweight versions, since lightweight guns would produce an excessive amount of recoil and might also tend toward stock splitting and other mechanical problems. The .375 H&H magnum, the .458 Winchester magnum and the 10-gauge shotguns are the best known heavyweights. Personally, I maintain that the matter of recoil is highly subjective and that anyone can learn to live with recoil if he takes enough time and trouble.

Adding weight to either a rifle or a shotgun is both a fairly simple, yet relatively complex undertaking. Since you cannot add much weight to either the barrel or the action, the additional weight has to be added to the stock. Every rifle and shotgun has a point of balance which is upset when weight is added to the butt stock. Hence, you have to live with a lightweight gun and learn to like recoil, or adjust yourself to a somewhat unbalanced gun which, at first, will seem butt-heavy and slow to nestle in the shoulder. Later, when you use a lighter gun, it will seem to be so light that it is likely to fly out of your hands; with a lighter shotgun, you almost certainly will overswing your targets.

The simplest way to add weight to a gun is to make or have

Balance and weight of Lawson-customized rifle is such that shooter may fire one-handed using thumbhole stock.

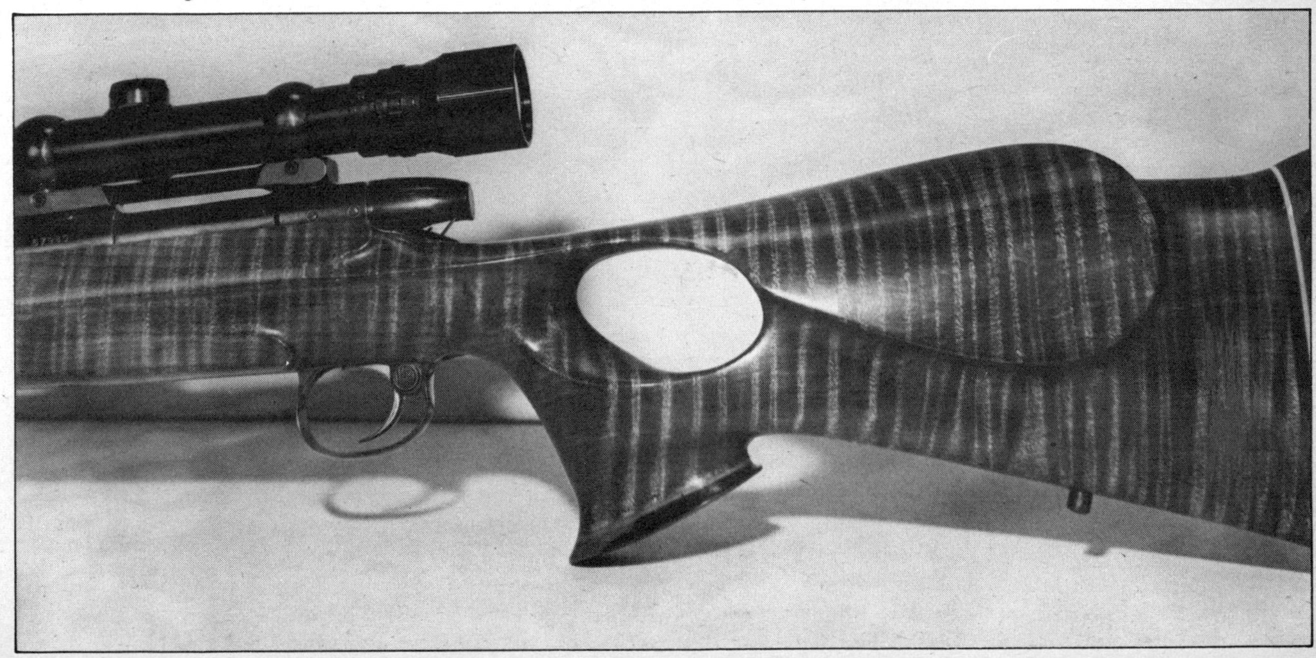

Weight difference between aluminum scope, above, and steel scope tube is measured in a few ounces.

made up a stock that has more dense and heavier wood than what you have now. You can buy a semi-inletted blank from Bishop, Fajen, or Paulsen, partially depleting your checking account while gaining as much as 1½ pounds. If a new stock is out of the question, you can resort to the old dodge of taking off the butt plate or recoil pad, augering a large hole into the butt, then filling the hole with molten lead.

Before you start pouring lead with gay abandon, here is a trick I learned from an old stockmaker. Fill the hole with unlubed cast bullets, remount the butt plate, and see if you now have too much weight. Adjust the weight by adding or removing cast bullets. Once you have determined the right amount of weight, weigh the bullets, then melt the same amount of lead so you can pour it into the new hole in the butt stock.

In doping out the location of the hole you need to drill or auger, don't make the mistake of using the hole that houses the takedown bolt in most shotguns and in some rifles. Pour lead into that hole, and someone will have his hands full drilling out lead when the day comes that the action has to come out of the wood.

The recommendation often is made that switching butt plates, recoil pads, grip caps and other accoutrements will take off or add a few ounces, but a few ounces are better than nothing. At least, that's the way you hear it told. Well, it ain't necessarily so, as the old song says.

I weighed a couple of Pachmayr rubber recoil pads, two plastic butt plates, and two steel butt plates. One was an old Niedner plate, the other a butt trap plate by Albright Products. The rubber recoil pads came in as the heavyweights, the plastic butt plates and the steel plates were almost evenly matched, the difference being as little as one-tenth of an ounce! Even if every bit of weight is important, keep in mind that the rubber recoil pads will add comfort to your shooting.

A few ounces of weight can be gained or lost in working over a rifle. For instance, you might switch the steel scope mounting blocks and replace them with aluminum blocks, or perhaps swap a lightweight aluminum model for a steel tube scope.

Some twenty years ago, a friend who did stockwork as a hobby dreamed up a way so some weight could be added to a rifle without upsetting the balance too much. Just how well this worked out I don't know, but not having heard screams of dismay from the owner of that lightweight rifle, I assume that it worked reasonably well.

Rubber recoil pad, at right, turned out to be the heavyweight of the butt plates. Removal of plastic or metal butt plate from stock and installation of recoil pad may add as much as four ounces to rifle.

With the barreled action removed from the stock, the thickness of the wood below the barrel channel is measured. If it is at least one-inch thick, better is 1¼, carefully remove some wood from the barrel channel. This space then is filled with molten lead. Once this has hardened, the surface is roughed a bit and leveled if necessary. Then the entire length of the channel is glassbedded. About a pound of weight can be added this way. Since this additional weight is not concentrated in one area but distributed a fair bit, this should not affect the balance of the gun, especially if some lead has been added to the butt stock.

The expensive way of adding weight to a rifle is to have the gunsmith install a heavier barrel or one that is not as tapered as the original, perhaps even a shade longer. Only a few ounces can be gained that way, and by the time costs are considered, it probably would be cheaper to have a custom rifle made up, doing as much of the work yourself as you are capable of doing.

Some campfire sage once remarked that gun weight is just the opposite of people weight. He pointed out that adding a couple of ounces of weight here and there to a rifle or shotgun is real work, while it is all too easy for you or me to gain a couple of pounds.

Weight reduction for rifles is a relatively common requirement, but shotgun surgery is not as frequent, according to most gunsmiths. There are several ways of paring off ounces, but be forewarned that too light a rifle in a heavy caliber can turn into a real shoulder pounder. Granted, a 7½-pound rifle seems to weigh eight or more pounds after you have carried it all day and after scaling a mountain or two in quest of sheep or goats. But remember that a seven-pound rifle will settle faster on a target than one that weighs only six pounds, and that recoil and even muzzle blast can become downright nasty.

I saw such a rifle some years ago. It was a beauty made up by one of the leading stockmakers and anyone should have been delighted to have that sleek beauty in his gun rack. But then I had a chance to shoot that .270, the kick and blast were so bad that I gave up after two rounds. The rifle, with scope, sling and four rounds of ammo, weighed just a shade over 6¼ pounds.

Replacing the steel floor plate with one of aluminum is simple. Another half ounce can be pared off the weight of a bolt action rifle by drilling out the bolt handle knob. Remember to centerpunch, and lock the bolt safely into the vise of the drill press. It is best to start with a smaller drill bit, then repeat the drilling with a slightly larger bit. Be sure to measure the depth to which you can drill safely without having the drill bottom out to leave an ugly hole.

If this happens, cut off the bolt knob, and install a new one, but only after you have completed your drilling. Although brazing sometimes is suggested for such a job, it is much better to weld such a joint. After drilling and installing the new knob, degrease the hole and use touch-up bluing.

Another ounce or two can be lopped off the weight of a rifle by either replacing the steel trigger guard with one of aluminum or by contouring the old one. This is not a difficult job, but does take considerable care so the symmetry of the trigger guard is maintained. The job is done best with a file, although a grinder removes the metal a lot faster. Either method requires planning and laying out with a scribe so that the end result is not only utilitarian, but pleasing to the eye. Many gun shops have bits and pieces of military surplus rifles

on hand and are willing to part with some of the stuff. Such parts as trigger guards and butt plates often can be converted into something useful. Being of good quality steel as a rule, they make ideal pieces for practicing such jobs as filing, grinding or buffing.

Sixgun weight can be reduced a bit by re-shaping the frame somewhat. For instance, you can regrind so that the square butt becomes a round butt, the trigger guard can be trimmed and slimmed, or can be cut to become what sometimes is called a combat trigger guard. The hammer can be skeletonized a bit, but I doubt the little bit of weight that can be trimmed in this manner makes much difference.

To tackle this job, drill holes into the hammer, making certain enough metal is left between the holes so fractures due to stress and metal fatigue will not occur. Use the hardest drill bit you have, since it means you can avoid having to anneal the hammer before you start to drill. If the hammer must be annealed before drilling, it also must be hardened again after you are done with the drilling. This type of hammer work was popular when fast draw was in vogue, but the demand for skeletonized hammers seems to have reached an all-time low.

One job that is not in the realm of most home gunsmiths is the tapering of a barrel and the installation of a muzzle brake. Such a major operation can take quite a few ounces off the weight of a rifle and requires some skill on the lathe. Essentially, it begins with removal of the barrel from the action, then removing the bluing and any sights or scope blocks. Then fasten the barrel shank into the chuck of the headstock, and with the help of a tapering attachment, begin to remove steel from the barrel. If the barrel becomes too slender, it will become whippy and accuracy will go down the drain. Once the barrel has been tapered to your satisfaction or to specs, the muzzle end is threaded for the brake. If the barrel is to be shortened, this should be done before it is tapered. I have used a number of rifles with muzzle brakes and have found that nearly all of them reduce recoil or kick quite effectively. However, most of them, by directing the muzzle blast laterally and somewhat backwards, also increase noise somewhat. In short, you may reduce the weight of a rifle, but you also may sacrifice shooting comfort and perhaps even accuracy.

Gunsmithing literature is singularly lacking in suggestions on how to add or reduce gun weight. As a matter of fact, none of the standard books even mention this facet of gunsmithing, either the professional or the hobby kind.

Back in the early Sixties, the term "mountain rifle" or "sheep rifle" began to appear in print. Usually, such a rifle was described as being short-barreled with a severely tapered tube, a custom stock with the fanciest, lightest and most stable wood, a fixed-power scope, no sights, a light carrying strap. Every so often, a skeletonized steel butt plate would show up in these articles. Invariably, the gun was described as a tack driver, and usually would weigh in the neighborhood of six to 6½ pounds. It was a dream gun to carry, it was fairly accurate, but muzzle jump was so bad that it took too long to recover the sight picture.

Tolerable rifle weight, recoil and handling qualities of a big game rifle are subjective and what fits you and is to your liking, may or may not fit me or anyone else. So before you decide on adding or chopping off weight, be certain that this is really what you want.

Winchester factory drilled hole in bolt handle of Model 70 .375 H&H bolt at left. Drilled version is a shade lighter than non-drilled. Bolt assembly from Mauser M-98, below, without drilled handle, weighs only slightly more than Model 70.

Chapter 17

BASICS OF STOCK REFINISHING

Minimum Equipment, Experience And Time Are Required With These Instructions

REFINISHING A STOCK is undoubtedly the easiest, yet the most rewarding home gunsmithing project anyone can tackle. Refinishing requires a minimum of equipment and, perhaps best of all and seldom mentioned, refinishing of a stock can be done in stages as time permits. I have refinished a stock and done some minor repairs in five evenings, working no more than three hours per evening.

There is a variety of reasons for refinishing. Worn finish is the most frequent, although a lot of shooters and hunters take pride in a battered, worn stock. What these gents do not understand is that the wood finish offers protection to the wood, and that unprotected wood undergoes some unexpected changes. Gun oil, permitted to soak into the fibers, will make the wood pulpy — maybe not in a month

Danger of stock or finish damage is minimized if home gunsmith will stick with recognized products designed for stock use.

or two, but certainly within a year. Wood, no matter how well cured and dried, is also prone to cupping, twisting and warping once the protective skin of the finish has worn off. No matter what kind, the finish tends to protect the surface of the wood from nicks and scratches. It also prevents one from getting wood slivers in his hands.

When finishing or refinishing, this also is the time to repair minor damages, clean the checkering, and perhaps install sling swivels or a recoil pad. The latter two jobs can be done without refinishing the stock unless the original wood finish of the stock chipped and cracked when drilling or sawing. Chipping can be prevented by using a sharp drill bit, while trimming the butt stock is best done with a saw with the finest teeth you can get. This will give you a smooth cut and forestall chipping the finish.

To refinish a rifle stock, remove all of the hardware, recoil pad and spacer, sling swivel studs, and magazine floor plate, so you have only the wood left. If the stock has an inletted monogram escutcheon, leave it in place and cover it with masking tape cut to size. Removing any carefully inletted escutcheon all too often results in chipped or broken edges of the inletting which then must be repaired with considerable care. A simple checkering cradle, either purchased or knocked together from scrap wood, is ideal for working on a stock, whether you merely want to clean out the checkering or strip the old finish.

Since there are at least as many types of stock finishes as there are calibers, you may have to try one or more of the finish removers. Perhaps the most versatile stripping compound is the G96 Stock Finish Stripper which removes virtually all lacquer and varnish finishes easily. Synthetic finishes usually respond to the Birchwood-Casey stock finish stripping agent, but I have run into several finishes which had to be removed either by a strong commercial stripper, or by some odd-ball solvents. Silicone finishes, or stocks that have been wiped off with a silicone cloth and some of the silicone transferred to the finish, usually respond to naphtha, benzene, kerosene or gasoline. Some other solvents, such as chloroform, are either difficult to find or dangerous to use.

Old oil finishes, like those found on some military stocks, seldom respond to any of the stock finish removers, but will respond to some solvents. I've had fair luck with soaking the entire stock in alcohol; with methanol or methyl alcohol being the better choice if it is available. Only fair success was achieved with denatured alcohol.

I have heard about baking the oil out of the stock, but never have tried it. The stripped stock is wrapped in some absorbent paper such as cleansing tissues or paper towels, then further wrapped in aluminum foil. The whole thing is cooked at about 180 degrees in the oven. The paper wrapping allegedly absorbs the oil that is being driven out of the wood by the heat. The system makes sense — provided you have an oven large enough to handle a stock.

Because stock finishes vary so much, there is no single piece of advice anyone can offer about stripping the old finish. Some of the commercial varnish removers require

Stock must be rotated slowly while G96 stock finish stripper is sprayed on wood. Before finish is sprayed, all metal, plastic or rubber components are carefully removed from stock. Inletted escutcheons are masked.

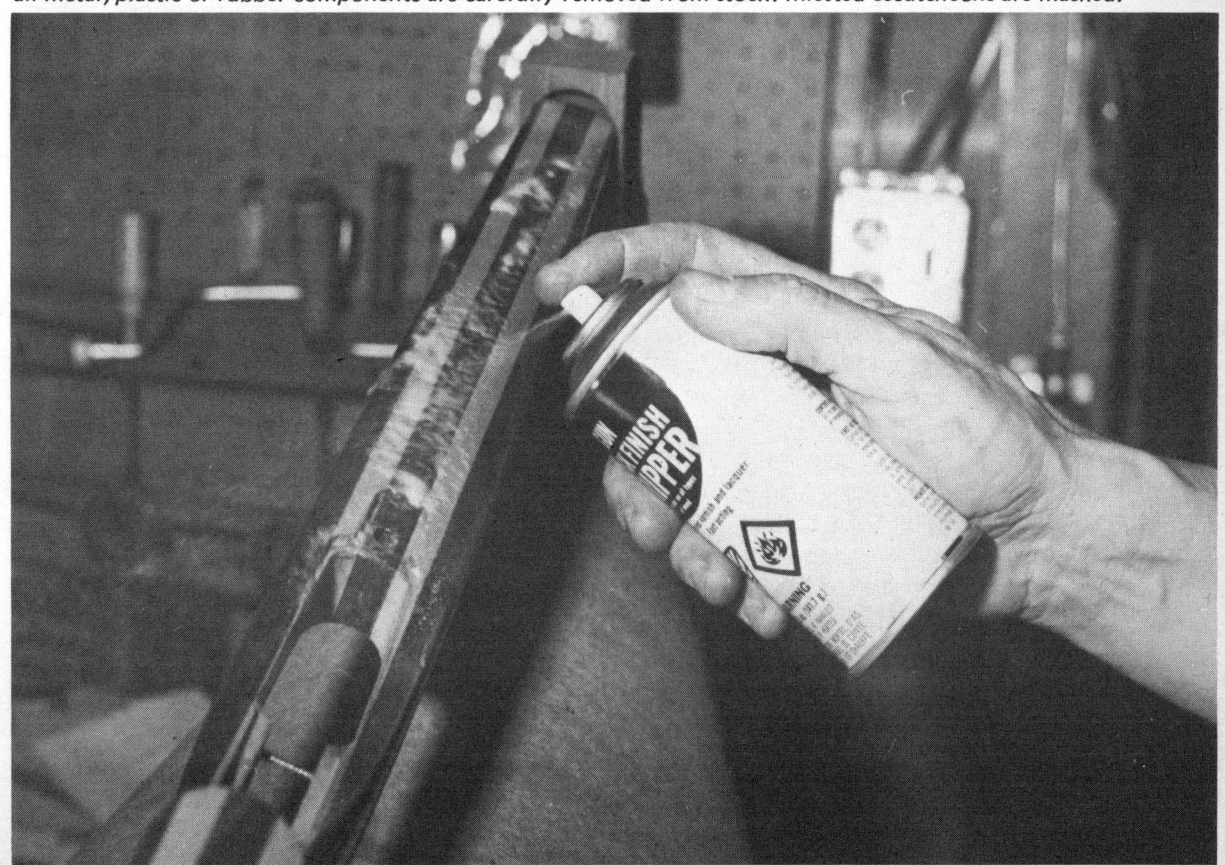

After entire stock has been stripped, the appropriate sealer and filler materials must be applied. There are a number of well-known brand names available to hobbyists.

Use of commercial tack rag is easiest way to remove sanding residue from stripped stock. Tack rag leaves no chemical which may harm sealer, filler or finish.

that the work be rinsed after the remover has done its work, while others are simply wiped off. I favor the latter kind. Giving the entire stock a bath not only is messy but almost impossible in my laundry sink which is just a bit larger than a postage stamp. Moreover, I like to be able to control the amount of moisture the wood absorbs. Too much moisture does not help the matter of sanding and raising the wood grain.

When working with any varnish or finish remover, keep tools, sandpaper and sanding blocks out of the way and cover your workbench with paper. Don't use newsprint, since some of these inks will transfer onto the bare wood — and let me tell you, that is a mess! A pair of rubber gloves is certainly indicated, at least for the standard varnish removers and also perhaps for the application of a stain.

Application of finish remover is done best with half an old T-shirt folded so no ends fly around as you apply the solvent or remover. I have found it best to apply two thin coats rather than one heavy one, since the first coat usually takes off all the readily accessible finish and those parts of the finish which are worn or ready to flake off. Let the remover do its work for the proper time, then wipe it off with a clean rag. Apply the second coat and wait a minute or two longer than the instructions require.

By trial and error, I have found what I think is the best way to handle this matter of finish removal.

Strip the stock of all hardware, recoil pad, spacers, grip caps and all such doodads. Lock the stock in the checkering cradle, cover the bottom of the cradle with brown wrapping paper or cut-open grocery sacks. Lock the cradle with the stock in the swivel base vise. This not only allows you to rotate the stock, but also gives you ready access to some of the hard-to-reach areas such as the cheekpiece.

Once all of the finish has been removed from the stock, you are ready to raise the grain. If some of the finish remains, apply some more finish or varnish remover on those resisting areas, then wipe off with a circular motion and a fair bit of pressure, turning the rag so that the old remover does not make contact again.

To raise the grain, use a clean, soft cloth. Soak it in warm water, wring out slightly so it doesn't drip, then apply to the wood. Let it sit for a few minutes, soak again, wring out and keep going until the entire stock has had this warm bath. Let dry for several hours — depending on temperature and humidity — then start sanding the whiskers raised by the dampening of the wood. It is a matter of opinion whether or not a sanding block is desirable. I tried sanding blocks, both the store-bought kind and the homemade ones and found I could not control the sanding enough to suit me. So now I have a pile of sanding blocks, but seldom use them.

If warm water is not handy, you can get similar results

After each application of stripper, softened finish may be removed with steel wool. More than one coat may be necessary and care must be exercised to place only clean steel wool against stripped wood.

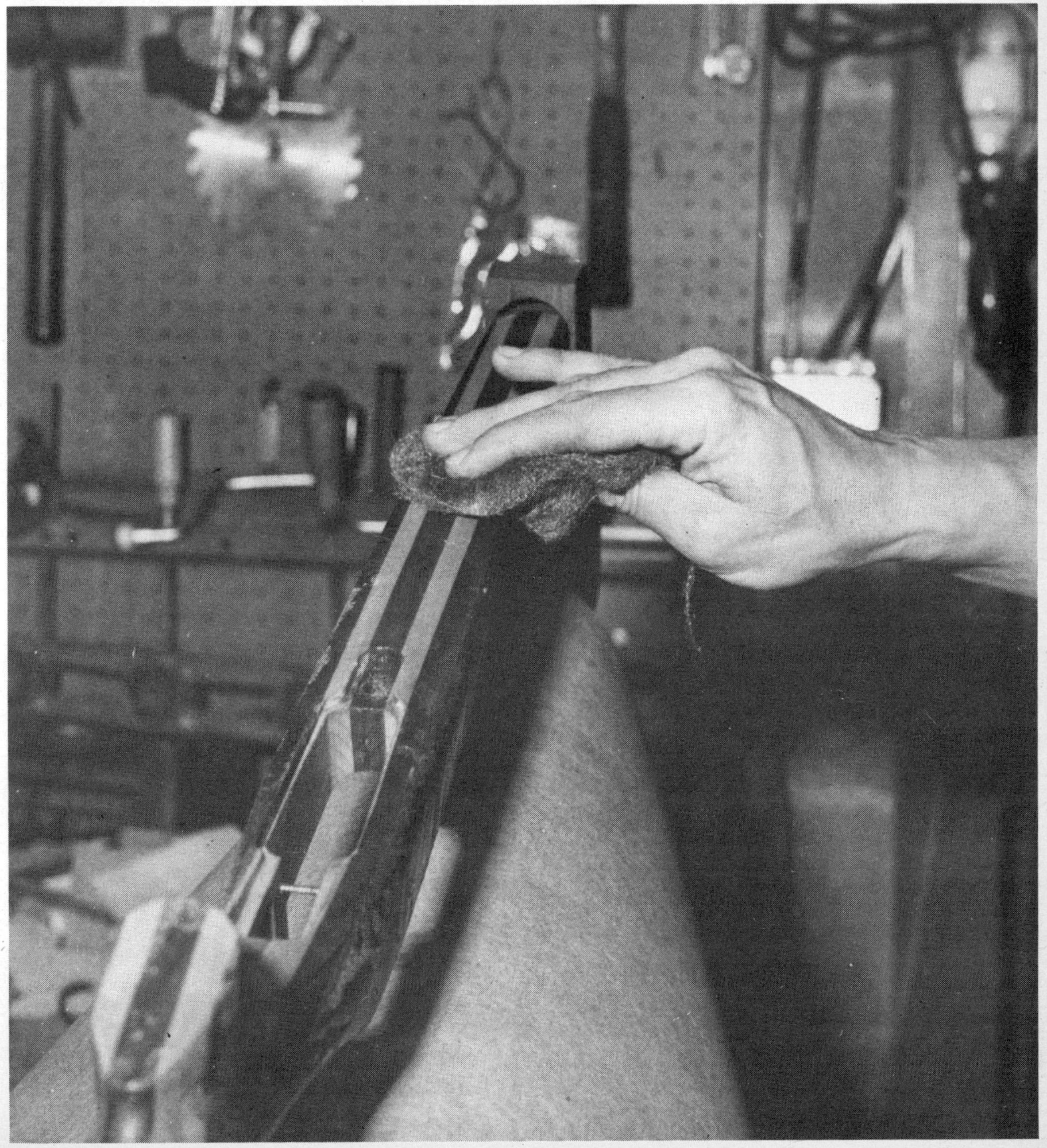

by using denatured alcohol. When using chemical solvents or compounds, be sure to have adequate ventilation and observe the cautionary statements on the labels.

When buying sandpaper, get at least three grades. Three sheets of each grade should allow you to finish at least one or two stocks in style. The sandpapers usually called "finish" grade or "finishing paper" are what you want. The non-clogging Adolox papers from Brownell's are even better, since they wear a bit longer and also cut the whiskers of the wood faster and better while not clogging as much as the run-of-the-mill wet-or-dry papers.

Generally, four grits or grades of roughness are available and you should have at least three of them. As a rule of thumb, the higher the grit number, the finer the grit. On Brownell's Adolox papers, the No. 0 designation is the same as 80 on other papers, No. 3/0 is identical to 120, 6/0 is the corresponding number for 220, while 8/0 grit, the finest, is the same as 280 grit. Adolox, by the way, does the same job as sandpapers, but consists of aluminum oxide grains, hence it lasts longer. Although more costly per sheet, it is actually cheaper, since it outlasts sandpaper by quite a bit.

Cut sandpaper sheets to size by folding them, grit side out, then cutting the inside of the paper with a sharp knife.

Always sand in the direction of the grain of the wood. Cross sanding invariably leaves horrible marks on the wood which either cannot be removed at all or with considerable difficulty. Sanding around sharp edges, such as the cheekpiece, should be done with care so that the contour is not broken. Checkered areas also must be sanded with TLC — tender loving care.

To clean checkering, either the cut or the impressed type, use the varnish remover as outlined above, then clean the lines of the checkering with a toothbrush. Although the recommendation is often made that an old toothbrush will do the job, one look at the bent and broken bristles should convince you that a new toothbrush is indicated. I found that tapered toothpicks are just the ticket for cleaning out cruddy checkering. Under no circumstances resort to wire brushes or wire wheels — they will certainly damage the checkering.

Before you begin to raise the grain of the wood — sometimes called whiskering the wood — go over the stock carefully. Any small repairs should be made now, such as raising dents or repairing small cracks.

The majority of dents will respond to the hot water with rag treatment. Be sure to remove all of the finish, then apply to the area a piece of soft, clean rag soaked in hot water and wrung out. As soon as this cools off, replace it with another hot-water-treated cloth. Usually, two such applications are sufficient to raise the grain and bring the wood back up to its former level. Let the area dry fully, then sand, starting with the coarsest grit paper. When smooth, repeat the wet cloth treatment, let the wood whisker, then dry sand it with the next finest grit. Repeat this with the finest grit paper. By that time, the wood should be glass smooth.

This dent raising can be done when the stock is to be refinished completely, or with the finish removed only in the area of the dent. If the latter is the case, simply sand smooth, and when dry and smooth, refinish only that area.

This is the usual advice but there is a slight catch to it. Thanks to the new epoxy and plastic finishes, this combining of new and old finish can produce some horrible looking results. Since an analysis of the finish now on the stock is not possible, you and every stockmaker in the country can start playing a guessing game. Frankly, I got so sick and tired of guessing what some other guy might have used to finish a stock, factory or custom, that I now simply strip the finish off the stock, and if the original repair is large enough, refinish the whole stock from butt to schnabel forend.

Hairline cracks and even bigger ones should be repaired at this point. As mentioned in the chapter on glassbedding, Acraglas without floc makes a great bonding medium for such cracks and splits.

Begin by removing all finish right down to the bare wood. Depending on the size of the crack or split, you have to decide which way you want to go. Use denatured alcohol to degrease the wood in the split and around it. Do not attempt to chisel or undercut the split the way you'd repair a plaster wall. If the crack is large, see if you can open the crack more simply by twisting the two ends of the stock or the area of the crack. Do this gently so that you won't split the wood any more. If the crack does open a bit, pad one end of the stock heavily and hold it in the padded jaws of the vise. Make your bonding agent, and if the crack is large, add some matching color to the agent. Holding one end of the stock in the vise, twist the break open and with the free hand apply the bonding agent as deeply as possible. The wood must be dry and grease free, so be sure to let it air dry completely after swabbing it with the denatured alcohol.

Acraglas, by the way, is Brownell's trade name for a glassbedding compound especially designed for gunsmithing work. The other bonding agent favored by some experienced gunsmiths and stockers is epoxy cement. A number of those are on the market, and most are similar in action and setting qualities.

It is possible to add a bit of color to the epoxy glue before it is forced into the crack and the bond then can be sanded and handled the same way the rest of the stock is being treated.

Acraglas or epoxy glue also can be used for other stock repairs. A later chapter covers reworking a military stock. A great many of these stocks have all sorts of unnecessary hardware on them. Removed, they leave unsightly holes in the wood. Fill those areas with Acraglas or epoxy glue, sand them, perhaps stain, then finish and you'll have difficulty finding this sort of repair once the stock has been completely refinished. Screws holding the grip cap and sling swivel studs can be securely seated with Acraglas and I have used it to anchor silver escutcheons in stocks.

One trick is mentioned in Bob Brownell's book, *Gunsmith Kinks*. In some of the stock cracks and splits, it often is difficult to force enough of the bonding agent into the split, even when the split is opened by twisting. One gunsmith simply turned the nozzle of the air compressor hose on it and that worked out fine — except that the shop, bench, wall and ceiling then needed cleaning.

Repairs such as these should be clamped or held together in some fashion until the bonding agent has a chance to set. Because this sort of stock damage occurs most frequently in the wrist of the stock, clamping is difficult at best. A better bet is some of the heavy-duty rubber bands sold for that purpose or, if you can find an old inner tube, cut your own rubber bands.

A bit easier to use is fiberglass filament tape. Use the widest tape you can find and pull it tight, applying the tape right over the bonding agent. I found that the areas where the tape sticks to the bare wood sand out fine and the tape does not stick to epoxy glue or Acraglas.

Despite what the instructions say, I leave such repairs alone for no less than twelve hours and find that a longer period seems to be even better, although both of these chemical fasteners have supposedly set fully in less time. After the tape or rubber bands are removed, sand the repair smooth and raise the grain of the wood in that area as outlined above.

One trick that works well for larger repairs is to mix Acraglas with wood dust. This gives the Acraglas the texture of wood, the wood dust coming from the various stock repairs I do. A cabinetmaker's rasp, also known as patternmaker's rasp, makes lots of fine sawdust that can be saved, then used for such repairs. The addition of a bit of wood dust also makes such repairs more amenable to accepting stains.

In raising the grain then knocking the whiskers off, the suggestion often is made that fine steel wool will do a better and faster job than sandpaper. Since a steel wool pad will conform to the stock's high and low spots better than sandpaper, this would seem to be an excellent suggestion. At least I thought so once, many years ago.

The steel wool did a great job knocking off the raised grain, but it also deposited a lot of fine steel wool fibers all over the stock, especially into the inletted areas where it was difficult to get the steel fibers out. I first tried an air hose with only mediocre results, then a magnet, and finally a tack rag.

If you have compressed air and get the bright idea of blowing the accumulated sanding dust off the wood, don't! Most compressors and portable tanks contain residual amounts of moisture and you really don't need a fine mist of dirty water all over the final sanded stock.

Tack rags are handy to have around the shop and you can either make them yourself if you like messing around with

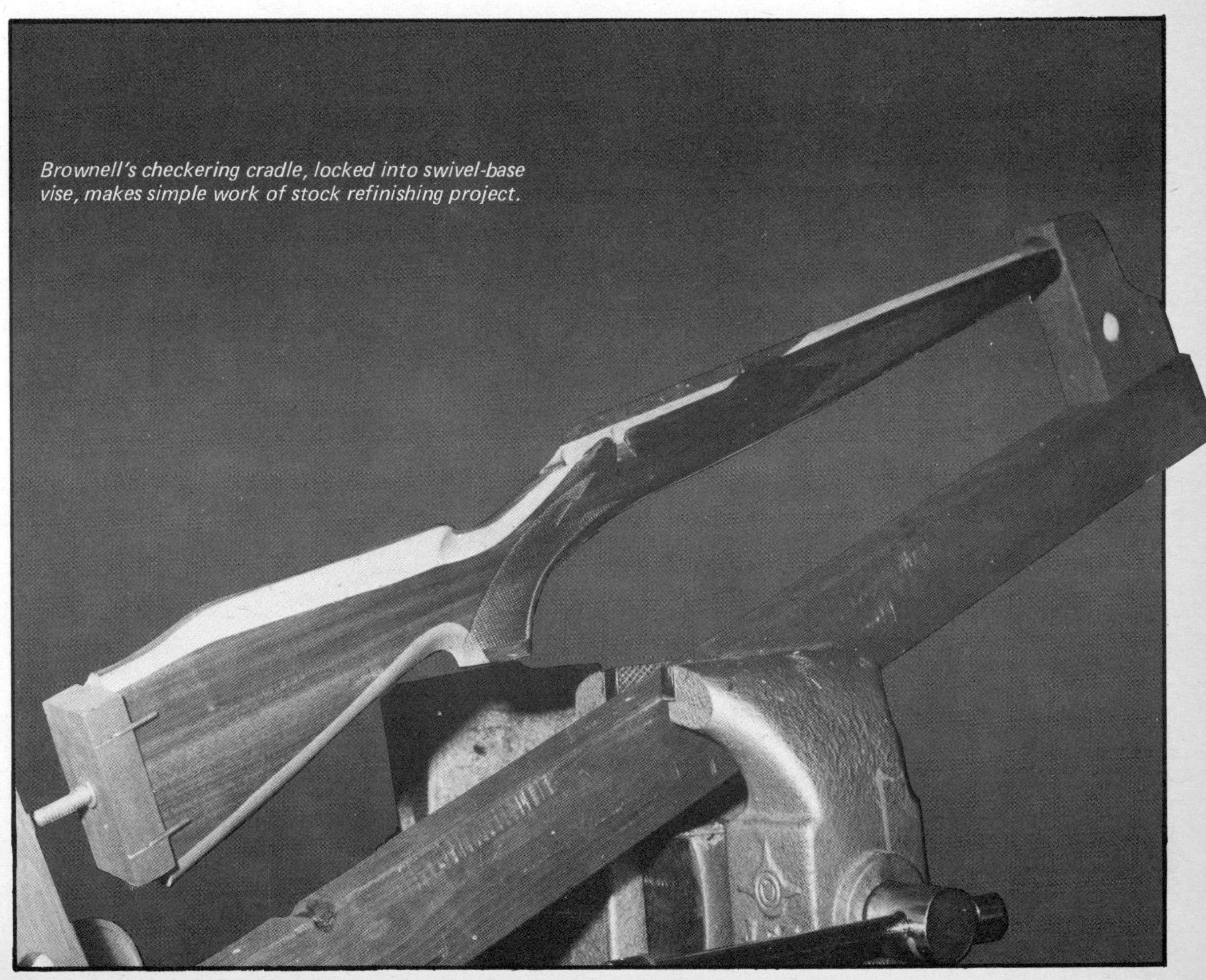

varnish, or buy them for less than a buck. They last well, especially if kept clean and stored in an air-tight jar.

Some woods are extremely dense, others have open pores. The latter need filling of the pores and don't let anyone tell you that the wood dust left from the sanding is more than enough filler material for such woods. Having tinkered with restoring antique furniture and furniture refinishing, I long ago learned that the open wood pores, even those of the most dense wood, require sealing and, in most cases, filling.

As long as moisture has access to even the tiniest area of wood, it will enter. The wood, on the other hand, being a conductor of moisture, will guide moisture farther and farther into the wood fibers. This means that pores of the wood must be sealed as well as filled. The sealing will improve the moisture resistance of the wood, while the filler will give the wood the required smooth surface for the finish to hold. The simplest of the sealers is that old marine standby, spar varnish. Buy the best grade you can find, then dilute it with either naphtha or white gas. It should have the consistency of water. When stirred properly, this mixture will show no sediment in the bottom of the can or bottle.

Before mixing gas and varnish, check the label on the varnish can — some varnishes are not fully soluble in gas or naphtha. In this case, use the solvent recommended by the varnish maker.

To apply sealer, be sure all areas of the stock have been given their final sanding and that all dust has been removed with a tac rag. Sealer is best applied with a two-inch varnish brush with the stock held in the checkering cradle. More than ninety percent of the stocks I have worked on absorbed the sealer like a sponge. The trick is to cover all areas of the stock using smooth, long strokes of the brush. Apply enough sealer to leave areas moist until the sealer has been soaked into the wood. Once the resins of the sealer have set in the wood, absorption of the sealer will stop. You will need plenty of clean, dry rags to wipe the stock down as dry as you can get it.

Areas where metal and wood meet must be cleaned with special care. Buildup of the sealer may prevent proper seating of the barrel or the trigger guard. If the varnish hardens before you wipe it off, you have to sand those areas again before going on with the filler.

The sealer coat prevents moisture from entering the wood, but it does not give the smooth surface needed for a good stock finish. To get that smooth finish, a filler must be used on all areas of the stock that will be finished. This means that the barrel channel and the area where the action or the trigger guard are inletted are now completed as far as you are concerned.

Dem-Bart or G96 both offer compounds which fill the dual role of sealer and filler. If you will only be doing one or two stocks, these commercial products are time savers and can prevent some messy home-mixing of sealer and filler material. Birchwood-Casey has a stock filler that does the job but you have to use a sealer before applying the filler.

Fillers are usually classified as soft or paste type and as hard fillers. It is the latter that is required for stock work. The soft fillers, useless on gun stocks, are most often used to patch nail holes in plaster, or plaster board and to fill in the holes made by finishing nails or countersinks.

The hard fillers dry hard, while the soft or paste fillers take forever and two days to dry.

For those who like to experiment, here is a well-tested filler formula, but messy to make up: spar varnish, best grade, ten parts by weight; silica, finest grade, forty parts by weight; mineral spirits, add as needed.

To mix, use a two-pound coffee can, thoroughly cleaned and dried in the oven. Pour the varnish into the can, add a little of the silica and mix well with either a spatula or an old kitchen spoon. Keep adding small amounts of the silica powder and keep stirring. Add powder slowly to avoid lumping.

Once most, if not all, of the silica has been mixed into the varnish, add the mineral spirits or the best grade turpentine you can find. Add only enough mineral spirits to produce a smooth paste. The filler can be stored in any glass jar that can be sealed tightly and should be stirred every so often so the silica does not settle on the bottom, becoming rock-hard.

Before using the filler, mix again thoroughly, then remove only a small quantity for your work. I use one of those plasticized paper tubs from cottage cheese to mix the filler with whatever stain I want to add. Burnt umber is probably as good as anything else. Try three parts by weight with the above formula. If you ask twelve guys what coloring they use, you'll get a dozen different answers. When the filler has the color you think is just right, add a bit more solvent and stir again until the filler is more liquid than paste. You are now ready to apply the filler to the stock. It is handy to have a piece of scrap stock wood to check the coloring of the filler.

Remove only enough filler for one stock and never put left-over filler back into the storage jar. Application of the filler is again with a two-inch varnish brush. If the sealer has been removed completely from the brush, you can use the same brush for the filler.

For those who have done some fine woodworking jobs or perhaps even some stockwork, the omission of flame or heat when talking about raising the grain must be apparent. If you are in a hurry and can be sure you will do a perfect job, it is permissible to flame the stock after moistening the wood. This can be done by means of an old-fashioned blowtorch, an electric heat gun or the flame of the gas burner on the kitchen stove.

The trick, of course, is to make sure that the flames reach every square millimeter so that the wood grain is raised uniformly. If the grain is not raised this way, you start out with a botched-up job.

Most of the old-time stockmakers favor sealing the end grain. This means that the sealer coat also should be applied to the butt end of the stock where the recoil pad or the butt plate goes when the job is finished. The sealer coat can be left off in the areas where you will be using a glassbedding compound.

Brownell's offers five different water soluble stains for stock work and finishing, one of them being resorcin brown. W.E. Feldman describes a method of using this stain to obtain the Japanese suigi finish that seems to be better and easier to achieve than the torching required by the traditional suigi method.

He suggests that when raising the grain, you use a solution of resorcin brown rather than plain water for the moistening. Dry with an electric heater, then sand down as usual. Raise the grain this way at least five times, then finish the stock with oil.

The trick in raising the grain is to wait until the moistened wood has dried completely. If you begin to sand before that dryness level has been reached, you not only will mess up the wood, but will clog the paper prematurely. When putting sandpaper or any other abrasive material to wood, remember that the appearance of the final finish depends entirely on the quality of the work that serves as the basis of the finish.

The matter of fuming stocks has been almost forgotten and reference to this method of imparting some additional color to light-colored stocks is usually found only in old gunsmithing books.

Light or blond woods, in contrast to oak or walnut, contain little tannic acid; so when raising the grain, use a strong tea rather than plain water to moisten the rag. Tea is just full of tannic acid, and once the stock has absorbed some of it, proceed with the fuming by placing the stock into an airtight cupboard or wooden box, leaving a dish of strong ammonia in the bottom of the cupboard or box. In a few days the desired golden brown coloring is achieved and one may proceed with the rest of the finishing.

Knowing Your Finishing Materials And How To Use Them Is An Important Phase!

The range of popular stock finishes seems almost as unlimited as the variety of rubbing compounds, right.

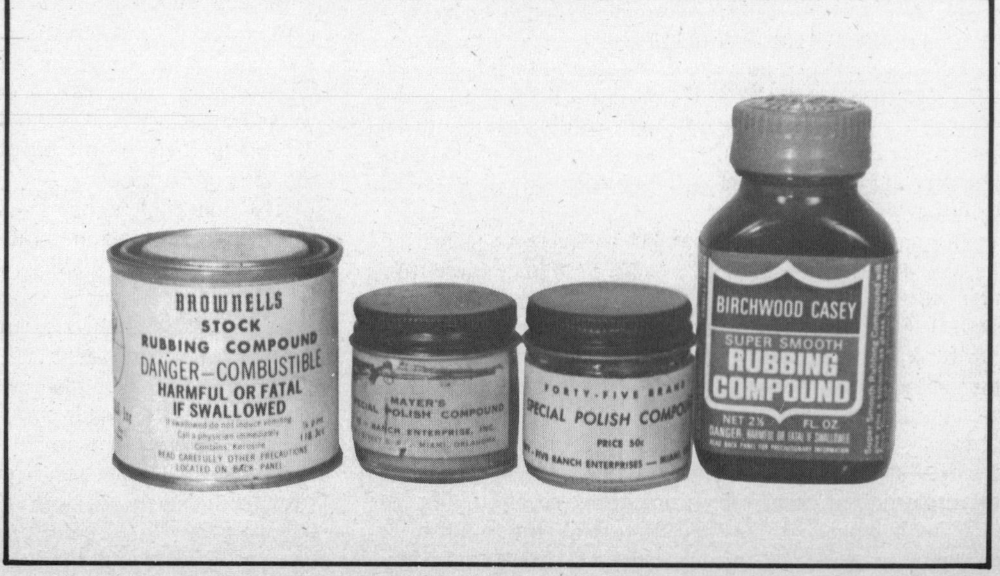

C OMMERCIAL STOCK finishes can be broken down into three classes: lacquers or varnishes, oil finishes, and plastic finishes. Repairing scratches, dents and worn spots on a stock finished with either varnish or oil is not too difficult and even your first attempt should be successful.

Since oil-finished stocks are the easiest to repair as far as finishes go — and since some of the tricks of the trade originated with this finish — let's start with patching up the finish on such a stock. Lin-Speed oil is probably the most widely used stock finishing oil. Chances are your stock was finished originally with this product. But even if the oil finish on that scratched stock comes from a can that was labeled Boiled Linseed Oil or perhaps London Finishing Oil the method is the same and the two oil finishes won't fight.

Start with a little Lin-Speed oil on your fingertips, applying it to the area to be repaired. The Lin-Speed oil not only will remove some of the surface dirt and grime, but will soften and penetrate the old finish. The ball of your thumb is a good rubbing medium since the heat of the hand and the friction will tend to soften the old finish and permit a little bit of the new oil to flow into the old finish. If the repair gets too dry, add a few more drops of Lin-Speed and keep working on the area until a perfect blending of the finishes has taken place. Wipe clean, polish with a soft cloth and perhaps one of the stock preservatives. That's it!

Dents that cannot be raised, often can be repaired by an old trick that I learned many years ago from the late John Buhmiller, the barrelmaker. Clean out the dent with a nut pick or the point of a knife, but do not cut the wood. Apply a few drops of shellac — it is best to use white rather than orange shellac for most stockwork — then sand the dent and the area around it, starting with 4/0 paper and working up to perhaps 8/0 grit paper. Occasionally you may have to add a couple of drops of shellac. Pretty soon the shellac and the dust from the sanding combine and fill in the dent which then can be refinished with whatever finish was on the stock originally.

When the time comes that an oil-finished stock must be cleaned, use a lint-free cotton rag. Sprinkle some methyl alcohol on it — ethyl is better, but harder to get and more expensive — and wipe the stock down. Using the same rag, add a few drops of either boiled linseed oil or Lin-Speed, wipe down again, leaving just a trace of oil on the stock. Do not let the oil sit on the stock. Wipe it off with a clean, dry cloth.

Varnish and lacquer finished stocks are repaired almost as easily but you may have to try several solvents. Some varnishes and other similar finishes will respond to alcohol, others will react to turpentine or other solvents used in the paint and varnish field. Once you have discovered what solvent is needed for the finish, wipe the damaged area lightly with a soft cloth and a few drops of solvent rubbed over the area. In most cases, this will soften the finish coat and permit it to run together.

If this does not work, you will have to resort to touching up the damaged area with spar varnish. If the area is on the

If the home gunsmith has use of a checkering cradle or other device to hold stock, spraying stock finish, such as Tru-Oil, is simplified. Care is exercised to apply finish evenly and prevent running.

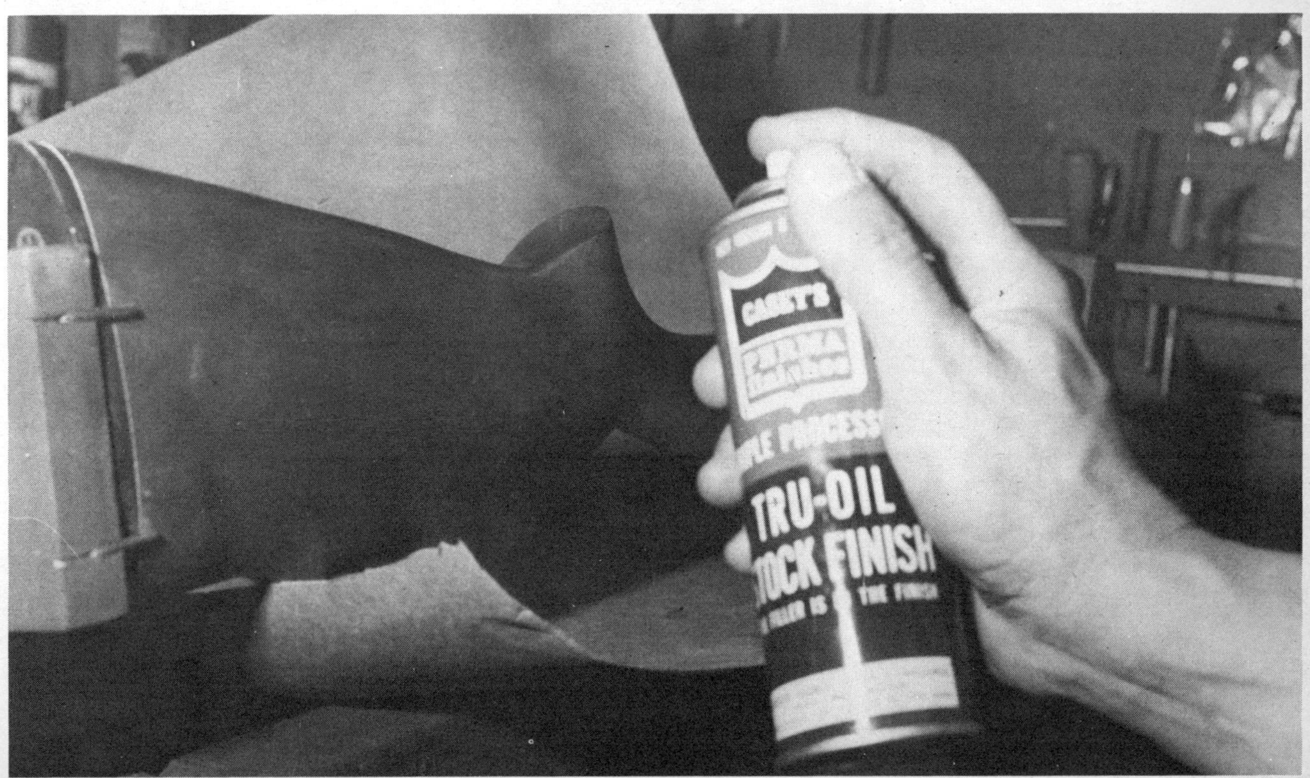

large side, you may have to sand with a fine grit paper, apply another coat of varnish, and repeat two or three times until the spot has blended in fully.

Patching the plastic stock finishes — those based on one of the polyurethane compounds — sometimes can become a nightmare. This happened to me when I sprayed some of the aerosol polyurethane finish on a stock also finished with what was supposed to be a poly compound. First the finish turned almost soft, then it hardened and ended up looking like a pale, dried prune. Unfortunately, not all plastic finishes are based on polyurethane, and the sundry plastic finishes are not all soluble in the same solvents.

I talked this problem over with gunsmiths as well as stockmakers, and the consensus of opinion is this: You must have a great deal of luck if, when attempting to repair plastic finishes, you happen to hit on the solvent that will not only allow you to soften the old finish, but also will hold the finish either with the same base or with another base.

Most of the pros who do stock and finish repair work agree it is best to strip the stock completely and start with the bare wood. Not only are the results more uniform, but there is less chance of messing up a stock. In the long run, it also is cheaper and less time consuming to start all over.

More paper and printer's ink has been devoted to the various types of stock finishes than to any other subject matter in the firearms field. There are gunsmiths, stockmakers and gun writers who will swear an oil finish is the only way to go; others will tell you that the oil finish bit is vastly overdone, that a French polish or finish is better than anything else. Then there are the gents who will sell you the idea that a varnish finish is best, that it beats everything else by a country mile. Some fellows prefer the sundry plastic finishes, others favor any of the more exotic finishes, many originating in the furniture finishing field. The oil and varnish finishes are the easiest to repair and maintain, and I believe that this consideration is often the deciding one in selecting a stock finish.

Most fillers have their specific solvent, so the filler made for lacquer may dissolve when a coat of varnish is applied. A real old-fashioned paint and varnish store probably has several types of fillers on hand and the proprietor can inform you about each. This, however, is seldom the case in hardware stores and other such shops and you could wind

Clear, walnut or other polyurethane finishes are available from such manufacturers as G96.

up with the wrong stuff. For this reason, I suggest getting your stock finishing supplies from a specialty house catering to gunsmiths. All of the plastic and epoxy finishes I have used contained their own filler material, often in suspension with the finish itself. All you must do is try to spray all areas of the stock evenly.

During stock refinishing I either mount the stock in the checkering cradle or suspend it on a long and rather stiff wire from the ceiling. Both systems have advantages and disadvantages. The cradle may block some parts of the wood from being reached by a spray finish. Thus, hanging the stock seems to be the answer, except that there should be a backing sheet of paper behind the stock somewhere so that the spray is confined to the job and the paper. Too much spray on a hanging stock means that runs are almost guaranteed.

I prefer the oil finish to look at and handle, but usually wind up doing a varnish finish since I rarely have the time to tackle a proper oil finish. A poor one, that has been rushed and forced, is worse than a layer of paint slapped on a hunk of wood.

I never have counted the different ways an oil finish can be done and even gunsmiths who have done oil stocks for years disagree as to the best way of doing an oil finish. I favor a final sanding after the filler has dried. Then I use a little bit of oil, such as Lin-Speed, applied to the palm of my hand and the ball of the thumb, and spread it on the stock, working it in well until the entire stock has an extremely light coat of oil.

Continue to rub fast and hard, until the stock no longer is oily or sticky, then set it aside to dry. Unless you build a drying cabinet heated with a light bulb or live in Arizona where it is hot and dry, this drying can take days or even a week.

Traditionally, you then take the finest pumice or rottenstone you can find, mix it either with a bit of water or with some cutting oil, apply the paste and again rub like hell. Wipe off, let dry, and start over again with the oil, then rottenstone treatment, repeating until the wood has a deep sheen and a dull gloss to it. I did one stock some years ago this way and it took twenty-seven applications of oil to get the stock finished to my satisfaction. Like fine hand-checkering, a good oil finish is time-consuming and tedious.

Almost as good is the varnish finish that has been hand rubbed. Known as Dull London Oil Finish, London Oil Finish, or by similar names, you again use a filler, and sand smooth. Apply a thin, even coat of the best outdoor spar varnish you can buy. Let dry fully, then sand down with fine sandpaper, remove all dust, repeat the varnish coating and sanding. Then apply boiled linseed oil or Lin-Speed, and continue as outlined for the oil finish.

French polishing, as used on antique furniture, is similar to the varnish oil job, except that the varnish is not brushed

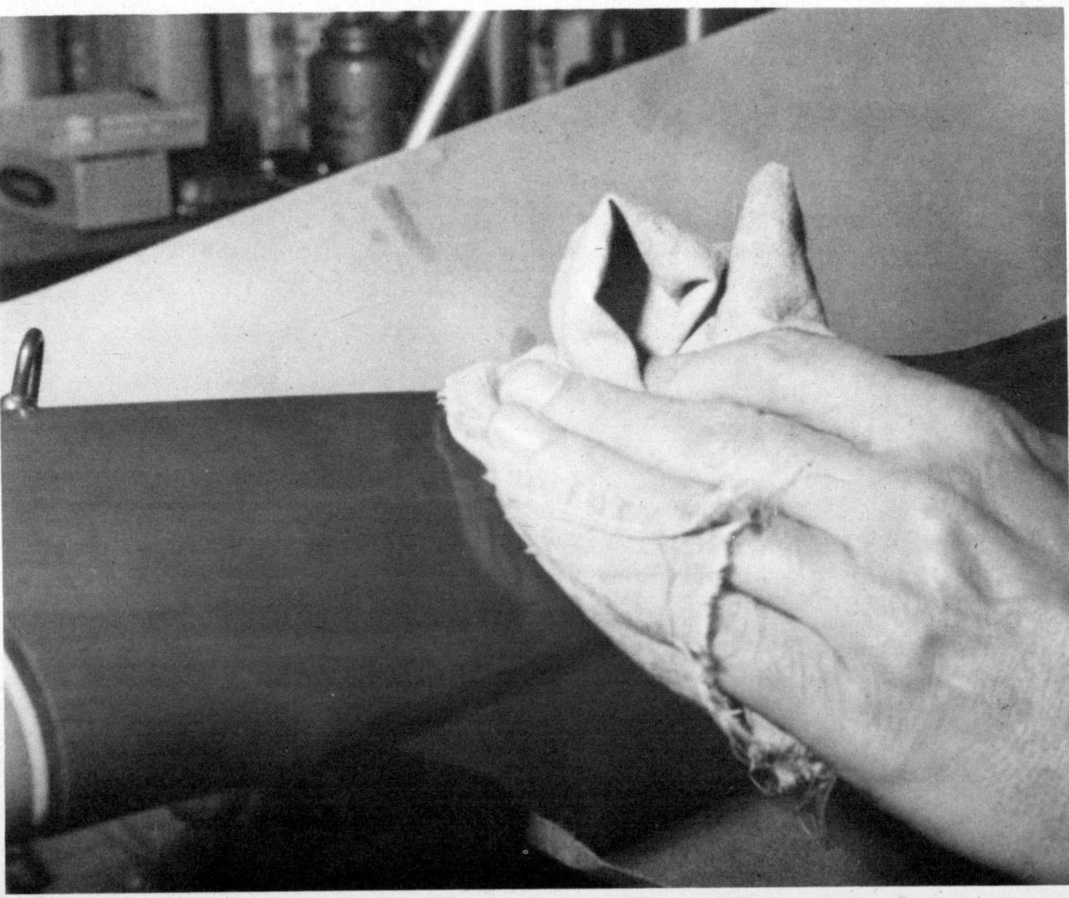

Fine steel wool or fine sandpaper is used between coats of oil. Sandpaper residue is easier to remove.

on but is applied with a cloth pad, preferably cheesecloth. This allows application of a thin varnish layer. Some fellows like to stick a cotton pad into the cloth pad so that more varnish can be held in the pad.

Rub the stock until entirely covered with varnish, then let it dry fully. Some stockers apply several coats this way, simply putting one coat on top of the other, while others sand between coats. The latter method gives a somewhat better finish, taking more time and work, of course.

The simplest must be the varnish finish. The finest outdoor spar varnish — sometimes cut with boiled linseed oil — is applied to the stock, then permitted to dry. One school likes to sand between coats of varnish, the others simply apply one or two more coats, let dry, then use the stock.

Shellac and lacquer finishes are similar to the varnish finishes, except that the shellac finish does not last long and looks like the devil when compared to the varnish finish. Most lacquer finishes are borrowed from the piano manufacturers and give the finish you'd expect on a Steinway Baby Grand — nice and shiny but useless as a finish for a rifle that will be used.

A mixture of equal parts of white shellac and boiled linseed oil is another quick finish which is easy to use, lasts long, and permits the grain of the wood to show perhaps a bit richer than the wood actually is. Apply it with a pad, a few drops at a time, until the stock is covered, then rub or use a buffing wheel. Repeat four or five times, making certain each coat is fully dried before starting the next application.

Plastic finishes come in aerosol spray cans as well as for brush application, but the brush system gives me a more even finish than the spray. This may be due to lack of spraying experience. Flecto Verathane is a good finish which

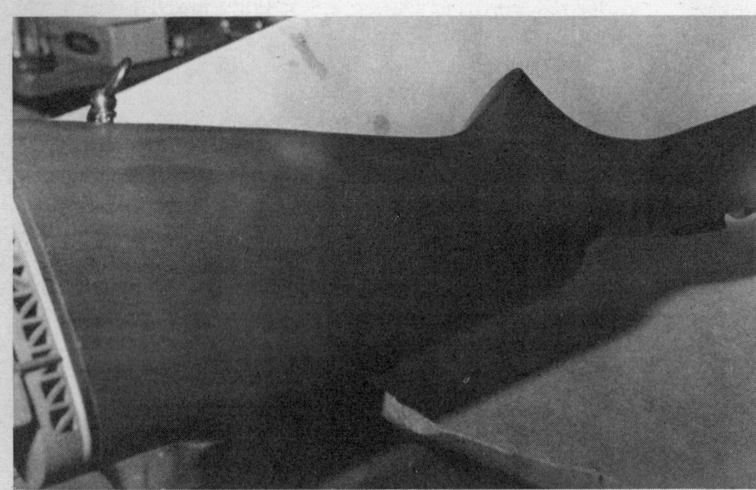

Stock at left was treated with three coats of spray and fine sandpaper. Sanding dust is best removed with tac rag which may be made of cheesecloth saturated with thinned varnish, or readily purchased.

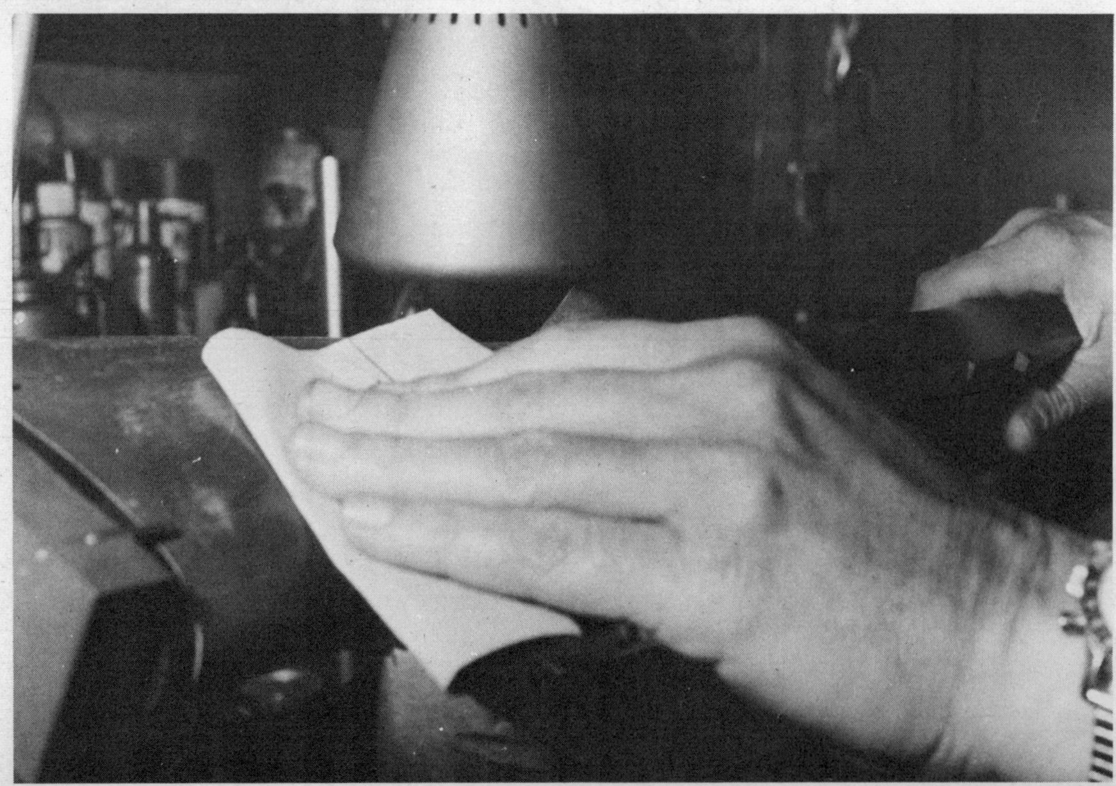

has good resistance to abuse, but other brands have given equally good service on rifle and shotgun stocks that see a great deal of use.

Birchwood Casey Tru-Oil is not an oil finish and contains its own filler. I favor brush application over the aerosol can, since the nozzle of these cans tends to clog and it is not always possible to clear the nozzle fully. Thanks to its special chemistry, this finish will not allow the sun to affect the coloring of the wood under the finish. It can be hand rubbed if so desired. The directions call for the use of fine steel wool and for the sake of trying it, I did so. I promptly went back to sandpaper.

The G96 polyurethane aerosol finish gives a fine, smooth finish, and the walnut colored type may be considered on light-colored stocks if darkening of the grain is desired. The cans are marked either Plain or Walnut and this affords a clue as to which to use with a given stock.

I have no idea where this old-time method of finishing a muzzleloader stock originated, but it works like a little charm. Take three ounces of best grade boiled linseed oil, add one ounce of turpentine, shake well, then add a few drops of vinegar until the mixture turns cloudy. Use only a little of it at a time and rub in well. The finish lasts well and keeps looking good.

Brownell's glassbedding compound, Acraglas, has been discussed earlier in this book. I have never tried using Acraglas for stock finishing, but there is a cult of professional gunsmiths who believe this stuff is the answer to all stock-finisher woes. Stocks finished with Acraglas

have a long-lasting, durable finish that offers a great deal of eye appeal.

A gun that sees a fair bit of use usually has the barrel swabbed out, perhaps the fingerprints are wiped off the steel and that's about it. As mentioned I use a G96 silicone gun mitt on steel and wood. Every so often, especially after getting a stock wet, I dry the wood, then give it a coat of stock preservative. A number of these products are specially marketed for gun stocks.

I can't say I approve of what a former crony of mine does with his rifle stocks. He slaps a coat of Simonize on them, then power buffs them.

Sometimes furniture waxes are used for that purpose, but never even think about using a household product that claims to make scratches disappear! It contains solvents which will soften the base of the finish, and while the scratch disappears, so does the base of the varnish or shellac and with it some of the finish you were trying to beautify.

Working with wood is a rewarding experience and the results of a refinishing job are well worth the time and trouble. But a word of warning: The chemistry of these specialized finishes is changing and improving constantly. With the changes of the product also comes changes in handling. Even if you are using the best and have used it before with complete success, read the directions before you start. If there are special precautionary statements or warnings on the label, bottle or can, heed them...some solvents are highly volatile, some are quite flammable, and a few of them can produce allergic reactions.

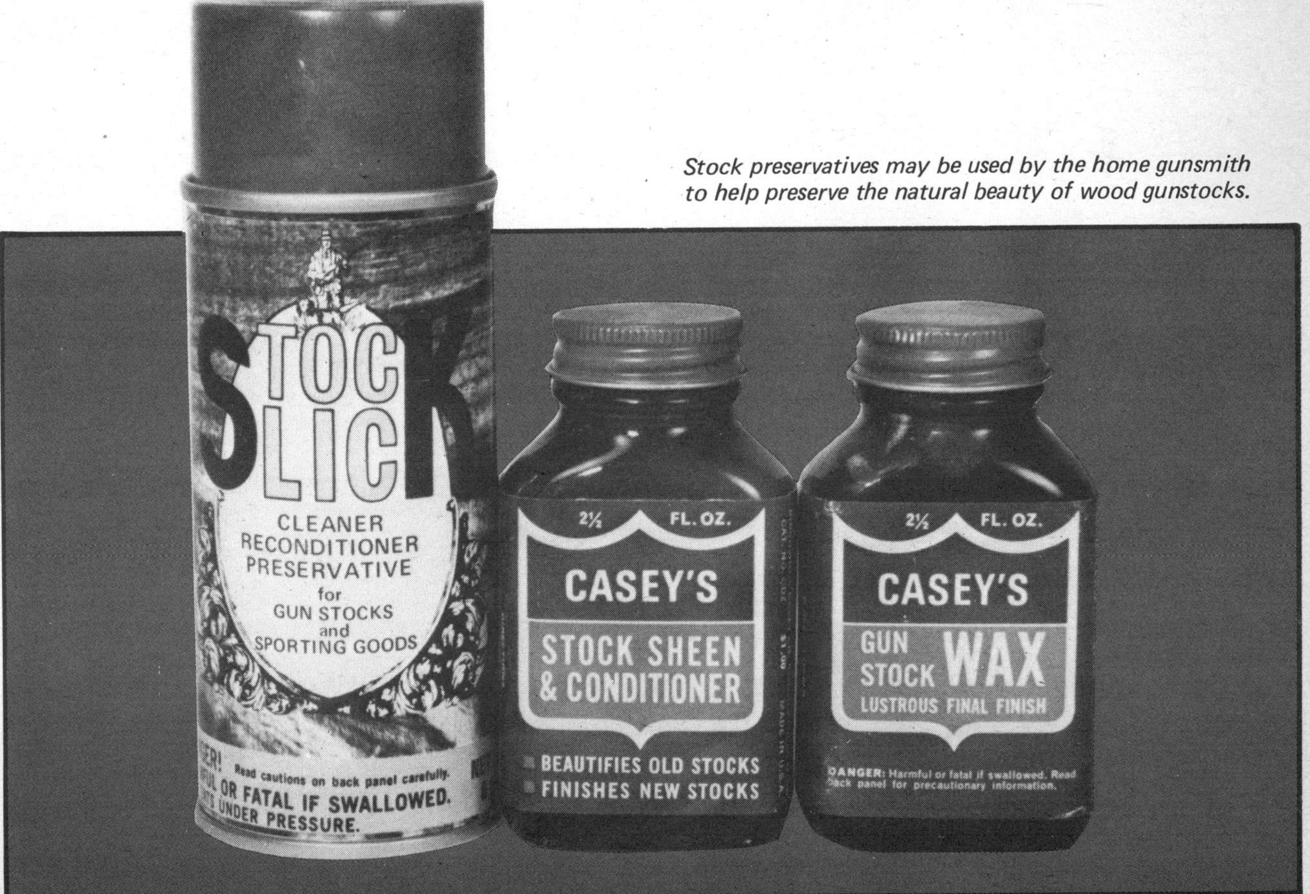

Stock preservatives may be used by the home gunsmith to help preserve the natural beauty of wood gunstocks.

Chapter 18

SPORTERIZING THE STOCK

There's Top Wood In Some Of The Military "Clubs" That Can Be Converted To Today's Fashions

The sporterized stock on the right started out life looking much like the other two military pieces at left. Text describes the ten-hour transformation of wood.

THE HOME gunsmith who likes to work with stocks is a lucky gent. Surplus military stocks still are available, and quite often can be bought for a mere pittance, like two for five bucks. The next time you find a bargain like this — and many gun shops have stacks of these old stocks — lug a couple home.

A lot of these stocks were made when good-to-excellent wood was the rule rather than the exception, and quite a few originally were oil finished and rubbed down with tender loving care. I grant you that their configuration may resemble that of a fence post, that the pistol grip is more utilitarian than handsome, but there is a lot of darned good wood going to waste.

The first rule when working with military surplus stocks is to save the hand guards, all metallic doodads that were on the stock, and if the long forend is cut off, save that wood for plugs you will want to fashion to fill in the larger holes left in the wood when the hardware is removed. Much of the hardware can be reshaped and used again. With some patience the steel butt plate can be converted into a Niedner plate or perhaps into a trap butt plate.

In this case, both the stock and the action started out as military arms. Both have been modified.

A few minutes spent in comparing a modern factory stock and a military type should show you quickly where to start with the stock surgery. If the butt of the stock is too clubby and the pistol grip looks like it was made for Big Foot, get out the wood rasp. A great deal of butt stock shaping can be done with various power sanders, from the sanding disc on an electric hand drill to the belt sanders.

When using a sander of any kind, remember to keep the work moving — or if using a hand-held sander, keep the sander moving. When slimming down the sides of the butt-stock, it is best to start at the top or comb, run the sander along from butt to wrist, then make the next sanding cut right below it, trying to avoid overlaps. Repeat this on the other side of the buttstock, then see how much you have trimmed off and how much more wood has to come off to give the stock more eye-pleasing lines.

It is a simple matter to give a military stock a bit of extra class. There is the matter of a contrasting forend tip, for instance. I favor cutting off the forend just fourteen inches ahead of the trigger guard. There is no rule about cutting the forend and the tip square, so why not cut a forty-five-degree angle, slanting it one way or the other?

Before grabbing the dovetail saw, remember that the wood tip adds anywhere from two to three inches to the length of the forend. To add the classy look to the stock, you can add a white or a black spacer, use either a contrasting or exotic wood, or perhaps even a hunk of scrap wood that comes from some other stock. Stock suppliers, like Fajen and Bishop, have specially selected forend tips, or you can buy them from such sources as Brownell's. See Chapter 19 for more details.

Some military stocks have finger grooves in the forend. I have tried filling these with plastic wood and other types of gunk, and while they can be filled this way, finishing these

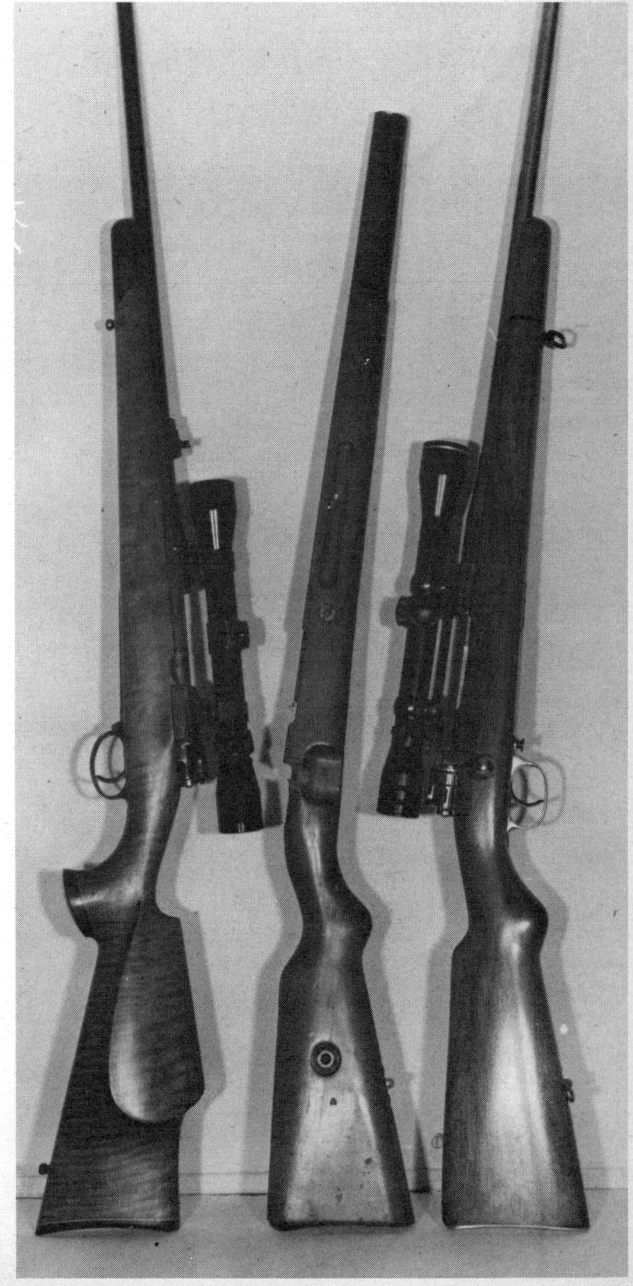

Military wood may be modified in any of several configurations, to suit the shooter/owner.

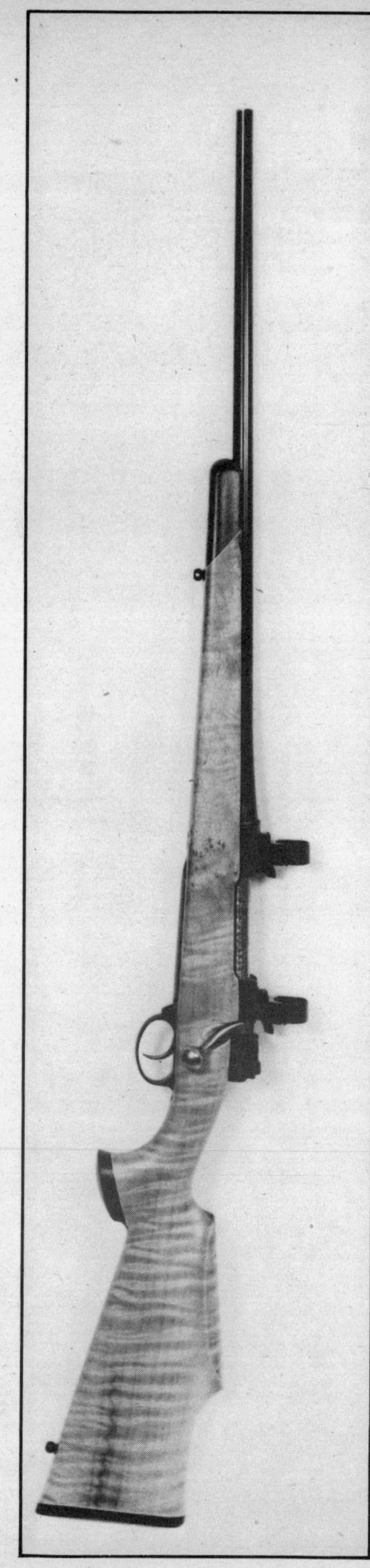

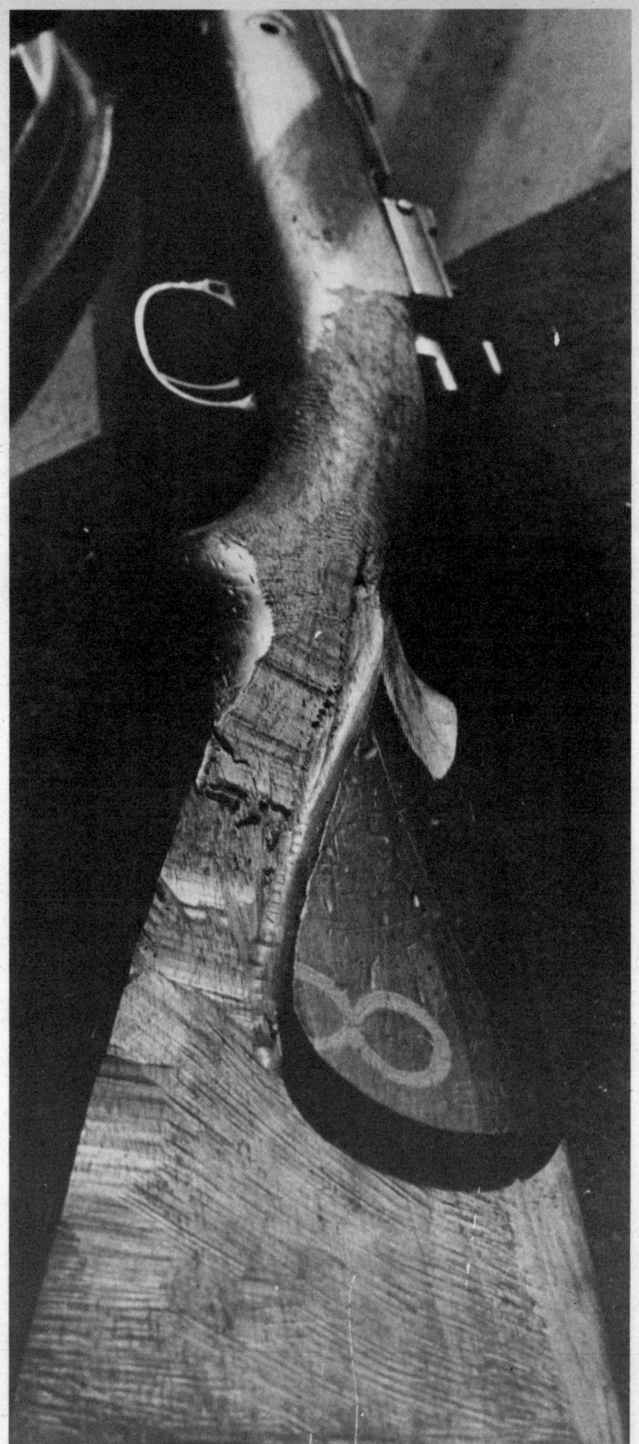

Left-handed shooters may be accommodated with surplus rifle stocks as demonstrated at left. The piece above is having a cheekpiece added with the help of some careful rasp work, along with grip checkering.

patch jobs is something else. I never have been able to fill these finger grooves so the stock doesn't look like a refugee from the scrap pile. After some trial and error whittling, I found most of these stocks have ample forends. Thus, the depth of these grooves can be reduced somewhat by slimming down the forend.

If a spokeshave is handy and you know how to use it,

HOME GUNSMITHING DIGEST

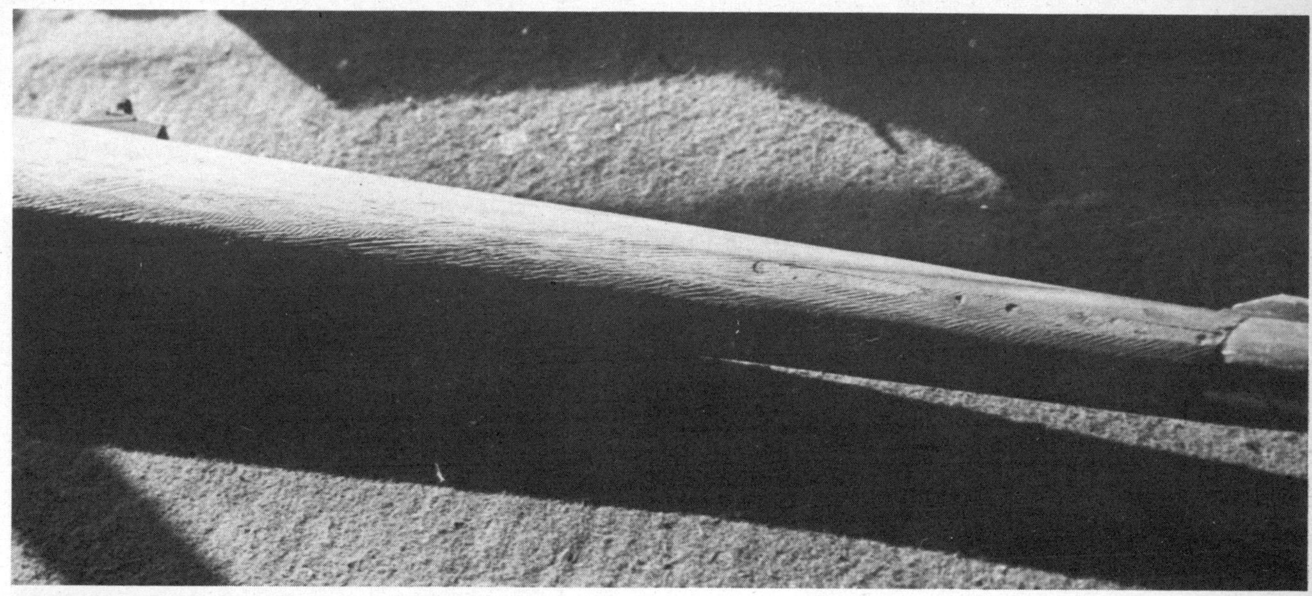

Reshaping the forend is done with wood rasp, shown in progress above. After final coat of new finish, surplus military rifle stock is hung up to dry, right.

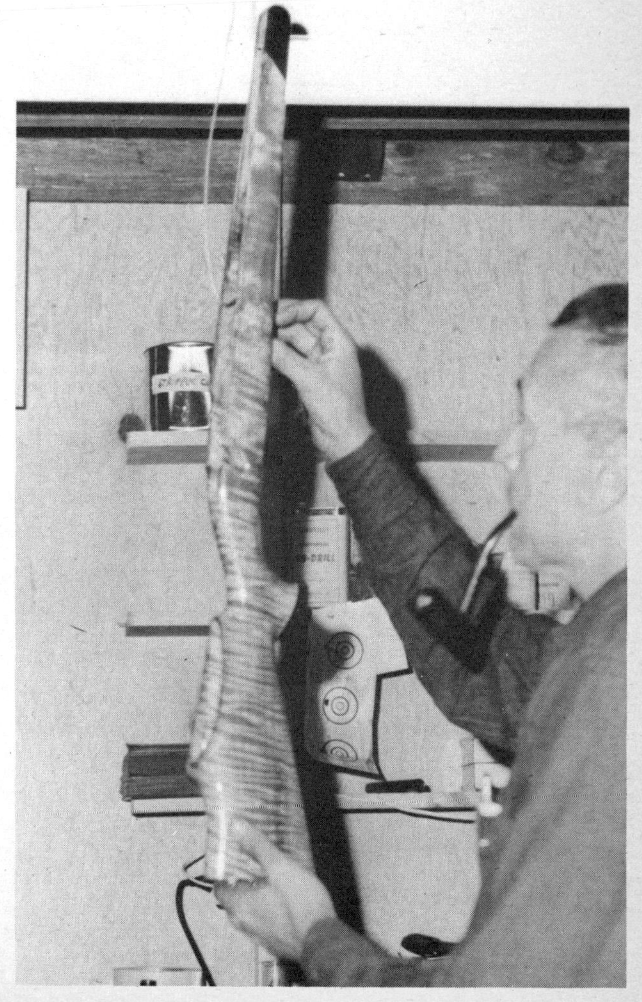

this will do a neat job trimming down the forend enough to make the finger grooves less visible. Any of the various power sanders also will do the trick. As a last resort, you can use a wood rasp, then a cabinet file to smooth out the rough cuts of the rasp.

For rough cuts on stocks, Stanley Surform files are another good way of shaping wood fast and with ease. A jack plane can be used to shape a forend, provided you are skilled in handling such a tool. Block planes won't do an even enough job and tend to cut high and low spots which then require a lot of sanding.

If the forend is too slender to allow removal of the finger grooves by shaving off excess wood, you still can shape the forend so the stock looks more like a custom job than a relic of bygone wars.

Military stocks usually are endowed with cross bolts, sling keepers which are recessed into the butt stock, and other hardware which is more utilitarian than handsome. Some sling swivels can be reworked, then re-installed, but the cuts in the stock are there to stay — at least for a while.

Specialty lumber yards where only woods for furniture are sold often have small sheets of thin veneer which can be used to cut patching covers. Cut the cover for such a patch to just fit the outside dimensions. Instead of building the hole up with wood and glue, use your fiberglass stock bedding compound to hold the cover and its base. Making such a patch is similar to making a Dutchman in carpentry work. If you can't find veneer, you can try your hand at cutting your own, using either a surgical scalpel, fine-toothed veneer saw or a tenon saw.

If you want to get rid of the cross bolt, carefully remove it from the stock, then fill holes with plugs cut with the plug cutter, using the cut-off stock pieces. The addition of a recoil pad and a grip cap, both offset with white line spacers, is often enough to hide the parentage of the military stock.

Many surplus stocks have sundry markings burned into the wood. These marks usually are not too deep and will disappear with the usual sanding or when a rasp is used in shaping the stock.

If you live in country where Osage orange grows, you can make handsome grip caps and forend tips from well-seasoned hunks of that wood. A great many other woods of local origin can be used in small quantities. If you live near a commercial stockmaker, you may find that he will be happy to part with some of the cut-offs that usually wind up in his scrap bin.

Should you feel the need, there is no trick to adding a

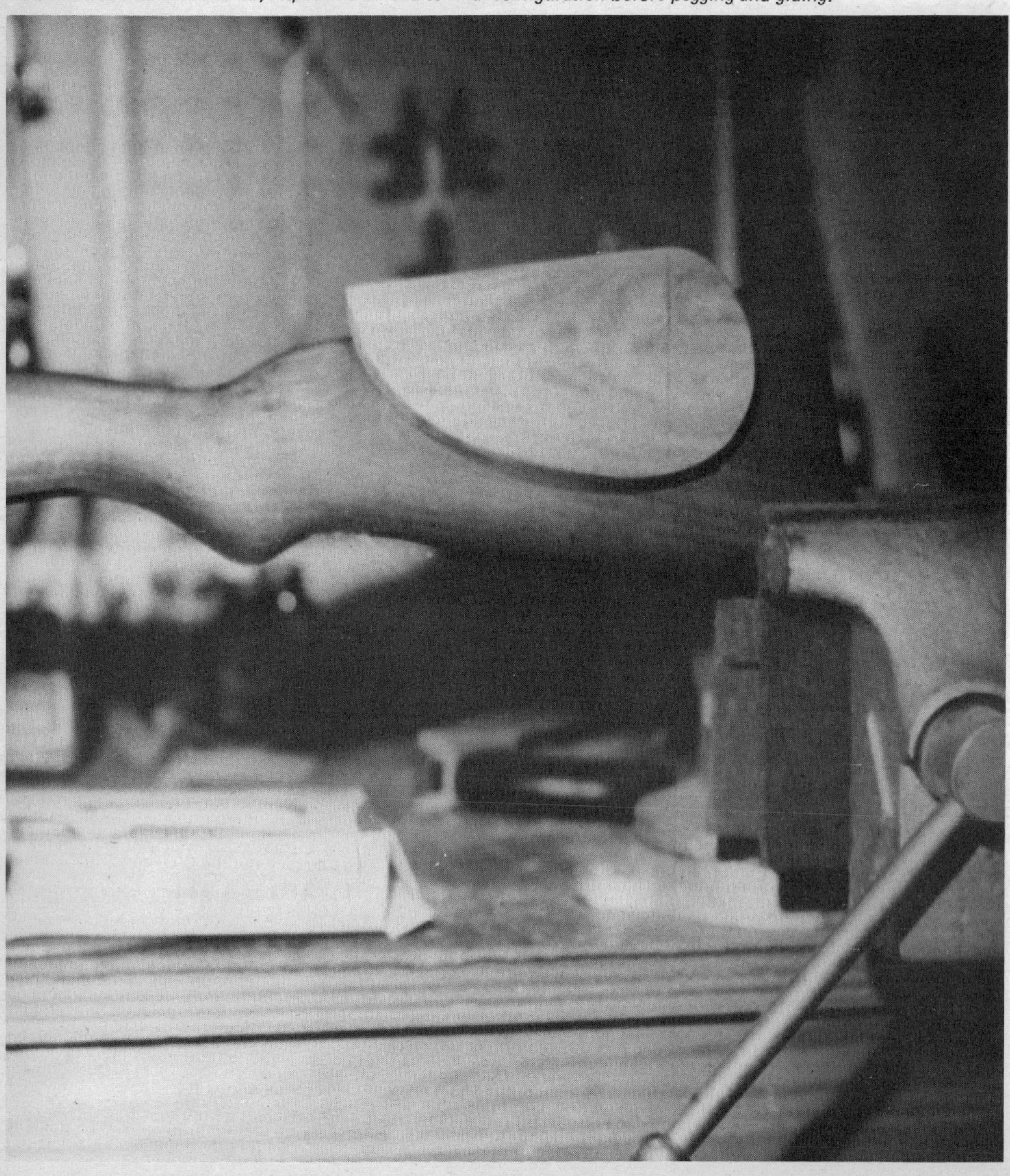

A Roberts cheekpiece may be added to your military stock, if it suits your fancy. Cheekpiece is added to stock somewhat oversized, rasped and sanded to final configuration before pegging and gluing.

Roberts cheekpiece. These are carefully shaped and sanded additions that can be added to most stocks and shaped so well by rasping and sanding that most fellows won't believe that that nice sporter stock was once a military stock and that the cheekpiece was added later.

You can seat a Roberts addition on the stock with a short length of dowel or two and some glue or glassbedding compound. Better yet, inlet the cheekpiece a bit. A sharp chisel is used for the inletting. Undercutting is not essential, especially if you use dowels and glassbedding compound. If, however, you want to rely on fit alone, careful undercutting becomes essential, using white glue, cabinetmaker's glue or glassbedding compound.

Once any such stock addition has been permanently placed, sand it smooth, raise the grain and refinish it to suit your taste. Many surplus stocks are of light wood. These can be stained to resemble walnut, or can be treated to the ammonia fuming outlined in an earlier chapter. I've had little luck in adding striping or color to the stock additions. I now stain the whole stock to a medium walnut, then give

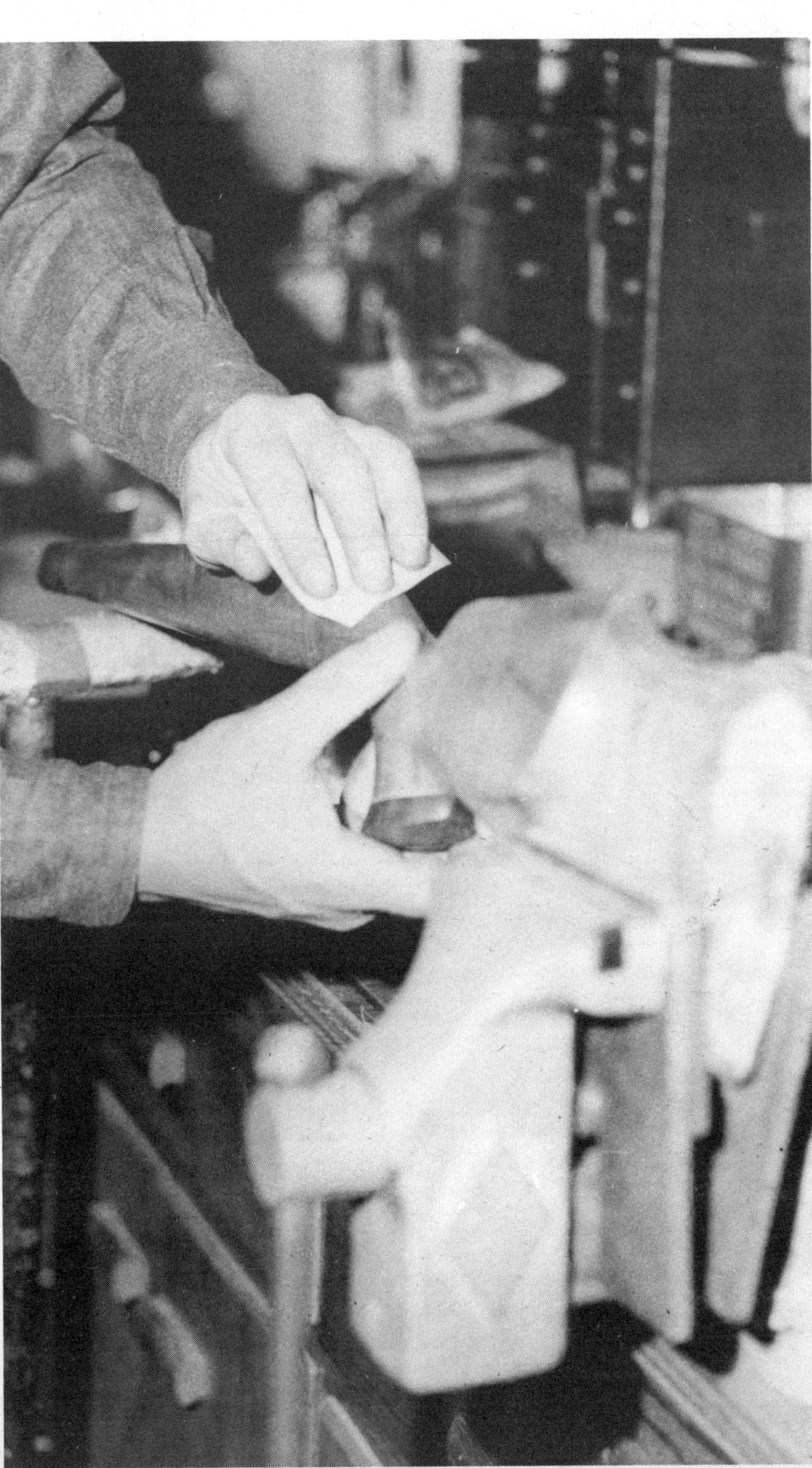

Careful application of cheekpiece, along with described sanding and finishing techniques, results in beautiful custom stock appearance.

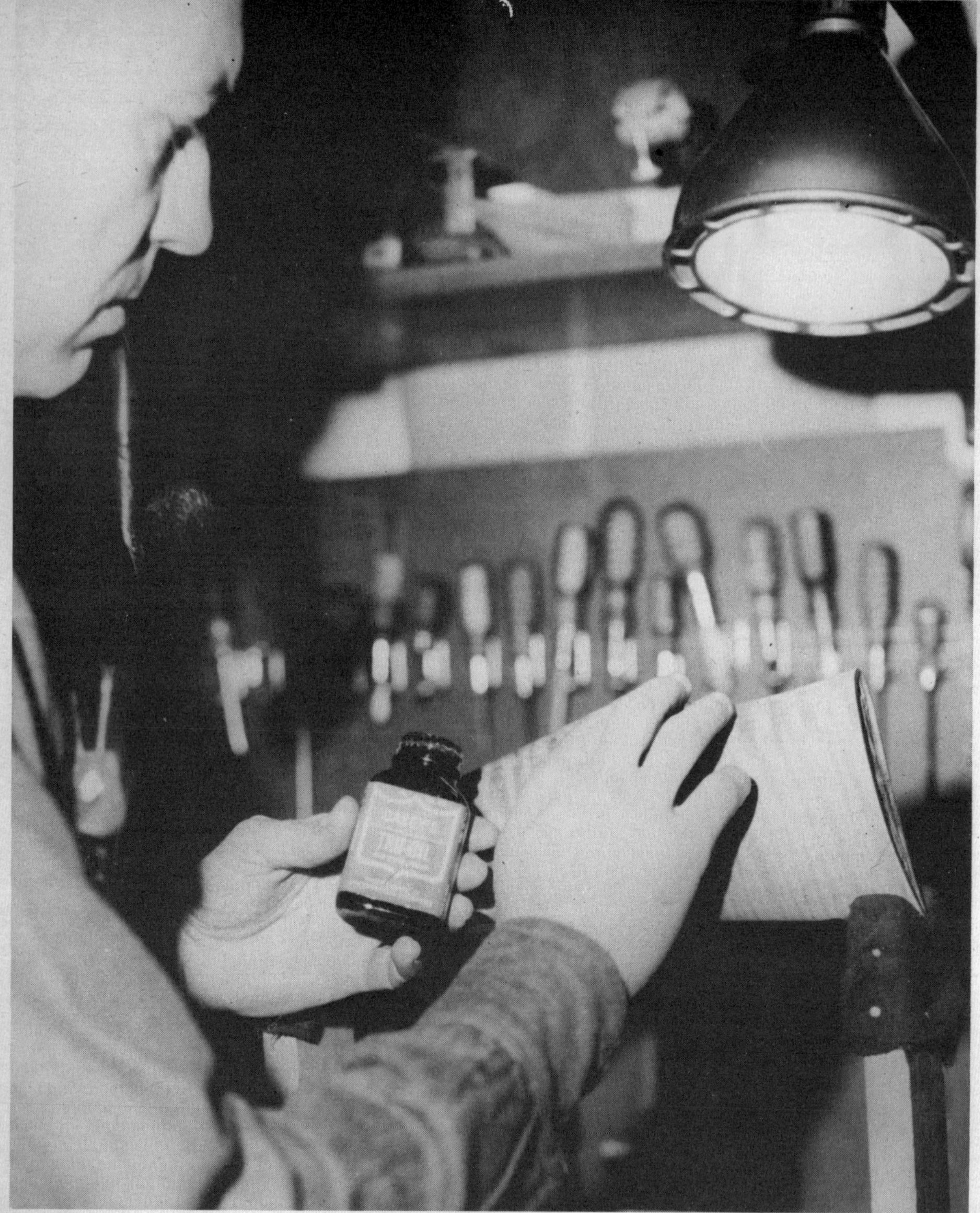

Final application of oil finish is hand-rubbed into wood and allowed to dry.

the wood a slow oil finish as described earlier.

There is a better than even chance that the inletting in the barrel channel and the action area must be altered so the stock will accept the action and barrel contour to be used. I favor glassbedding the action areas to begin with, since the wood may have been exposed to prolonged oil soaking which could make it soft. The strength of the glassbedding is well worth the time and trouble, especially if you have taken pains in reworking the stock.

After the barrel channel has been inletted, don't forget to seal the pores of the wood in any area where the original finish has been disturbed or removed. Sealing the pores is not required if the area is being glassbedded.

If you want to try your hand at checkering, a surplus

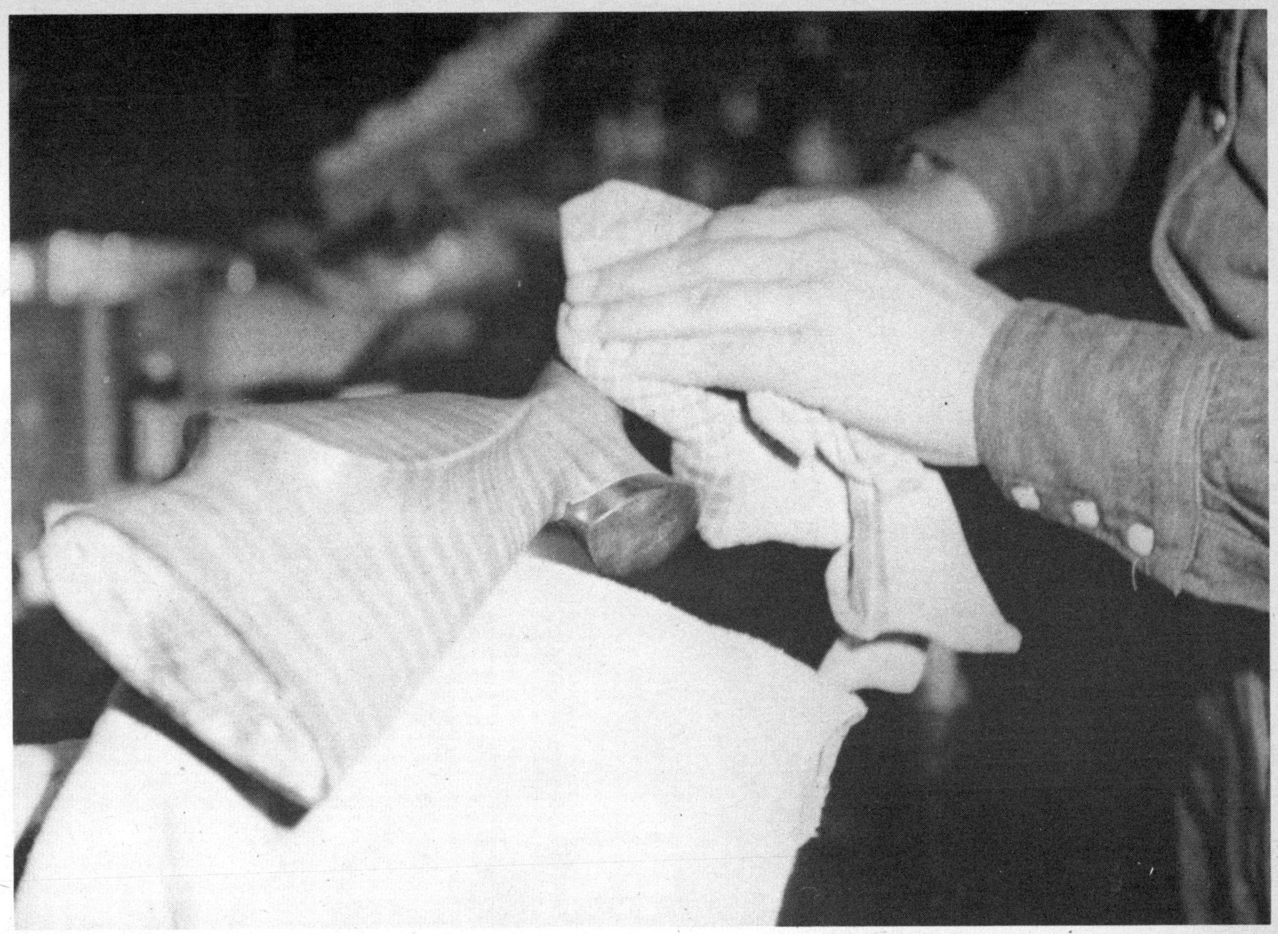

Special stock wax application will produce truly custom appearance for military wood. Military surplus stocks provide the home gunsmith with plenty of raw material for experimenting with checkering and finishes.

stock is a good way to start. Checkering is done after the final finish has been applied and when the stock is finished completely, except for installation of the hardware, recoil pad, et al.

I prefer to remove all such items as sling swivels and recoil pads before I start to refinish a stock. Thus, I can concentrate on finishing the wood and don't have to worry about scratching the bluing on a swivel or leaving an unsightly mark on a recoil pad. However, I seem to be outvoted here, since many professionals and quite a few amateur stockmakers leave everything on the stock.

Fashions in stocks change almost as rapidly as ladies' hemlines. Twenty years ago, exotic inlays and light wood were the fashion. Then the inlays faded from the picture and nobody in his right mind had a light finish put on a stock. Now, inlays are coming back, and although the light finishes have not set the shooting world on its collective ear, they won't lead to a loss of your voting rights.

Like checkering, I never have tried my hand at inlays — except once when I was all steamed up about a custom stock I was making. I had spent entirely too much money for the semi-inletted stock, then added inlays.

Unfortunately, my enthusiasm exceeded my skill considerably and the result was a miserably botched stock that had to be redone by a professional.

I long have felt that you don't give a new driver a Rolls Royce and that inlay work should perhaps be tried on an inexpensive stock, such as a revamped military stock. Inlays are inexpensive, but custom stocks are not. The inlays made by Lee Estes are excellent and can be bought from Brownell's, who also can furnish the needed tools if you don't have them.

Reworking a military stock has more advantages than drawbacks. I would hesitate to try some of the things I've done with surplus stocks on blanks or semi-inletted stocks that cost a week's pay. I've tried various finishes on surplus stocks; I have modified butt plates and learned to install recoil pads on surplus stocks. I've learned woodworking to a degree that far exceeds the skills I'd have acquired had I started with a good hunk of wood.

Over the years, I've collected a number of these stocks that nobody wanted, refinished and rebuilt them. Now I find that I prefer the looks of some of these stocks to some of the commercial jobs.

Chapter 19

GRIP CAPS, SPACERS & FOREND TIPS

These Simple Decorative Touches Can Add Inexpensive Personality To Your Firearm

Wood intended for grip spacers usually comes drilled for easy installation, while tip blocks are unmarked.

FOR LESS than ten bucks, you can customize most any rifle or shotgun stock. The simplest start is to add a grip cap. You need only to drill a hole into the flat base of the pistol grip and seat a woodscrew. Such grip caps are available in steel, plastic and horn. Some can be installed as they come from the supplier; others can stand some polishing.

Before starting the screw, run it over a piece of moist soap or a candle stump, then seat the screw, using a screwdriver with a blade that fits the screw slot. If you are adding a grip cap to extend the length of the pistol grip, you can add a spacer or two. The spacer can be made from wood or plastic, with plexiglass, especially colored plexiglass, being used most widely.

One or more spacers can be added to a butt plate or a recoil pad. These are fastened in place with the same screws that hold whatever you have on the butt now. Again, plastic spacers are used most widely, black and white

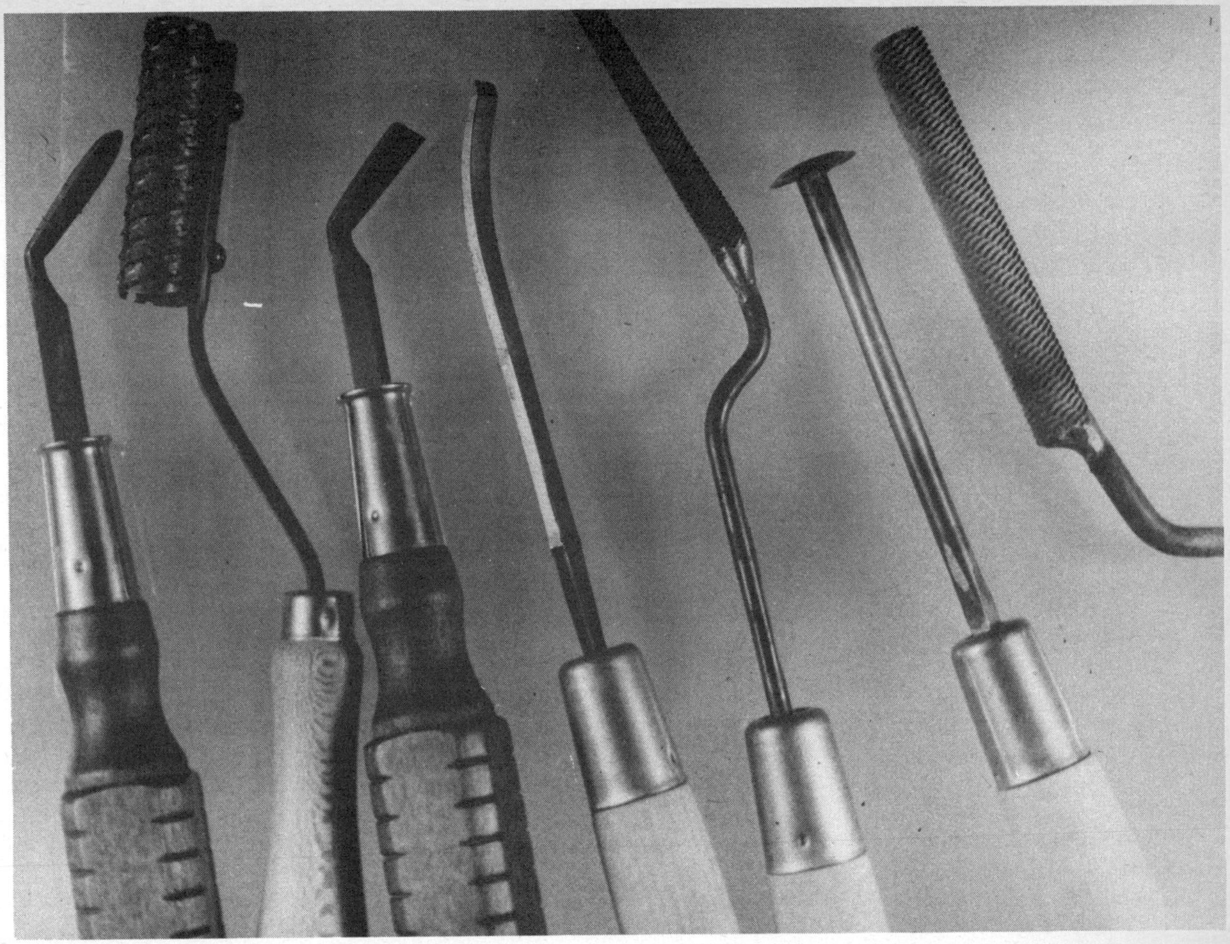

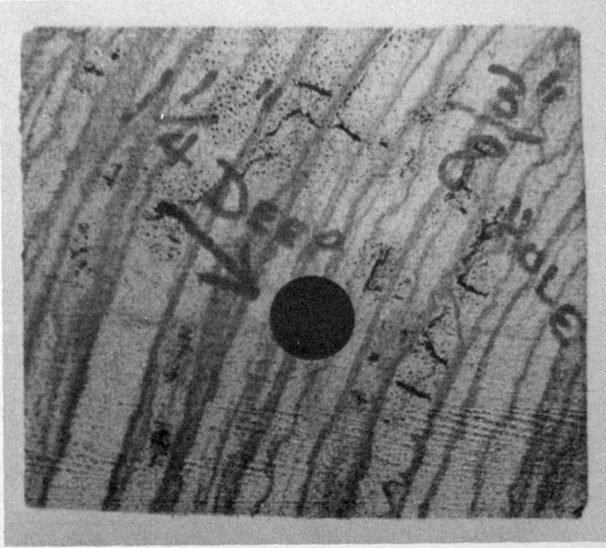

Stock tools used for inletting and shaping are also valuable when forming new forend tip.

predominating. These spacers are slightly over-sized and must be trimmed to fit the contour of the stock and the recoil pad or butt plate.

Wood grip caps are installed by various means. Some stockers simply glue them in place after shaping them, using either an epoxy glue or Acraglas; others use two beheaded nails as fastening pins. Still others install a blind dowel into the cap and the pistol grip. A blind dowel is one that does not show on the side of the job that is visible.

Most commercially produced forend tips and wood grip caps are made from exotic woods. Many of these woods must be protected from the influences of humidity and temperature, so when they reach you, many have a layer of wax on them. Once the wax has been removed so the wood can be shaped, sanded and finished, the exotic woods have the tendency to check. This is not the fault of the supplier, but is natural with such woods. Thus, if you have to put the job aside for a while, apply a coat of oil or wax over the unfinished areas of these exotic wood parts. Thin wood butt spacers should be treated in the same manner. Once these woods have been final sanded, sealed and filled, then finished, the checking tendency will cease.

Installation of a contrasting wood forend tip is relatively simple. As mentioned in the preceding chapter, I favor a distance of fourteen inches from the front of the trigger guard to the point where a new forend tip will start. Keep in mind that the addition of a forend tip will add between two and four inches to the length of the stock, so you decide how long you want the forend tip, then work backward to the length of the actual forend.

Before you decide what length you want the forend and how long the tip should be, remember that you can slant

Spacers come oversized; dowel holes are not always centered.

Wood pieces from previous stock work are saved for future use as spacers and forend tips.

the joint of the two woods any way you want. Keep in mind, however, that the wood for the tip must be large enough for your plans. If, for instance, you like the appearance of the German schnabel forend design, there is nothing to stop you from shaping the new tip in this manner.

To enhance the appearance of the contrasting forend tip, one or two wood spacers often are added. These contrast in color from the new tip and the stock itself. Spacers can be bought, or if you have a bandsaw, you can cut your own. Use a guide on the saw table so the final wood thickness of the spacer is uniform, with the thicker spacers measuring 0.1185-inch, the thinner ones 0.0660-inch.

Before making the first cut in the wood for the tip,

locate the exact center of the end cut that will fit against the forend of the stock. Once you have decided how much angle you want at the joint of the tip and stock, cut the stock, then measure the thickness of the wood there. A one-quarter-inch dowel is more than adequate for holding tip, spacer and forend together. Locate the center of the cutoff forend, then drill a one-quarter-inch hole from one-half to a full inch deep.

Next, inspect the wood block that will be the new tip. If the joint between it and forend will be slanted, mark a matching line to determine whether there is enough wood on top of the block to permit cutting out the barrel channel. If not, you may have to move the tip upward, thus changing the location of the hole for the dowel. For this

Length of forend may be measured from forward edge of trigger guard; other stockers measure along barrel channel.

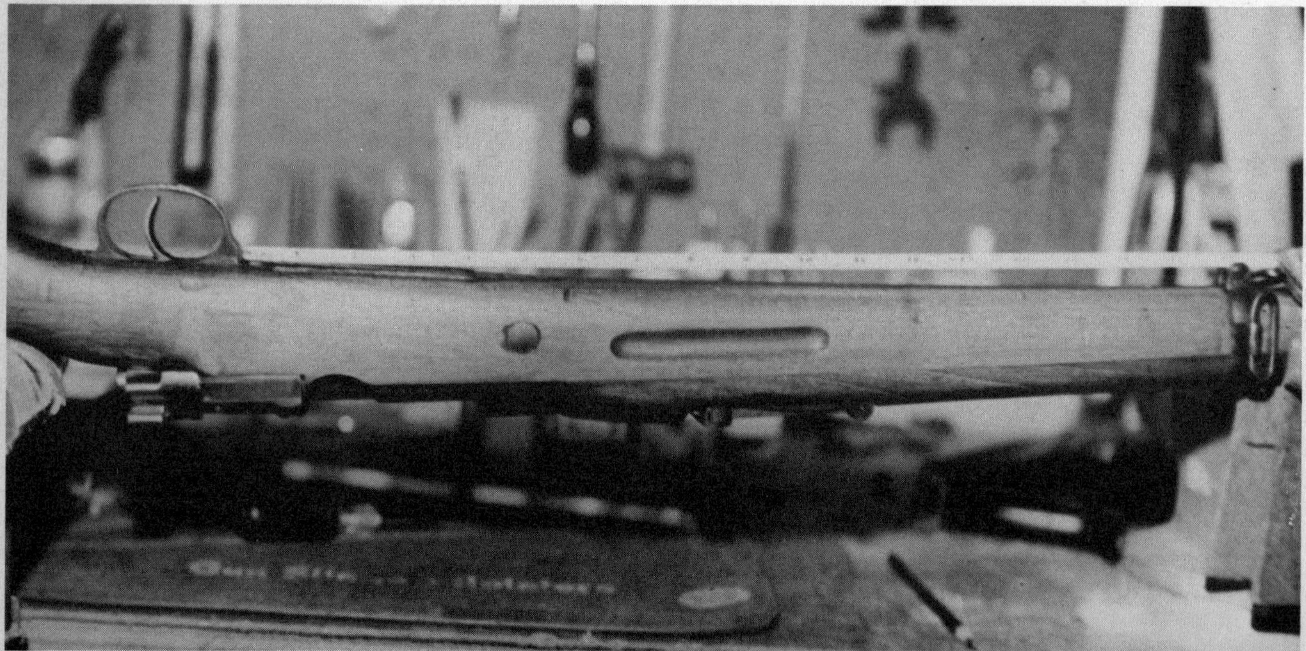

HOME GUNSMITHING DIGEST

Cut-off forend is drilled, dowel is inserted, cemented and allowed to set.

reason, the hole is not drilled until the position of the tip is fixed.

Depending on the length of the new tip and how far the dowel extends into the forend, cut the dowel. Use a hardwood dowel, preferably maple. Chamfer the end with a chamfering bit and brace, or sand the ends of the dowel on a belt sander to get the chamfered ends. Make five or six grooves in the side of the dowel, running parallel to each other the full length. These grooves make it possible for air to escape while the dowel is being forced into the two holes and the adhesive used takes up whatever free space there is.

Grooving also can be done spirally and it is said that this gives somewhat better holding power to such a glued joint. The grooving can be done with any sharp tool.

White glue is good, epoxy glues are better, and Acraglas stock bedding compound is best for fastening darned near anything to anything, from forend tip to spacers and screws.

Set the dowel into the forend with whatever adhesive you have decided to use and let the job sit overnight. When dry, slip the spacers, if you are using any, over the dowel, then set the block of wood that will become the tip. Position the wood so grain runs in the right direction, then mark the upper surface of the block for the barrel channel. Usually you can measure the depth of the channel at the very end of the forend so you know how far to cut down in the block in forming the channel.

Make two shallow cuts with a dovetail saw to delineate the width of the channel. Use a straight gouge chisel to remove the first wood from the channel area. I find it easiest to take the block of forend tip wood off and lock it into the well-padded jaws of the bench vise to make the preliminary cuts. Later, when roughing out of the channel is completed, I place the block back on the dowel. With the butt of the stock supported, either on a stand or on the bench, I lock the block once more into the vise so that I can run the Quickcut inletting tool, a scraper or a rasp along the length of the channel.

Glue the spacers and the forend tip block on the dowel, making certain the adhesive makes contact with all touching wood surfaces. Clamp together and let the adhesive set for at least twelve hours.

As soon as you start shaping the forend tip block, you'll find out how well you have prepared the glue joint. For quick removal of a lot of wood I opt for a sanding disc on the one-quarter-inch electric drill. The line between the stock and the forend should flow smoothly and about ninety percent of this rough shaping can be done with a sanding disc. The larger hand-held belt sanders cut too fast for careful shaping. Bench model belt sanders are better, although handling the long stock may turn out to be a bit more work than you bargained for.

If any special features are to be added to the forend tip, this is the time to do so. Mentioned was the schnabel forend and now is the time to find one, make a sketch, then copy it. Sand smooth, and I mean perfectly smooth, then raise the grain, sand, raise the grain again and sand smooth — as outlined in an earlier chapter.

Remember what was said about the checking of exotic

Sanding disc chucked into electric drill will provide rapid method of shaping new forend tip.

wood, so be sure to use wax or oil if the work has to rest for any length of time. The forend tip and spacers are finished in the same way the rest of the wood is finished.

Horn butt plates, grip caps and forend tips are elegant additions. I like the looks of them, but in contrast to other materials, horn needs care once in a while. Since horn dries out, then cracks and chips, a light wipe-down with a drop or two of a good quality non-gumming oil is in order several times a year.

Steel grip caps and butt plates should also be given a light coat of oil every so often. I found that the G96 silicone mitten does a good job, and I use this mitten routinely for wiping down all of my guns, going over wood and metal alike.

Plastic grip caps, if made of tenite, can be buffed and polished. According to Bob Brownell, you wet-sand lightly with No. 400 mylar abrasive, using ample amounts of water. Follow this with a 600 mylar sanding, again using lots of water. Use a rough paper towel to burnish the surface. For a still better polish, Brownell suggests No. 555 Polish-O-Ray on a loose muslin wheel.

Rosewood tips, grip caps, and even spacers usually are waxed heavily to prevent checking. Denatured alcohol is a good solvent for wax, and surfaces to be glued should have as much of the wax removed as can be wiped off with a solvent soaked rag or large patch. It is best to repeat the wax-removing job several times because the wax usually used is quite stubborn and resists removal with considerable tenacity.

The purists among stockmakers, both professional and amateur, like to stress that the harmony of a gun could be damaged if the wood of the newly installed forend tip is too unlike in grain or not unlike enough in coloring to the rest of the stock. If the combination of colors is too garish and bothersome, you can always strip off the finish and restain the offending parts of the wood.

Since some of the exotic woods are not too well known, a short description seems in order:

Zebra wood: A cream-colored wood with black

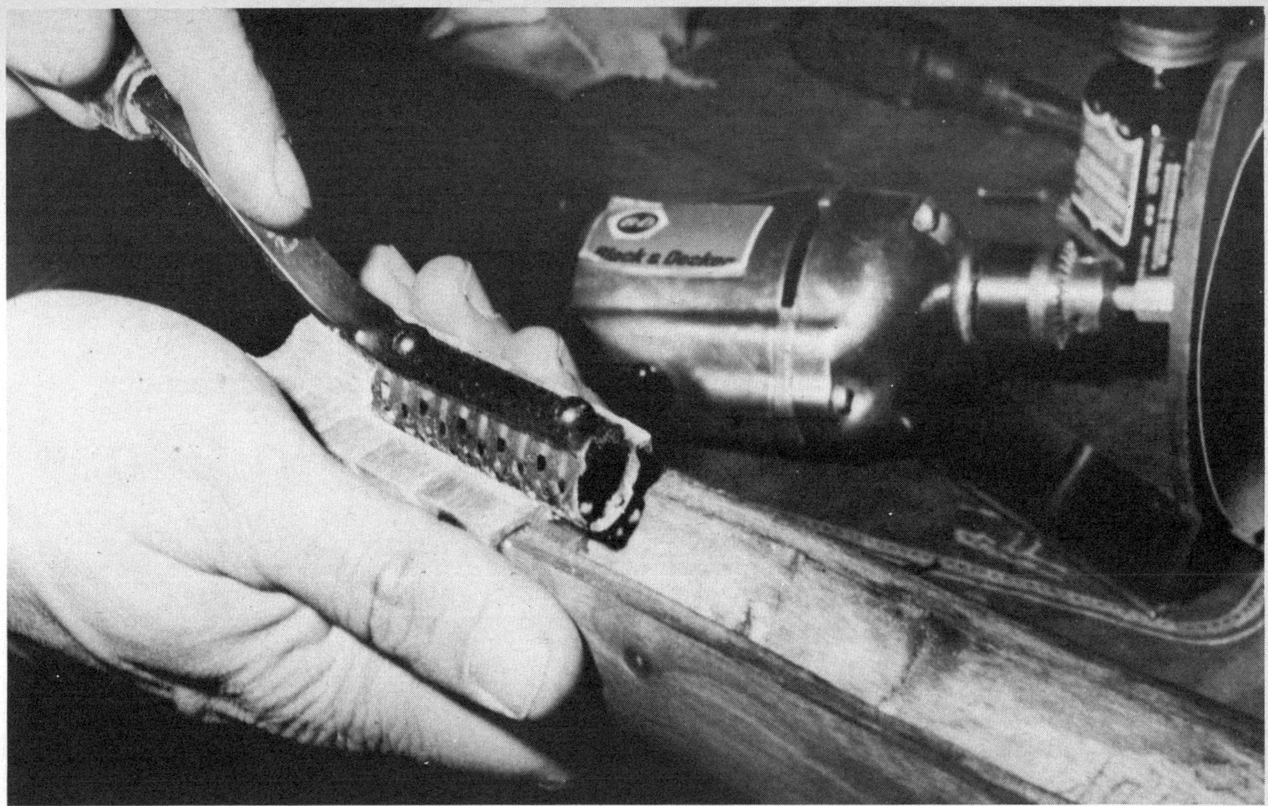

After shaping outside of newly-installed tip, barrel channel must be inletted. In this step, extra care must be taken to prevent binding and loss of accuracy. Frequent trial fitting of action is necessary.

lengthwise stripes. Use a sharply diagonal cut to emphasize the grain of this wood. Matching forend tip and grip cap give a stock an unusual, yet pleasing appearance.

Rosewood: A dark wood that takes a nice polish, usually nicely figured, more on the purple side, and not as dark as ebony. Blocks usually have quite a bit of color contrast, are heavily waxed.

Cocobolo wood: A tough, close-grained wood, having beautiful figure with darker streaks. Smith & Wesson offers this wood as an option in their special Magna grips.

Walnut wood: Most blocks have outstanding color and figure. This wood often is used by the pros when working with a special walnut stock.

Redwood burl: A bird's-eye figured wood with good coloring. Most often used for grip caps and forend tips.

Myrtle wood: A light wood with good figure that makes excellent, strongly contrasting grip caps and forend tips. Most myrtle is deeply grained, making stocks and stock additions quite stunning.

Inlays, contrasting woods for tips and caps, caps, and spacers, as well as the inletting tools needed are available from such sources as Brownell's and Mittermeier. Brownell's maintains a good supply of select woods and inlays at all times.

Completed installation job presents smooth-flowing appearance enhancing the beauty of any rifle stock.

Chapter 20

THE PROS AND CONS OF GLASSBEDDING

Bedding Your Favorite Rifle In Glass May Or May Not Improve Accuracy

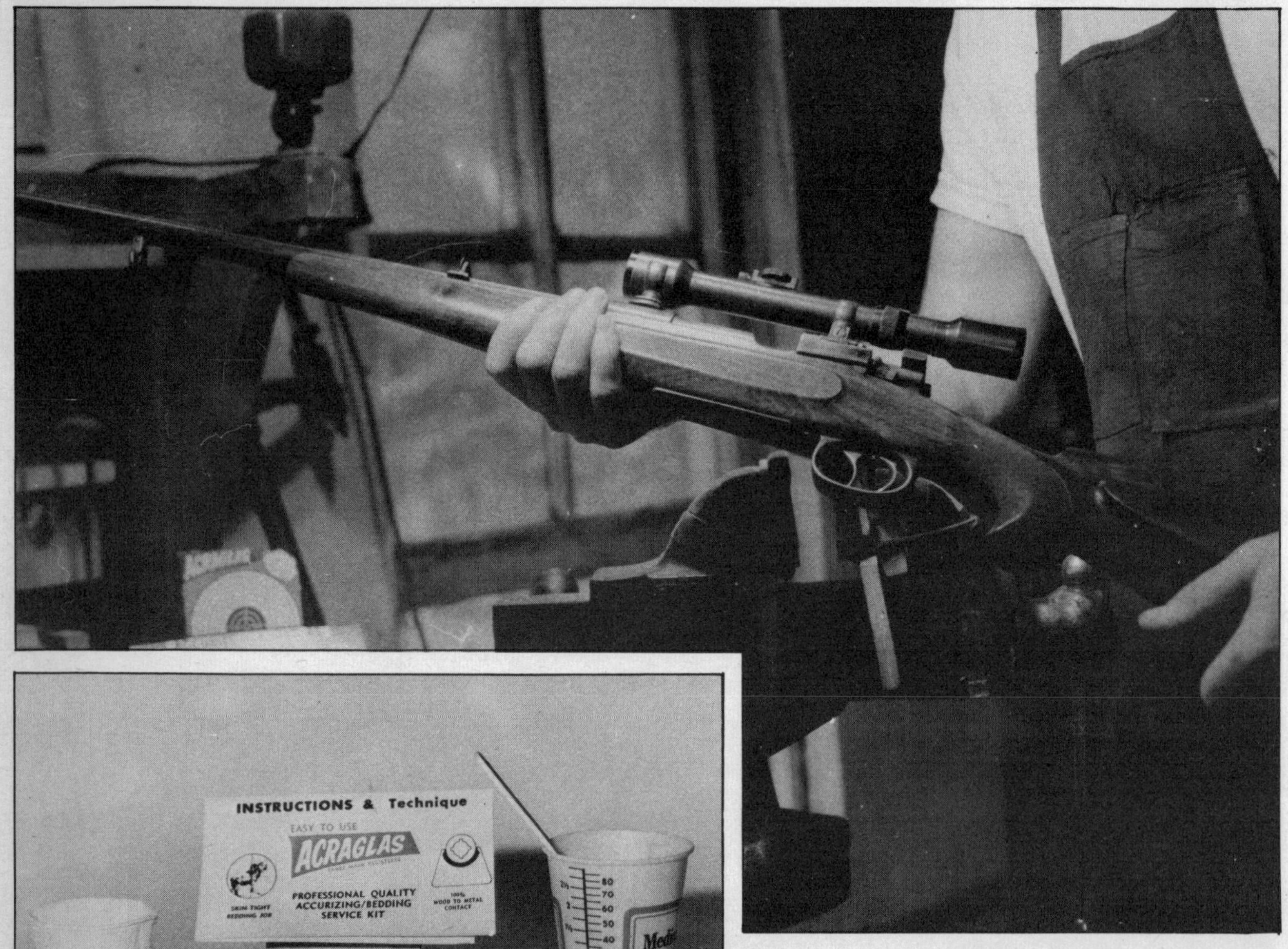

Pre-World War I sporter rifle, above, had absorbed moisture in forend, adversely affecting accuracy. Glassbedding instructions must be carefully followed.

UNLESS THE WOOD in the barrel channel of a rifle has been specially treated, the wood will absorb moisture from the air. This results in warping, cupping and pulling of the wood and invariably you'll discover this state of affairs just before you want to take this particular rifle on a hunting trip.

The degree with which a piece of wood will take on moisture depends on how long and well it was seasoned, how well the exterior of the wood has been finished and made moisture-resistant and the degree of ambient atmospheric humidity. If a rifle suddenly goes sour, there are three possible causes. A scope block and ring might have come unhitched or perhaps a screw or two sheared or loosened from recoil. The bedding screws may be loose or, in areas where there is a high degree of humidity, the wood soaked up some of the moisture. Since the exterior of the wood is normally protected, it is most probably due to the fact that the barrel channel either has not been finished at all, or the sealer coat of varnish or shellac was simply not adequate to protect the wood from the moisture in the air.

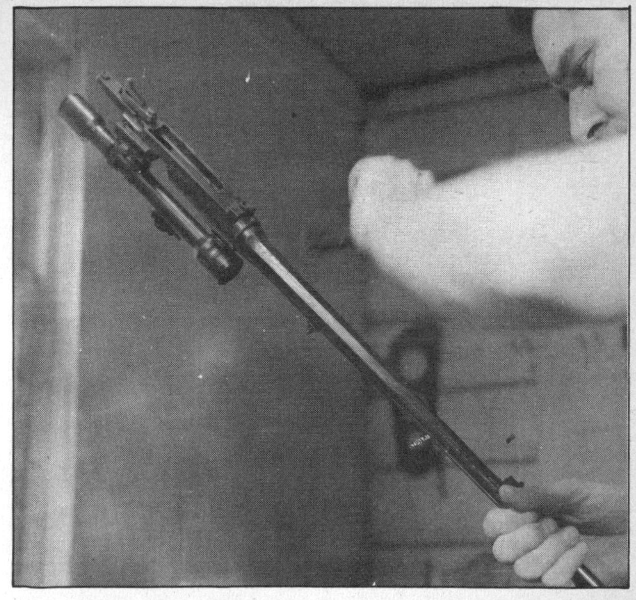

Barreled action is removed from stock and release agent is carefully applied to metal, upper right. With stock in padded vise, long strips of masking tape form trough above barrel channel. Removing excess wood from barrel channel, right, demands caution and sharp chisel, as described in text.

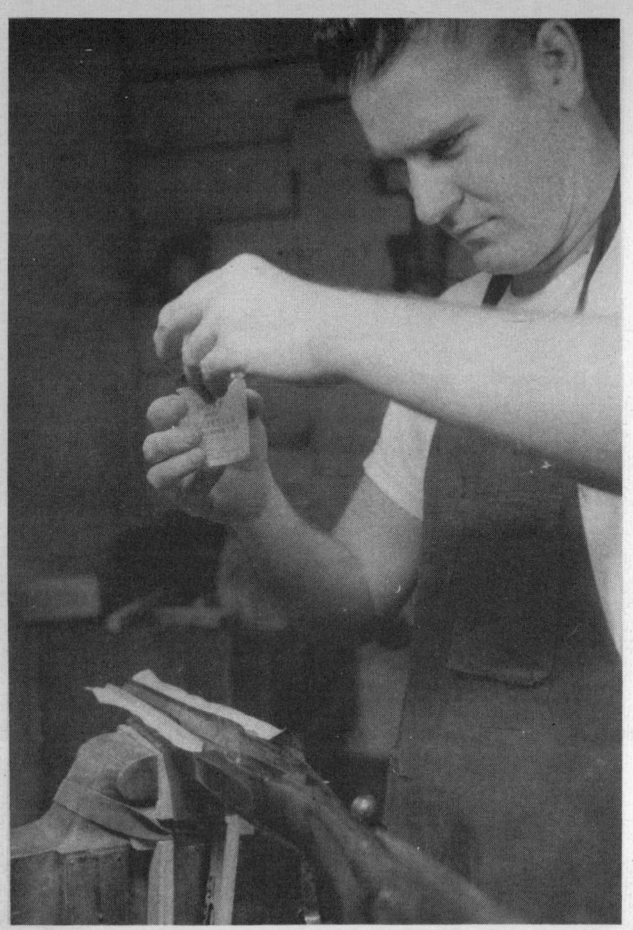

Coating the barrel channel with some sort of sealant is important and most firearms manufacturers take care of this during the stock-finishing process. However, there is always an outside chance that the job was not done properly or that there was not enough sealer used to protect the wood completely. If stock warpage does occur, or if you suspect that the wood pores were not sealed and did absorb moisture, take a critical look at the rifle. A straightedge along the stock and one on top of the barrel will give you the first indication that something has gone sour.

One custom rifle with a very light and tapered barrel gave me fits for a while before I discovered what was wrong. The unfinished barrel channel had soaked up moisture from a very damp midwest summer and although the straightedge did not indicate stock warping, the barrel did. By placing the butt on the floor and looking straight down the barrel, I could actually see how the slim barrel was being pushed out of the channel by the warped wood. Warpage was so extensive that I decided to go all the way and glassbed the barrel and the inletted action.

A great many stockmakers, and this includes some of the top names in the field, resort to glassbedding every so often. It is true that a properly inletted stock should not need it, except perhaps in the area of the recoil shoulder where glassbedding adds needed strength. The blessing of fiberglass, however, also leads to some misuses. A lot of fellows simply went the path of least resistance; they whittled away enough wood for any action and barrel, saving lots of tedious handwork and time, then simply glassbedded the rifle instead of doing a careful job to begin with.

Correct timing must be strictly observed as bedding material is mixed and applied. After mixture is stirred, floc material is added, left, and stirred again. Compound is applied with wood spatula from kit.

I prefer to glassbed the action area of any rifle that develops more recoil than the .30/06, especially when I expect to use that rifle a great deal for hunting big game. Barrel channels that have warped are glassbedded, as are the stocks of most of my varmint rifles for the sake of improved accuracy. Rifles with fully free-floated barrels also are treated in this manner since I want to be absolutely certain that there will be no cupping or warping of the forend.

Glassbedding is not a very complicated process, despite what some writers have said on the subject. As with most other jobs, lay out your work first, read and then reread the instructions, taking the work step-by-step. It is true that glassbedding compounds will set hard as a rock and you must use a release agent unless you want to face a miserably messy job. Beyond that, there is no great trick to glassbedding a barrel channel, an action or both. The whole job, from beginning to end, should not take you more than two hours or so, including cleanup time.

There are several good glassbedding compounds on the market, and all of them work on more or less the same principle. I did my first bedding job with Bob Brownell's Acraglas, found it easy to handle and perfectly satisfactory. I stuck with it for some twenty bedding jobs. In recent years, several of these epoxy compounds have been offered in gel form which is said to be somewhat easier to use. However, two of these gels take too long to set and others have a poor shelf life. I don't recommend them.

A package of Acraglas sells for about five bucks and there is enough in each such package to take care of two rifles. As long as you keep the leftover stuff from the first bedding without mixing it, you can store the unmixed ingredients for a long time. In addition to the bedding compound, you will need your heavy bench vise with well-padded jaws to protect the stock from being marred. Screwdrivers that fit the slots of the bedding screws are needed, as is a small and well-sharpened wood chisel to whittle away wood. A roll of masking tape, some pieces of fine sandpaper and a few hunks of fine steel wool are the essentials for the job. If you have a Dremel tool, you'll find it useful. If you work carefully and slowly you may not need any of the touch-up wood finishes, but it is nice to have some on hand in case you do mess up the finish of the wood here and there. If the stock you are about to bed has been oil finished, some Casey Tru-Oil should be on hand.

As mentioned earlier, begin by reading the instructions, then go over them a second time to be sure you have not missed any of the finer points. Let me stress again that you need not rush. Be sure to mix your ingredients as directed. The mix will set fairly fast, but not quite as fast as you may have heard.

Start by removing the stock from the barreled action. If the gun is scoped, you can leave the scope in place or remove it as you please. If the stock bedding screws need touch-up bluing or any other kind of attention, now is the time to tend to that job.

As with everything else, there is a right and a wrong way to remove a barreled action from the stock. Here is how the pros do it: Lock the gun into the padded jaws of the bench vise with the barrel downward. This allows you to see the bedding screws when you start to loosen them. Work slowly and keep one hand clamped around the barrel and forend so that when the last thread of the screws are turned out, the action will drop out of the stock. If the barreled action fits so snugly into

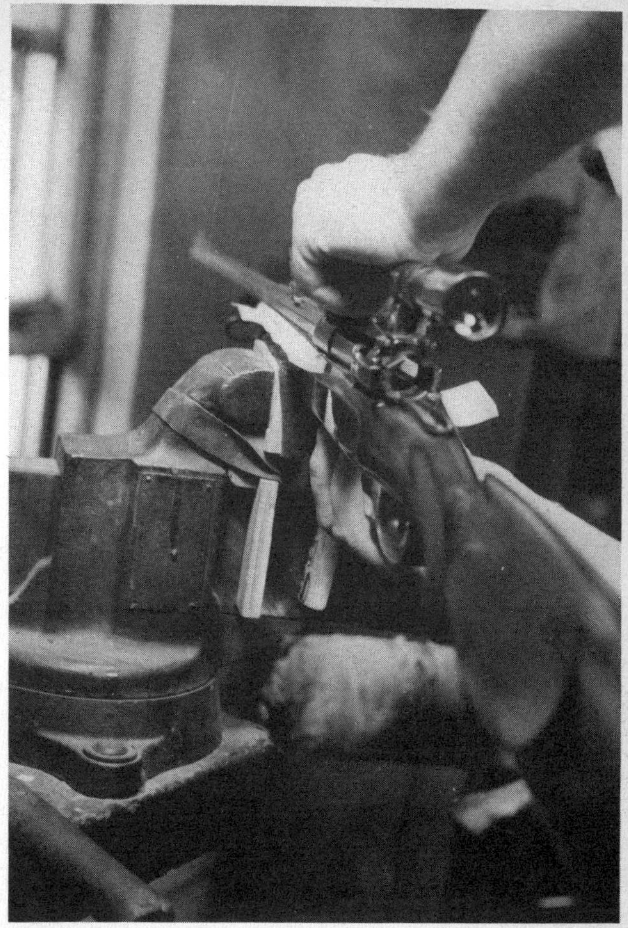

After bedding compound has been spread as uniformly as possible, barreled action is pressed down into stock, above. Bedding screws are then fully tightened down.

the wood that you cannot budge it by simply pushing on the barrel near the forend tip, give the barrel a tap or two with a rawhide mallet. Some stockmakers prefer to lock the barrel itself into the padded vise jaws, then support the butt with a bench or simply swivel the vise so that the butt of the stock rests on the bench top.

Once the steel and wood have been separated, take a good long look at the points where wood and steel make contact. Trouble spots are usually quite easily seen. If they are not readily visible, use some inletting blue — Jerrow's Inletting Blue is a good choice — and apply a small amount of the gunk to the action and barrel where the steel makes contact with the wood. The dye will be transferred once the barreled action is again seated in the wood. The now-blue-black areas of the wood show you right away where there is heavy pressure on the wood from the steel. At those pressure points, some wood must be removed and this is a matter of trial and error. Chisel, file or scrape away a bit of wood from the dyed

wood area, then check fit of steel and wood again. Keep doing this until all such pressure spots have been eliminated.

If you don't have any inletting blue, you can make some yourself. Add a little bit of lamp black to cold cream or mix a small amount of Prussian Blue to vegetable shortening. If these products are not available, you have to resort to very slow and careful wood removal in the pressure area. Remove just enough wood to have a loose fit between wood and steel. What wood is removed at this stage of the bedding will eventually be replaced by Acraglas, which will set and conform to the steel contours.

If the rifle barrel was free floated, you can apply Acraglas to the entire length of the barrel channel. If the barrel was not free floated and you want to have it so, you must remove enough wood from the barrel channel to free the barrel fully. If you don't want to have the barrel free floated, scrape away enough wood to free the barrel, then fill the entire barrel channel with Acraglas.

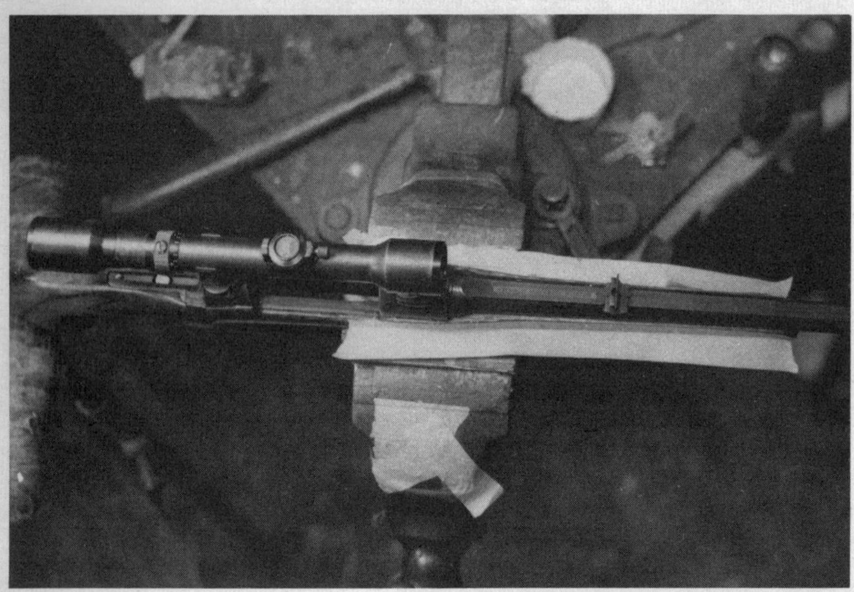

Left: Some of the glassbedding compound has oozed out of barrel channel but is held within bounds by the masking tape trough.

Area under action is generally slowest to harden and must be checked before removal of barrel is attempted. Temperature and humidity influence hardening rate.

Should you want the whole barrel fully bedded and only the forward three or four inches of the forend free floated, here is a trick straight from a professional. Bed the barreled action in the newly applied Acraglas. Tighten all bedding or stock screws with care, then turn the rifle upside down in the vise so that the top of the barrel is upside down, trigger guard up. Make certain that the gun is locked securely in the vise and that the butt is properly supported. Now take a three to four pound weight and with the help of some tape or nylon fishing line, fasten the weight to the barrel in the area where the Acraglas makes contact with the barrel. Let the job dry completely in this manner. The result is that you have a fully bedded barrel and action except that the first few inches of the barrel are free floated where the steel enters the area of the barrel channel.

Start your glassbedding by carefully coating all metal parts that will contact the bedding compound with release agent. This includes the action, magazine, barrel, recoil lug and the bedding screws. The release agent is important and enough of the stuff comes with each package of Acraglas that you need not stint. If you are unlucky enough to get steel and bedding compound to make contact without the release agent, you will have an awful time cleaning up and removing the compound from the steel. To avoid having the bedding screws stick in the bedding compound, use plenty of release agent, making certain that all the threads of the screws are amply covered. Another way of getting this done is to use an ample amount of petroleum jelly so the screws will not set in the bedding compound. Should you somehow miss getting release agent or petroleum jelly on the screws and you find that they are locked tight, try heating the tip of the screws with your small soldering iron. Get the screws warm, but not hot, and they usually can then be turned out with the ratchet of your brace.

After removing all the wood that needs to be cut away, use masking tape on the outside of the forend, so that the tape forms a small trough. Make certain that you have enough tape fastened in place. Too much is easily trimmed off, but using too little means a last minute patch job on the tape trough.

Make up the fiberglass mixture, following the directions to the letter. There is a small vial of stain with each Acraglas package which may be added to give the mixture some color. Go easy on the stain as too much cannot be removed and a little of the stuff will do a lot of staining. Stir in the stain if you feel that you want to use it, then add the floc. In adding the floc, which is the glass compound, follow directions precisely. When you start mixing the compound, watch the timing. After adding the floc, stir the mix until it is creamy smooth. Spread the bedding compound, using the paddle that comes with the Acraglas, until the mix is evenly spread throughout the barrel channel and the recoil shoulder where the recoil lug contacts the shoulder. Press the barreled action into the mixture and tighten the bedding or stock screws.

Now let the job rest for several hours. By that time the surplus Acraglas will have oozed out of the barrel channel and can then be peeled off with a dull knife or a spatula. If the

To facilitate removal of barreled action from hardened bedding compound and stock, insertion of wooden dowel into chamber will make lifting simpler. Excess compound and masking tape may be removed prior to this step.

Work carefully and slowly during stock clean-up phase. Fine sandpaper on sanding block, followed by fine steel wool will remove traces of glass.

bedding compound has not settled fully, let the job sit longer and try again. The speed with which Acraglas or any other such compound sets depends on temperature and humidity and there is no way this can be rushed. Attempts to remove the excess too early or doing any other work on such a fresh bedding job will, in all probability, lead to an unsatisfactory job.

After the surplus fiberglass mixture is removed, I prefer to wait another twenty-four hours before doing any further work on the bedding. Under conditions of high humidity, very high or low temperatures, I prefer to let the Acraglas set thirty-six hours. If the Acraglas was mixed properly, you should be able to clean off accidental drippings, the surplus from the channel and action area, and do whatever stock finish retouching might be needed.

Remove the stock again and clean the release agent from all the metal parts. As mentioned before, if you have a very tight fit, use a rawhide mallet to tap the barreled action out of the stock. Remove the masking tape and clean off whatever Acraglas sticks to the stock where it should not be. Use very fine steel wool to remove any of the bedding compound that might stick to the steel. If you work carefully, you probably won't need to resort to any touch-up bluing. Use spot remover to get rid of the pink release agent and either alcohol or warm water to remove the green release agent. Some users of Acraglas have found that spots of the compound respond easily to a treatment with vinegar, and this is the suggested way to clean up hands and fingernails.

Spots of fiberglass that do not respond to scraping with a dull knife can be removed with very fine sandpaper. A bit of

Tru-Oil stock finish from the aerosol can will prove helpful to touch up the finish that might wear off during that operation.

Reassemble the rifle, tighten the bedding screws, clean up the bench and you have completed your first glassbedding job. Glassbedding jobs are plentiful once you learn how to handle the stuff and have gained some confidence in doing a job that is said to be so tricky that it had best be left to the professionals.

Here are a few of the more routine jobs for which I have found Acraglas useful: Bedding the recoil shoulder of a rifle that was kicking so hard that it began to wear out the recoil shoulder of the stock; glassbedding a side by side or an over/under shotgun; flowing small amounts of Acraglas into stock cracks to seal the crack permanently; anchoring inlays and grip caps with Acraglas; and sling swivel studs that have worked loose are refastened permanently with this. I have even repaired some of my pet tobacco pipes which developed cracks in the bowls with Acraglas with complete satisfaction.

Over the years I have kept a scrapbook of tricks I've heard about using a glassbedding compound. Here are several of them. When pouring or spooning the Acraglas into the action area of the stock, and to prevent having the stuff flow into the trigger mortise, use modeling clay. Acraglas won't stick to it and the clay is easily removed once the compound has set. Patternmakers used beeswax for the same purpose, while others have used tightly packed, nonsterile cotton.

If all the voids have not been filled on the first bedding, and before adding more Acraglas, be sure to remove all of the release agent where you want to add bedding. Very good results can be obtained from a second bedding and one gunsmith found that he gets excellent results by leaving out the floc completely. As mentioned above, go easy with adding stain to the Acraglas, as it is very easy to get the mix too dark. One stockmaker used the sawdust from his bench to add to the Acraglas. It worked like a charm and made the

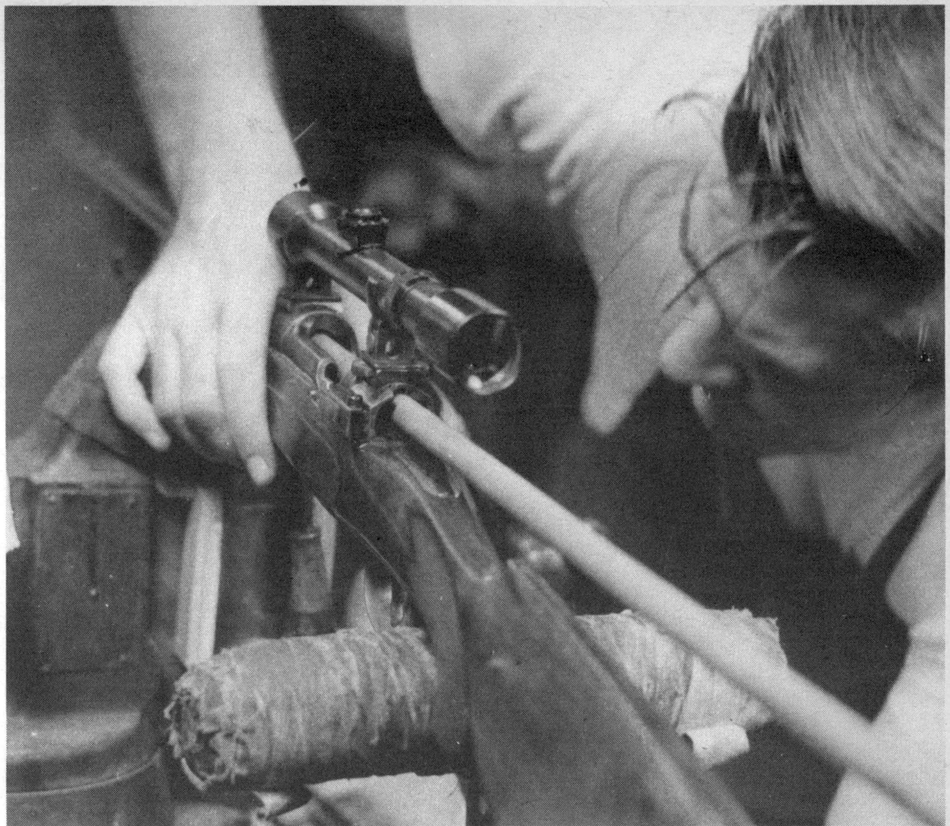

bedding look like wood. Taking the action out of the stock is made easier if the bolt is removed. To offer a better handle, use a two-foot length of dowel rod that has one end chamfered. Inserted into the rear bridge, it provides a perfect handle to lift the action with one hand, the barrel with the other.

To get the proper fit when bedding the recoil lug, some experienced gunsmiths have found that covering the front and sides of the recoil lug with the elastic electrician's tape gives just the right amount of relief when the screws are set. Apply enough release agent to the tape so that you won't have to dig and scrape the Acraglas out later on. Of course, the tape is peeled off before reassembly.

Needing only small amounts of Acraglas every so often, I first halved, then quartered the suggested amounts and still wound up pitching too much of the bedding compound out. One of the small, double-ended measuring spoons liberated from the kitchen is just what the doctor ordered. I can make up what I need in the precise proportions without having mixture left over. One user of the Brownell product reports that leftover Acraglas can be put in the freezer. Thaw out, then use as if it were freshly mixed, according to him. I have no idea how long Acraglas can be kept that way, but if its worked overnight, it should also be usable a week later as long as it is kept in a frozen state.

I have used Acraglas for a great many rather unconventional jobs around the gun room and the house. Any and all loose screws in wood can be reset with the stuff. Mixed with powdered aluminum or steel filings, it makes a dandy filler. On jobs where a strong glue joint is needed, I use Acraglas. For anchoring a contrasting wood block to the stock forend, it is hard to beat the bond that you can get with Acraglas.

Brownell's Acraglas bedding compound kit will set the home gunsmith back only about five bucks but will provide many times that value in accuracy.

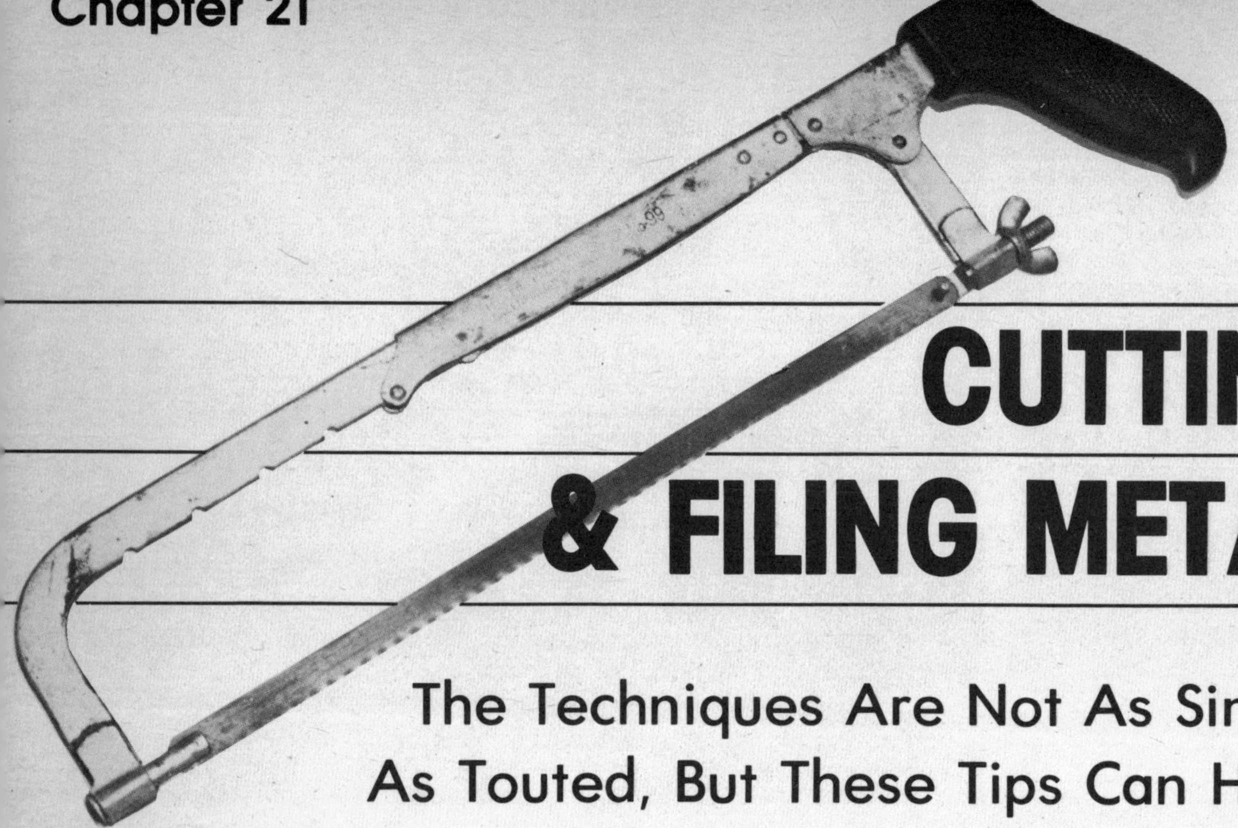

Chapter 21

CUTTING & FILING METAL

The Techniques Are Not As Simple As Touted, But These Tips Can Help!

MACHINISTS WHO have learned their trade well can take a chunk of steel and one hacksaw and cut themselves the neatest, truest and smoothest V-block you have ever seen. We mortals, less endowed with those skills, may run into trouble trying to whack off a piece of drill rod.

While you must learn the handling of the hacksaw and master the creation of an even and perhaps square cut yourself, a few pointers about hacksaws in general and hacksaw blades in particular are in order.

When buying a hacksaw frame, you have the choice of a fixed frame and an adjustable type, the latter being the better choice. Hacksaw blades range in length from eight to twelve inches, and the adjustable frame can accommodate any of these lengths, while the fixed frame can accommodate only one specific size. While the eight-inch

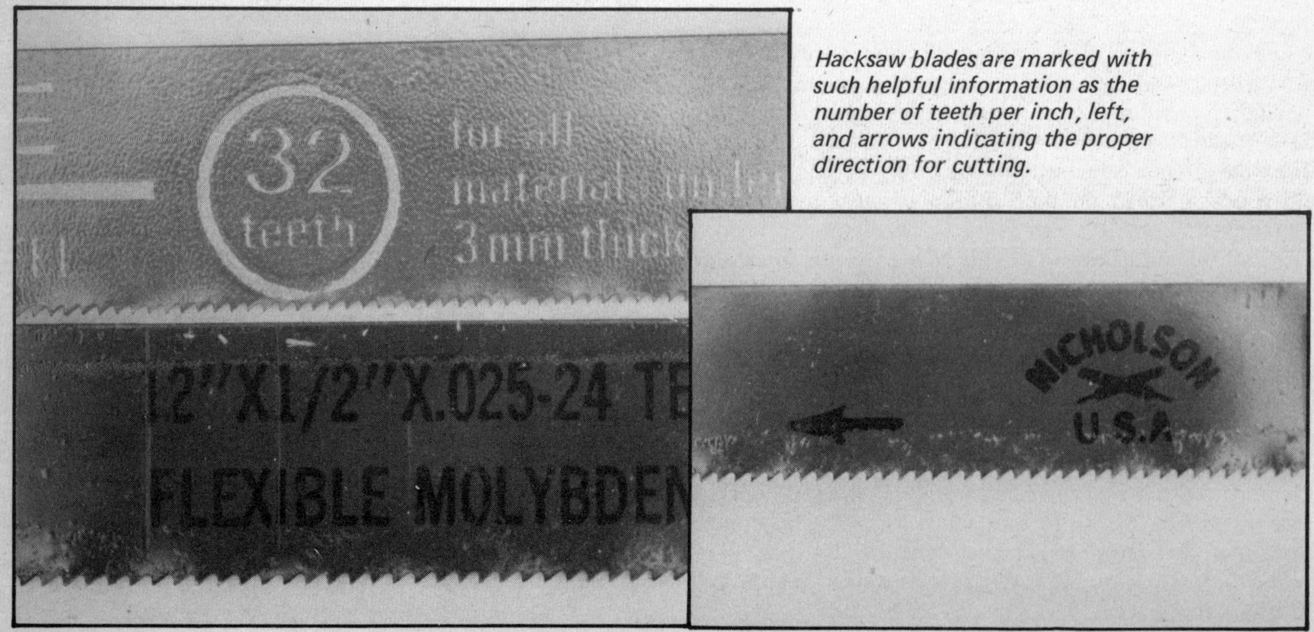

Hacksaw blades are marked with such helpful information as the number of teeth per inch, left, and arrows indicating the proper direction for cutting.

Cutting rods of harder materials may be done on edge of grinding wheel.

Small cut-off wheels, such as those designed for Dremel Moto-Tool, will cut most materials easily.

blade is adequate for most jobs, there are just enough jobs that come up where a twelve-inch blade would be handy. Hence, I favor the adjustable frame, and usually buy only longer blades.

Hacksaw blades are offered in three types or styles: the all-hard, the semi-flex, and the flexible back blade, with the latter the best choice as far as I'm concerned. On this type of blade only the teeth are hardened, and thanks to the soft back of the blade, the blade binds less often and there won't be as much blade breakage. The number of teeth per inch on the blade governs its ultimate use, and this is one of the secrets of doing good work with a hacksaw — selecting the right blade and not being afraid to switch blades when changing the type of stock you want to cut.

Soft metals, cast iron, bronze and the like are cut best with blades having fourteen teeth per inch. Tool steel, drill rods, high-speed steel and high-carbon steel are cut best with a blade that has eighteen teeth per inch, while twenty-four per inch blades are a good bet for cutting brass, copper, pipe and angle iron. The blade with thirty-two teeth per inch is usually reserved for cutting thin sheet metal, tubing and other thin stock.

Any metal to be cut should be locked into the bench vise. Thin-walled stock should be sandwiched by wood blocks, the blocks being cut with the metal at the same time. The saw blade is set into the frame so the teeth face forward; most of the better blades have a directional arrow that shows in which direction the teeth are to face.

Using a hacksaw is simple once the mechanics of cutting metal are understood. The hacksaw blade cuts on the forward stroke, and clears chips from the teeth on the

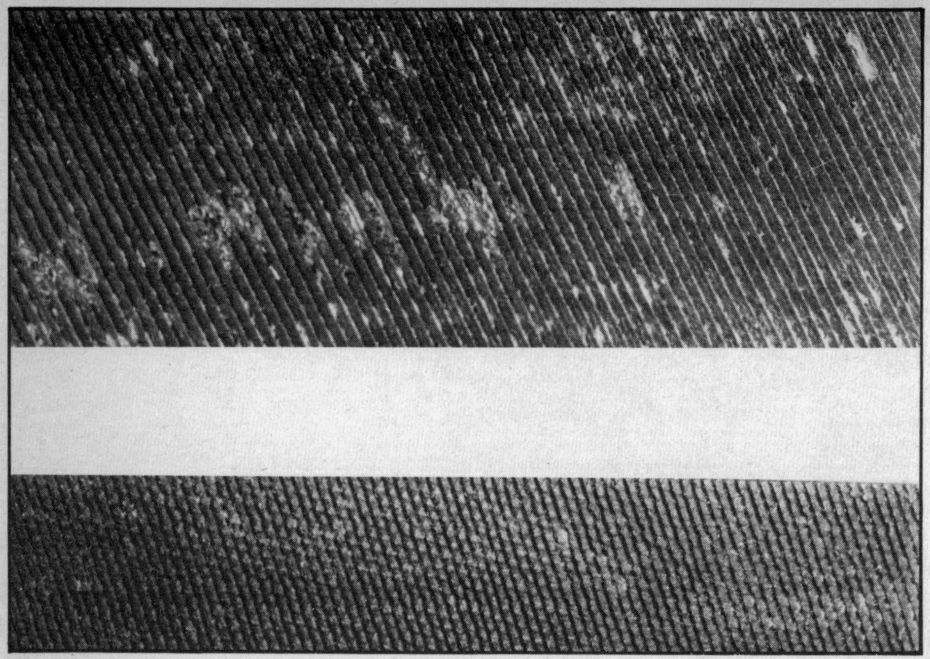

Single-cut file teeth, above, and double-cut file, below, left. Double-cut teeth have self-cleaning action when properly used.

backward stroke. If the saw binds or is pinched, you probably don't have enough pressure on the blade during the forward strokes. Use light pressure on the saw until the cut is well started. When starting a cut, use the thumb to guide and steady the blade. This not only establishes the cutting line, but helps keep the blade at the required ninety-degree angle to the work.

In drilling metals, cutting oil is used to reduce friction and the generated heat. A couple drops of cutting oil applied every so often to the cut being made by a hacksaw will make cutting easier and faster.

One of the most important tools on my bench is a jeweler's saw. The one I use is sold by Brownell's as a gunsmith bench saw. I like it a bit better than the conventional jeweler's saw since the blade is stiffer, hence does not break. A set of fine and extra-fine blades makes this a versatile tool. This saw can be used dry, since most of the cuts made with it do not go through very thick or heavy stock.

Every so often you find that some long pin or rod is so hard that cutting with a hacksaw is considerable work. In such cases, use the edge of the grinding wheel, making certain you quench the hot cut so as not to draw the temper and soften the material unduly.

If the stock isn't too thick, you can use the Dremel Moto-Tool with a cut-off wheel. The abrasive wheels are handy to shorten screws and pins, but the smaller wheels are not suitable for cutting heavy stock. When using a cut-off wheel of any kind, or when using the bench grinder for this purpose, wear eye protection and a plastic face

File card, left, or brush is essential item for home gunsmith's shop and should be used to clean file teeth. File-tapering steel rod is facilitated by locking stock in lathe chuck, as shown below.

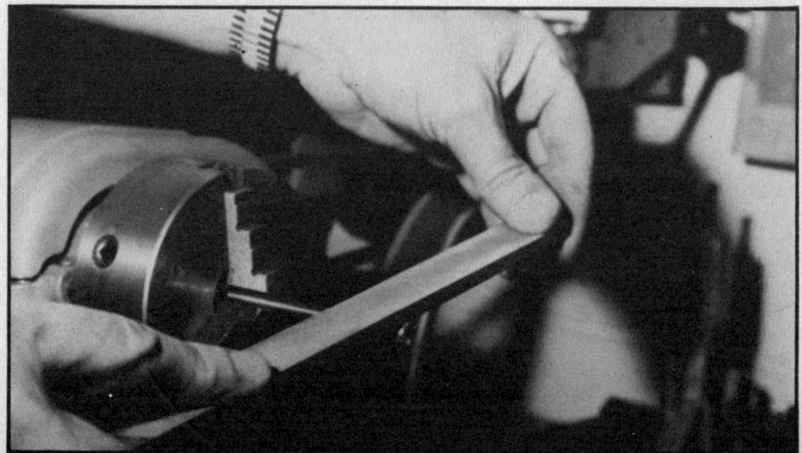

HOME GUNSMITHING DIGEST

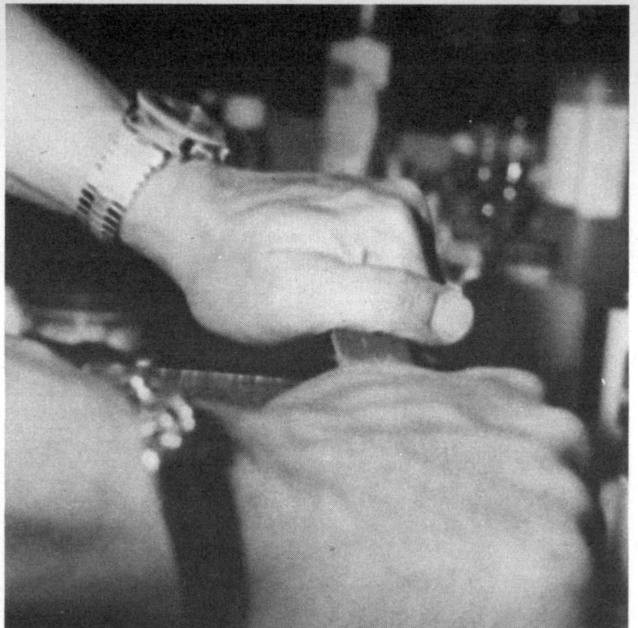

shield. A thin wheel, when forced, can shatter and the flying pieces become dangerous missiles. Larger cut-off wheels can be used in any electric drill or on a drill press.

Depending on the type of cut-off wheel, the speed at which the wheel should be run usually is marked on the package and on the wheel; this speed should not be exceeded. Thus, speed reduction on the pulleys of the drill press may have to be made. If the stock being cut with a wheel is thick, don't try to force it, but take several shallow cuts.

You may note a wobble in the wheel. This disappears once the wheel begins to cut and has entered the material. No lube is used with cut-off wheels and, depending on the hardness of the material being cut and the cutting speed used, wheels may need to be replaced often.

Round stock of all types can be cut accurately and quickly on a lathe with a cut-off wheel or tool. If this is not available, you can use any other cutter to reduce the circumference of the work, then cut the rest with a hacksaw. Most cutting operations on the lathe must be set up so the work is supported in the head stock on one end, with a steady rest and perhaps a follower rest at the other end.

A lathe, drill press or even an electric drill can be used — the latter only if the work is short — to polish, file or trim the cut edge. A slight chamfer is needed if, for instance, a piece of rod is to be threaded. The chamfering or slight tapering is essential for the threading die to get the proper bite in the metal.

Although cutting metals is not difficult, a slight goof is often impossible to correct. Many mistakes made in metal working can be traced back to the fact that the job was not marked suitably or the markings were wiped off accidentally.

A can of layout blue will last a lifetime and once you have used it, you will wonder how you ever got along without it. Layout blue is brushed onto whatever you need to mark, then permitted to air dry. Pencil, felt pen and scribe marks are readily visible and won't rub off, yet it washes off easily with denatured alcohol.

In marking round or hexagonal stock, be sure to mark the entire circumference of the cut to be made, since you may want to rotate the work so the weight of the cut-off piece doesn't bind the saw. Square or rectangular stock should be marked with a machinist's square; if the edges are not square, true them off if you can. Should you feel this is beyond your capabilities, take the piece to a machine shop and have it trued off on a surface grinder.

Anyone can take a file to a piece of metal stroke the file across the surface, and mess up the job royally. Filing is an art that requires practice, but once you have mastered it, you won't forget it. The body of the file is first cut to give it the required number and size of teeth, then is hardened. The tang — the part where the handle goes — is not hardened to keep it from breaking when pressure is applied. Six different types of cuts are used, with teeth either single or double cut. The number of teeth per inch gives the file its name and application.

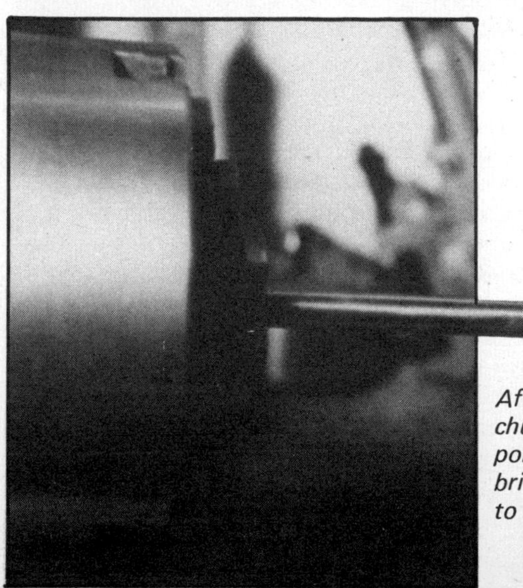

After filing chucked rod, polishing cloth brings stock to mirror finish.

Using a strip of abrasive cloth in the same manner as a shoe rag, a bright polish on round stock is obtained.

Type of Cut	Number of Teeth per Inch
Rough Cut	20
Middle Cut	25
Bastard	30
Second Cut	40
Smooth Cut	50-60
Dead Cut	100 or more

Single-cut files are used for hard metals, and special files are made for some specific metals. For the average home shop, a set of good files can be used for most jobs if the files are cleaned properly and cared for.

When a file has no teeth on one side, it is said to have a "safe" side and this can be used for such cuts as the dovetails for a sight. Files come in a variety of shapes, and a set of fine Swiss or needle files is handy to have on the bench. These files need not be set into handles, but larger files should have handles since a slip from the steel shaft can produce a painful and slow-healing wound in the palm.

A file card or file brush is essential; even if you can't see that the teeth of the file are clogged, believe me, they are and need cleaning.

Experienced machinists sometimes fall into the evil habit of knocking the edge of the file against the vise, or worse yet, on the ways of the lathe. That is the easiest and also the fastest way to mess up a good file or a lathe bed. To slow down clogging of the file cut, run a piece of blackboard chalk over the teeth until they seem to be filled with chalk dust.

Good files are an investment and should be treated as such. I tried just once to make do with some cheap files, and the darned things were so poorly hardened they didn't even make up into decent chisels and were finally converted into screwdrivers. Files should be hung up so they don't touch each other. Tossing them into a drawer is not the way to treat a good tool.

Running a file back and forth over a hunk of steel would seem to be a simple matter. Unfortunately, it is not quite as simple as it sounds. Basically there are three types of filing. Straight filing means that the file is pushed either straight with or at a slight angle to the piece being filed. In straight filing, the file will cut only on the forward stroke, and the file should be lifted off the work for the return stroke.

In draw filing, you grasp the file at both ends, then push and draw the file across the surface being worked. Draw filing is done best with a mill file for a fine finish. This type of filing is used to remove tool marks created by another file, a lathe or a milling cutter. The classic way to position a file for draw filing is at a right angle to the work, but a smoother finish can be achieved by angling the file slightly. Apply moderate pressure with the file, and change the contact point often so the same teeth aren't being used constantly. Softer metals, such as aluminum, brass and copper will clog a file very quickly, so don't forget to clean the file frequently and chalk the teeth as needed.

Uneven hand pressure on the front and rear of a file as well as rocking the file creates major problems. Rock the file just a few times across a flat, narrow edge of some piece of scrap in the vise, then put a straight edge on it and see how the flat line is now convex. A convex surface also is indicative of the file not being held level and square to the work. In checking to see if an edge or angle is true, you need not only a machinist's square but something that will act in lieu of a surface plate. If you have a drill press, chances are its table was ground. If so, you can use this as a surface plate.

An inexpensive surface plate can be made with a piece of half-inch-thick plate glass. Have the edges ground, then set it on a level surface. You now are the proud owner of a surface plate that cost one-tenth the price of a commercial type.

Lathe filing is the simplest type of filing which one can master quite quickly, providing he has a lathe. I've never had much luck with lathe filing on the Unimat, but the bigger tools such as a small armature lathe that runs six inches or bigger are suitable for most lathe filing jobs. The headstocks on the big production machines usually are too high and too large for comfortable filing. With smaller lathes, such as the six-incher, the problem may be that the stock that needs work is too big for the headstock.

In lathe filing the file is not held steady, but is stroked forward, then lifted and brought back. Angling the file slightly will help to clear the file of chips and will aid in getting a ridgeless finish. If the work to be lathe filed is long, it must be supported in one or more locations with the steady rest, a follower rest or both.

A fine finish can be achieved if a piece, after filing, is polished while running in a lathe. For steels and other hard metals, strips of aluminum oxide abrasive cloth are used, while non-ferrous metals are polished with strips of silicon carbide cloth. Run the lathe at about 5000 revolutions per minute surface speed, and if a tail stock is used be sure that the center is not too tight against the work. If running on centers, do not forget to lubricate them.

Start polishing with 80 grit cloth, and use 120 or finer grit for the final polishing. Some machinists feel a few drops of oil on the polishing cloth give a better and smoother finish, while others prefer to use three or even four grits for their dry polishing.

The gunsmithing field requires a number of special files. Mentioned were the fine needle files which come in a variety of shapes. These files usually are not equipped with handles, since they aren't meant to remove large quantities of metal, but are designed primarily for shaping small areas. The dovetail or sight slot files usually have two safe sides. The screw slot files also have two safe sides, these being the wide sides of the file body.

If you become interested in filing — and many consider this to be a metalworking art form — find a master machinist who is willing to let you watch. I've seen such a man take a round barrel and, with nothing more than three files and a small machinist square, convert that round tube into a hexagonal barrel which retained its cylindrical shape in the action area. Since filing motion comes from the shoulder, it is important to have the vise and your shoulders at the right level. For removing metal quickly, a fair bit of pressure must be exerted on the file, hence you often will see that master filers stand on a little platform at their vise. That extra two or three inches gives them the leverage needed for rough filing.

Filing a straight line is difficult. One way to be sure you follow the scribed line is to clamp the work into the vise so the piece being filed is just a hair above the jaws of the vise. If the jaws of the vise are not long enough, use some bar stock on both sides of the work for holding the work and as a filing guide. Thin stock will vibrate and screech under the file, so clamp with bar stock and let the surface project out of the clamping stock just enough to get the filing done.

Frequently the first-time filer will assume his file is worn out when it does not cut. It takes a long time and quite a bit of work to wear out a file, so more than likely, the file teeth are clogged. Sometimes the suggestion is made to oil the teeth lightly to prevent clogging, but when the file is permitted to rest, the gummed oil and metal chips will cut down on the effectiveness of the file. The use of a wire wheel on either an electric drill, drill press, or a grinder often will clear the clogged teeth of a file, especially when filing a soft metal such as aluminum.

In contrast to sandpaper where a sanding block or the fingers bear down on the paper, emery cloth never should be backed with anything, least of all your fingers. If you apply pressure to the emery cloth, then put a straight edge on the work, you almost certainly will have ridges and waves. On rounded surfaces, emery cloth is used much like a shoeshine cloth. On the lathe and drill press, the cloth or strip is held the same way, against the pressure of the turning work, and the strip is "walked" up and down the work. A conventional sanding block sometimes is used with emery cloth when the surface to be polished is quite large, but this is a job for an expert polisher with a skill level few of us can hope to attain.

Although the gunsmith is not often faced with the question as to the precise degree of hardness a piece of steel might have, a file can be used to estimate the hardness.

Metal hardness is tested on several different scales, such as the Rockwell and the Brinell. Each of these has several sub-scales. The one most frequently used in gun work is the Rockwell C scale. Using the corner of a sharp file, stroke across the metal you are testing and note the resistance

your file encounters. On steel that is thought to be extremely hard, never use the teeth on the face of the file, since the steel could ruin the teeth. Although this is only a guide, the estimate is quite close to actual measurements once you have learned to gauge the resistance the metal offers the file teeth.

Estimated Metal Hardness Test With File

What Happens	Rockwell C Scale approx.
With slight pressure, file removes metal	20
Some degree of resistance is felt on file as it cuts	30
Metal is cut with difficulty	40
File barely cuts metal	50
File slides over metal without cutting it	57

This guide is accurate enough for 99.9 percent of the gunsmithing you are likely to tackle. The Ames Precision Machine Company produces a small portable hardness tester which is suitable for relatively small pieces of work. The larger units cost several thousand dollars and belong in a production shop or on the bench in an inspection lab.

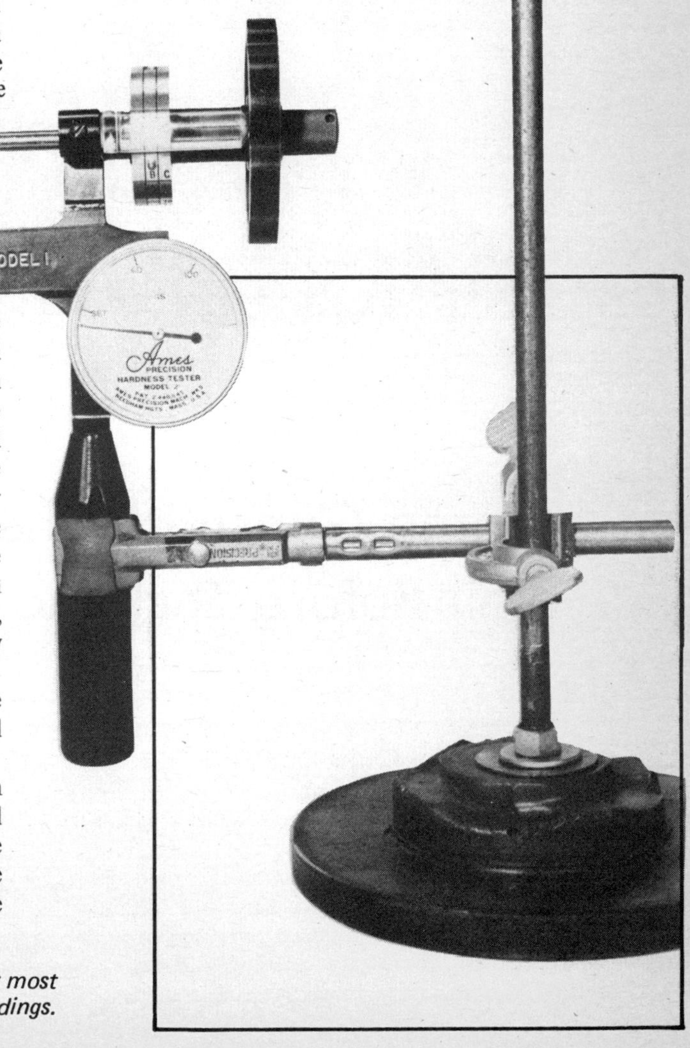

Ames Hardness Tester is an expensive item for most gunsmiths, but gives precise metal hardness readings.

Chapter 22

DRILLS, TAPS, DIES & WHAT TO DO WITH THEM

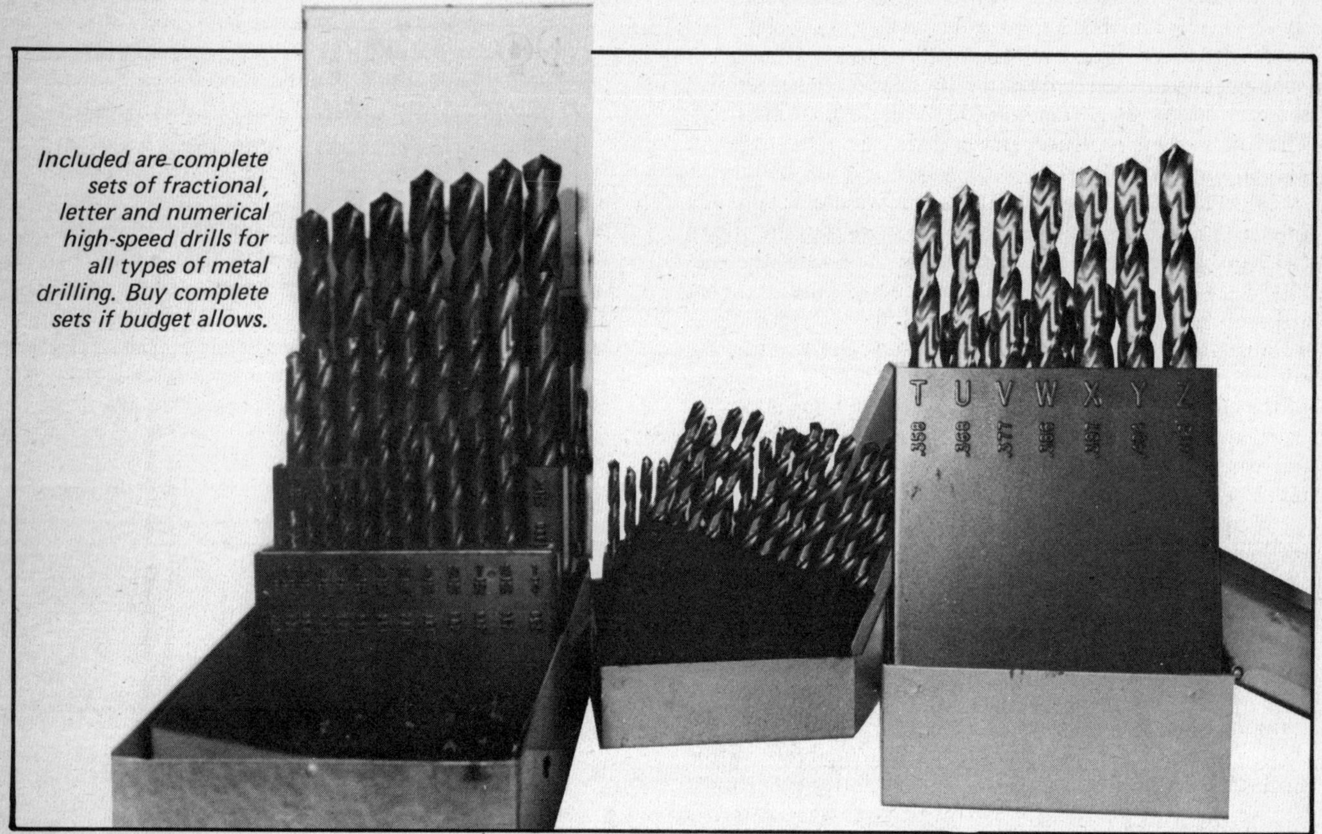

The Home Gunsmith Should Learn His Lessons Well Before Tackling Expensive Projects!

IF YOU EXPECT to do much drilling, you need an electric drill as the basic minimum. The usual quarter-inch drill is barely adequate, and a much better investment is either a three-eighths or a half-inch drill, complete with a stand.

If permanent installation of a stand is not possible, make provisions to clamp the stand to the bench top, although mounting with bolts is better so the clamps won't be in the way — and they usually do get in the way at the most critical times.

A bench-mounted drill press is a worthwhile investment, since it has much more versatility than any portable drill. When buying a drill press, be sure to get the instruction manual with it so you can study the pulley arrangements for either speeding up or slowing down the spindle. As a general rule of thumb, drilling holes in wood and other woodworking jobs call for the drill to run at near-maximum rpms, while for metalworking, the drill must be slowed down.

Most drill presses have step-type pulleys and the motor mount can be moved back and forth to make spindle speed changing easy. When the belt runs from the large pulley on

the motor shaft to the small one on the spindle, you will get maximum rpms, while the spindle will run at minimum rpms when the belt goes from the small pulley on the motor shaft to the large one on the spindle.

The run-of-the-mill drills available in most hardware stores are just that. They can be used for some wood drilling and for making holes in some metals, but for precision work in either medium, such drills will wear rapidly and more than likely will burn out when either run or fed too fast. Brad point drills are fairly expensive, but will outlast most other drills, even when working with tough stock woods. For woodworking of any kind, I favor those drills over most other kinds, excepting cabinetmaker's drills.

Never attempt to use a drill bit designed for wood on metal and vice versa. Wood drill bits come in fractional sizes, and special ones can be bought which allow you to use a bit larger than a quarter inch in a quarter-inch electric drill. Drill bits designed for metal drilling come in three designations plus metric. Twist drills are sold either as single units or in sets. I suggest that you start with the most complete set you can afford.

DRILL DESIGNATIONS

Numerical: The smallest one is the No. 80 drill which has a diameter of 0.0135-inch, while the largest one carries the No. 1 and measures 0.228-inch. The difference in size from one number to the next is not uniform in this system.

Alphabetical: Goes from letter A to letter Z, or from 0.234 to 0.413-inches. Here too there is no uniformity in the increase or decrease in size, hence you must measure or check the table to get the size of a specific letter drill.

Fractional: This designation starts with a one-sixty-fourth-inch drill which measures 0.0156-inch and goes on up to drills larger than four inches. Increments are one-sixty-fourth of an inch in sizes up to about two inches.

Metric: Size increments are 0.1mm from the small 0.5mm drill to the 10.0mm drill, and drills larger than 10mm come in 0.5mm increments. Until use of the metric system becomes more widespread, don't bother getting a metric set of twist drills.

Medium hard steels, such as those found in many firearms receivers, are drilled best with special cobalt drills. These, as well as many other specialized drills, can be bought from Brownell's, Mittermeier and others. For steels with a Rockwell rating higher than 40 on the C scale, solid

Drill Sizes

Size	Dec.	Size	Dec.	Size	Dec.	Size	Dec.
80	0.0135	49	0.073	20	0.161	I	0.272
79	0.0145	48	0.076	19	0.166	J	0.277
1/64	0.0156	5/64	0.0781	18	0.1695	9/32	0.2813
78	0.016	47	0.0785	11/64	0.1719	K	0.281
77	0.018	46	0.081	17	0.173	L	0.290
76	0.02	45	0.082	16	0.177	M	0.295
75	0.021	44	0.086	15	0.18	19/64	0.2969
74	0.0225	43	0.089	14	0.182	N	0.302
73	0.024	42	0.0935	13	0.185	5/16	0.3125
72	0.025	3/32	0.0938	3/16	0.1875	O	0.316
71	0.026	41	0.096	12	0.189	P	0.323
70	0.028	40	0.098	11	0.191	21/64	0.328
69	0.0292	39	0.0995	10	0.1935	Q	0.332
68	0.031	38	0.1015	9	0.196	R	0.339
1/32	0.0313	37	0.104	8	0.199	11/32	0.34375
67	0.032	36	0.1065	7	0.201	S	0.348
66	0.028	7/64	0.1094	13/64	0.203	T	0.358
65	0.035	35	0.11	6	0.204	23/64	0.359
64	0.036	34	0.111	5	0.2055	U	0.368
63	0.037	33	0.113	4	0.209	3/8	0.375
62	0.038	32	0.116	3	0.213	V	0.377
61	0.039	31	0.12	7/32	0.21875	W	0.386
60	0.04	1/8	0.125	2	0.221	25/64	0.3906
59	0.041	30	0.1285	1	0.228	X	0.397
58	0.042	29	0.136	A	0.234	Y	0.404
57	0.043	9/64	0.1406	15/64	0.2344	13/32	0.4063
56	0.0465	28	0.1405	B	0.238	Z	0.413
3/64	0.0469	27	0.144	C	0.242		
55	0.052	26	0.147	D	0.246		
54	0.055	25	0.1495	1/4	0.250		
53	0.0595	24	0.152	E	0.250		
1/16	0.0625	23	0.154	F	0.257		
52	0.0635	5/32	0.15625	G	0.261		
51	0.067	22	0.157	17/64	0.2656		
50	0.07	21	0.159	H	0.266		

Drill size (inches)	DRILLING SPEED (RPMs)			
	Brass	Cast iron	Mild steel	Stainless steel
1/16	12,000	6,000	4,800	3,000
1/8	6,000	3,000	2,400	1,500
1/4	3,000	1,530	1,200	1,000
3/8	2,000	1,000	815	500
1/2	1,530	760	610	380
5/8	1,220	610	490	300
3/4	1,000	500	400	250
7/8	875	440	350	220
1	760	380	300	190

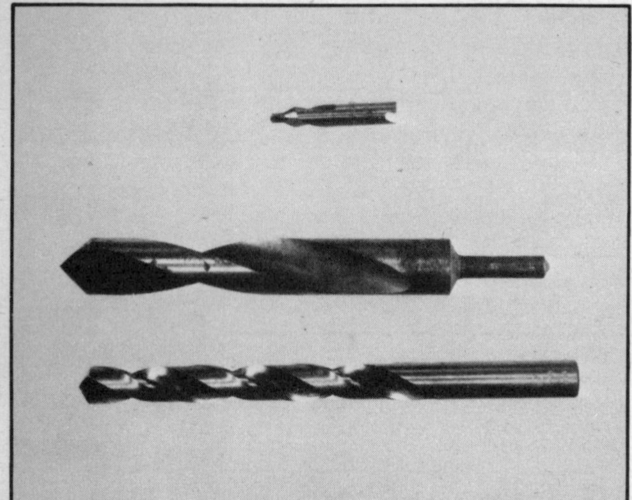

Above (from top): Countersink used in lathe work; a wood bit with its recessed shoulder; high-speed drill for use in metal. (Right) Bolts and hold-down bars are needed to hold vises or the work securely on table of a drill press.

carbide drills are the best choice. Because of their high cost, buy only what you need when you need it. Carbide-tipped twist drills will sometimes do the job and are less costly, but these bits must be handled with care when bottoming out since they tend to snap off.

Carbon steel twist drills are probably the cheapest ones and will not last long, especially when drilling fairly hard wood or steel. The high speed or HS drills have greater versatility and will last longer than the less expensive ones.

A drill must not only be sharp, but also run true, that is, at a ninety-degree angle to the drilling surface. Hard steel being drilled must be clamped into the drill press vise or held solidly in some other way, since the pressure of the drill on the steel can shift the work or even force the drill off its path. If this happens, an oval rather than a round hole is the result. Truth to tell, few machinists are good at regrinding drill tips. Despite numerous attempts at

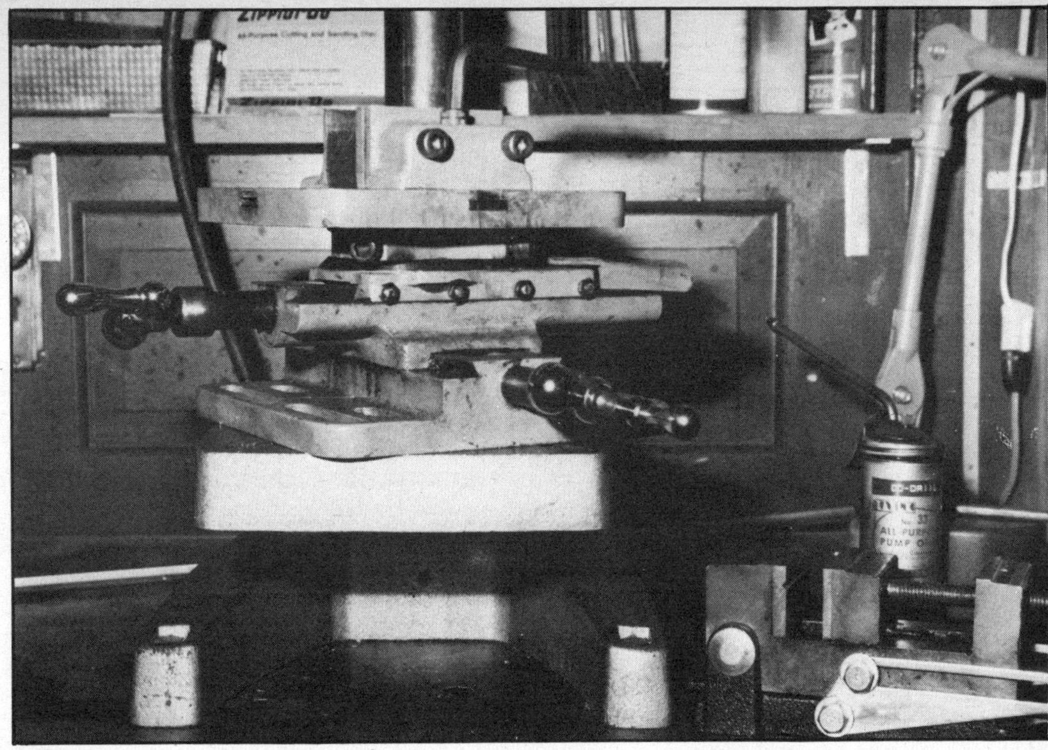

Essential for some jobs is compound vise. The smaller machinist vise on bench holds small parts; it can be bolted to table of drill press.

sharpening bits, I never have gotten a good point on any bit, even when using the allegedly goof-proof drill sharpening stands or holders. The electric drill tip sharpeners which work somewhat like electric pencil sharpeners are useless. If you can master the art of sharpening a drill bit with a grinding wheel, you then can give the drill tips whatever special angle you need or want.

The angle of the two cutting blades of the drill tip govern the ultimate use of the bit to some extent. Generally, for thin sheets of materials or very hard ones, an eighty-eight-degree angle is suggested for sharpening a drill bit. A sixty-eight-degree angle is usually indicated for production use where drills one quarter inch or smaller are used, while the fifty-nine-degree tip is the one most widely used for general shop use, and a forty-nine-degree tip angle is recommended for soft metals such as copper.

A trick I learned from an old-time carpenter for drilling wood or making such things as loading blocks, is to mark each point where the bit is to enter, then use a large nail to start the hole. This, of course, is essentially the same thing as using a centerpunch when drilling metal. Centerpunching is important, whether drilling into a flat or a round surface. If the metal to be drilled is extra hard or thick, many machinists use a slightly smaller drill bit to start the hole. In drilling through thin stock or sheet metal, be sure that the work not only is anchored securely, but that there is a wood backing board under the area where you expect the drill to bottom out.

Running spindle speed for wood and metal was mentioned earlier in this chapter. Smaller drill bits should

Work to be drilled is locked into 3-jaw chuck of lathe, drill is locked into chuck in tail stock, which is moved so drill slowly makes contact with the rotating work.

be operated at higher spindle speeds than the bigger bits, HS drills are the most widely used ones.

A few words should be said about drill presses and the accessories needed. If a new machine is not within your budget, shop around for a used model. When you find one that looks reasonably good — and there is a motor with it — ask to see it in operation. A bent spindle throws the whole machine out of whack and, if a drill locked into the chuck

goes around like an egg beater, stay clear of the tool unless you want to tackle a spindle replacement job. Though not difficult to switch, you have to have the correct spindle for the tool, and finding the right one may be a time-consuming job.

The table of most drill presses is slotted as well as grooved. The slots are used to anchor vises, clamps and other holding gadgets with bolts and nuts, while the grooves serve as bases for the sliding vises which are handy for milling, engine turning and other jobs. A machinist's vise is essential, and the Atlas Universal Compound vise, though fairly costly, is one piece of equipment you should have. Some drill presses have a tilting table which might be a nice feature, but I've never felt the need for it.

New drill presses must be wired, while a used one might well have a motor with it. Some of the home shop machines have cut-off switches installed, others come without. Much depends here on what kind of stand you have, buy or make. Some machinists favor the dead-man's switch, which is foot operated. Remove the weight from the switch and the machine shuts off; it will not start again until the required weight is again placed on the switch. I found such a foot release switch more of a hazard and general nuisance, so did away with it. But you have to judge for yourself.

A couple of box or open-end wrenches for the hold-down bolts, a ballpeen hammer to drift wedges into place, a chip brush and a couple of oil cans round out the needed equipment.

When drilling metal, always use a lube; cutting oil is the best choice. I have used a number of other lubes, but keep coming back to Brownell's Do-Drill which I also use on the lathe. Keep the drill press table clean of chips and spattered oil and clean the column every so often. To keep the table

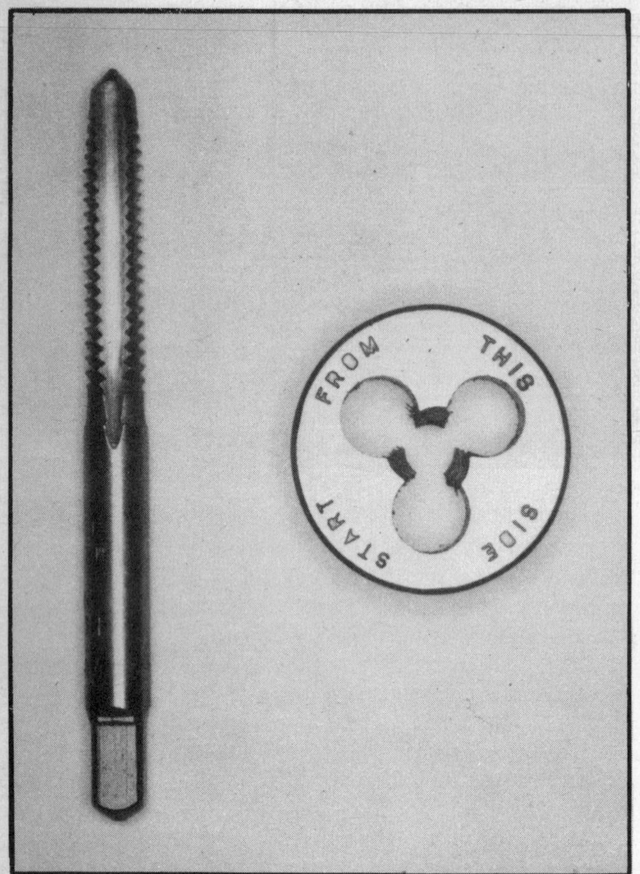

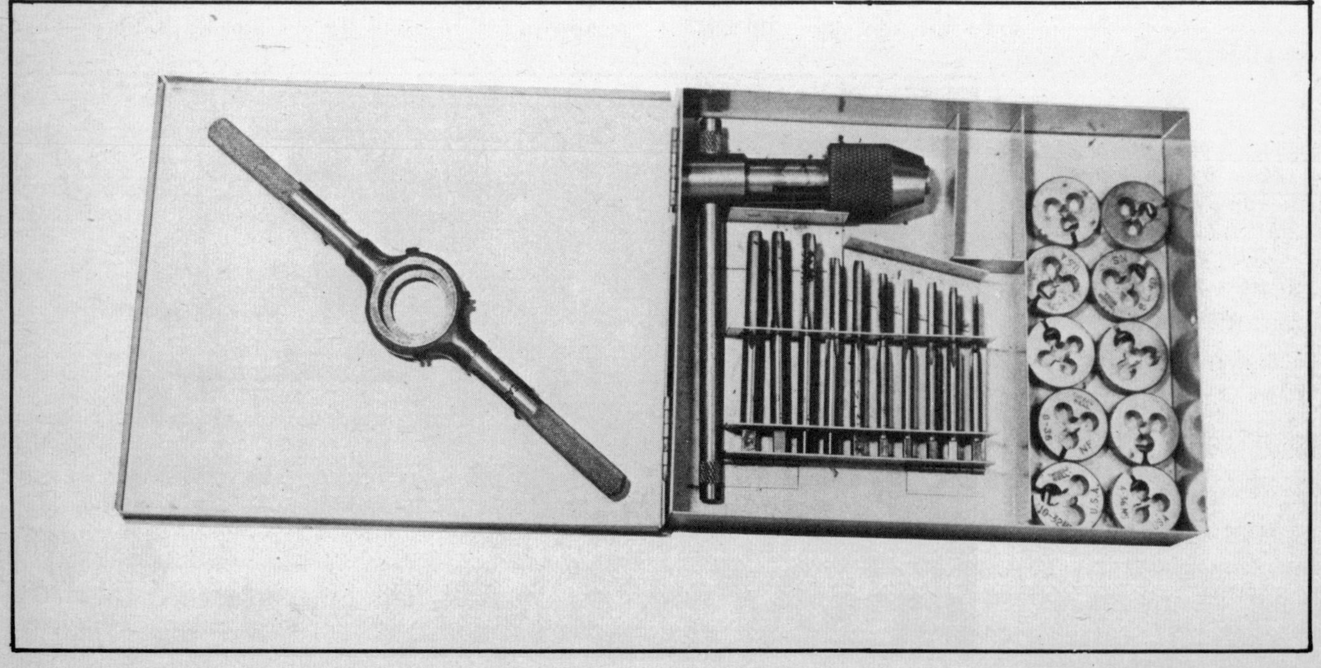

Left: The tap cuts internal threads, die cuts externally. Both are hand operated. Note marking on die. On reverse side is thread designation. (Below) Small tap/die set is adequate for most jobs. Buy only taps, dies needed.

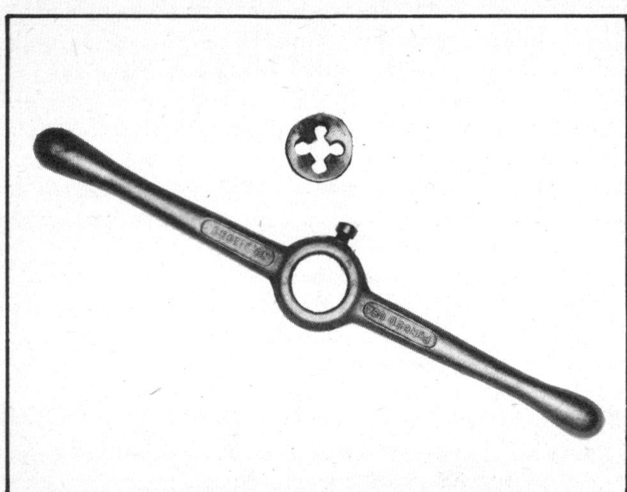

Die is locked into die stock for threading, is held in
place with set screw with screw bottoming into a small
hole in side of die. Lock securely so die can't slip.

sliding and all parts rust free, I use liberal amounts of
WD-40 which I keep on the bench in a spray can.

Deep hole drilling calls for special drills and techniques,
but gun work usually doesn't call for this type of job. The
same can be said for reamers. Most of the holes you will
need to drill will go into and perhaps through relatively thin
metal. Deeper holes seldom are drilled out true and even
more infrequently come out perfectly aligned. These holes
are finished with a reamer, which is a fluted metal cutting
tool. As reamers are hand-turned, it is best to use a tap

wrench and exert only slight downward pressure. Never try
to run a reamer in a drill press or an electric drill, and leave
chambering reamers to the professionals.

A lathe allows you to do a considerable amount of
horizontal drilling, reaming and boring, as well as making
inside threads. If the lathe is equipped with a gear shift
lever, changing the turning speed of the lathe is simple. But
if there is no lever, all of the gears must be changed in order
to change the turning speed.

I made the mistake of holding out for a lathe without
the automatic gear changer, and now spend more time
changing gears than running the lathe.

Most lathe operations also must be lubed, and one can
use either a cutting oil like Brownell's Do-Drill, or a
semi-solid lube called Lubri-Cut. I began using the latter
some years ago, when I was doing some major shop jobs on
my little six-inch lathe. I liked it so well I now use it a great
deal, especially on jobs where I want to reduce oil
spattering.

In contrast to the drill press where the spindle rotates
and moves the drill bit into the work being drilled, on the
lathe the work is held in the spinning chuck, and the drill,
set into the non-rotating tailgate chuck, is moved against
the revolving work.

Cutting an internal or external thread, or recutting a
damaged one is a job that can be learned easily and one that
will be needed every so often. The internal thread cutter,
called the tap, is important in gunsmithing, since holes
drilled for scope or sight installation must be threaded for
the mounting screws. The process of making those internal
threads is called tapping, and only hand-held taps are used
— this in contrast to machine tapping. Since the trueness of

SCOPE MOUNT SOCKET SCREW SET — B-Square Co., Box 11281, Ft. Worth, Tex. 76109

REDFIELD RING (32) 5-44 x .235	LEUPOLD RING (16) 8-40 x .275	RUGER RING (24) 6-40 x .275	WEAVER SAKO RING (16) 6-40 x .25	WEAVER TIP-OFF CLAMP (4) 6-48 x .313	IMPORT RING (8) 6-32 x .25
REDFIELD LEUPOLD BASE (12) 6-48 x .235	REDFIELD LEUPOLD BASE (3200 RING) (10) 6-48 x .295	REDFIELD LEUPOLD BASE (12) 6-48 x .345	REDFIELD LEUPOLD BASE (3 each) 6-48 x .395 / 6-48 x .550	B-SQUARE SCREWS SPECIAL ASS'T (12)	WEAVER BASE (8) 8-40 x .245
REDFIELD BASE (4) 8-40 x .250	REDFIELD BASE (4) 8-40 x .315	REDFIELD BASE (4) 8-40 x .505	WEAVER BASE (10) 6-48 x .180	WEAVER BASE (8) 6-48 x .255	WEAVER BASE (10) 6-48 x .288

Left: (above) Pitch gauges are used to check thread size. At top is U.S. thread pitch gauge, in center is one for British threads, at bottom is one for metric measurement. (Right, above) A box of assorted gun mounting screws can be used not only to complete jobs, but also to check the threads. This B-Square set features socket head screws.

the threads is vital, most gunsmiths do not use the tap by hand, but use the drill press or a special tapping wrench that is locked into the chuck of the drill press.

The tap's square end is set into a tap wrench for most jobs, but if precision is called for, the B-Square Tru Tapper is the tool to reach for. Essentially, this is a tap wrench with a centered sliding rod, the upper end of which is locked into the chuck of the drill press. Thus, the tapper will run into the hole at the same angle as the drill; and tapping is done by rotating the Tru Tapper back and forth, using cutting oil.

The precision job required for sight or scope mounting calls for precision taps. Taps found in hardware shops may be fine for working on a lawnmower, but their design is not suitable for gunsmithing work, even if the correct size. In precision tap sets — the only ones worth having on the bench — each size tap is represented by three different taps. These are the taper tap, the plug tap and the bottom tap. The taper tap is used to start the thread in the hole. It is ground to a long taper which acts as a guide for the tap in the hole. The taper tap has a self-guiding cutting bevel, but this doesn't mean that it can't cut a hole crooked if started that way.

The long taper tap doesn't reach far into the drilled hole, and the plug tap then is used to finish the threading. For blind holes — holes which do not bottom out such as scope mounting holes — a special bottom tap is needed to cut the thread to the bottom of the hole. The tap itself is square at the bottom so it does not cut deeper.

The tap cuts internal threads, while the die makes external threads. Split dies are better, since they are easier to start squarely on the work. When threading a rod, taper the end where you want to start the threads. The chamfer or taper can be put on either by filing while the stock is turning in a lathe, or with a grinder. The die is held in the holder known as the die stock, and dies are marked as to which end goes toward the work. To start the die, hold the palm of one hand on top of the die which is locked into the die stock. Be sure that the die starts squarely with the work. Use plenty of cutting oil and work slowly. Rotate the die stock one-half to three-quarters of a turn clockwise, then turn it counterclockwise to break the chips. Cut slowly, use oil and break and clear the chips frequently, especially when cutting a long thread. Check your work often by turning the die off the threads.

When buying taps and dies, you can either buy the various sets available, or you can buy only what you actually need. Special taps and dies for gunsmithing can be bought separately from Mittermeier, Brownell's and from the B-Square Company. Thread designations are given in number of threads per inch. The metric and the British Whitworth threads are little used in gunsmithing.

Threads are a science in themselves, but you will encounter only three major designations: NF which indicates National Fine; NC referring to National Coarse; and NS or UNS for National Standard, where threads of less than 0.25-inch are designated in fractions. NEF is the abbreviation for National Extra Fine, and is seen on taps and dies for some gunsmithing jobs, such as 5/16x32 NEF.

Compressed air is a boon to the gunsmith, but when blowing chips away from freshly cut work, shield your eyes. When running the first nut on an external thread, be sure to get all of the chips out of the threads, then use oil or lube on the nut or bolt. If you forget this lubrication, it is possible to freeze the thread as it is being turned out. That means a wrecked job.

Dies larger than half-inch are seldom needed for any home gunsmithing jobs, and you are getting into a different

Threading tool or cutter on lathe has been moved back to show the threaded stock for custom loading die.

Threading job has been oiled so the friction of turning stock will not damage the tool.

ball game with the larger taps and dies. Threading pipe requires special dies, of course, but essentially the same techniques are required. Knowing how to thread pipe comes in handy when you want to make light stands for photo floods or stands for chronograph screens, and many other jobs.

Every so often you may find that someone drilled and tapped a hole, but you have no idea what thread size was used. For small screws, fall back on your assortment of scope and sight mounting screws. Start the screw by hand and see if it threads easily. If it does and there is no side play, you hit the nail right on the head. If the screw won't budge, chances are the hole was drilled and tapped for a smaller diameter screw or a different thread. You then must keep trying screws and see which one threads easily into the hole. If the hole is large, try the same approach with a larger screw. Professional machinists use go and no-go gauges, called thread plug gauges, but their use is so limited in gunsmithing that you probably won't find them in shops.

Determining the thread size of a screw or bolt is done with a screw pitch gauge. These gauges consist of a series of notched blades of different thicknesses, and each blade's notches correspond to the thread cut by a standard tap. When you get a perfect match of the notches on the blade and the threads on the bolt or screw, you simply look at the blade and the thread identification is marked for you to read off.

You may find that you need to make a hole into a length of round stock, but that none of your drills are large enough and/or long enough. Using either a compound vise or a machinist's vise, mount the work to be drilled on the table of the drill press. Then, using a slightly undersized drill bit, drill the hole to the required depth. Without touching the setup of the work being drilled, replace the drill bit with a boring bar of the required size. Set it into the chuck of the spindle, then measure the boring bar cutter and set it so that the first cut is a roughing cut. Measure the hole, adjust the boring cutter if needed, then make the final cut.

I prefer to tackle such jobs on the lathe where a boring setup is arranged horizontally rather than vertically as it is on the drill press. With the lathe you can bore tapered holes also, but this calls for a good working knowledge of the lathe. External tapering on a lathe can be done two ways: a slight taper adjustment is usually built into the tail stock, or a special tapering attachment is added to the lathe which allows you to set up many styles and types of external tapers.

Depending on your lathe, the available cutting attachments and cutter holders, plus your skill, the lathe is hard to beat as a thread cutting machine in the home workshop. If an automatic gear changer is on the lathe, changing the threads you want to cut becomes as simple as flicking on a light switch. There is no easier way to thread loading dies than with a lathe. Any job that can be done on a screw machine can be run on many of the smaller lathes. A special threading tool bit can be mounted in the boring bar for internal threading. The threading bit has the same shape and rake as a regular or external threading tool.

When cutting threads on the lathe, either inside or out, the work must be lubed. The most uniform distribution of cutting oil is obtained by dipping a clean two-inch varnish brush into a pan of cutting oil, then lightly touching the spinning work, thus transferring cutting oil to the cut being made. In setting the lathe up to turn a specific size thread, remember that the tool also must be adjusted for machining speed so that the cutting bit does not burn out when used on a piece of hard steel that is turning too rapidly.

If I sound prejudiced in favor of a lathe, I plead guilty. I learned my lathe lore the hard way, making every mistake in the book, plus a few which must have set some sort of record.

But can you think of any other home shop tool that allows you to cut right hand threads, then, with a twist of the wrist, cut the same thread left-handed?

Chapter 23

TECHNIQUES FOR BROWNING

The Methods Used By Early Gunsmiths Have Changed Little In The Modern Age

A concentrated solution of baking soda seems to be the only way to degrease steel properly prior to browning. None of usual degreasing agents seem to accomplish it.

LIKE BLUING, browning is a rusting process, but that is where all similarities between the two techniques end. From what we have been able to learn about the old-fashioned methods of browning a barrel or other metal parts of a gun, the gunsmiths of that earlier period used any and all methods to get a light covering of rust going on metal. Of course, the trick is to get an even coat of rust, then build up that coat step by step.

Let's assume that all of the polishing has been done. For bluing — hot, cold or touch-up — you'd then degrease the job with one of the special preparations offered for that purpose: acetone, alcohol, or most any other solvent that attacks grease. Since cold bluing sticks to steel prepared in this manner, the reasoning would be that the same hunk of steel should respond to browning after being similarly degreased. It does not!

The job most often encountered is browning a barrel and it is essential that the cleaned and degreased metal stays that way. So make up a couple of acid-free wood plugs, from maple dowel rod. Shape them so one end of each plug fits securely into the bore of the barrel. Shaping the plugs is best done on a sander, but with a sharp knife you can shape a plug almost as well, provided you sand it afterward to achieve a tight seal. The plugs not only prevent accidental browning of parts of the bore, but also act as handles for the work while being manipulated.

Degreasing the hunk of barrel I wanted to brown was tougher than I had anticipated. The usual degreasing agents degreased the metal, or at least that is what I thought. The first application of the browning solution quickly showed I had not removed all the grease. Puddling of the browning solution was quite severe.

Minimum equipment is needed for browning, unless of course you want to do your own polishing. A high polish of the steel is essential and the better the finish, the better the final result.

After making up the plugs, fashion two hangers from wire coat hangers so that the barrel can be suspended while drying. Hanging the barrel up in this manner also makes it easier to apply the browning solution. For the carding, it is best to remove the barrel from the hanger contraption.

You'll need a browning or rust-inducing agent. I found

Left: Hardwood plugs from dowel need not be long, but must be tapered to drive into the barrel. (Right) The Dixie preparation works, but process must be repeated a number of times for the desired finish.

that the Dixie Gun Works product — simply called Browning Solution — does the job well and fairly quickly, provided the surface is one hundred percent grease-free.

Before settling on the Dixie preparation I went through a stack of sundry browning formulas. The old-timers used just about anything that induced rust, from strong and weak acids to a ten percent solution of table salt, sea water, if it's handy — in short, anything that produces rust can be used to brown a barrel.

With this in mind, I degreased and tried a fifteen percent solution of table salt. The solution puddled like mad and results were so spotty that I washed the barrel in hot water, dried it, and took it back to the buffing wheels. I went through a number of degreasing agents with little luck, then decided to try some of the other products. Among those were pure household ammonia and several cleansers. Then, following suggestions by Turner Kirkland who heads up Dixie Gun Works, I made up a hot concentrated solution of ordinary baking soda. That finally did the trick after the barrel had been treated twice with hot water baths that way, drying in between.

The simplest way to apply whatever browning solution you decide on is by means of a cotton patch or ball. With the barrel degreased and perfectly dry, apply the browning solution sparingly and as evenly as possible. If there is extensive puddling, the degreasing job was not complete and it is best to start all over again. Let the first application of the rusting agent sit on the work for at least eight hours, but a twelve-hour interval is even better.

Carding is the term that describes the removal of rust. Carding can be done by means of wire wheels which are grease-free, or by means of a wire handbrush, or by fine steel wool. The steel wool must be degreased as outlined in the chapter on bluing; remember that burning off grease from steel wool must be done outdoors. Rub lightly until all of the surface rust is gone and until you are down almost to the shiny metal again. Suspend the work again on the wire hangers, holding the job in place by means of the wooden plugs used to close off the bore of the barrel.

After twelve hours, card the job and apply more rusting solution, continuing until the work shows an even brown. In doing two barrels this way, I found that it is best to repeat this step ten to twelve times.

After buffing and degreasing as outlined in the text, the piece of barrel is ready for the first coat of browning solution. If puddling occurs, it means starting over.

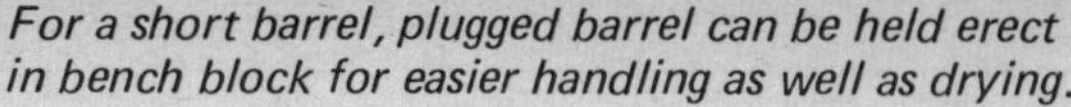

Once a satisfactory brown has been achieved, the work is washed in very hot water to stop the rusting action, dried and the newly browned part can be given the final treatment.

The browned part — dried and still warm to the touch from its hot bath — is given a coat of beeswax. Some gunsmiths favor raw linseed oil or a mixture of this oil and beeswax. Antique guns often have a fairly glossy finish on the browned metal parts. This was accomplished by lightly lacquering the surfaces. The major trouble with this coating is that it scratches quite easily, leaving ugly marks on the work. A great many twist barrels were treated this way to give them eye appeal, but for hunting, such a final coating is just about useless.

Roy Dunlap recommends a thinned marine spar varnish coat, applied with a spray gun. I believe that this would work, but I have had reasonably good results with two coats of the wash shellac used in furniture refinishing and polishing. Use steel wool between coats, and if the browning job is not brown enough, you can add a bit of coloring to the shellac to deepen the coloring of the finish.

There are as many browning solutions as there are gunsmiths who do restoring work of antique guns or who work only with black powder guns. Mention was made of a ten percent solution of table salt. The tincture of iodine used on small scratches as disinfectant does a neat job, but the stuff is fairly expensive and the number of applications on a big job, such as a barrel, runs into a fair bit of change.

The suggestion often is made that a bit of acid etching, after polishing, helps to get the rusting started. A twenty-five percent solution of hydrochloric acid often is mentioned, but this is a bit strong to keep around the shop. A weaker, five to seven percent, solution might be better and is not nearly as hard on fingers and clothing.

Light acid etching — sometimes called pickling — speeds the rusting process, but also makes perfect degreasing more troublesome. Rottenstone with slaked lime in a tumbling rig often is suggested. While a cartridge case tumbler could be used for the smaller parts, amateur gunsmiths usually don't have a tumbler large enough for barrels. A light acid etching with boric acid can be used. This method is the better choice since the boric acid, though etching the metal, also is removed quite easily.

A weak lukewarm solution of ammonium chloride was used by early black powder gunsmiths. This method works fairly rapidly, but when the final coat is applied and after carding, the work must be heated until it scorches paper to set the rusting. The trick here is to apply a coat of oil. Just about any kind seems to work, but perhaps linseed oil would be best. Oil the barrel, then heat — a reverse process of oil or wax being applied after browning is completed. The hot metal will permit entry of some of the oil and this may explain the sheen of some of the old browned barrels.

If a lot of browning is to be done, a sweat box should be constructed. This is a simple wooden box, perhaps lined with sheet metal, where steam from a couple of kettles or pans containing water can be sent into the box. The sources of steam must have a heat supply, and the roof of the box should slant backward to prevent condensation dripping on the work. Once a part has been given the ammonium chloride treatment, it is parked in the sweat box for about one day. The temperature maintained in the box should not drop below 70 degrees Fahrenheit.

After-rusting is the common problem with browning jobs. Essentially, this is merely a continuation of the rusting or browning process. To stop after-rusting, wash or even boil the newly browned parts in hot water, then dry thoroughly and coat them as outlined above.

Thanks to a growing interest in old shotguns, the question of how a twist barrel is browned will be covered briefly here. The formula given here comes from R.H. Angier who claims to have received it from the U.S. Bureau of Standards. A total of at least eight passes should be made and each of them will produce a slightly different coloring. Carding or removal of surface rust must be done with dry brushes or wheels and after carding, the work is boiled in water, the solution being applied while the metal is still warm from the bath. Roy Dunlap claims this solution, when applied for too long, will blue a part rather than brown it. He also states that it is best if the parts are kept warm and the solution is applied while the metal is warm. Bluing results if parts are boiled after carding, and if the treatment is continued, the finish will be black. I have never tried this method, therefore cannot comment on its merits.

The solution consists of: antimony trichloride, 4 parts;

ferric chloride, crystals, 4 parts; gallic acid, 2 parts; distilled water, 1 part.

J.P. Stelle and William B. Harris give several formulae, as does Angier, for special browning solutions, but I feel that some of the methods and formulae are too complex for the home shop.

After I had tried most of the methods outlined in this chapter, I talked with a gunsmith who specializes in repairing black powder guns. Every so often, if someone induces him to come off the range and back into the shop, the man will build custom flintlocks. Asked about his method of browning steel, he handed me a gallon jug of ordinary cider vinegar!

Polish, degrease, and apply the cider vinegar, let the work sit for at least twelve hours, card the surface rust, and start the cider treatment again. In about two weeks, and after careful carding, there will be a deep brown finish on all parts. After stopping the rusting process by means of a hot bath, and while the parts are still hot, he applies any old wax polish he has handy. The wax then is buffed lightly and the job looks like that proverbial million bucks.

Experience has shown that a browning solution that works well on one type of steel may not work on other steel. Moreover, since the color is not uniform from gun to gun, and since methods of preparation vary somewhat from shop to shop, nobody has yet developed that perfect browning solution that works on every piece of steel or iron. It does seem to be agreed that metal parts which are kept warm if not hot during the entire process seem to take the browning more quickly and uniformly.

If patches appear on the finish, or if puddling occurs as you are applying the wet cotton sponge, I can guarantee you that your degreasing was incomplete. Best bet: Go back to the buffing wheels after you have prevented any after-rusting. Rebuff lightly, just enough to remove the rust and get back that high luster with which you started.

If you have the facilities and the acid, surface etch as outlined above, then degrease and start all over again with the first layer of rust.

It seems to make relatively little difference how you induce rust formation, as long as it is uniform, the carding is right, and the after-rusting is stopped completely. If you miss one little step, you will have your hands full for some time to come. It will mean disassembly of the gun, and starting the hot water bath affair again. Whatever finish was given to the barrel after the rusting process was completed will have to be repaired or removed totally and reapplied.

The trick in browning is to let the work sit for eight to twelve hours, the longer time being the better, to get an even browning or rusting. At least, that's the way it worked when I used the Dixie Browning Solution and after I learned to leave well enough alone for some time.

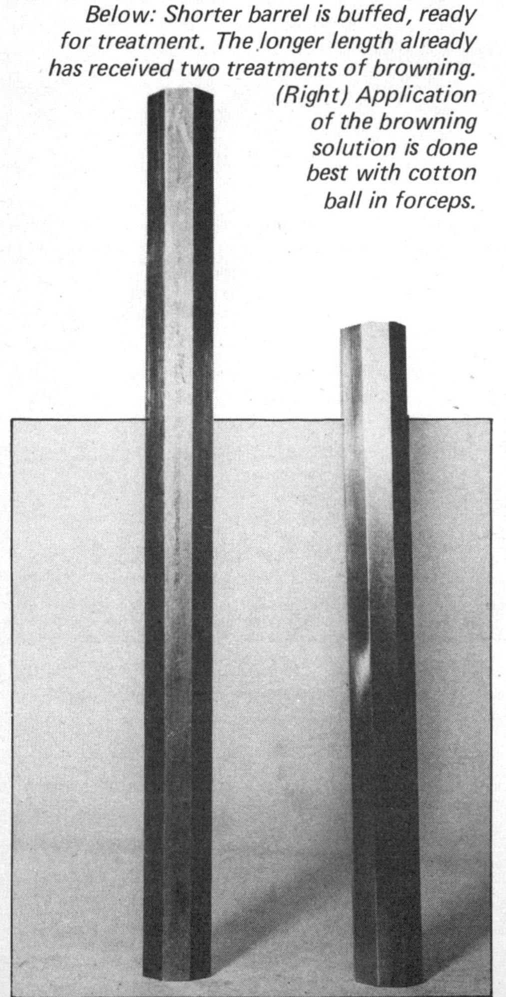

Below: Shorter barrel is buffed, ready for treatment. The longer length already has received two treatments of browning. (Right) Application of the browning solution is done best with cotton ball in forceps.

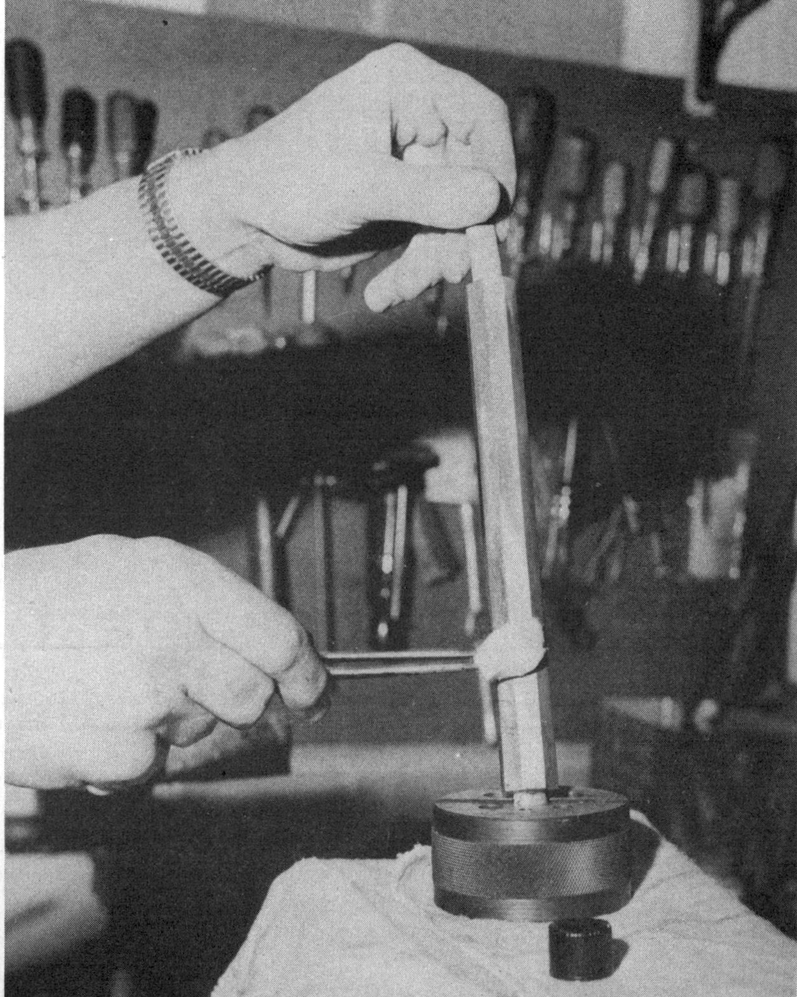

Chapter 24

THE 30-MINUTE CAP & BALL PISTOL

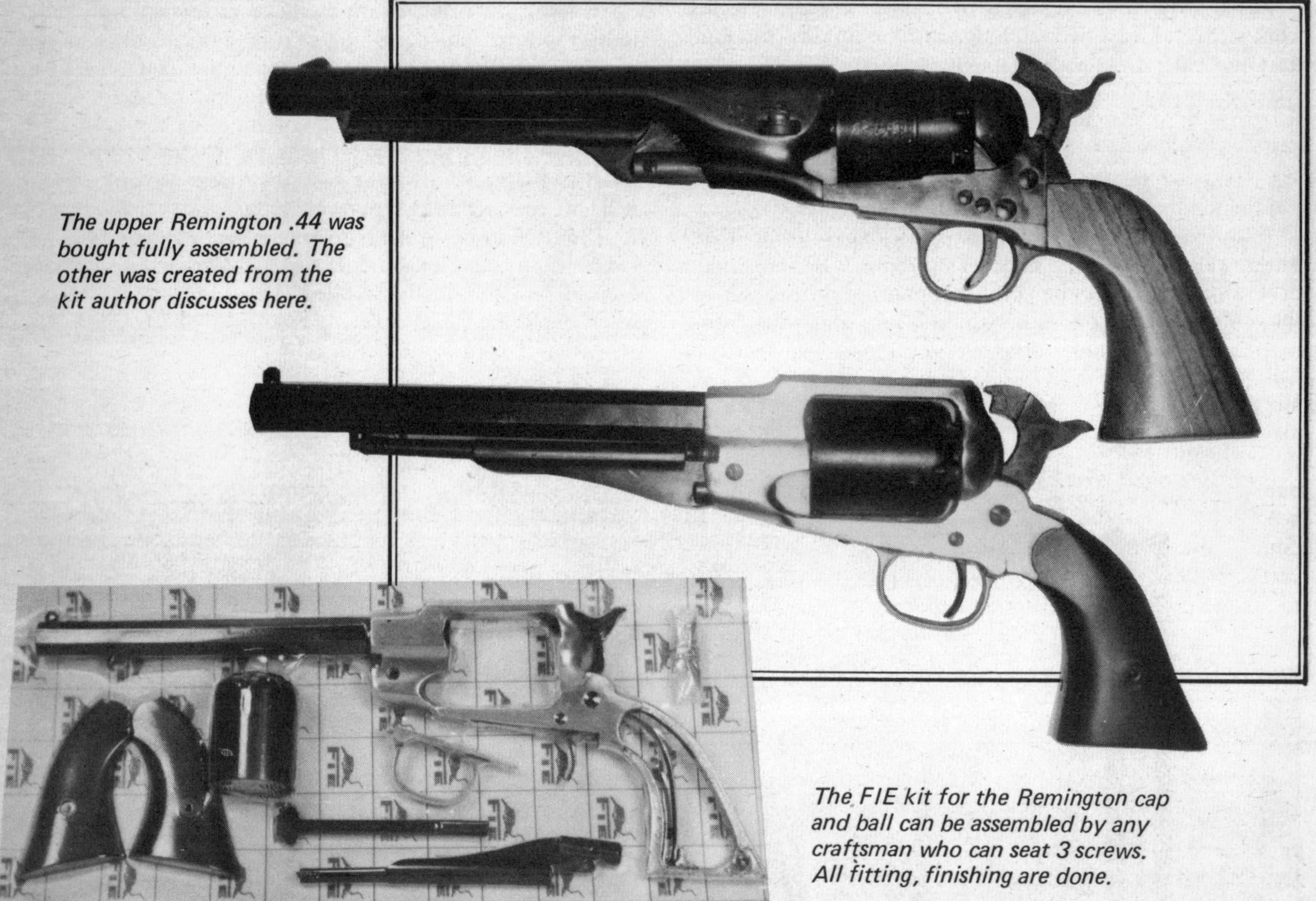

The upper Remington .44 was bought fully assembled. The other was created from the kit author discusses here.

The FIE kit for the Remington cap and ball can be assembled by any craftsman who can seat 3 screws. All fitting, finishing are done.

A Kit Such As This Gives You An Opportunity To Test Your Newly-Acquired Knowledge

FOR THE WOULD-BE home gunsmith, it might be well to begin with a project that can give you some help in the way of instructions and techniques. One of the many kits available today might be the answer, since they employ the more simple gunsmithing techniques, yet give one an opportunity to develop the skills he will use on more complicated projects at a later time.

Kits for black powder guns come in all sizes and shapes, and there is a wide choice when it comes to the degree of difficulty involved in assembling a specific kit.

There are long gun kits, as well as derringer kits, that require some woodworking; others also require basic knowledge of draw filing and metal polishing. There are other kits you can assemble with ease, but you have to sand

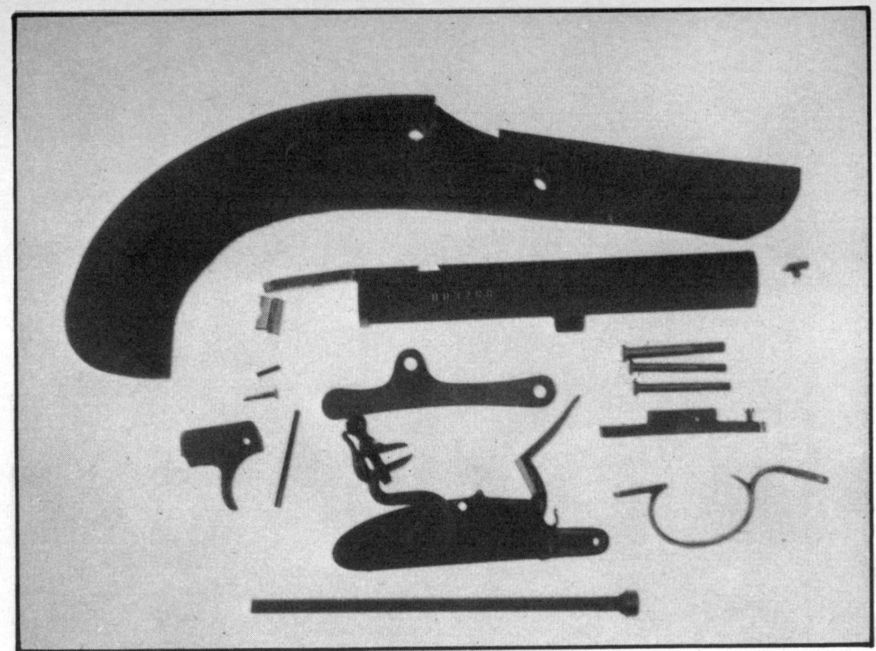

Flintlock kit from the same importer requires minimal assembly skills. The lock has been pre-tuned for finished gun to function smoothly.

the stock, stain and finish it with the supplied materials.

A rather unique kit for a .44 caliber Remington cap and ball revolver is offered by Firearms Import & Export of Miami. For under $60, you get a gun that can be ready for loading and shooting in less than thirty minutes.

All parts of the gun are neatly packaged in a plastic bubble pack and the instructions are easy to follow. You need only one screwdriver which, should the need arise, can double as a light mallet when turned around. All metal parts have been factory buffed, brass parts are polished, and

the rest of the parts are blued.

The earlier FIE kits called for do-it-yourself assembly of the cylinder stop, the trigger and cylinder stop springs, while the newer kits have these parts already assembled in the gun.

In such a kit, the next assembly step is the trigger guard. Move the rear edge of the brass guard underneath the ledge in front strap and push the guard back a hair; this will align the screw hole in guard and frame. A total of three screws must be seated during the entire assembly, and all of them

Newer kits from FIE are assembled at the factory to the point shown. Trigger guard installation is next.

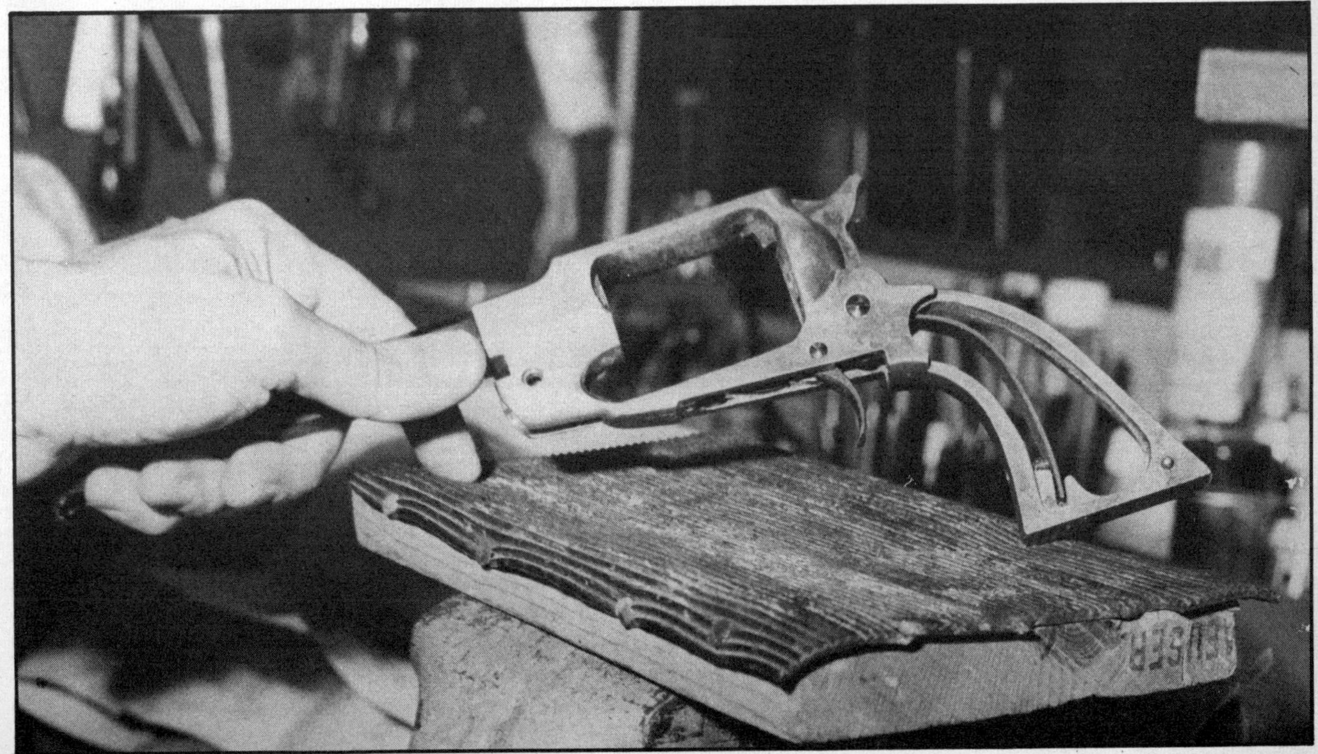

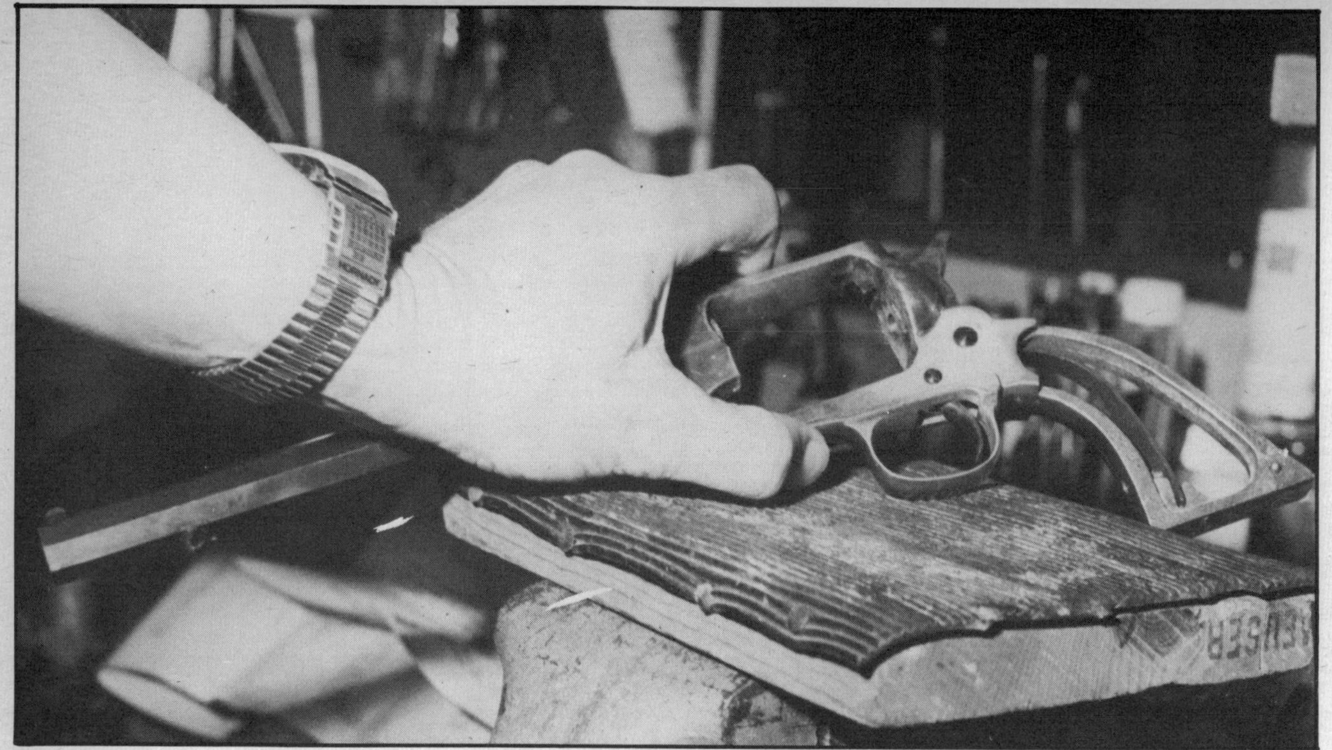

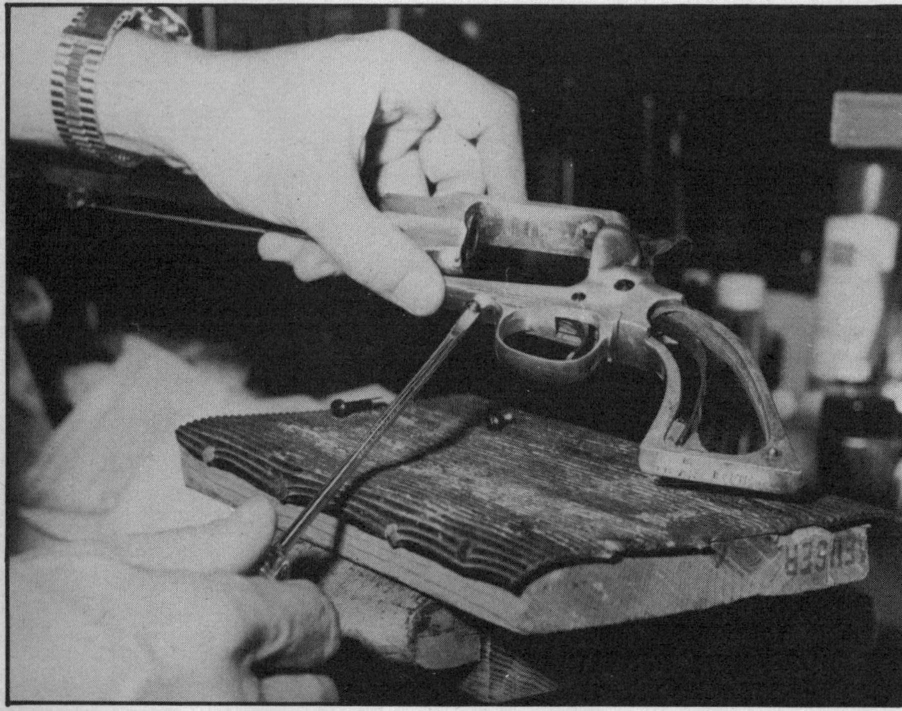

Above: Slide rear edge of the trigger guard to rear until it slips under lip of the frame. (Left) Seat the screw that anchors the guard to the frame.

should be seated firmly but not too tightly. The longest screw eventually will hold the grips together, the shortest will hold the trigger guard where it belongs. The screw left over is used to anchor the rammer-loading lever assembly in the frame.

Next, insert the cylinder pin, place the hammer on half-cock, and slide the cylinder into the frame. Once the cylinder has slipped into place, hold it there with the cylinder pin which is pushed rearward. Insert the ball rammer, move up the loading lever and keep pushing it just a bit until the holes align, then seat the screw. Mount the already finished wood grips and the total elapsed time for the assembly is about twenty minutes, which includes time off for pipe lighting and dog ear scratching, plus a phone call or two.

Should this be your first black powder venture and some of the descriptive terms are unfamiliar, don't worry. With the exceptionally clear and easy-to-follow directions comes an exploded view of the gun. In the instructions, each numbered part is described, the numbers corresponding to those used in the exploded drawing. There seems to be no way that anyone could goof in assembling the FIE kit gun.

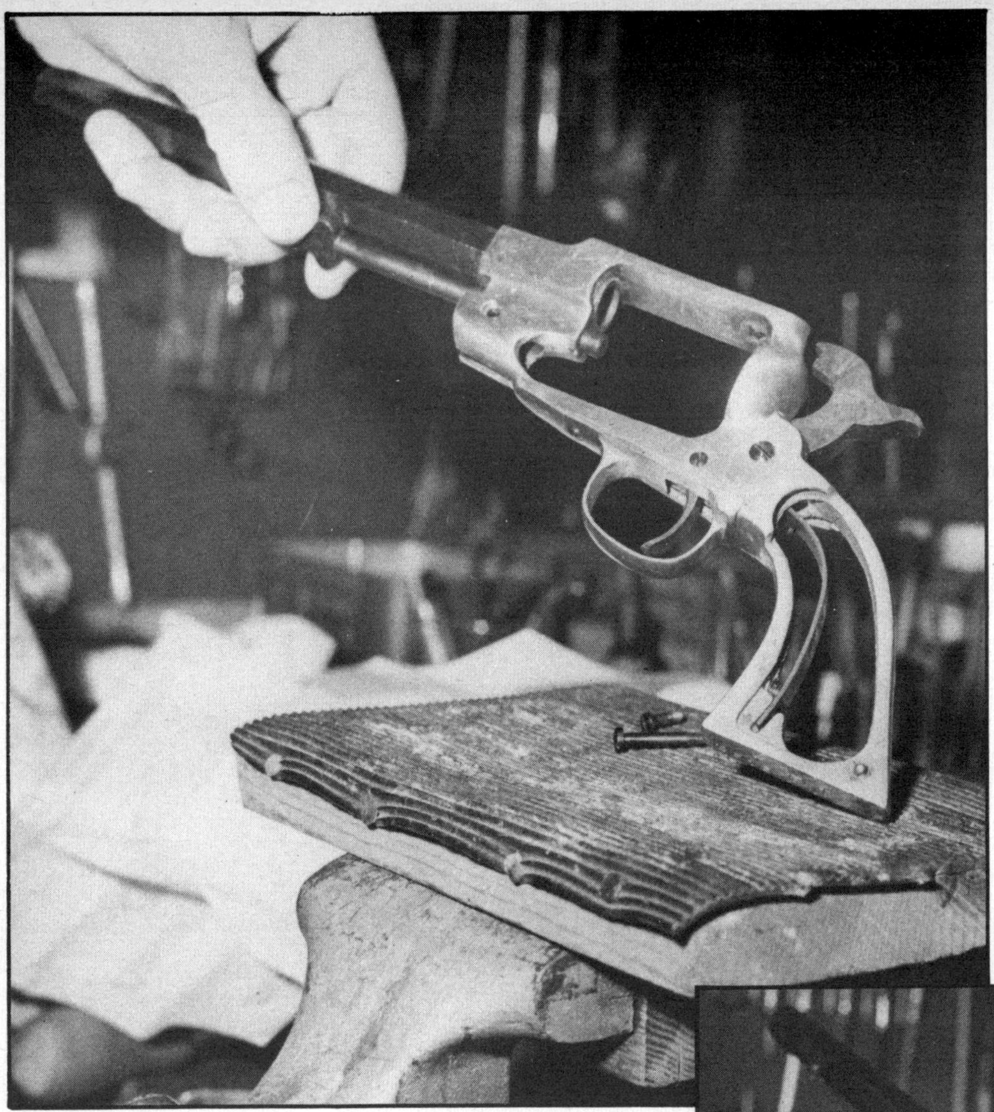

Left: Insert cylinder pin, place hammer on half-cock. Slip cylinder in position, hold it there with cylinder pin. (Below) With cylinder in place, hammer on half-cock, check rotation and indexing of the cylinder.

This revolver compares favorably with a replica that sells for almost twice as much and a little adroit polishing could make this Italian import a handsome addition to anyone's black powder armament. The barrel is eight inches long, and the assembled gun weighs two pounds, nine ounces. Color case-hardening on the hammer is well executed, as is all of the bluing and the well-polished brass frame. Like most black powder six-guns, trigger pull varies quite a bit, with the mean average of ten pulls reading just fifty-two ounces. Nipples already were installed, but the only remaining job was to clean and degrease the gun before loading and firing.

Buying a pre-assembled kit, especially a revolver kit, has the advantage that the gun has been factory timed, and that locks have been tuned to some extent. Kits that require more work on the part of the home gunsmith — and I generally recommend these to the more experienced fellow who has not only a collection of hand-tools but also some power tools — have the advantage that the assembler has a chance to study and learn the mechanics of the gun or lock, and that he can learn to tune his gun.

The vast majority of black powder kits come with fairly complete instructions, but there are some which require a

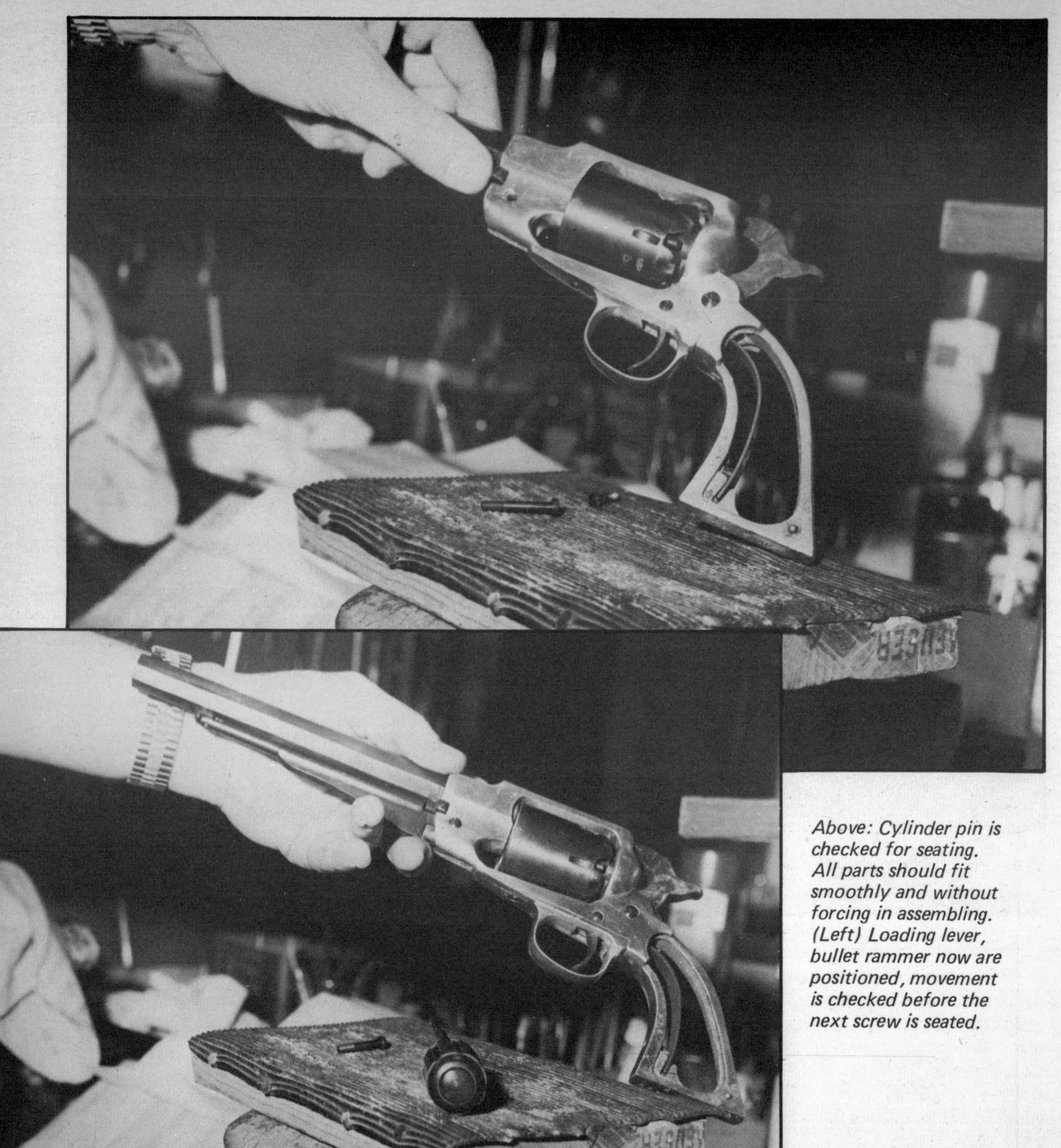

Above: Cylinder pin is checked for seating. All parts should fit smoothly and without forcing in assembling. (Left) Loading lever, bullet rammer now are positioned, movement is checked before the next screw is seated.

considerable amount of shop knowledge and assembly savvy. One kit I tackled some years ago required the hardening of parts, color case-hardening, draw filing and polishing of most parts, plus bluing and some degree of wood finishing.

Assembling kits of almost any type can become a fascinating hobby. Invariably, the first gun, especially when total assembly and woodwork are required, usually doesn't have the eye appeal later jobs will have, but don't let that worry you. At least one of us keeps that first effort handy to show off his obvious craft improvements and my small collection of home-built and finished guns shows the evolution of my gunsmithing skills.

But be forewarned: kits can be habit forming. Usually, you start with a simple kit, complete it, and although you swore that you'd never tackle another project like it when you were having all sorts of problems, the finished gun makes you forget your promise. So you get a slightly more

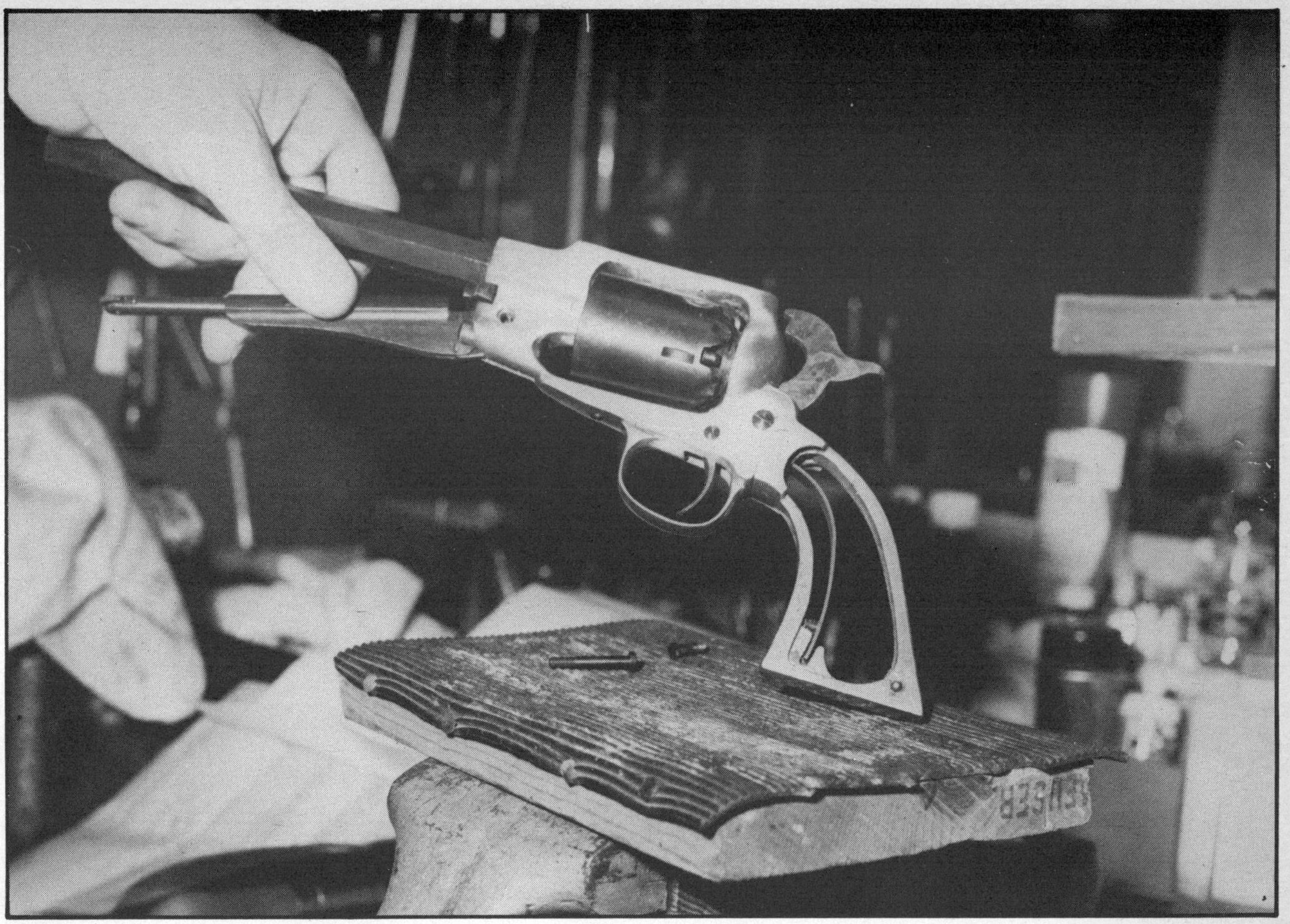

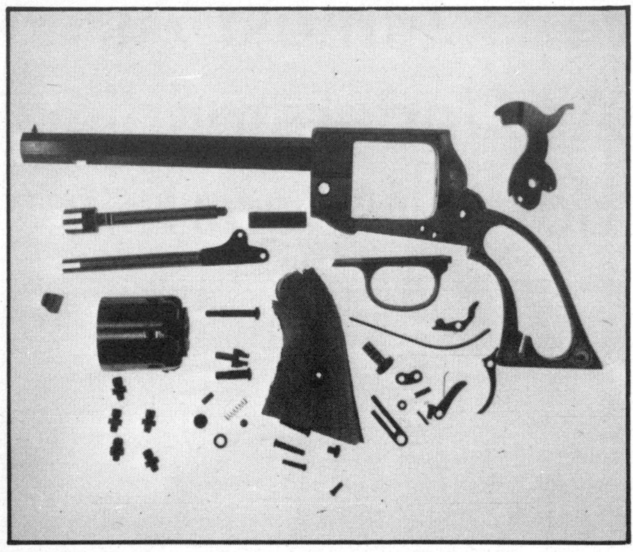

Above: Manipulation of the rammer helped to slip parts into position so final grip could be seated. With the installation of the grips, the gun is ready to shoot. (Left) Kit from Dixie Gun Works calls for much more work, including filing, fitting, finishing, bluing.

complex kit, and complete it. Then you discover that you can buy locks, barrels, stocks or even stock blanks, plus semi-finished furniture, and before you know it, you have graduated from the kits to an advanced form of gunsmithing.

When you get the kit fever, or reach the stage where you buy the basic and unfinished parts and fashion your own guns from them, you will have to decide which way you want to go. Purists will encourage you to follow in their footsteps and build nothing that isn't the truest replica of a vintage gun.

Others, who are equally skilled in the shop and on the range, will tell you to build whatever you want, that design and functionality are more important than slavishly following the designs of some long-dead gunmaker. I tried both ways, and ended up copying and modifying the work of others so the results of my labors are in no way comparable to the originals. I feel I have more leeway this way, that I can try new ideas, and if I goof I can always palm it off as something new I'm trying to dream up.

It isn't too difficult to make the transition from black powder kit to smokeless guns, and from there to making your own custom rifle or handgun. Relatively little home gunsmithing is done on shotguns, excepting of course those designed for black powder, but there is always room for improvement. Maybe you will design or make that new type of gun we've all been waiting for.

Chapter 25

A MATTER OF MEASUREMENT

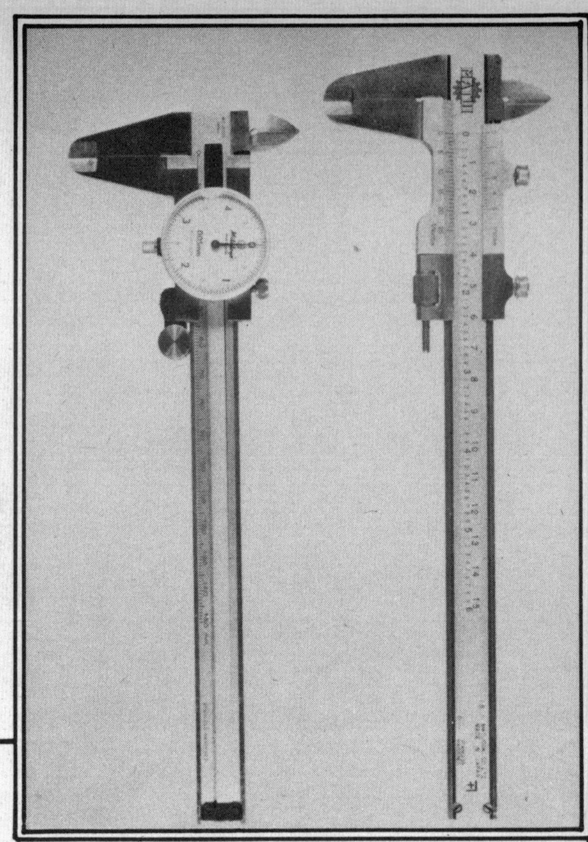

You can learn to read a vernier scale, but direct reading instruments are simpler and more certain since readings are not dependent on interpretation.

How To Measure Is Almost As Important As Understanding What It Means!

Micrometers come in many sizes and styles, making them suitable for a multitude of measuring tasks.

IT MAKES little difference if a forward sling swivel stud is located 1-7/8, 2 or 2-1/16 inches from the forend tip of the stock. But when working with a lathe or a drill press, that one-eighth-inch on one side and one-sixteenth-inch on the other side suddenly loom large.

Gunsmiths usually measure in thousandths of an inch which, in the decimal system, translates to 0.001 — frequently you will see measurements of 1/10,000 or 0.0001-inch.

We have three means of measuring the smaller divisions of an inch: the machinist's ruler, the vernier caliper and the micrometer. The ruler is seen most often in the fraction version where each scale is divided into 1/4, 1/8, 1/16, 1/32 and perhaps 1/64 inch. Unless you have the eyes of a hawk, you probably will need a magnifier to read the small divisions, and there is always the chance that you may misread or miscount the number of divisions.

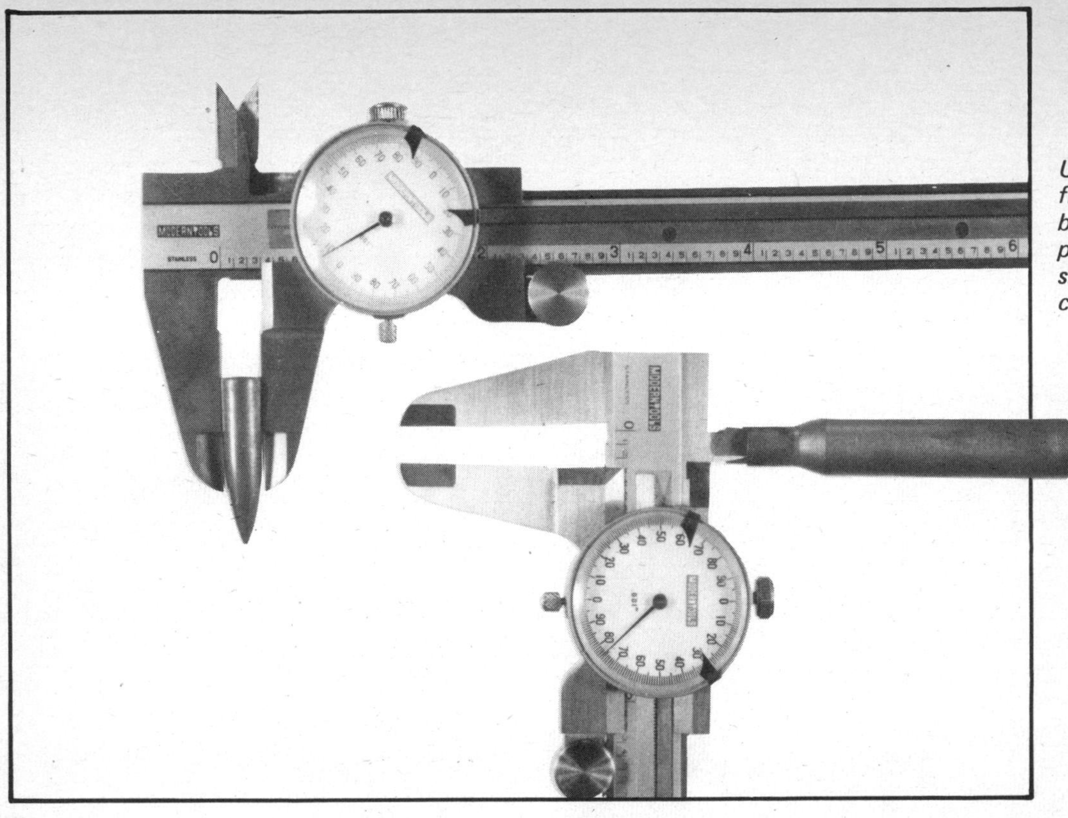

Use of vernier scale's flat jaws to measure bullet diameter, with pointers on other side used to measure cartridge case mouth.

The vernier caliper, like the micrometer, comes in two basic styles: on one, the actual measurements are read off with a micrometer thimble or vernier scale and you must learn how to read the divisions properly. Both the caliper and micrometer also are available as direct-reading tools.

Some eighteen years ago, four of us were running pressure tests in a major ballistics lab. As the crusher came from the gun, we each used the one micrometer that was at hand, and each wrote down his readings. These then were checked against the proper tables. When we compared our findings, not one of us agreed with the other fellows. The differences resulted from the reading of the micrometer; since then I've used only direct-reading measuring tools.

The vernier caliper has a great degree of versatility, but has the drawback of not being as accurate a measuring device as the micrometer or mike. The forward jaws are used to measure inside diameters, such as a case mouth. Within limits, this side of the vernier also is used to measure such things as length of case neck. The slide of the vernier, as it extends outward from the body of the tool often is used as a depth gauge.

The mike has flat anvils on both contact measuring surfaces, therefore lending itself to most measuring jobs. A number of special mikes are on the market, and though usable for gun work, they are usually more expensive and nothing can be gained by buying one of them over the standard mike.

The direct-reading vernier and the direct-reading mike

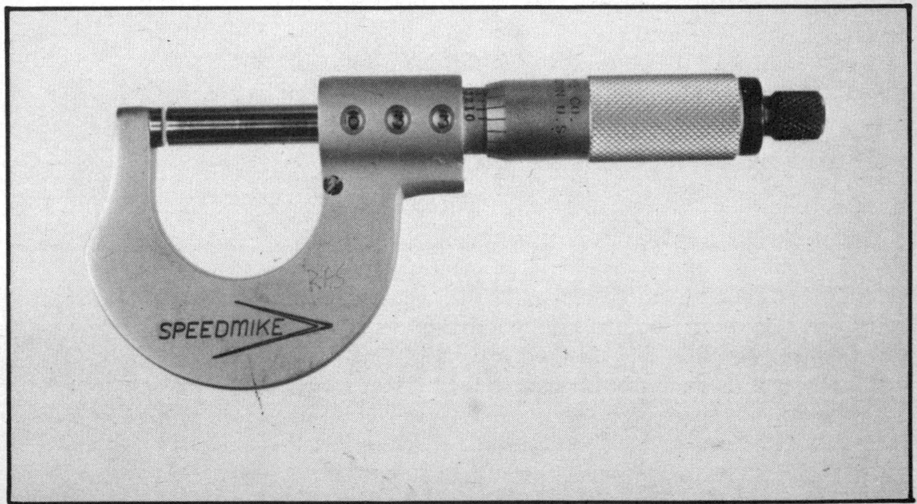

Direct reading Speedmike by Slocomb is an accurate and easily handled precision tool.

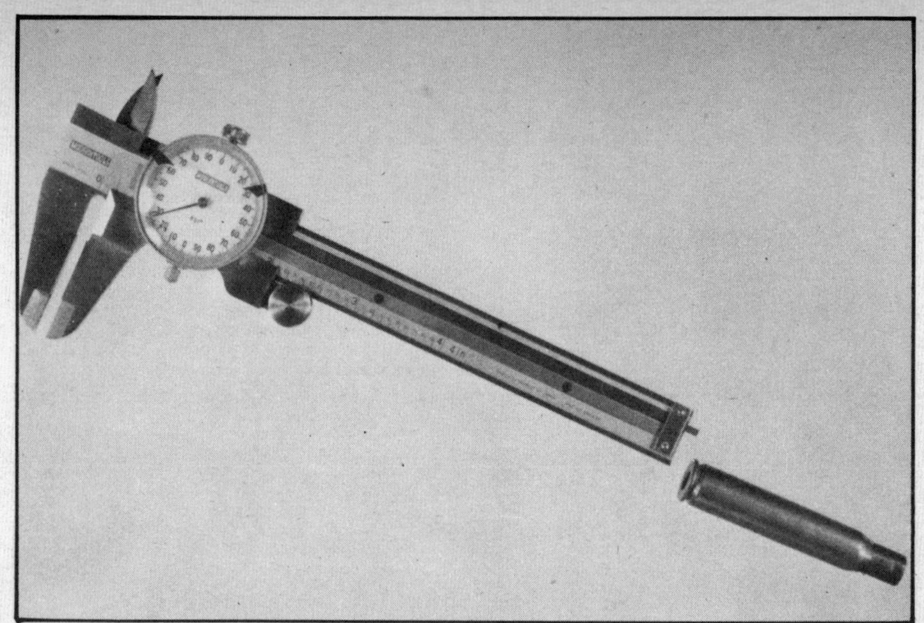

Vernier scale also may be used to measure primer pocket depth.

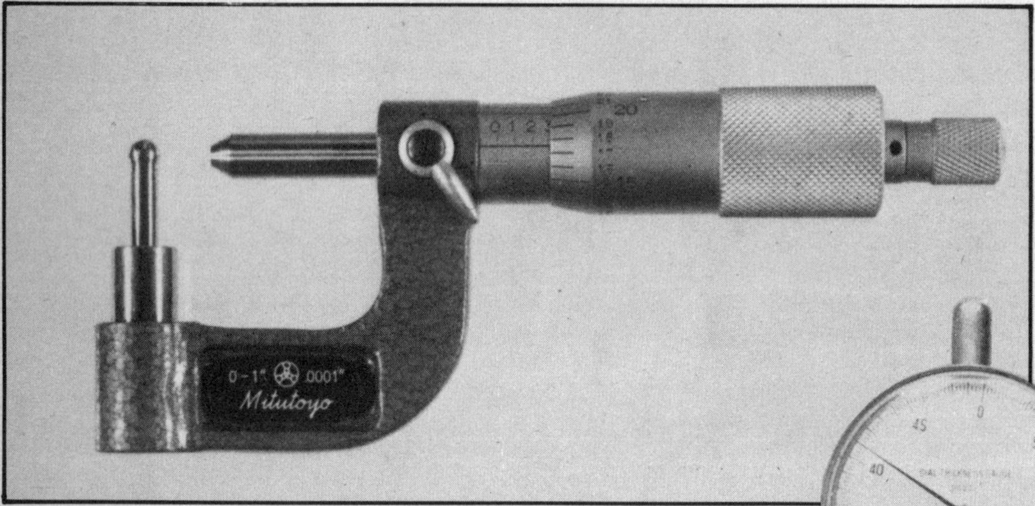

This specialty mike, like others, can be used but has limited applications. Quadra thickness gauge, below, is an extremely sensitive measuring tool.

have taken over, not only with hobby gunsmiths and reloaders, but in machine shops and engineering offices where only a decade ago the use of a direct-reading measuring tool was considered with something less than favor.

Another advance in measuring is the dial indicator. Dial indicators measure thickness, length and width. They also are used to check surface flatness as well as the concentricity of bullets and cartridge cases. You can rig up dial indicators for many jobs, including checking case length and verifying the overall length of a loaded round.

The B-Square Company offers a number of specially designed tools for the handloader, all of them featuring dial gauges. Thickness micrometers with dial gauges, used widely in the paper industry, are handy to check such measurements as the rim thickness of a cartridge case, especially since they must be accurate to 0.00025-inch.

Although not used often, two other types of gauges must be mentioned here. The small hole gauges and the telescoping gauges are invaluable for precision machine work, such as chambering, threading barrels and other such

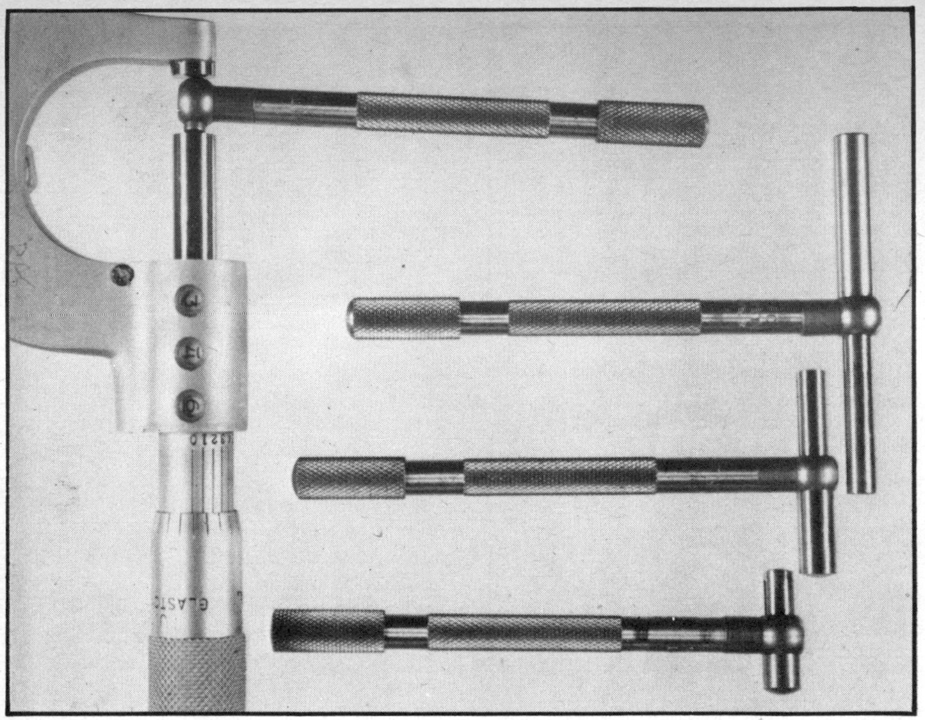

Telescoping gauges come in many sizes, but only the small sets are needed in gunsmithing work.

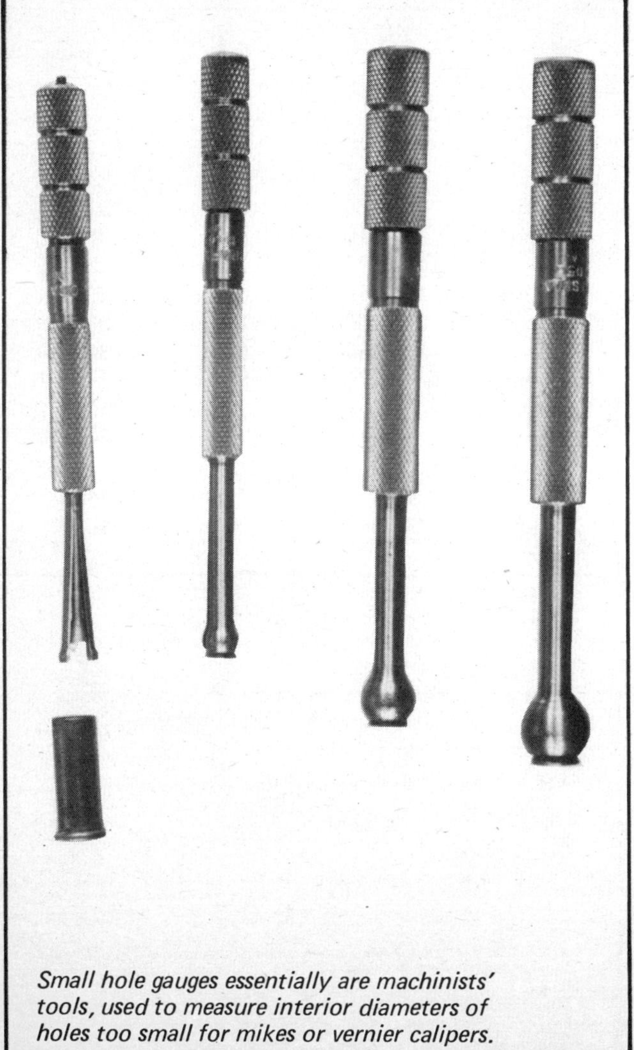

Small hole gauges essentially are machinists' tools, used to measure interior diameters of holes too small for mikes or vernier calipers.

jobs. The small hole gauge slips into the bore of a rifle, and is allowed to expand until there is a snug feel. The gauge is then locked. The measurement of the bore is made by measuring the expanded ball on the gauge with a micrometer or a vernier caliper.

Telescoping gauges may have one fixed and one spring-loaded plunger, or two spring-loaded plungers. Again, with the plungers compressed, the gauge is inserted into the hole or tube to be measured; when the gauge feels snug against the walls of the item being measured, the plungers are locked in place. As with the small hole gauge, measurement is taken from the contact points of the gauge.

Screw pitch gauges and their uses have been discussed in an earlier chapter. Added here are the feeler gauges which are useful for many jobs. The better ones have a more sophisticated locking mechanism for the blades, and the gauges themselves sometimes are called lead thickness or simply thickness gauges.

Vernier calipers and micrometers give readings in decimals of an inch. Thus, a one-quarter-inch drill measured with either of these devices will read 0.25. The conversion from fraction to decimal is almost automatic with most of us, when the measurement readily is translated from one system to the other. A mike reading of 0.00359-inch is not readily translated into a fraction, while most of us have to stop and figure out that three-sixty-fourths is the same as 0.46875-inch. For some reason, even the most recent engineering drawings give dimensions in fractions as well as in decimals of an inch.

The metric system, used almost everywhere except in the United States, is a simple system based on units of ten. There are ten millimeters (mm) in one centimeter (cm), and 10cm make up one decimeter (dm), and ten of those make up one meter (m). One millimeter is about the same as one-twenty-fifth of an inch and, expressed in decimals, that is 0.03937079 which is usually shortened to 0.039-inch. The metric system uses only decimals — not fractions — for

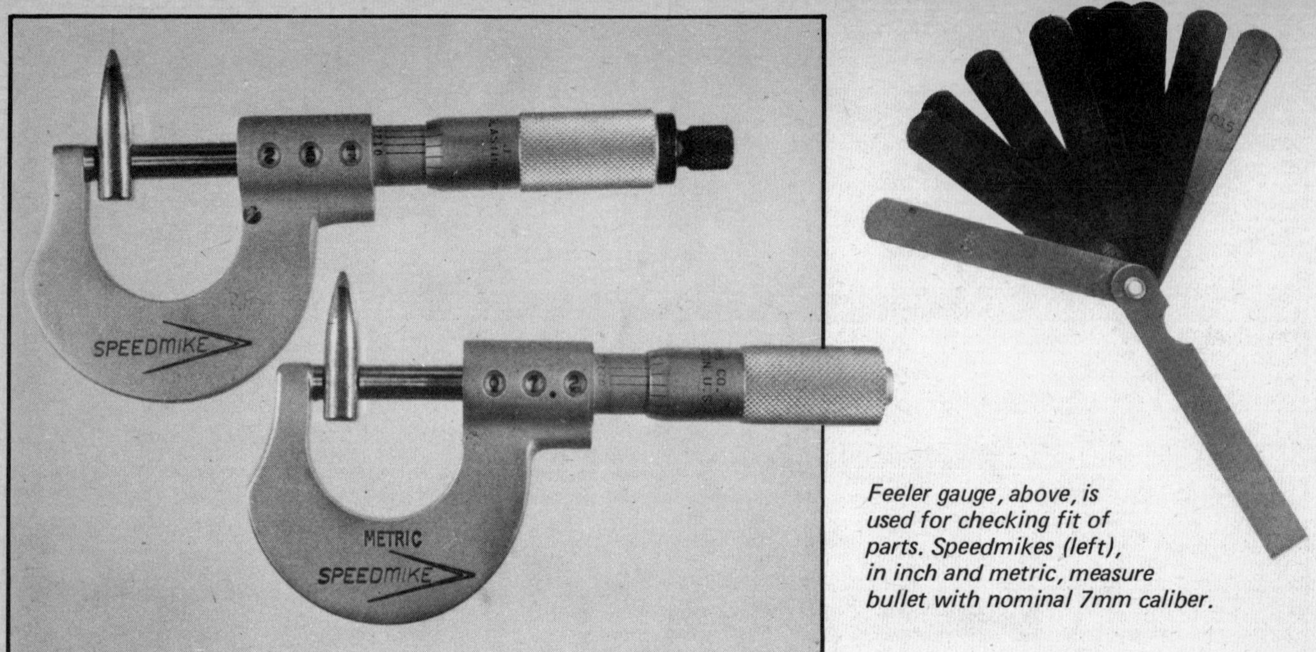

Feeler gauge, above, is used for checking fit of parts. Speedmikes (left), in inch and metric, measure bullet with nominal 7mm caliber.

instance, 1.5 meters is one meter and five decimeters or fifty centimeters.

The standard measure of length in the metric system is the meter; in the weight system, the basis is the kilogram (kg) which is equivalent to 2.2046 pounds. There are 1000 grams (g) in 1 kg, one gram is the same as 15.432 grains (gr), and one ounce translates into 28.35 grams.

The following tables and conversion factors included in this chapter will help to clarify the relationship between our current system of weights and measures and the soon-to-come metric system. Although the conversion is certain to cause some confusion, as does any radical change, the metric system is much easier to handle and the complexity of the fractional system will disappear once the metric system is accepted.

Conversion Factors for Metric Units

grams (gm) to grains (gr) . . . . .multiply by 15.43
grains (gr) to grams (gm) . . . . .multiply by 0.0648
kilogram (kg)/cm^2 to psi . . . . .multiply by 14.223
psi to kg/cm^2 . . . . .multiply by 0.07031
atmospheres to psi . . . . multiply by 14.70
psi to atmospheres . . . . multiply by 0.06804
ft/lbs to kg/m . . . . multiply by 0.1383
kg/m to ft/lbs . . . . multiply by 7.233
meters (m) to feet (ft) . . . . multiply by 3.281
ft to m . . . . multiply by 0.3048
inches to m . . . . multiply by 0.254
millimeters (mm) to inches . . . . multiply by 0.394

Weight Equivalents

Avoirdupois pound . . . . 7,000 grains
Avoirdupois ounce . . . . 437.5 grains
gram (gm) . . . . 15.43 grains
milligram (mg) . . . . 0.015 grains
pound avdp. . . . . 453.5 gm

Metric Cartridge Conversion

Metric	Inches	Metric	Inches
4 mm	.157480	7.7 mm	.303149
4.3 mm	.169291	7.8 mm	.307086
4.5 mm	.177165	7.9 mm	.311023
5 mm	.196850	7.91 mm	.311416
5.5 mm	.216535	7.92 mm	.311809
5.6 mm	.220470	8 mm	.314960
6 mm	.236220	8.15 mm	.320855
6.35 mm	.249999	9 mm	.354330
6.5 mm	.255905	9.1 mm	.358267
7 mm	.275590	9.3 mm	.366141
7.5 mm	.295275	9.5 mm	.374015
7.56 mm	.297637	10.35 mm	.407479
7.6 mm	.299212	10.75 mm	.423227
7.62 mm	.299998	11.15 mm	.438965
7.63 mm	.300093	11.2 mm	.440940
7.65 mm	.301180	11.25 mm	.462201

Fractional Inches to Millimeters

Inches	mm	Inches	mm	Inches	mm	Inches	mm
1/64 =	.397	17/64 =	6.747	33/64 =	13.097	49/64 =	19.447
1/32 =	.794	9/32 =	7.144	17/32 =	13.494	25/32 =	19.844
3/64 =	1.191	19/64 =	7.541	35/64 =	13.890	51/64 =	20.240
1/16 =	1.587	5/16 =	7.937	9/16 =	14.287	13/16 =	20.637
5/64 =	1.984	21/64 =	8.334	37/64 =	14.684	53/64 =	21.034
3/32 =	2.381	11/32 =	8.731	19/32 =	15.081	27/32 =	21.431
7/64 =	2.778	23/64 =	9.128	39/64 =	15.478	55/64 =	21.828
1/8 =	3.175	3/8 =	9.525	5/8 =	15.875	7/8 =	22.225
9/64 =	3.572	25/64 =	9.922	41/64 =	16.272	57/64 =	22.622
5/32 =	3.969	13/32 =	10.319	21/32 =	16.669	29/32 =	23.019
11/64 =	4.366	27/64 =	10.716	43/64 =	17.065	59/64 =	23.415
3/16 =	4.762	7/16 =	11.113	11/16 =	17.462	15/16 =	23.812
13/64 =	5.159	29/64 =	11.509	45/64 =	17.859	61/64 =	24.209
7/32 =	5.556	15/32 =	11.906	23/32 =	18.256	31/32 =	24.606
15/64 =	5.953	31/64 =	12.303	47/64 =	18.653	63/64 =	25.003
1/4 =	6.350	1/2 =	12.700	3/4 =	19.050	1 =	25.400

Millimeters to Decimal Inches

mm	Inches	mm	Inches	mm	Inches	mm	Inches
.01 =	.00039	.34 =	.01339	.67 =	.02638	1. =	.03937
.02 =	.00079	.35 =	.01378	.68 =	.02677	2. =	.07874
.03 =	.00118	.36 =	.01417	.69 =	.02717	3. =	.11811
.04 =	.00157	.37 =	.01457	.70 =	.02756	4. =	.15748
.05 =	.00197	.38 =	.01496	.71 =	.02795	5. =	.19685
.06 =	.00236	.39 =	.01535	.72 =	.02835	6. =	.23622
.07 =	.00276	.40 =	.01575	.73 =	.02874	7. =	.27559
.08 =	.00315	.41 =	.01614	.74 =	.02913	8. =	.31496
.09 =	.00354	.42 =	.01654	.75 =	.02953	9. =	.35433
.10 =	.00394	.43 =	.01693	.76 =	.02992	10. =	.39370
.11 =	.00433	.44 =	.01732	.77 =	.03032	11. =	.43307
.12 =	.00472	.45 =	.01772	.78 =	.03071	12. =	.47244
.13 =	.00512	.46 =	.01811	.79 =	.03110	13. =	.51181
.14 =	.00551	.47 =	.01850	.80 =	.03150	14. =	.55118
.15 =	.00591	.48 =	.01890	.81 =	.03189	15. =	.59055
.16 =	.00630	.49 =	.01929	.82 =	.03228	16. =	.62992
.17 =	.00669	.50 =	.01969	.83 =	.03268	17. =	.66929
.18 =	.00709	.51 =	.02008	.84 =	.03307	18. =	.70866
.19 =	.00748	.52 =	.02047	.85 =	.03346	19. =	.74803
.20 =	.00787	.53 =	.02087	.86 =	.03386	20. =	.78740
.21 =	.00827	.54 =	.02126	.87 =	.03425	21. =	.82677
.22 =	.00866	.55 =	.02165	.88 =	.03465	22. =	.86614
.23 =	.00906	.56 =	.02205	.89 =	.03504	23. =	.90551
.24 =	.00945	.57 =	.02244	.90 =	.03543	24. =	.94488
.25 =	.00984	.58 =	.02283	.91 =	.03583	25. =	.98425
.26 =	.01024	.59 =	.02323	.92 =	.03622	26. =	1.02362
.27 =	.01063	.60 =	.02362	.93 =	.03661	27. =	1.06299
.28 =	.01102	.61 =	.02402	.94 =	.03701	28. =	1.10236
.29 =	.01142	.62 =	.02441	.95 =	.03740	29. =	1.14173
.30 =	.01181	.63 =	.02480	.96 =	.03780	30. =	1.18110
.31 =	.01220	.64 =	.02520	.97 =	.03819	31. =	1.22047
.32 =	.01260	.65 =	.02559	.98 =	.03858	32. =	1.25984
.33 =	.01299	.66 =	.02598	.99 =	.03898	33. =	1.29921

Metric Units of Measure and English Equivalents

1 millimeter (mm) = ... (about 1/25") 0.03937079 in.
10 millimeters = 1 centimeter (cm) = ...0.3937079 in.
10 centimeters = 1 decimeter (dm) = ...3.937079 in.
10 decimeters = 1 meter (m) = ...39.37079 in.
or 3.2808992 feet, or 1.09361 yards
10 meters = 1 dekameter (dam) = ...32.808992 feet
10 dekameters = 1 hectometer (hm) = ... 109.36 yards
10 hectometers = 1 kilometer (km) = ... 0.6213824 mile
10 kilometers = 1 myriameter (mym) = ...6.213824 miles
1 inch = ...25.4 mm or 2.54 cm
1 foot = ... 304.8 mm or .3048 m
1 yard = ... 91.14 cm or .9114 m
1 mile = ...1.609 km
1 square centimeter (sq cm or cm^2) .... 155 sq. in.
1 square inch = ... 6.452 sq. cm.
1 cubic inch = ...16.393 cu. cm.
1 cubic centimeter (cu cm, cc or cm^3) .... .061 cu. in.
1 cubic decimeter = ... 61.023 cu. in. or .0353 cu. ft.
1 liter (l) = ... 1 cu. dm or 61.023 cu. in.
1 cubic foot = ... 28.317 l
1 gallon = ... 3.785 l
1 kilogram (kg) = ...2.2046 lbs.
1 pound = ... .4536 kg.

Conversion of Inches to Millimeters

In.	0	1/16	1/8	3/16	1/4	5/16	3/8	7/16	1/2	9/16	5/8	11/16	3/4	13/16	7/8	15/16
0	0.0	1.6	3.2	4.8	6.4	7.9	9.5	11.1	12.7	14.3	15.9	17.5	19.1	20.6	22.2	23.8
1	25.4	27.0	28.6	30.2	31.7	33.3	34.9	36.5	28.1	39.7	41.3	42.9	44.4	46.0	47.6	49.2
2	50.8	52.4	54.0	55.6	57.1	58.7	60.3	61.9	63.5	65.1	66.7	68.3	69.8	71.4	73.0	74.6
3	76.2	77.8	79.4	81.0	82.5	84.1	85.7	87.3	88.9	90.5	92.1	93.7	95.2	96.8	98.4	100.0
4	101.6	103.2	104.8	106.4	108.0	109.5	111.1	112.7	114.3	115.9	117.5	119.1	120.7	122.2	123.8	125.4
5	127.0	128.6	130.2	131.8	133.4	134.9	136.5	138.1	139.7	141.3	142.9	144.5	146.1	147.6	149.2	150.8
6	152.4	154.0	155.6	157.2	158.8	160.3	161.9	163.5	165.1	166.7	168.3	169.9	171.5	173.0	174.6	176.2
7	177.8	179.4	181.0	182.6	184.2	185.7	187.3	188.9	190.5	192.1	193.7	195.3	196.9	198.4	200.0	201.6
8	203.2	204.8	206.4	208.0	209.6	211.1	212.7	214.3	215.9	217.5	219.1	220.7	222.3	223.8	225.4	227.0
9	228.6	230.2	231.8	233.4	235.0	236.5	238.1	239.7	241.3	242.9	244.5	246.1	247.7	249.2	250.8	252.4
10	254.0	255.6	257.2	258.8	260.4	261.9	263.5	265.1	266.7	268.3	269.9	271.5	273.1	274.6	276.2	277.8
11	279.4	281.0	282.6	284.2	285.7	287.3	288.9	290.5	292.1	293.7	295.3	296.9	298.4	300.0	301.6	303.2
12	304.8	306.4	308.0	309.6	311.1	312.7	314.3	315.9	317.5	319.1	320.7	322.3	323.8	325.4	327.0	328.6
13	330.2	331.8	333.4	335.0	336.5	338.1	339.7	341.3	342.9	344.5	346.1	347.7	349.2	350.8	352.4	354.0
14	355.6	357.2	358.8	360.4	361.9	363.5	365.1	366.7	368.3	369.9	371.5	373.1	374.6	376.2	377.8	379.4
15	381.0	382.6	384.2	385.8	387.3	388.9	390.5	392.1	393.7	395.3	396.9	398.5	400.0	401.6	403.2	404.8
16	406.4	408.0	409.6	411.2	412.7	414.3	415.9	417.5	419.1	420.7	422.3	423.9	425.4	427.0	428.6	430.2
17	431.8	433.4	435.0	436.6	438.1	439.7	441.3	442.9	444.5	446.1	447.7	449.3	450.8	452.4	454.0	455.6
18	457.2	458.8	460.4	462.0	463.5	465.1	466.7	468.3	469.9	471.5	473.1	474.7	476.2	477.8	479.4	481.0
19	482.6	484.2	485.8	487.4	488.9	490.5	492.1	493.7	495.3	496.9	498.5	500.1	501.6	503.2	504.8	506.4
20	508.0	509.6	511.2	512.8	514.3	515.9	517.5	519.1	520.7	522.3	523.9	525.5	527.0	528.6	530.2	531.8
21	533.4	535.0	536.6	538.2	539.7	541.3	542.9	544.5	546.1	547.7	549.3	550.9	552.4	554.0	555.6	557.2
22	558.8	560.4	562.0	563.6	565.1	566.7	568.3	569.9	571.5	573.1	574.7	576.3	577.8	579.4	581.0	582.6
23	584.2	585.8	587.4	589.0	590.5	592.1	593.7	595.3	596.9	598.5	600.1	601.7	603.2	604.8	606.4	608.0

Conversion of Inch Decimals to Millimeters

Hundredths of an Inch	0	1	2	3	4	5	6	7	8	9
0	0	0.254	0.508	0.762	1.016	1.270	1.524	1.778	2.032	2.286
10	2.540	2.794	3.048	3.302	3.556	3.810	4.064	4.318	4.572	4.826
20	5.080	5.334	5.588	5.842	6.096	6.350	6.604	6.858	7.112	7.366
30	7.620	7.874	8.128	8.382	8.636	8.890	9.144	9.398	9.652	9.906
40	10.160	10.414	10.668	10.922	11.176	11.430	11.684	11.938	12.192	12.446
50	12.700	12.954	13.208	13.462	13.716	13.970	14.224	14.478	14.732	14.986
60	15.240	15.494	15.748	16.002	16.257	16.510	16.764	17.018	17.272	17.526
80	20.320	20.574	20.828	21.082	21.336	21.590	21.844	22.098	22.352	22.606
90	22.860	23.114	23.368	23.622	23.876	24.130	24.384	24.638	24.892	25.146

Chapter 26

SECRETS OF GUN POLISHING

Patience, Combined With Practice, Can Give Your Gun That Million Dollar Look!

REPEATED MENTION has been made that any finish applied to metal is only as good as the polishing job with which you start. Polishing is an art in itself, and if you never have tried it, you'd best have a pro do it to avoid messing up a fine gun.

Most gun shops and some firearms companies make it clear that they offer two or three types of metal finishes. The first might be called Standard or Hunter grade; then there is the slightly better grade often called either the Deluxe or Custom finish; and then there is the Super Deluxe or Master finish. All three of these finishes have the metal parts dipped into the same tank of bluing solution. Since there is usually quite a cost difference, that extra something must be found in the polishing. Essentially, polishing is an abrasive process, in which you start with a fairly coarse grit of polishing medium and gradually work toward a satin finish of the metal by re-polishing with finer and finer grits of abrasive.

Because there was no space for camera at left side of buffer, this photograph illustrates unsafe practices: rotation of wheel is wrong and user is not wearing gloves. For this wrong-way illustration, hammer being buffed was refugee from author's scrap box.

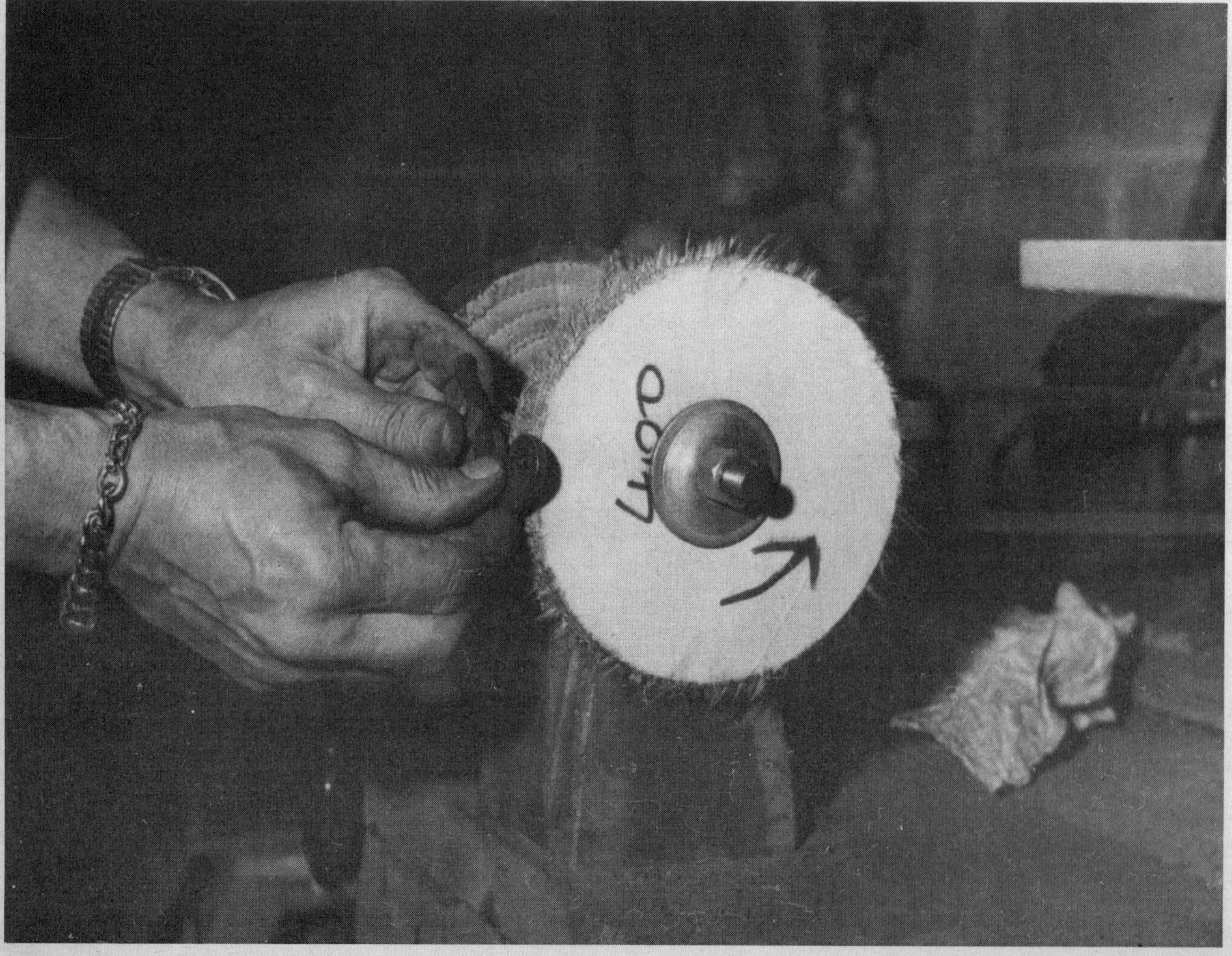

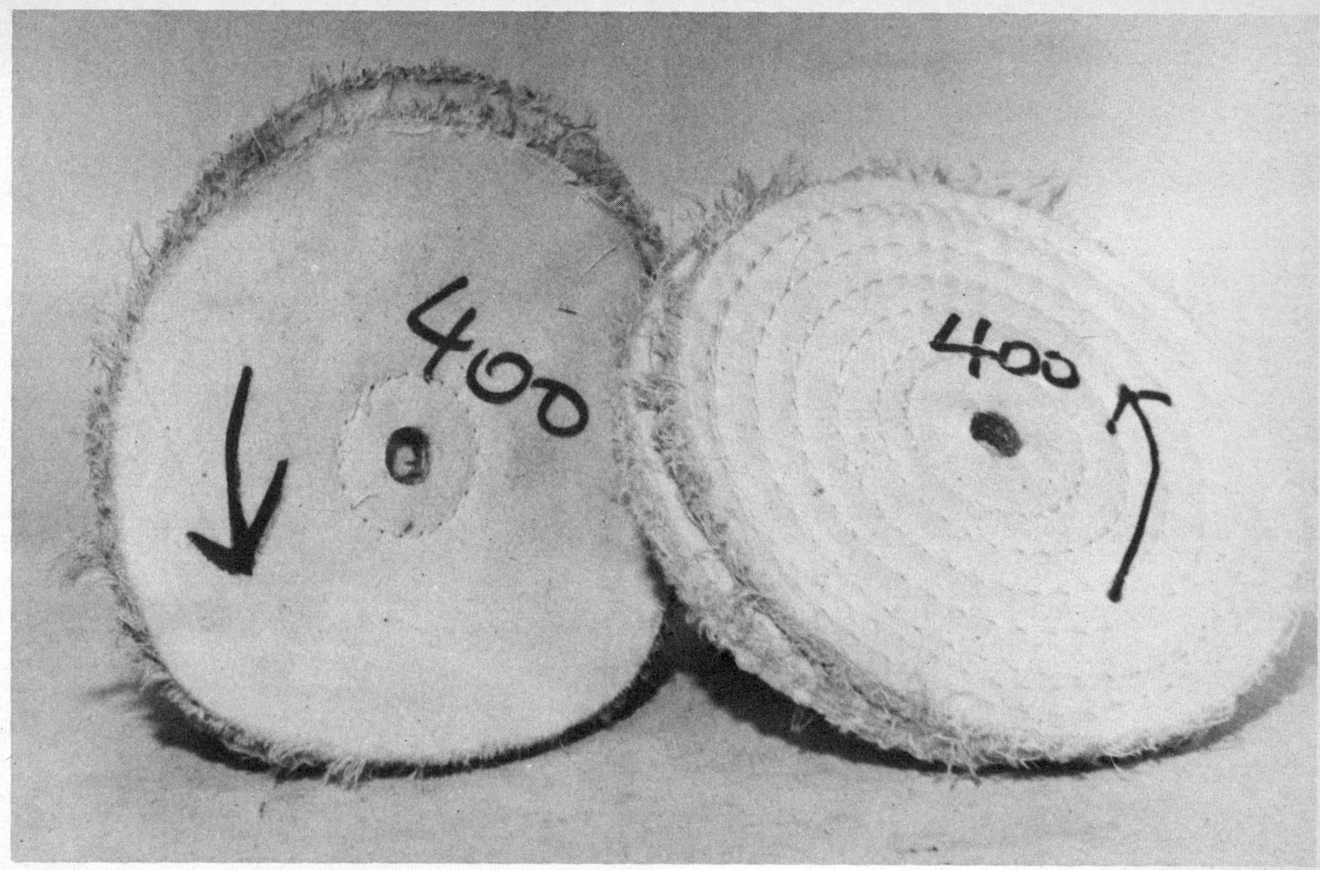

Note that grit and direction of spin are indicated on the loose muslin wheel at left, and on stitched muslin wheel at right.

The polishing head or wheel may be composed of one of several different materials. Felt wheels usually are compressed, but some gunsmiths favor a wooden wheel with felt stripping fastened to it. Felt buffing bobs or heads for the Dremel Moto-Tool are great for getting into tough spots such as trigger guards and are essentially similar to the wheels that you buy. With muslin wheels, you can have the layers of muslin stitched together to give you a firm wheel, or just loosely held together, with the loose muslin wheels being used to finish each step of the polishing process.

To confuse things a bit more, there also are some highly specialized wheels, such as the old-fashioned leather wheels. Wire wheels for matte finishing and carding, as well as for rust removal where you need a lot of cutting action, also are used. For this I suggest a fine and a medium wire wheel. The very coarse wheel should be reserved for garden tools and other such items where a little bit of scoring won't harm the item being polished.

All wheels come in several sizes, the size needed being governed by the size of your buffer, arbor, or the motor shaft and how high the motor may be mounted on the bench. The six-inch wheels are probably the best choice for the hobby gunsmith, with the eight-inch size being the maximum. Also important is the size of the arbor — the shaft on which the wheel sits and spins around. Wire wheels, like grinding wheels, must be driven at certain speeds and like the grinders, they also have a maximum and a minimum rating of revolutions per minute.

The power your motor delivers also governs the size of the wheel you should use. Most of the motors have a spindle speed rating which, for most one horsepower motors, runs around 1750 rpm. Most of the one-quarter and the one-half horsepower motors have a similar spindle speed, and that means using a six-inch wheel. The eight-inch wheels are suitable for 1hp motors for grit abrasives.

Buffing wheels must run true and felt wheels especially must have square edges. Wear a wheel, or get one that is not true on the edges, and it becomes a nightmare, especially when buffing sharp edges or screw holes. When a wheel must be squared or a particular grit must be removed from either a felt or a muslin wheel, you will need a clean dressing stone used to dress grinding wheels. The crystolon rubbing brick sold by Brownell's is a good choice. Since they are not expensive, I always get two of them, keeping one "clean" for the buffing wheels, using the other on my grinders.

Aside from the various felt bobs for the power tools and a couple of wire wheels, you will need the following basics for polishing:

Three six-inch wheels, three-eighths-inch wide, with a

Solid felt commercial wheel, left, compared to homemade wheel at right. To make your own, cut pine board into circle, drill center hole, then use white glue to attach felt insulation on wheel, using wide rubber bands as clamps to hold felt strip until dry. When the felt wears down, it is a simple matter to replace it with another strip.

one-half-inch hole for the arbor. In technical lingo, you will be buying three 6x3/8x½-inch stitched muslin wheels. Eight 6x3/8x½-inch loose muslin wheels also will be required.

Mount three of the stitched muslin wheels on the arbor. Turn on the motor and note in which direction the wheels move. To polish, the wheel must turn clockwise away from the operator, and if the wheel spins the wrong way, you will not get a satisfactory finish. Rotation of the arbor can be switched around on the motor or the wiring of the motor can be reversed, depending on the motor you have. Incidentally, liberated motors from old refrigerators are easy to find, won't bust the piggy bank, and they last, which makes them a favorite with gunsmiths.

Once you have the wheels running in the right direction, mark them on the side of the muslin with a directional arrow and the number 140. I prefer a felt marking pen since it doesn't wear off, but you can use any type of marker that you have handy as long as the marking will not be obliterated by using the wheels.

Next take four 6x3/8x½-inch loose muslin wheels, mount them, mark the directional arrow so that they, like the stitched ones, can be remounted to run in the same direction. Instead of marking them with the number 140, mark the loose wheels with the number 240, thus denoting the finer grit that will be used on those wheels.

Loose muslin wheels must be freed of loose threads. Mount the wheel, hold the edge of an old file or the square shank of a screwdriver squarely in front of the spinning wheel. With a slow, steady motion, bring the edge to bear squarely on the wheel. Clouds of dust and loose threads will come out, but this won't take long. The edge of the wheel — the side that will be used to apply the polish — is known technically as the periphery, incidentally.

If you are after the best finish possible, the rest of the loose muslin wheels or buffs are used with No. 400 grit. Again, mark the grit number and direction of spin on the side of the wheel, then de-fringe it as described above.

The matter of polishing compound comes next. When I first tried my hand at polishing gun parts prior to cold bluing them, I messed up a perfectly nice Model 98 action by using the wrong buffing compound which I had bought in a hardware shop. With the action hanging over my bench as a gruesome reminder of my lack of knowledge, I called for technical help.

The oft-mentioned Bob Brownell was not always a purveyor of gunsmithing tools, but started out as a bluer in a back room somewhere, then ran a bluing shop for a number of years. Naturally, he recommended his own product, called Polish-O-Ray. I tried it and have been hooked on it ever since.

Polish-O-Ray comes in four grits: No. 140, No. 240, No. 400 and there is even a No. 500, which is ultra fine and is used only for the super-deluxe jobs. This buffing compound comes in two-pound foil tubes, and once the tube is opened, you have to dream up ways of keeping it soft. It can be resoftened, but it is much better to prevent hardening. After getting some good advice on keeping the stuff usable for a year or so — all of the ideas were from gunsmiths — I came up with a system that has kept Polish-O-Ray in perfect condition for better than two years.

Each tube comes with a plastic bag so that the shelf life of the product can be extended. Raiding the kitchen cupboard, I found a large Tupperware container with an airtight seal lid.

Put about one or two inches of water into the bottom of the container, mark each of the plastic bags with an indelible marking pen to show the grit number, then fold the mouth of the bag over after sticking the tube of Polish-O-Ray inside. Once in a while I change the water since the standing water in the sealed container acquires a rather pungent odor, but the polishing compound remains properly soft.

To charge the periphery of a wheel, bring the exposed

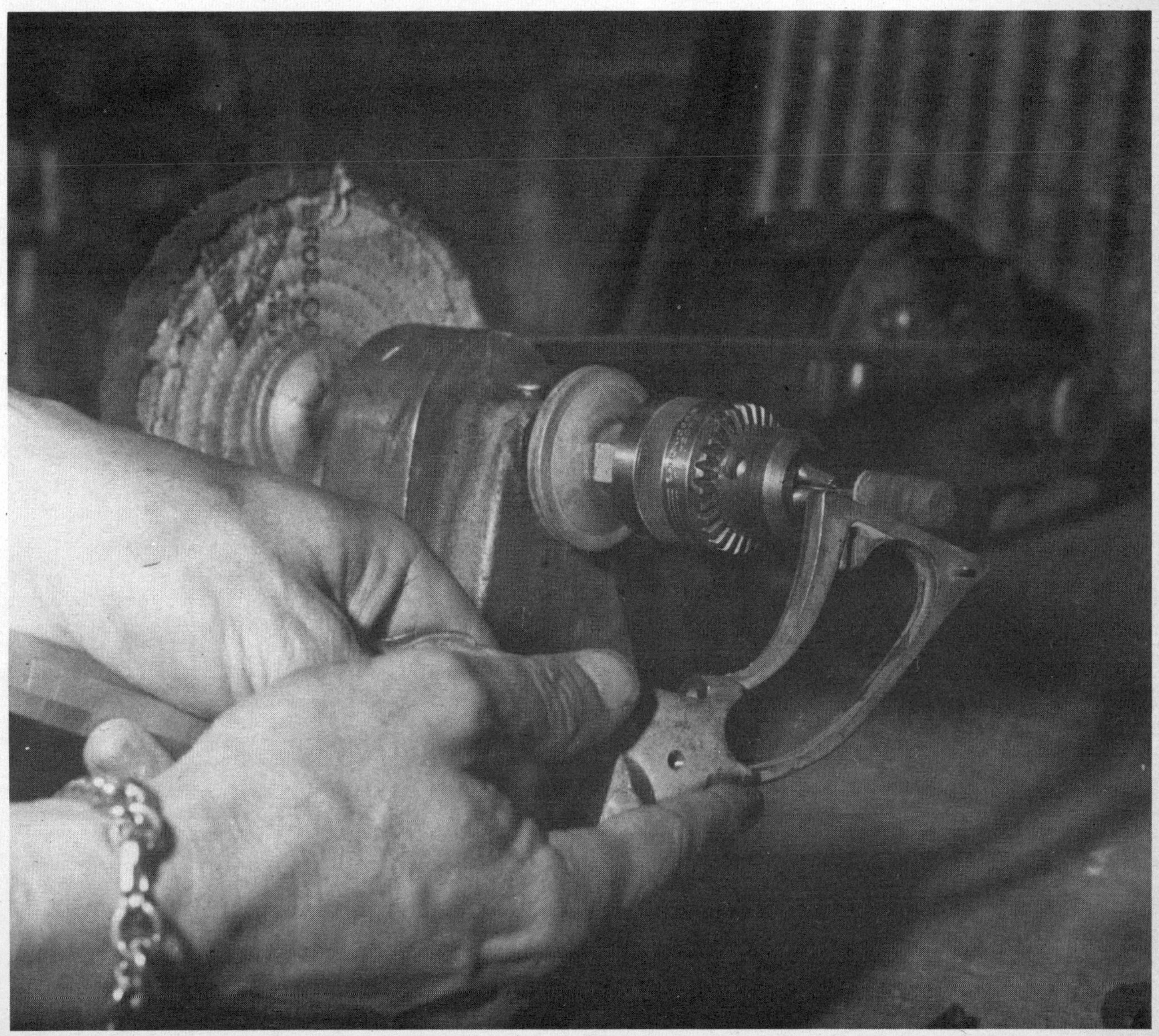

Again, rotation of wheel is wrong and gloves are missing; but positioning of buffer/sander precluded correct camera angle and the handgun grip frame was strictly a scrap-box item.

Aluminum oxide strip glued to sanding drum of Moto-Tool does quick work in cleaning up rough spots not easily reached with a felt bob in chuck running from polishing head.

THE CONTENTS OF THIS KIT are ideal for: Smoothing & polishing molds, dies & castings; Blending in; Relieving stress concentration areas; Polishing out fatigue lines; Cleaning contacs & electrodes; Damaskeening; Removing rust, heat-marks, excess solder and spotweld burns and Micro-deburring. Use light work pressures. Limit speed to 25,000 R.P.M. or less and mandrel overhang to ½ inch or less.

C (coarse texture) Green—Upper Left.   M (medium texture) Brown—Upper Right.

F (fine texture) Red—Lower Left.   XF (extra fine) Light Green—Lower Right.

SIZE NUMBER	Cratex Shape and Dimensions		PRICE		HOW TO RE-ORDER
			EACH	PER 100	
2	TAPERED EDGE WHEEL	⅝" Dia. x 3/32" thick	8c	$4.00	Add Grit Texture Letter to Size Number as: No. 8-C, No. 8-M, No. 8-F, No. 8-XF, etc.
8	CYLINDER POINT	¼" Dia. x ⅞" long	11c	5.50	
9	BULLET POINT	½" Dia. x 1" long	11c	5.50	
10	BULLET POINT	⅜" Dia. x ⅝" long	12c	6.00	
64	STRAIGHT WHEEL	½" x ⅛" x 1/16" hole	8c	4.00	
74	STRAIGHT WHEEL	⅞" x ⅛" x 1/16" hole	11c	5.50	
85	STRAIGHT WHEEL	1" x 1/16" x 1/16" hole	17c	8.50	Sold through leading Industrial Supply Distributors
3	WHEEL MANDREL	⅛" shank	40c	4.44 dz.	
4	POINT MANDREL	⅛" shank	30c	3.36 dz.	

Selection of rubberized abrasive points and wheels should be on hand at all times since they have many shop uses.

Small bobs are used in the Dremel Moto-Tool, while larger ones may be used in a drill press, the extra chuck on a buffer, or on hand-held electric drill.

end of your polishing compound toward the wheel as it rotates toward you. Apply some pressure to the wheel with the polishing compound, but there is no need to press so hard that the wheel collapses. Use just enough pressure so the wheel will take on the buffing compound. When the periphery begins to show the color of the compound, let the wheel spin while you take a breather. This allows the compound to harden somewhat.

Then again bring the stick of polishing compound to bear on the periphery of the wheel. This time, not only use pressure on the stick, but give a little bit of a circular motion to the stick while applying pressure. This will charge the periphery of the wheel. Again rest the wheel at this point to allow the polishing compound to harden on the wheel. If you start polishing while the compound is still soft on the wheel, you will not get an even finish, since the compound wears off rapidly.

After using a wheel loaded with a certain abrasive, the wheel has to be reloaded with the same grit used before. Never mix grits. Trying to remove the compound from a wheel so it can be used with another grit is guaranteed to lead to grief.

Remember the mention made that, before bluing, you must remove the last vestige of grease from the steel to be blued? One way to keep finger or skin oils off

Triple aught steel wool pad attached to split hardwood dowel makes quick work in smoothing out rough spots. Can be used dry or with fine grinding compound and oil mix. Minimum rpms allows better control for metal removal and polishing.

the metal you are polishing is to use cotton gloves as the professional does. Whenever you pick up an action, a slide or any part that is about to be polished and buffed, wear gloves! Wear them when handling the polished part, even when not running the wheels.

In going from one grade of grit to the next finer one, never polish in the same direction. Make certain that your new buffing direction is at a ninety-degree angle to the previous one. If you look at the first polishing with a magnifying glass, you will see that the polishing really does show marks, and all of the marks hopefully run parallel to each other. The next grit is used to buff out these marks, and hence must be run at right angles to the earlier buffing.

Good buffing and polishing constitute an art that must be learned by doing it, not just once, but repeatedly. There are dozens of jobs, like the ejection port of the .45 ACP, that require special handling. Bob Brownell's dissertation on the subject in his *Gunsmith Kinks* is well worth reading, then rereading.

Let me cover some points here that come under the heading of "wish I had known that when...." The felt bobs used with the Dremel Moto-Tool can be used in other chucks, and you can get felt bobs, either already mounted on a mandrel or mountable so you can change bobs and therefore grits. These mandrels can be used in the drill press when the speed of the spindle is adjusted, or can be mounted in a chuck that is screwed onto the arbor of your polisher or wherever you have the wheels mounted. Rough spots, such as castings found in an unassembled kit gun, can be polished out with special polishing sticks. If these are not available, then use the aluminum oxide cloth which comes in three grits. These strips can be held by a piece of hardwood dowel which has been split at one end to a depth of about 1¼ inches. This dowel then is set into the chuck of the drill press or, if your electric drill has a speed adjustment, can even be used in that tool.

Another split dowel, equipped with a steel-wool pad that has been degreased, can be used to remove rough surfaces, as well as some pitting and rust. If you feel you must use the lathe chuck for your polishing, be sure to clean the lathe bed and ways so that all grit and abrasive dust are removed before the lathe is used again.

When a wheel has been used for a while and you have been adding buffing compound, there is going to be a buildup in some areas of the periphery; the low spots will be loaded, while the flat areas will be lacking the compound. Now is the time to clean off the wheel with the truing brick. If the wheel is not trued, it will chatter, and the results will be waves in the polished work.

Buffing requires the use of both hands. Sooner or later, especially when the work is not brought straight against the turning buffing wheel, the wheel will grab and the piece about to be polished will be spun out of your hand. The answer to that and also to tired feet is a heavy rubber mat. Your feet will appreciate it, and when a part does land on the mat, you won't have to worry about filing nicks out of a sight base or some other small part that took off. If you plan to do a fair bit of buffing and polishing, rig up a dust collector that works on the suction system similar to those you see on saws and planers. When polishing, a respirator mask is recommended.

Felt bobs come in many sizes and shapes. They are inexpensive and a good collection of them will save the day for you, especially when you get into some of the tricky areas in polishing some shotguns and the more esoteric rifles. If buffing intrigues you so much that you want to

Rubberized polishing points come in many shapes and grits, and are nearly ideal for working in tight areas where it is easier and more certain to move the tool against the work — since it is easier to control tool, speed and area being polished.

Another safety feature that,
if you'll pardon the pun,
never should be overlooked
are safety glasses. Again,
however, gloves are missing.

tackle other jobs, don't get carried away and start to buff collector's guns. Rebluing such a gun automatically deflates its value.

Remember, too, that any polishing job requires complete disassembly of the gun to be buffed. Most rifles and nearly all shotguns present few difficulties, but with some of the semiautomatic pistols, the job can become hairy. Some of these guns contain little springs hidden away. In such cases, you will wish that your bench was less cluttered and your floor cleaner. I know whereof I speak.

Some parts are polished on one side only and quite often the factory inspection glosses over such things as the inside of side plates of six-guns. I get good results by first using No. 240, then No. 400 grit, but experienced hands at this game just give the piece a couple of passes over the 400 grit wheel or felt bob and get excellent results.

On the whole, it is better to make several light, even passes rather than one hard pushing pass. If you stop for even one second during such a hard push pass, look out! That wheel may not look like it is loaded with abrasive, but take a look at such a polish job. High and low spots are all too apparent.

In an earlier chapter, mention was made of filing and polishing on a lathe. If you can master the art of draw filing, you may discover that a good draw filing job often is as good as a good buffing job, especially on octagonal barrels which are a lot harder to polish than to draw file. Long barrels require a continuing motion from muzzle to breech over the wheel. It is quite easy to bobble here and there, and if this happens, either slow down the speed at which you move the work, or try to correct goofs by draw filing.

Some six-guns have tight chambers and a judicious pass or two with a felt bob and some No. 240 grit polishing compound should relieve the chamber enough for easy chambering and ejection of the fired brass. If you have a drill press or a large electric drill, it is a good idea to use one or the other, since this allows you to set the cylinder squarely under the spindle of the press or right under the drill. Work with care and be sure that the felt bob enters at a ninety-degree angle. Check your work frequently to be certain that not too much metal is being polished off.

Before tackling gun buffing, I decided to practice on some scrap stock. I mentioned this to a friend who runs a gunshop, and he invited me to help myself to parts from his scrap bucket. There was an old floor plate complete with trigger guard, a hunk of busted barrel, screws, sights — a wild array of useless junk that was just right for learning the art of buffing. These scrap parts have served over and over again, for learning to grind and contour the same trigger guard over and over again, and to draw filing a barrel. That same barrel later served me well when I tackled my first drilling and tapping job.

Sometimes you will find that what looks to be a good bluing job was just that, not because of the quality of the bluing but because of good polishing prior to bluing. This is easy to see if you take an old length of barrel and strip the bluing and rust off it — sometimes you can even see how the work was polished and which way the job was handled.

Buffing is not difficult, it just takes patience and practice!

Percussion hammer, below left, first was cleaned up, rust polished out, then surface polished with 140-grit Polish-O-Ray. Note the parallel polishing marks left by the 140-grit. Next came polishing with 240 and 400-grit Polish-O-Ray, below right.

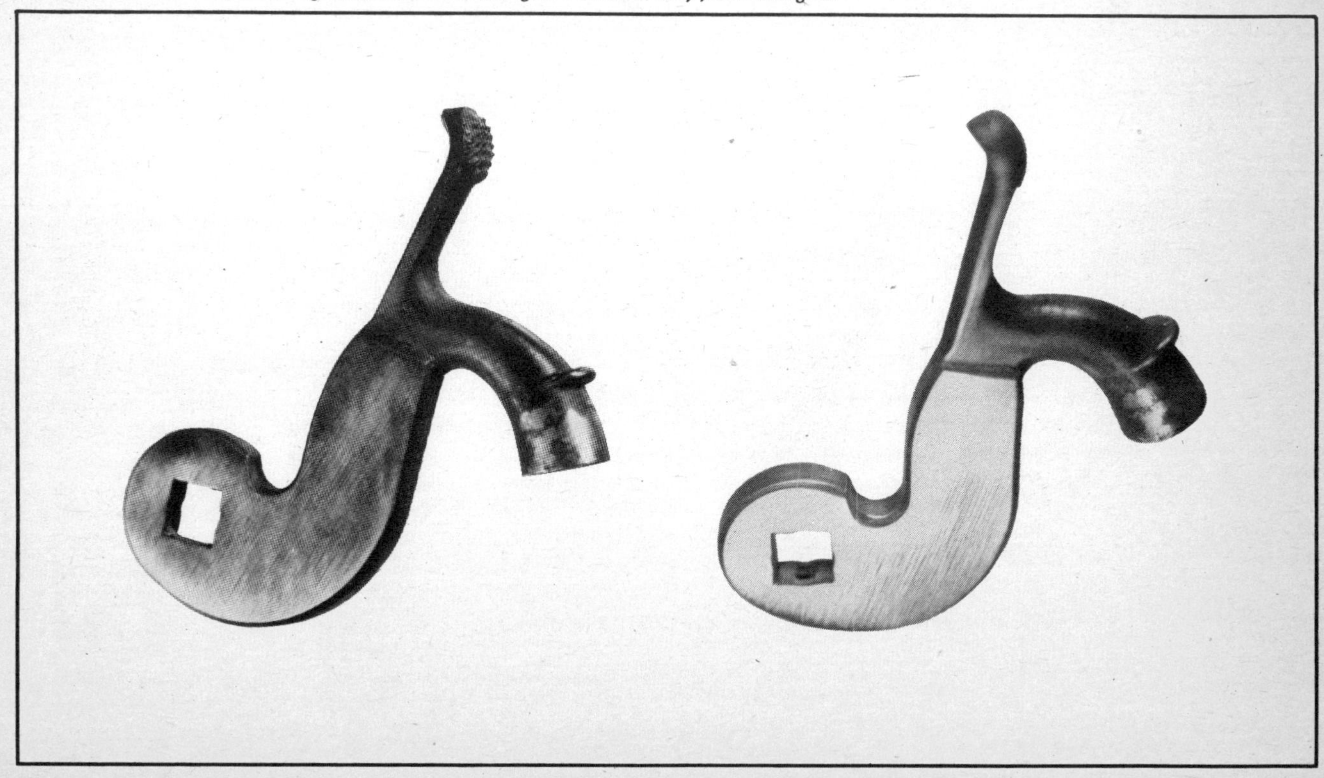

Chapter 27

FROM TWO WRECKS, ONE RIFLE

Cannibalization Is The Name Of The Game For Some Obsolete Models

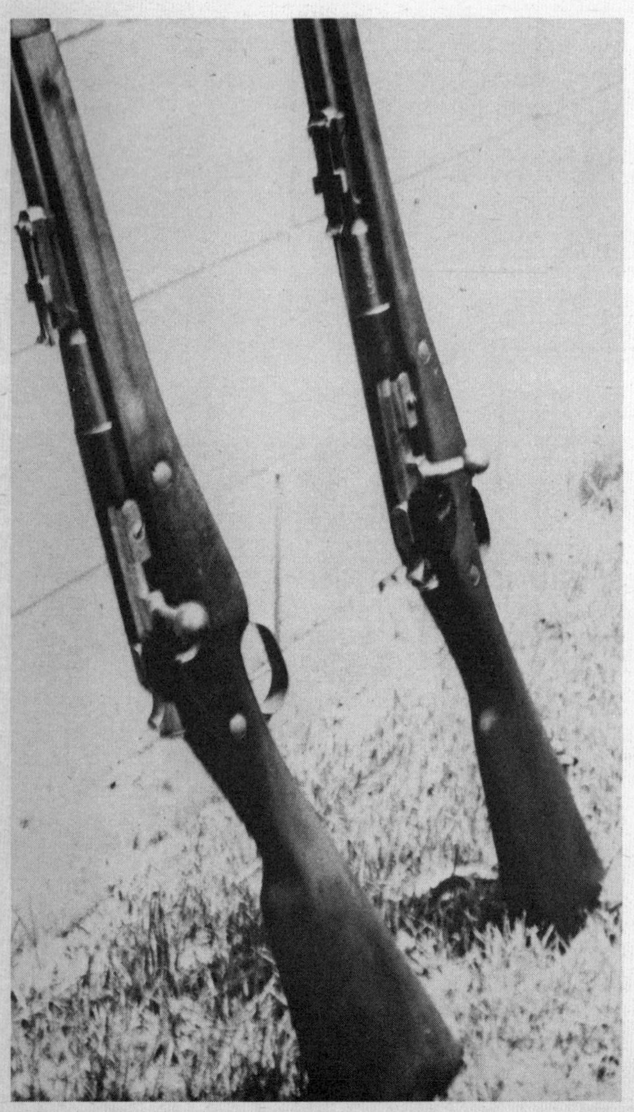

FOR THE hunter, shooter and gun collector, the years immediately following WWII were good ones. Military rifles, some relatively new as well as obsolete models, were plentiful and cost so little that you now must wonder why you didn't buy more of them in those days.

Building a fine, representative collection of military rifles would have been simple and could have been accomplished without having to float a second mortgage. A catalog from that period shows, for instance, an early Japanese Murata being offered for $45, while a cutaway Lee-Enfield, used for teaching purposes, carried the ridiculous price tag of $24.50!

At that time, I became interested in military rifles, especially early ones, but did not have enough foresight to buy good representative specimens to build a collection. I simply accumulated them with the idea that someday I'd get them all organized, then fill in the voids as the occasion arose.

Among the more interesting of the early bolt action rifles are the French Lebels and the Berthier, with the variations of the Kropatchek being added to confuse things a bit.

Going back in the developmental history of the bolt action design is interesting, especially when you can examine the efforts of the various designers and see how one borrowed from the other, while the latter improved on a design feature he borrowed from the other fellow.

Two Lebel-Remington rifles, one with a cracked receiver, the other badly butchered, to be combined into one sporter.

One of two Lebels at left had had some rather unique stock customizing work performed in the past. Above: Brass drift and hammer remove forend cap.

The one French rifle I found I was missing was the Remington Model 1907-15. The Berthier is a modification and improvement of the Lebel, and the Berthier was improved by the Remington Model 07-15 design. Gone is the tubular magazine which has been replaced by a three-shot Mannlicher clip, but the two-piece bolt remains, as do some of the other features of the basic action. The original rifles were chambered for the 8mm Lebel round, but in 1934, the Remington 07-15 was given a new lease on life, when it was rechambered for the 7.5mm rimless cartridge which was designed for use in the light machine guns. The cartridge is known usually as the 7.5x54MAS cartridge.

After several years of searching and waiting, no such Lebel-Remington had appeared on the scene, so I decided to buy the first one I could find, regardless of condition. I got my wish. The rifle, with near mint stock and barrel, had a deep split in the forward bridge of the receiver, thus precluding any idea of shooting my latest acquisition.

A few months later, I found another Remington 07-15 that had been reworked by someone who thought he knew

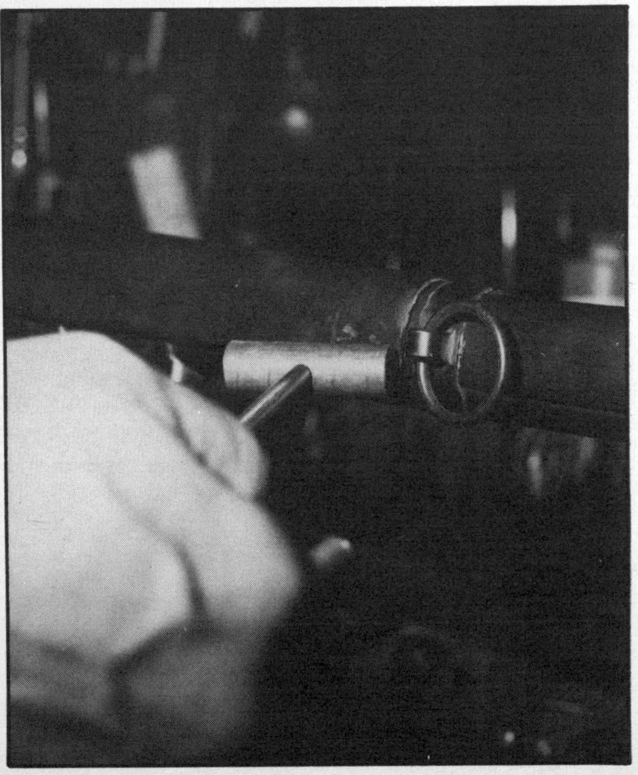

Careful use of brass hammer will remove rear barrel band.

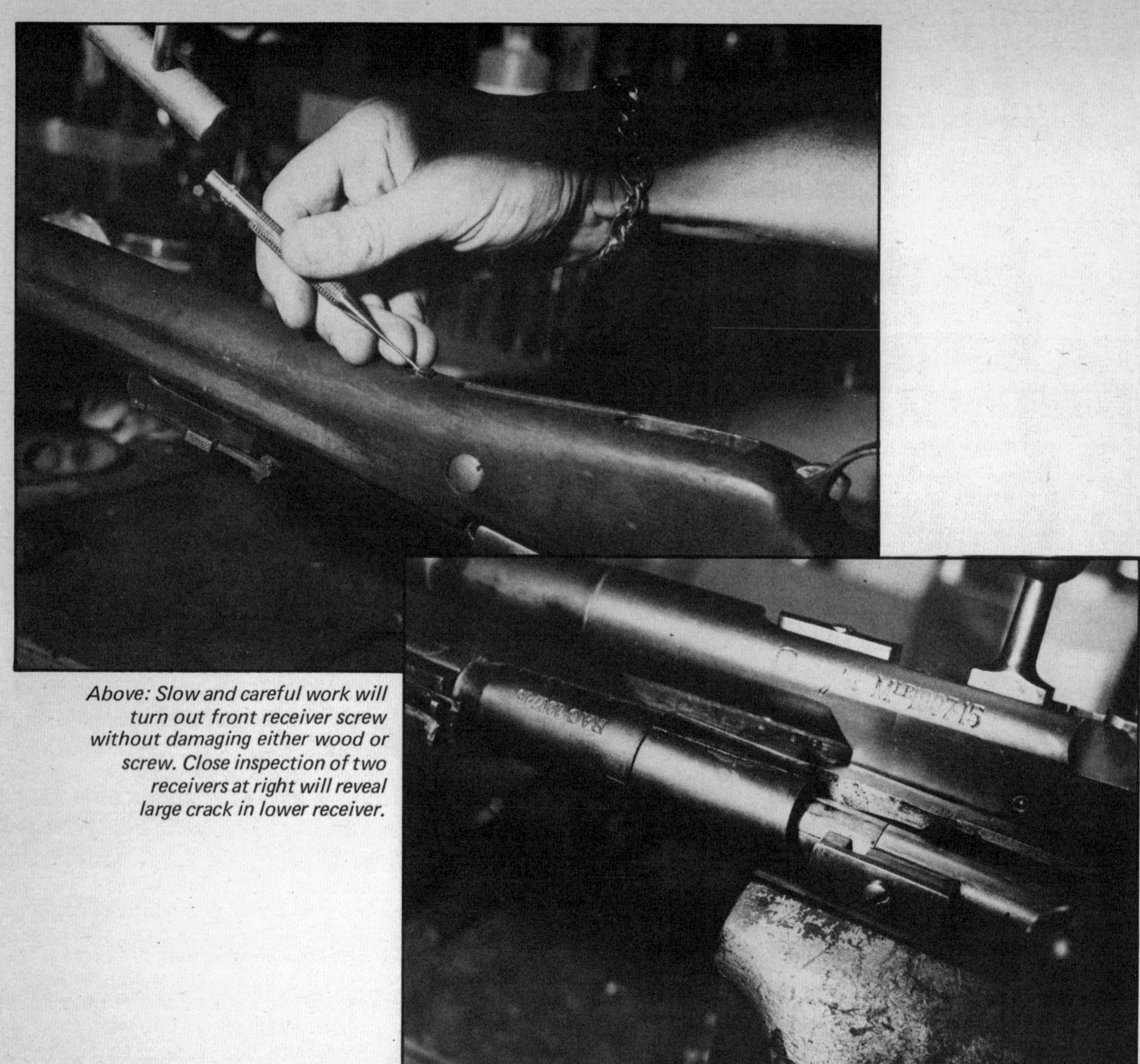

Above: Slow and careful work will turn out front receiver screw without damaging either wood or screw. Close inspection of two receivers at right will reveal large crack in lower receiver.

what he was doing. The barrel had been chopped off, the forend had been reworked, the barrel innards resembled a sewer pipe, but the action was all in one piece, including the bolt which had been doctored.

The next step would be cleaning and stripping both guns, then swap actions and stocks so I eventually would have one good Lebel-Remington rifle.

If you have never torn a gun apart for which take-down instructions are not available, these tips might help you and should also prevent you from having to carry your gun to the local 'smith in a brown paper sack. In tearing a number of guns apart that lacked instructions or even exploded views, I found that the following happened invariably: (a) the mechanism functioned before, but did not after reassembly or (b) some of the pins, screws or springs, which once were in the gun, apparently had lost their home during the assembly process. With more care, I solved these specific problems.

When these rifles were rechambered, the cleaning rods were replaced by stacking swivels. I removed the hardware from the forend by depressing the retaining springs, then drifted the forend cap and barrel band off with a brass drift. I turn the rifle so I can apply even force to the bands. If this is not done, the bands will tip or cant and the result will be chewed wood.

Most rifles are held in the wood by two stock screws, one forward of the trigger guard, the other to the rear of it. Remove the rear screw, which should present no problem. The front screw does not have the conventional screw slot, but requires a tool similar to the spanner used to remove firing pin bushings from double-barrel shotguns.

Forgetting about special tools, take a small punch and a

Left: Cocking piece on right was messed up by unknown inexpert gunsmith. Same bolt and action, below, with trigger group, magazine and springs removed.

light hammer; by alternating where the punch is placed, you can turn out the wood screw.

On the right side of the action, just behind and slightly below the bolt knob, you should find a large machine screw. As you turn that screw out, keep your left hand under the trigger guard. The screw must be removed fully, and once freed, will permit the entire trigger guard, trigger and the springs to come out of the rifle. Some rifles of this type may have the Mannlicher-type clip which is inserted into the action from below.

To remove the bolt, proceed as follows: Unscrew the large machine screw on top of the bolt. Move the bolt slightly rearward, until the bolt head is located in the machined cut. Depending on the condition of the rifle, accumulated grease, and the original fit, the bolt head may turn with ease or stick in place as if glued.

Note that there are two forward locking lugs. Using the brass drift, and holding the drift on the lug on the right side of the bolt face, turn out the bolt head. Note that it cams into the bolt body and that the hole in the head lines up with the hole from which you just removed the bolt screw.

If you find that the bolt head will not turn, try some Bust Rust. Jamming the bolt rearward does not help, since it does not permit the rotation of the bolt head which is needed to separate the two pieces of the bolt.

Up to this moment, the job of combining two wrecks so that I'd have one usable rifle was fairly simple. If there had been a gunsmith around with a properly equipped shop, my labors on this project would have been finished, except for reassembling all the bits and pieces and making sure that no parts were left over.

The barrel of these Remington rifles has an outside

*Cracked receiver with bolt inserted but unlocked.
Bolt screw is shown fully seated in removable bolt head.*

*Bolt removed from action with
bolt screw partially backed out.*

diameter of 1.175 inches where the barrel seats into the receiver ring and it tapers, within two inches, to 0.964-inch.

The rear sight appears to sit on two bands which almost completely encircle the barrel. Since there was no evidence that these bands were screwed onto the barrel, I assumed that they were silver soldered in place.

To remove such sights, use a propane torch and play the flame all around the sight base or bands, making certain the flame is kept in motion and isn't too large.

You could now use three hands — one to keep the torch going, one to hold a brass drift and one to hold the hammer used to pound on the brass drift which is held against the rear edge of the sight base or band.

Once the silver solder has softened, drift the sight out of its position, and slip it down the barrel with the drift. Make sure to wait a spell before removing the sight fully, as it's hot!

Once the sight has cooled, slip it off the barrel and keep it with the rest of the parts.

Barrel removal comes next and here is where things get a bit sticky, literally and figuratively. A gunsmith should be able to turn the barrel out of the action, provided he has a heavy-duty barrel vise. There are a number of tricks that make it possible to remove a barrel from an action, but most military rifles will resist any such efforts. One of the oldest tricks — and one that is not recommended — is the use of a lathe and a Stilson wrench. As far as I am concerned, that is just about the fastest way to mess up a lathe bed and an almost sure way of springing the rifle's action.

If no gunsmith is available, you have to make up your own barrel vise, which is covered in another chapter. Remove the barrel from the action, do whatever barrel and action swapping is needed, then screw one or the other barrel back into the action.

You'd think screwing a barrel into an action is about as difficult as dropping a freshly cast bullet that you had picked up prematurely, but it's not. Just running the barrel into the action is simple, but getting the right fit is something else. A lot of actions and barrels have a mark, the index or witness mark, that shows one how far the tube

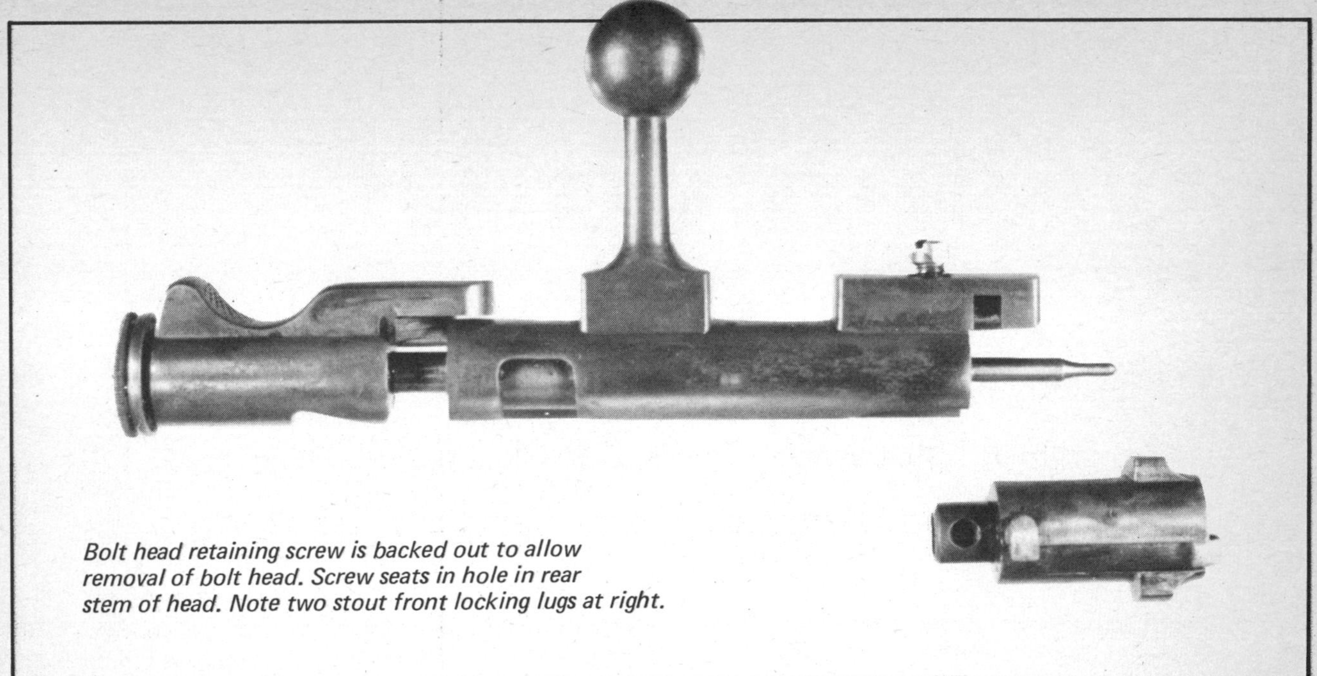

Bolt head retaining screw is backed out to allow removal of bolt head. Screw seats in hole in rear stem of head. Note two stout front locking lugs at right.

gets screwed into the action. If, like me in this instance, you have no intention of shooting the rifle, simply running the threads together until the barrel is locked in place is good enough. This is provided the sights are now on top of the barrel and not underneath. Remember to mark the gun — a piece of tape on the butt stock is sufficient — to indicate the gun has not been headspaced and checked, therefore should not be fired. Headspacing is a job for the pro and never should be attempted with live ammo.

Reassembly of this or any other rifle shouldn't present any problem. Remember that 99.9 percent of all parts on nearly all guns fit together snugly, that there is usually a point where one part bears on another which then transfers its work or energy on yet another part.

If things don't go together smoothly, remember how the thing came apart. It is true that a light tap or two might be indicated once in a while, but wildly beating a part is not

the way to tackle the job at hand, if you don't want to be known as a hammer mechanic.

Somewhere between taking the rifle apart and putting it together again, you probably will have to clean the crud and grease of a couple of decades out of the action, parts and springs. The simplest way is to use a bluing tank. You can either buy the tank, have one made locally, or make something suitable yourself.

The easiest, least costly and also longest lasting tank of this type I've had was one I built some years ago. It is fifty inches long, eight inches wide and high, made from common pine shelving. I glued and nailed the surfaces on the boards, then used marine fiberglass inside and out to cover the thing. It holds hot water and cleaning solvent without leaking.

To clean the parts, I dump them in the tank and let them sit there for a spell. Various industrial solvents, hot water and detergent, plus a number of specialized solvents are on the market. Usually marketed as degreasers or solvents, sometimes as bluing removers, they all do the trick. Particularly cruddy parts may need scrubbing with an old toothbrush, a hand-held wirebrush or even a piece of steel wool.

Rinse clean, let air dry, then lightly lube and assemble...or as the instructions usually say so blithely: *Assemble In Reverse Order.*

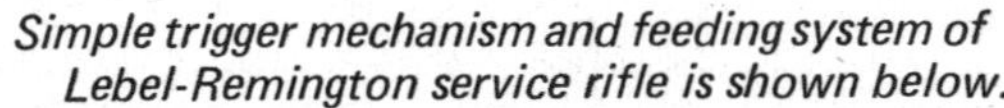

Simple trigger mechanism and feeding system of Lebel-Remington service rifle is shown below.

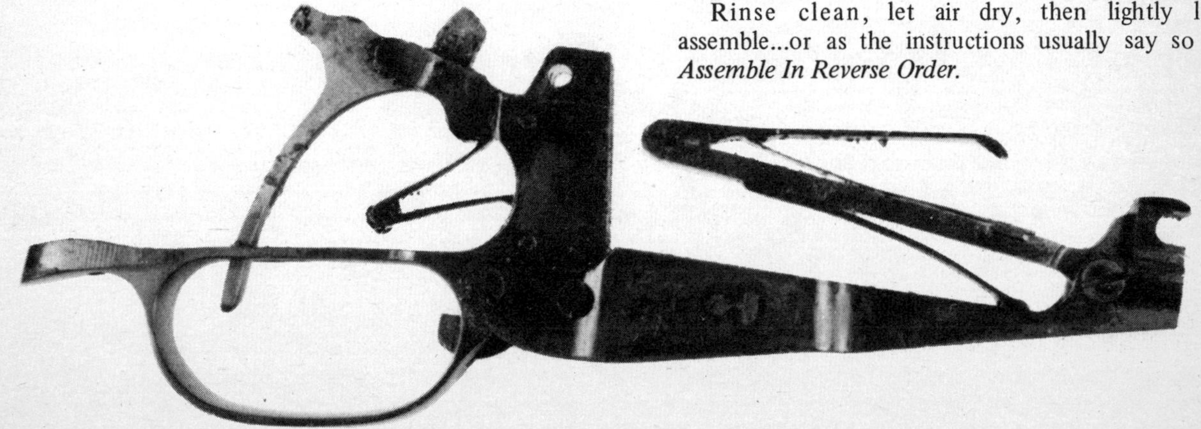

Chapter 28

BASICS OF GLASS STOCKING

Fiberglass May Lack Beauty, But It Has Strength And Character For Hard Use!

ONE OF THE latest wrinkles in benchrest shooting is the fiberglass stock. Since several jillion wood stocks have been salvaged by glass-bedding barrel channel and action, this move from bedding to stock was a natural progression. Fiberglass has a number of advantages over wood when it comes to the matter of adding a handle to a barreled rifle action.

Unlike wood, fiberglass is completely stable. It will not warp, twist or cup; nor will it absorb moisture, then surrender it when the atmospheric humidity disappears and temperatures rise. Fiberglass is much lighter than wood and appears to be at least twice as strong. It also is easier to work with than wood, and any goofs are corrected easily with fiberglass. The one real drawback is that fiberglass lacks the eye appeal of wood, it cannot be checkered, and while inletting is identical to inletting a wood stock, the exterior finish cannot be applied by either the home gunsmith or a professional gunsmith. The exterior finish is best applied by a car painter!

Chet Brown pioneered the fiberglass stock and is the head honcho of the Brown Precision Company (5869 Indian Avenue, San Jose, California 95123), producers of fiberglass stocks for nearly every purpose. Stocks are offered for benchrest and target rifles, as well as for hunting

Fiberglass stock by Chet Brown is lightweight, rugged, impervious to most dings, ready for sling and recoil pad installation.

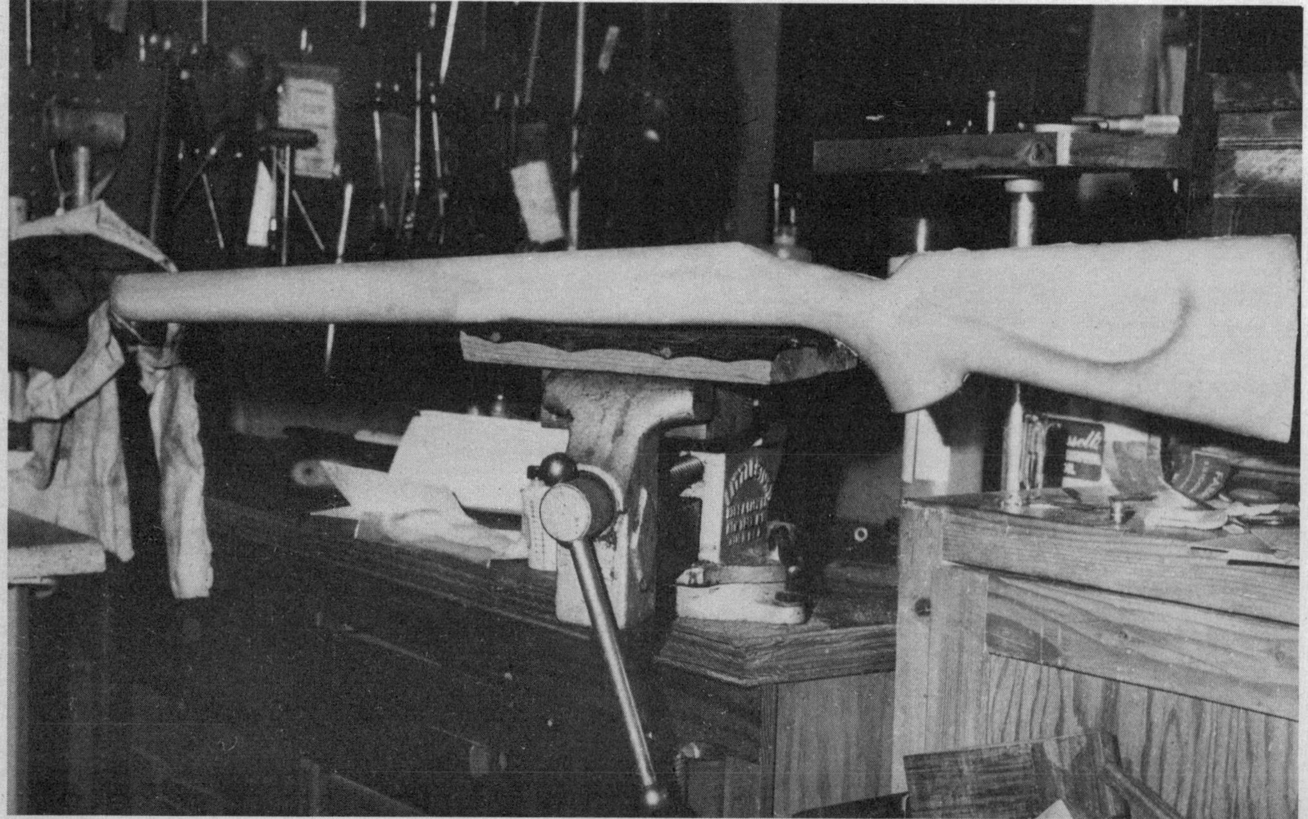

Factory wood stock taken from Remington Model 700 7mm Magnum, scales 2¼ pounds with pad and swivels.

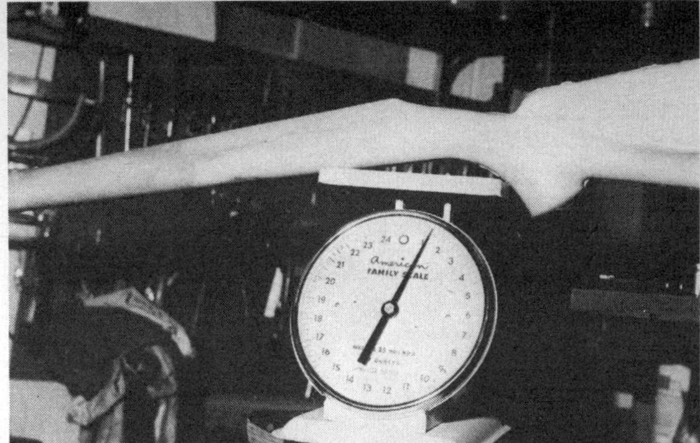

Fiberglass stock designed to replace wood on M700 weighs a pound less than wood, plus a few ounces for addition of recoil pad and two sling swivels.

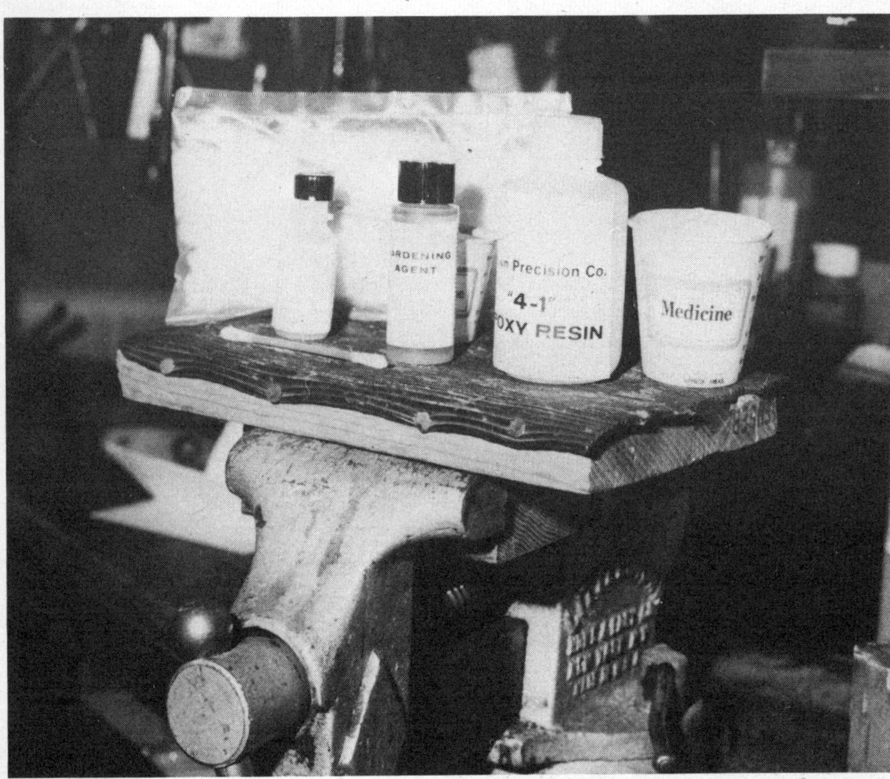

The home gunsmith should have a little practice before tackling a bedding job with fiberglass stock, although instructions and materials are included with kit.

rifles, and you can order most stocks directly from the firm. If someone does not want to tackle the job of restocking a rifle, send the barreled action to Brown, tell him exactly what you want and the kind of finish desired. They'll do all the work for you for a reasonable charge.

The stocks are semi-inletted and still show mould marks on the outside when Brown ships that new rifle handle to you. Inletting is simple, since fiberglass can be sanded, cut with a knife, filed, or trimmed with most any type of a cutting tool that fits into the area. The barrel channel on the stock with which I worked was almost fully inletted and needed only a few strokes with some fairly coarse sandpaper to finish that part of the job.

Once the action is seated, the barreled action should be parallel with the top and the sides of the stock when the bedding is completed. The trigger should be located in the center of the trigger cutout in the stock and should extend downward the same amount it does in a wood stock. There should be no contact between stock and trigger, safety, bolt handle, bolt release or the guard screws, and only the rear surface of the recoil lug should make contact with the stock. Inletting should be deep enough so barrel and action are seated in the stock to about one-half their total depth.

When inletting is completed, locate one of the guard screw holes, then drill a slightly oversized hole through the stock. Seat the guard screw lightly and check the alignment of metal and fiberglass once more. Remove all the metal, and sand the barrel channel and the inletted action area with coarse sandpaper, preferably No. 80 or even a coarser grit. Be sure to give all areas the required roughness or teeth

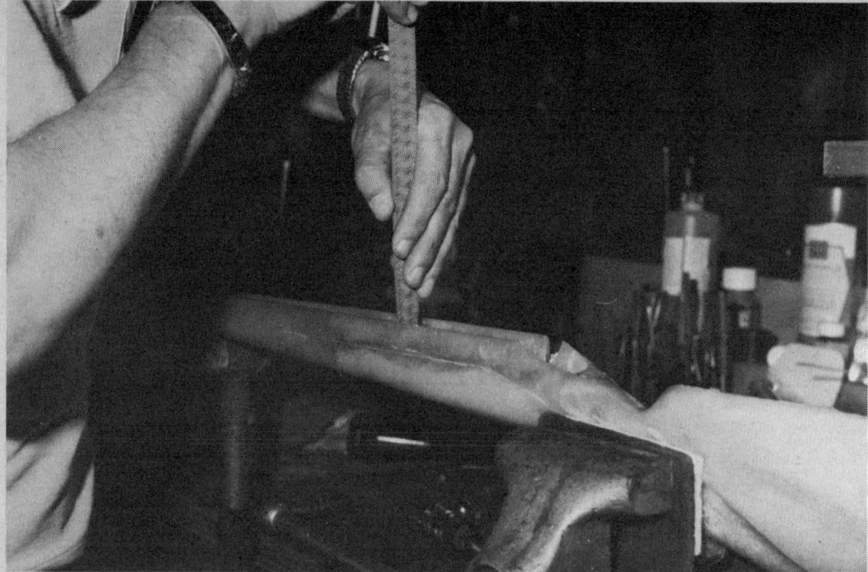

A coarse file such as used to sharpen chainsaws will remove excess fiberglass rapidly.

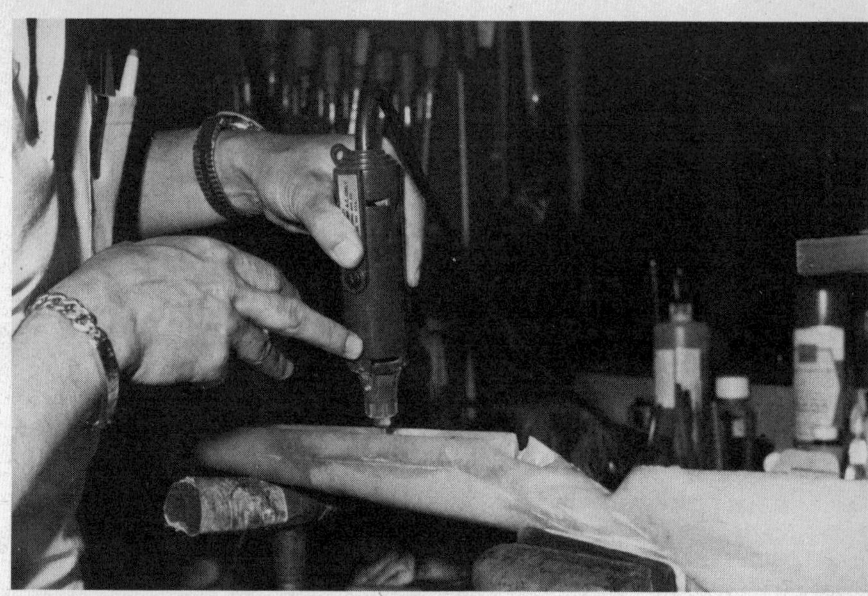

Barrel channel is relieved by use of Dremel Moto-Tool. Method is similar to that required for inletting wood stock, described elsewhere in this book.

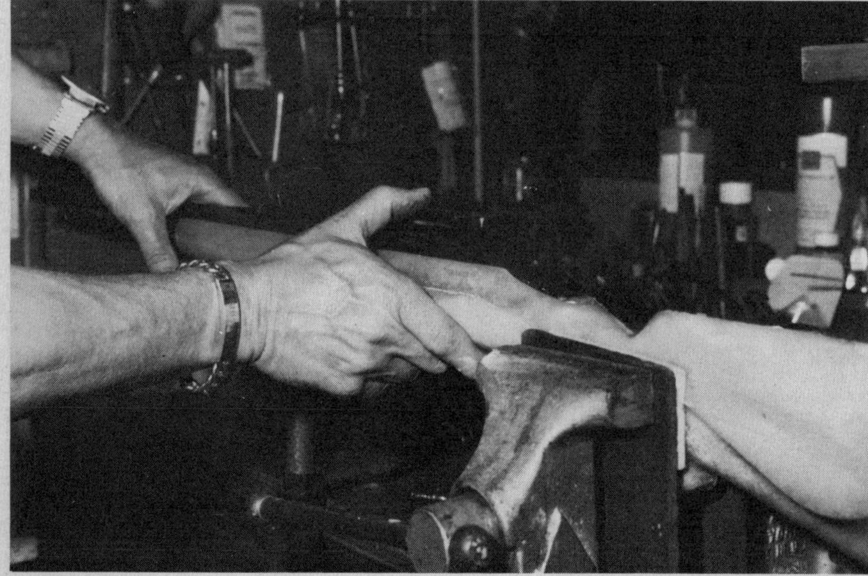

Little inletting was necessary to fit action into fiberglass stock. Despite ruggedness of material, padded jaws are mandatory.

HOME GUNSMITHING DIGEST

so the bedding compound will have the needed bonding surfaces.

The glass-bedding process used for fiberglass stocks is the same one as described elsewhere. My stock arrived with the required glass-bedding materials, but any of the other epoxy glass-bedding compounds can be used, such as Devcon, Microbed, Acraglas, etc. Do not forget the release agent, and use liberal amounts of it. Tape all holes shut with Scotch or masking tape. Bed the barreled action and let the fiberglass harden fully. When the bedding compound is solid, remove the barreled action again and drill the guard screw holes. If need be, file out the bolt cut-out on the stock.

Inlet and bed the trigger guard, then remove it so you can start finishing the outside of the stock. Usually, the exterior surface of the stock has small pinholes from the casting of the stock. If the hole is small and shallow, use a ground-down nail, ice pick or a dental pick to roughen up the bottom of the hole. Use some of the glass-bedding epoxy compound to fill these holes, and when the material has fully hardened, sand it smooth.

For slightly larger holes — and none of them will be much larger than the head of a dressmaker's pin — outline the holes with a regular lead pencil. Look the stock over on all sides under a good light, then fill those holes either with car body putty or with an unthinned car lacquer primer. Rub whatever filler material you use into the holes with your fingertips.

If you sanded the stock or filled small holes prior to filling those pinhead holes, be sure to get all the sanding dust off the stock and out of the holes; a blast of compressed air will make this easy. Wipe the stock down with a Tac rag to remove all sanding dust. Work as much of the putty or primer into the holes as you can. The aim is to get all the air out of the holes, so work the filler material well into any and all holes. Let dry fully, then sand down with No. 120 or 180 dry paper. Remove all the dust and check the stock again for holes.

If there is still evidence of holes or any of those filled recently have not been filled completely, repeat the putty or primer treatment. Since the primer material has a built-in shrinking factor, it may be necessary to repeat filling the holes.

The recoil pad comes next. Since benchrest rifles are classified by weight, Chet Brown prefers to use the Pachmayr No. 200 pad, since it is possible to hollow out the inside of the pad and thus cut an ounce or two off the weight of the finished rifle. The butt where the pad is installed is rather porous and even a bit rough, but the entire area should be sanded down with No. 80 grit or coarser sandpaper. Using an epoxy glue, seat the recoil pad and fashion a clamp for it with heavy rubber bands. When the glue is fully cured, shape and sand the recoil pad so the contour of stock and pad match.

On most of these stocks you can see where the moulds were joined and this line, as well as any other area not perfectly smooth, must be sanded down. Start with No. 180 dry sandpaper, then dust and go over the stock with No. 240 grit paper.

If you know something about car painting and finishing, you probably can finish the rest of the stock work without too much trouble. Lacking such knowledge, I followed Chet Brown's advice and took the stock to the nearest car body repair shop and had the painter there finish this project. Essentially, you first mask all parts which you don't want painted, sand and fill again, then prime and have it painted with whatever color strikes your fancy.

Although the finished rifle — the original barreled action in the Brown fiberglass stock — weighs 1¼ pounds less than the original Model 700, the recoil of that 7mm Magnum appears to be somewhat reduced. I use this rifle for mountain hunting where gun weight is an important consideration, and the fiberglass stock, despite considerable wear and tear, looks as good today as it did when I put the rifle together.

Best of all, there is little likelihood that the stock ever will require refinishing and dent raising. Fiberglass can take the beating without showing the traces of it.

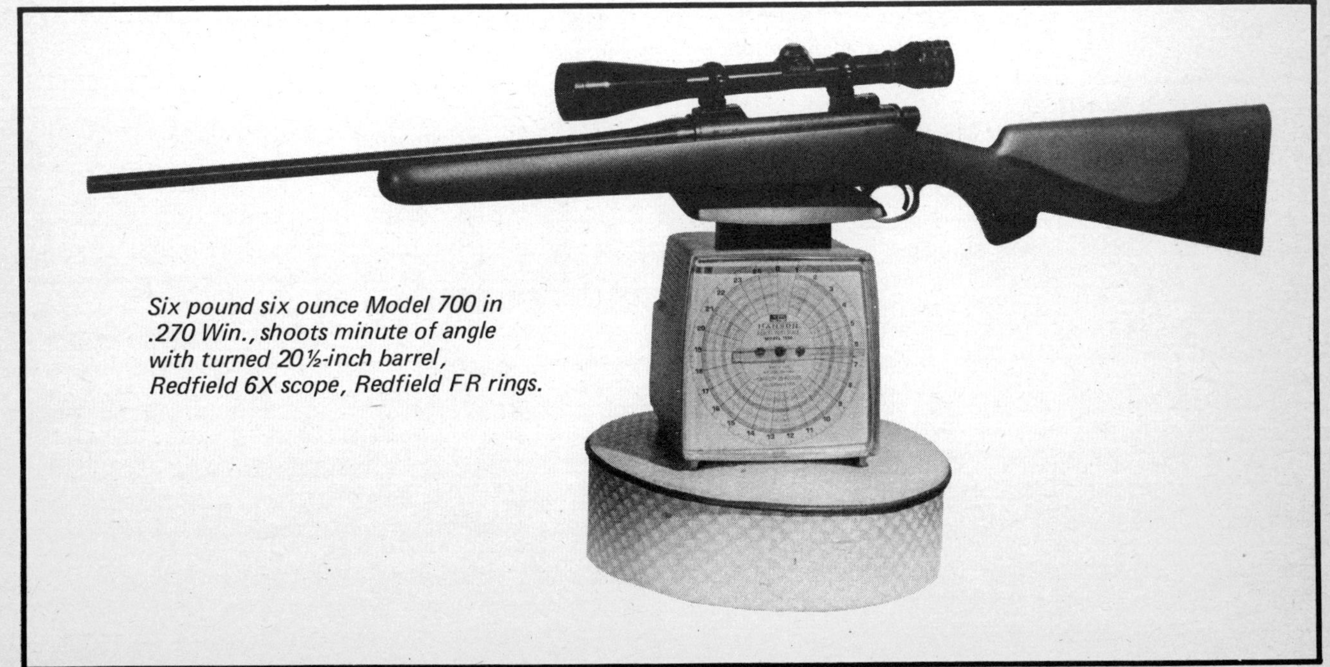

Six pound six ounce Model 700 in .270 Win., shoots minute of angle with turned 20½-inch barrel, Redfield 6X scope, Redfield FR rings.

Chapter 29

Most front sight beads are threaded into shotgun barrel and, with proper care, may be turned out without damage to metal. Alternatively, bead may be left in place, and sight ramp may be drilled out to help anchor new ramp.

SIGHTS FOR SLUG GUNS

You Can Develop That Ancient Scattergun Into A Big-Game Getter At Minimum Cost

MORE AND more states are requiring that medium and big game be hunted with a shotgun firing slugs. Hand in hand with this, hunters have discovered that the shotgun slug is a highly effective projectile at the shorter ranges, especially when shooting through brush at a fast-moving and often heavy-muscled game animal.

In the past several years, our firearms manufacturers have paid attention to this trend and most of them now offer special slug barrels for many of their models. These slug barrels have rifle-type sights which allow the shooter to aim his shot, thus getting better accuracy than he could from the traditional bead shotgun sight.

These barrels are fairly expensive and are not available for some of the older model shotguns, especially those which have been discontinued. This means then that the hunter either has to make do with whatever sight he now has on his shotgun barrel, or he buys a new shotgun with which barrel swapping is possible. But there is yet another alternative: install rifle-type sights yourself.

The simplest of these sights is known as Slug Site (3835 University Ave., Des Moines, Iowa 50311) and can be installed on any type of shotgun in less than five minutes; it also can be removed, and remounted as often as the need arises. Essentially, this sight consists of a pre-shaped sheet

steel stamping of the basic sight, which has a rear sight notch and a front bead with a red dot. Both ends of the sight can be bent by means of pliers, thus sight adjustment is possible, although it is a matter of trial and error rather than simply clicking a knob one way or the other.

The instructions that come with the Slug Site are complete and detailed, and mounting the sight takes only minutes, since the sight is fastened by means of an adhesive backing strip.

A pointer or two from my own experiences with this

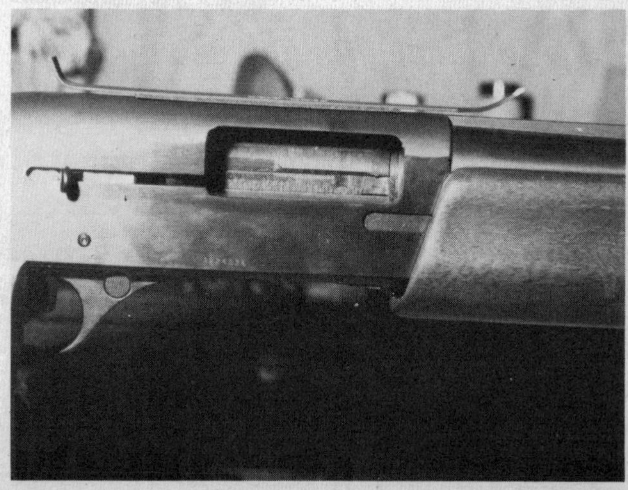

With the protective covering of the adhesive still in place, the Slug Site is positioned on the receiver.

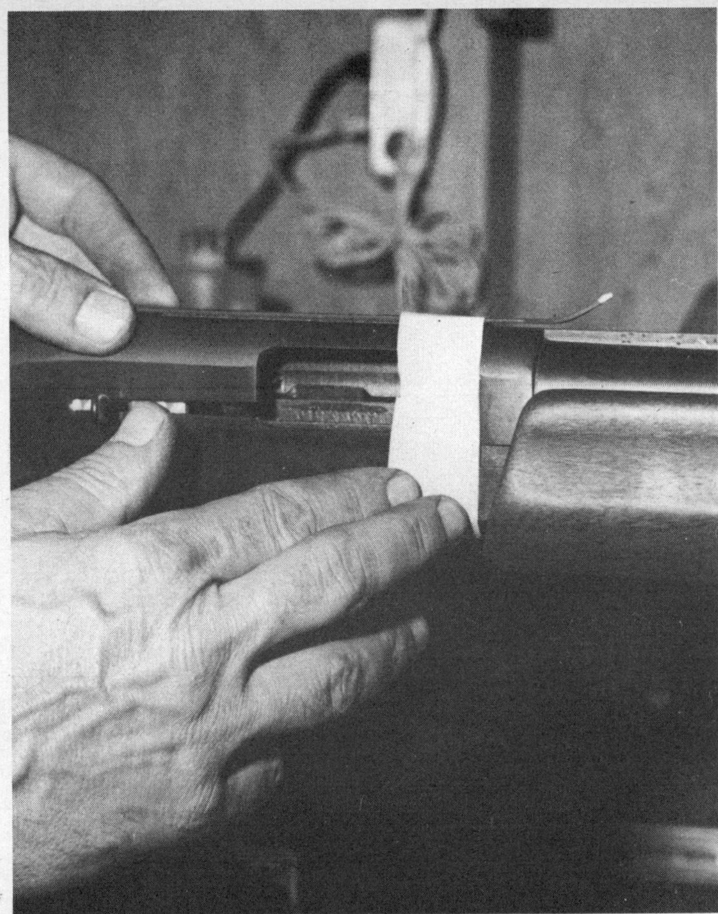

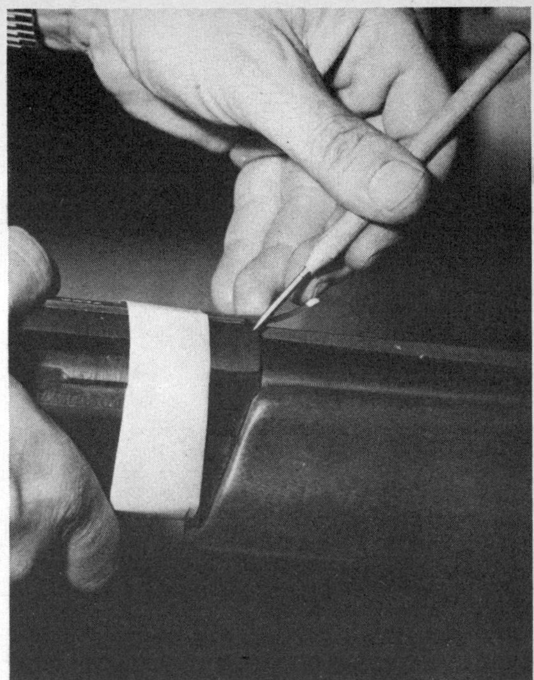

Adhesive tape (left) holds Slug Site on gun as it is shouldered and sighted. Once sight location has been set, light line is scribed on receiver, (above) facilitating repositioning after removal.

sight might be in order. If you are far-sighted, the Slug Site should be mounted on the barrel since, when receiver-mounted, it might be too close to the eye. Before peeling off the protective covering from the adhesive, I position the sight where I think I want it, then tape it lightly into place with masking tape. This allows me to mount the gun to the shoulder and see just how eye and sight line up.

For repeated mounting and removal of the sight on the same gun, I scribe a light line on each side of the forward end of the sight so that repositioning it does not require a great deal of time and attention as to the precise location wanted.

Unlike rifle actions and barrels in which there is plenty of steel to drill and tap for mounting sight bases, most shotguns have thin-walled receivers and even thinner-walled barrels, hence drilling and tapping is not recommended unless you have a great deal of experience doing this type of work.

Some years ago the late John Dewey, a top-rated gunsmith and benchrest shooter, used a small ramp front sight and a folding leaf rear sight to produce what he called the Fine Line shotgun sights. The sights were made by Marble Arms, and Dewey made up a high front and rear ramp on which the Marble sights were set by means of a dovetail. The ramps were held in place by two pre-shaped sight bands. One end of the band fitted into a machined slot, and the other side of the band was held in place by two 8-48 screws.

Despite the interest in this type of sight, no manufacturer currently offers a package deal containing a front and rear sight and a suitable means of fastening these sights to the barrel. Dewey accomplished the fastening by using shaped spring stock 0.025-inch thick, so that the sight band had enough spring in it to allow secure fastening. Such a sight band can be made easily from flat spring stock, and

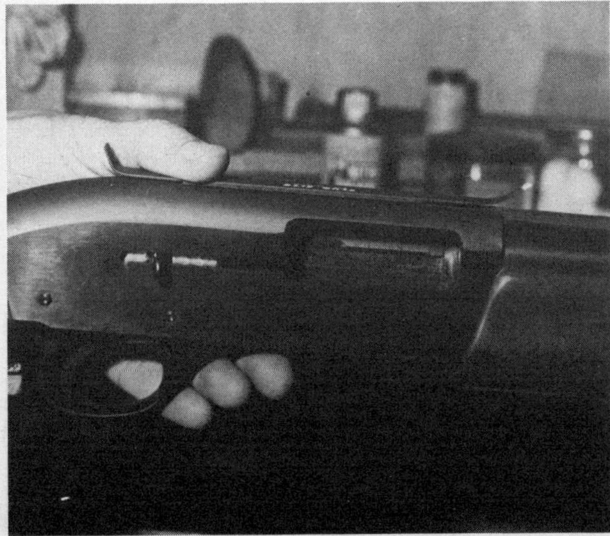

Slug Site in position and ready for use.

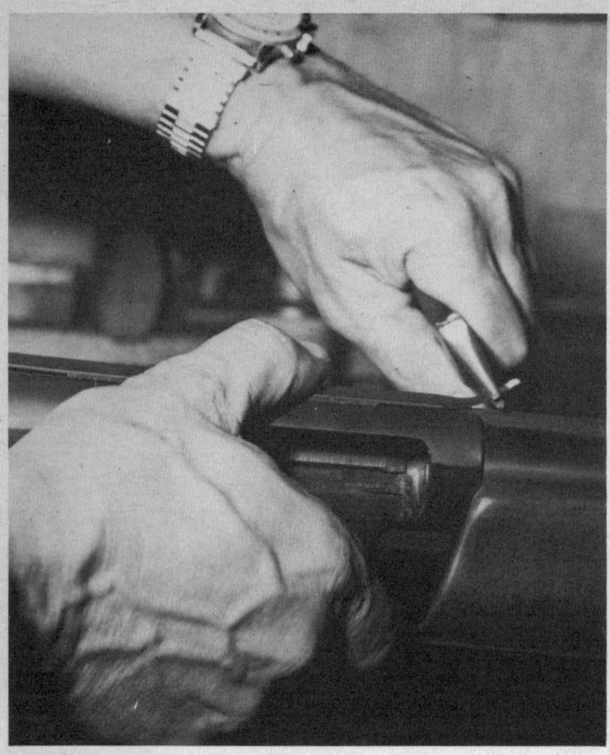

Adjusting the Slug Site (left) is a matter of simply bending metal with pliers — bit of tape on pliers will protect sight finish. Dewey Fine Line front sight is secured by barrel band, without drilling and tapping.

rather than inserting one end into a machined cut, two sets of screws could be used on each of the elevated sight blocks.

Yet another way to create sight bases is to use the Williams ramps, either the Streamline or the Shorty model. The Streamline ramp is designed to be sweated on and can be used as a front ramp without the hood. The Shorty ramp, which can either be screwed on or fastened by means of silver soldering, which is the way to go here, is a bit too long for rear base use. Cut it flush front and rear, use touch-up blue, and sweat it into place. The dovetail slot of the Shorty will accept any type of rear sight you care to install.

The issue rear sight found on the M1 carbine has been used as a rear sight for a slug gun on several occasions. Here, a sight base is fashioned by using one-eighth-inch sheet steel which is rolled across a steel mandrel to give it the needed contour.

It is best to start by making the rear sight so that, once the height is determined, you can figure out the right height for the front ramp and sight.

The following method of doping out sight heights works well and will enable you to order the correct height front sight and also will assure you that the first shots will be right on target:

1. Locate where you want the rear sight, then measure the outside diameter of the barrel at that spot. Divide that figure by two.

2. Figure out the minimum height of the rear sight, then add this to the figure obtained above in (1). This is for open sights and if you want to use a peep sight, add 0.125-inch to the figure.

3. Measure the OD of the barrel at the muzzle, and divide this by two.

4. Subtract the figure you got in (3) from the figure you arrived at in (2).

The figure obtained in (4) is important, since both the Marble and the Williams overall sight/ramp heights tables list sight and base heights available; these tables are based on the above way of doping the heights.

If you want a particularly high front and rear sight, use shim stock of equal heights for both bases. Shim stock of varying thickness can be obtained from Brownell's, and some such stock can be made in your own shop. Hacksaw blades that have outlived their usefulness are easy to fashion into the desired shapes.

Silver solder the shim stock to the base of the sight or ramp, blue and polish, then silver solder this into place. Use a clamp to hold sights in place while doing the soldering.

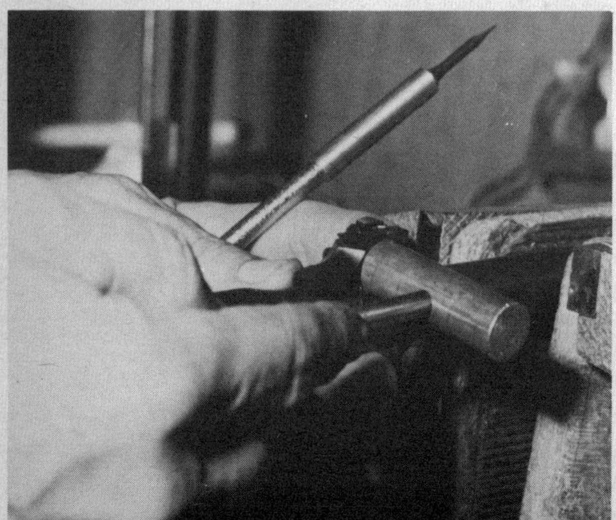

Brass mallet is used to tap mounted front sight onto shotgun barrel.

HOME GUNSMITHING DIGEST

Receiver removed (left), rear sight is positioned on barrel. Before final tightening of front sight band screws (below), front and rear sights are tapped into correct alignment.

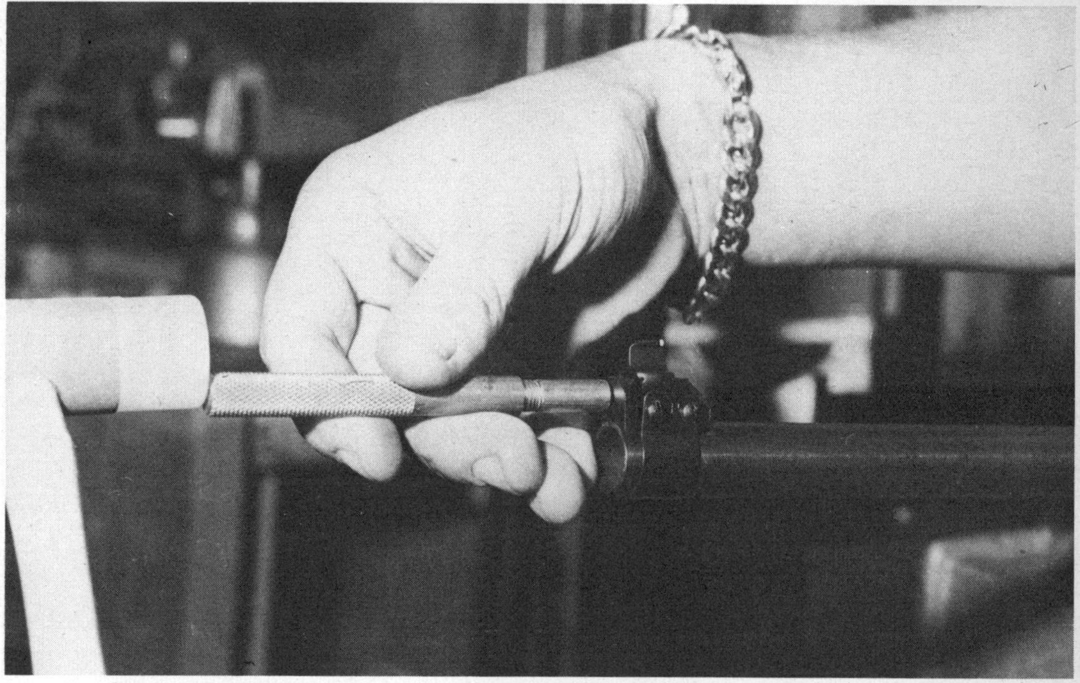

If you don't have a machinist's clamp or don't feel like improvising some sort of clamp, try the B-Square sight soldering jig which fits any bore you are likely to encounter.

Most gun shops have boxes and boxes of old sights stashed away. Some of them have come off various guns at one time or another, others are commercial sights which did not sell. Such scrap boxes contain untold treasures and you can often buy several pounds of sights for pennies.

It should be mentioned here that some shotgun actions, barrels, and even ribs can be drilled and tapped successfully and without too much trouble. Such drilling requires the use of a precision drill press with a stop to limit spindle movement. As a general rule of thumb, it requires three or four threads to hold a sight. Measure the length of that many threads on a screw, thus predicting the depth of the drilled and tapped hole.

If this is more than you care to cope with, or you are not certain about the thickness of the metal you need to drill into, take the gun to the gunsmith. It is much cheaper in the long run to spend a couple of bucks to have the holes drilled and tapped than to ruin a good gun.

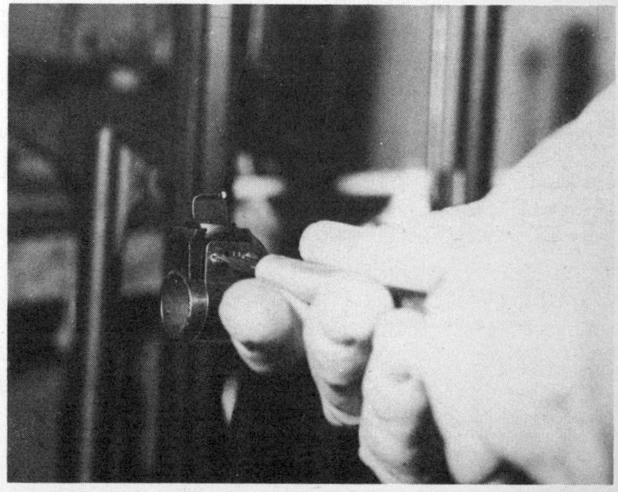

Screws must be cinched down completely to withstand the shock of firing. Sight position may be lightly marked before returning shotgun to scattergun mode.

Chapter 30

THE BASICS OF GUNSTOCK SURGERY

With Minimum Tools, You Can Make A Club More To Your Liking

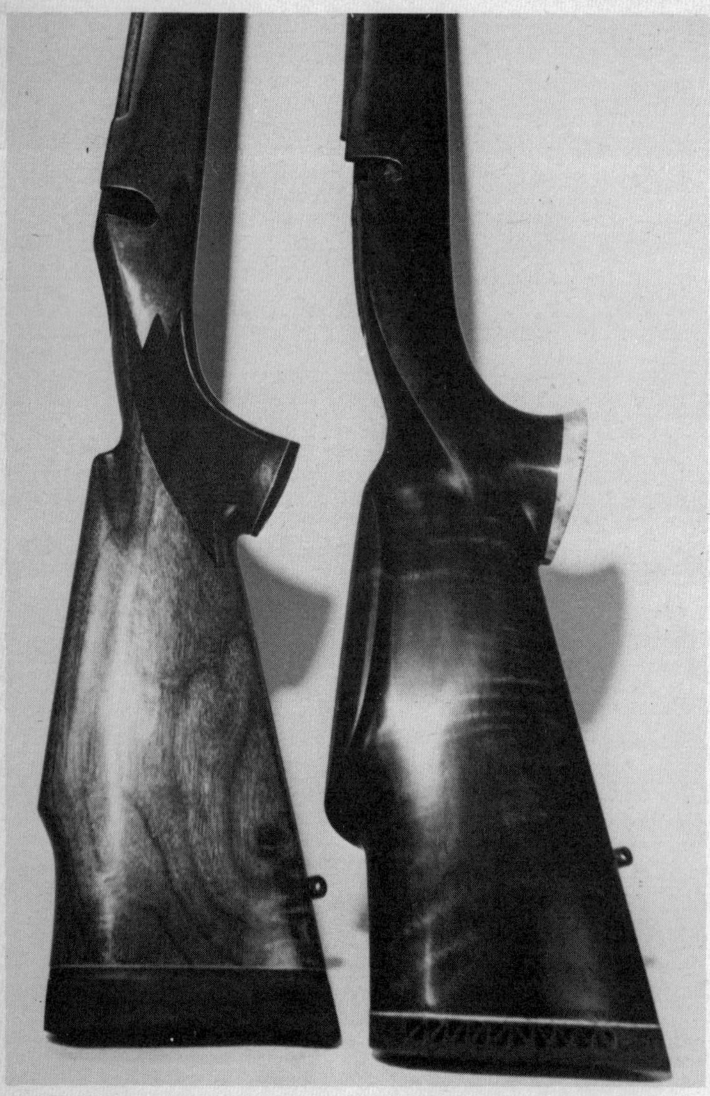

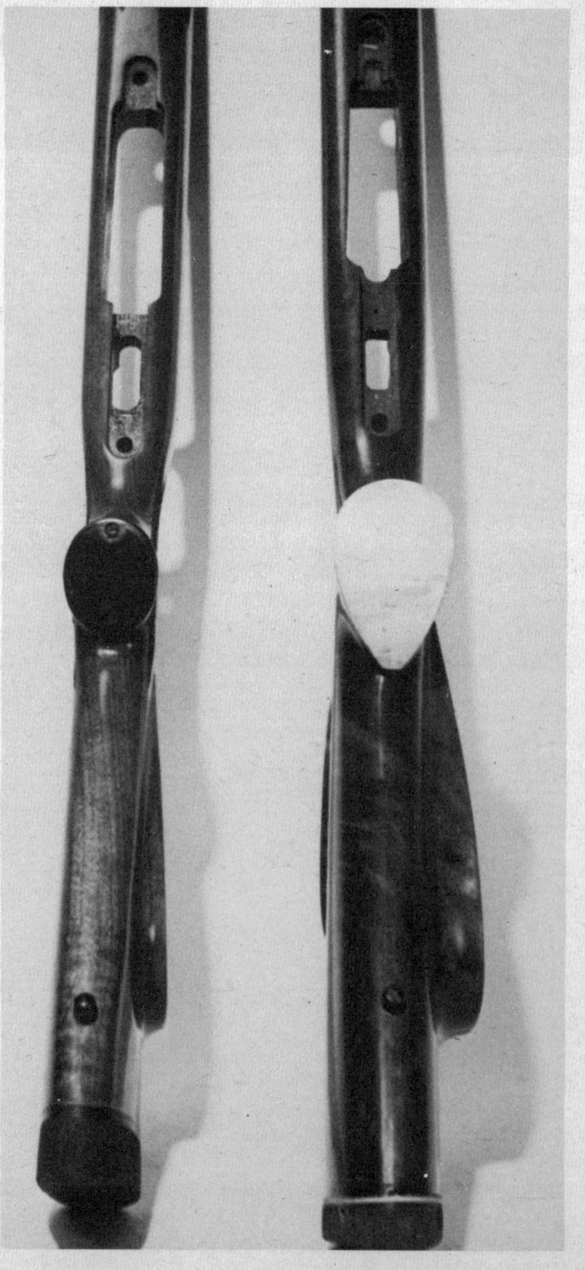

Two views of two stocks, one ready for some wood surgery. Stock at left is from M700, at right, wildcatted 8mm magnum. Note excessive width of stock and cheekpiece.

EVERY SO often you get a stock for a shotgun or a rifle that, although it fits you, is either too heavy or has design features which make it look like a pregnant elephant.

Such an overweight lack of graceful lines becomes painfully clear when the monster stock is compared, side by side, with the elegant lines of another stock. If that sight scares you, get out the files and the wood rasps, clear off the sander and get to work.

One such monster stock came with an 8mm wildcat rifle I obtained some years ago. The ballistic performance and recoil were almost identical to that of the recently introduced 8mm Remington magnum, so it was natural that I'd compare the stock of that Model 700 with the stock that came with that wildcat rifle. With the barreled action removed from the wood and only the sling swivel studs and the rubber recoil pad left in place, the lines of the stocks were compared.

The wildcat stock had a contrasting wood forend tip and pistol grip cap, the latter with an excessive forward swing which is sometimes known as the California pistol grip. There also was a vastly overgrown cheekpiece of the rollover kind, with the buttstock almost a half-inch thicker at the butt than any other rifle stock in my battery. Compared with the Remington stock which weighed 2¼ pounds, the wildcat stock tips the scales at three pounds three ounces, or thirty-six versus fifty-one ounces!

Though a bit heavier and somewhat squarer, the stock forward of the pistol grip did not lend itself to much slimming down, since the barrel of the rifle was somewhat thicker and heavier than that of the Model 700 and the

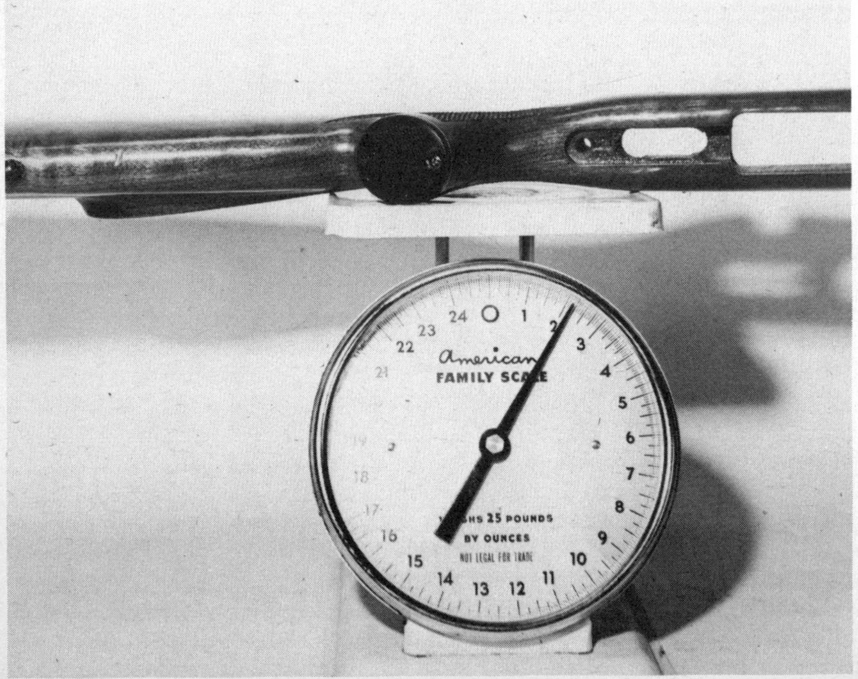

Wildcat rifle stock weighed in at three pounds three ounces before alteration, above, while M700 stock was a comfortable 2¼ pounds.

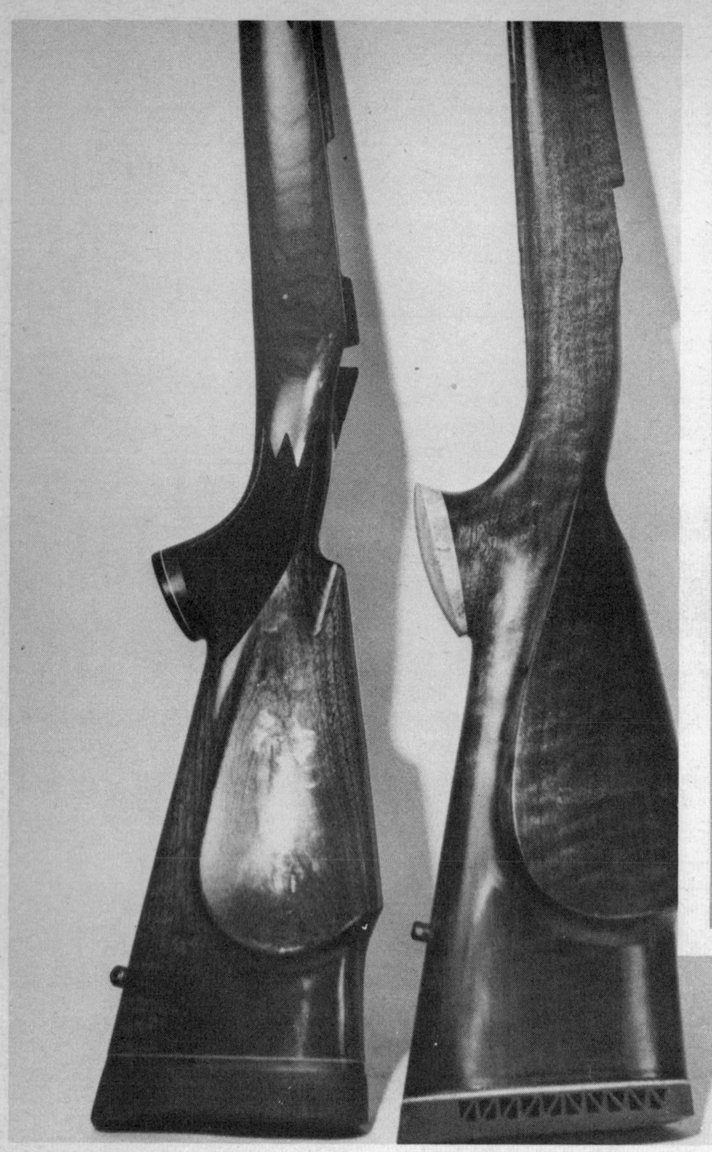

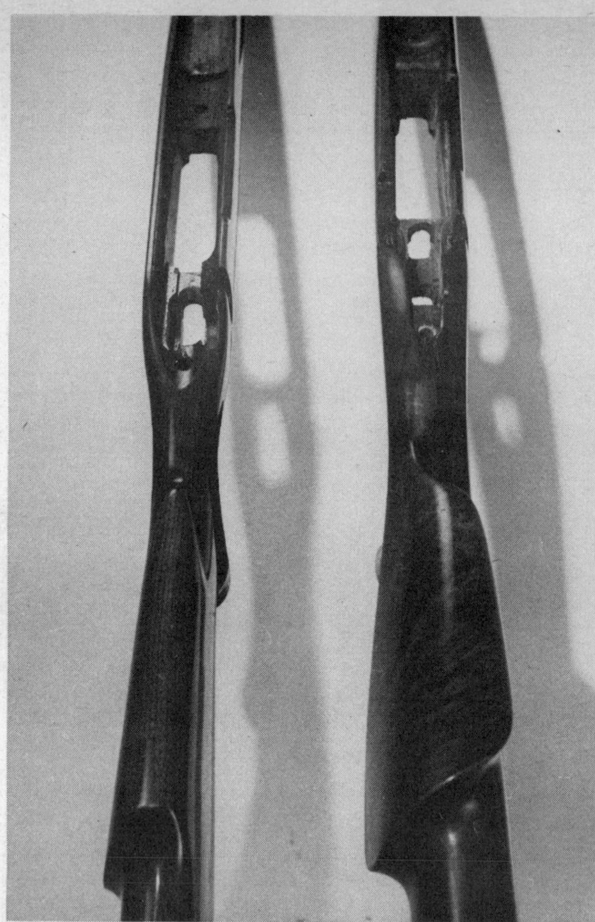

Two more photos which illustrate the club-like appearance of the 8mm custom stock before alteration.

lines of the forend were not excessively heavy or clumsy. An inch-by-inch comparison of the two stocks, then a comparison with several other stocks clearly pointed the way: The pistol grip would have to be slimmed down, but would have to retain its basic teardrop shape. The extra-heavy cheekpiece would have to be slimmed down, while the rollover section would have to be sharply reduced in size or perhaps removed completely. The right side of the buttstock also would come in for some wood removal, and I guesstimated that about a half pound of wood could come off the stock without making it appear lopsided or too slim.

If you have woodworking files and rasps on hand, you can use them. The Dremel Moto-Tool, with a handful of sanding drums and the needed mandrel, removes a lot of wood in a hurry, but keep the tool moving or you'll sand deep gouges into the stock which would be difficult to remove.

The power tool that most stockmakers use and that I favor is the Rockwell-Delta bandsander. With two different strips of sanding paper, you can whittle down a stock in minutes and then final sand it in a jiffy. Here, too, be sure to keep the work moving along the belt or you will find out just how efficient the tool is.

A word of caution about belts: You can buy your sander in a lot of stores or order it from such a source as Brownell's, but chances are extra belts or special grits cannot be bought in the local hardware store. If you go the belt sander route — and I recommend it for a great deal of metal polishing and metal removing as well as for stock work — order the special belts offered by Brownell's. I keep a stock of at least six belts of each type on hand so I don't run out.

Before using the first file, rasp or sandpaper, remove the barreled action from the rifle. Also remove any and all metal such as sling swivel studs. I prefer to remove the recoil pad, too, although some stockers leave it in place. I feel that it is easy enough later on to re-shape the pad, and with it off the stock, I don't have to worry about it making contact with the belt sander.

If you never have yanked a recoil pad off a stock, you may have some trouble doing so. With the stock under a good, strong light, tip or tilt the butt at about forty-five degrees.

Text describes method of using support blocks and hand tools required for weight-reducing job.

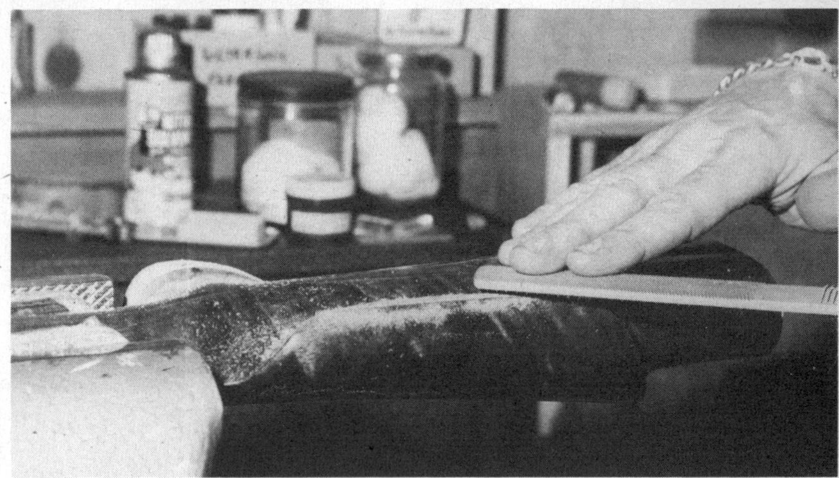

Flat side of four-in-hand rasp roughs out new shape of cheekpiece, right. Below, sanding wheel on Dremel Moto-Tool rounds pistol grip, reducing excessive sweep.

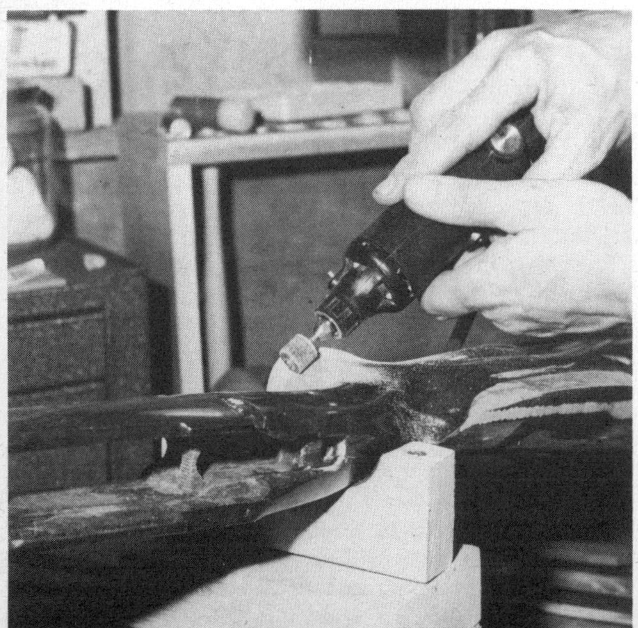

Look for scars in the rubber where the screws were seated. Use a screwdriver with a slender, round shank, making certain the tip is squared off properly. To make penetration of the screwdriver through the rubber recoil pad easier, apply either a dab of case lubricant from the reloading bench or some Vaseline to the blade and shank of the screwdriver. Once the blade makes contact with the head of the screw, gently rotate the blade of the screwdriver until the blade slips into the slot of the screwhead.

Almost invariably, the heads of the screws are so badly chewed up that they should not be used again. Dan Bechtel, head honcho of the B-Square Company, has been a fervent advocate of socket head screws for years. He has used such screws for fastening rubber recoil pads, and when the wrench is ground from its hex shape to the round, the scars left in the rubber will be almost invisible.

Since using a rasp or file requires a certain amount of pressure, don't try to use a checkering cradle for your stock surgery. Instead, use the machinist's vise with well-padded jaws, and support the stock on the bench, working on the end that has the major part of the support on the bench.

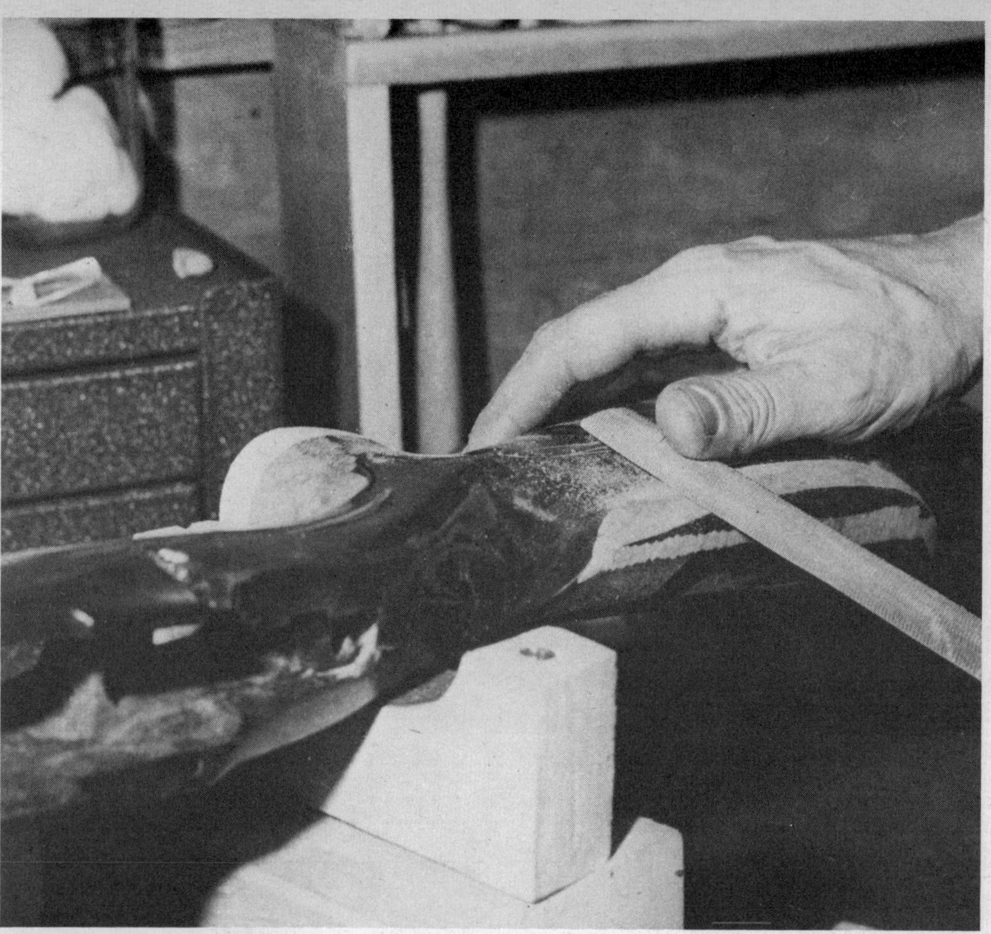

Rollover cheekpiece, right, is reduced by flat rasp; smooth file is next. Below, reduced pistol grip receives final shape with half-round.

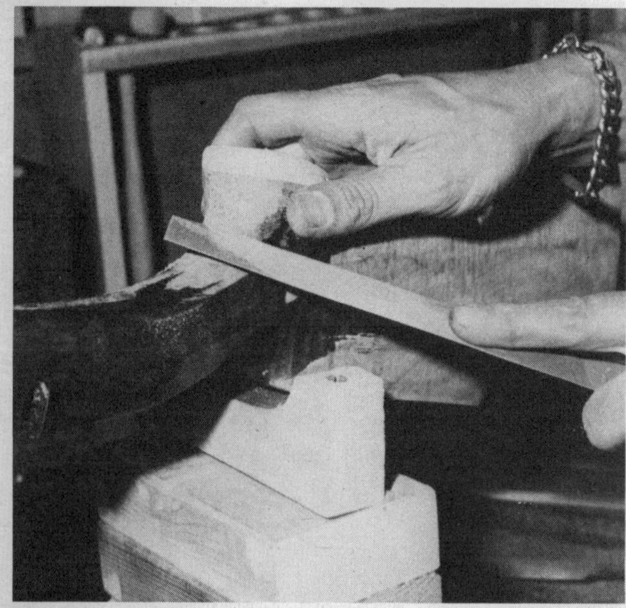

When locking the forend or the inletted area of the action into the vise, you don't need much pressure to hold the work.

Be careful in tightening the vise. It is easy to crack thin forends and action areas, especially on the lighter sporter stocks. Level the stock by eye, then measure the distance between butt and bench. Scrap blocks of 2x4 nailed together make good support blocks. You can pad the top block with some rags, rubber padding or felt, or again using scrap lumber, you can make up a piece of wood that is shaped to fit the stock, screw it on a 2x4 block, then pad this support piece.

My cosmetic surgery session started with the over-grown pistol grip. Since I wanted to retain some of the original shape of the contrasting wood, I started with a four-in-hand rasp, then switched to a half-round pattern maker's cabinet rasp, and finished with a half-round cabinet file.

Nicholson, one of the oldest houses making fine files, offers the Magicut file which is quite suitable for removing wood as well as steel, leaving a nice, smooth finish. This file, as well as the cabinet file, was used for eighty percent of the filing on the stock.

Once a new shape for the grip was determined, I took the stock over to the belt sander. Running a coarse grit, I removed the rollover feature, then flipped the stock over so that the rest of the rollover and the right side of the butt could be sanded. Once most of the excess wood had been removed, I switched to a fine-finish belt, and went over the areas previously sanded on the belt sander.

The Remington stock was kept on the bench for constant comparison purposes, and my stock measurements were made with a ruler. Stock calipers are handy, but not really essential, and in a pinch, you can even use your vernier calipers for some of the measurements.

Because of the fairly hefty recoil developed by the 8mm wildcat, I left the cheekpiece more or less alone, restricting

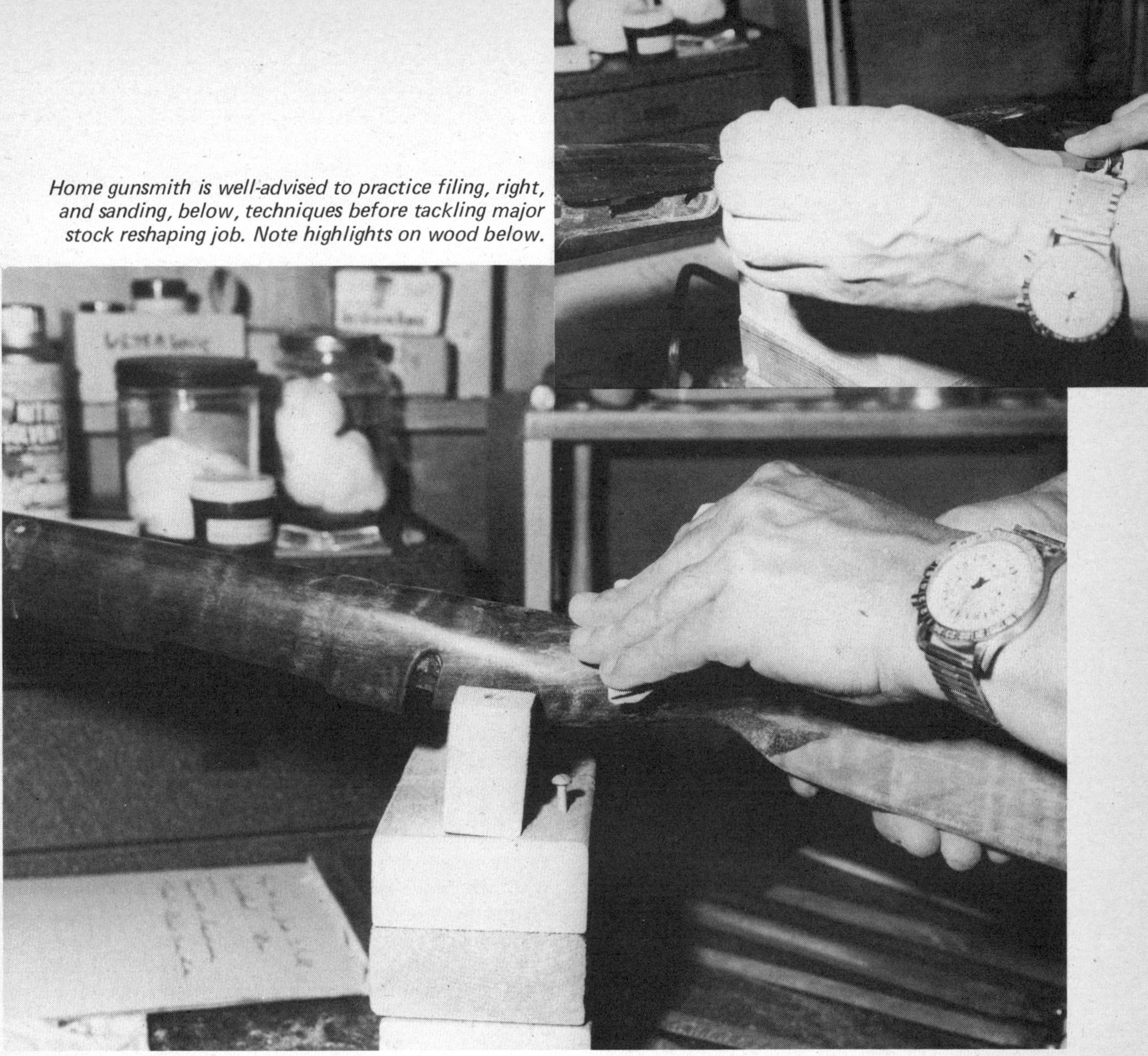

my filing, sanding and rasping to reshaping it without removing too much wood.

After the buttstock had been shaped, I went back to the pistol grip. With the Dremel Moto-Tool and a sanding drum, I shaped the contour of the pistol grip where the half-round files and rasps did not give me a smooth enough curve. Here you reach a point where you must make a decision.

I prefer to sand smooth at this point so that I can get an overall view of the pistol grip. With a soft pencil, I mark the areas where more wood should be removed, this being done with a fine half-round file. Some stockmakers simply shape with either a rasp, sander or cabinet file and check the configuration of the job at this stage of the beautifying process. It helps to mount the stock to the shoulder every so often, even if there is no recoil pad in place. If the lack of a pad bothers you, use a couple of strips of masking tape to hold the pad in place for the shouldering. Remember that the stock has to fit you and please you, so work and

shape to your desire and forget about classic lines, Monte Carlo stock and all the other features we hang on our stocks.

You will note that I began my stock surgery without removing the old finish. The finish left on the stock serves to protect the wood from stains and dirty hands. Once the stock was shaped to my satisfaction, the old finish would be stripped off and the stock refinished.

Before final sanding, I reassembled the gun, again taping the rubber recoil pad in place, but not bothering with remounting the scope. I wanted to determine whether I needed to make any changes in the stock and only actual shooting would tell me just how well my handiwork had panned out. During the original stockwork, the action area of the rifle had been glass-bedded, and test firing from the machine rest showed that the barrel channel had not warped to any appreciable degree. The five five-shot strings showed me that the stock surgery had not affected the quality of the stock handling, nor did I feel any more recoil

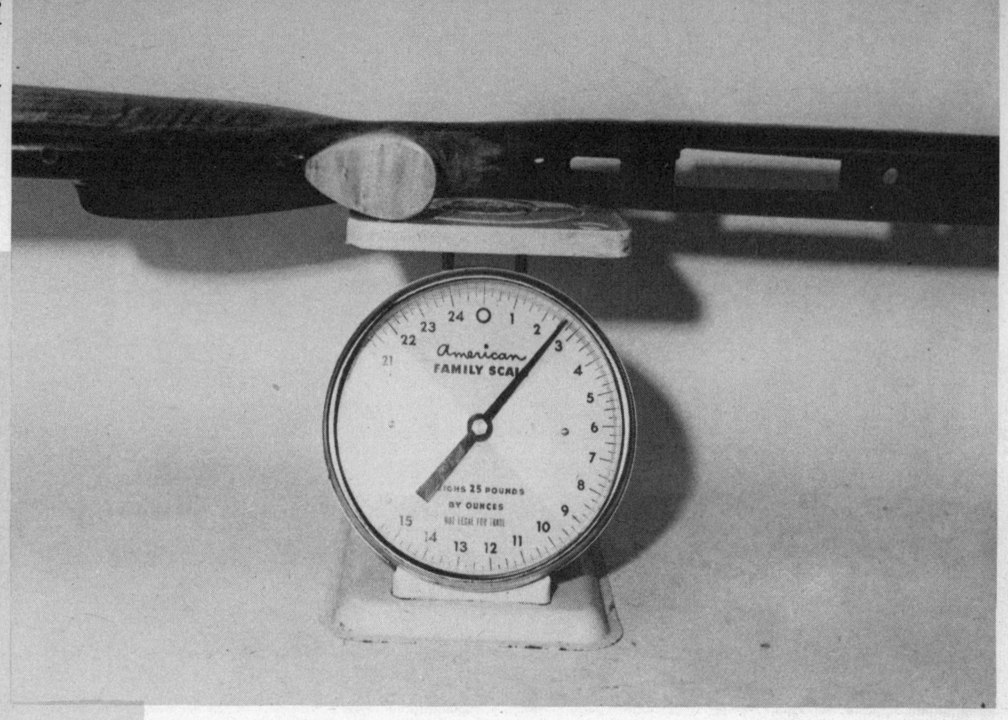

After most excess wood is removed, stock shows about half pound less weight, right. Pistol grip and buttstock, below, show thinner profile.

than before the stock configuration was changed.

The fact that the rollover cheekpiece had been removed did not affect the handling of the rifle from the bench, and the five-shot strings from the offhand, kneeling and sitting position did not change my thinking. I was well satisfied with the stock surgery I had performed.

I did make some slight changes in the shape of the pistol grip, then final sanded the stock areas where I had removed wood. Just a shade under a half-pound of wood was removed and I feel that the new shape of the stock, although a bit unusual, is pleasing to the eye.

When working with a semi-finished stock, or perhaps even a stock blank, shaping and wood removal are somewhat easier, since you don't have to concern yourself with the work of some other fellow. For instance, the contrasting wood forend, though attractive enough in color and wood grain, was not shaped to what I considered eye-pleasing form.

Instead of putting wood rasp to wood at the very tip of the contrasting forend tip, I used a light plastic hammer inside the barrel channel. Although it didn't wobble or flop around, it did show signs of being doweled in place.

Since the rubber recoil pad showed traces of having been fastened not only with two screws but also with some of the leftover glass-bedding compound, it stood to reason that whoever stocked the rifle, also used the fiberglass-epoxy mix to anchor the forend tip.

Any pressure applied at the very tip of the wood could have produced a fracture of the wood so a new forend tip might have been required. Since it then would have meant three different woods in one stock, I left the forend alone.

Perhaps, one day, when I can find a barrel that fits the barrel channel of that stock so the barrel can be clamped into the stock to serve as support while sanding, I'll tackle that job. I would then either create a schnabel forend or perhaps just sand the tip round. Until that day comes, I can live with the stock shape as it is.

When you buy wood files, make sure the hardware clerk really sells you wood files. Few files are equally at home on wood and steel, and few files are marked as to their intended use. They might have some nondescript stamping

More trimming could be done around pistol grip and on cheekpiece, as indicated by these two views of stock.

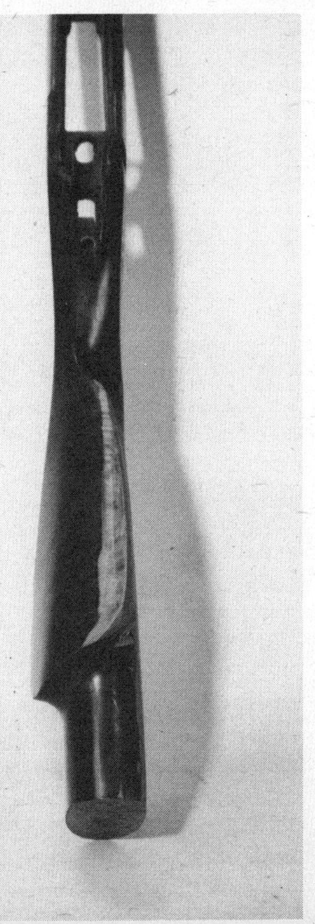

on them, such as *smooth,* which doesn't help to identify its use. Again, suppliers catering to the professional stockmakers are the best sources for tools and other materials you might want or need. I feel that the belt sander has greater versatility than disc sanders or even orbital sanders.

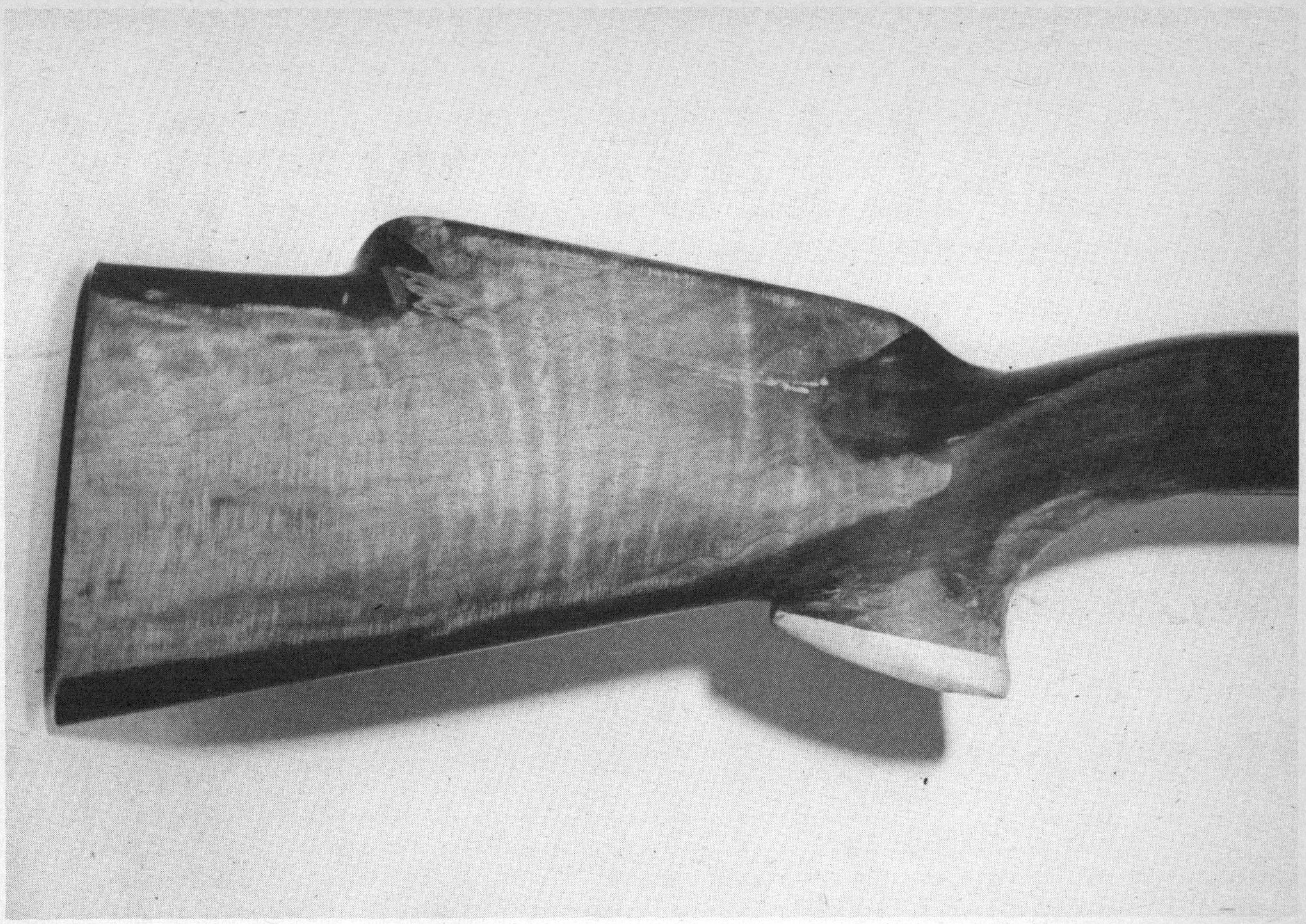

The various sanding wheels as well as the rasp-like wheels or drums are a great help, but because of their relatively small size, extra care must be taken, since it is difficult to control just how much wood is removed with each pass of the power tool. However, for getting into those tight spots, the hand-held tool with a sanding or rasping head is hard to beat.

A versatile woodworking tool is marketed by Stanley Tools. Known as Surform, the plane with the interchangeable blades has the widest appeal, but there is nothing wrong with either the Surform round file or the flat file. The flat file also has interchangeable blades, while the blade for the round file can be unscrewed from the handle and a new blade inserted. These Surform blades for plane and flat file come with regular-cut and fine-cut teeth in the flat configuration and only in the regular cut in the half-round shape.

Reshaping a stock or parts of a stock is not difficult and requires only a handful of tools. If you follow through on your ideas of what you want to have the stock look like, you should not encounter any problems. The nice thing about working with wood is that goofs usually can be corrected, sometimes with just one or two strokes of a rasp.

Chapter 31

A REAL LIGHTWEIGHT

Here Are Some Steps That One Hunter Took To Reduce His Load In The Field!

Omission of usual pistol grip saved two ounces, with slight shortening of action lever.

IT WAS MISERABLE — cool weather, then an afternoon snow of a foot or two, then warming for the next two days.

During the snow, Dennis Lambert sat near a hastily built fire on a Western Colorado hillside with his deer-hunting companion. As the two warmed and dried a little, they discussed ways to make hunting more pleasurable and more efficient. That was when Lambert decided to try to lighten his gear burden as much as possible, but have it remain reliable and serviceable.

Earlier in this volume, a chapter discussed means of lightening rifle weight. Many of us think about it, but the advantages never become real, until you've been lugging that rifle through the mountains or a swamp.

Lambert, a hunter who resides in Southern California, is like most of us flatlanders: He tends to hurt a lot, when he's carrying a big load and fighting the thin air of mountain heights. The story of how he went about lightening that load is not unlike a lot of others, but here is how he went about it:

"Over the past two years, I have refined most of my gear, although there is still room for improvement. Finally came time for my rifle to get a close scrutiny and see how it could be lightened.

"I wanted a light, handy rifle with big-game capabilities and as flat a trajectory as possible. I chose the time-tried .270 Winchester as the cartridge."

The term handy rifle, infers short and light, but for this

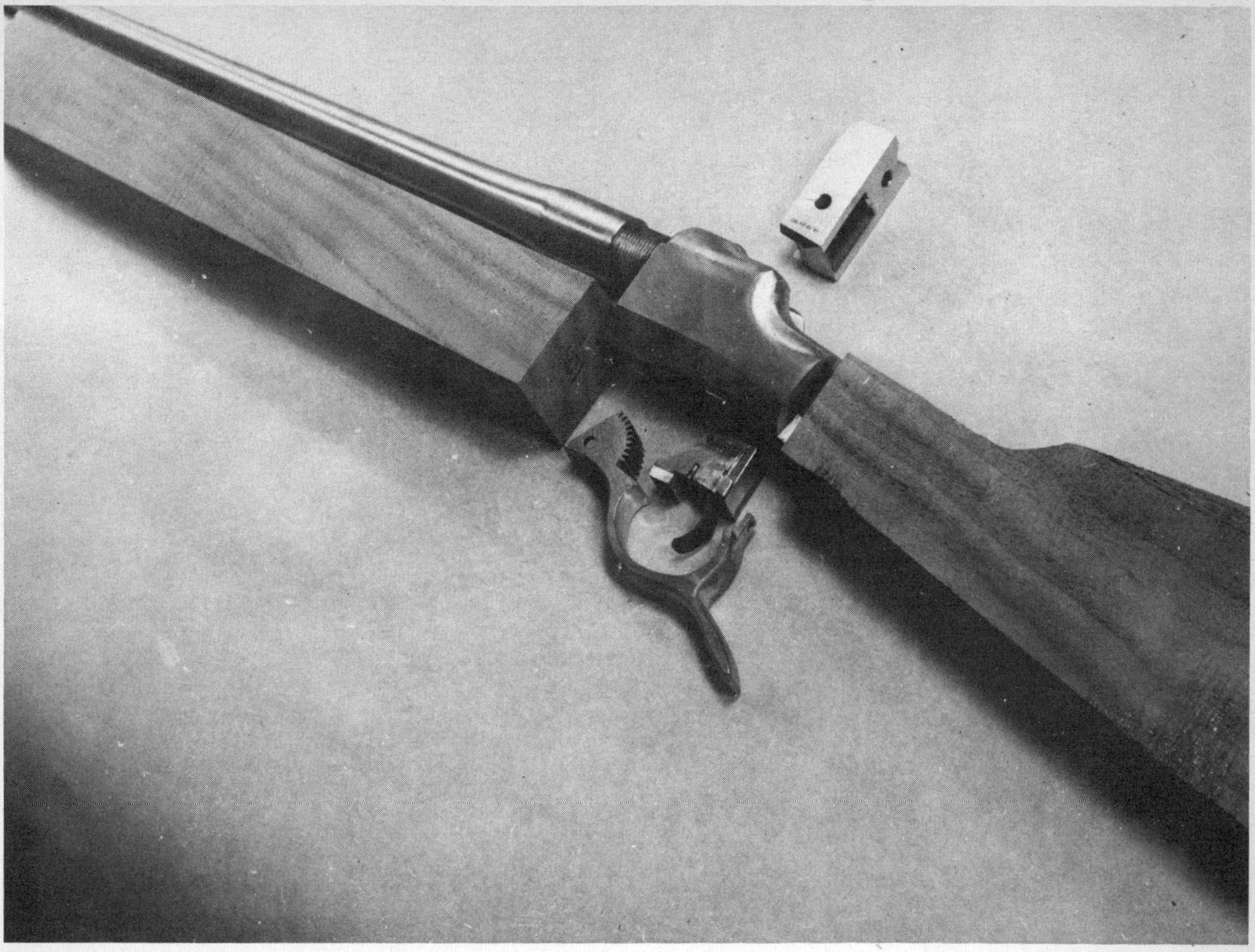

project light weight was of prime importance. On many occasions Lambert had carried a light 8½ to nine-pound scoped rifle and wished for a rifle the size and weight of a Model 94 or the average .22 rimfire. His goal was to build a 5½-pound .270.

For his purposes, the length was almost as important as the weight. Slung over your shoulder, a short rifle does not hang up as often as a longer piece and, when carried through the thick brush, also is less likely to slow one down. When climbing those loose shale slopes or navigating around the rimrock, a short, light rifle is pretty handy, either slung or for a one-hand carry.

"I looked at all of the available rifles capable of handling the .270 and compared weight and overall length for a given barrel length. It didn't take much research for a single-shot falling block rifle to rise to top place in this comparison. Then I had to weigh the advantage of successive shots with my preset goals."

Think back over the venison you have brought home and see if the pattern is similar: On nondangerous game, most successful kills are connected on the first shot. If you miss the first shot, you probably will miss the next twenty. Usually the first well-placed shot will anchor or slow the game allowing a little time for a quick second shot.

"Now I knew that if I selected a single-shot, I must be prepared mentally and physically for a well-placed first shot, then, if necessary, a hurried follow-up shot. With practice, I found this could be done," Lambert says.

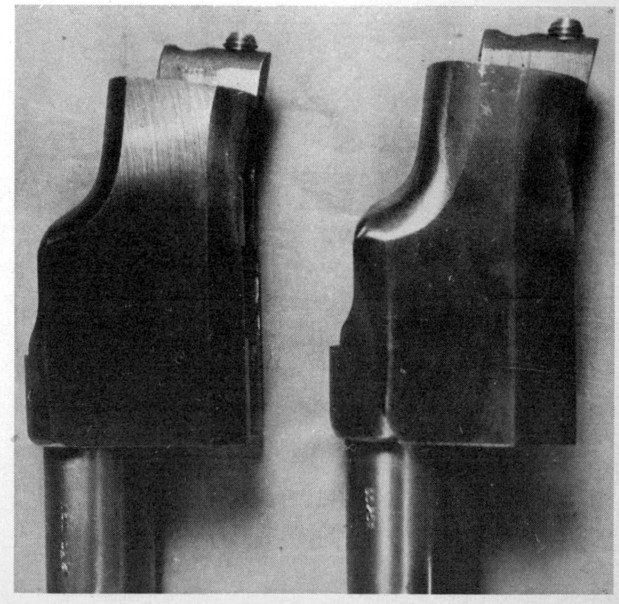

Above: Basic components of custom featherweight rifle as they appeared at start of project, a modified Riedl single-shot. Metal machined from sides of action as compared with right of two shown below.

Unassembled action components, above, clearly shows
rack and pinion gear system which actuates breechblock.
Right: Barrel set up in milling machine which removed
four ounces without loss of strength or rigidity.

Follow-up shots can be made rapidly if need be; not as
quickly as an experienced man with a bolt, pump or lever,
but quickly. If you don't believe this, take your favorite
single-shot rifle — preferably a .22 — practice a little at
continuous reloading and firing at a target to gain
familiarity and technique, then challenge a friend to a
plinking match. Choose a set number of rounds so he must
reload his magazine at least twice. You will be surprised at
the outcome. You can load and fire faster from a
single-shot than from a repeater, if the repeater must be
reloaded. Now that friend Lambert wasn't burdened by the
thought of only one chance at his target, he was ready to
proceed.

Using a single-shot, one can gain up to six inches of
barrel with the same overall rifle length as compared to a
bolt action.

Now for the rest of the problem: light weight. There are
only a few ways to reduce weight without sacrificing
strength. For help in this area, Lambert contacted James
and Roger Riedl, operators of the Riedl Rifle Company in
Westminster, California. They are builders of extremely fine

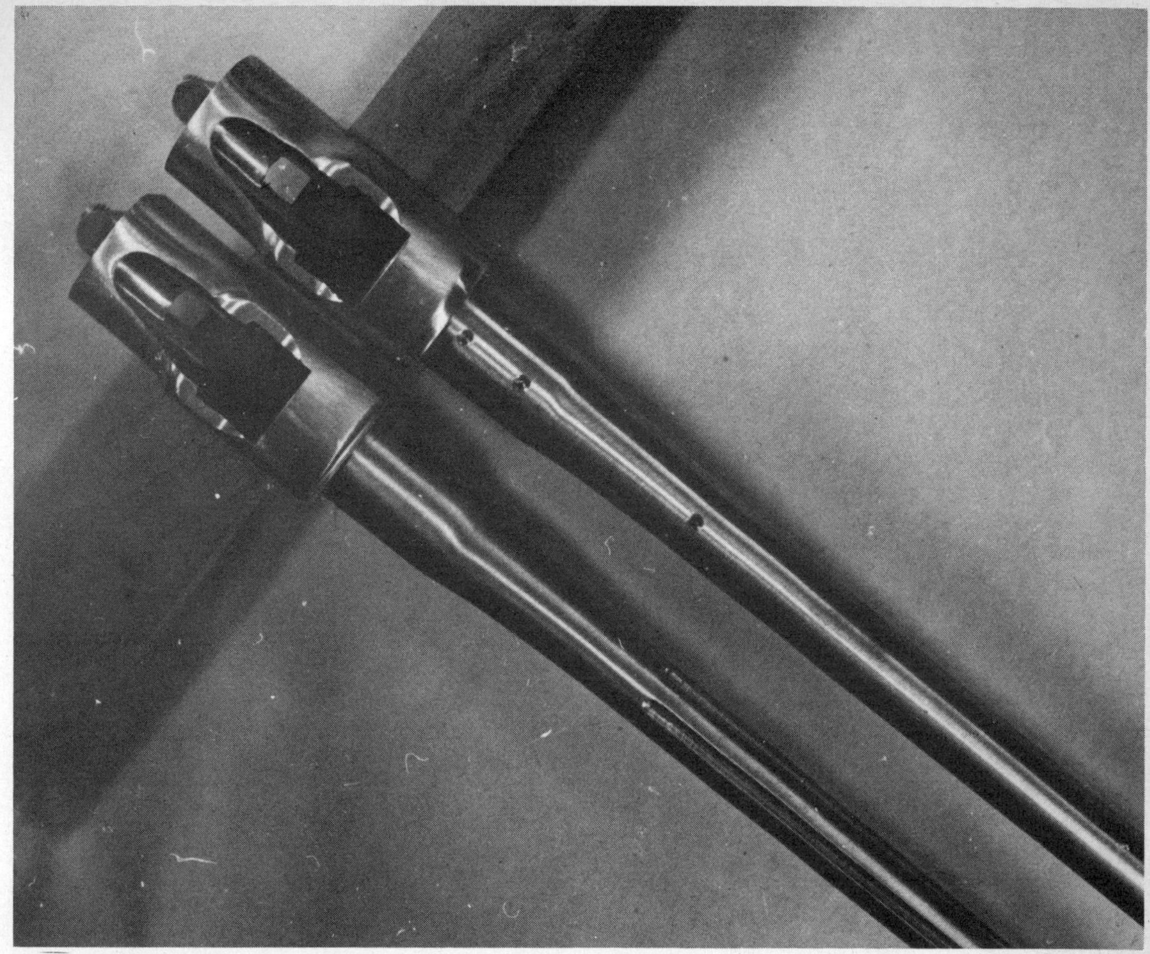

Six flutes cut in barrel to lighten, are visible on lower barrel. Flutes were cut on milling machine, .200" wide by .080" deep, milled from five inches ahead of action to within one-and-a-half inches of muzzle..

custom single-shot rifles on their own action at a competitive price. They tossed around many ways to lighten a rifle. Basically there are three areas to reduce weight: wood, action and barrel.

"Roger Riedl and I went through several hundred available stock blanks of claro walnut — California black walnut — to find a piece of strong, straight-grained wood that seemed to be the lightest.

"For the stock design, I chose a straight pistol grip similar to the M94 Winchester, which saved a couple of ounces. I also wanted the forend rather full to give me something to hang onto and a wide butt similar to that of a shotgun to distribute the recoil over a larger area. A six-pound rifle — even a .270 — can kick in a poorly designed stock.

"With the exterior dimensions for the forend and buttstock chosen, the only place to remove wood is from the interior, and that is exactly what Riedl did. He drilled large diameter holes into the buttstock and routed out the forend. The resulting stock is a clean-looking, well-shaped, strong stock that, due to the Riedl stock design, is not punishing to shoot.

"James Riedl is the machinist. We went over many methods to reduce the weight of the action without jeopardizing strength. Fortunately, the Riedl single-shot

action is extremely beefy, capable of handling any cartridge we might want. The Riedls have even barreled and chambered their action for some of the big .50, .577 and .60 cartridges now available.

"We started reducing action weight by routing out the inside and shortening the finger lever — we lost about one ounce here. We then milled down the sides of the action and removed some material from inside the front and rear."

This still left an action with side walls as thick or thicker than those of most other current single-shots. This process took about five more ounces from the weight. The three-eighths-inch diameter stock through-bolt was reduced by one-third its length, saving almost another ounce. The completed action was reduced to thirty-six ounces from forty-seven ounces; almost a twenty-five percent reduction.

The barrel is where most gunsmiths tend to remove most of the rifle weight, but it is where one can lose some desirable qualities, such as barrel rigidity. One can reduce weight by just lopping the end off of the barrel or by turning it down until it looks like a soda straw. On the No. 3 barrel used, Lambert and the Riedls found they could reduce the weight by about 1-1/3 ounces per inch.

"For my rifle, I chose a twenty-two-inch barrel. This gave me a short rifle without compromising too much velocity with a .270. Several more ounces can be removed

Rifle builder James Riedl tested lightweight single-shot .270 across Teal Chronograph, as discussed in text. Three-power Leupold scope sight added but eight ounces to overall weight, mounted on rings and base by Conetrol.

without sacrificing rigidity of the barrel by fluting, similar to the cylinder of a revolver. This technique is starting to be used by some serious target shooters. James Riedl did a fine job of fluting from about five inches in front of the action to within about 1½ inches of the muzzle. He used six flutes about .200-inch wide and about .080-inch deep. This removed four more ounces.

The completed rifle weighs about 5.9 pounds. With scope and rings, it weighs about 6¾ pounds. This is not quite as light as the goal, but the concept of a light, handy rifle was accomplished.

"Had I chosen a slimmer barrel, the overall weight could have been reduced to below 5½ pounds, including scope and rings. I chose Conetrol rings for sleekness and light weight, and a Leupold 3X eight-ounce scope for light weight and all-around performance. When I have a variable scope, I usually set it at about 4X and leave it there, so the fixed power scope has one less adjustment for me to worry about. I may change to a Leupold 4X scope for the

increased magnification and field of view, since there is only a slight increase in weight," Lambert says.

The trio took the rifle to the range for a trial run and it performed beautifully. They chronographed a series of reloads composed of Winchester brass, CCI primers, Sierra 130-grain bullets and 4350 and 4831 powder with a 23.3-inch barrel on the rifle. A moderate load, then a near-maximum load was chronographed for these four possible combinations.

They then shortened the barrel length to 22.0 inches from 23.3 inches and rechronographed. The maximum load for each powder lost less than thirty feet per second. The moderate loads for both powders exhibited a slight increase in velocity, fifteen and twenty-five feet per second, respectively, which none of the three can explain.

The average velocity for near-maximum loads for 4350 and 4831 were 3210 and 3160 fps, respectively, in the twenty-two-inch barrel without any signs of excessive pressure. Lambert considers these velocities appropriate for

Bottom and top views of completed .270 lightweight, left and above, show open action of Riedl single-shot. Completed rifle with scope tipped scales at 6¾ pounds.

the intent of the rifle. Incidentally, they chronographed the loads using the new hand-held Teal velocity-reading digital chronograph with excellent accuracy.

The weight breakdown of the component parts is tabulated below:

PART	STANDARD WEIGHT	NEW WEIGHT	% DECREASE
Wood	2.18 lbs.	1.48 lbs.	32%
Complete Action	2.92 lbs.	2.20 lbs.	25%
Barrel (No. 3)	24" 2.83 lbs.	22" 2.45 lbs.	13%

As can be determined from the table, the best place to reduce additional weight would be the barrel, and this was where the weight was lowered. Lambert's goal was as high a performance as possible, both in rigidity and velocity, and

he chose the No. 3 twenty-two-inch barrel as a compromise. A larger bore diameter — .308 or .338 — also would reduce the weight.

"A session at the range with a proposed hunting load using 130-grain Noslers and 4350 produced five-shot groups measuring less than two inches. At one hundred yards, the smallest three-shot group was less than an inch with 55 grains of 4350. I plan to use this load with a little more refining for my hunting load.

"As the rifle neared completion, we already were talking about the next mutation: a takedown rifle with interchangeable barrels. I think a .338 Winchester/.270 Winchester combination would be almost a perfect combination for my North American trip.

"James and Roger Riedl's rifle can be made to accommodate both head sizes easily and already they have plans for a takedown feature.

"So we are off on another project, but not before I try this one out on a planned elk hunt this Fall and possibly a few mule deer," Lambert reports.

Admittedly, the project outlined here is pretty involved for the home gunsmith, but it does give an idea of what can be done to create a weight reduction. Some of the steps can be taken in your home shop, but I'd suggest you be fully confident of your own abilities before you started working on a really expensive rifle or one that is dear to your heart!

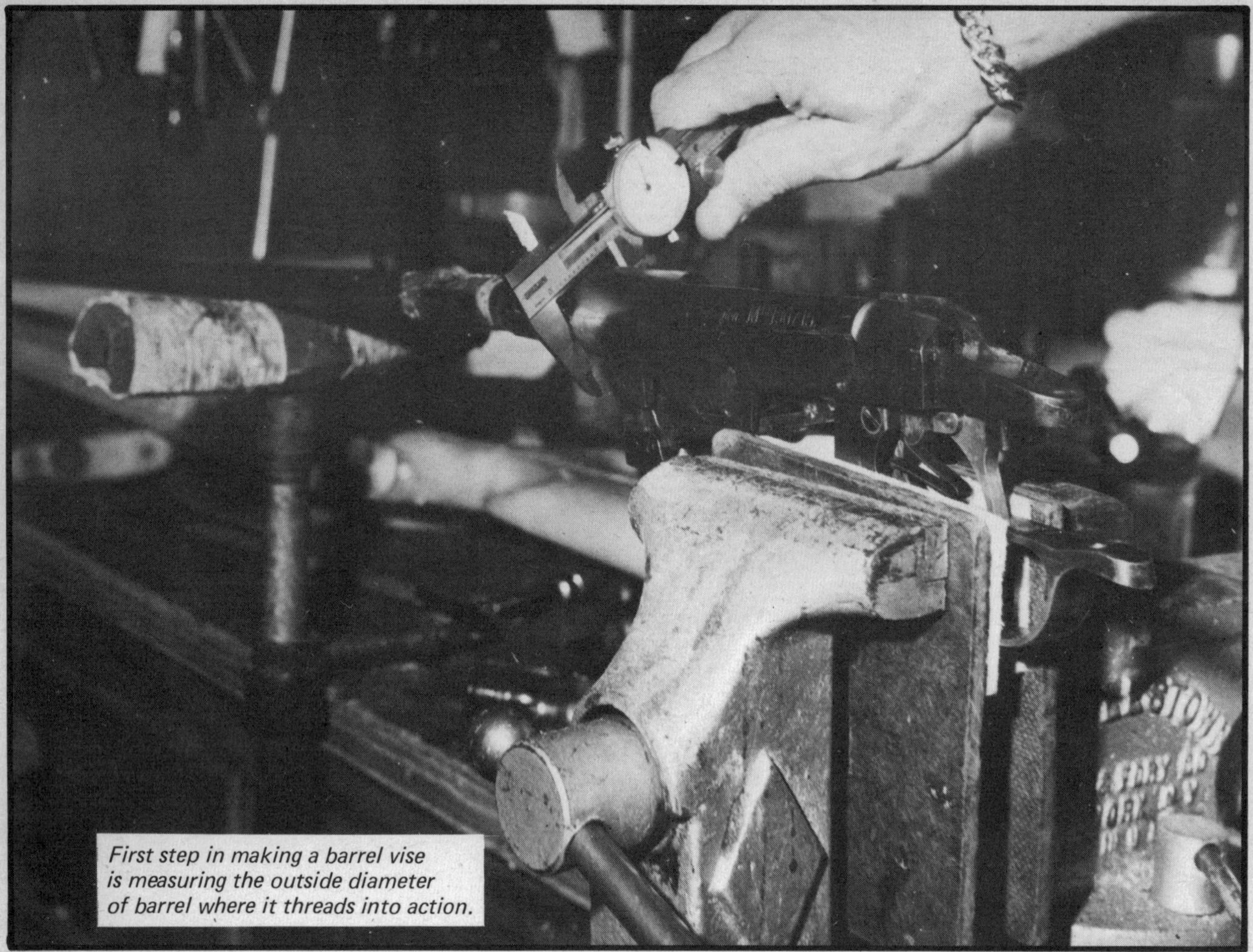

Chapter 32

First step in making a barrel vise is measuring the outside diameter of barrel where it threads into action.

TREATING THE TOUGHS

There Are Some Home Gunsmithing Chores That Verge On Impossible, But These Tips May Help!

As IS USUALLY the case in such books as this, I've made reference to several jobs that may seem simple enough in the telling, but when you get down to doing the actual work, you'll tend to wonder whether I know what I'm talking about. Nothing seems to work.

That's the reason for this particular chapter. It is meant to cover some of the chores mentioned in passing that require more thought and method than was contained in the original reference.

The treatment for tough chores that I outline here should be of help and, hopefully, you won't go through life cursing me and demanding your money back from the publisher of this particular tome.

BARREL REMOVAL

Jerking a barrel off an action is really a job for a gunsmith who has the equipment for the job, plus the experience of tackling the job. Once a barrel has been yanked off an action, the day will come when the same

Left: Broken military stock is squared off to be converted into barrel vise. Below, drill press ensures accurate drilling of hardwood block for larger barrels.

barrel goes back on the action or perhaps the barrel is replaced. Mention was made earlier of the index or witness mark often found on the action and the barrel. Screw the barrel into the action until it is seated snugly and the two marks should line up with a minimum of trouble. Of course, if a barrel has been set back, or you have a replacement, the original witness mark on the action becomes meaningless. At any rate, the witness mark is only a guide, and you still have to check the headspace.

Most military rifles have the barrels turned into the actions so hard you can anticipate problems in barrel removal. On the other side are the lever action rifles which often have rather soft actions. They tend to spring and bend out of shape the moment you put a wrench to them to turn the barrel out.

Of all the shop equipment the amateur really doesn't need, barrel vises and action wrenches must lead the way. First of all, commercial wrenches and vises will cost somewhere from $125 to $160, not counting the extra bushings. If you are a skilled machinist and have access to the power tools and the needed steel, you can make one or both of these tools, but for most us mortals, that is a job beyond our skills and capabilities.

Before removing a barrel from an action, the scope must be removed. I prefer also to remove the scope blocks and, if there is one, the rear sight. If the front sight is screwed into place, I take it off, too. The shank of the barrel is where the threads seat in the mating threads of the action, and the chamber is just ahead of the shank. Barrel contours vary, not only in the chamber area, but for the whole length of the tube. You may have a perfectly straight barrel where the thickness of the chamber and the outside diameter

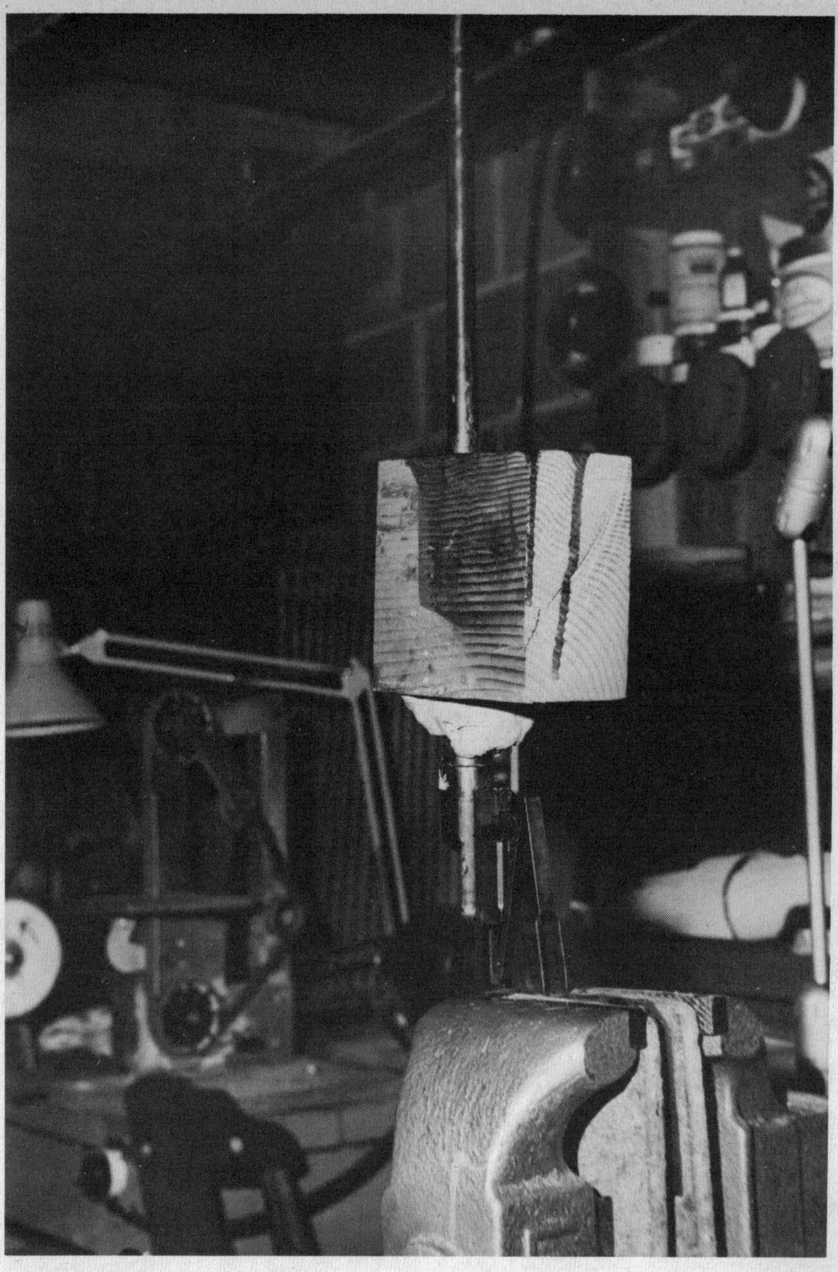

Text describes method of applying putty or wax dam under 2x4 block for large-size barrel vise.

(OD) at the muzzle are identical, you may have a severely tapered barrel, or anything in between.

The way to separate barrel and action is to lock the barrel at the chamber end into some sort of holding device, set a large wrench on the action, after removing the bolt, of course, then heave on the wrench. The barrel supposedly will hold still while you turn the action off the barrel. At least, that is what the books say.

I remember a good friend who was a master gunsmith and who sweated, cussed, then sweated some more for five hours trying to yank a barrel off one of my rifles — and he had been at the gunsmithing game for some thirty years at that time.

Let's look at that holding device just mentioned. You start with the best, heaviest swivel-base machinist's vise you can afford. I opt for jaws at least four inches wide, although you can live with the three-inch jaws if you are not going to be doing much work calling for lots of power, such as barrel removal, draw filing and other such jobs.

Into the jaws goes the barrel vise which is contoured internally to the shape and OD of the barrel at the chamber. When seated in the barrel vise, the action just clears the one edge of the vise.

Here the swivel feature of the bench vise becomes important. With the barrel held in the barrel vise which, in turn, is locked into the bench vise, rotate the bench or machinist's vise so the barrel extends over the bench, while the action overhangs the front of the bench so that the wrench can get the needed purchase on the action. You'll need plenty of elbow room for the job, so don't work yourself into a corner.

What is a barrel vise? After inspecting a dozen or so of them and admiring the stuff they are made of and the ingenuity of the makers, I'd say a barrel vise is a gadget that

Homemade barrel vise with barrel locked in bedding compound.

is supposed to but seldom does hold any contour barrel without slipping, moving or scratching the barrel, while three other guys heave away on the wrench fastened to the action.

For about two bucks you can make a barrel vise, or you can buy one for $30 or so. Both of them are almost certain to permit the barrel to slip and spin at will — it ain't supposed to, but it does. The commercial barrel vise is offered with special bushings, such as for the Enfield, the Springfield, the Model 70 Winchester, the Mauser and perhaps some other barrel contours. You also can buy blank or undrilled bushings which you then drill out, ream and polish in the hope one will fit and hold the barrel.

To prevent slippage of the barrel in the barrel vise when the pressure is applied to the action, rosin traditionally is sprinkled into the barrel vise. Sometimes it does the trick, then there are the times when rosin seems to help the barrel spin like a top. There is always the chance that one or two small hunks of rosin will be as hard or even harder than the bluing or even the steel. I have one barrel that looks like it has been worked over with a metal checkering file — and the action is still on that barrel.

One of the best-known barrel removal methods is known as the rope trick. Use one-half-inch nylon rope, anywhere from three to six feet in length. Make either a loop or an eye with one end of the rope and let it hang free near the action. The rope then is wound around and around the barrel until the rope is used up and the loop or eye won't budge. Lock the action into a heavy machinist's vise with padded jaws, then insert a three-foot length of one-inch pipe through the loop and yank. Resting the end of the pipe where it goes through the loop against the barrel gives extra leverage. Rumor has it that barrels will come out that way.

Instead of rosin, one enterprising gunsmith uses double-faced tape, wrapping it around the barrel in the critical area. Locked into the barrel vise, he swears that even military tubes won't be able to resist the pressure.

Bushings for barrel vises have been made from aluminum bar stock and tubing, from Cerrosafe casting metal, and even from split copper tubing and plumbing pipe. The name of the game is to stop the barrel from rotating in the barrel vise under any and all conditions, since a barrel that moves in the vise simply will not release the action.

The simplest but a bit messy way of making up a barrel vise is to drill a hole into a block of wood, then glass-bed the barrel in the hole.

If the vise is to be used only once or twice, you can get along with using two pieces of softwood, such as pine. Make sure the board does not have any knots. Cut the board to the width of the jaws of your machinist's vise, and on the bottom, make a rectangular cutout so the cross-bar of the bench vise fits into the boards. In short, the design is the same as that used to make up pads for the vise.

Mark the contour of the barrel on both boards, doing your drawings within one-half-inch of the top of the board. Then, using wood chisels, saws and sandpaper, prepare two inletted areas in the boards so the barrel is now gripped in the contoured area; the inletting should extend to at least half the thickness of the board. Apply either a glass-bedding release agent or a light layer of Rig Grease to the barrel, make up a small batch of Acraglas, and fill that inletted area with the stuff.

Let it sit until hard, then fill in the rest of the inletted channel. If you try to fill the whole area in one session, chances are that you will have too much glass-bedding compound. If you spill in too much of the stuff, you will have a hard-to-clean-up mess.

Once the bedding compound is solid, remove the barrel and degrease or remove all of the release agent. Then apply rosin to the barrel, lock the barrel and home-made barrel vise into the machinist's vise as tightly as possible. Now apply the wrench to the action and heave-ho.

Dissolving a bit of the rosin in turpentine eliminates the scratching problem, and this solution, once the turpentine evaporates, seems to have even greater non-slip tendencies.

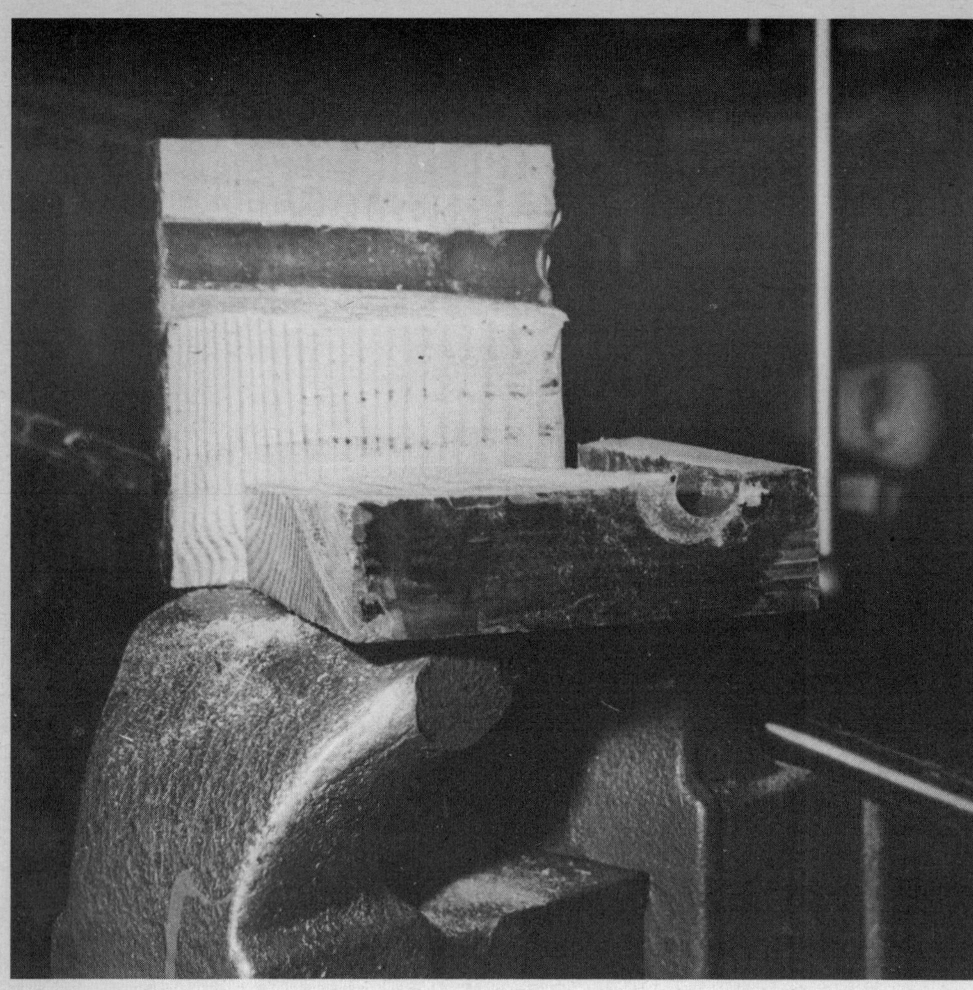

Acraglas has hardened
and 2x4 block has been
cut with crosscut saw.

If the barrel is too thick at the chamber end or you don't want to bother with cutting and chiseling, when making the vise from two hunks of scrap board, you can use nearly any block of wood. I have made up these vises from cutoff buttstocks, from busted military stocks, from pieces of 2x4, and from hardwood cutoffs rescued from the scrap bin at the lumberyard. Hardwood is better than softwood, with oak the best choice.

Measure the OD of the barrel where it threads into the action, and also the OD of the barrel where the block of wood ends. Put the block on the bench, place the barrel on it so only the action sticks out over the block on one side, make a chalk mark on the barrel to indicate where you want to measure the OD of the tube. The hole you want to drill through the width of the board should be slightly larger than the largest OD measurement of the barrel. Since the tube probably tapers, go by the largest measurement, with the extra space being filled out later with Acraglas.

Drill through the block completely, put release agent or a light coating of Rig on the barrel, move the block so it sits just a shade away from the forward edge of the action. Block off any possible flow of Acraglas with either a wax or a putty dam, then fill the hole with glass-bedding compound, again doing the filling in two stages. Remember that the bedding compound tends to run when made up too thin and poured too rapidly.

Once the barrel has been bedded fully in the block of wood, cut the block apart with a saw, and there is your custom barrel vise. Apply rosin to the inside of the bedding, wipe the release agent off the barrel, lock the whole shebang into the bench vise and get out the big wrench.

There is no doubt in my mind that the easiest way to remove a barrel from an action is to take it to a gunsmith. But we don't have one in my neck of the woods, so it's a do-it-yourself proposition, whether I like it or not.

Once you get the hang of it and learn how to make up a barrel vise, barrel removal is no longer an ornery chore to be avoided at all costs.

REMOVAL OF SILVER SOLDER

There seems to be no question about the usefulness of silver solder as a permanent bond between metals. Because so little heat is required to create a good bond, silver soldering is important in gunsmithing work, since excessive or extensive heating of parts could affect the composition of the metals being joined.

As easily as silver solder flows and makes reliable joints and bonds, the removal of old silver solder has stumped many gunsmiths and more than one barrel has been ruined by the careless use of a flame to melt off that sticking solder.

Silver solder is used most often for installing sights on barrels, and removal of these sights is quite simple. Gently play the flame from a propane torch over the base of the sight, keeping the flame moving and hitting all sides of the sight base. Use a medium-size flame, and in a minute or two, silver solder will come bubbling out from under the

With wood block and barrel locked in bench vise, pipe wrench is tightened on action and pulled.

sight base. Tap the sight with a brass mallet or hammer to dislodge it completely. If there is some slight resistance to the removal, it means that not all of the silver solder has liquified, so re-apply the flame and try again in a minute or two.

With the sight off the barrel, there is silver solder left on the base of the sight as well as on the barrel. Since the sight will be re-installed at some future time, you simply leave the hardened solder on the sight base. When the time comes, add some flux, heat, add some more solder and watch it flow to make the desired joint. But the solder on the barrel must be removed and it's not easy. Heating the barrel so the solder can be wiped off is often suggested, but don't do it!

Getting silver solder to the state where it can be wiped off requires a considerable amount of heat. This, in turn, means the crystalline structure of the metal being heated will undergo changes. Wire wheels, grinders and buffers only make things worse; acids will etch the barrel, but won't affect the silver to any great extent.

Residue of old silver solder job
resists removal attempts; must be
taken off before rebluing, left.
Careful file work is necessary
to ensure complete silver removal.

After fighting the problem and seeking help from some professionals with little or no luck, I decided to ask Bob Brownell, the gent who has forgotten more about gunsmithing than most of us could learn in two lifetimes.

According to Brownell, silver solder removal ranks among the most troublesome jobs in the gunsmithing field, and few of the pros know how to go about it. Essentially, here is what Brownell suggested, and when I tried it on a couple of barrels, it worked like a charm:

Lock the barrel into the padded jaws of your bench vise so you can draw file from the muzzle toward you. Needed are a couple of small hand files for fairly light layers of silver solder, and for heavier layers of silver, it is best to use a bastard, second-cut and fine-cut file. For thin layers of silver, the second-cut and the fine-cut should be adequate.

Holding the file at a ninety-degree angle to the bore and using one hand on the handle and the other hand at the tip of the file, stroke the teeth of the file over the accumulated silver, applying just enough pressure to the file for the silver to come off in the form of dust. Rotate the barrel so you draw file all areas where there is an accumulation of silver solder.

Emery cloth strip is used to polish area of barrel which has had silver solder removed, prior to touch-up bluing.

There are always high and low spots where the silver accumulated, with the high areas usually being at the edges where the base of the sight made contact with the barrel. Check for these high and low spots with your fingertips. Use the coarsest cut file first, until the area feels smooth. Then use the next finer cut file to remove file marks and whatever silver solder is left on the barrel. If you use only two files, you should have a perfectly smooth barrel without any traces of accumulated silver. The file marks should be barely visible, but should not be felt when you run a fingertip across them. If three files are used, finish up with the finest file that you have.

Final polish with No. 180 grit emery paper, following it with 240 grit if an extra-fine finish is required.

Degrease fully, then apply the touch-up bluing compound of your choice. Once this has dried, use a pad of very fine steel wool to polish and burnish. If you want a bit of gloss on that touch-up area, add a few drops of fine oil to the steel wool, but do not use this oil treatment until you are satisfied about the quality of the touched-up area. If there is quite a bit of difference between the old and new bluing, you might try a second coat of touch-up bluing.

One of the barrels I draw filed to get rid of the silver solder would not give me a satisfactory blending of colors. Using a degreaser and bluing remover, I wiped off the area, extending it a bit, then followed with denatured alcohol, which was dried with a quick shot of compressed air. The first application of touch-up bluing did the trick, and the final polish with oil and steel wool gave me what I consider a perfect job.

RANDOM GLEANINGS

A trick I learned from an old cabinetmaker has been useful so often that I've wondered why nobody else ever has come up with the idea. You lube a drill that enters metal, you use cutting oil when cutting a hunk of drill rod

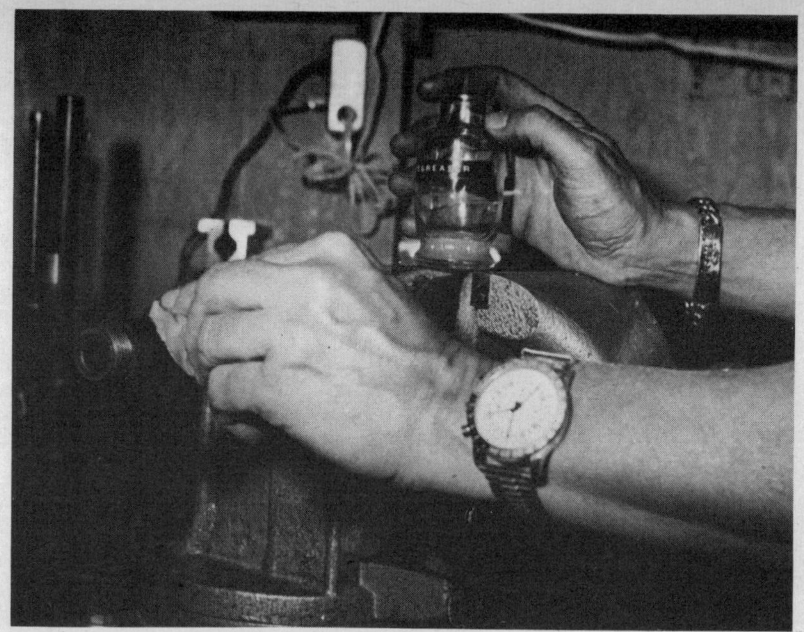

Metal work, right, is degreased before application of touch-up bluing. Below: Cotton ball soaked in bluing solution is rubbed briskly over damaged area to blend in with original bluing.

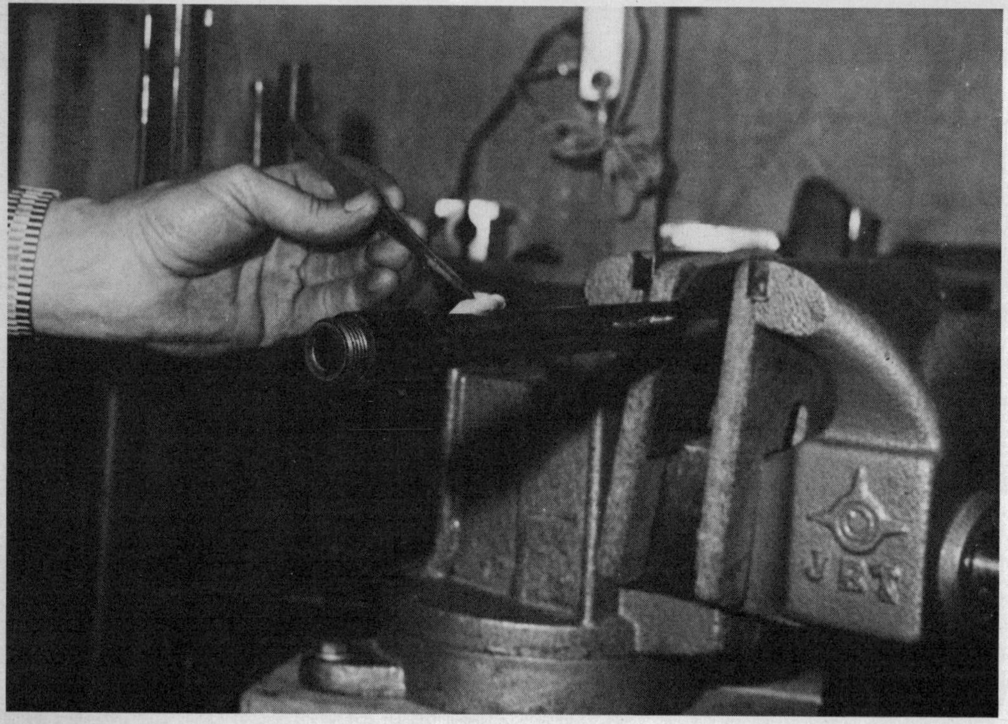

off with a hacksaw, why then not use a lube for seating a wood screw?

Find a small piece of soap or a candle stump, run the threads of the screw over the soap or the wax. Dry soap is good, slightly moistened soap is even better. This is a handy trick when seating the screws that hold butt plate, recoil pad, grip cap, or even sling swivel studs.

If you are a shotgunner, you know that snap caps for single and double-barrel guns are essential items. There is nothing wrong with having one in the chamber of a pump or autoloader, but somehow, there never are enough snap caps around the shop. The next time you make up your favorite glass-bedding compound, you can make a bunch of snap caps.

The plastic hulls are most suitable for this. Trim each of them with a sharp knife to 1.125 inches. Spread some release agent on a piece of scrap board and stand your cases like soldiers on the board. Pour the extra bedding compound into the hulls, let harden, and you have snap caps that will last a long time.

Old files can be used to make a lot of tools. Since finding a file-hardening compound proved to be impossible, I contacted Bob Brownell. From his bag of professional tricks, he pulled out the following:

Combine equal parts of baking flour, bone black and charred leather dust from the local shoe repair shop. Add a good dose of plain table salt and water to make a thick paste.

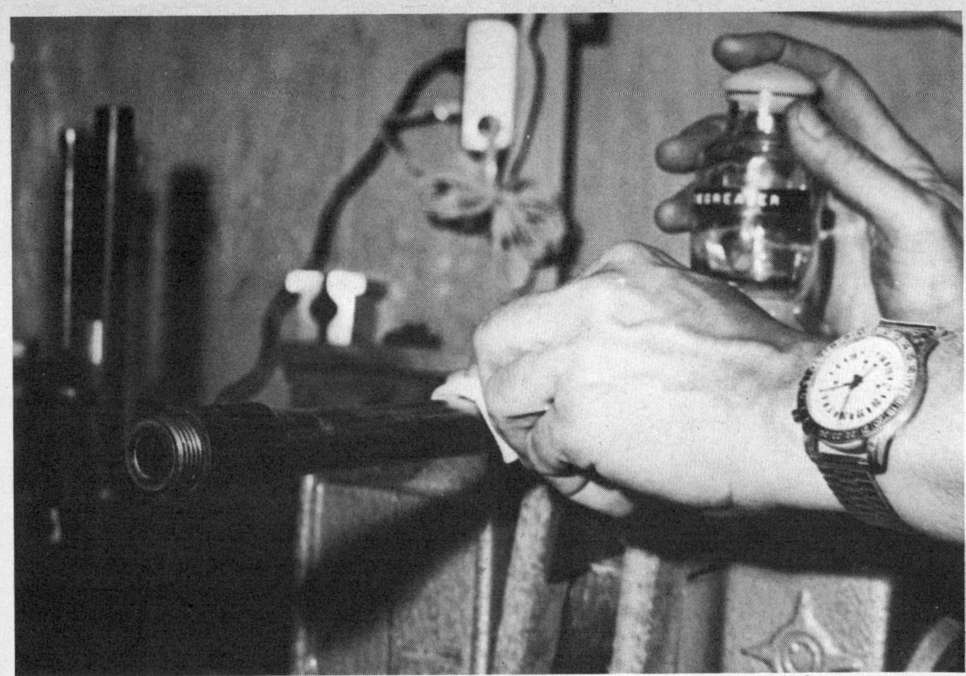

Wipe off touched up area of barrel after bluing is dry. Repeat application, if necessary, left. Final step includes burnishing reblued area with fine steel wool.

Heat the file slowly, then dip it into the paste, piling some of the paste onto the file. Slowly heat the file, but not enough to blister the paste. When the file shows a healthy red color, bend it to the desired shape. Again heat to red hot, then quench the file in brine. The paste, thanks to the charred leather, really stinks, especially when it gets too hot and burns. Once you get a noseful of some of the gunsmithing gunks that are being used, you will understand why so many of the pros favor outlying shops with large windows. That charred leather does more than just clean your sinuses.

Mention was made elsewhere of layout blue, the stuff you use to paint work with so you can see the scribe marks later. A can of the stuff will last a lifetime, but it is not always found readily.

A light copper coating will do the same job and such a wash coat is easily wiped on whatever it is you need to mark. Use four ounces of copper sulfate in eight ounces of water, which makes a cold saturated solution; add one ounce of sulfuric acid, stir and apply a thin layer, let dry and have fun.

If you don't want to mess around with mixing the above stuff, try Brownell's Oxpho-Blue. Apply a thin coat with saturated cleaning patch, let dry and wipe off lightly with clean patch. Most other instant blues also work, if you wipe them off before they set fully.

Making special clamps for repairing cracked gun stocks sometimes is easier in a big shop where lots of metal scrap can be found. Then there is the usual suggestion to cut one-inch strips from an old inner tube and use these rubber bands to apply pressure. Or instead of wasting time looking for an inner tube to cut up, one also can use 3M Scotch filament tape. You can buy it in drug stores. It makes great packages at Christmas time, and the rest you can use in the shop for your own projects.

When filing and sawing small metal parts, one must protect the surface of the part you're working on so that

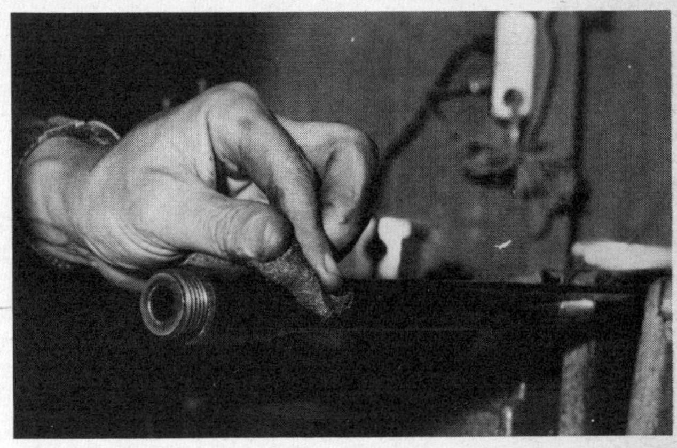

the vise doesn't leave unsightly marks on it. The padded vise jaws don't hold parts well enough for filing and sawing, and trying to get vise marks out later on can be a real pain. Set the piece you're working on into the vise lightly and note exactly where the pressure points of the jaws will be. Then use a felt marking pen to note the spot. Heat up the propane torch, apply a drop or two of silver solder to the marked spots, then let it harden, and you can lock the part into the vise and not worry about marring it. To remove the silver solder, heat the spot, and the solder will run right off, if you didn't use more than one or two drops.

If you ever have to fasten a vise, drill stand, or any other device that will exert torque, onto soft wood boards, you will find that the holding nuts with the washer on the underneath side pull tight, but sooner or later will develop play. Eventually you'll have oval holes and that means the holding power of that section of the bench or stand has gone down the tube.

Use one-eighth-inch flat bar stock scraps, drill a hole slightly larger than the bolt used for holding down whatever you are fastening, run the bolt through the hole in the bar stock and cinch tight. The bar stock applies and distributes pressure to the board from underneath and there is no wear on the holes in the wood.

Chapter 33

I N WRITING A book such as this, one tends to wonder whether he has kept his prose simple enough that the beginning gun tinkerer can understand it.

This question called for a bit of consideration and I contacted Hal Swiggett down Texas way to discuss the problem — if there was one.

"We might try my son, Vern," the senior Swiggett suggested. As it turned out, Bob Gustafson of Thompson/Center had just sent him a kit for a Hawken rifle. Friend Hal didn't have the slightest idea when he was going to have an opportunity to put the kit together.

"I'll tell him he can have the finished muzzleloader, if he will keep a record of what he does, as he's assembling it," Hal Swiggett suggested. "He's just getting interested in

"Have I made some kind of mistake?" seems to be the expression on novice gunsmith Vern Swiggett's face.

THE MAKING OF A GUN TINKERER

Using The Instructions Outlined Earlier, A Rank Amateur Proves His Abilities

Here's proof that a total beginner can build a functioning muzzleloader.

Plenty of sandpaper, instead of a wood rasp was used during the stock building, working slowly but surely.

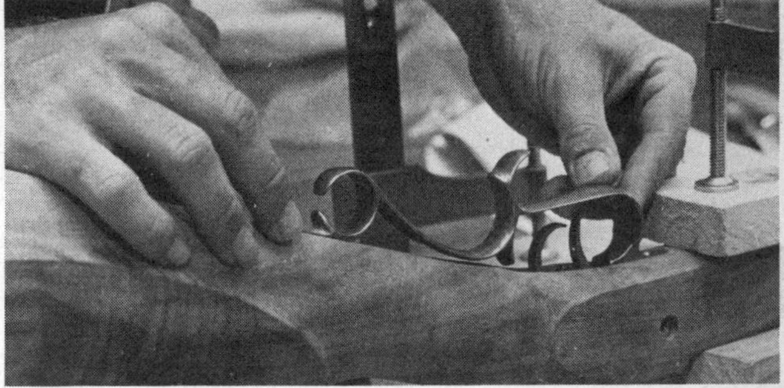
The metal trigger guard had to be stretched slightly but the instructions from Thompson/Center covered it.

black powder shooting, so he'll read anything he can, including your manuscript."

"If you don't think it'll seem we're a little heavy on black powder," I suggested.

"Muzzleloader shooting is the hottest thing in the country right now," Swiggett declared. "It's a natural."

So we agreed on a run-through. Vern Swiggett picked up the rifle kit on a Sunday, along with the reading material. Monday found him visiting a neighborhood hardware store. He asked the clerk to supply him with everything necessary to build the rifle. As suggested throughout this tome, he ordered good-quality tools, figuring he would have use for them later. If not, any error of workmanship certainly couldn't be blamed on inferior equipment.

Vern Swiggett had never built anything. He had no wood or metal-working experience whatever, so this was to be a

real honest-to-goodness test of instructions versus the inexperienced.

That he read and did well is beyond question, as can be seen by the finished product.

But now let's let Vern tell how it was done:

"The Thompson/Center Hawken kit rifle is completed! I took it to the range yesterday and shot it a few times. I was able to get a tight group but, unfortunately, wasn't able to sight it in because I didn't understand how the sight worked" — Vern has used iron sights little in his life and wasn't familiar with the basics of moving the rear sight the way the bullet impact point needed to be moved — "until after I had left the range, but I think next time I will be able to zero it right where I want it.

"After I had shot two or three times a man who was shooting a pistol a few feet away came over and asked,

Three holes must be drilled in the stock to install trigger guard.

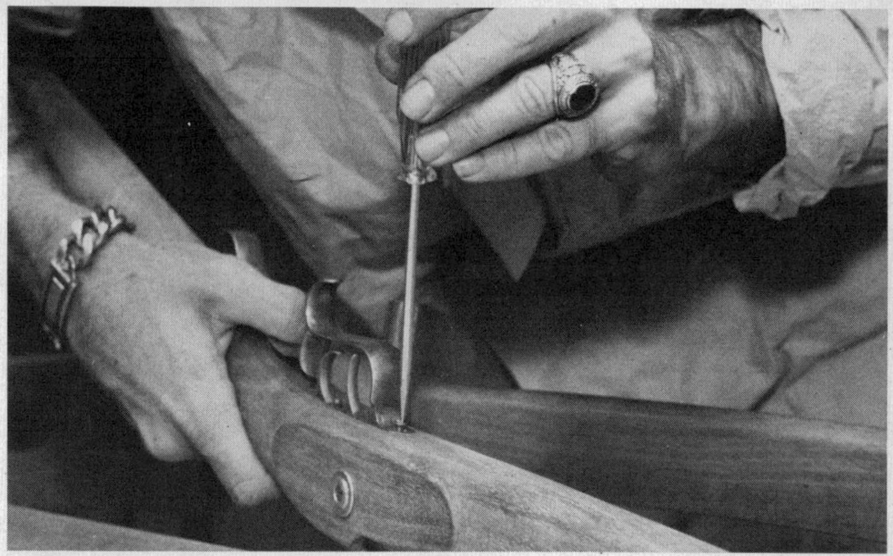

The trigger guard is temporarily placed for further wood work.

Last tang screw is tightened down before wood removal begins. The builder found it necessary to take off a good deal of wood from this section of stock.

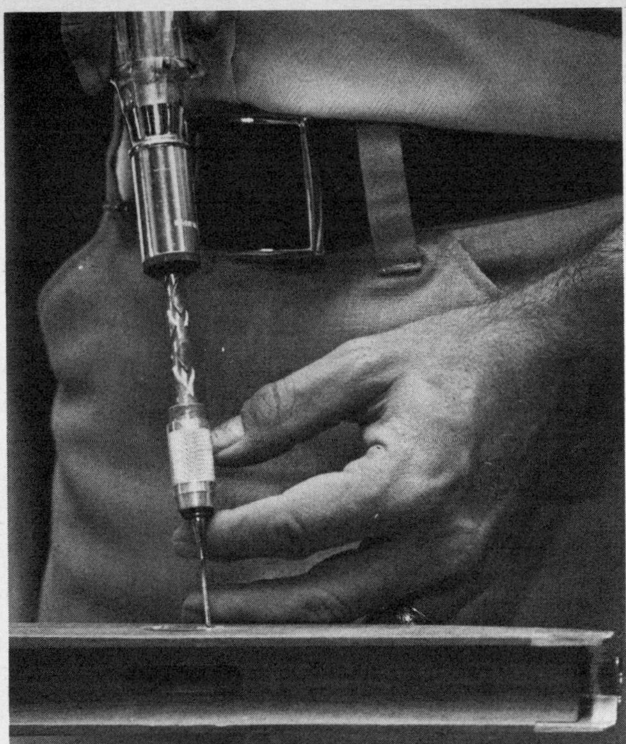

Escutcheon holes must be drilled with precision.

'How much does it weigh?' All I could think about was the rifle and told him eight or nine pounds. As it turned out, his interest was in the weight of the .50 caliber round ball.

"Thinking back over some of the things that were significant when I constructed the rifle, my initial impression was that there was going to be an awful lot of work to do to make it special. I read the instructions many times before starting work. Actually, before I did any work at all, I went to a neighborhood hardware store and bought all of the tools the instructions suggested, including a Surform rasp, a regular half-round rasp, a round rasp, a mill file and several different grades of sandpaper. I also bought

three large clamps and a 2x8-inch plank about twenty-four inches long.

"After studying the photographs in the instructions, I clamped the plank to my worktable. To this I clamped the rifle stock. I began near the butt plate on the side where the patch box is inletted at the toe. Using coarse sandpaper wrapped around a block of wood, I sanded until the brass and wood flowed together evenly, continuing across the comb, down onto the cheekpiece and finally to the bottom on the other side.

"I relied heavily on coarse sandpaper, medium, too, rather than much use of the rasps. I figured by using this method it would take a little longer, but reduce the danger of taking off too much wood in one spot as is easily possible with rasps. Perhaps on another rifle I might be able to take some shortcuts, but on this first one I felt like the careful way was the best way.

"When I got to the underside of the cheekpiece, I used the round rasp. With it I was able to smooth out the sharp edges. I also used medium-grade sandpaper wrapped around the rasp to make a smooth-flowing line underneath that cheekpiece.

"I continued to work the remainder of the wood with the various grades of sandpaper. In areas where a large amount of wood needed to come off I did resort to a rasp. One of the areas where the rasp was used by itself was around the tang.

"Before working this part of the rifle stock I drilled two one-eighth-inch holes and set the tang. Not until this was done did I work with rasps and sandpaper to remove a considerable amount of wood — enough to make the wood and metal flow smoothly together as if it were a single piece.

"This part of the work I enjoyed a lot, because I wanted to make the lines of my Hawken as delicate as possible. Where the wrist flowed back to the cheekpiece I could get that delicacy. There was a good deal of wood to be removed around the trigger guard, which added to this appearance. But most of the work was done on top.

"The lock flats on both sides caused some trouble. I'm sure more time could have been spent on them, but I'm

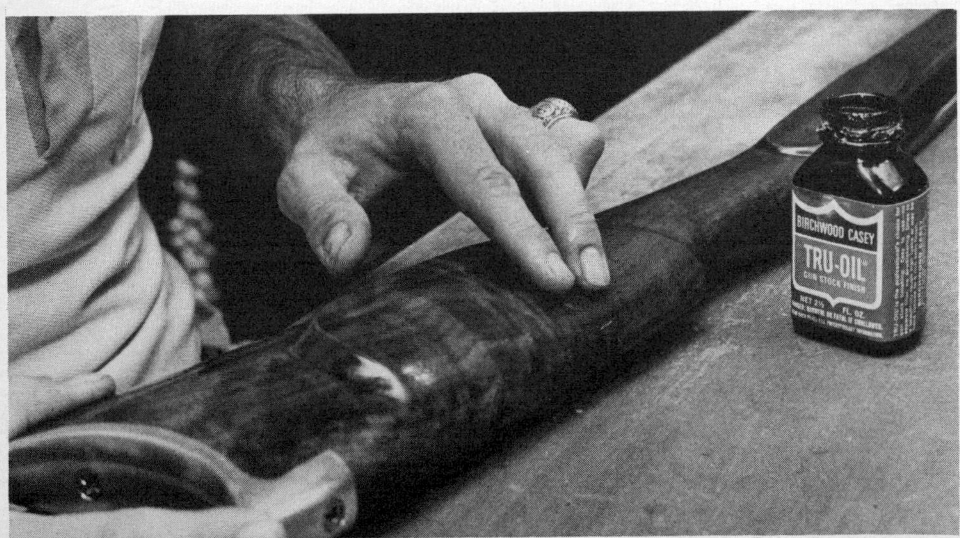

Tru-Oil finish was applied in four coats by hand. Glossy finish was not to builder's preference.

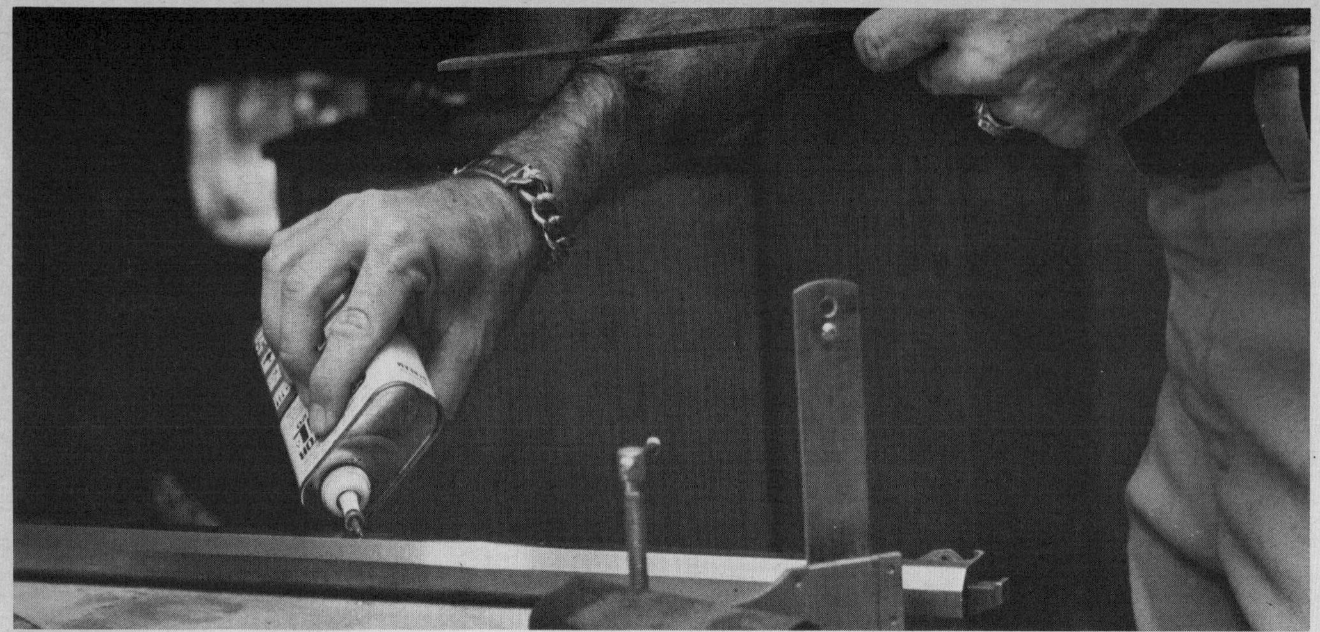

An application of machine oil to the hexagonal barrel eased filing chores, above. Final mirror-finish polish was done with emery cloth wrapped around file. Swiggett feels mirror finish is not necessary for browning process.

satisfied and as they say, 'beauty is in the eye of the beholder.'

"The problem with the lock flats is that they need to be kept even in depth as well as equal in length and shape. The round rasp was used quite a bit here, along with sandpaper. This wasn't difficult, but required a good deal of rasping, along with clamping and unclamping to view the other side. Only through extreme caution could the two sides be kept equal.

"After I progressed past the locks, the forearm was pretty well finished. Sanding was all that was necessary as there was no shaping to be done. The thing here, again, is to keep the wood flowing smoothly into the brass forend cap. It needed only a little refining.

"A little drilling in the forend was necessary where the escutcheons were inset. These are one-sixteenth of an inch holes. Here I set the brass before sanding so as not to overdo, leaving brass edges exposed.

"Underneath, three, three-thirty-seconds of an inch holes are required. One is necessary to secure the trigger. The other two are for securing the trigger guard. These, as with the other drilling, are easy by simply setting the metal in place, marking the center of the hole, removing the metal and drilling. There was no difficulty other than needing to stretch the trigger guard a bit to fit the inletting, but this was mentioned in the instructions and wasn't alarming.

"I tried to follow the instructions faithfully and was preoccupied with the woodwork. I couldn't imagine there being much work to finishing the metal. Looking back, there is as much work involved — and of equal importance — in finishing the metal as the wood.

"After the stock was completed, I installed the various pieces to make sure everything fit. Satisfied everything was as it should be, each piece was removed and the real stock finishing undertaken."

First, a really fine grade of sandpaper was used to go over the entire stock to make sure it was as smooth as possible. After wiping the stock with a clean cloth, young Swiggett applied a warm, damp cloth to wet the wood evenly without saturating it. Only a few minutes were necessary for it to dry and the stock felt quite rough again. After going over it with fine sandpaper wrapped around a block of wood, it felt much smoother than before.

"Since it worked so well one time, I decided a second dampening was in order, so I went through the same procedure again," Vernon Swiggett says.

"I then applied walnut-colored filler. This was applied with a cloth, then rubbed against the grain with a piece of burlap to force it into the grain. Light rubbing with fine steel wool removed the excess filler after it dried.

"Going to Birchwood Casey's Muzzle Loader and Stock Finishing Kit, I applied one coat of Colonial Red stock finish. I wanted a slightly reddish color but not a painted appearance. I followed the instructions for both the walnut filler and the Colonial Red stain.

"Next came four coats of Birchwood Casey True Oil gun stock finish. The instructions said to apply liberally with the fingers. On the first coat I did just that. I applied too much because I did get some runs. It took time and work to remove those runs and redo what I should have done right the first time.

"After the four coats of finish my stock really looked beautiful. It was shiny, glossy, but this was not what I wanted. I was hoping to get a satin, hand-rubbed appearance. I made another trip to the neighborhood hardware store and bought a pound of pumice; nothing but

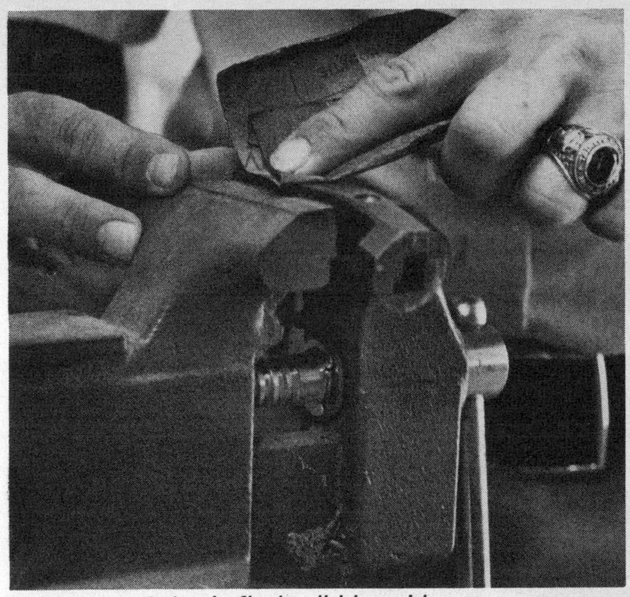

The tang needed only final polishing with emery paper.

Degreasing and browning the barrel was done in home garage as shown. See text for details of process.

Above: At the proper temperature for browning, the barrel is hot enough so that drops of water dance on the surface. At left, muzzle gets initial swabbing.

white, crushed, powder-like stone. I used the instructions with the pumice along with those included with the finishing kit."

Linseed oil was applied to a clean cloth, then that cloth powdered with pumice. Shaking off the excess not absorbed by the linseed oil, Swiggett rubbed the stock, with the grain. Clean linseed oil was used to wipe off the remaining granulation. He next used a dry cloth to dry off the stock. The result was a hand-rubbed, oil-finished stock.

Birchwood Casey's stock finishing kit affords the user a choice: the varnished, glossy look or the hand-rubbed finish, by taking it a step farther. Stock finishing took approximately sixteen hours; some of this time was spent to correct mistakes.

"Now that the stock is finished I thought I had it made

because all I lacked was the draw filing, polishing and browning of the metal pieces. Those steps sure sounded simple.

"But I had put in approximately nine hours on draw filing and polishing, while browning took another four hours. Almost as much time as on the stock."

Draw filing the barrel required concentration and some endurance. The barrel was clamped in place as suggested in the instructions, each flat draw filed and polished before going to the next one. Each flat took approximately one hour to finish.

"I worked the mill file back and forth with about four-inch strokes until the entire flat was covered. The idea is to remove the diagonal machine marks and replace them with parallel filing marks. The concentration comes in keeping the file flat in order not to destroy the sharp edges between the flats.

"I did encounter one problem not mentioned in the instructions. My file seemed to leave equally hideous marks as the ones I was trying to remove. I decided to use a bit of oil on the surface being filed. This worked and gave me the

HOME GUNSMITHING DIGEST

desired finish. Apparently the oil remedied whatever was causing my trouble."

Polishing is done by wrapping various grades of emery cloth around the mill file and polishing the flat, back and forth. After the finest grade of emery cloth is used, the final step is to rub thoroughly with a high grade of steel wool.

"The tang was so near finished that I didn't file it at all — just polished it with emery cloth.

"There were a few scratches I was unable to get out completely even after some eight hours or so on the barrel, but most of these scratches disappeared in the browning process which leads me to believe perhaps I devoted too much time and attention in trying to get a mirror finish.

The barrel does need to be smooth and there cannot be any gouges or deep scratches, but it does not have to be polished like a mirror."

Polishing completed, Swiggett again assembled the rifle to make sure everything fit and all that remained to be done was the browning. This required another trip to that nearby hardware store to purchase a propane torch.

Using the plum brown furnished with the Birchwood Casey Muzzle Loader Kit, Swiggett relied heavily on the instructions, which show how common wire coat hangers can be bent to support a heavy barrel, while heat is being applied with the propane torch. Those same instructions carefully explain how to check for the proper temperature of the metal before applying the browning solution.

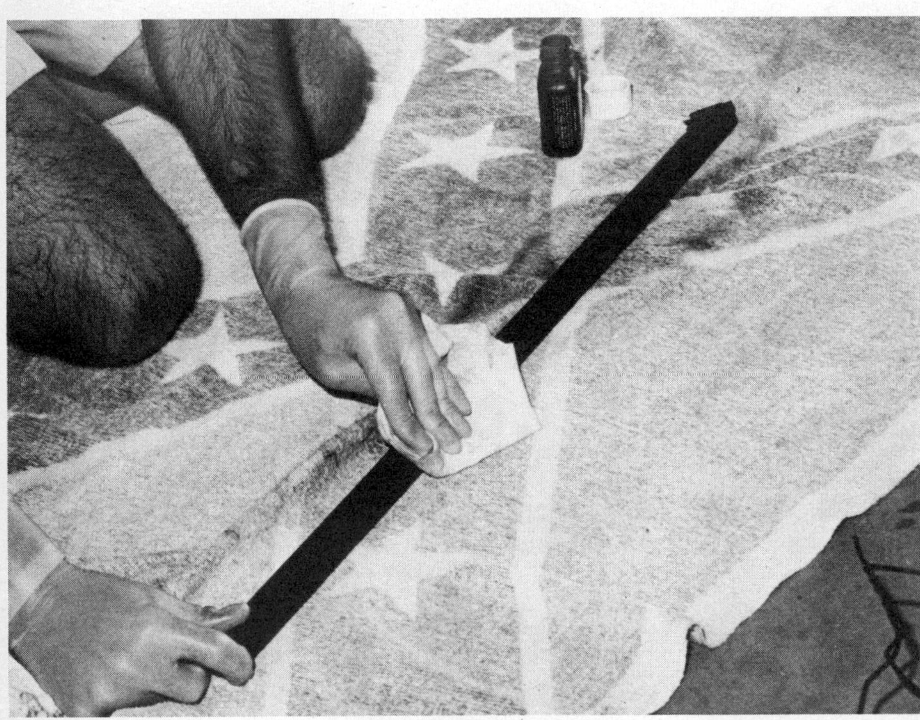

Barrel is allowed to cool to handling temperature and cleaned with damp rag. Note surgical gloves.

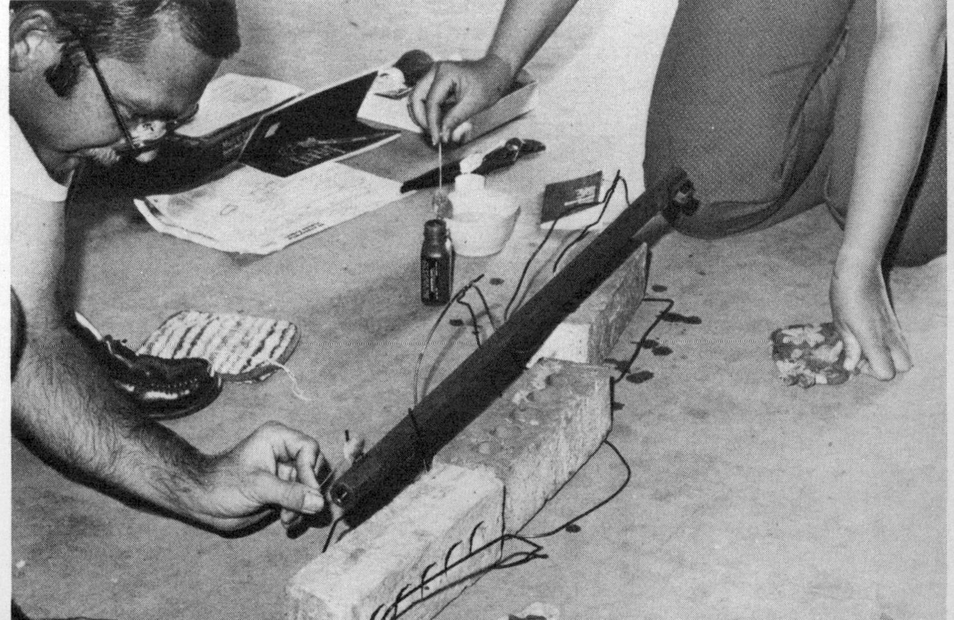

Four coats of plum brown were applied to barrel for color.

Phillips screwdriver is placed in muzzle to rotate barrel.

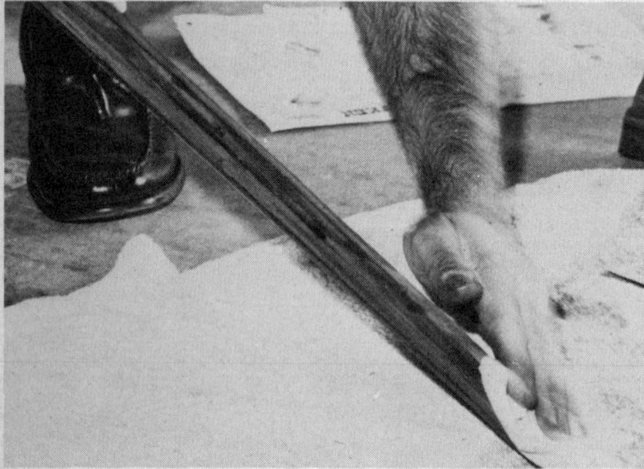
Browning residue is easily wiped off barrel, above.

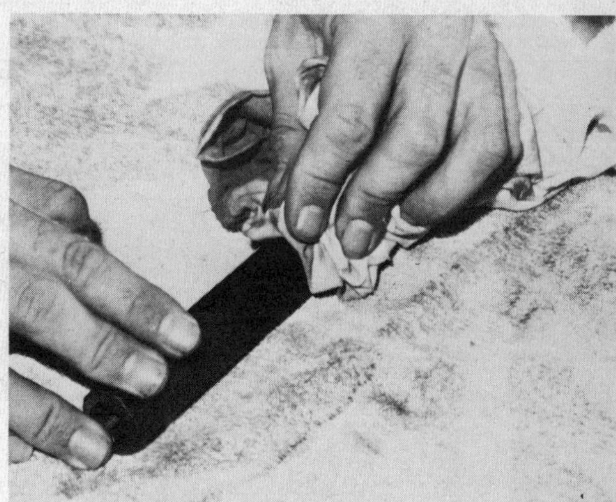
Barrel is thoroughly cleaned with damp rag.

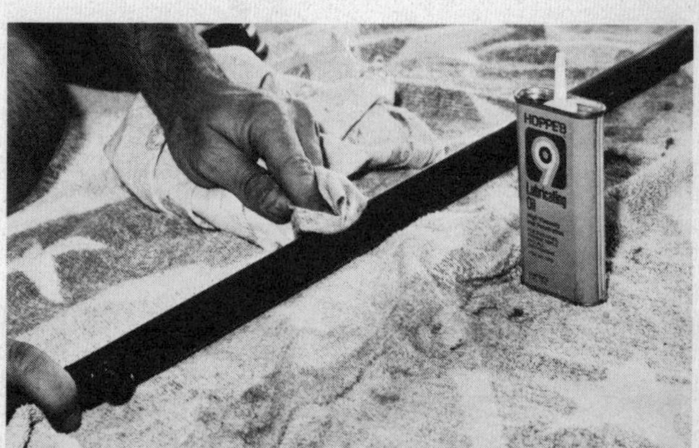
After cleaning, barrel is given good coat of gun oil.

more exciting than anything else going on in the neighborhood at the time; their three children grabbed ringside seats to watch the show.

Swiggett used a screwdriver in the muzzle, as Linda used pot holders on the other end to rotate the barrel, making each side accessible for easier swabbing.

After a thorough going over with the Birchwood Casey plum brown, the barrel was allowed to cool enough to handle. Handling was with surgical gloves to avoid further degreasing, then the barrel was wiped with a damp cloth. It

The instructions emphasized that the metal should be degreased before it is heated and the browning solution applied. Any fingerprints or oily spots on the metal will not take the browning stain equally, so all that hard work in draw filing and polishing would be lost. A bottle of cleaner-degreaser is furnished with the Birchwood Casey kit.

Vern Swiggett placed the barrel on the little stands made from coat hangers, per the instructions. Heating the barrel with the propane torch took a bit longer than expected, but Swiggett did tend to overheat it a bit a time or two and had to wait for it to cool. The criteria seems to be the sizzle test, better described as a small amount of water on the heated surface. If it remains on the metal and evaporates slowly, the metal is too cold. If it immediately vanishes in a puff of steam, it is too hot. At the ideal temperature, the water will sizzle and dance about as it evaporates. When the tiny amount of water danced and sizzled, Swiggett swabbed on the plum brown formula.

Making every effort to apply the solution evenly while the barrel was at a constant temperature, Swiggett's wife, Linda, grabbed a swab and helped out. All this was taking place on the cement-surfaced garage floor and proved far

looked horrible, as if the job was all wrong — until wiped off with that fairly damp cloth. The barrel was heated four times all told, with four coats of plum brown, to get the beautiful finish acceptable.

After the fourth and final swabbing, the barrel again was wiped with the damp cloth to remove those last deposits left from the browning, then a liberal coat of Hoppe's gun oil was applied and rubbed in. Hoppe's was handy at that moment, but any good oil serves the purpose and beeswax can be used for this final step by rubbing it on the still-warm barrel. This same browning process was used on the tang and sights.

Small parts of muzzleloader are polished with steel wool and browned in same manner as barrel.

Factory finished Thompson/Center Hawken rifle, above, compared to kit version. Early factory model shown was manufactured with case-hardened steel trigger guard, while kit and later factory jobs feature brass guard.

Bob Gustafson, left, of Thompson/Center company, talks over blackpowder kit building with Swiggett.

All that remained was to put the parts together, remove the steel working screws in the stock and replace them with the brass screws provided. The steel screws were in tight and there was some difficulty in removing them, but it was accomplished with no disastrous results.

Another minor difficulty would have been encountered had not Vern Swiggett been an aspiring black powder shooter already owning a rifle: No nipple wrench was provided with the kit. This could prove a disappointment to a kit purchaser, since the finished rifle is of little value without the nipple installed.

The Thompson/Center Hawken assembled in shooting condition, the ramrod was next. This consisted of installing the brass tips on the furnished dowel with epoxy cement, then sanding until the wood and metal felt and appeared as one piece.

The ramrod was finished in the same manner as the stock. It is of a different type of wood, therefore has a slightly different appearance, but it turned out real well.

Cleaning the bore before that first shot, Swiggett found a black substance in the barrel, which probably came from some of the browning solution getting in through the nipple vent. But the rifle fired on the first attempt.

Swiggett was a bit amazed at hitting the target with his first shot, as there are no instructions on how to install or adjust the sights. Thompson/Center should consider adding a bit more info here, as only experienced iron sight users know how to move the rear sight in the direction the bullet needs to be moved.

The would-be gunsmith also feels some of the instructions should be more detailed for folks like himself who never have undertaken such a project before. The knowledgeable workman will read only what he wants or needs, but the beginner will soak up every detail then still do a few things wrong. There is no way he can be given too much advice.

"I didn't know what was expected of me when I began. I certainly didn't have any prior experience working with wood or metal, yet I was able to get a shootable rifle with approximately twenty-nine hours of effort. Anyone with any skill or experience should be able to complete this kit considerably quicker." That is Vern Swiggett's opinion. At

A beautiful firearm at less cost, the completed Thompson/Center .50 caliber Hawken kit rifle, viewed from lock side.

HOME GUNSMITHING DIGEST

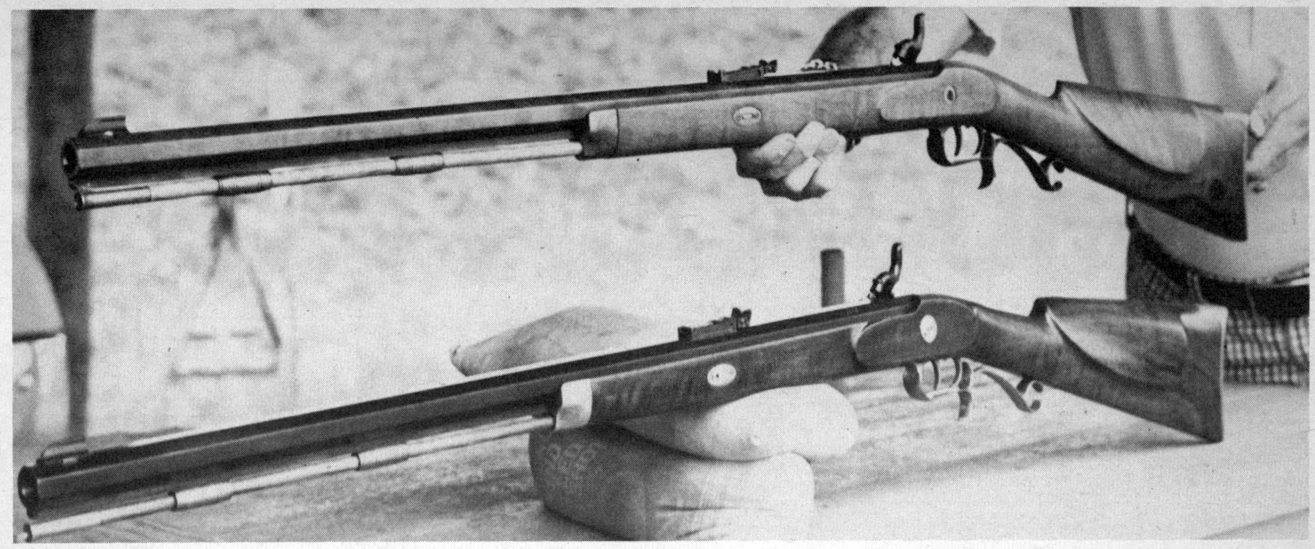

The Hawken kit gun, below, turned out to have a better looking piece of stock wood than older factory-built model.

any rate, he finished up with a truly beautiful Thompson/Center .40 Hawken from his kit.

It is better-finished than my factory rifle, and I hesitate to say this, because the finish of Thompson/Center products has never been in question. On the other hand, Thompson/Center employees can't put in twenty-nine hours to finish each rifle as Vern did on his.

The cost of materials — not including the kit — ran to almost $50. Vern Swiggett didn't own a single item necessary and bought only top-quality tools since he figured they would be cheapest in the long run; sooner or later they will come in handy for something else.

The final test of any rifle is in how it shoots. This .50 Thompson/Center Hawken is producing five-shot groups at fifty yards averaging almost an even 1¾ inches. This is with .490 balls, Thompson/Center patching lubricated with Maxi-Lube and 85 grains of Gearhart-Owen FFg. Some groups are bigger, of course, but a good many are smaller. The tightest so far is five-shots in 1-3/8 inches at fifty yards. And the rifle is cleaned after each five-shot string.

This particular Thompson/Center Hawken kit is available in .45 or .50 and in percussion or flint.

Young kit builder declared after first shot, "Nothing fell off, the stock didn't crack, the browning didn't blow and I was able to hit what I aimed at." Could a gunsmith ask for more?

Chapter 34

CAMOUFLAGE YOUR HUNTING GUN

Basic Materials And Techniques Can Make You Invisible To Your Game

In its normal state, deeply-blued and highly-polished double-barrel side-by-side shotgun stands out with painful clarity against camouflaged hunting jacket and hat. Some hunters remember to hide everything but their guns.

SOME OF THE things hunters do make little or no sense as far as I am concerned. Mind you, I'm not knocking the hunter — heck, I have hunted from one end of the country to the other and in a few other spots in this world — but some things just don't make sense.

Take the duck or goose hunter: He gets duded up in camouflage pants and mud-colored hip boots, dons a camouflage jacket and cap, smears camouflage paint on his face, wears camouflage gloves and even sticks two camouflage bandannas in his pocket, then uses a brightly blued shotgun! Okay, so duck hunters are as crazy as trout fishermen.

But the fellow who stalks the wily turkey and collects his Thanksgiving dinner is a real hunter! He, too, gets decked out in clothing that darn near makes him invisible; clothing that breaks up his outline so that it's hard to spot him if and when you encounter him in the woods. But he too carries a gun that's visible one hundred yards away.

Varmint hunters, especially those who use calls adroitly, have to stay hidden so that the incoming varmint won't be able to spot the danger. Again, we — yes, I hunt ducks, geese, turkey and varmints plus a few other critters — get all decked out in camouflage clothing, but nothing is done to make our guns less visible.

If you hunt in snowy territory, you wear white and the gun you pack on these trips is camouflaged, even if the camouflage job consists only of a coat of white paint or some two-inch-wide tape wrapped around the gun. Why not camouflage your gun for other types of hunting?

Of course, a number of camouflage methods have been tried on guns over the years but, until recently, I never encountered one that was really satisfactory. First, there was camouflage cloth that was wrapped around the gun and glued into place. The wrapping never lasted much longer than one or two hunting trips, and getting the old stuff off and putting new material on became a chore.

Local duck hunters use a variation of this method, wrapping strips of burlap around the barrels of their guns and taping the burlap into place. This works reasonably well on doubles, but the idea falls flat on its face when you try that stunt with a pump or an autoloader.

Then, there were a few Teflon-coated and OD-painted guns on the market, but few hunters bought them and this idea also passed on. Living in an area where duck and goose hunting is a way of life, I had shopped around for a good way to camouflage my duck gun. I figured if I could ever find a good method, I'd later use the same camouflage system for my combination turkey gun, and maybe a varmint rifle.

Before the last hunting season, I doped out a way of camouflaging a gun and what I found out about it while tackling the job sold me on the idea of dressing up a couple of my other guns that way. Basically, you can do the job in three evenings, providing the various layers of paint and gunk dry completely in that time. You will need the following:

LPS Instant Cold Galvanize. Depending on the gun, one or maybe two cans will do the job. I used just a dab of the second can on the gun illustrated, but put the rest of the second can to good use by spraying the bottom of a trash can that had seen better days.

Rust-oleum paint in brown, green and yellow in eight-ounce cans. I found the brush-on paint easier to use than the aerosol spray, since the brush allows you greater control of the paint applied.

Krylon, an acrylic spray coating, one or two cans.

Total cost of all the materials mentioned is under $10. The LPS Instant Cold Galvanize and the Krylon spray are best applied out-of-doors, unless you have adequate space and ventilation in your workshop. If you do use the Krylon spray indoors, be sure there are no open pilot lights or the possibility of any sparks near the area you're working in — and refrain from smoking, since the vapors from Krylon spray may ignite explosively.

Depending on the type of action on the gun you want to work on, your camouflaging job will vary a bit. I don't suggest getting spray or paint on the action bars of a pump gun, for instance, and an autoloader will require a slightly different treatment than a bolt-action gun.

On bolt-action rifles, it is best to treat the wood separately from the barrel action. The barrel channel need not be painted or treated, but this might be a good time to see if the barrel channel is waterproof. If not, a sealing coat of shellac or varnish can be applied.

The ejection port of a varmint bolt-action is not big enough to worry about camouflaging, but the bolt handle should be treated. Remove the bolt from the action and spray only the bolt handle — you can either mask the remainder of the bolt or, with careful spraying, cover only the bolt handle. To prevent binding of the action, the bolt itself, of course, should not be treated.

Gas vents on the action should be plugged with a match or toothpick before spraying or painting, and the ejection port

Problem: Find the camouflaged shotgun in picture.

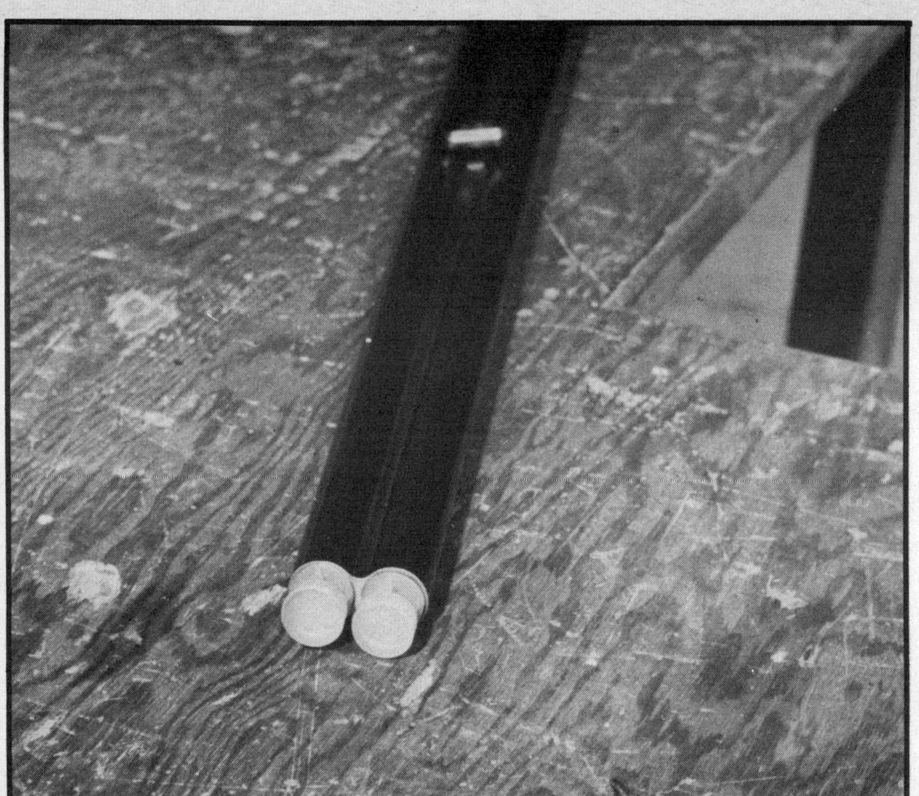

Plastic shot wads make ideal plugs in shotgun muzzles to prevent any spray paint from entering barrels. Wooden dowels may be used with rifles.

should be plugged or masked before you begin operations. Smoothbore barrels are best plugged with a suitable plastic wad with plastic shot collar to avoid getting any spray into the barrel, and rifle barrels can be plugged with a dowel whittled to fit like a cork. If the dowel is permitted to project a few inches from the muzzle, the dowel also will serve as a handy handle while manipulating spray can and gun at the same time.

The side-by-side shotgun was camouflaged without being stripped or taken down, and single-barrel shotguns — of the top-break variety — revolvers and semiautomatic pistols need not be taken down either.

As long as you avoid a too-enthusiastic application of either the LPS or the Krylon spray around functioning parts, they still will operate properly. The safety, top-lever, triggers and sling swivels on the side by side were checked for smooth functioning after both spray applications and there were no problems. With semiautomatic pistols, be sure that the slide, hammer and magazine release, as well as the safety, are fully functional after each spray coat.

You may wonder about the sling swivels on the side by side, but I like a sling on a shotgun — especially a duck or goose gun. A sling leaves my hands free for a bag of blocks, lunch and shooting box.

Before you actually begin to camouflage the gun, take a look at the sundry pieces of camouflage clothing you own. Note that not only the design, but also the colors vary — especially the background color. Colors on the current military camouflage suits contain quite a bit of green, the coloring being designed to match the verdant jungle growth of Vietnam.

Select your paint and the pattern to match your clothing

Fast-drying cold galvanize acts as base for further painting. Spray paint should be used outdoors or in well-ventilated workshop. Avoid any open flame.

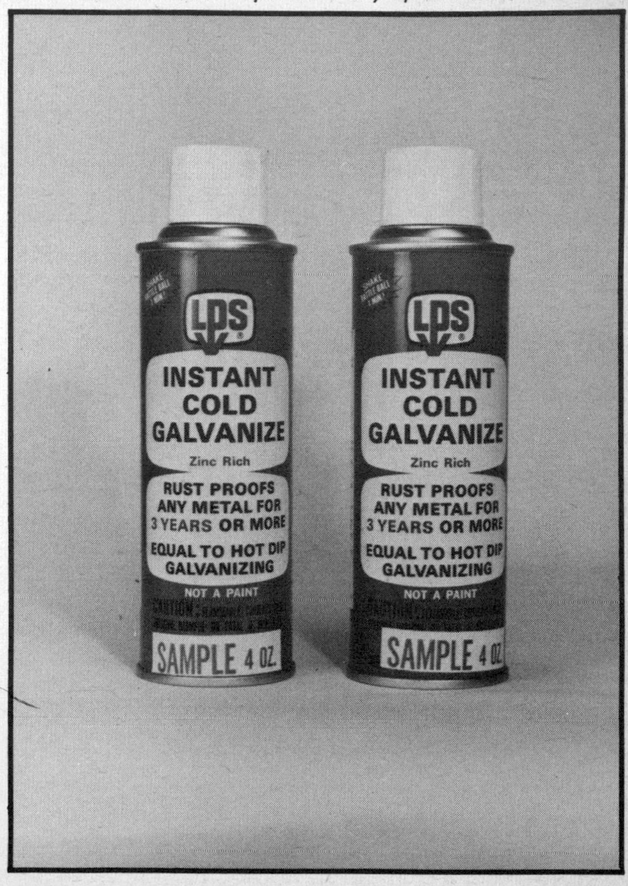

Cold galvanize material should be sprayed on all surfaces to be painted. Close firearm action and mask working surfaces.

and also the area where you'll be using the camouflaged gun. The color best known as dead grass does not match the gray-greens you encounter when calling coyotes in Texas and, conversely, the green used by the varmint hunter will not match the muddy-brown of the Maryland goose hunter's terrain.

Begin the job by cleaning the gun internally and externally, being sure to remove all traces of gun oil, grease, solvent and dirt from all external parts of the gun. If, for instance, some dirt is left in the checkering, you will find it almost impossible for the LPS galvanize or the paint to adhere. If the checkering has filled in with dirt and the accumulated crud of ages, use an old toothbrush to remove all foreign matter. Before using the LPS spray, be sure that no dust has collected on the gun and that all parts are bone-dry.

The LPS Instant Cold Galvanize is said to rustproof any metal for three or more years. This spray is not a paint, but actually bonds with the metal to which it is applied, setting up an electromechanical action that fuses ninety-five percent of a pure zinc compound to the steel. The LPS product prevents rusting underneath the camouflage paints, and the zinc deposit effectively withstands over 3000 hours of saltwater exposure.

Holding the nozzle about a foot from the gun, spray lightly in long, sweeping strokes. Keep the spray can in constant motion when applying the LPS, or you'll end up with heavy blobs of the galvanize in some spots. The spray will be dry to the touch within five minutes — at least on a bright breezy day with low humidity.

This quick drying enables you to turn the gun over within a short period of time and complete the spray job on the other side. Check the functioning parts — if the gun has not

Rust-oleum paint colors may be selected to blend in with area and season most likely to be hunted.

paint in these cans has been thoroughly mixed, you can begin to blend your own colors by mixing varying amounts of yellow with brown and with green.

Yellow mixed with dark brown gives you a color very close to dead grass, and yellow plus forest green gives you a light green, the final color depending on the ratio of the two basic colors used when making the mix.

The yellow/brown mix, when combined with the yellow/green mix, gives yet another color suitable for the camouflage job. Yellow alone is not suitable for use as a camouflage color, and the dark brown and deep green should be used sparingly.

When you start painting, remember that the basic idea behind a camouflage job is to break up the distinctive outline of an object, and an irregular placement of paint splotches is better than a uniform distribution.

Never work with a brush that is too full of paint, and in such areas as the checkering, use the dry-brush technique. Here, the fibers of the small brush contain just a little bit of paint, for if too much paint is used, you will fill in the checkering. Use the same dry-brush method around screwheads, taking care not to fill in the screwhead slots, or the serration of the safety and similar points.

There is no need to use too much paint on this job. The LPS spray serves as a base and, if you have done a reasonably even job in spraying on the galvanize, can serve as a background color for your camouflage painting.

been taken down — after half an hour has elapsed, then let the work dry overnight or at least six hours.

For the most durable job, I favor two separate but light applications of the LPS Instant Cold Galvanize, letting each application dry the recommended time.

The Rust-oleum paints come next. Our local hardware store had only three of the basic colors: yellow (659), chestnut brown (977), and forest green (1282). Once the

Using camouflage jacket as a pattern guide, various colors of Rust-oleum are applied with brush. Author describes in text the array of custom colors which may be obtained from mixing three paints; basic brown, forest green and yellow.

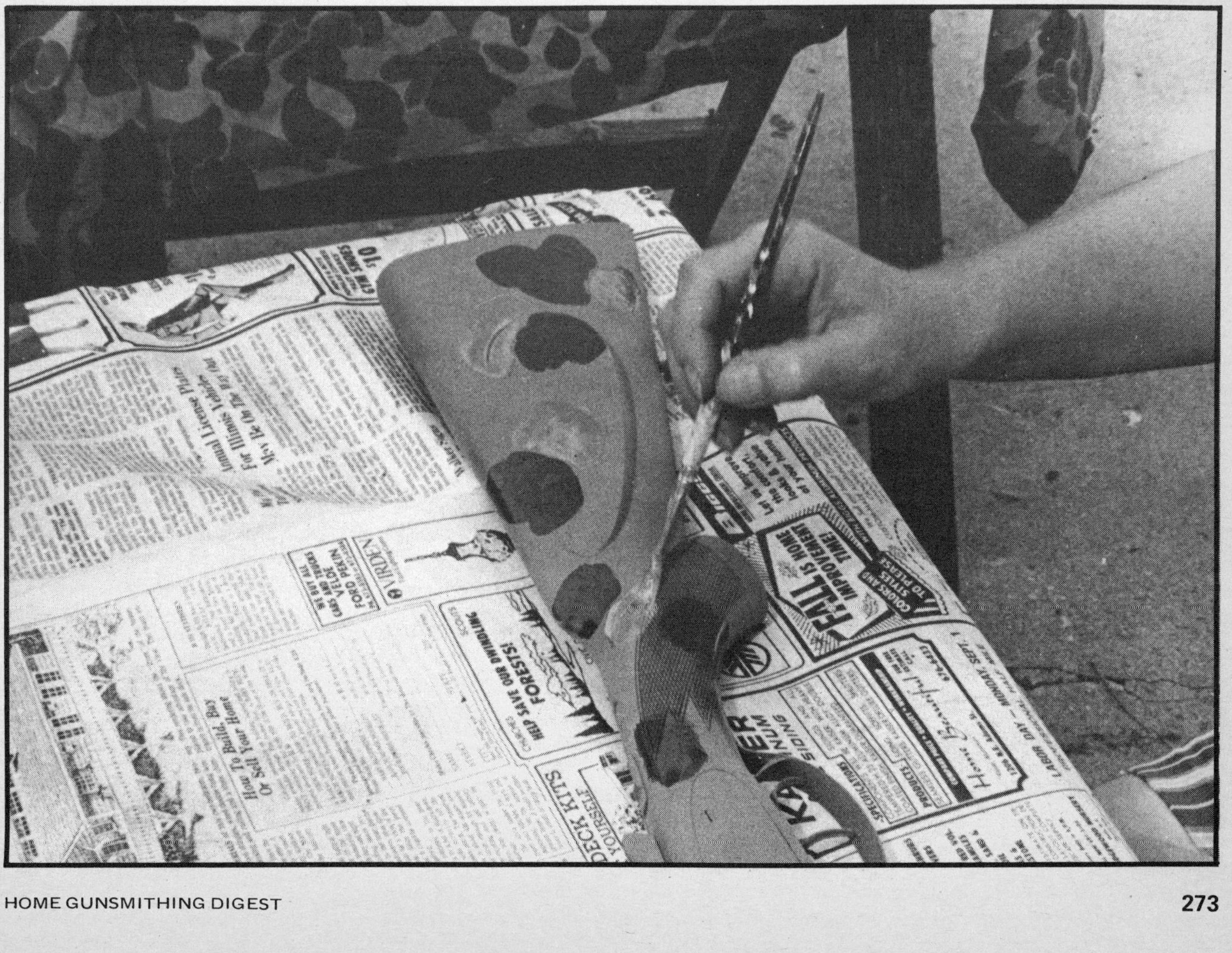

Clear acrylic spray coating is applied to all painted surfaces to form protective coating.

The Rust-oleum paints do a good job in covering and a single coat of the various colors will be sufficient. I found it easiest to start at the butt of the shotgun, using a camouflage jacket as a guide for some of my splotches of paint. Keeping in mind the basic aim is to break up the outline of the gun, carry some of the splotches of paint over the comb, and from the cheekpiece down into the butt stock.

Whenever wood meets metal or metal meets metal, bring the paint almost to the junction of the two meeting parts, then continue the paint splotch in the same way on the other side of the junction. In this way, there is no chance for any paint to run down inside and gum up the works.

As you proceed toward the muzzle, you'll find that you refer back to the camouflage jacket less frequently and are proceeding at a faster pace with the various colors. Just be sure to vary the size and shape of the various color splotches, as well as the juxtaposition of the colors.

If the humidity is low enough, you may find that the butt is dry enough to the touch for you to start the other side in a short time. If not, leave the painted side uppermost and finish the job as soon as the paint has dried sufficiently.

You may have used Rust-oleum in aerosol cans for other jobs and found it easier and faster to apply to such things as outdoor furniture. But in camouflaging a gun, it is too difficult to control the amount of spray when you're working with small splotches of color, and you may end up with too much paint on critical areas of the gun. Although there is a broad spectrum of colors to choose from, especially in larger paint stores, the colors are too clear and bright for the effect you want to create, and blending of the liquid paints is the only answer.

As soon as all of the Rust-oleum paint has dried thoroughly — and this will vary with the temperature and humidity — spray the entire paint job with the clear acrylic. Usually, twenty-four hours is sufficient time for the Rust-oleum to dry, but in our area of high humidity it took longer.

When using the acrylic spray, be sure to cover all areas that were painted. The Krylon provides a permanent protective coating for the Rust-oleum paints. It dries clear and stays that way, sheds dirt and effectively seals all porous surfaces.

Unpainted sections of the gun, such as the recoil pad, need not be sprayed. Use the same technique with the Krylon as you did with the LPS spray, long sweeping motions with the nozzle of the can about a foot from the surface of the gun. The trick with the acrylic spray is to get enough spray on the surface without creating runs or sags.

For best results, the manufacturer of Krylon suggests that this be applied when the temperature is between seventy and eighty degrees. When the temperature is within this range, the Krylon dries almost immediately and you can place the gun on a flat surface and give first one side and then the other a light application of the Krylon.

Check the functioning of the gun after the first application of Krylon, then inspect it carefully from butt to muzzle to be sure that all painted areas have been covered. In good light you will be able to detect a subtle difference in areas still not covered by the Krylon. Apply a second light coat of the Krylon, paying particular attention to the uncovered spots you have noted.

Once the last treatment has dried, check the functioning again, then take the invisible gun hunting. Of course, I can't promise anyone that he'll bag more ducks, call in more coyotes, or collect his Thanksgiving gobbler the first hour out, but such a camouflage job is just one more item that will work in your favor.

After clear acrylic has thoroughly dried, shotgun is broken down into basic groups, excess paint is removed and action is worked to ensure free-movement of all parts.

Chapter 35

TRICKS OF THE TRADE

These Hard-Learned Shortcuts May Save You Hours Of Frustration And Labor!

YOU CAN HAVE a barnful of machine tools and do fair to middling work, while some other guy, with nothing more than a dozen files, will do jobs that make both of us green with envy. Everybody who works with tools sooner or later develops certain habits and methods of doing things that make life easier and speed the job. Since gunsmiths depend on manual skill and a good dose of technical know-how for their living wages, it cannot be too shocking to learn that some have mastered the art of doing a job in half the time it takes another.

Here is a collection of tips I have gathered here and there.

FROZEN SCREWS

With stuck screws and taps, before taking a chance and shearing off the screwhead, use a liberal dose of Bust Rust, an aerosol penetrating oil made by Jet-Aer Corporation. Let it work for at least ten minutes, then give the stuck screw or tap another shot and wait a few minutes more. In nine out of ten cases whatever is stuck will come out easily. If this still doesn't work, use either an impact driver, or the drill press.

Chuck the suitable screwdriver into the chuck of the press, then set the work into a machinist vise, making certain that the vise is anchored to the table of the drill press. Seat the blade in the slot of the screw, then without the power, turn the belt of the drill press or, if that is not within easy reach, simply grasp the chuck of the drill press and see if the screw won't turn out. If you don't have Bust Rust, Coca Cola will do nearly as good a job.

For frozen screws, spray on a shot or two of Bust Rust, wait a few minutes, and in most cases the screw will turn out just the way it says in the books.

PORTABLE COMPRESSED AIR

Not everybody can have compressed air in the shop. I needed my compressor on the indoor range to water down the dirt backstop, and did not want to go the cost of a second compressor. For less than $20, I bought one of the small portable air tanks, hooked a hose onto it, and now have portable compressed air. The tank can be moved from place to place, and taking it out to the range to fill takes only a minute. If you don't have a compressor, your local gas station probably will let you fill your portable tank, especially if you buy your gas there.

Any heat treating or welding requires oxygen, plus some other gas. The large tanks are way too big for the average shop, and rental of tanks has become so costly that it is almost cheaper to buy the tank. Used tanks often can be found advertised in the classified section of the local paper, and believe it or not, you are entitled to an ownership certificate. If you ever move, especially over long distance, you may find that the mover will not move such tanks. You can sell the tanks and often at a price higher than you paid originally.

HOMEMADE DUMMY ROUNDS

To check the feeding of any firearm, never use live ammo, especially indoors. Outdoors it may be permissible, but watch where that barrel is pointed. Dummy rounds, made by Winchester, can be bought, or you can make your own if you are a handloader.

As you full-length size the case, it will decap the case automatically. Seat that spent primer right back into the primer pocket, but clean the pocket first. Check overall length of the case, and trim it if needed. Then seat a suitable bullet to the required depth. A dab of paint, either on the base or better yet on the bullet nose, will identify the round as a dummy. Nail polish does just fine for this.

TARGET-KISSING ROUNDS

Once or twice a year I also buy two or three lipsticks of as bright and varying colors as I can find. I lightly run the bullet tip of a live round over the lipstick, then shoot that round. The result is a transfer of lipstick to the target paper. Let's say you want to sight-in an '06 with a 150, a 165 and a 200-grain bullet. Normally, shooting at the same target means you have to hike down to the one-hundred-yard target butt after every shot to mark it on the target. The lipstick smear sometimes can be seen through the spotting scope if the light is right; it can certainly be seen when you have the target in front of you. This little trick will show just where each of the loads will print without having to adjust the scope or the sights.

COLLIMATOR SPUDS

I have often wondered why so many of us who possess collimators use those handy gadgets only on scopes. They work just as well with iron sights, peep sights and such optical sights as Weaver's Qwik-Point. And for the long range handgunner, a collimator is a necessity.

Spuds for collimators are available for most calibers, but not all. Emergency spuds can be made from drill rod, with only the center of the rod being turned down and polished. Since you cannot fit a spring into the spud end that fits into the barrel, machine a collar into it so the part of the spud that fits into the muzzle extends between 1.5 and 2.0 inches into the barrel. Break the edges lightly on both ends with a file, while the cut-off spud runs in the lathe. On long work, use a steady rest, turning on centers if the rod is thick enough.

LEATHER LAPPING

Lapping with leather is an old machinist's trick. A well-worn belt that has seen better days is good for that purpose, but I found that tanned hide from deer or even caribou works well. A super-fine finish can be put on round stock in the lathe by using leather which is amply covered with ordinary talcum powder. For the first few passes a few drops of Do-Drill cutting oil with Bon-Ami works wonders. Wipe clean, use another hunk of leather lightly sprinkled with talcum, and add talcum as it wears off.

Chamber lapping can be done that way, too, but here it is best to lock the barrel into a vise and use a length of drill rod that has been split so the leather will hold. If you start with steel wool and some fine lapping compound, leather with Bon-Ami, then talcum, you will give that chamber the mirror look.

VISE HEIGHT

Depending on your posture and taking into consideration the height of most workbenches, mounting the vise on the bench will mean one of two things. For sawing, the lower level is just right, but for precision work and for filing small pieces, the bench top and vise will be too low.

Using a hunk of scrap board suitable for your needs, nail a piece of 2x4 on the base. Cover with rubber matting, and you have a work surface that is a bit easier to manage, especially if the eyes are no longer what they were thirty years ago.

Some lumberyards have cut-off ends of two-inch-thick hardwood planking. Scraps of that stuff often can be had

Although not as efficient as a compressor, a portable compressed air tank does have the advantage that for a few bucks you have a limited amount of compressed air in your shop.

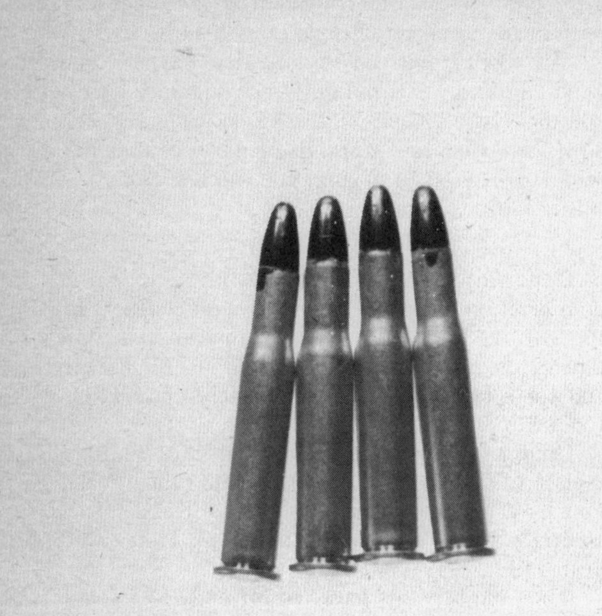

Winchester-Western now produces dummy rounds in most calibers that are available from Brownell's. If, however, you are a handloader, you can make your own: just leave a spent primer in the case, and mark them as dummies with nail polish or India ink on the bullet nose. If bullet weight, style also should be recorded, and it's a good idea, use an engraver or even just a metal scribe.

for the asking and are worth having in the shop. One never knows when they may come in handy. For instance, when I wanted to do some draw filing on the big machinist's vise, I had problems. Thanks to my six-foot frame, and the standard height bench, I not only was uncomfortable while filing, but had a devil of a time seeing what I was filing. Then I discovered that hunk of hardwood scrap under the bench. It took only a few minutes to sand the thing down, drill some holes for the bolts that would hold the vise on the hardwood board as well as on the bench. Now four bolts hold the board, and four bolts from the vise go through the plank and also through the top of the bench — neither vise nor hardwood plank will ever budge, especially since I used Loc-Tite on the bolts and nuts that hold the whole shebang in place.

WORKBENCH RENEWAL

When I was thinking about building the last workbench, I mentioned it to a neighbor. He had fallen heir to a considerable length of bowling alley flooring. Although I don't bowl, I had heard about these hardwood floorings and the few guys who had been able to latch on to some of the stuff were as happy as bunnies in the pea patch. We hauled, dragged, cussed and sweated a piece of that flooring into my shop. It's good, but it isn't hardwood, and I knew I'd have to replace the top one day.

In talking the problem over with the lumberyard head honcho, he made a near brilliant suggestion. Every yard sells hardwood parquet flooring by the bundle and sometimes the bundles break. These cannot be sold, since they might be slightly damaged.

For all of five bucks I got the better part of such a bundle of hardwood flooring, and installed it right on top of the bench. That was the fastest way of adding life to a bench which sees a lot of hard use and wear.

CHAMBER, BORE OBSTRUCTIONS

The most frequently encountered bore or barrel obstruction is caused by a dry cleaning patch that becomes unhitched from the tip of the cleaning rod. Depending on the estimated location of the stuck patch, stand the gun up so either muzzle or breech are accessible, whichever is closer to the barrel obstruction. Slowly dribble either bore solvent or a light gun oil into the bore so it will soak the patch fully. Then drive it out with a cleaning rod, using either a commercial device that holds the rod centered in the bore or making one from a cartridge case that has the head cut off with a tube cutter.

Then there is the case that comes unglued in the chamber, the base or head being ejected nicely and the rest of the body stuck in the chamber. If the chamber has not been pitted, the case usually will come out by a relatively simple method.

Whenever possible, remove the bolt. Spray the butt end of the case with one or two liberal blasts of Bust Rust, wait a few minutes, then force a slightly oversized patch into the case while turning the cleaning rod to the right or left. Once the patch is lodged, try first to continue the rod in the direction you started it. Sometimes it will turn out, sometimes it won't. If not, switch the direction of the cleaning rod motion.

Another method that works more often than not, involves the use of Cerrosafe, the chamber casting metal. Seat a patch one inch or less ahead of the case mouth with a cleaning rod equipped with a button tip. Melt the Cerrosafe and, using a funnel, pour the casting metal into the case until full, wait until the metal hardens, then push from the muzzle with a rod. Presto! Out pops the case.

Remember what was previously said about freeze fit of metal parts? Reverse that thinking and do what I saw a gunsmith do some years ago. He had a de-headed case stuck in the chamber, and being away from his shop, he had to improvise. He packed dry ice around action and chamber — be sure to wear gloves for this — and pretty soon the dry ice had shrunk the case enough for it to slip right out of the chamber.

Another 'smith, Jerry Yorks, one day encountered a Marlin Model 93 in .38-55 that suffered from the same malady. Out in hunting camp you don't have Cerrosafe nor is there dry ice handy. Taking a six-inch length of baling wire, he bent it into the shape of an ice tong, with the ends of the wire bent slightly outward and hammered flat between two rocks. Push this emergency stuck case remover through the case neck so it will expand to catch the case neck.

Either push this hook with the case out with a rod, working the rod from the muzzle with the usual care, or use a string or anything else to catch the hooks at the base or curve. Pull the stuck case out that way. Make certain that the hook ends have no sharp burrs to scratch the chamber. Steel spring is better for this, but usually is not found in a hunting camp. Unless the case is really stuck, this will do the trick.

If the above remedies fail, you still have some other choices. A thread tap, if handy and of the proper size, often will save the day. Select a tap that is large enough to get a good bite inside the case, but which will not cut through the case and damage the chamber walls.

A 3/8x16 taper tap is a good choice for .30/06, .270 Winchester and similar calibers. This only works on bolt action rifles since the tap has to be inserted from the breech end. Carefully run the tap into the broken-off case until it holds firmly, then use a stiff cleaning rod to knock out tap and case, with the rod being inserted from the muzzle.

Again, a shot of Bust Rust before starting the tap will make it much easier to push case and tap out.

For an elevated work surface, try this: nail a piece of rubber mat to a block of scrap board which, in turn, is nailed to a length of 2x4. The block of 2x4 then can be locked into the jaws of a vise providing a higher work surface and reducing the element of fatigue.

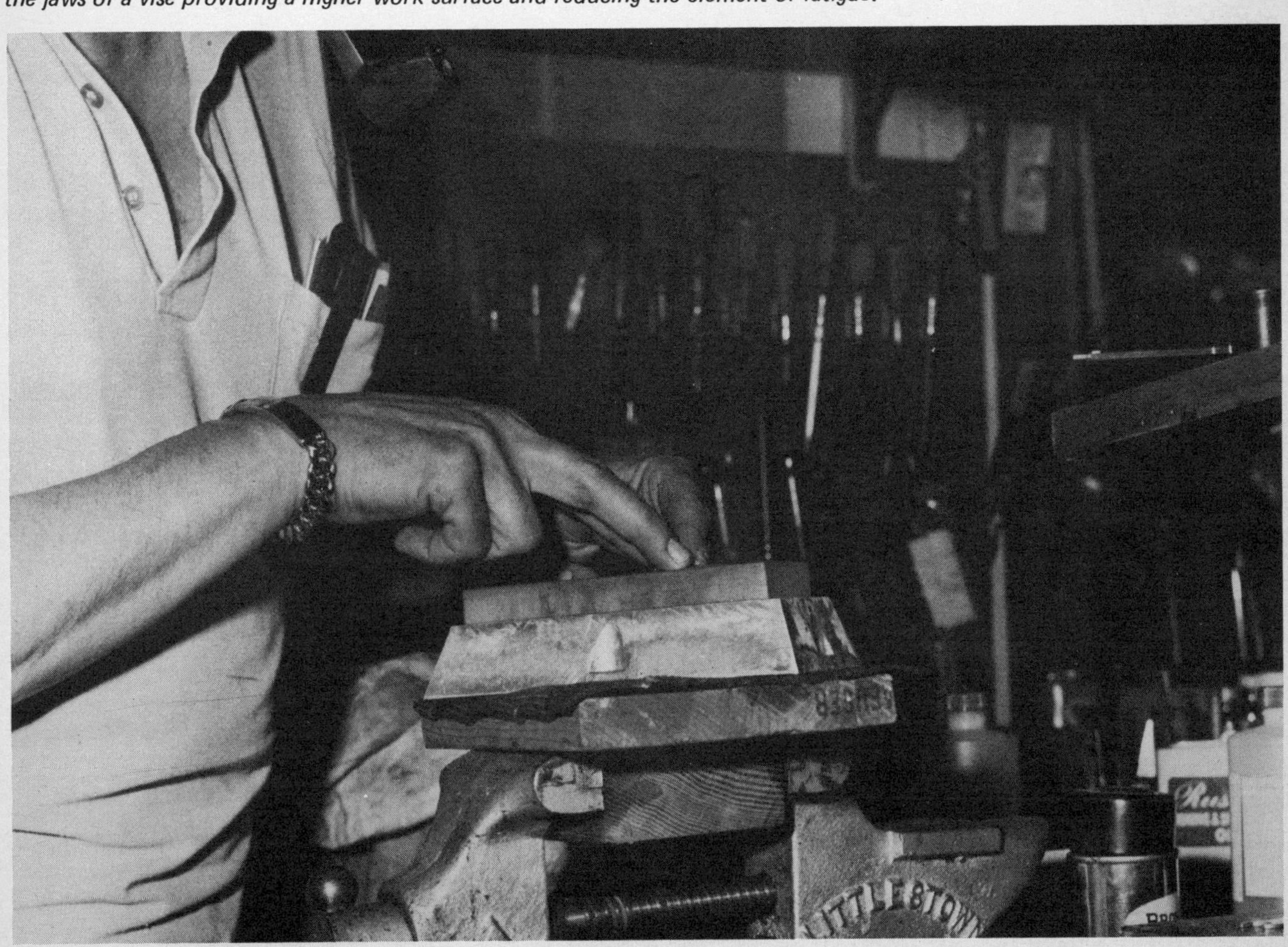

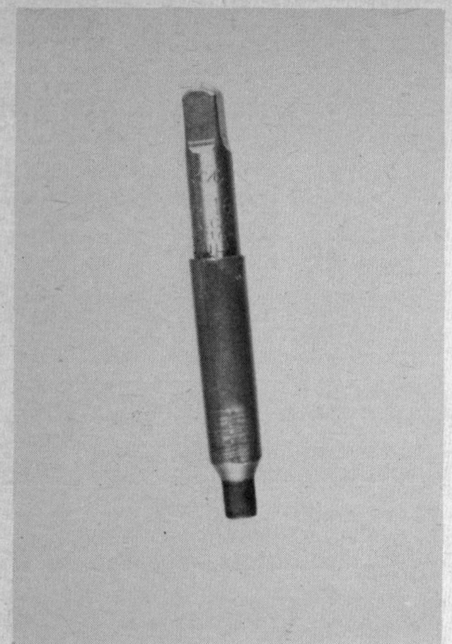

Although chainsaw file is preferred, 3/8-16NC thread tap essentially does the same thing as the chainsaw file.

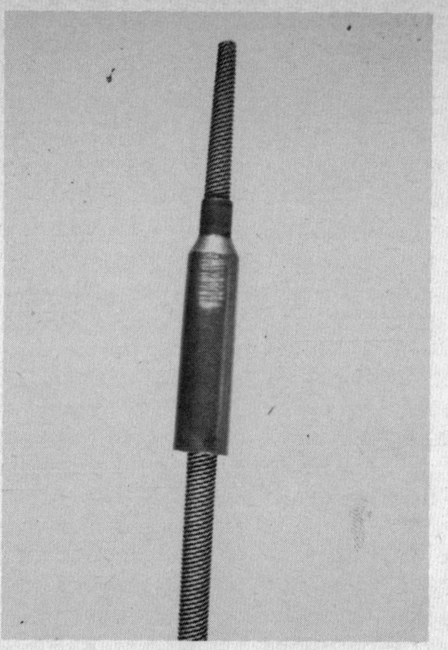

Round chainsaw file inserted from rear of stuck case was turned until teeth bit into neck, then one tug did it.

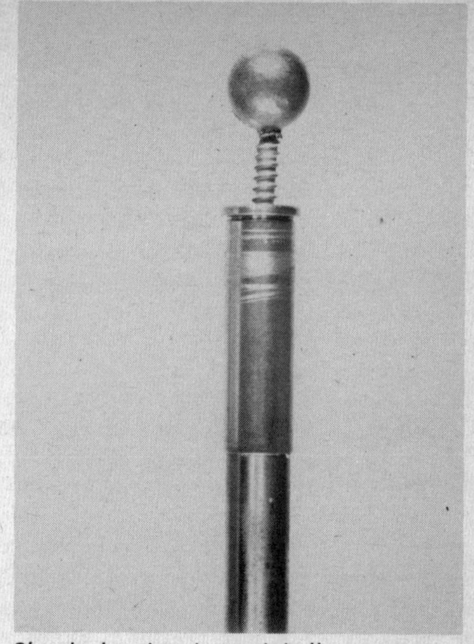

Simple, handmade stuck-ball remover made from modified wood screw, .357 magnum case and length of drill rod.

Much trickier is the often used method that involves heating the action lightly so the metal expands somewhat. Since the steel of the action will get warm before the brass, or so it is hoped, the stuck case often will come out, especially when previously tapped as outlined just now. But save this method as the last resort. You have to be extremely careful not to alter the temper of the steel.

If the case is big enough — that is, the neck has enough diameter — try a round file. This can be one of the standard round metal files, or even a chainsaw file. Turn it into the brass of the case from the breech end, pound file and case out from the muzzle with a cleaning rod.

CENTER-PUNCH, SCRIBING AID

Sometimes you will run into a rifle receiver that simply resists all efforts of scribing or even center-punching. Stop by the nearest machine shop and ask for some of the discarded lathe tools or cutters. The center-punch is ground to about a sixty-degree angle, then polished really bright on the belt sander or the wheel so tools will not shatter; surface imperfections on such hard steel will break the metal like glass when struck on one end while resting against hard steel at the other.

MUZZLELOADER OBSTRUCTIONS

There is not a black powder shooter around who, at one time or another, did not have a ball stuck way down where it resists all attempts of goosing it out. If the caliber is large enough, take a good-sized flat-head wood screw. Either silver solder a suitable length of drill rod to the head of the screw or perhaps even tap and drill the head, cutting a suitable thread also into the end of the drill rod. Drop it forcefully on the ball, then turn the screw and rod to the right until the screw threads have a good purchase in the lead of the ball. Pull the ball out, then save the rod. With such insurance, you'll never need it, again!

Another trick — provided there is no powder charge in the barrel — is this: Make certain nobody is in front of the muzzle, then put the rifle on a bench, and turn out the nipple. Apply the muzzle of a powerful airgun to the hole, where the nipple is threaded into the action, then fire the airgun without a pellet or BB. It does the trick every time, I've been told, and it sure beats making up the rod-screw gimmick outlined above.

STIPPLING TOOL SUBSTITUTE

In an earlier chapter I mentioned metal checkering and stippling. One source for a stippling tip is a lathe tool, ground as outlined above for center punching. If you use one-quarter-inch lathe bits, they can be set into a brass hammer which makes the job of stippling quite a bit easier and a lot less fatiguing. Drill holes into the hammer face about 0.75-inch deep, round off the lathe bits on the grinder, then set with an arbor press.

If you don't have an arbor press, open the jaws of your machinist's vise until whatever you want to force-fit slides into the jaws. Then simply tighten the jaws of the vise. It's not as impressive as having an arbor press standing around, but it does the trick.

DRILL PRESS TABLE EXTENSION

Every so often, I find that the table of my ancient drill press is just too small for whatever job I have to tackle. Someone pointed out that extruded aluminum in flanged channel form costs only a few bucks. The hunk I liberated from a contractor was six inches wide and five feet long, which I later cut to thirty inches.

When placed over the hole in the center of the table, a bolt and piece of bar stock can be used to anchor the aluminum bar, the same way drill press vises and other machine tools are locked into place. You can fasten all sorts of clamps and, since the aluminum is thick enough, I find that I can drill and tap it for special fixtures and jigs.

One day I used that piece of aluminum stock on the bench to lay out a scope mounting job and found that it had a great deal of shop versatility when it came to working on jobs which had to be anchored while being marked or worked on.

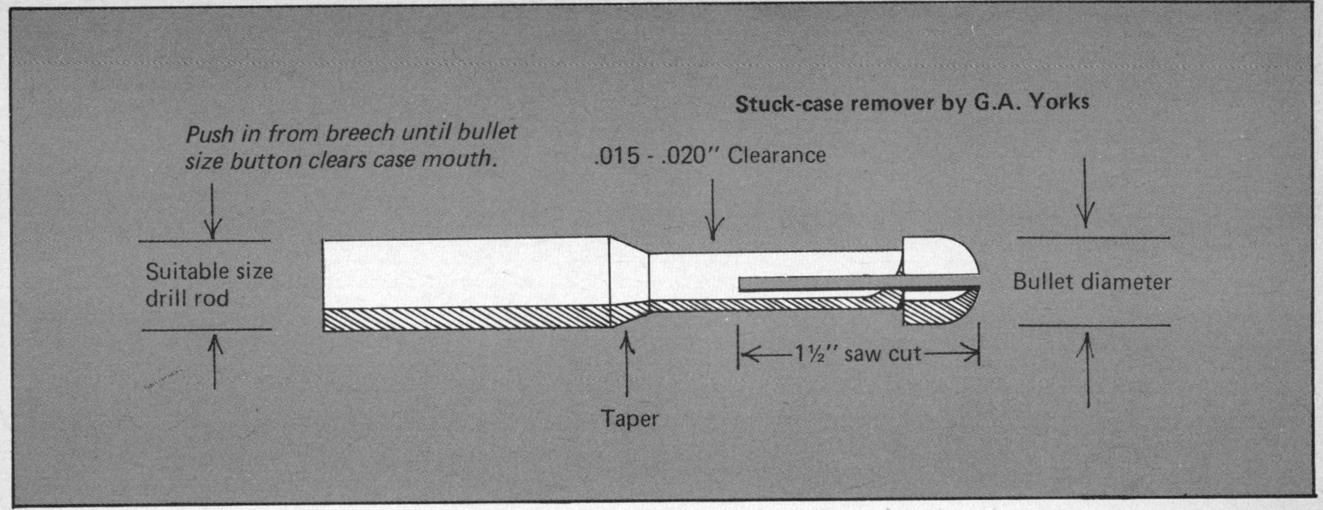

Spread the head end with a screwdriver enough so it has to compress a bit to pass through the case neck and will expand to outside neck size, then tap out from muzzle with rod. The sharp corner of the head should be broken just enough so it isn't sharp to prevent chamber damage or scratching. All turning should be done before making the saw cut. Almost any steel rod will have enough spring in it to do the job, but drill rod comes in fractional sizes so that one can pick a rod size close enough to bullet diameter so there's little turning for diameter and clearance.

UNJUGGING PISTOL CHAMBERS

Being a pistol collector with a limited budget, I sometimes buy guns most collectors won't touch. Some of them need tender loving care and lots of cleaning, others need grips, a spring or screw here and there, while others might be referred to as total wrecks with some charity. In short, a lot of my bench time is spent doctoring these selfloaders.

If and when the time comes that the latest addition to the collection seems to be in firing condition, I load her up and see what happens, keeping at least a couple of pairs of fingers crossed during the test firing. She feeds and fires, but the fired case will not extract. Of course, the chamber should have been checked with the gun taken down. Like most of us, I have perfect 20:20 hindsight. Strip the gun and proceed!

If the chamber is not too badly jugged, push out the fired case with a rod from the muzzle, then drive out the primer and run a 9/64-inch drill through the primer pocket of the case. Insert a 6-32x1¼ machine screw through the case, then tighten a 6-32 nut against the head of the cartridge case.

Remove the barrel from the gun, chuck the shank of the 6-32 screw into the drill press, then apply a dab of medium valve-grinding compound to the cartridge case. With the drill press running at low speed, hold the barrel with the finger and slide the chamber up and down the case for several minutes. Keep the barrel moving at all times and add valve grinding compound as it needs replenishing.

Use a patch soaked with solvent to clean out the chamber, making certain that all the gunk is removed from the chamber, as well as the inside and outside of the barrel. Reassemble the gun and test fire.

In most cases, you will have to repeat the outlined steps, but this time use fine valve-grinding compound. Make up a second cartridge case, since the brass wears, thanks to the valve-grinding compound and therefore will be undersized. If the chamber was a real mess, you may have to use first coarse, then medium and finally fine valve-grinding compound with three different cartridge cases.

FRONT SIGHT HEIGHT FINDER

I have never quite figured out how some of the fellows

White-out pencil used by typists to correct mistakes or white china marker can be used to bring out stamping and other markings on firearms for photographic purposes.

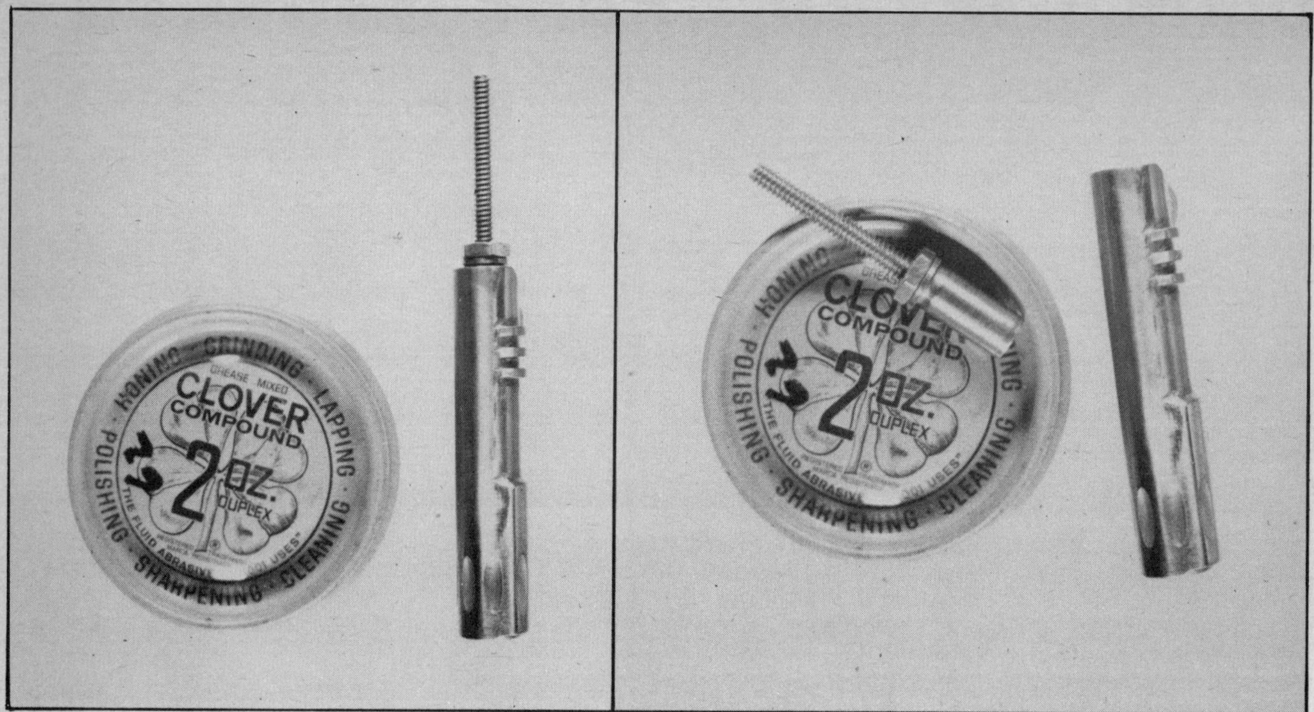

| Homemade polishing reamer for jugged chamber is simple to make and requires only a few minutes. The same tool also can be used to relieve chamber tightness in revolvers. | Chamber polishing tool should be used with fine valve-grinding compound. Depending on how badly chamber is jugged, different grades of compound may be needed. |

who dream up sights arrive at the suitable height for the front sight. Years ago, when banging around with an old single-shot rifle, I knocked off the front sight and despite searching, never found the blamed thing on the range. The local hammer mechanic who claimed to be a gunsmith, was unable to help, so the rifle was racked up and forgotten until I moved.

Nobody I knew had a twin of the rifle so we could measure the height of the front sight. Rather than buying six or eight and try them by placing them on the muzzle end of the barrel while the rifle was locked and leveled in the vise, I came up with this idea: Take a length of wire — even a straightened paper clip will do — run it around the muzzle, and twist the ends together with pliers. Let the end stick straight up in the air, get to the rear sight and take a look. Keep clipping lengths of twisted wire until the front sight takes up just half the space of the rear peep, or fits right into the V-cut or whatever the rear sight has as a sighting method. Now measure the height of the twisted wire from the steel of the barrel up and that's the sight height you need or want.

BLACK POWDER BALL REMOVER

Just about every black powder shooter, at one time or another, will ram the ball into the barrel, all the way down, then discover the powder charge *does not* go on top of the ball.

Commercial worms, termites, stuck ball pullers or whatever are always somewhere else when you discover you goofed. Take a roundhead wood screw, file the sides of the head flat so that the head will be more or less square, but leave the screw slot alone. Then drill out the primer pocket of a .357 magnum case, insert the screw so the head is inside the case. Run silver solder into the case and into what used to be the primer pocket.

An 11/32 drill rod with a bit of solder will hold nicely in the case, but be sure the rod is long enough for the length of your barrel.

Drop this creation down the tube. The weight of the rod, case and screw should cause the tip of the screw to penetrate the stuck ball. Turn the rod clockwise until the screw gets a good bite, then pull.

Instead of drill rod, you can use hardwood dowel rod, and use the silver solder only to join cartridge case and screw. Taper the end of the dowel so that the case can be solidly jammed onto the dowel.

COLOR SIGHT INSERTS

Adding a dab of red color, or some orange glow paint to the front sight of a handgun to improve the sight picture is one way of doing the job, but those dabs of paint don't last long.

One local police officer licked that problem neatly. Most bars and restaurants use plastic swizzle sticks, so do your thing at the beanery where they use red swizzle sticks. Cut a piece to size with a sharp knife and file out a suitable notch from the front sight, using a Swiss file and perhaps one with a safe side like that used for cutting dovetails. A drop of glue helps. The six-gun that was equipped with a red front sight insert for me by the local minion of the law has been well used for some three years, yet the sight insert looks new and shows no signs of wanting to pop out.

DIRECTORY OF TRADE SOURCES

CLEANING & REFINISHING SUPPLIES

A 'n A Co., Box 571, King of Prussia, PA 19406 (Valet shotgun cleaner)
Armite Labs., 1845 Randolph St., Los Angeles, CA 90001 (pen oiler)
Armoloy Co. of Ft. Worth, 204 E. Daggett St., Ft. Worth, TX 76104
Birchwood-Casey, 7900 Fuller Rd., Eden Prairie, Minn. 55344 (Anderol, etc.)
Bisonite Co., Inc., P.O. Box 84, Kenmore Station, Buffalo, NY 14217
Blue and Gray Prods., Inc., 817 E. Main St., Bradford, PA 16701
Jim Brobst, 299 Poplar St., Hamburg, Pa. 19526 (J-B Compound)
GB Prods. Dept., H & R, Inc., Industrial Rowe, Gardner, MA 01440
Browning Arms, Rt. 4, Box 624-B, Arnold, Mo. 63010
J. M. Bucheimer Co., Airport Rd., Frederick, MD 21701
Burnishine Prod. Co., 8140 N. Ridgeway, Skokie, Ill. 60076 (Stock Glaze)
Caddie Products Corp., Div. of Jet-Aer, Paterson, NJ 07524 (the Cloth)
Chem-Pak Inc., Winchester, VA 22601 (Gun-Savr. protect. & lubricant)
Chopie Mfg. Inc., 531 Copeland, La Crosse, Wis. 54601 (Black-Solve)
Clenzoil Co., Box 1226, Sta. C, Canton, O. 44708
Clover Mfg. Co., 139 Woodward Ave., Norwalk, CT 06856 (Clover compound)
Dri-Slide, Inc., Industrial Park, 1210 Locust St., Fremont, MI 49412
Durango U.S.A., P.O. Box 1029, Durango, CO 81301 (cleaning rods)
Forty-Five Ranch Enterpr., 119 S. Main St., Miami, Okla. 74354
Gun-All Products, Box 244, Dowagiac, Mich. 49047
Frank C. Hoppe Div., P.O. Box 97, Parkesburg, Pa. 19365
J & G Rifle Ranch, Box S 80, Turner, MT 59542
Jet-Aer Corp., 100 Sixth Ave., Paterson, N.J. 07524 (blues & oils)
Kellog's Professional Prods., Inc., P.O. Box 1201, Sandusky, OH 44870
K.W. Kleinendorst, 48 Taylortown Rd., Montville, N.J. 07045 (rifle clg. cables)
LPS Res. Labs. Inc., 2050 Cotner Ave., Los Angeles, Calif. 90025
LEM Gun Spec., Box 31, College Park, Ga 30337 (Lewis Lead Remover)
Liquid Wrench, Box 10628, Charlotte, N.C. 28201 (pen. oil)
Loner Products, Inc., P.O. Box 219, Yorktown Heights, NY 10598
Lynx Line Gun Prods. Div., Protective Coatings, Inc., 20626 Fenkell Ave., Detroit, MI 48223
Marble Arms Co., 420 Industrial Pk., Gladstone, Mich. 49837
Micro Sight Co., 242 Harbor Blvd., Belmont, Ca. 94002 (bedding)
Mill Run Prod., 1360 W. 9th, Cleveland, O. 44113 (Brite-Bore Kits)
Mirror-Lube, P.O. Box 693, San Juan Capistrano, CA 92675
New Method Mfg. Co., Box 175, Bradford, Pa. 16701 (gun blue)
Northern Instruments, Inc., 6680 North Highway 49, Lino Lake, MN 55014 (Stor-Safe rust preventer)
Numrich Arms Co., West Hurley, N.Y. 12491 (44-40 gun blue)
Outers Laboratories, Box 37, Onalaska, Wis. 54650 (Gunslick kits)
Radiator Spec. Co., 1400 Independence Blvd., Charlotte, N.C. 28201 (liquid wrench)
Realist Inc., N. 93 W. 16288 Megal Dr., Menomonee Falls, Wis. 53051
Reardon Prod., 103 W. Market St., Morrison, IL 61270 (Dry-Lube)
Rice Gun Coatings, 1521-43rd St., West Palm Beach, FL 33407
Rig Products Co., Box 279, Oregon, Ill. 61061 (Rig Grease)
Rusteprufe Labs., Sparta, WI 54656
Saunders Sptg. Gds., 338 Somerset, No. Plainfield, NJ 07060 (Sav-Bore)
Schultea's Gun String, 67 Burress, Houston, TX 77022 (pocket-size rifle cleaning kit)
Service Armament, 689 Bergen Blvd., Ridgefield, N. J. 07657 (Parker-Hale)
Silicote Corp., Box 359, Oshkosh, Wis. 54901 (Silicone cloths)
Silver Dollar Guns, P.O. Box 475, 10 Frances St., Franklin, NH 03235 (Silicone oil)
Sportsmen's Labs., Inc., Box 732, Anoka, Minn. 55303 (Gun Life lube)
Taylor & Robbins, Box 164, Rixford, Pa. 16745 (Throat Saver)
Testing Systems, Inc., #5 Tenakill Pk., Cresskill NJ 07626 (gun lube)
Texas Platers Supply Co., 2453 W. Five Mile Parkway, Dallas, TX 75233 (plating kit)
Totally Dependable Prods., Inc., P.O. Box 277, Zieglerville, PA 19492
C. S. Van Gorden, 120 Tenth Ave., Eau Claire, Wis. 54701 (Instant Blue)
WD-40 Co., 1061 Cudahy Pl., San Diego, CA 92110
West Coast Secoa, 3915 U S Hwy. 98S, Lakeland, FL 33801 (Teflon coatings)
Williams Gun Sight, 7389 Lapeer Rd., Davison, Mich. 48423 (finish kit)
Winslow Arms Inc., P.O. Box 783, Camden, SC 29020 (refinishing kit)
Wisconsin Platers Supply Co., see: Texas Platers Supply Co.
Woodstream Corp., P.O. Box 327, Lititz, Pa. 17543 (Mask)
Zip Aerosol Prods., 21320 Deering Court, Canoga Park, CA 91304

CUSTOM GUNSMITHS

Walter Abe, Abe's Gun Shop, 5124 Huntington Dr., Los Angeles, CA 90032
Ahlman Cust. Gun Shop, R.R. 1, Box 20, Morristown, Minn. 55052
Amrine's Gun Shop, 937 Luna Ave., Ojai, CA 93023
Anderson's Guns, Jim Jares, 706 S. 23rd St., Laramie, WY 82070
Antique Arms, D. F. Saunders, 1110 Cleveland Ave., Monett, MO 65708 (Hawken copies)
R. J. Anton, 874 Olympic Dr., Waterloo, IA 50701
Dietrich Apel, P.O. Box 473, Star Rte., Newport, NH 03773
Atkinson Gun Co., P.O. Box 512, Prescott, AZ 86301
E. von Atzigen, The Custom Shop, 890 Cochrane Crescent, Peterborough, Ont., K94 5N3 Canada
Bacon Creek Gun Shop, Cumberland Falls Rd., Corbin, Ky. 40701
Bain and Davis Sptg. Gds., 599 W. Las Tunas Dr., San Gabriel, Calif. 41776
Joe J. Balickie, Rte. 2, Box 56-G, Apex, NC 27502

Wm. G. Bankard, 4211 Thorncliff Rd., Baltimore, MD 21236 (Kentuckys)
Barta's, Rte. 1, Box 129-A, Cato, Wis. 54206
Roy Bauer, c/o C-D Miller Guns, St. Onge, SD 57779
Bennett Gun Works, 561 Delaware Ave., Delmar, N.Y. 12054
Irvin L. Benson, Saganaga Lake, Pine Island Camp, Ontario, Canada (via Grand Marais, MN 55604)
Gordon Bess, 708 River St., Canon City, Colo. 81212
Bruce Betts Gunsmith Co., 100 W. Highway 72, Rolla, MO 65401
Al Biesen, W. 2039 Sinto Ave., Spokane, WA 99201
Roger Biesen, W. 2039 Sinto Ave., Spokane, WA 99201
John Bivins, Jr., 200 Wicklow Rd., Winston-Salem, NC 27106
Ralph Bone, 4118-19th St., Lubbock, TX 79407
Boone Mountain Trading Post, Averyville Rd., St. Marys, Pa. 15857
Victor Bortugno, Atlantic & Pacific Arms Co., 4859 Virginia Beach Blvd., Virginia Beach, VA 23462
Breckheimers, Rte. 69-A, Parish, NY 13131
John P. Brown, Jr., 3107 Elinore Ave., Rockford, IL 61103
L. H. Brown, Brown's Rifle Ranch, 1820 Airport Rd., Kalispell, MT 59901
Lenard M. Brownell, Box 25, Wyarno, WY 82845 (Custom rifles)
E. J. Bryant, 3154 Glen St., Eureka, CA 95501
David Budin, Main St., Margaretville, NY 12455
George Bunch, 7735 Garrison Rd., Hyattsville, Md. 20784
Samuel W. Burgess, 25 Squam Rd., Rockport, MA 01966 (bluing repairs)
Leo Bustani, P.O. Box 8125, W. Palm Beach, Fla. 33407
Cameron's Guns, 16690 W. 11th Ave., Golden, CO 80401
Carter Gun Works, 2211 Jefferson Pk. Ave., Charlottesville, VA 22903
Ralph L. Carter, Rt. 1, Box 92, Fountain, CO 80817
Cassell Gun Shop, 813 S. 12th, Worland, WY 82401
R. MacDonald Champlin, P.O. Box 74, Wentworth, NH 03282 (ML rifles and pistols)
Mark Chanlynn, Bighorn Trading Co., 1704-14th St., Boulder, CO 80302
N. C. Christakos, 2832 N. Austin, Chicago, IL 60634
Jim Clark, Custom Gun Shop, 5367 S. 1950 West, Roy, UT 84067
Kenneth E. Clark, 18738 Highway 99, Madera, Calif. 93637
Cloward's Gun Shop, J. K. Cloward, 4023 Aurora Ave. N., Seattle, WA 98102
Crest Carving Co., 14849 Dillow St., Westminster, Ca. 92683
Philip R. Crouthamel, 513 E. Baltimore, E. Lansdowne, PA 19050
Jim Cuthbert, 715 S. 5th St., Coos Bay, Ore. 97420
Dahl's Custom Stocks, Rt. 4, Box 187, Schofield Rd., Lake Geneva, WI 53147
Dahl's Gunshop, 6947 King Ave., Billings, MT 59102
Homer L. Dangler, Box 254, Addison, MI 49220 (Kentucky rifles)
Davis Gun Shop, 7213 Lee Highway, Falls Church, VA 22046
Dee Davis, 5658 So. Mayfield, Chicago, Ill. 60638
Jack Dever, 8520 N.W. 90, Okla. City, OK 73132
R. H. Devereaux, 475 Trucky St., St. Igance, MI 49781
Dominic DiStefano, 4303 Friar Lane, Colorado Springs, CO 80907
Bill Dowtin, P.O. Box 72, Celina, TX 75009
Drumbore Gun Shop, 119 Center St., Lehigton, PA 18235
Drummond's Gun Shop, 123 E. 4th St., Williamsport, PA 17701
Charles Duffy, Williams Lane, W. Hurley, N.Y. 12491
John H. Eaton, 8516 James St., Upper Marlboro, MD 20870
Gerald D. Eisenhauer, Rte. #3, Twin Falls, Ida. 83301
Bob Emmons, 238 Robson Rd., Grafton, OH 44044
Bill English, 4411 S. W. 100th, Seattle, Wash. 98146
Ken Eyster, Heritage Gunsmiths Inc., 6441 Bishop Rd., Centerburg, O. 43011
N. B. Fashingbauer, Box 366, Lac Du Flambeau, Wis. 54538
Ted Fellowes, Beaver Lodge, 9245-16th Ave., S.W., Seattle, Wa. 98106 (muzzle loaders)
H. J. and L. A. Finn, 12565 Gratiot Ave., Detroit, MI 48205
Jack First, The Gunshop, Inc., 44633 Sierra Highway, Lancaster, CA 93534
Marshall F. Fish, Rt. 22 North, Westport, NY 12993
Jerry Fisher, 1244—4th Ave. West, Kalispell, Mont. 59901
Flynn's Cust. Gunsmithing, 3309 Elliott, Apt. B, Alexandria, LA 71301
Larry L. Forster, Box 212, Gwinner, ND 58040
Frazier's Custom Guns, Jay Frazier, Box 8644, Bird Creek, Alaska 99540
Clark K. Frazier/Matchmate, RFD 1, Rawson, OH 45881
Freeland's Scope Stands, 3737—14th Ave., Rock Island, Ill. 61201
Fred's Gunsmithing & Firearms Co., 214 Holly Ct., Darien, IL 60559
Fredrick Gun Shop, 10 Elson Drive, Riverside, R.I. 02915
R. L. Freshour, P.O. Box 2837, Texas City, TX 77590
Frontier Arms, Inc., 420 E. Riding Club Rd., Cheyenne, Wyo. 82001
Fuller Gunshop, Cooper Landing, Alas. 99572
Gentry's Bluing and Gun Shop, P.O. Box 984, Belgrade, MT 59714
Ed Gillman, Valley View Dr., R.R. 6, Hanover, PA 17331
Dale Goens, Box 224, Cedar Crest, NM 87008
A. R. Goode, Rte. 3, Box 139, Catoctin Furnace, Thurmont, MD 21788
Charles E. Grace, 10144 Elk Lake Rd., Williamsburg, MI 49690
George T. Gregory, Rt. 2, Box 8G, Plymouth, CA 95669 (saddle rifles)
Griffin & Howe, 589 Broadway, New York, N.Y. 10012
H. L. Grisel, 61400 S. Hwy. 97, Bend, OR 97701 (rifles)
Gun City, 504 Main Ave., Bismarck, ND 58501
H & R Custom Gun Serv., 68 Passaic Dr., Hewitt, N.J. 07421
Paul Haberly, 2364 N. Neva, Chicago, IL 60635
Martin Hagn, Kalmbachstr. 9, 8115 Kochel a. See, W. Germany (s.s. actions & rifles)
Chas. E. Hammans, Box 788, Stuttgart, AR 72160
Harkrader's Cust. Gun Shop, 825 Radford St., Christiansburg, VA 24073
Rob't W. Hart & Son Inc., 401 Montgomery St., Nescopeck, PA 18635 (actions, stocks)

Hal Hartley, 147 Blairs Fork Rd., Lenoir, NC 28645
Hartmann & Weiss KG, Rahlstedter Str. 139, 2000 Hamburg 73, W. Germany
Hubert J. Hecht, 55 Rose Mead Circle, Sacramento, CA 95831
Edw. O. Hefti, 300 Fairview, College Sta., Tex. 77840
Iver Henriksen, 1211 So. 2nd St. W., Missoula, MT 59801
Wm. Hobaugh, Box M, Philipsburg, MT 59858
Hodgson, Joseph & Assoc., 1800 Commerce St. 7S, Boulder, CO 80301
Richard Hodgson, 5589 Arapahoe, Unit 104, Boulder, CO 80301
Hoenig-Rodman, 6521 Morton Dr., Boise, ID 83705
Hollis Gun Shop, 917 Rex St., Carlsbad, N.M. 88220
Bill Holmes, 2405 Pump Sta. Rd., Springdale, AR 72764
Ernest Hurt's Specialty Gunsmithing, P.O. Box 1033, (820 E. Broadway), Muskogee, OK 74401 (bolts and breechblocks)
Hyper-Single Precision SS Rifles, 520 E. Beaver, Jenks, OK 74037
Independent Machine & Gun Shop, 1416 N. Hayes, Pocatello, Ida. 83201
Jackson's, Box 416, Selman City, TX 75689
Paul Jaeger, 211 Leedom St., P.O. Box 67, Jenkintown, PA 19046
J. J. Jenkins, 375 Pine Ave. No. 25, Goleta, CA 93017
Jerry's Gun Shop, 9220 Ogden Ave., Brookfield, Ill. 60513
Bruce Jones, 389 Calla Ave., Imperial Beach, CA 92032
Jos. Jurjevic, Gunshop, 605 Main St., Marble Falls, TX 78654
John Kaufield Small Arms Eng. Co., 7698 Garden Prairie Rd., Garden Prairie, IL 61038 (restorations)
Kennedy Gun Shop, Rt. 6, Clarksville, Tenn. 37040
Monte Kennedy, P.O. Box 214, Kalispell, MT 59901
Kennon's Custom Rifles, 5408 Biffle, Stone Mtn., Ga. 30083
Kerr Sport Shop, Inc., 9584 Wilshire Blvd., Beverly Hills, Calif. 90212
Kesselring Gun Shop, 400 Pacific Hiway 99 No., Burlington, Wash. 98233
Vern Kitzrow, 2504 N. Grant Blvd., Milwaukee, WI 53210 (single shots)
Don Klein Custom Guns, Box 277, Camp Douglas, WI 54618
K. W. Kleinendorst, 48 Taylortown Rd., Montville, NJ 07045
J. Korzinek, RD #2, Box R, Canton, PA 17724 (riflesmith)
L&W Casting Co., 5014 Freeman Rd. E., Puyallup, WA 98371
Sam Lair, 520 E. Beaver, Jenks, OK 74037
Maynard Lambert, Kamas, UT 84036
LanDav Custom Guns, 7213 Lee Highway, Falls Church, VA 22046
Alain Laquieze, P.O. Box 26087, New Orleans, LA 70186 (foreign long guns)
Harry Lawson Co., 3328 N. Richey Blvd., Tucson, Ariz. 85716
John G. Lawson, 1802 E. Columbia, Tacoma, Wa. 98404
Gene Lechner, 636 Jane N.E., Albuquerque, NM 87123
LeDel, Inc., Main and Commerce Sts., Cheswold, Del. 19936
Mark Lee, Ken's Metal Finishing, 2333 Emerson Ave. N., Minneapolis, MN 55411
Leer's Gun Barn, R.R. #3, Sycamore Hills, Elwood, IN 46036 (repairing and sight fitting)
Art LeFeuvre, 1003 Hazel Ave., Deerfield, Ill. 60015
LeFever Arms Co., R.D. 1, Lee Center Stroke, Lee Center, N.Y. 13363
Lenz Firearms Co., 1480 Elkay Dr., Eugene, OR 97404
Al Lind, 7821—76th Ave. S.W., Tacoma, WA 98498
Max J. Lindauer, R.R. 2, Box 27, Washington, MO 63090
Robt. L. Lindsay, 9416 Emory Grove Rd., Gaithersburg, Md. 20760 (services only)
Ljutic Ind., Box 2117, Yakima, WA 98902 (Mono-Wads)
Llanerch Gun Shop, 2800 Township Line, Upper Darby, Pa. 19083
Jim Lofland, 2275 Larkin Rd., Boothwyn, PA 19061 (SS rifles)
London Guns, 1528—20th St., Santa Monica, CA 90404
McCormick's Gun Bluing Service, 609 N.E. 104th Ave., Vancouver, WA 98664
Bill McGuire, 1600 N. Eastmont Ave., East Wenatchee, WA 98801
R. J. Maberry, 511 So. K, Midland, Tex. 79701
Harold E. MacFarland, Star Route, Box 84, Cottonwood, Ariz. 86326
Monte Mandarino, Box 26087, New Orleans, LA 70186 (Penn. rifles)
Marcos Gunsmithing, 547 Main St., Paterson, NJ 07501
Marquart Precision Co., Box 1740, Prescott, AZ 86301
Martel's Custom Handguns, 4038 S. Wisteria Way, Denver, CO 80237
E. H. Martin's Gun Shop, 937 S. Sheridan Blvd., Lakewood, CO 80226
Mashburn Arms Co., 1218 N. Pennsylvania, Oklahoma City, OK 73107
Seely Masker, Custom Rifles, 261 Washington Ave., Pleasantville, NY 10570
Mathews & Son, 10224 S. Paramount Blvd., Downey, Calif. 90241
Maurer Arms, 2366 Frederick Dr., Cuyahoga Falls, Ohio 44221 (muzzleloaders)
Eric Meitzner, Rte. 1, Northfield, MN 55057
Miller Custom Rifles, 655 Dutton Ave., San Leandro, CA 94577
Miller Gun Works, P.O. Box 7326, Tamuning, Guam 96911
C.D. Miller Guns, Purl St., St. Onge, SD 57779
Earl Milliron, 1249 N.E. 166th Ave., Portland, Ore. 97230
Mills (D.H.) Custom Stocks, 401 N. Ellsworth, San Mateo, Calif. 94401
Wm. Larkin Moore, 2890 Marlics St., Agoura, CA 91301
Larry Mrock, 4165 Middlebelt, Orchard Lake, MI 48033
Natl. Gun Traders, Inc., 225 S.W. 22nd Ave., Miami, Fla. 33135
Clayton N. Nelson, R.R. #3, Box 119, Enid, OK 73701
New England Custom Gun Serv., P.O. Box 473, Star Route, Newport, NH 03773
Newman Gunshop, 119 Miller Rd., Agency, Ia. 52530
Nu-Line Guns, Inc., 3727 Jennings Rd., St. Louis, Mo. 63121
O'Brien Rifle Co., 324 Tropicana No. 128, Las Vegas, Nev. 89109
Warren E. Offenberger, Star Route, Reno, Oh 45773 (ML)
Pachmayr Gun Works, 1220 S. Grand Ave., Los Angeles, Calif. 90015
Charles J. Parkinson, 116 Wharncliffe Rd. So., London, Ont., Canada N6J2K3
Byrd Pearson, 191 No. 2050 W., Provo, UT 84601
Bob Pease Accuracy, P.O. Box 787, New Braunfels, TX 78130 (benchrest)
John Pell, 410 College Ave., Trinidad, CO 81082
Pendleton Gunshop, 1210 S. W. Haley Ave., Pendleton, Ore. 97801
C. R. Pedersen & Son, Ludington, Mich. 49431

Al Petersen, Box 8, Riverhurst, Sask., Canada S0H3P0
A. W. Peterson Gun Shop, 1693 Old Hwy. 441, Mt. Dora, FL 32757 (ML rifles, also)
Phillip Pilkington, P.O. Box 2284, University Station, Enid, OK 73701
Ready Eddie's Gun Shop, 501 Van Spanje Ave., Michigan City, IN 46360
R. Neal Rice, Box 12172, Denver, CO 80212
Ridge Guncraft, Inc., 234 N. Tulane, Oak Ridge, Tenn. 37830
Rifle Ranch, Jim Wilkinson, Rte. 5, Prescott, AZ 86301
Riedl Rifles, 15124 Weststate St., Westminster, CA 92683
Rifle Shop, Box M, Philipsburg, MT 59858
W. Rodman, 6521 Morton Dr., Boise, ID 83705
Carl Roth, 4728 Pineridge Ave., Cheyenne, WY 82001 (rust bluing)
Royal Arms, Inc., 10064 Bert Acosta, Santee, Calif. 92071
Murray F. Ruffino, Rt. 2, Milford, ME 04461
Rush's Old Colonial Forge, 106 Wiltshire Rd., Baltimore, MD 21221 (Ky.-Pa. rifles)
Lewis B. Sanchez, Cumberland Knife & Gun Works, 5661 Bragg Blvd., Fayetteville, NC 28303
Sanders Custom Gun Serv., 2358 Tyler Lane, Louisville, Ky. 40205
Sandy's Custom Gunshop, Rte. #1, Rockport, Ill. 62370
Saratoga Arms Co., R.D. 3, Box 387, Pottstown, Pa. 19464
Roy V. Schaefer, 965 W. Hilliard Lane, Eugene, OR 97404
N.H. Schiffman Cust. Gun Serv., 963 Malibu, Pocatello, ID 83201
Schuetzen Gun Works, 624 Old Pacific Hwy. S.E., Olympia, WA 98503
Schumaker's Gun Shop, 208 W. 5th Ave., Colville, Wash 99114
Schwartz Custom Guns, 9621 Coleman Rd., Haslett, Mich. 48840
Schwarz's Gun Shop, 41-15th St., Wellsburg, W. Va. 26070
Shaw's, Rt. 4, Box 407-L, Escondido, CA 92025
Shell Shack, 113 E. Main, Laurel, MT 59044
George H. Sheldon, P.O. Box 489, Franklin, NH 03235 (45 autos & M-1 carbines only)
Shilen Rifles, Inc., 205 Metropark Blvd., Ennis, TX 75119
Harold H. Shockley, 204 E. Farmington Rd., Hanna City, IL 61536 (hot bluing & plating)
Walter Shultz, R.D. 3, Pottstown, Pa. 19464
Silver Dollar Guns, P.O. Box 475, 10 Frances St., Franklin, NH 03235 (45 autos & M-1 carbines only)
Simmons Gun Spec., 700 Rogers Rd., Olathe, Kans. 66061
Simms Hardward Co., 2801 J St., Sacramento, Calif. 95816
Fred Sinclair, 1200 Asbury Dr., Box 302, New Haven, IN 46774
Skinner's Gun Shop, Box 30, Juneau, Alaska 98801
Markus Skosples, c/o Ziffren Sptg. Gds., 124 E. Third St., Davenport, IA 52801
Jerome F. Slezak, 1290 Marlowe, Lakewood (Cleveland), OH 44107
Small Arms Eng., 7698 Garden Prairie Rd., Garden Prairie, IL 61038 (restorations)
John Smith, 912 Lincoln, Carpentersville, Ill. 60110
Smitty's Gunshop, 308 S. Washington, Lake City, Minn. 55041
Snapp's Gunshop, 6911 E. Washington Rd., Clare, Mich. 48617
R. Southgate, Rt. 2, Franklin, Tenn. 37064 (new Kentucky rifles)
Fred D. Speiser, 2229 Dearborn, Missoula, MT 59801
Sport Service Center, 2364 N. Neva, Chicago, IL 60635
Sportsmens Equip. Co., 915 W. Washington, San Diego, Calif. 92103
Sportsmen's Exchange & Western Gun Traders, Inc., P.O. Box 603, Oxnard, CA 93030
George B. Spring, 9 Pratt St., Essex, CT 06426
Jess L. Stark, 12051 Stroud, Houston, TX 77072
Keith Stegall, Box 696, Gunnison, Colo. 81230
Victor W. Strawbridge, 6 Pineview Dr., Dover Point, Dover, NH 03820 (antique arms restoring)
W. C. Strutz, Rte. 1, "Woodland", Eagle River, WI 54521
Suter's House of Guns, 332 N. Tejon, Colorado Springs, Colo. 80902
Swanson Custom Firearms, 1051 Broadway, Denver, Colo. 80203
A. D. Swenson's 45 Shop, P.O. Box 606, Fallbrook, CA 92028
T-P Shop, 212 E. Houghton, West Branch, Mich. 48661
Talmage Ent., 43197 E. Whittier, Hemet, CA 92343
Taylor & Robbins, Box 164, Rixford, Pa. 16745
Gordon Tibbitts, 1378 Lakewood Circle, Salt Lake City, UT 84117
Daniel Titus, 119 Morlyn Ave., Bryn Mawr, PA 19010
Tom's Gunshop, 4435 Central, Hot Springs, AR 71901
Trinko's Gun Serv., 1406 E. Main, Watertown, Wis. 53094
Herb. G. Troester's Accurizing Serv., 2292 W. 100 North, Vernal, UT 84078
Dennis A. "Doc" Ulrich, 2511 S. 57th Ave., Cicero, IL 60650
Brent Umberger, Sportsman's Haven, R.R. 4, Cambridge, OH 43725
Upper Missouri Trading Co., Inc., Box 181, Crofton, MO 68730
Roy Vail, R. 1, Box 8, Warwick, N.Y. 10990
Milton Van Epps, Rt. 69-A, Parish, NY 13131
VanHorn-Abe, 5124 Huntington Dr., Los Angeles, CA 90032
J. W. Van Patten, Box 145, Foster Hill, Milford, Pa. 18337
Vic's Gun Refinishing, 6 Pineview Dr., Dover, NH 03820 (antique arms restorations)
Walker Arms Co., R. 2, Box 73, Selma, AL 36701
Walker Arms Co., 127 N. Main St., Joplin, MO 64801
R. A. Wardrop, Box 245, 409 E. Marble St., Mechanicsburg, PA 17055
Weatherby's, 2781 Firestone Blvd., South Gate, Calif. 90280
Wells Sport Store, 110 N. Summit St., Prescott, Ariz. 86301
R. A. Wells, 3452 N. 1st, Racine, Wis. 53402
Robert G. West, 27211 Huey Ave., Eugene, OR 97402
Western Gunstocks Mfg. Co., 550 Valencia School Rd., Aptos, CA 95003
Duane Wiebe, 426 Creekside Rd., Pleasant Hill, CA 94563
M. C. Wiest, 234 N. Tulane Ave., Oak Ridge, Tenn. 37830
W. C. Wilber, 400 Lucerne Dr., Spartanburg, SC 29302
Williams Gun Sight Co., 7389 Lapeer Rd., Davison, Mich. 48423
Bob Williams, c/o Hermans-Atlas Custom Guns, 800 E St. N.W., Washington, DC 20004
Williamson-Pate Gunsmith Service, 6021 Camp Bowie Blvd., Ft. Worth, TX 76116

Wilson Gun Store Inc., R.D. 1, Rte. 225, Dauphin, Pa. 17018
Thomas E. Wilson, 644 Spruce St., Boulder, CO 80302 (restorations)
Robert M. Winter, Box 484, Menno, SD 57045
Lester Womack, Box 17210, Tucson, AZ 85710
Yale's Gun Shop, 2618 Conowingo Rd., Bel Air, MD 21014 (ML work)
Mike Yee, 4700-46th Ave. S.W., Seattle, WA 98116
York County Gun Works, RR 4, Tottenham, Ont., L0G 1W0 Canada (muzzleloaders)
Yukon Firearms Service, P.O. Box 36, Carcross, Yukon, Canada
Russ Zeeryp, 1601 Foard Dr., Lynn Ross Manor, Morristown, TN 37814

GUNS & GUN PARTS, REPLICA AND ANTIQUE

Antique Gun Parts, Inc., 1118 S. Braddock Ave., Pittsburgh, PA 15218 (ML)
Armoury Inc., Rte. 202, New Preston, CT 06777
Artistic Arms, Inc., Box 23, Hoagland, IN 46745 (Sharps-Borchardt replica)
Carter Gun Works, 2211 Jefferson Pk. Ave., Charlottesville, Va. 22903
Darr Tool Co., P.O. Box 778, Carpinteria, CA 93013 (S.S. items)
Dixie Gun Works, Inc., Hwy 51, South, Union City, Tenn. 38261
Federal Ordnance Inc., 9643 Alpaca St., So. El Monte, CA 91733
Fred Goodwin, Sherman Mills, ME 04776 (antique guns & parts)
Log Cabin Sport Shop, 8010 Lafayette Rd., Lodi, OH 44254
Lever Arms Service Ltd., 771 Dunsmuir, Vancouver, B.C., Canada V6C 1M9
Edw. E. Lucas, 32 Garfield Ave., East Brunswick, NY 08816 (45/70 Springfield parts)
Lyman Products Corp., Middlefield, CT 06455
Markwell Arms Co., 2414 W. Devon, Chicago, IL 60645
Numrich Arms Co., West Hurley, N.Y. 12491
Replica Models, Inc., 610 Franklin St., Alexandria, VA 22314
S&S Firearms, 88-21 Aubrey Ave., Glendale, N.Y. 11227
C. H. Stoppler, 1426 Walton Ave., New York, NY 10452 (miniature guns)
Upper Missouri Trading Co., 3rd & Harold Sts., Crofton, NB 68730
C. H. Weisz, Box 311, Arlington, VA 22210
W. H. Wescombe, P.O. Box 488, Glencoe, CA 95232 (Rem. R.B. parts)

GUN PARTS, U. S. AND FOREIGN

Badger Shooter's Supply, Box 397, Owen, WI 54460
Behlert Custom Guns, Inc., 725 Lehigh Ave., Union, NJ 07083 (handgun parts)
Philip R. Crouthamel, 513 E. Baltimore, E. Lansdowne, Pa. 19050
Charles E. Duffy, Williams Lane, West Hurley, N.Y. 12491
Federal Ordnance Inc., 9634 Alpaca St., So. El Monte, CA 91733
Fenwick's Gun Annex, P.O. Box 38, Weisberg Rd., Whitehall, MD 21161
Jack First, The Gunshop, Inc., 44633 Sierra Highway, Lancaster, CA 93534
Greg's Winchester Parts, P.O. Box 8125, W. Palm Beach, FL 33407
Hunter's Haven, Zero Prince St., Alexandria, Va. 22314
Walter H. Lodewick, 2816 N.E. Halsey, Portland, OR 97232
Numrich Arms Co., West Hurley, N.Y. 12491
Pacific Intl. Merch. Corp., 2215 "J" St., Sacramento, CA 95816 (Vega 45 Colt mag.)
Potomac Arms Corp. (see Hunter's Haven)
Martin B. Retting, Inc., 11029 Washington, Culver City, Cal. 90230
Sarco, Inc., 323 Union St., Stirling, NJ 07980
Sherwood Distr. Inc., 18714 Parthenia St., Northridge, CA 91324
Simms, 2801 J St., Sacramento, CA 95816
Clifford L. Smires, R.D., Box 39, Columbus, NJ 08022 (Mauser rifles)
N. F. Strebe Gunworks, 4926 Marlboro Pike, S.E., Washington, D.C. 20027
Triple-K Mfg. Co., 568-6th Ave., San Diego, CA 92101 (magazines, gun parts)

GUNSMITH SUPPLIES, TOOLS, SERVICES

Albright Prod. Co., P.O. Box 1144, Portola, CA 96122 (trap buttplates)
Alley Supply Co., Carson Valley Industrial Park, Gardnerville, NV 89410
Ames Precision Machine Works, 5270 Geddes Rd., Ann Arbor, MI 48105 (portable hardness tester)
Anderson Mfg. Co., P.O. Box 3120, Yakima WA 98903 (tang safe)
Armite Labs., 1845 Randolph St., Los Angeles, Cal. 90001 (pen oiler)
B-Square Co., Box 11281, Ft. Worth, Tex. 76110
Jim Baiar, 490 Halfmoon Rd., Columbia Falls, MT 59912 (hex screws)
Behlert Custom Guns, Inc., 725 Lehigh Ave., Union, NJ 07083
Al Biesen, W. 2039 Sinto Ave., Spokane, WA 99201 (grip caps, buttplates)
Bonanza Sports Mfg. Co., 412 Western Ave., Faribault, Minn. 55021
Brookstone Co., 125 Vose Farm Rd., Peterborough, NH 03458
Bob Brownell's, Main & Third, Montezuma, Ia. 50171
W. E. Brownell, 1852 Alessandro Trail, Vista, Calif. 92083 (checkering tools)
Maynard P. Buehler, Inc., 17 Orinda Hwy., Orinda, Calif. 94563 (Rocol lube)
Burgess Vibrocrafters, Inc. (BVI), Rte. 83, Grayslake, Ill. 60030
M. H. Canjar, 500 E. 45th, Denver, Colo. 80216 (triggers, etc.)
Chapman Mfg. Co., Rte. 17 at Saw Mill Rd., Durham, CT 06422
Chase Chemical Corp., 3527 Smallman St., Pittsburgh, PA 15201 (Chubb Multigauge)
Chubb (see Chase Chem. Co.)
Chicago Wheel & Mfg. Co., 1101 W. Monroe St., Chicago, Ill. 60607 (Handee grinders)

Christy Gun Works, 875-57th St., Sacramento, Calif. 95819
Clover Mfg. Co., 139 Woodward Ave., Norwalk, CT 06856 (Clover compound)
Clymer Mfg. Co., 14241 W. 11 Mile Rd., Oak Park, Mich. 48237 (reamers)
Colbert Industries, 10107 Adella, South Gate, Calif. 90280 (Panavise)
A. Constantine & Son, Inc., 2050 Eastchester Rd., Bronx, N.Y. 10461 (wood)
Dave Cook, 720 Hancock Ave., Hancock, MI 49930 (metalsmithing only)
Cougar & Hunter, G 6398 W. Pierson Rd., Flushing, Mich. 48433 (scope jigs)
Alvin L. Davidson Prods. f. Shooters, 1215 Branson, Las Cruces, NM 88001 (action sleeves)
Dayton-Traister Co., P.O. Box 593, Oak Harbor, Wa. 98277 (triggers)
Dremel Mfg. Co., 4915-21st St., Racine, WI 53406 (grinders)
Chas. E. Duffy, Williams Lane, West Hurley, N.Y. 12491
Peter Dyson Ltd., 29-31 Church St., Honley, Huddersfield, Yorksh. HD7 2AH, England (accessories f. antique gun coll.)
E-Z Tool Co., P.O. Box 3186, 25 N.W. 44th Ave., Des Moines, la. 50313 (lathe taper attachment)
Edmund Scientific Co., 101 E. Glouster Pike, Barrington, N.J. 08007
F. K. Elliott, Box 785, Ramona, Calif. 92065 (reamers)
Forster Products, Inc., 82 E. Lanark Ave., Lanark, Ill. 61046
Keith Francis, P.O. Box 537, Talent, OR 97540 (reamers)
G. R. S. Corp., Box 1157, Boulder, Colo. 80302 (Gravermeister)
Gager Gage and Tool Co., 27509 Industrial Blvd., Hayward, CA 94545 (speedlock triggers f. Rem. 1100 & 870 pumps)
Gilmore Pattern Works, P.O. Box 50231, Tulsa, OK 74150
Gold Lode, Inc., 181 Gary Ave., Wheaton, IL 60187 (gold inlay kit)
Gopher Shooter's Supply, Box 278, Faribault, MN 55021 (screwdrivers, etc.)
Grace Metal Prod., 115 Ames St., Elk Rapids, MI 49629 (screw drivers, drifts)
Gunline Tools Inc., 719 No. East St., Anaheim, CA 92805
H. & M. 24062 Orchard Lake Rd., Box 258, Farmington, MI 48024 (reamers)
Half Moon Rifle Shop, 490 Halfmoon Rd., Columbia Falls, MT 59912 (hex screws)
Hartford Reamer Co., Box 134, Lathrup Village, Mich. 48075
Paul Jaeger Inc., 211 Leedom St., Jenkintown, PA. 19046
Jeffredo Gunsight Co., 1629 Via Monserate, Fallbrook, CA 92028 (trap buttplate)
Jerrow's Inletting Service, 452 5th Ave., E.N., Kalispell, MT 59901
Kasenite Co., Inc., 3 King St., Mahwah, N.J. 07430 (surface hrdng. comp.)
J. Korzinek, RD #2, Box R, Canton, PA 17724 (stainl. steel bluing)
LanDav Custom Guns, 7213 Lee Highway, Falls Church, VA 22046
John G. Lawson, 1802 E. Columbia Ave., Tacoma, WA 98404
Lea Mfg. Co., 237 E. Aurora St., Waterbury, Conn. 06720
Lightwood & Son Ltd., Britannia Rd., Banbury, Oxfordsh. OX1 68TD, England
Lock's Phila. Gun Exch., 6700 Rowland Ave., Philadelphia, Pa. 19149
Marker Machine Co., Box 426, Charleston, Ill. 61920
Michaels of Oregon Co., P.O. Box 13010, Portland, Ore. 97213
Viggo Miller, P.O. Box 4181, Omaha, Neb. 68104 (trigger attachment)
Miller Single Trigger Mfg. Co., R.D. on Rt. 209, Millersburg, PA 17061
Frank Mittermeier, 3577 E. Tremont, N.Y., N.Y. 10465
Moderntools Corp, Box 407, Dept. GD, Woodside, N.Y. 11377
N&J Sales, Lime Kiln Rd., Northford, Conn. 06472 (screwdrivers)
Karl A. Neise, Inc., 5602 Roosevelt Ave., Woodside, N.Y. 11377
Palmgren Prods., Chicago Tool & Eng. Co., 8383 South Chicago Ave., Chicago, IL 60167 (vises, etc.)
Panavise, Colbert Industries, 10107 Adelia Ave., South Gate, CA 90280
C. R. Pedersen & Son, Ludington, Mich. 49431
Ponderay Lab., 210 W. Prasch, Yakima, Wash. 98902 (epoxy glass bedding)
Redford Reamer Co., Box 40604, Redford Hts. Sta, Detroit, MI 48240
Richland Arms Co., 321 W. Adrian St., Blissfield, Mich. 49228
Riley's Supply Co., 121 No. Main St., Avilla, Ind. 46710 (Niedner buttplates, caps)
Ruhr-American Corp., So. Hwy #5, Glenwood, Minn. 56334
A. G. Russell, 1705 Hiway 71N, Springdale, AR 72764 (Arkansas oilstones)
Schaffner Mfg. Co., Emsworth, Pittsburgh, Pa. 15202 (polishing kits)
Schuetzen Gun Works, 624 Old Pacific Hwy. S.E., Olympia, WA 98503
Shaw's, Rt. 4, Box 407-L, Escondido, CA 92025
L. S. Starrett Co., Athol, Mass. 01331
Texas Platers Supply Co., 2453 W. Five Mile Parkway, Dallas, TX 75233 (plating kit)
Timney Mfg. Co., 2847 E. Siesta Lane, Phoenix, AZ 85024
Stan de Treville, Box 33021, San Diego, Calif. 92103 (checkering patterns)
Twin City Steel Treating Co., Inc., 1114 S. 3rd, Minneapolis, Minn. 55415 (heat treating)
Will-Burt Co., 169 So. Main, Orrville, OH 44667 (vises)
Williams Gun Sight Co., 7389 Lapeer Rd., Davison, Mich. 48423
Wilson Arms Co., 63 Leetes Island Rd., Branford, CT 06405
Wisconsin Platers Supply Co., see: Texas Platers
W. C. Wolff Co., Box 232, Ardmore, PA 19003 (springs)
Woodcraft Supply Corp., 313 Montvale, Woburn, MA 01801

HANDGUN ACCESSORIES

A. R. Sales Co., P.O. Box 3192, South El Monte, CA 91733
Baramie Corp., 6250 E. 7 Mile Rd., Detroit, MI 48234 (Hip-Grip)
Bar-Sto Precision Machine, 633 S. Victory Blvd., Burbank, CA 91502
Behlert Custom Guns, Inc., 725 Lehigh Ave., Union, NJ 07083
C'Arco, P.O. Box 308, Highland, CA 92346 (Ransom Rest)
Case Master, 4675 E. 10 Ave., Miami, Fla. 33013
Central Specialties Co., 6030 Northwest Hwy., Chicago, Ill. 60631

D&E Magazines Mgf., P.O. Box 4579, Downey, CA 90242 (clips)
Bill Dyer, 503 Midwest Bldg., Oklahoma City, Okla. 73102 (grip caps)
Essex Arms, Box 345, Phaerring St., Island Pond, VT 05846 (45 Auto frames)
R. S. Frielich, 396 Broome St., New York, N.Y. 10013 (cases)
Laka Tool Co., 62 Kinkel St., Westbury, L.I., NY 11590 (stainless steel 45 Auto parts)
Lee Custom Engineering, Inc., 46 E. Jackson St., Hartford, WI 53027
Lee Precision Inc., 4275 Hwy. U, Hartford, WI 53027 (pistol rest holders)
Los Gatos Grip & Specialty Co., P.O. Box 1850, Los Gatos, CA 95030 (custom-made)
Matich Loader, 10439 Rush St., South El Monte, CA 91733 (Quick Load)
W. A. Miller Co., Inc., Mingo Loop, Oguossoc, ME 04964 (cases)
No-Sho Mfg. Co., 10727 Glenfield Ct., Houston, TX 77096
Pachmayr, 1220 S. Grand, Los Angeles, Calif. 90015 (cases)
Pacific Intl. Mchdsg. Corp., 2215 "J" St., Sacramento, CA 95818 (Vega 45 Colt comb. mag.)
Pistolsafe, Dr. L., N. Chili, NY 14514 (handgun safe)
Platt Luggage, Inc., 2301 S. Prairie, Chicago, Ill. 60616 (cases)
Sportsmen's Equipment Co., 415 W. Washington, San Diego, Calif. 92103
M. Tyler, 1326 W. Britton, Oklahoma City, Okla. 73114 (grip adaptor)
Whitney Sales, Inc., P.O. Box 875, Reseda, CA 91335
Dave Woodruff, Box 5, Bear, DE 19701 (relining and conversions)

HANDGUN GRIPS

Crest Carving Co., 8091 Bolsa Ave., Midway City, CA 92655
Fitz, 653 N. Hagar St., San Fernando, CA 91340
Gateway Shooters' Supply, Inc., 10145-103rd St., Jacksonville, FL 32210 (Rogers grips)
Herrett's, Box 741, Twin Falls, Ida. 83301
Mershon Co., Inc., 1230 S. Grand Ave., Los Angeles, Calif. 90015
Mustang Custom Pistol Grips, 28715 Via Montezuma, Temecula, CA 92390
Robert H. Newell, 55 Coyote, Los Alamos, NM 87544 (custom)
Rogers Grips (see: Gateway Shooters' Supply)
Safety Grip Corp., Box 456, Riverside St., Miami, Fla. 33135
Jean St. Henri, 6525 Dume Dr., Malibu, CA 90265 (custom)
Schiermeier, Box 704, Twin Falls, ID 83301 (Thompson/Contender)
Sile Dist., 7 Centre Market Pl., New York, N.Y. 10013
Southern Gun Exchange, Inc., 4311 Northeast Expressway, Atlanta (Doraville), GA 30340 (Outrider brand)
Sports Inc., P.O. Box 683, Park Ridge, IL 60068 (Franzite)

MUZZLE-LOADING GUNS, BARRELS OR EQUIPMENT

A&K Mfg. C., Inc., 1651 N. Nancy Rose Ave., Tucson, AZ 85712 (ctlg. $1)
Luther Adkins, Box 281, Shelbyville, Ind. 47176 (breech plugs)
American Heritage Arms, Inc., Rt. 44, P.O. Box 95, West Willington, CT 06279 (rifles)
Anderson Mfg. Co., P.O. Box 3120, Yakima WA 98903
Armoury, Inc., Rte. 202, New Preston, CT 06777
Beaver Lodge, 9245 16th Ave. S.W., Seattle, WA 98106
John Bivins, Jr., 200 Wicklow Rd., Winston-Salem, NC 27106
Blue and Gray Prods., Inc., 817 E. Main St., Bradford, PA 16701
G. S. Bunch, 7735 Garrison, Hyattsville, Md. 20784 (flask repair)
Butler Creek Corp., Box GG, Jackson, WY 83001 (poly patch)
CAI, Conversion Arms, Inc., P.O. Box 449, Yuba City, CA 95991 (stainl. steel BP shotshell adaptors)
Cache La Poudre Rifleworks, 111 So. College, Ft. Collins, CO 80521 (custom muzzleloaders)
Challanger Mfg. Co., 118 Pearl St., Mt. Vernon, NY 10550
R. MacDonald Champlin, P.O. Box 74, Wentworth, NH 03282 (custom muzzleloaders)
Chopie Mfg. Inc., 531 Copeland Ave., LaCrosse, WI 54601 (nipple wrenches)
Classic Arms Intl., Inc., 20 Wilbraham St., Palmer, MA 01069 (BP guns and kits)
Connecticut Valley Arms Co. (CVA), Saybrook Rd., Haddam, CT 06438 (kits also)
Earl T. Cureton, Rte. 2, Box 388, Willoughby Rd., Bulls Gap, TN 37711 (powder horns)
DJ Inc., 1310 S. Park Rd., Fairdale, KY 40118
Leonard Day & Co., 316 Burt Pits Rd., Northampton, MA 10160
Dixie Gun Works, Inc., P.O. Box 130, Union City, TN 38261
EMF Co., Inc., Box 1248, Studio City, CA 91604
Eagle Arms Co., Riverview Dr., Mt. Washington, KY 40047
Euroarms of America, Inc., 14 W. Monmouth St., Winchester, VA 22601
The Eutaw Co., Box 608, U.S. Highway 176W, Holly Hill, SC 29059 (accessories)
Ted Fellowes, Beaver Lodge, 9245 16th Ave. S.W., Seattle, Wash. 98106
Firearms Imp. & Exp. Corp., 2470 N.W. 21st St., Miami, Fla. 33142
Marshall F. Fish, Rt. 22 N., Westport, NY 12993 (antique ML repairs)
Clark K. Frazier/Matchmate, RFD. 1, Rawson, OH 45881
C. R. & D. E. Getz, Box 88, Beavertown, PA 17813 (barrels)
Golden Age Arms Co., 14 W. Winter St., Delaware, OH 43015 (ctlg. $2)
A. R. Goode, Rte. 3, Box 139, Catoctin Furnace, Thurmont, MD 21788 (ML rifle bbls.)
Green River Forge, Ltd., P.O. Box 885, Springfield, OR 97477 (Forge-Fire flints)
Harper's Ferry Arms Co., 256 E. Broadway, Hopewell, VA 23860 (guns)
Hopkins & Allen Arms, #1 Melnick Rd., Monsey, NY 10952
International Arms, 23239 Doremus Ave., St. Clair Shores, MI 48080
JJJJ Ranch, Wm. Large, Rte. 1, Ironton, Ohio 45638
Art LeFeuvre, 1003 Hazel Ave., Deerfield, Ill. 60015 (antique gun restoring)
Les' Gun Shop (Les Bauska), Box 511, Kalispell, Mont, 59901
Lever Arms Serv. Ltd., 771 Dunsmuir, Vancouver 1, B.C., Canada

Log Cabin Sport Shop, 8010 Lafayette Rd., Lodi, OH 44254
Lyman Products Corp., Rte. 147, Middlefield, CT 06455
McKeown's Guns, R.R. 1, Pekin, IL 61554 (E-Z load rev. stand)
Judson E. Mariotti, Beauty Hill Rd., Barrington, NH 03825 (brass bullet mould)
Markwell Arms Co., 2414 W. Devon, Chicago, IL 60645
Maurer Arms, 2366 Frederick Dr., Cuyahoga Falls, OH 44221 (cust. muzzleloaders)
Mowrey Gun Works, Box 28, Iowa Park, TX 76367
Muzzleloaders Etc., Inc., Jim Westberg, 9901 Lyndale Ave. S., Bloomington, MN 55420
Numrich Corp., W. Hurley, N.Y. 12491 (powder flasks)
Ox-Yoke Originals, 130 Griffin Rd., West Suffield, CT 06093 (dry lubr. patches)
Penna. Rifle Works, 319 E. Main St., Ligonier, PA 15658 (ML guns, parts, ctlg. $1.50)
A. W. Peterson Gun Shop, 1693 Old Hwy. 441 N., Mt. Dora, FL 32757 (ML guns)
Richland Arms, 321 W. Adrian St., Blissfield, MI 49228
Rush's Old Colonial Forge, 106 Wiltshire Rd., Baltimore, MD 21221
Salish House, Inc., P.O. Box 27, Rollins, MT 59931
H. M. Schoeller, 569 So. Braddock Ave., Pittsburgh, Pa. 15221
Scott and Sons, P.O. Drawer "C", Nolanville, TX 76559
Sharon Rifle Barrel Co., P.O. Box 106, Kalispell, MT 59901
Shiloh Products, 37 Potter St., Farmingdale, NY 11735 (4-cavity mould)
C. E. Siler Locks, Rt. 6, Box 5, Candler, NC 28715 (flint locks)
Ken Steggles, 77 Lower Eastern Green Lane, Coventry, CV5 7DT, England (accessories)
Ultra-Hi Products Co., 150 Florence Ave., Hawthorne, NJ 07506
Upper Missouri Trading Co., 3rd and Harold Sts., Crofton, NB 68730
R. Watts, 826 Springdale Rd., Atlanta, GA 30306 (ML rifles)
W. H. Wescomb, P.O. Box 488, Glencoe, CA 95232 (parts)
Thos. F. White, 5801 Westchester Ct., Worthington, O. 43085 (powder horn)
Williamson-Pate Gunsmith Serv., 6021 Camp Bowie Blvd., Ft. Worth, TX 76116
York County Gun Works, R.R. #4, Tottenham, Ont. L0G 1W0, Canada (locks)

REBORING AND RERIFLING

P.O. Ackley (see: Max B. Graff, Inc.)
Atkinson Gun Co., P.O. Box 512, Prescott, AZ 86301
Bain & Davis Sptg. Gds., 559 W. Las Tunas Dr., San Gabriel, Calif. 91776
Fuller Gun Shop, Cooper Landing, Alaska 99572
Max B. Graff, Inc., Rt. 1, Box 24, American Fork, UT 84003
Bruce Jones, 389 Calla Ave., Imperial Beach, CA 92032
Les' Gun Shop, (Les Bauska), Box 511, Kalispell, MT 59901
Morgan's Cust. Reboring, 707 Union Ave., Grants Pass, OR 97526
Nu-Line Guns, 3727 Jennings Rd., St. Louis, MO 63121 (handguns)
Al Petersen, Box 8, Riverhurst, Saskatchewan, Canada S0H3P0
Schuetzen Gun Works, 624 Old Pacific Hwy. S.E., Olympia, WA 98503
Siegrist Gun Shop, 2689 McLean Rd., Whittemore, MI 48770
Snapp's Gunshop, 6911 E. Washington Rd., Clare, Mich. 48617
R. Southgate, Rt. 2, Franklin, Tenn. 37064 (Muzzleloaders)
J. W. Van Patten, Box 145, Foster Hill, Milford, Pa. 18337
Robt. G. West, 27211 Huey Ave., Eugene, OR 97402

RIFLE BARREL MAKERS

P.O. Ackley Gun Barrels, Max B. Graff, Inc., Rt. 1, Box 24, American Fork, UT 84003
Atkinson Gun Co., P.O. Box 512, Prescott, AZ 86301
Ralph L. Carter, Rt. 1, Box 92, Fountain, CO 80817
Christy Gun Works, 875 57th St., Sacramento, Calif. 95819
Clerke Prods., 2219 Main St., Santa Monica, Calif. 90405
Cuthbert Gun Shop, 715 So. 5th, Coos Bay, Ore. 97420
B. W. Darr, Saeco-Darr Rifle Co., Ltd., P.O. Box 778, Carpinteria, CA 93013
Douglas Barrels, Inc., 5504 Big Tyler Rd., Charleston, W. Va. 25312
Douglas Jackalope Gun & Sport Shop, Inc., 1048 S. 5th St., Douglas, WY 82633
Federal Firearms Co., Inc., Box 145, 145 Thomas Run Rd., Oakdale, PA 15071
C. R. & D. E. Getz, Box 88, Beavertown, PA 17813
A. R. Goode, Rte. 3, Box 139, Catoctin Furnace, Thurmont, MD 21788
Hart Rifle Barrels, Inc., RD 2, Lafayette, N.Y. 13084
Wm. H. Hobaugh, Box M, Philipsburg, MT 59858
David R. Huntington, RFD #1, Box 23, Heber City, UT 83032
Kogot, John Pell, 410 College Ave., Trinidad, CO 81082 (custom)
Gene Lechner, 636 Jane N.E., Albuquerque, NM 87123
Les' Gun Shop, (Les Bauska), Box 511, Kalispell, MT 59901
Marquart Precision Co., Box 1740, Prescott, AZ 86301
Nu-Line Guns, Inc., 3727 Jennings Rd., St. Louis, Mo. 63121
Numrich Arms, W. Hurley, N.Y. 12491
Al Petersen, The Rifle Ranch, Box 8, Riverhurst, Sask., Canada SOH3PO
Sanders Cust. Gun Serv., 2358 Tyler Lane, Louisville, Ky. 40205
Sharon Rifle Barrel Co., P.O. Box 1197, Kalispell, MT 59901
Ed Shilen Rifles, Inc., 205 Metropark Blvd., Ennis, TX 75119
W. C. Strutz, Rte. 1, "Woodland", Eagle River, WI 54521
Titus Barrel & Gun Co., R.F.D. #1, Box 23, Heber City, UT 84032
Wilson Arms, 63 Leetes Island Rd., Branford, CT 06405

SIGHTS, METALLIC

B-Square Eng. Co., Box 11281, Ft. Worth, Tex. 76110

Behlert Custom Sights, Inc., 725 Lehigh Ave., Union, NJ 07083
Bo-Mar Tool & Mfg. Co., Box 168, Carthage, Tex. 75633
Maynard P. Buehler, Inc., 17 Orinda Highway, Orinda, Calif. 94563
Christy Gun Works, 875 57th St., Sacramento, Calif. 95819
Jim Day, 902 N. Bownen Lane, Florence, SD 29501 (Chaba)
E-Z Mount, Ruelle Bros., P.O. Box 114, Ferndale, MT 48220
Firearms Dev. Lab., 360 Mt. Ida Rd., Oroville, CA 95965 (F. D. L. Wonder-sight)
Freeland's Scope Stands, Inc., 3734-14th Ave., Rock Island, Ill. 61201
Paul T. Haberly, 2364 N. Neva, Chicago, IL 60635
Paul Jaeger, Inc., 211 Leedom St., Jenkintown, PA 19046
Lee's Red Ramps, 34220 Cheseboro Rd., Space 19, Palmdale, CA 93550 (illuminated sights)
Jim Lofland, 2275 Larkin Rd., Boothwyn, PA 19061
Lyman Products Corp., Rte. 147, Middlefield, Conn. 06455
Marble Arms Corp., 420 Industrial Park, Gladstone, Mich. 49837
Merit Gunsight Co., P.O. Box 995, Sequim, Wash. 98382
Micro Sight Co., 242 Harbor Blvd., Belmont, Calif. 94002
Miniature Machine Co., 212 E. Spruce, Deming, N.M. 88030
Modern Industries, Inc., 613 W-11, Erie, PA 16501
C. R. Pedersen & Son, Ludington, Mich. 49431
Poly Choke Co., Inc., P.O. Box 296, Hartford, CT 06101
Redfield Gun Sight Co., 5800 E. Jewell St., Denver, Colo. 80222
Schwarz's Gun Shop, 41 - 15th St., Wellsburg, W. Va. 26070
Simmons Gun Specialties, Inc., 700 Rodgers Rd., Olathe, Kans. 66061
Slug Site Co., Whitetail Wilds, Lake Hubert, MN 56469
Sport Service Center, 2364 N. Neva, Chicago, IL 60635
Tradewinds, Inc., Box 1191, Tacoma, WA 98401
Williams Gun Sight Co., 7389 Lapeer Rd., Davison, Mich. 48423

STOCKS (Commercial and Custom)

Abe and VanHorn, 5124 Huntington Dr., Los Angeles, CA 90032
Adams Custom Gun Stocks, 13461 Quito Rd., Saratoga, CA 95070
Ahlman's Inc., R.R. 1, Box 20, Morristown, MN 55052
Don Allen, Rte. 1, Northfield, MN 55057 (blanks)
Anderson's Guns, Jim Jares, 706 S. 23rd St., Laramie, WY 82070
R. J. Anton, 874 Olympic Dr., Waterloo, IA 50701
Dietrich Apel, Star Route 2, Newport, NH 03773
Austrian Gunworks Reg'd., P.O. Box 136, Eastman, Que., Canada, J0E 1P0
Jim Baiar, 490 Halfmoon Rd., Columbia Falls, MT 59912
Joe J. Balickie, Custom Stocks, Rte. 2, Box 56-G, Apex, NC 27502
Bartas, Rte. 1, Box 129-A, Cato, Wis. 54206
John Bianchi, 100 Calle Cortez, Temecula, CA 92390 (U. S. carbines)
Al Biesen, West 2039 Sinto Ave., Spokane, Wash. 99201
Stephen L. Billeb, Rte. 3, Box 163, Bozeman, MT 59715
E. C. Bishop & Son Inc., Box 7, Warsaw, Mo. 65355
John M. Boltin, P.O. Box 1122, No. Myrtle Beach, SC 29582
Brown Precision Co., 5869 Indian Ave., San Jose, CA 95123
Lenard M. Brownell, Box 25, Wyarno, WY 82845
E. J. Bryant, 3154 Glen St., Eureka, CA 95501
Jack Burres, 10333 San Fernando Rd., Pacoima, CA 91331 (English, Claro, Bastogne Paradox walnut blanks only)
Calico Hardwoods, Inc., 1648 Airport Blvd., Windsor, Calif. 95492 (blanks)
Dick Campbell, 365 W. Oxford Ave., Englewood, CO 80110
Winston Churchill, Twenty Mile Stream Rd., Rt.1, Box 29B, Proctorsville, VT 05153
Cloward's Gun Shop, Jim Cloward, 4023 Aurora Ave. N., Seattle, WA 98102
Crane Creek Gun Stock Co., 25 Shephard Terr., Madison, WI 53705
Crest Carving Co., 8091 Bolsa Ave., Midway City, CA 92655
Custom Gunstocks, Dick Campbell, 365 W. Oxford Ave., Englewood, CO 80110
Dahl's Custom Stocks, Rt. 4, Box 187, Schofield Rd., Lake Geneva, WI 53147 (Martin Dahl)
Jack Dever, 8520 N.W. 90, Oklahoma City, OK 73132
Charles De Veto, 1087 Irene Rd., Lyndhurst, O. 44124
Bill Dowtin, P.O. Box 72, Celina, TX 75009
Reinhart Fajen, Box 338, Warsaw, Mo. 65355
N. B. Fashingbauer, Box 366, Lac Du Flambeau, Wis. 54538
Ted Fellowes, Beaver Lodge, 9245 16th Ave. S. W., Seattle, Wash. 98106
Clyde E. Fischer, Rt. 1, Box 170-M, Victoria, Tex. 77901
Jerry Fisher, 1244-4th Ave. W., Kalispell, MT 59901
Flaig's Lodge, Millvale, Pa. 15209
Donald E. Folks, 205 W. Lincoln St., Pontiac, IL 61764
Larry L. Forster, Box 212, Gwinner, ND 58040
Horace M. Frantz, Box 128, Farmingdale, N.J. 07727
Freeland's Scope Stands, Inc., 3734 14th Ave., Rock Island, Ill. 61201
Dale Goens, Box 224, Cedar Crest, N.M. 87008
Gary Goudy, 263 Hedge Rd., Menlo Park, CA 44025
Gould's Myrtlewood, 1692 N. Dogwood, Coquille, Ore. 97423 (gun blanks)
Charles E. Grace, 10144 Elk Lake Rd., Williamsburg, MI 49690
Rolf R. Gruning, 315 Busby Dr., San Antonio, Tex. 78209
Half Moon Rifle Shop, 490 Halfmoon Rd., Columbia Falls, MT 59912
Harper's Custom Stocks, 928 Lombrano St., San Antonio, Tex. 78207
Harris Gun Stocks, Inc., 12 Lake St., Richfield Springs, N.Y. 13439
Hal Hartley, 147 Blairsfork Rd., Lenoir, NC 28645
Hayes Gunstock Service Co., 914 E. Turner St., Clearwater, Fla. 33516
Hubert J. Hecht, 55 Rose Mead Circle, Sacramento, CA 95831
Edward O. Hefti, 300 Fairview, College Sta., N. Tex. 77840
Herter's Inc., Waseca, Minn. 56093
Klaus Hiptmayer, P.O. Box 136, Eastman, Que., Canada J0E 1P0
Richard Hodgson, 5589 Arapahoe, Unit 104, Boulder, CO 80301
Hollis Gun Shop, 917 Rex St., Carlsbad, N.M. 88220
Henry Houser, Ozark Custom Carving, 117 Main St., Warsaw, MO 65355
Jackson's, Box 416, Selman City, Tex. 75689 (blanks)

Paul Jaeger, 211 Leedom St., Jenkintown, Pa. 19046
Johnson Wood Products, Rt. 1, Strawberry Point, IA 52076 (blanks)
Monte Kennedy, P.O. Box 214, Kalispell, MT 59901
Don Klein, Box 277, Camp Douglas, WI 54618
LeFever Arms Co., Inc., R.D. 1, Lee Center Stroke, Lee Center, N.Y. 13363
Lenz Firearms Co., 1480 Elkay Dr., Eugene, OR 97404
Philip D. Letiecq, RD 2, Homer, NY 13077
Al Lind, 7821 76th Ave. S.W., Tacoma, WA 98498 (cust. stockm.)
Bill McGuire, 1600 N. Eastmont Ave., East Wenatchee, WA 98801
Gale McMillan, 28638 N. 42 St., Box DY72 - Cave Creek Stage, Phoenix, AZ 85020
Maurer Arms, 2366 Frederick Dr., Cuyahoga Falls, OH 44221
Leonard Mews, Spring Rd., Box 242, Hortonville, WI 54944
Robt. U. Milhoan & Son, Rt. 3, Elizabeth, W. Va. 26143
C. D. Miller Guns, Purl St., St. Onge, SD 57779
Mills (D.H.) Custom Stocks, 401 N. Ellsworth Ave., San Mateo, Calif. 94401
Nelsen's Gun Shop, 501 S. Wilson, Olympia, Wash. 98501
Oakley and Merkley, Box 2446, Sacramento, CA 95811 (blanks)
Maurice Ottmar, Box 657, 113 E. Fir, Coulee City, WA 99115
Pachmayr Gun Works, 1220 S. Grand Ave., Los Angeles, CA 90015 (blanks and custom jobs)
Paulsen Gunstocks, Rte. 71, Box 11, Chinook, MT 59523 (blanks)
Peterson Mach. Carving, Box 1065, Sun Valley, Calif. 91352
Phillip Pilkington, P.O. Box 2284, University Station, Enid, OK 73701
R. Neal Rice, Box 12172, Denver, CO 80212
Richards Micro-Fit Stocks, P.O. Box 1066, Sun Valley, CA. 91352 (thumb-hole)
Carl Roth, Jr., 4728 Pineridge Ave., Cheyenne, Wy. 82001
Matt Row, 19258 Rowland, Covina, CA 91723
Royal Arms, Inc., 10064 Bert Acosta Ct., Santee, Calif. 92071
Sanders Cust. Gun Serv., 2358 Tyler Lane, Louisville, Ky. 40205 (blanks)
Saratoga Arms Co., R.D. 3, Box 387, Pottstown, Pa. 19464
Roy Schaefer, 965 W. Hilliard Lane, Eugene, OR 97404 (blanks)
Shaw's, Rt. 4, Box 407-L, Escondido, CA 92025
Hank Shows, The Best, 1202 N. State, Ukaih, CA 95482
Walter Shultz, R.D. 3, Pottstown, Pa. 19464
Sile Dist., 7 Centre Market Pl., New York, N.Y. 10013
Six Enterprises, 6564 Hidden Creek Dr., San Jose, CA 95120 (fiberglass)
Ed Sowers, 8331 DeCelis Pl., Sepulveda, CA 91343 (hydro-coil gunstocks)
Fred D. Speiser, 2229 Dearborn, Missoula, MT 59801
Sportsmen's Equip. Co., 915 W. Washington, San Diego, Calif. 92103 (carbine conversions)
Keith Stegall, Box 696, Gunnison, Colo. 81230
Stinehour Rifles, Box 84, Cragsmoor, N.Y. 12420
Surf N' Sea, Inc., 62-595 Kam Hwy., Box 268, Haleiwa, HI 96712 (custom gunstocks blanks)
Swanson Cust. Firearms, 1051 Broadway, Denver, Colo. 80203
Talmage Enterpr., 43197 E. Whittier, Hemet, CA 92343
Brent L. Umberger, Sportsman's Haven, R.R. 4, Cambridge, OH 43725
Roy Vail, Rt. 1, Box 8, Warwick, N.Y. 10990
Weatherby's, 2781 Firestone, South Gate, Calif. 90280
Frank R. Wells, 350-C E. Prince Rd., Tucson, AZ 85705 (custom stocks)
Western Gunstocks Mfg. Co., 550 Valencia School Rd., Aptos, CA 95003
Duane Wiebe, 426 Creekside Rd., Pleasant Hill, CA 94563
Bob Williams, c/o Hermans-Atlas Custom Guns, 800 E St. N.W., Washington, DC 20004
Williamson-Pate Gunsmith Service, 6021 Camp Bowie Blvd., Ft. Worth, TX 76116
Robert M. Winter, Box 484, Menno, S.D. 57045
Fred Wranic, 6919 Santa Fe Ave., Huntington Park, CA 90255 (mesquite, French and black walnut blanks)
Mike Yee, 4700-46th Ave. S.W., Seattle, WA 98116
Russell R. Zeeryp, 1601 Foard Dr., Lynn Ross Manor, Morristown, TN 37814

TRIGGERS, RELATED EQUIP.

M. H. Canjar Co., 500 E. 45th Ave., Denver, CO 80216 (triggers)
Custom Products/Neil A. Jones, 686 Baldwin St., Meadville, PA 16335 (trigger guard)
Dayton-Traister Co., P.O. Box 593, Oak Harbor, WA 98277 (triggers)
Flaig's, Babcock Blvd. & Thompson Run Rd., Millvale, PA 15209 (trigger shoe)
Gager Gage & Tool Co., 27509 Industrial Blvd., Hayward, CA 94545 (speedlock triggers f. Rem. 1100 and 870 shotguns)
Franklin C. Green, Rt. 2, Box 114-A, Montrose, CO 81401 (electronic trigg. system)
Bill Holmes, 2405 Pump Sta. Rd., Springdale, AR 72764 (trigger release)
Paul Jaeger, Inc., 211 Leedom St., Jenkintown, PA 19046
Michaels of Oregon Co., P.O. Box 13010, Portland, OR 97213 (trigger guards)
Miller Single Trigger Mfg. Co., R.D. 1 on Rte. 209, Millersburg, PA 17061
Viggo Miller, P.O. Box 4181, Omaha, NB 68104 (trigger attachment)
Ohaus Corp., 29 Hanover Rd., Florham Park, NJ 07932 (trigger pull gauge)
Pachmayr Gun Works, 1220 S. Grand Ave., Los Angeles, CA 90015 (trigger shoe)
Pacific Tool Co., P.O. Drawer 2048, Ordnance Plant Rd., Grand Island, NB 68801 (trigger shoe)
Richland Arms Co., 321 W. Adrian St., Blissfield, MI 49228 (trigger pull gauge)
Sport Service Center, 2364 N. Neva, Chicago, IL 60635 (release triggers)
Timney Mfg. Co., 2847 E. Siesta Lane, Phoenix, AZ 85024 (triggers)
Melvin Tyler, 1326 W. Britton Ave., Oklahoma City, OK 73114 (trigger shoe)
Williams Gun Sight Co., 7389 Lapeer Rd., Davison, MI 48423 (trigger shoe)

Bibliography

Ackley, P.O.; *Home Gun Care & Repair;* Stackpole, 1969.

Angier, R.H.; *Firearms Blueing and Browning;* Stackpole, 1936.

Baker, Clyde; *Modern Gunsmithing,* (2nd Ed.); Small Arms Technical Publishing Co., 1933.

Bish, Tommy L.; *Home Gunsmithing Digest* (Vol. I); DBI Books, Inc., 1970.

Brownell, Bob; *Gunsmith Kinks;* Brownell's, 1969.

Burch, Monte; *Outdoorsman's Workshop;* Winchester Press, 1977.

Chapel, Charles Edward; *Gun Care and Repair;* Coward-McCann, 1943.

Cooley, R.H.; *Complete Metalworking Manual;* Arco Publishing Co., 1967.

Dunlap, Roy; *Gun Owner's Book of Care, Repair and Improvement;* Outdoor Life/Harper & Row, 1974.

Dunlap, Roy F.; *Gunsmithing;* Stackpole, 1963.

Frazer, Perry D.; *Elementary Gunsmithing,* Stackpole, 1958.

Hatcher, J.S.; *Hatcher's Notebook;* Telegraph Press, 1957.

Howe, James V.; *The Modern Gunsmith;* Funk & Wagnalls, 1934.

Howe, Walter; *Professional Gunsmithing;* Small Arms Technical Publishing Co., 1946.

Johnson, Harold V.; *General Industrial Machine Shop;* Charles A. Bennett Co., 1970.

Kennedy, Monty; *Checkering and Carving of Gunstocks;* Stackpole, 1962.

Linden, Alvin; *Restocking a Rifle;* Stackpole, 1969.

Linden, Alvin; *Shaping Inletted Blanks & Notes on Model 70 Winchester;* Stackpole, 1958.

MacFarland, H.E.; *Gunsmithing Simplified;* Combat Forces Press, 1953.

MacFarland, H.E.; *Introduction to Modern Gunsmithing;* Stackpole, 1965.

McCarthy, Willard J., and Smith, Robert E.; *Machine Tool Technology;* McKnight & McKnight Publishing Co., 1968.

National Rifle Association; Firearms Assembly I, *Guidebook to Shoulder Arms;* NRA, 1972.

National Rifle Association; Firearms Assembly II, *Guidebook to Handguns;* NRA, 1972.

National Rifle Association; *Gunsmithing Guide;* NRA, 1971.

National Rifle Association; *NRA Illustrated Firearms Assembly Handbook* (Vol. I); NRA, 1968.

National Rifle Association; *NRA Illustrated Firearms Assembly Handbook* (Vol. II); NRA, 1969.

Newell, D.A.; *Gunstock Finishing and Care;* Stackpole, 1966.

Nonte, George C.; *Pistolsmithing;* Stackpole, 1974.

Stell, J.P. & Harrison, William B.; *Gunsmith's Manual;* Samworth, 1945.

Tanner, Hans; *Petersen's Basic Gun Repair;* Petersen Publishing Co., 1973.

Vickery, W.F.; *Advanced Gunsmithing;* Small Arms Technical Publishing Co., 1955.

Walker, Ralph T.; *Hobby Gunsmithing;* DBI Books, Inc., 1972.

Walker, Ralph T.; *Black Powder Gunsmithing;* DBI Books, Inc., 1978.

Whelen, Townsend; *Amateur Gunsmithing;* NRA, 1924.

Whelen, Townsend; *Small Arms Design & Ballistics;* Small Arms Technical Publishing Co., 1945.

Williams Gunsight Co.; *How to Convert Military Rifles* (1st Ed.), Williams Gunsight Co., 1959.

Williams Gunsight Co.; *How to Convert Military Rifles* (3rd Ed.), Williams Gunsight Co., 1961.

Williams Gunsight Co.; *How to Convert Military Rifles* (6th Ed.), Williams Gunsight Co., 1969.